A History
of
The Robert Cochrane Tradition

*A Critical and Biographical account
of the
Clan of Tubal Cain*

*A Legacy lived
through
The Round of Life*

Tubal's Mill

For

Roy Bowers aka Robert Cochrane
February 1931- June 1966

May your quest herein reveal itself in Truth.

THOTH PUBLICATIONS
Markfield, Great Britain

Copyright 2024 Shani Oates

All rights reserved. No reproduction, copy or transmission of this publication may be made without written permission. No paragraph of this publication may be reproduced, copied or transmitted save with the written permission or in accordance with the provision of the Copyright Act 1956 (as amended).
Any person who does any unauthorised act in relation to this publication may be liable for criminal prosecution and civil claims for damages.

The Moral Rights of the Author have been asserted.

A CIP catalogue record for this book is available from the British Library.

Cover design by Shani Oates

ISBN 978-1-913660-40-6

Printed and bound in Great Britain

Published by Thoth Publications
Copt Oak Cottage, Whitwick Road, Markfield, LE67 9QB

Web address: www.thoth.co.uk
email: enquiries@thoth.co.uk

"Nothing is purely good or evil, these are relative terms that man has hung upon unaccountable mysteries (. . .) to my particular belief, the goddess, white with the works of Good is also Black with works of darkness, yet both of them are compassionate, albeit the compassion is a cover for the ruthlessness of Total Truth. Once we deviate from the search for Truth, then our works are nothing, our lives as the winter winds. It speaks for itself, outside systems, religious beliefs, beyond and before the grave."

~Robert Cochrane (1931-1966)~

Revised & Abridged Edition
Plough Monday 2018

A Dedication to Fate: Baldr's Draumar.

1. Once were the gods | together met, And the goddesses came | and council held, And the far-famed ones | the truth would find, Why baleful dreams | to Baldr had come.

2. Then Oðin rose, | the enchanter old, And the saddle he laid | on Sleipnir's back; Thence rode he down | to Niflhel deep, And the hound he met | that came from hell.

3. Bloody he was | on his breast before, At the father of magic | he howled from afar; Forward rode Oðin, | the earth resounded Til the house so high | of Hel he reached.

4. Then Oðin rode | to the eastern door, There, he knew well, | was the wise-woman's grave; Magic he spoke | and mighty charms, Til spell-bound she rose, | and in death,

The Wise-Woman spake:

5. *"What is the man, | to me unknown, That has made me travel | the troublous road? I was snowed on with snow, | and smitten with rain, And drenched with dew; | long was I dead."*

Oðin spake:

6. *"Way-tamer my name, | I am Slain-tamer's son; Speak thou of hell, | for of heaven I know: For whom are the benches | bright with rings, And the platforms gay | bedecked with gold?"*

The Wise-Woman spake:

7. *"Here for Baldr | the mead is brewed, The shining drink, | and a shield lies o'er it; But their hope is gone | from the mighty gods. Unwilling I spake, | and now would be still."*

Oðin spake:

8. "*Wise-woman, cease not! | I seek from thee All to know | that I fain would ask: Who shall the bane | of Baldr become, And steal the life | from Oðin's son?*

The Wise-Woman spake:

9. "*Hoth thither bears | the far-famed branch, He shall the bane | of Baldr become, And steal the life | from Oðin's son. Unwilling I spake, | and now would be still.*"

Oðin spake:

10. "*Wise-woman, cease not! | I seek from thee All to know | that I fain would ask: Who shall vengeance win | for the evil work, Or bring to the flames | the slayer of Baldr?*"

The Wise-Woman spake:

11. "*Rind bears Vali | in the western halls, And one night old | fights Oðin's son; His hands he shall wash not, | his hair he shall comb not, Til the slayer of Baldr | he brings to the flames. Unwilling I spake, | and now would be still.*"

Oðin spake:

12. "*Wise-woman, cease not! | I seek from thee All to know | that I fain would ask: What maidens are they | who then shall weep, And toss to the sky | the yards of the sails?*"

The Wise-Woman spake:

13. "*Way-tamer thou art not, | as erstwhile I thought; Oðin thou art, | the enchanter old.*"

Oðin spake:

14. "*No wise-woman art thou, | nor wisdom hast; Of giants three | the mother art thou.*"

The Wise-Woman spake:

15. "*Home ride, Oðin , | be ever proud; For no one of men | shall seek me more Til Loki wanders | loose from his bonds, And to the last strife | the destroyers come.*"[1]

Hela, by Karl Ehrenberg

Acknowledgments

Sincere thanks to Judith & Peter of the *Museum of Witchcraft* in Boscastle, and to Simon Costin, its Curator, for their joint assistance and time given to searching for specific documents, so needful in this history of Cochrane's Tradition. CTC's gratitude to them is immeasurable. Their generous permission to share and reproduce those vital documents made this publication possible. Equally, CTC acknowledge the great gift granted by Ashley Mortimer, Sarah Kay, and Julie Payne at the Doreen Valiente Foundation – *Centre for Pagan Studies*, whose equally generous permission to quote freely from Doreen Valiente's prolific archive is without precedent.

CTC especially offer their deepest thanks to Ken Rees for his crucial advice and research on the historical events and personages concerned. Likewise the Clan treasure the archival knowledge and sterling advice gifted to them by the indefatigable Clive Harper whose patient assistance and enthusiasm were vital to this project. To the inimitable Stuart Inman, esteemed and dear friend CTC offer their sincere appreciation for sharing his knowledge of persons and events referred to throughout this biography.

A further debt of gratitude is extended to dearest Kin in the US, to Jane and Arnett Taylor for their invaluable first-hand knowledge of Craft histories concerning CTC during the 1970s-80s, and for sharing their documents and letters pertaining to those matters stateside. To the best and most stoic of friends Chris Reibling, CTC offer eternal appreciation for his patience and tact when presenting needful proofreading advice. And last, but not least, CTC thank Roy, John, Doreen, Bill, Bobbie, and J &V, and all beloved Kith and Kin past and present, without whose legacy, knowledge, input, records, permissions and kind exchanges, none of this would ever have materialised or been relevant.

"Whatever Madame le Guiden has in store – the Law is that you will overcome - and in the overcoming find spiritual strength."

~ Robert Cochrane

Contents

Introduction   12

1 Death: Ouroboros

I) Of Vision and Veil

Feeding the Demon and the Saint	13
Mystical Abode of the Mighty Dead	19
The Five point Star of Love and Death	23
Frith, Faith & Fealty – Overcoming of Fate	25
The Arte of Seeing	32

II) Nomenclature

The Pellar Within	38
Sweet Child in Time	47
The Lore of the People	59
Of Craft, Clan,	
Old Compton & Charlie Cardell	70
Never the Twain	98
A Real People	105

III) The Roots of Chaos

Gardnerian Myth	112
Lucifer: A spectre within the Clan?	
Chaos Reigns	

2 Re-Birth: The Eternal Mask

IV) The Phantom Royal Windsor Coven

Tattered Oaths and False Identity	142
Ghosts in the Machine.	163
An Entangled Web	184
A Fine Ruse	201

V) The Regency & 1734

A Compact Broken, A Compact retained	214
From Ashes Rise	221
A Speculative Craft	227
An Operative Craft	243
A Shift from the Shadows	259
1974: A Royal Jewel	277

3 Love/Maternity: Fruition & Union

VI) The Eternal Pilgrim

1734 & Joe Wilson	284
Immortal Wisdom	295
Of Clan & Compass	299
The Celestial Rose	305

4 Maturity: Realisation of Truth

VII) The Lapwing

The Ancient Keltic Church	309
Castles Made of Sand	330
A Cuckoo in the Nest	341
Media Sorcery!	356
Sleight of Hand	364

5 Wisdom: Mirror of the Muse

VIII Evolution

The Roebuck in the Thicket	380
Ground Zero	392
A Giant is Slain	409

IX) Epilogue — 424

Appendices — 426

Bibliography — 427

LIST OF ILLUSTRATIONS FOR TUBAL'S MILL

Hela	6
Three Mothers – Carrawbrough	18
Memento Mori – Shani Oates	21
Spirit of Sacrifice – Shani Oates	22
Norns (1889) Johannes Gehrts	29
Three Mothers – Lorenz Frolich	32
The Seiðkona - Vardlokkur	36
Robert Cochrane In Caving Gear	39
Gundustrup Cauldron	94
Swing System – Threshing Poles	108
Metaphysical Poem - Robert Cochrane	129
Triune Horn-ed God - Shani Oates	134
AAA Scan of Oath to Thames Valley Coven	143
Text of Cochrane's Instructions	269
Letter from Cochrane to Ronald White	269
Windsor Heraldic Insignia	280
Plantagenet Boar Insignia	280
Ermine chart	283
Cochrane's Signature & Sigil	283
E. J. Jones Summer 2003	304
Frau Gode	305
Irminsul	308
Hand-staff and Arrows	328
E. J. Jones & Shani Oates 1999	343
Nemesis - Shani Oates	407
She will gather you up Home again.	423

Please note the selected sections of Evan John Jones' letters, handwriting samples and other documents referred to throughout, that were previously published separately under the title of ***Tubal's Mill Legend***, are now included in this revised publication.

Introduction

Robert Cochrane referred to *'the muck of ages,'* and of the need to cast it off in order to bring new light and hope to the Craft, free of its delusions and deceits. Taking his advice, CTC open the pages of its history to share a true understanding of what Robert Cochrane's Tradition *actually* is. Sourced from *within*, the candid reality reveals its true place in the past, present and future of the Craft.

Without prejudice this biographical account spans fifty years of Clan history, challenging previous beliefs set down in error by those who know the least, and by those with much to gain. Sometimes, these have been one and the same. Written by outsiders beyond the bounds of its Lore, Law, and Covenants, their speculative accounts add nothing to its truths, but they do obfuscate them.

Through controversy and biased misrepresentation, incidents not of the Clan's making, past or present, were defined by those without authority or qualification. Factual accounts prompted and supplemented by necessary critique restore the balance, offering craft researchers and interested practitioners a unique insight into the people and the craft of The Clan of Tubal Cain.

CTC *share* that singular perspective, frequently ignored in the voices of others whose personal motivations led them to declare a different history for the Clan. No good purpose is served by the suppression of certain uncomfortable facts that find no origin within the Clan, which may surprise those unfamiliar with those facts. For those already aware of its troubled history, the information found in this biography will bring true insight.

Robert Cochrane's works and Tradition at no point ceased or diverged, but are maintained through his own *People of Goda, of the Clan of Tubal Cain,* and nowhere else. It is whole, complete in and of itself. Contrary suggestions forwarded by others, being without foundation, are duly dismissed. CTC stand by what *is*, and defend that reality. If this shakes down a house of cards, remember, it was built by others. CTC exact a duty born in gyfu; a charge to *'take all we are given, and give all of ourselves.'* 'The Work' is all that matters.

1 Death: The Ouroboros

I) Of Vision and Veil

Feeding the Demon and the Saint

Clan systems are those communities that have thrived upon the recognition of a Head-Kinsman, who acts as priest, king and warrior in defence and support of his people, in all matters of life and death, law and duty, judicial and spiritual. In order to hold that position, *something other* is said to have alighted upon them, a vital force perceived as the luck, or welfare of that Clan. It is an intrinsic Virtue imbued through time and upheld in name. This Fate, is understood as ambivalent at worst, and at best, beneficent, so long as the Head-Kinsman is just, and acts within the *rightness of things.* Conversely, where that person fails to uphold the ethic of the Clan they represent, that Fate is at best ambivalent and at worst maleficent. The Head-Kinsman is bound through oath and Covenant to their Clan, and to the over-arching spirit that guards and guides that Clan. This Virtue known to those who follow the lore and customs of Northern Tradition as *Hamingja*.

A special transmission leaves the Head-Kinsman upon death, to seek another worthy to hold it in lineal succession. It may, leave that person if required or desired by extreme or necessary circumstance. Thereafter, it is irrefutably absent from them. Hamingja carries the very literal meaning of *fate that walks in the shape/form of.....,* and its mystery and ability to shape-shift, one to another, is relative to each one chosen in succession to bear it. It is a light, a beacon of force – an invisible mark, recognised by those it is known to, and sensed even by those who do not. Witnessed in the eerie darkness, this glow of ages is the fleeting vestigial ether – Fate, the Mother of all things, shifts even the gods.

All members of a dedicated Clan have access to that Virtue, and partake freely of it, but do not hold it, though each will of course hold individual Virtue as an imbued spiritual force, aligned as one within it. This may synthesize into a well-bonded collective, fashioning a strong, harmonic equilibrium. Formidable on all fronts, such a Clan would readily face all challenges presented in life and death; by fate and fortune; and of the gods and men. Again, this view is one preserved within the Clan's distinctive Mythos and remains significantly divergent to countless others within the Craft.

Other concepts similarly deviate, retaining the integrity of earlier faiths and beliefs absorbed by the cumulative and continuously evolving Egregore of the Clan. The Clan of Tubal Cain's rites, duties and Law are passed from one Head-Kinsman to another, in linear succession. Cochrane's widow authorised Evan John Jones alone to continue their Tradition with her blessing under Clan Law. A Clan has only *one* Head-Kinsman. Historically, and factually, as an entity greater than the sum of its parts, a Clan may encompass subgroups *within*, but never as fractured entities *without*.

These idiosyncratic beliefs and developments must nonetheless be set within the greater context of Clanship in order to realise the bonded significance inherent in this vibrant, though archaic social unit. Visionary insight encourages a deeper understanding of the relevance held by the three sets of Mysteries (male, female and priestly) within some Clanships - the Clan of Tubal Cain explicitly. To maintain contextual significance, a brief exploration of the development of Clanships in Northern Europe and England is necessary at this point, in order to make better sense of what follows.

Historical examples of tribal systems across Iron Age Germania and Scandinavia, commonly demonstrate a three class system. Comparable to the roles adopted by the more archaic caste system of India, these were void of the lack of democratisation enforced there. Each Clan had a provider level: the farmers or manual labourers that generated sustenance; above them, a warrior class existed only to protect and defend its people. Residing above all, a Clan was governed through an elite or noble class of priests, teachers, kings and law-makers.

In particular, the Scandinavian Clan or *ätter (ætt)*, expressed a much envied social group based on common descent, a belonging to, or, by formal acceptance/adoption into that particular family, witnessed at the 'þing.'[2] Clan is a very specific term that determines a group of people united by actual or perceived kinship and descent. Kinship based bonds may often be purely symbolical in nature, where all people within the Clan share a *given* (common) ancestor to bind

---

[2] (thing=assembly of law) http://en.wikipedia.org/wiki/Norse_mythology

their identity and cohesion as a family. Because this ancestor is not always human, they may be referred to as an atavistic totem.

Historic Clans survived in a mutual state of *gyfu* - an exchange of protection and providence for the whole Clan, executed through a *Dryghten* (lord/laird/earl/jarl). Affiliation to that lord required that each oath-bound family was obliged to support their named Clan with a promised force of arms. Hence a slight towards one member, becomes a slight to all. Clans are generally described as kinship based subgroups of tribes. Non-blooded personages within the Clan were bound alongside blood relatives through a shared allegiance to their liege lord and his lady as Head-Kinsmen, forming a family unit built on loyalty and trust.

Dynastic lineages or houses engaged systems where succession was not an automatic birth-right, but acquired by election, most commonly through the Tanist appointment, or by force of arms, an extreme measure, much frowned upon unless circumstance of dishonour or dissatisfaction occurred in a duly appointed elected leader. It was and remains essential that any leader must exhibit the combined abilities of priest, warrior and judge. Without these, he is deemed unfit to lead.

Though all Clans are often a smaller part of a larger society or tribal chiefdom under the jurisdiction of a King, this particular and most noteworthy exception to the *blooded* family construct is the aforementioned *ätter*, which commonly exists outside the accepted societal norm. Cochrane explained this through his inimitable poesis: *"So we come to the heart of the people, a belief that is based upon eternity, and not upon social needs or pressures."* [3]

Because Celtic language groups of peoples are defined literally by their physical blood families, they remain quite distinct in their comparison to the Germanic based traditions of Scandinavia where virtue was prized above blood. This meant that adoption into a Clan was possible by recognition of particular valour. That grant of admittance would otherwise remain closed to those outside familial blood ties or marriage. Denied lineage by conventional means of literal 'kin' tied in 'blood,' a kindred person may be recognised,

---

[3] Oates, S. *Star Crossed Serpent III* (UK: Mandrake of Oxford 2016) #2 Cochrane to Wilson 12th Night 1966 p 405

accepted and adopted into that family to create an extended, bonded community.⁴

Each Clan attains further definition through the primal aegis of its named ancestral or deific benefactor, by whose Frith⁵ all are held in allegiance to the current Head-Kinsman. As representative of every member of that Clan, he is able to trace his people historically back to their founding aegis. Henceforth, the *People* of that Clan, adopt a suffix of either *ing* or *ung* to that named principle, which distinguishes them as being *of* it. This is a belong*ing* in the *spirit of the blood,* and its bond is of a different reciprocity entirely.

Temples, mounds and areas of sacred landscapes were frequently dedicated to specific gods, which may in some cases reflect the ancestral name given to a Clan family. In both cases, the people and the land are named for the god under whose aegis they place themselves. The people are *not* named *for* the land they traverse - another distinct factor denoting Clan. Drawing diverse folk from many areas, of separate lands in some cases, together, they form a rich collective, a People.

Roaming historically as wanderers, mercenaries, pirates and pioneers, movement occurred as necessity demanded, often far from their Homeland Hearth. Kinship is bound in spirit, rather than blood. Their lands *are (in) their* blood and bone, their gods *are their* breath and tears. They owe duty to their Head-Kinsmen and they follow the Law of the People. To break this bond renders that person an exile, an out-cast from their People – a person of no worth or consequence. Operative as a precedent system in the Northern lands for hundreds of years immediately prior to medieval feudalism, it was, in so many ways superior to it.⁶

Honouring that bond takes a simple, profound form. Germanic peoples once congregated in natural woodland groves, not dissimilar to their fellow Celtic speaking lowland tribes though rarely, if ever, did they concede to temple constructions. Offerings, given as *Blót,* or *Sumbel* formed the genus of worship by all ancient Germanic and Scandinavian peoples, resembling cognate practises of

---

⁴ http://en.wikipedia.org/wiki/Germanic_peoples
⁵ Peace, friendship, and well-being in an ordered and civil society of people.
⁶ http://fmg.ac/Projects/MedLands/ENGLAND,%20AngloSaxon%20&%20Danish%20Kings.html

those other tribes east and west of them. Occasionally, a pile of rough stones known as a *horgr* demonstrated a crude, iconic altar.

When discussing these sacred matters with E.J.J., specifically how the Abrahamic *Curse of Cain* within CTC's Mythos is manifest, he responded bluntly. He expected that knowledge on the sacrificial role of the Priest King was commonplace within the Craft. It is not. He explained that when speaking of curses intrinsic to certain myths and fables, one should first *mark* the law, then consider its consequence in Fate, wherein:

> The curse of *Ol' Tubal* lies in the management of the Clan itself. You are stuck with it until you feel the need to download it on someone else and when you do, you'll get a tremendous feeling of lightness and relief. In the end you find if you let it, it will rule your entire life and that quite simply is, the 'curse.' [7]

Pragmatic as ever, E.J.J. added that, although the mantle is heavy, it could also be a blessing. It was simply a paradox. E.J.J. strongly believed that all leaders should bear conviction of thought and deed, belief and action. On that perspective, his advice was very direct:

> You don't have to justify your work to anyone – this is how we work, and this is what we believe in, and it is no-one else's business. They either accept that or they don't, as must you. [8]

Equally keen to promote the gnostic premise that lays great emphasis upon self-reliance and responsibility, E.J.J.' maxim was to: *'take thyself as lamp;'* this he stressed unceasingly. Each person must tread their own path and not walk in the shoes of another; the details of a journey may not be duplicated, but must be unique to the individual concerned.

Quite independent of status, knowledge is one of the most precious gifts offered to humankind. Each person should sustain, enflesh and honour its priceless legacy to inspire those who follow, paying it forward for all *Wayfarers*. For readers of *The White Goddess*

---

[7] Oates, S. *Tubal's Mill: Legend* (UK: Create Space, 2016) Personal Correspondence from EJJ to SLO November 1999 (L20)
[8] Oates, S. *TM: Legend* (UK: Create Space, 2016) Personal Correspondence from EJJ to SLO September 2001 (L21)

by Robert Graves, let it be known, we are each avowed to be the *Roebuck* to the very end.

> The efficacy of religion lies precisely in what is not rational, philosophic or eternal; its efficacy lies in the unforeseen, the miraculous, the extraordinary. Thus religion attracts more devotion according as it demands more faith; that is to say, as it becomes more incredible to the profane mind. The philosopher aspires to explain away all mysteries, to dissolve them into light. Mystery on the other hand is demanded and pursued by the religious instinct; mystery constitutes the essence of worship, the power of proselytism.
>
> ~ Henri Frédéric Amiel [9]

Through Robert Cochrane and those who came before him, their Work, Tradition and Legacy of and for the People, is of CTC alone – none other. These sacred things demand freedom from the whispers of intrigue and from the mire of entanglement. The *People of Goda, the Clan of Tubal Cain*, give this testament, they ask: *"Would ye know more?"*

CARRAWBROUGH : COVENTINA'S WELL.

---

[9] http://www.bartleby.com/library/prose/218.html

Elegy for a Dead Witch

To think you are gone, over the crest of the hills,
As the moon passed from her fullness, riding the sky,
And the white mare took you with her.
To think that we will wait another life
To drink wine from the horns and leap the fire.
Farewell from this world, but not from the circle.
That place that is between the Worlds
Shall hold return in due time. Nothing is lost.
The half of a fruit from the tree of Avalon
Shall be our reminder, among the fallen leaves
This life treads underfoot. Let the rain weep.
Waken in sunlight from the realms of sleep.[10]

~ Doreen Valiente

The Mystical Abode of the Mighty Dead

I know that I hung on a windy tree nine long nights,

~ Havamal

The abode and Castle of this form or facet of the ultimate (multi-faceted) Godhead is named by Cochrane as *Caer Ochran*, and described as the *One in Seven'* upon the Hill, the Plough/Haywain again above, spinning always around them in cognate terms of Qabalism's *Three Negative Veils*. Madame la Guiden raises Her flag upon the Nowl, Her standard blazing in the sky, the mirror, as above so below. The Guiden pole is likewise the Distaff of the Great Spinner & Weaver, Her staff bears the flax (substance) of all threads (Fate) *Spun by a Woman (Norn) who sings to the Moon.* This is a folk myth that refers very much to the indwelling feminine spirit of the Mill itself.

Symbols within the Clan are frequently disguised as numbers and in this instance refer to an entirely different principle. Within his correspondence to Norman Gills, Cochrane keenly described himself

---

[10] Valiente, Doreen. *Rebirth of Witchcraft* (UK: Hale: 1989) p 136

as a man to whom his ancestors spoke and as Magister of a small Clan. He described its operation as a magickal group along the *seven and one* basis, not the expected, much promulgated thirteen. These obscure features are quite unique to the Craft as taught by Robert Cochrane.

His expression of *a seven and one Clan,'* does *not* refer in any way to the amount of people in his group. Repeated in error, possibly by those unaware it was a misconception instigated by others without claim to actual knowledge of Clan matters. Naturally, anyone who stands outside the bounds of a tradition, is without the benefit of its mentorship and praxis, a matter which automatically disqualifies them from offering anything other than opinion.

Cochrane gave a poetic description of the Clan's Compass to Bill Gray when he referred specifically to its gnostic alchemy as the *Order of the Sun.* Having some traceable origin in the holy and Sophianic magickal processes, it maintains archangelic order – namely, how 'Seven become One,' and how 'All are One and One is All.' These virtues form points marked around the boundary of the working area, or Dancing grounds, to denote the Compass as it is laid, where Seven + One = Eight. One other makes nine - the 9th gate, the Void beyond the Bridge – *'Out of Time, Out of Place.'*

These knots, obvious to the eye, are ruled by Sun, Moon and by the Stars. As the year turns and spins through the seasonal round, our Compass follows the cultural pattern of a Northern Tradition. Somewhat differently, those of the Wica / Wicca (hereafter referred to jointly as Wicca unless referencing Gardner's era specifically to avoid a clumsiness in the text) on the other-hand, follow a lunar pattern of 13 moons. Numerous books on Wicca use the number 13 to work through that annual cycle, consisting of monthly instruction etc.

Cochrane held a critical regard for the principles of divine and sacrificial kingship, though assuredly not in the popularly adopted Frazerian sense. He preferred the Northern understanding that brings balance through *gyfu*, being the exchange of reciprocity. That shift occurs in symbiosis, when one thing becomes another, pivoted upon the self as axial altar.

Of course, Cochrane acknowledged the Tau Cross in like manner of the Kerm/Holm Oak, highlighting the historical sacrifices at Uppsala and other sites, but makes a clear distinction between acts of physical sacrifice in purpose and context within the Clan Mythos. Averse to dogma, his commentaries are free of irrelevant or inappropriate incantation, scripted theatre, and of working ritual by rote, or in absent repetition. Cochrane strongly advocated the need for inspiration and surrender to the Nine Muses of the Moon.

A favourite topic of conversation he had with Bill Gray concerned the Marion Cults of the 12th century and the Templar code that had served the vital gnostic elements of mysticism exiled by exoteric Christianity. For Robert Cochrane, that divine relationship was the highest and most supreme gift above all else - the evolution of the self. Anything that fell short, was in his eyes, a weakness of man.

> Western Europe, morally and socially, has advanced more without the Old Craft and its attendant superstitions, than it ever did with them.[11]

For the People of Goda, Robert Cochrane remains a teacher, guide, trickster, poet and *vitki*. These titles slip easily over his frame.

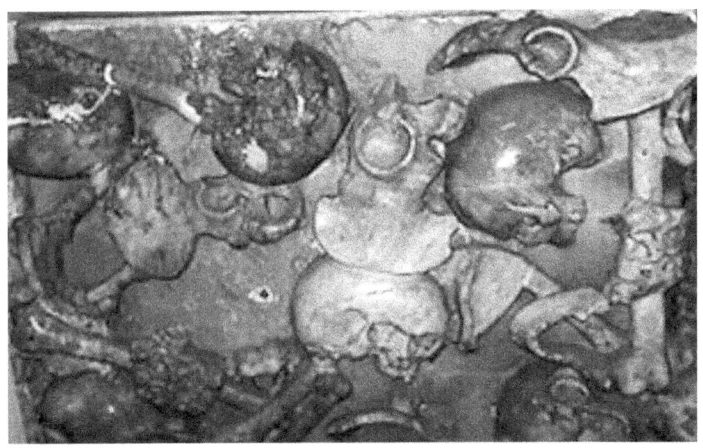

1931-1966 Memento Mori!

---

[11] 'The Craft Today.' *Pentagram* November 1964, reprinted in *Star Crossed Serpent III*, Shani Oates (UK: Mandrake of Oxford. 2016) p 278

Houzle

To all kin, past, present & future. In that congress do we partake the Houzle:

Thou who art clad in white.
Thou art asked to come and appear.
To fill the horn cup with favour,
love abundant every day.
White Queen, thy blessing
give to this sacramental Wine,
In thy wonderous name.
Motta thee,
Grammercie."

"All wise, twisted, crooked horned god.
Father overnight and (thou who art) equal to Fate
Herself.
Grow forth as Ye hear the summons to arms.
Hear the sacred Bell and look upon our Art.
Grief I suffer, pain have I without thee.
Superior Lord, therefore be this night,
together with thy beloved gathering.
Bless our lives and the sacred bread,
with Love Might and Wisdom.
Motta thee.
Grammercie

The Five Point Star of Love and Death

When regarding the Seasonal Rites of the Compass, both Robert Cochrane and E.J.J. made frequent reference to the Five-fold placement of the stages and way-markers of life. Reality is constructed from the fusion of experience generated through the mythic elements of cultural tradition that inform it. Belief and Faith (being of Mind and Memory) are twin pillars that embolden the *round of life* as emotive and empirical mirrors to its reality. By honouring the Covenant of the Clan, its people evolve through principles bound under the Aegis of the Law are: honour, mercy, duty and compassion. Seen as an exchange of Love, it is neither Sacred nor Profane. Both feed it. Both draw from it. Human beings are born as seekers unto life; we find love, acquire wisdom, mature in its sharing and then we die! That is Fate. But what of Destiny?

> Become at one with truth and you must surely die. Take up the works of truth and you are a condemned man, for the human race as a whole does not want truth, but the comfort of illusion. We are still babies suckling at a breast whose milk is poisonous, yet we think that we flourish upon poison. Truth, no matter how we interpret it, feeds demons as well as saints.[12]

Death –	Change/ Paradigm shift
Birth –	Regeneration/Resurrection
Love –	Desire, Ambition, Possession
Maturity –	Reason and Resolution
Wisdom –	Evolution. Release.

Between these five points all purpose is engineered by Fate, to which we either surrender or resist. Friction between these opposing poles creates the dynamic causality of life. Marking a pattern that interweaves aspiration and disappointment with experience, shifts are actuated from one stage to another. Just occasionally, an exceptional person will enter the field of being to challenge everything that is believed.

---

[12] Oates, 2016. *SCSIII* Op. Cit. Cochrane to Bill Gray #VI p 207

Through chaos and grief, upheaval and turmoil, remarkable individuals become influential catalysts for great paradigm shifts, sweeping away the dusty mores of stagnantion, breathing new life into the arts and sciences. Their gift of genius propels humankind into a higher level of universal evolution. Such a person is often a hero. In this biography, Robert Cochrane was that heroic anti-hero.

Aligned to the principle force of Truth, Robert Cochrane knew exactly what course his life would take, what his Faith would exact of him, and that it would *"gather him up home again."* The Craft world is much the richer for his gifts, and for his divine fire, the inspiration of true genius.

Death, seen by many as inimical to life, finds better expression as an allegory of the eternal battle waging between metaphysical forces. In a dualistic sense, aspirants and pilgrims witness an archaic principle of light, opposed only by the primal void. As a motif that repeats vis-à-vis timeless myth, it finds context in conflict where every reality finds embodiment through manifest symbol. Understood like this, conflict and the divine cause are one. The Halls of the Mighty Dead welcome those who fall in life. Gathered in the Wild Hunt, we ride with the host, seeking more of our kith and kin amongst the raging hoards.

> All mystical thought is based upon one major premise: the realisation of Truth as opposed to illusion. The student of the mysteries is essentially a searcher after Truth, or, as the ancient traditions described it – wisdom. Magic is only a by-product of the search for Truth, and holds an inferior position to Truth. Magic, that is the development of total will, is a product of the soul in the search for ultimate knowledge. It is an after-thought upon a much larger issue, the ability to use a force that has been perceived while searching for a more important aim within the self. No genuine Truth can be written down or put within an intellectual frame-work of thought. The truths are to be participated in during comprehension of the soul. Truth of this degree is not subject to empirical thought and is only apparent to the eye of the beholder, and to those who have followed a similar path of perception. [13]

---

[13] 'The Craft Today.' *Pentagram* November 1964. Reprinted in *Star Crossed Serpent III*, Shani Oates (UK: Mandrake of Oxford. 2016) p 278

Frith, Faith & Fealty - The Overcoming of Fate

Naked Truth — no less. This begins where life meets death, for in that flash, all that has passed is brought to the fore; in an instant, memory engulfs the mind with its own subjective history. And, so it was, that on Midsummer's Eve 1966, a man resolved to seek his Fate, to overturn his errant blindness, to grasp again the rope that binds true. His seeking brought him before the Pythoness - the Sybil, most terrible and most fair; for, *"He would know more…"*

Invoking the *faerie rade*, he sought an audience under the auspices of Madame *la Guiden*, a trial by which he might overcome the doom he felt about him.[14] But, the Lady called him hither. Roy Leonard Bowers (aka Robert Cochrane) slipped into a coma, unable to withstand the lethal effects of natural and prescription medicines consumed to speed him on his way. Suspended for nine days in no man's land, he died in a hospital bed without regaining consciousness. His controversial death fifty years ago has raised many theories regarding his Craft. As one of its most gifted exponents, his legend has no equal.

These tragic events reveal his frustrated genius, and the anarchic timbre of a tormented poet. Daring to eat from the table of the gods, his ravenous soul drank eagerly of Oðin's honeyed mead as inspiration intoxicated his mind and body with sacred manna. Error and strife had soured his life, a gift from Eris, whose threads held great torment in their weave. Though inflamed by an innate sense of injustice, he nonetheless beheld precious moments of grace. Catching sight of the philosopher's stone, the ripening of wisdom's fruit within haunted him as a lost gift, much lamented. Regretfully, he recalled his sense of loss: *"Glimpsing the grail, but twice, I lost all."* [15]

Those who look to his inspired works, gifted by the Muse, see only genius, undeniable by its light. Through the eternal manifest, there is a perennial philosophy within Cochrane's work; where the stream flows true, it serves still. To begin to know something of the man within the time and tide he lived, an exploration his words and works is essential.

---

[14] Gavin Semple - *A Poisoned Chalice*
http://www.clanoftubalcain.org.uk/A_Poisoned_Chalice.pdf
[15] Oates, 2016. *SCSIII* Op. Cit. Cochrane to Norman Gills. #12 p 402

During the phenomenon of the *swinging sixties*, a huge groundswell of philosophy, spiritualism, astro-sciences and political anarchy actuated greater freedoms of religion and occult practice. Their influences collectively nurtured the vibrant context that fashioned Cochrane into a forthright seeker. He firmly believed that answers are ever within reach of those who seek them in earnest. As his story unravels, others may begin to understand the roots of his unique logic.

Intensely charismatic and self-assured, his easy, persuasive charm drew men and women equally into his company. Doreen Valiente recalled that when she eventually met him in 1964, she'd considered him to be intensely charismatic and *"strikingly handsome."* [16] His ready contempt and smouldering arrogance were amplified by a strongly contentious nature and few tried to see the real person beneath the layers of frustration and anger. Since his death, it became apparent this was tolerated only when it served the best intentions of his peers within the Craft. For many, it proved to be an increasingly impossible trial as tolerances on all sides collapsed. Falling then into a quagmire of delusion, his unrelenting provocations accelerated his eventual alienation from all but his closest friends.

He was and remains a fascinating and exemplary figure. Possessed of a keen wit and a fascinating sense of otherness, many gravitated towards his orbit. Robert Cochrane was a powerful leader, a trendsetter, a natural *mover and shaker* whose innovations continue to reverberate throughout our modern-day world and all realms of occulture. Unprecedented in his time, Cochrane held a preponderance to veer heavily upon an ancestral stream that drew deeply of folk traditions and cultural praxis. This was in contradistinction to both the neo-Pagan ideologies presented through Gerald B. Gardner's Wica, and the heavily dogmatic occulted realms of the pallid Magus adopted by so many in his era. [17]

---

[16] Valiente, Doreen. *Rebirth of Witchcraft* (UK: Hale 1989) p 117

[17] It is uncertain as to whether Gardner initially celebrated the full 8 Sabbats or the 4 Celtic fire festivals only in the 1950s. Doreen Valiente was certainly asked in 1952 to write a Yule ritual. Other members have said that before 1957, only 4 were practised. Gardner himself claimed the Yule ritual of Doreen's was of ancient heritage. Gardner believed that the solar festivals (equinox's + solstices) were a Mediterranean or Middle Eastern import, despite many others who've pointed to the North and the Vikings. Many say that the fire festivals are older than the solar ones, yet many of the Neolithic and megalithic monuments are aligned to the equinoxes and solstices, as well as to the fire festivals and the lunar phases (at Stonehenge primarily.). Nomadic 'Celts' marked a return cyclical pattern between pasture and corralling in the spring and autumn months. Saxons and Vikings were

Ever the archetypal enigma, Cochrane was the true Aquarian man, (in the cosmic sense, his birth-sign not withstanding), the humble anti-hero was also the strutting peacock, the arrogant and bombastic autocrat, the child seeking approval, the fool as devil's advocate. He was hardly the type to shy away from confrontation. And in his short term as Magister of his Clan, he encountered a great deal of that. Above all else, his sought to re-establish the British Mysteries.

Striving to accomplish this task generated only friction and conflict, souring his vision of a thriving Craft, rich in culture and tradition. The cultivation of a People within the old Clan based communities and faiths of his ancestors, preoccupied and honed his focus. As Gardner's naturist cult grew into a popular community of Wicans basking in the glow of a pan-European Celtic revival, Cochrane's idiosyncratic objective presented an almost quaint incongruence.

Frustrated by what he perceived as a lost opportunity to fully embrace pre-Christian lore and custom, Cochrane felt compelled to act. Proud of his own endeavours, it was important to him that others became aware of an alternative way to truly live one's tradition. To that end, periodic references were made to his Clan, *the People of Goda* and also to an earlier coven throughout his various correspondences. Slender evidence suggests he and his wife Jane may have attended meetings held by *The Thames Valley Coven* before re-settling in Slough.

Recently discovered information suggests a slim possibility of a link between a London coven assembled by someone called Arthur Everley and *The Thames Valley Coven*. Though evidence is scant, and nothing conclusive, its purpose within this schema unfurls organically. Ken Rees has some knowledge of this coven, relayed to him by Ruth Wynn Owen, of the popular staged events and meetings held in Everley's wonderful garden, where *"The White Goddess, amongst other texts"* were freely discussed. [18]

Around this time, in an early letter to Bill Gray, Cochrane casually remarked upon the passing, decades previously, of a coven in

---

proud to celebrate solar festivals (reviving them after invasion, it was a vital facet of life with fate). Hence a complete and seasonal sequence of festivals is inherited.

[18] Ken Rees, 2017. Personal Correspondence. Imbolc

old Windsor town. Cochrane gave a charming description of his mother as a young girl who had known the coven's last surviving member. Referred to by him as 'Mrs' Blomfield, this real life Lady died in the middle of the 20th century.[19] He claimed that at least two (unnamed) ancestors were hanged for witchcraft, matters Cochrane's nephew has justifiably denied. Cochrane's widow, also repudiated these claims to several people after his death. The needful circumstances of those denials should be respected; only those involved know the truth of that claim, for, or against.

As indirect assertions, they may even be true in the generic sense; the matter is of deeper interest to anyone who studies the *spiritual reality* of a *blooded* tradition, and intuits laterally all inferences thereof. That imperative proved central to Cochrane's eccentric perception of hereditary lineages within the Craft, and why he embraced their intrinsic virtues to formulate initiatory experiences for those dedicants drawn to it.

He stated how, when a mere child himself, *Diana* had sealed his doom, sensing that She'd plucked him for Her own, to attend Her instruction of service.[20] As Ultimate Truth, She remained an unattainable abstract, Transcendent, harsh in Her unwavering ambivalence of him; yet gloriously imminent in symbolic form as a physical link to his metaphysical concept of Her.

> Some groups seek fulfilment in mystic experience - this is correct if one does not forget the duty of *involvement* - the prime duty of the wise. It is not enough to see The Lady, it is better to serve Her and Her will by being involved in humanity, and the process of Fate (The single name of all Gods is *Fate*).
>
> In fate, and the overcoming of fate is the true Graal, for from this inspiration comes, and death is defeated. There is no fate so terrible that it cannot be overcome - whether by a literal victory gained by action and in time, or the deeper victory of spirit in the lonely battle of the self, Fate is the trial, the Castle Perilous in which we all meet to win or to die -Therefore, the People are concerned with Fate - for humanity is greater than the Gods', although not as great as the Goddess. When Man triumphs, fate

---

[19] Oates, 2016. *SCSIII* Op. Cit. Cochrane to Gills #3 p 292
[20] Valiente, Doreen. *The Rebirth of Witchcraft* (UK: Hale, 1989) p 121

stops and the Gods are defeated - so you understand the meaning of magic now. Magic and Religion are aids to overcome Fate, and Fate is a cradle that rocks the infant spirit. [21]

How should the blessing of a good fate be conveyed? Cochrane once thanked Norman Gills warmly, acknowledging the gift of three crossed owl feathers bound to a hag-stone. [22] In that acknowledgement, Cochrane left Gills in no doubt he knew very well its traditional and historical significance. Void of 'death and rebirth' in the Round of Life, the hag-stone blessing is symbolised with the runic ϕϕϕ - *Life, Love and Wisdom*, and with *Flags, Flax and Fodder*. In other words, *food, clothes and shelter* — the basic rudiments of life. If you have these and the love of another united in the fourth 'ϕ,' then you are most blessed indeed. Clans had, since ancient times sworn oaths of kinship and allegiances upon such this most gravid stone, the

---

[21] Oates, 2016. *SCSIII* Op. Cit. Cochrane to Gills. #3 p 292
[22] Oates, 2016. *SCSIII* Op. Cit. Cochrane to Gills. #1 p 289

tomb, the hearth, and portal of rebirth: *"The mystery of woman is virgin, mother/hag in one person."*

Cochrane's passion for his *'dark and terrible'* Muse is unprecedented in the Craft. He declared her to be a harsh mistress, the Pale Leukothea who bears little resemblance to the *White Goddess* so beloved of others. On a superficial level, those least familiar with both, might easily mistake one for the other. For anyone of the People, privy to deeper aspects of Clan lore, they bear no resemblance whatsoever. As Supreme Godhead, She is the cold, ruthless *femme fatale*. She is *Fate, beyond Fate,* the absolute and total *Truth* manifest through Wyrd .

She is the Hidden Void, the Chasm, the Cauldron, the *force* of all things manifest through the *form* of the *God*. She is the One who binds his Fate and holds his Faith She is also, Grace. Her hidden aspect is Nox, shadow spectre of dark wisdom, from whom is drawn the *Child of Compassion,* the illuminator and guide to humankind. Adhering more closely to cultural roots, She manifests through the Northern Tradition as Hulda (Huldra), commanding the Skies and Compass axis. Flying hither in Her train upon the bitter winds of Winter, deceased souls are gathered home upon Her wild geese.

"Her Mirror is the Moon, the Greater Light" From which, via reflection: *"All women become a Lesser Light."* This shining, silver disc, is universally known to millions as the arcane and luminous symbol of Her transience, Her imminence and Her Transcendent presence. This emblem becomes Her literal *standard*, blazing aloft in the night sky, a poetic metaphor manifest as *Alba Guiden,* the Pale Leukothea – Diana, who seizes all in Her talons, beholden as *Her darling crew* ! Each man, raises himself by allegiance to Her banner, Her silver standard guarded by the *Man in the Moon,* the eternal wanderer, likened to Cain, whose personage within the Craft, is again - all things to all men.

An attendant Mythos is ever the key. The act of raising a (horn) cup to the Moon, affirms each host as hunter, vanquished to Her cause, affirming one's own troth to Her, in dedication and faith, held in allegiance as witness to Her Banner of Truth. The Guiden's [23] ability to wax and wane displays the absolute nature of Truth, for,

---

[23] Originally from the French, meaning small, banner for light horsemen, it became an English battle standard/heraldic crest.

"What is true today, may not be true tomorrow." And also, *"Behind the Illusion, is a greater Illusion still."*

Here, Cochrane refers to the fact that beyond Her Mirror, (a reflected image is false, therefore reflected light is illusory having no light of its own, so) is only shadow, the Dark, the Void. As an *Absolute Truth*, this holds all the fear and dread given to it. In fact, as the sum total of all nightmares and horrors the mind is capable of projecting, it is the *greater Illusion still*. Of his Clan, Cochrane declared himself the Trickster and Master – *"the 'devil in fact,"* asserting therein how the occult truth mirrored the outer plane, where the Creatrix reigns supreme upon the Inner plane.

Very much misunderstood, this vital tenet expresses the dynamic of their relationship. *He* leads at *Her* behest, subject to her aegis only. Serving Her as Master, he is manifest where She is Hidden, the symbiotic thread is a clear conduit for Truth, carrying the ancestral links forward, through all magicks and work. Years hence, it will no doubt be called into question, by those unscrupulous enough to set such virtue aside in vain folly.

Cochrane's oblique explanations for Craft deities were a stark contrast to the rising popularity of the Triple Goddess favoured by the Wica - of a Maid, Mother and Crone. Cochrane's elevation of the nebulous and ambiguous forms of female divinity, set him apart from those who promoted a more popular, but generic, goddess, whose prosaic form held no warmth for him. Declaring absolute authority and majesty for the divine female as manifest within woman born, his exceptional perception placed him in direct contradistinction to the commonplace attitude of rampant misogyny. The burgeoning sexual liberation of the 1960s had failed to expel that social inequality.

Forced to insist repeatedly upon his own distinction of Her as remote, primal, an absolute singularity, Cochrane believed She held a unique Triune Virtue, with an attendant religion that embraced Her through Wyrd. Cochrane lauded Her as *The Three Mothers* as a gentle introduction to the Norns, or the Fates, again manifest through womankind. As above, so below; always. The Godhead's feminine virtues are presented through the microcosmic forces of Wyrd, a view shared wholeheartedly with Evan John Jones. Cochrane explained Her status without ambiguity:

To my particular belief, the Goddess, white with works of good, is also black with works of darkness, yet both of them are compassion, albeit the compassion is a cover for the ruthlessness of total TRUTH. Truth is another name for godhead. Male or female it doesn't really matter, what matters is the recognition of neither good nor evil, black or white, but the acceptance of truth as opposed to illusion. [24]

The Arte of Seeing

---

[24] Oates, 2016. *SCSIII* Op. Cit. Cochrane to Bill Gray #VI p 207

Amergin, Bard of the Milesians, claimed the Land of Ireland in his magnificent lay, describing seer-ship and transvection as a mythic mnemonic. Cochrane emphasised the importance of the first five lines, with intuited explanations. Adopted later for mythic analogy, he instructed Joe Wilson in a letter to study that text most carefully as a key to the Mysteries.[25]

I am a stag: of seven tines,   (who survives the flood)
I am a flood: across a plain,   (that destroyed the world)
I am a wind: on a deep lake,   (of god moving o'er a desolate world)
I am a tear: the Sun lets fall,   (the sorrow of fate)
I am a hawk: above the cliff,   (the child who survived the flood)
I am a thorn: beneath the nail, (sacrifice, the weight of duty/gyfu)
I am a wonder: among flowers,   (for I am resurrection)
I am a wizard: who but I   (for I alone transform)

Sets the cool head aflame with smoke?

I am a spear: that roars for blood,
I am a salmon: in a pool,
I am a lure: from paradise,
I am a hill: where poets walk,
I am a boar: ruthless and red,
I am a breaker: threatening doom,
I am a tide: that drags to death,
I am an infant: who but I
Peeps from the unhewn dolmen, arch?
I am the womb: of every holt,
I am the blaze: on every hill,
I am the queen: of every hive,
I am the shield: for every head,
I am the tomb: of every hope."

Convinced this poem was a vital clue to the history of ancient Britain, its people and its lore, Cochrane remained cautious of uncritical analysis. He rejected another version of the *Song of Amergin,* translated by Robert Graves in his highly controversial poesis: *The White Goddess,* describing it as thoroughly mangled in order and meaning, and therefore of no use. Believing it had lost its

---

[25] Oates, 2016. *SCSIII* Op. Cit. Cochrane to Joe Wilson #4 p 388

magical intent, it was Cochrane's wish to see the complete work restored. His own idiosyncratic grasp of the text differs vastly from the following version by Graves.

> I am a wind on the sea,
> I am a wave of the ocean,
> I am the roar of the sea,
> I am a bull of seven battles,
> I am a hawk on the cliff,
> I am a teardrop of sunlight,
> I am a gentle herb,
> I am a boar enraged,
> I am a salmon in a pool,
> I am a lake in a plain,
> I am the vigour of man
> I am the meaning of poetry,
> I am a spear on the attack,
> I am the god who fires your mind. [26]

Stating that: *"Vowels are a sacred tree sequence from the north,"* whence Oak, Ash and Thorn refer obliquely to (runic) names of the Three Elemental Mothers, Cochrane considered they were manifest through the 4th rune, of fire, which he assigned to the *'alder god, Bran, Baal, [Loki] lower magic, fertility and death.'* Cochrane referred to the Wind as the Shekinah, acknowledging an associative motif employed in the descriptive roles ascribed to mythical solar avatars from the Christos through to Baldr, Llew, and Buddha. To show his own application of these forms in metaphysical terms, he instructed Wilson that:

> We teach by poetic influence, by thinking along lines that belong to the world of dreams and images. There is no hard and fast technique, no laid down scripture or law, for wisdom comes only to those who deserve it, and your teacher is yourself seen through a mirror darkly, [gnostic premise at the heart]. The answers to all things are in the [four realms] Air-Inspiration, and the Winds [disr/nornir] will bring you news and knowledge if you ask them properly. The Trees of the Wood [runes] will give you power, and

---

[26] Revised edition of Robert Graves *The White Goddess* (UK: Faber and Faber Limited 1961). It appears here under the principle of 'Fair Use.'

the Waters of the Sea will give you patience and omniscience, since the Sea is a womb that contains a memory of all things [marah], the sea of dreaming true, beyond the void, the dreamscape of the akashics. [27]

Cochrane's mythopoeic composition demonstrates his syncretic use of vital principles gleaned from the five initial lines of Taliesin's poem, to express *The Round of Life,* from birth through death, and into a sublime state beyond it. Musing upon them, it is easily seen how they emphasise the significance of all five stages relative to the rich unyielding cycle of life through: re-birth/*life;* youth/*love;* maturity/*fruition; wisdom;* death/*resurrection.*

Exploring that construct yet further, Cochrane shifts its significance again, grafting those precepts into a discussion of the hand, the five vowels through which it informs the language of the Craft and of the *Five Rings of Arte*. Finally, Cochrane summarises the use of sonic keys as the hand upon the door, offering this *Call to the Vǫlur* as one's birth-right, literally, borne of a very different Craft. Ancestral Craft holds those valorous spirits close, alongside the living; they were not perceived as the distant dead. It is completely unlike the magician's circle of arte where spirits are subjugated to the power of the cross through the auspices of an Abrahamic faith.

More importantly, in a letter to Bill Gray, Cochrane adamantly denied that his Craft was associated with base necromancy, or that his works demanded the selling of one's soul to spirits in Faustian acts of vanity. This crucial perspective contradicts popular opinion fuelled by more recent pronouncements from those who have failed to understood Cochrane's true intent. However, Cochrane did not disagree that his method of prophecy relies upon a metaphysical *otherness* which assumes direct converse in the consultation of the Vǫlur in spirit.

Christian glosses noted throughout interpretive translations of sagas and legends by Snorri Sturluson for example (assuming any written form was ever true to the heathen oral traditions of Northern Europe), have generated a tremendous disservice to subsequent understanding of their beliefs. The realms of the gods and of spirits were mutable and transitory. One of the last sagas to be translated

---

[27] Oates, 2016 *SCSIII* Op. Cit. Cochrane to Wilson # 3 pages 369-372

from Icelandic into English was the *Völuspá*. Written to preserve older, oral forms within a *Christianised* Iceland, the *Völuspá* combines variations sourced from two separate manuscripts: *Codex Regius* and *Hauksbók*. Snorri Sturluson refines further the Heathen and Christian themes in his version of the Eddas.

Reading the Sagas in their current form, one is left with a clear impression of the realms of heaven and hell, the dualism of god and the devil, where the Craft is the repository of the devil and all his works; a perspective very demonstrative of the mind-set of the scholarly monks of the 11-13th centuries. Within the Craft, the legacy from that combined vision is so engrained, many refer to the ancestral spirits as *The Mighty Dead*. When summoning those ancestral spirits, the Clan utilise the skills mastered in the arte of Seiðr; and so the role of the Vǫlur, lives on. Cochrane explained a little of this to Joe Wilson, stating how:

> The real mystery is only uncovered by the individual, and cannot be told .... I understand that in the past the Maid would wear a cloak sewn with little silver discs that the people would gaze upon – and she acted as a medium for the people as they reflected upon her cloak.[28]

Cochrane's description is compatible with an historical description of a Vǫlva engaged in Seiðr and with a rite performed by Charles Cardell. In confirming the authenticity of this rite to Joe Wilson,[29] Cochrane revels in a precious tradition hallowed still by the old families of the Old (true) Craft, where a priestess, taking the role of 'Maid' would don her special cloak to act as Seiðkona, the Seeress for her People. Held at a point where '*two streams meet;*' it placed the Seiðkona centrally upon a High Seat, where she and her attendants

---

[28] Oates, 2016. *SCSIII* Op. Cit. Cochrane to Joe Wilson #4 p 388
[29] Ibid.

could engage *Galdr* to induce trance and prophesy. Contra to more familiar forms of Indo-European spell craft and sorcery, Anglo-Saxon, Norse, Slavic and Icelandic charms were meant to be sung. The word galdor/galdr literally means incantation. Sorcery, that is, singing to the dead, is refined in the *Valgaldr* form.

Calling to deified, ancestral spirits, engages both forms as a way of manoeuvring the forces of will, nature and desire within a vocational and sometimes reverential manner. It is very distinct from the baneful manner adopted by western sorcery, that finds its base within dualistic or Abrahamic faiths. This is perhaps the best example of the natural expression to utilize both high and low forms of theurgy and thaumaturgy, together, without distinction.

Though Cochrane spoke openly of the Maze, of fasting, and of a sequence of dedicated occult keys, he described his re-discovery of a cultural heritage, and of renewed relationships of a very different kind. He had observed that truth is rarely as welcome as hope supposes it should be.

How later groups that sprang up after his death, including *The Regency,* 1734 and *Y Plant Bran,* were each influenced by Cochrane's works to a greater or lesser extent in each case, is most ably demonstrated by those people best qualified to do so – *themselves,* that is, by their own writings and works. Overwhelming media saturation and opinion upon its works, even if sincerely meant, labours under natural handicaps. CTC persevere, expressing in simple terms an optimism that a better understanding may be reached through factual certainty. Fertile ground is offered for growth.

> It is an honour, therefore, to stand firm, to resist, to meet force with force, these are considered works of virtue, but it is hard work. For defending your honour with toil is not the same as possessing it in peace. Nor is being moved by virtue the same as enjoying virtue. What virtue wins by toil, wisdom enjoys; and what is ordained, counselled, and guided by wisdom is accomplished by virtue.
>
> ~Bernard of Clairvaux

II) Nomenclature

The Pellar Within

Highlighting his personal status and purpose, Robert Cochrane brought a raw primality to the popular perception of the Craft. To fully comprehend this will require an exploration of parameters he might recognise. Even familiar comments if repeated and used out of context, can lead to false assumptions. Cochrane's self-defining declaration has all too frequently been used to confirm him as, 'witch.' It does not. Read carefully, the opposite is true.

> I describe myself as a Pellar. The People are formed in clans or families and they describe themselves by the local name of the Deity. I am a member of the People of Goda - of the Clan of Tubal Cain. We were known locally as 'witches,' the 'Good People.' 'Green Gowns' (females only). 'Horsemen,' and finally as 'Wizards. [30]

Cochrane typifies in these few lines how his *People* are *perceived by others*. These are not self-defining terms of choice. Frustrated by the lack of attention to the fact that *who his people really are* and how they should be referred to, remains a mystery to most, therefore open to unacceptable speculation. He confirmed that 'Witch' *was never* used as a term by those of the Craft about themselves. [31] Employed by others, it is a term that displays a lack of understanding with regard to the nature of works engaged. Underscoring perfectly what he actually *is* by nature, choice and belief, he explains the nature of the beast:

> What do witches call themselves? They call themselves by the name of their Gods. I am Od's man, since the spirit of Od lives in me. [32]

---

[30] Oates, 2016. *SCSIII* Op. Cit. Cochrane to Wilson # 3 pages 369-372

[31] In a curious you-tube interview, Monmouth appropriates this view as Ronald White's. Yet there is no document or letter to verify this view was shared by him before or after Cochrane's death. In this interview, Monmouth refers to several instances that absolutely contradict it, confirming in fact, the opposite. See *The Secret History of the Royal Windsor Coven & the Regency with John of Monmouth.* 9 Sep 2012 - Uploaded by WitchtalkShow https://www.youtube.com/watch?v=WpAAmBpF0Us

[32] Oates, 2016 *SCSIII* Op. Cit. Cochrane to Bill Gray # V p 267

And, even more explicit is:

> Now, what do I call myself. I don't. Witch is as good as any, failing that 'Fool' might be a better word. I am a child of Tubal Cain, the Hairy One.[33]

Witch is as good as any and worse than none! In other words, he is reiterating what he said earlier – that *'witch' is a name used by others for him and his kind*. As a descriptive, it does not even begin to touch how he perceived himself - that *fool* is closer than witch ever could be. He affirmed, again and again that all terms used for the people of his Clan are equally false. Without equivocation, he declared in whose tutelage he resided, and under what belief he cast his banner, and by what ethos he chose to abide under.

In terms of a magico-historical Mythos, this 'standard' has been overlooked for many decades. Studies of the role and virtue of his eponymous deity should prove immensely rewarding.[34] Cochrane defined all *labels as pointless* and irrelevant. Sharing Cochrane's preference for anonymity, his Clan remain all and none of these. Attention is better focussed on all matters that deepen both interest and knowledge of Cochrane's words and works throughout this very personal biography, than on names.

Beginning with the forge of making, the creative arte of the smith, after all, within the Clan's Mythos, anvil, smith and pellar are connected as immutable forms, both literally and figuratively. The historical root stem they share is astonishing; nomenclature not withstanding – what then lies beneath given titles?

Circumstantial usage has validated the modern use of the term *pellar*, and some have claimed it is relative to *expellar*; a person whose role is akin to an exorcist. However, this retrospective

---

[33] Ibid.
[34] Oates, 2016 *SCSIII* Op. Cit. See Appendices

attribution, presented rather obviously as an extension of duties pertinent to the original pellar role in the craft, is somewhat fanciful. Natural associations are clearly defined within its etymology where 'ex' is a prefix generating a thing of need; it is made manifest in: *e*xpression and also, *e*xpedient.

A mistaken attribution for the term *pellar* has led some people to assume that Robert Cochrane and Taliesin are the same person. They were most assuredly very different people! Taliesin, not Cochrane described himself as a pellar involved in a tradition oriented in the West Country. Discussion of this terminology and its misplaced application is exampled in a letter to Robin-the-dart from Evan John Jones:

> Not surprising that [Robin-the-dart] comes up with a middle-eastern connection for Pellar because there is a connection between Gypsy craft and the old English craft from way back. In fact, if you look at it carefully, there's a lot of common ground concerning the Gypsy Black Madonna and the Dark Goddess of the Clan, so somewhere along the lines, someone must have taken something from someone else, and woven it into their beliefs. [35]

These beliefs expose one of the founding elements of Cochrane's Tradition, formulated from within the gnostic stream of mystical Craft. As a term, *ex-pellar* shifts from beyond all those artificially imposed limitations upon the functions and purpose of a *pellar*. Each is not in conflict with the other, and may therefore serve in tandem. Initial familiarity with one particular usage may have ingenuously stimulated exclusive purpose and function, inimical to the other.

In time, the more obscure term and usage may simply have fallen into obscurity; yet it is the latter that remains more active in current perception. This then begs the same understanding of the etymology and use for 'witch'— and is probably the reason Robert Cochrane declined its use as a descriptive term in preference for *pellar*, a more generic term applied to cunning-men everywhere, and in specific circumstances hide-bound within a Tradition, to *priest*. Placed in context, Cochrane expounded *wisdom* as the lure:

---

[35] Oates, 2016 Op. Cit. *TM:Legend* Personal Correspondence from E.J.J. to SLO. 14th December 1999. (L1:p 2 of 7)(EJJ,L1)

(…) since talking about the People (we describe ourselves as such),(…) we come to the heart of the People, [of] a belief that is based upon eternity, and not social needs or pressures - the 'witch' belief then is concerned with wisdom, our true name then is the People and wisdom is our aim.[36]

Time has not shifted the way *The People of Goda* define themselves, though it is now clear that as Clans-folk, the way others refer to them has found new and interesting descriptions. Media characteristically follows common parlance, where everything is too easily popularised and absorbed. This propensity to shrink language effectively removes distinctive terminologies - the devil is in the detail, after all.

There has been a curious tendency to refer to Cochrane's Clan Tradition, that is *The People of Goda, of the Clan of Tubal Cain,* as he named it, by inappropriate terminology that fails to assert its singular position. In fact, the terms, Cochranite and Cochranian, properly suggest a generic form that has become far removed from the usage implied by Prof. Hutton when he first coined them within research material intended for future publication two decades ago.[37]

Muddled nomenclature applied by people outside CTC's Tradition, once taken up and applied generically, became acceptable for popular use by others, which established an impression that bears no relativity to it in reality. Over the past few years CTC have worked hard to provide examples throughout various publications to rectify the lack of previous knowledge available on matters fundamental to 'identity.'

Drawing directly upon the strength of personal authority to define who and what a Clan properly is and how those mechanics manifest with CTC, requires no further justification. Explaining that in terms that can be readily taken up to replace those used inappropriately when CTC is referred to by others, is something this chapter works to toward achieving.

Striving to be more than figures of authority for and of Cochrane's Tradition, it is essential to share that knowledge to assist

---

[36] Oates, 2016 *SCSIII* Op. Cit. Cochrane to Wilson # 2 pages 365-369
[37] Hutton, Professor Ronald. *The Triumph of the Moon* (UK: OUP. Press. 1999) p 317 which states quite clearly the true voices of 'public authority' – only members of the clan may pronounce upon it – and these two elders had the experience and authority to do so.

in the preservation of the customs and lore of this land, in mind and memory for generations to come. In depth explanations help to make sense of everything, including the history of those involved - even the nomenclature.

Dealing first of all with those terms applied indiscriminately by others when referencing CTC, the use of a name is a bonded adoption and literal entitlement under the law, be that where it pertains to a clan, a tribe or to society in general. Numerous traditional craft groups, *influenced* and *inspired* by Cochrane's works, are just that, no more, no less. They cannot be *of* a Tradition they are not Inducted into.

The Clan of Tubal Cain is a closed tradition, which means a seeker must be *Admitted,* with full rites and celebration. This status is not negotiable. Without the inherent vows of admittance, one is outside any particular tradition. No amount of semantics alters this premise. These tenets ensure support for the truly genuine seekers of the Mysteries that enshroud its legacy. For seekers of the profound, admission is not achievable by *desire alone, but in action.*

This remains a common truism having accordance with a number of rites that imbue a sense of belonging, of kinship and brotherhood, from the simple Christian *Rites of Confirmation* to the more elaborate *Rites of Initiation* into Freemasonry. Official histories of these traditions and their variant works are recorded by academics and upheld by the scholarly world. There are no circumstances by which conjecture and rumour are acceptable for inclusion. Facts must be supported with material evidence that is subject to rigorous analysis for content and context. The discipline requires verifications of authenticity where genuine sources are a treasure to be mined. With regard to Cochrane's works, Prof. Hutton astutely advises his readers that: *"The most reliable sources of information derive from two people who worked regularly with Cochrane — Doreen Valiente and Evan John Jones."* [38]

CTC defer to these two people at all times, citing their invaluable works throughout this biography. Students of the Craft have lost much in their unwitting adherence to biased advice from others who have knowingly undervalued their testimonies. Both Valiente and Jones, as direct sources to that tradition, have been

---

[38] Hutton, 1999. Op. Cit. p 317

habitually overlooked for those less qualified, when consultations or advice were required.

> Throughout the history of humanity, there have been myths, schools of wisdom and teachers who have shown a way to attain a working knowledge of esoteric thought and philosophy by using inference rather than direct method to teach the approaches to Cosmic Truth. [39]

During his assessment of Traditional Craft as it evolved in the late 1980-90s, Prof. Hutton applied a similar descriptive mode to Robert Cochrane's Tradition, to the one Cochrane had applied to Gardner viz – Gardnerian. The term Cochranian, if understood and used correctly should *imply* working *within* his authorised legitimate, and initiatory, hereditary line. Upheld in that way, it stands in opposition to how non-initiates develop those works merely *inspired or influenced* by those Traditions, and practised outside of them.

Those original categories were put forward almost two decades ago by Prof. Hutton for *The Robert Cochrane Tradition* and further traditions Prof. Hutton and others had been led to believe were founded from it. Formulated on information supplied by his sources, those assessments are basically flawed. Because those terms were created according to levels of influence and inspiration, they require significant factual revision. Due to semantic abuse they no longer apply:

1. 'Cochranian' – *"Had his [Cochrane's] career as a witch been longer and more stable, it is extremely likely that 'Cochranian' witchcraft would have become a readily identifiable strain of witchcraft."* [40]

In reality this term was relevant only at the time when Prof. Hutton applied it according to the dubious and limited information he received from non-Clan members regarding Cochrane's Tradition. Prof. Hutton went on to describe how:

---

[39] 'The Craft Today.' *Pentagram* November 1964. Reprinted in *Star Crossed Serpent III*, Shani Oates (UK: Mandrake of Oxford. 2016) p 278
[40] Hutton, 1999. Op. Cit. p 317 Ken Rees was amongst several sources *not* consulted, who may have offered more factual information for Prof. Hutton to draw from. His knowledge and that of others who may have also have contributed better advice, was directly discouraged, or not brought to Prof. Hutton's attention by his main source on the theme of traditional craft.

2. *"A direct continuity of the Cochrane Tradition"* was provided by his closest (Cochrane's) friend, E. J. Jones. [41]

3. *"A third tradition, 1734 is rooted in Cochrane's work originating in a correspondence (. . .) with Joe Wilson."* [42]

4. With regard to Cochrane's *"complex legacy, one part of it (was) represented by the London-based group known as 'The Regency,' a tradition 'according to some,' * was formed to carry on 'Cochrane's Tradition,'" "It lasted until 1974, and former members and guests have subsequently given birth to a number of different groups."* [43]

During the few years prior to publication of *The Triumph of the Moon*, Michael Howard had been Prof. Hutton's primary source and consultant, supplemented by brief and sometimes indirect contact with Marian Green, Doreen Valiente and Evan John Jones. Another researcher, Ken Rees, who had worked closely with Ronald White in the mid-1970s, explains that Prof. Hutton was not fully informed by his main source (Howard). Rees claims *The Regency* did not properly cease until around 1976 although Ronald White and George Winter had stepped back from the London Scene in 1974. They had planned to move to Shropshire within a few years.[44]

Prof. Hutton firmly acknowledged Valiente's close involvement with all the relevant people made her a superior and accurate source, and one able to cite meticulously recorded details of their ventures in her Notepads.

> Doreen Valiente has described Robert Cochrane as: *'perhaps the most powerful and gifted personality to have appeared in modern witchcraft,'* and she is probably better placed than anybody else to make such a judgement. [45]

---

[41] Hutton, 1999. Op. Cit. p 317
[42] Hutton, 1999. Op. Cit. p 317
[43] Hutton. 1999. Op. Cit. p 460 See ref 31, p 318 *Light from the Shadows'* by Gwyn [aka Michael Howard] plus personal comments by Michael Howard 28th Nov. 1997 & 25th June 1998
[44] Ken Rees in a personal communication, expressed his belief that Prof. Hutton *"didn't always talk to the right people."* Michael Howard (Hutton, 1999 Op. Cit. p 318) is cited by Rees as "a weak source." August/2006 For a more accurate account, see Rees, Ken. *Investigating the Regency* TC # 121
[45] Hutton, 1999. Op. Cit. p 318

Constant pressure to define and re-define the boundaries of Cochrane's Tradition, has stirred up prejudicial attention and some criticism from noted sections of the Craft Community external to the Clan. Their opinions have no bearing upon the matter. Likewise, it has not gone unnoticed by several other people in the Craft that the traditions of others are rarely, if ever, called into question in this way, nor pilloried into defending their own boundaries; nor are they subject to the same scrutiny and criticism.

For example, anyone devoid of an Initiatory status of *for any* line of Wicca, the *Feri-Tradition,* or the *Cultus Sabatti* could *not* claim one, nor could they pronounce opinion upon them and expect to be taken seriously. What is more likely, is that they would receive censure for their folly.

It is a normal and acceptable feature of Admission to receive exclusive status within a closed enclave of people, differentiated from those *without,* literally and figuratively. It would also be acceptable for any of those people to assert and defend those boundaries where necessary, and to expect the support of their peers when doing so. With regard to Wica, the matter is rather more complex as there are several different forms operating beneath that umbrella, of which G. B. Gardner represents the founding, initiatory line.

Of the many groups that follow his teachings in preference to other Wiccan modalities, some only may rightfully claim themselves to be Gardnerian, subject to certain proofs. That initiatory status distinguishes GBG's direct line from other generic forms within the popular Wiccan movement, initiatory or otherwise.

In like manner, within Traditional Craft (new or old) there are so many different forms, systems with family specific myths and folklore. Cochrane's Clan Tradition is specifically dedicated to its adherents as a People, with discreet esoteric practises that are protected by its exclusive rites of Admission.[46]

Those merely *influenced* by what they may have gleaned from its *exoteric* precepts, or who simply wish to work in a comparable manner may not rightfully refer to themselves as: *Cochranian,* or *Cochranite.* By the above criterion, those terms refer only to its own People and no others. As noted above, the terms,

---

[46] In Traditional Craft, Admission is the term used to distinguish an 'initiate', which has an altogether different association within its mysteries.

Cochranian/Cochranite were used by Prof. Hutton to identify that Tradition in less formal terms, to further distinguish those *of* Cochrane's direct lineage from those who might seek to appropriate it by assumption. As a general yardstick, this has served well for several years, but the explanation now requires stringent refinement.

Because Cochrane's line, Tradition and Clan *already possess a title* indicative of its unique and distinct status for those persons of Full Admittance - *The People of Goda of the Clan of Tubal Cain,* these terms present a misnomer, and are deemed inappropriate, To that end, CTC have set down the descriptive parameters that determine its tradition, and its distinction from all others it may have influenced to varying degrees.

The random usage of Prof. Hutton's term witnessed the inclusion of *rooted* to suggest a deeper attribution. The Clan respectfully insist that the terms *Clan* and *Cochrane Tradition* should be properly understood and applied, free of all previous bias and misappropriation. To avoid confusion:

> The only group that could possibly consider themselves as rooted in the *Robert Cochrane Tradition* is the Clan itself. Even those groups and/or covens which are maintained as satellites, that is, those who are oath–bound in troth to remain in allegiance to the CTC, would at best be considered as *deriving* from it. All we have we hold. Those alone would be able to demonstrate any requisite measure of influence and experience of and from that tradition. Only those *in* the tradition are *of* it. Naught else is *rooted* in his tradition, lacking direct nurture *and* continuity as *birthed from within.* [47]

Former members, irrespective of whether they left by choice, or were expelled or exiled from the Clan, are *beyond* it. Any former member who remains an individual practitioner, or moves on to join or assist in the generation of other groups as two former (exiled) Clan members, Ronald White and George Winter did within *The Regency,* do so, completely independently of the Clan, renouncing all former allegiance to it.

As individuals now standing outside the Clan tradition, they may not properly be described as having *derived from The Robert*

---

[47] Robin-the-dart. Candlemas 2016.

Cochrane Tradition, as all connections to it, are relevant only to the time anyone actual belongs within it. Equally, the term, *derived from*, does not extend to former members' works nor to subsequent traditions they might establish thereafter.

Derive and all its synonyms better describe self-propagation *within* the Clan as expansive kin-ship groups, avowed by allegiance. By default that excludes everything else. Only a person within the Clan, is able to say they are Clan; it keeps its Tradition solely within itself. This is why a Clan system is unique.

Joe Wilson's 1734 system typifies the strict definition - *influenced*, and then only in part, by the Clan's exoteric works and beliefs. Having *no* admittance to Robert Cochrane's Clan Tradition, its oath-bound structure, esoteric rites or personal mentoring, 1734 remains created via Clan sources that were *influential* and even *inspirational* to it. Clan is Clan, and nothing else is. 'One is one and all alone and ever more shall be so.'

Sweet Child in Time

Resuming focus upon *The People*, to all kin within Cochrane's Clan, his desire to shift with the passion of our ancestors, to reach out to them, should be fully appreciated. Grieving the scarcity of good apprentices, he was equally mournful of the surfeit of unworthy masters, superficial groups and media hype. Cochrane knew well and to his cost, how striving to be a leader was often at the cost of one's own evolution. More than once he expressed a desire to unburden himself from that heavy duty.

Tensions within the Clan that occurred when White and Winter joined, lasted until his death in 1966, which caused him to falter in his resolve to expand it further. More than once he contemplated abandoning the notion of bringing the Mysteries to more people, and to work instead with his magickal partner and wife, Jane. He conveyed his despondency to Bill Gray, explaining how (certain) members of his group held them back, and that he found the struggle to maintain his authority exasperating. He confessed how this distracted him, and caused him to distance himself from the group. Emphasising how weary he'd become of leading others, especially after the first group had fallen apart years before, he was barely able to disguise his contempt. In his closing comment to Bill Gray, Cochrane added that former brethren had *"gone over to Aradia,"* referring of course to Gardnerian Wica.

Cochrane conveyed to Gray the complete failure of certain Clan members to comprehend and appreciate his quest to revive those deeper Mysteries of the Craft he believed were overlooked and ignored for the pursuit of hedonism and spell craft. Spirituality and an acknowledgment of custom, culture and ancestry were almost non-existent. Thwarted by this under sight on their part, Cochrane became increasingly cynical about the neo-Pagan revival. It served no valid purpose that he could see; they had made no efforts to make it relevant to their 20th century needs, or understanding of science and the universe. Cochrane found himself at odds with their apathy and preference for non-historical twee nostalgia. And so it seemed to his companions, that he'd simply become progressively unreasonable and more susceptible to persistent, deepening melancholia. He turned ever inwards, to his Faith, and to the Mysteries.

> I am master of a small Clan, the devil in fact. I in turn recognise the authority of those who are higher than myself, and that authority, once stated, is absolute, do what we may.[48]

Consider Cochrane's second letter to Joe Wilson, dated as January 1966, in which he offers an explanation and some advice on specific virtues of discretion and silence that concern sub-rosa matters of one's Craft. Cochrane underscores the brevity of the matter:

> I will attempt to explain something of it to you [the Faith] – this will be a difficult task since talking about the People (we describe ourselves as such) is a matter that *every hereditary group trains out of its members*. The religion is even more mystical than most – so *words are very poor approximations* of what we actually discover or feel about our beliefs.[49]

Cochrane was a keen advocate of Shakespeare, whom he considered *"knew a thing or two,"* extoling the virtue of themes he

---

[48] Oates, 2016. *SCSIII* Op. Cit. Cochrane to Gray # VIII p 217
[49] Oates, 2016. *SCSIII* Op. Cit. Cochrane to Wilson #2 pages 365-369

believed accurately portray and preserve the purity of both rural witchcraft at its simplest in *The Merrie Wives of Windsor,* and paganism at its noblest and best in *King Lear.* [50]

> I have a wild theory that he [Shakespeare] spent some time in one of the more advanced clans; and that it was during his service that he first gave birth to his silver tongue. Nearly all of the witchcraft of the school I belong to, wraps its secrets in blank verse and kennings. Robert Graves writes a great deal of nonsense about many things (. . .) but he was absolutely accurate when he wrote that the protean goddess was the true inspirer of the poet. (. . .) The latter day Wica should read Shakespeare and throw Aradia overboard[51]

This candid statement denounces *all contrary opinion*, expressed by those who have ignored Cochrane's own stance on all matters relating to his Faith, of its Mythos and of his views regarding others following an entirely different path. An entire book could be written to counter every incorrect or inappropriate statement ever said or written about *The Robert Cochrane Tradition'*, using his own comments culled from letters and articles. Yet the duty and of that task must and should fall to those whose own path requires it.

Academics wishing to study and comment upon CTC's Tradition, especially its beliefs and tenets, might perhaps regard its true source as the key to understanding them. Without the key, attempts to interpret them are fruitless.

Nothing has been written by Clan members about its Tradition for almost two decades. Until recently, everything written, is by those outside, looking in, yet their endeavours cannot breach its depths or complexity.

Nothing is what it seems. Cochrane believed *"The nature of proof can only be shown by inference and of participation, not by intellectual reasoning."* The Clan Mysteries are revealed to the individual only through *direct* mystical contact, a purely gnostic and uncommon praxis in our post-modern era. Engagement rather than analysis – a concept entirely dissimilar to regulated and rigid dogma bound belief systems.

---

[50] Oates, 2016. *SCSIII* Op. Cit. Cochrane to Gray #X p 174
[51] Oates, 2016. *SCSIII* Op. Cit. Cochrane to Gray #IX p 182

Academia accepts it knows next to nothing of the Eleusinian Mysteries. Everything written and recorded of its rites arises from the perspective of an outsider. Opinion, no matter how learned, falls away when compared to any exposition, no matter how meagre, from an official exponent of those initiatory Mysteries. Only direct, first-hand accounts, that draw upon fact and provenance should set a valid base line for study.

With regard to the subjectivity of what is implicit, and therefore apparent only to an initiate of any mystery tradition, one researcher admitted that the very nature of factual evidence renders all speculative verbiage as: *"inadmissible for historical purposes;"* [52] Doyle White draws keen observation to a close, drafting instead, a biased conclusion founded upon his ability to reject those areas of conflict, dismissing evidence that potentially compromise the falsely conceived conclusion he settled on.

Naturally, Cochrane loved to play the fool and he loved to cast his grey magic to veil and obfuscate his vision and his work from those beyond the parameters of those he called kin. As a *Fool*, Cochrane advised Bill Gray how this trickster role established him as a true *"follower of Tubal Cain, the Hairy One."* Obviously, this is a matter of some lengthy discussion betwixt Cochrane and Gray.

In another response, Cochrane pressed upon Gray his view of the Craft as a repository of occult science, utterly distinct from paganism. He saw that modality as a religious pantheism, a reflection of god's manifest existence within the corporal world, though he conceded a source origin, common to all spiritual philosophies for it. [53]

> I do not ever think I can ever cross the line between them [pagans] and myself, since the basic philosophy is so very different. I really think it is time that a distinction was made between witchcraft and paganism (. . .) there is too wide a gap between religious faith and religious science. [54]

A variety of locations were required for the different themes relevant to Clan Rites, ranging from Hilltops to dense woodland, even caves and chapels. Fires were prepared as standard practice,

---

[52] Ethan Doyle White *An Elusive Roebuck* www.ethandoylewhite.blogspot.com
[53] Oates, 2016. *SCSIII* Op. Cit. #V Cochrane to Bill Gray p 267
[54] Oates, 2016. *SCSIII* Op. Cit. #VII Cochrane to Bill Gray p 271

centred within two or three designated areas more generally open to the winds and all elements. Deliberate use was made of gloriously dramatic locations. Included amongst his working areas, Cochrane referred to *Burnham Beeches in Berkshire, Wittenham Clumps in Oxfordshire, the Sussex Downs, Cheddar Gorge in Somerset and the Brecon Beacons in South Wales.*

Other areas mentioned in more recent years, are the haunts of those who have followed Cochrane's example in his search for suitable caves, Iron-Age hill forts and rocky outcrops. They *do not* tend to be those he frequented himself.[55] Dark, hooded robes were worn as the Clan paced or danced the Mill around each fire in turn, as the ritual demanded. Their ritual tools included knife, cord, whetstone, cauldron, human skull, a ladle, a cup or drinking horn and a forked staff called a Stang. The Clan use them still.

Cochrane's innovative approach and tangible *otherness,* attracted a number of respected occultists to work with him. His remarkable vibrancy had not gone unnoticed both by those who liked him, and by those who did not. Having an empathic awareness of how he affected those around him, Cochrane utilised it to great effect, manipulating their views in-line with his singular vision. His obsessive preference for working outside is now deemed indicative of his appreciation for animistic and arcane tribalism. Keeping ritual elements close to his chest, his predilection for intuitive workings were noted features, resulting in lengthy, highly experiential rites as raw as they were introverted.

Generating shifts of consciousness by impulsive inspiration, did nothing to ease the comfort of his peers, and this unsettled some of those who worked with him. As *Supreme Master of Ceremonies,* Cochrane orchestrated all players and though the results were undeniably intense, a significant majority of guests and members lacked familiarity with his free-fall format, frequently leaving them utterly fazed. Even so, to date, no-one present as a guest or member, at any of his rituals, has since found its measure elsewhere.

Eschatological and cosmological principles factored into the Clan's Mythos were gleaned from inspired, visionary experience, borne of the well-spring of the Companie engaged in the Work.

---

[55] For example, although the Stipperstones in Shropshire is an area often listed as one of his ritual sites, Cochrane never worked there, only the sites referred to here.

Pushing all boundaries of profound philosophical and theological enquiry, Cochrane endeavoured to preserve a core element of the mysteries to carry them forward into the next generation. He had sensed an acute deficiency of intuition (mystical comprehension) in the occult regimes he encountered, and realised how that paucity, along with a decadent crudity of approach for the old mysteries, had instigated their decline.

Without ingress, they began to fade into obscurity. Too few, he believed, were able to work their mazes and endure their trials. To better fit their attendant (archaic) legends in his own time, he was inclined to admit, "*I have had to break away from the Horn and Knife, and make them different. Moon and Mill brought back to Myth and Castle.*" [56]

During a Clan working, in which the Oxfordshire cunning-man known as Norman Gills had guested, a poetic vision was shared with Cochrane of a flaming sword, a metaphysical gift Cochrane acquired to advance his gnostic work through the *Gate of Fire,* and the *Serpent of Earth.* Cochrane heeded his friend's advice to utilise *'the power that draws both together'* by devising a very special Rite. Undertaken late in 1965, he felt all grievances suffered to that point were vindicated. Responding to these prophesies, he explains how much he is at odds with the eastern star of Christianity, preferring the *Mill* of his Northern ancestors.

> I honestly believe the Old Ones of Britain did not like their people taking up with foreign gods (. . .) and I have never heard of anyone getting results (. . .) who follow the walnut and the almond, rather than the rowan, the oak and the blackthorn. (. . .) Maybe our Lady will come down to earth once more and we can begin all over again [57]

Lamenting things absent from the Craft, including the ability to read signs, portents and the language of hand and eye, Cochrane desired to restore those mystical wisdoms gained in the five centuries between the age of enquiry (begun in the scholasticism of the 12th century) and its abrupt end in the Reformation of the 17th century.

In a letter to '*a*' Dear Norman, generally presumed to be Gills, Cochrane offered poetic consolation for a bereavement due to

---

[56] Oates, 2016. *SCSIII* Op. Cit. #3 Cochrane to Norman Gills p 296
[57] Oates, 2016. *SCSIII* Op. Cit. #2 Cochrane to Norman Gills p 293

love lost in a recent death. Though it remains unconfirmed which *Norman* Cochrane writes to, his words speak of an eternal tryst to come, in the *Golden Sunrise and Sunset,* as an example of a Traditional Craft sentiment.

A fascinating tenet of Traditional Craft Mysteries concerns the compassion of Prometheus, who, in his heroic intent to advance our race's evolution, invites the wrath of Nemesis upon himself. Such deeply considered origins were to Cochrane, profound truths upon which his die was inexorably cast. Being a thoroughbred non-conformist, his political views could never have won him an approved seat as a peer amongst a middle-class establishment quite content with the status quo. Cochrane's scathing candour frequently developed into parody, with some measure of resentment, he referred to them as: *"the good folk of the fashionable set (. . .) who take tea, have sherry and cake."*

In his eyes, they sought only the flaccid rudiments of passion and were less than tolerable. With gritted teeth, he attended their cocktail parties, book launches and gallery viewings hoping to procure their interest in his innovative vision. Unable to do so, Cochrane responded with scorn and contempt for theirs.

> I am pain, grief, sorrow and tears,
> The rack, noose and stake.
> The flayer and the flayed,
> The hunted and the hunter.
> The Head without a body,
> Thrust upon a stake.
> The body without a head,
> Hung upon a tree.
> Yea! All this, but still I am whole. [58]

Fated to depart this realm perplexed and bereft of mask, he was the proverbial, prodigal son. As a recluse at odds with himself and the world around him, he carried hope along his final pilgrimage that all could be different.

Falling foul of his increasingly irrational and autocratic mannerisms, friends and family abandoned him, one by one. With

---

[58] Oates, 2016. *SCSIII* Op. Cit. #5 Cochrane to Gills. *I am She* – Poem by Jane Bowers pages 331-333

nothing further to lose, he made his gambit. Exploiting his own absolute Faith in the Clan's Mythos, he invoked the Pale Faced Goddess, beseeching Her to witness his petition to complete the work he'd failed to achieve. Deliberately obtuse, Robert Cochrane's writings nonetheless remain exoteric to his Tradition, preserving their original integrity as an exclusive epiphany for each individual Journeyman.

Once more, without the esoteric keys to ensure true comprehension through an attendant mythoi, the variables of interpretation are vast. For the most part, he was addressing others familiar enough with his view to respond in kind, engaged in a two-person dialogue only, or who were so unfamiliar with the material, their responses would be as the student to the mentor, seeking further clues in the very precious and emotively distinct teacher/student dynamic. Open now to public scrutiny, their enigmatic mystery is nonetheless largely preserved.

> No genuine esoteric truth can be written down within an intellectual framework of thought. The truths involved are to be participated in during comprehension of the soul. Truth of this degree is not subject to empirical thought and is apparent only to the eye of the beholder, and to those who have followed a similar path of perception.[59]

Almost sixty years later, the Craft remains as divisive as ever on matters of Faith, belief and the nature of Truth. In common with countless other spiritual minds throughout history, Cochrane recognised Truth alone to be the one constant within all realms where illusion obfuscates the means by which man may come to know himself and know god. His expression of Truth as a sacred and divine tenet remains a controversial topic debated in forums today, where some detractors on the outside looking in, denounce his system of belief as disruptive and prone to chaos.

As operatives of those works on the inside looking out, the Clan are able to observe this perception as a misunderstanding of how change is a formidable catalyst for evolution. Cautioned often by E. J.

---

[59] 'The Craft Today.' *Pentagram* #2, November 1964. Republished in: Oates, 2016. *SCSIII* Op. Cit. p 278

J. about genuine commitment to a magickal path, he noted the true context for this principle, advising that:

> Once you embrace a dedicated magical path, you must live within its bounds and Mythos; to forget that mundane and profane are one, to step out from its boundaries, is to invite Chaos.[60]

Another generation has taken up his gauntlet, avowed to continue that quest with vigour, leading the Tradition ever forward a in accordance with its Ethos. More orthodox Craft modalities are not indulged by the freedoms afforded within Wicca and neo-Paganism, so have maintained a more *discreet* presence, highlighting the diverse factions within the Craft that repudiate the popular stereotypical image of it. Cochrane used the term *religious* quite discriminately, perhaps simply to inspire deeper, more spiritual connections within a Craft he believed had become detrimentally obsessed with spell-work and base 'magics.'[61]

Both Gerald B. Gardner and Robert Cochrane promoted their uniquely idiosyncratic occult philosophies as the tenets of religion, a fundamental concept rejected by many of their latter-day would-be practitioners and followers. Where Cochrane acquired his views and use of magick, is discussed in a later chapter.[62] Suffice to say he believed spell-craft to be trivial, a minor tool of circumstance rather than desire. Preferring the magick (sic) of a spiritual nature within the context of a mystical religion, he believed desire spurred the ardent pilgrim onwards in the quest for experiential Truth.

Nonetheless, religion is a harsh descriptive, wholly unsuited to many modern craft modalities. Primarily, this is because religion has come to typify an erring, proscriptive dogma and predominant intolerance, often to an unacceptable extreme. As a loaded term, religion tends to negate all things of a deeply spiritual nature, though Cochrane's advocacy of it as the measure of each seeker to rout falsity as a harmonic of devotion is naturally upheld.

---

[60] Personal communication between E.J.J. and S.L.O. August 2000
[61] Cochrane followed Cardells example, opting for the 'k' spelling to distinguish a higher form of occult belief and practise than the illusory form of stage 'magic.'
[62] In particular, his *grey magic*, something E. J. J. explained as a glamour of contempt for those he had a low opinion of, wished to keep on tenterhooks, or simply wished to throw off-track, even if it meant playing the fool. It is a traditional tool of art and one both E.J.J. and Robin-the-dart have similarly employed.

In what passes as Witchcraft today, there is as much illusion and unresolved desire as there is in the outside world. In the closed circles of some covens, there is greater bigotry and dogma than ever there was in many sections of the moribund Christian church. Many witches appear to have turned their backs upon the reality of the outside world, and repeat, parrot fashion, the rituals and beliefs that they know have little or no relationship with the 20th century and its needs. [63]

Cochrane believed wholeheartedly that it was better to traverse the path alone than follow anything that lacked Virtue, a qualitative power sourced in the divine. Every seeker is seduced to the occulted artes, even within Companie and Clan; no-one is immune. Ma'at is Cosmic Truth, beyond all mortal perception of it. Her virtue enflames real pilgrims to find expression of those divine principles and each seeker should take up the tools of the smith to forge their own destiny, to preserve honour and to destroy and release that which does not serve evolution in Truth, Love and Beauty.

Cochrane insightfully promoted the strength and purpose of womankind as a receptacle and conduit for a sacred mystery of divine origin. Cochrane and E.J.J. both believed the Maid of the Clan shaped and reflected the Egregore. They described this dynamic aspect of their Craft as:

> A repository for centuries of the deep feminine wisdom, the protector of the dispossessed female – in that it recognises her for what she is, man's total and absolute equal and the goddess' representative upon earth. [64]

Profoundly mystical, these principle expressions of gnostic elements severely marginalised his works, categorising them as 'challenging.' Cultic factions that continue to exploit specific conventions of modern witchcraft as a contrived heritage for the Craft, deem Cochrane's more natural perspective as contentious. Infused with custom based folk magics, the Craft includes certain

---

[63] 'The Craft Today.' *Pentagram* #2 Nov. 1964. Republished in Oates, 2016. *SCSIII* Op. Cit. p 278
[64] Oates, 2016. *SCSIII* Op. Cit. #6 Cochrane to Wilson. p 405

elements and certain praxes of witchcraft, but that does not mean it is predicated upon them.

Acutely aware of the loss of a real cultural heritage in every sense of the word, Cochrane lived each day as a prisoner sensible of that deprivation upon Craft teachings. Alluding often to this realisation as the subjective cause of his personal desolation, he made it his mission to re-claim all that he could through *the five artes of the blood*. The five artes are the higher principles of tradition he believed certain returning souls possessed, wise with imbued knowledge from former service on this particular path of pilgrimage.

Drawn like moths to a flame, a few brave souls engaged him in written correspondence. Not all have been published, remaining obscure; a mercy perhaps? The probability that other letters may occasionally turn up over the next few years should not be discounted. Each one reveals a little more of this very unique individual and his unparalleled devotion to his Craft.

Two letters, discovered in recent years amongst correspondence belonging to the author Robert Graves, depict a politically motivated, vulnerable and somewhat cynical enquirer. [65] Deftly, Cochrane fished that known authority on mythology, testing the waters. Probing, yet cajoling of Graves, the true value of these particular letters is found in their disclosure of the paradigm that sources his legacy, an unseen cipher almost.

Declaring himself to be both: *"a critic and admirer"* of Graves and his work, Cochrane dismissed much of it as mangled and next to worthless. [66] Despite his critique of Graves' poesis, 'The White Goddess' remains a fabulous and intriguing work. Focused almost exclusively upon Celtic mythopoeia, it is a volume incorrectly quoted as a text book for the beliefs of Cochrane's Tradition.[67] That remark could not be further from the truth. Valuing its methodology as a tool of poesis, Cochrane perceived in Graves' intuitive work, a perennial philosophy that appealed to his own assertion that Truth (neither male nor female) is the absolute Godhead. Cochrane

---

[65] The poet and author Grevel Lindop found these two letters from Robert Cochrane to Robert Graves in Majorca during his research for the republication of *The White Goddess*, a volume he edited. These letters are republished in *SCSIII* See Oates, 2016. Op. Cit. pages 200-207

[66] Oates, 2016. *SCSIII* Op. Cit. Cochrane to Wilson #1, December 1965. pages 364 & #12 to Norman Gills p 402

[67] Oates, 2016. *SCSIII* Op. Cit. Cochrane to Bill Gray # VI, 27th May 1964 p 207

declared that until others embrace this principle: *"We are all still babes sucking at the breast of poison."*

Hence it becomes essential to take up the duty to inform, to instruct – to direct towards Truth. The role of 'teacher' is to shield, guard, guide, coerce, tease and stimulate each student to seek beyond their boundaries, safely, where great revelations should entice them towards an understanding of what is NOT truth. By removing illusion, they stand alone to apprehend insights of *The Truth*, in its most Platonic sense.

Cochrane's attempts to explain his adherence to the Ethos of Service, bound in Faith to Fate, brought him only frustration. His mystical beliefs differed enormously from those expressed in the contemporary paganisms he witnessed everywhere around him. Absent of the specific element of *gyfu*, of paying back, and paying forward all that one has received, his directive to: *'Take all you are given, give all of yourself,'* was not widely met.

When describing the matter of Faith to Joe Wilson, Cochrane emphasised that he was not of the Wica. The distinction between what constitutes an hereditary *family* from an hereditary *group*, is determined by the reference to *a People*. By referring to himself as *'a member of the People,'* Cochrane stressed requisite discretion and an obligation to preserve the beliefs of their Faith, saying: *"Therefore, they do not talk about <u>themselves</u>."* [68]

Keen to assert theological differences across the occult spectrum, Cochrane discriminated between what was genuine and of use to his Craft, and those overtly quaint paganisms and superstitions inimical to it. Perhaps through E.J.J.' empathic explanation of how this manifests through a Mythos, clarity may be achieved in their understanding of Cochrane's principle distinctions between his beliefs, and those he believed were held by his neo-Pagan contemporaries.

> One thing they didn't have though, was the Castle of the Goddess, the place we developed and built, shaping it to our beliefs about where we go after death. Most held to a rather nebulous Summer-lands. They also accepted some of the old Gods and Goddess, as did we. But where we differed was in claiming that behind these,

---

[68] Oates, 2016. *SCSIII* Op. Cit. Cochrane to Wilson #2, 12th Night 1966 p 364

there was one supreme deity, and that the Old Ones were no more than aspects of this deity. To the many Gardnerians and pagans of that time, this was a total anathema, as there was nothing beyond them. And in some cases, having wandered off into the Celtic Otherworld, they came back with even more gods and goddesses. [69]

Beyond a fundamental overlap with other pathways into the Mysteries, Cochrane's Craft elevated *occulted* Virtue above all, explored through a spontaneous, trance-inducing regime. He'd perceived the tenets of Wica through those closest to him, brethren who'd once been his companions upon the lonely pilgrimage to gnosis.

Finding the philosophical and metaphysical differences too great, he declared all Wicans and pagans to be: *"Naught but dancing peasants."* By the few he'd encountered, all were judged harshly. He saw only a naïve expression of outmoded paganisms instead of another valid pathway through to the Mysteries, modelled by a few, but very sincere, dedicated initiates. Perhaps he had been unfortunate to know more of the former and too few of the latter.

The Lore of the People

Whether or not one chooses to believe in the validity of the research that strongly supports the actual existence of *The New Forest Coven* or not, for clarity within this exposition, it should be assumed that it did exist. Of course, this relates only to what Gardner created *after* leaving his parent coven, thereafter deemed Gardnerian. More properly named as *The Wica,'* the term was created by Gardner to describe his operative system of modern witchcraft. It remains an initiatory enclave, a distinction that separates it from more recent adaptations based upon it which now include similar movements under the all-inclusive term *Wicca*.

---

[69] Private letter to SLO from E.J.J. (EJJ,L2) See *'TM: Legend'* in the Appendices, where various extracts are scanned in for authenticity and provenance. This comment perfectly empathises the belief in a *'Singular god-head,'* a distinction that distinguishes it from notions of a Triplicity..

The original term 'Wica,' has acquired a qualifying date of 1939 by some Craft historians as the baseline for *all Craft traditions* that appeared after it. That date is deemed by them to indicate Gardner's interaction with his parent coven. That precedent led to the categorisation of everything created after this date as Wiccan (unless an earlier date or foundation proves otherwise of course). Obviously, this is a grand imposition.

The notion that Wicca predates the numerous Craft Traditions known to have their origins in the 18th century, fails dramatically to preserve the scant reserve a real history has provided. The proposed existence of the New Forest Coven prior to Gardner's creation of Wica ironically supports the prior existence of an alternative resource that should be cherished. It provides valid example of certain folk beliefs as discernible ritual praxes.

Traditions vary enormously across class, region and trade; they have no generic form to assert a constructed conformity of belief or praxis. What criteria would persuade opinion that *'The Robert Cochrane Clan Tradition,'* and other traditions within the Craft, are Wiccan, or conversely, are independent of it, and whether or not they are of more recent provenance than 1939, or 1951-4?

The mechanics of procedure are disclosed slowly. Where no provenance exists, works should be examined for theological inferences and philosophical intent. Hearsay and opinion are not valid factors for determining these matters.

Enquiring minds should seek factual validation. The directive to accept what we are merely told is patronising and generates only stagnation of knowledge. No sensible researcher should accept what is explained to them if devoid of authentic sources. Resource based, accountable research into any Tradition is relatively non-existent.

And yet several traditions truly abound with genuine historical precedents. A few years ago, Ethan Doyle White decided against a truly thorough analysis of materials and mythic precedents for his academic treatise on modern Craft traditions, choosing instead to simply apply the 'advisory yardstick' imposed by the 1939 benchmark. He shared with the Clan his soon to be published comparative account of Wicca alongside the *'Robert Cochrane Tradition.'* Implying that all forms of Craft are generically Wiccan,

Doyle White conceded a philosophical distinction only between, "*Thelema and Gardnerian Wicca,* " [70]

Certain systems were discussed in his treatise according to how he perceived their doctrinal theology; of course, Chaos Magick and Thelema are classic example of systems that purport to stand void of such inhibitive factors. Even so, they do adhere to strict pretexts of Law. Therefore, being exactly the opposite of Wicca, he accepted them as being operative *outside* the Classification of Wicca. As it can be argued that Traditional Craft, likewise, is equally devoid of 'set' theological doctrines, and is also subject to strict tenets of 'Law', then it must, by that same criteria, *fail* the Wiccan classification. Needless to say, Doyle White did not apply this logic as a sustained criteria across those systems he incorporated into his study.

There is another distinction to consider that concerns modern practitioners working in a *traditional* manner, who have studied the older crafts and customs of our forebears, be that ancestral lore from the 8th century or the 18th century. Would their works be deemed Wiccan simply because they were revived *after* 1939, and are therefore deemed to be younger than Gardner's Wica?

By the definitions and models employed by some academics, including Ethan Doyle White, then yes they would. As an error bound oversight, this example serves to bewilder, especially in consideration of the vast array of titles and sub-definitions as a means to form a comfortable demographic for labelling disparate groups that choose to stand outside the box.

Post-dating the 1939 Wican benchmark does not automatically imply a praxis as Wiccan! Wicca is defined *by its tenets, by ethic, perception* no less so than other traditions of craft, witchcraft and folk belief. Where these traditions clearly demonstrate a divergence from those of Wicca, they rightly avoid that classification. The arbitrary date is almost irrelevant except for establishing a chronological marker. Those who remain discreet concerning their tenets, cannot be assumed to belong to any category, and are voided from classification. With regard to how historic paganisms were perceived, the following commentary is particularly lucid on this account:

---

[70] Ethan Doyle White: October 2010 – Clan Forum discussion in which he presented his ideas.

The Germans differ much from these usages, for they have neither Druids to preside over sacred offices, nor do they pay great regard to sacrifices. They rank in the number of the gods those alone whom they behold, and by whose instrumentality they are obviously benefited, namely, the sun, fire, and the moon; they have not heard of the other deities even by report. [71]

For those followers of classical religions, it must have been an enormous shock to discover diversity and discretion concerning the beliefs of Clan and Cultic peoples, whose gods and their mysteries relied totally upon very personal and subjective beliefs. Archetypal, ancestral cults were the bedrock of belief and praxis. Holding a reverence for the ancestors and semi divine heroes (of the blood, literal and metaphysical through adoption) has informed many traditional branches of the Craft, and is what distinguishes it from Christianity - reverence of god through the intermediary of saints, and from Wicca - reverence for gods/esses directly.

Despite, differences in theology, the Teuton is generally deemed pagan (polytheistic), the classic Christian (monotheistic); yet both engage the revered dead, be they heroic ancestors, or saints, called upon to act as intermediaries for the divine. Both are distinct from Wicca, which is also (generally though not always) deemed polytheistic, but which does not generally employ or engage intermediaries, preferring to approach the gods directly.

Wicca and paganism share a belief in a host of otherworld elemental forms and forces, completely refuted and rejected by Christianity. Beholding the form invocations and prayers take, has also been a way academics have sought to classify diverse belief systems.

The following Assyrian prayer, could be described as having very *Christian* overtones, so, if lifted from its original *archaic pagan* context and used in a *post-Gardnerian* ritual (as it calls upon an intermediary, and in an obviously Christian manner), would it make that ritual, pagan, Christian, or Wiccan, according to the aforementioned criteria established by some academics

---

[71] Caesar: Gallic war 6.21

A Prayer for the Dying (Assyrian)

> BIND the sick man to Heaven,
> for from Earth he is being torn away!
> Of the brave man who was so strong,
> his strength has departed.
> Of the righteous servant, the force does not return,
> In his bodily frame he lies dangerously ill.
> But Ishtar, who in her dwelling,
> is grieved concerning him,
> descends from her mountain unvisited of men.
> To the door of the sick man she comes.
> The sick man listens!
> Who is there? Who comes?
> It is Ishtar, daughter of the Moon God!
> Like pure silver may his garment be shining white!
> Like brass may he be radiant!
> To the Sun, greatest of the gods, may he ascend!
> And may the Sun, greatest of the gods,
> receive his soul into his holy hands! [72]

As for ritual construct, ceremony is fundamentally universal, having recognisable patterns of *ingress, congress* and *egress*, requiring stages of opening, invocation, communion, dedication and closing. They may even share mutually inclusive elements of fasting, praying and sacrifice. On that premise alone, one cannot say a Hindu Puja consisting of these forms is Wiccan, any more than a Native Tribesman of the Americas, chanting and drumming around his fire, crying out to the sky father is Heathen! Pashupati is an archaic god-form underpinning many horned deific motifs, including *Agni* and *Ganesha*, much revered in the Hindu faiths.

The concept of Goddess Triplicities, (typically, as sets of 3 x3 are akin to the *Nornir* etc. From the *Tridevi Shaktis* to Hekate, Her most extreme forms of destruction, are found in *Kali/Durga* for the purity of the soul; Lakshmi for Creation through all forms of Love, through the hearth, fecundity and love; and *Sarasvati*, for Preservation, through all acts of Wisdom as spiritual knowledge. Male and female virtues of force and form enjoin the sustenance of

---

[72] http://www.sacred-texts.com/pag/ppr/ppr08.htm

the universe to abate the forces of Chaos via the maintenance of Law, - that is, by living in the *'rightness of things'* as a Universal tenet of belief, interpreted culturally, ethically and, finding expressing through all forms of Law and Lore.

There is a thread by which discovery of a commonality and shift from one belief system to another across Europe is possible, recognising the basic ethic, yet celebrating the diverse Mythic theology ascribed to them. Identifiable to men like Graves, a poet, and to historians such as Jane Harrison, who coined the term *Triple Goddess*, this knowledge is apparently far from common.

Hereafter, anyone in modern academia who says '*The Robert Cochrane Tradition*' must be Wiccan because it reveres a Horn-ed god and a Triple goddess, should re-visit their comparative religion studies. The differences reside not in how CTC *craft their gods*, but how CTC *craft their cultural perspectives* of them, in ethos and in their respective mythologies and mysteries, primarily; but in praxis, hardly at all. As a mitigating evaluation, it comes down to why, and what the focus is.

From Sumer to the Summer Isle, ritual form changes very little. Especially so in rites of fertility and of the hearth. Likewise, to announce that the observance of seasonal rites defines Traditional and Wiccan praxes within the same category, shared alongside other neo-Paganisms – again reveals an ignorance of lateral thinking.

To preserve a singular and unique identity requires constant vigilance to avoid sliding into anonymous homogeneity. Maintenance of a tradition as a thriving buoyant entity, requires provision for its growth and preservation and should not induce atrophy or degeneration. Always it must retain a relativity to the people and to time in order to evolve. Survival demands it must not stagnate; once it does, then that tradition no longer serves a useful place in society. Cochrane observed how:

> Symbols contain the seeds of their own revelation, the virtue [essence] of which changes with each group/era using it. [73]

---

[73] 'The Craft Today' *Pentagram* #2 Nov. 1964. Republished in Oates, 2016. *SCSIII* Op. Cit. p 278

Cochrane further supported the dictum that sigils have universal significance, and their expression within the Craft supports the mysteries that stimulate magickal comprehension:

> The Mysteries are also a means by which man may perceive his own inherent divinity; that students of the mysteries are seekers of truth and wisdom, with magick its by product, a secondary device of little real consequence.[74]

Because magick was intrinsically bound to the religious practices of prehistoric peoples, many rituals were considered incongruous for other cultures, whose resolution was to extrapolate only those specific elements of ritual magickal formulae deemed useful. Studying the archaic structure of magickal procedure in the following list, extrapolated from Akkadian ritual preparations, a pattern is readily observed of its preservation into modern formats.

Without compromise to expression or intent, its archaic formulae is found in ritual magic and in Wica. As the origin for this procedure precedes the 1939 benchmark by about 4,000 years, it can hardly be classified as Wiccan. And yet, by these criteria, Doyle White deems a system, 'Wiccan.'

- ❖ Fire and water were seen as purifying forces in a metaphoric and literal sense, in that they carried away or destroyed waste. They were not seen as pagan elementals in the modern understanding of these terms.
- ❖ The rituals were commonly performed at night under the stars, the archaic representatives of each relevant deity.
- ❖ Lamps/fire/torches to invoke deity to destroy waxen images. Fumigations to cleanse and purify air borne contagion cords for binding [metaphoric paralysis] all objects used burned and scattered to winds.
- ❖ Doors and windows blessed and dusted with flour extreme cases of death-wish - victim placed in a circle of flour [life essence of grain deities/shield against lesser spirits directed to perform ill acts]
- ❖ Standards raised to 4 compass/cardinal points.

---

[74] 'The Craft Today' *Pentagram* #2 Nov. 1964. Republished in Oates, 2016. *SCSIII* Op. Cit. p 278

- ❖ Asperge/cleanse/cense the area – use of bell and drum to 'frighten away spirits' – medieval clapping and classical theatre – cacophony abhorrent to them [opposite of harmonics]
- ❖ Pronounced attention fixated upon the Full moon [Nanna/Sin – lunar father/head of pantheon.]
- ❖ Psalms and prayers used then and now, continuously – biblical and Sumerian and Egyptian.
- ❖ Animal generally slaughtered after transference of spell to it – burned or buried with full funerary rites to appease queen of underworld – maintain balance of order/death meted.
- ❖ 'Lifting of hands' in gesture of supplication for invocations and prayers – eventual complex sequence of sigils and symbols to express – [mudra concepts/genuflection/evocation]

This format illustrates very succinctly particular archaic imperatives notable for their inclusion and continuance within many streams of magick. Cult images of deity/icons were believed to preserve the essence of the god in order to receive offerings and prayers, where again, identity was and continues to be made through analogy and metaphor.

A considerable number of sophisticated magickal concepts derived from the middle and near East formed the basis of modern Craft rituals. This is particularly evident in the awareness of the marking of the elementals at the four cardinal points which were once stellar and later attributed to the four winds.

The four Royal Stars, named *Watchers*, seen as guardians (e.g.: Kerubim) were evoked in high places. Their symbols were traced in the air with torches or ritual wands (symbolising air), as their sacred names were called out.

Parallels between these artes and those employed within the Craft of more recent centuries are self-evident. Witches and pagans are commonly depicted dancing or moving in circles and serpentine spirals, yet these were traditional cultural dances of the prehistoric world, preserved in folk custom and lore, frequently performed around either a fire or deific icon!

Folk-lore preserves the legends of faeries, with whom witches were associated after the 16th century, dancing in magical rings with each other, and on occasion, with humankind. Now as then, circles cast, be they gouged into the earth, created from flour, shells, stones, fire, or water, or envisioned in mind, are for celebration, prayer and worship, denoting the mindfulness of sacred space only. They offer no real protective value or purpose except in similar extreme circumstances to those observed in ancient times.

A space is charged by intent. The actions are merely theatre for the mind. Remember too, that many temples in the archaic world, were *round*! Annual narratives relating legends of folk history, are dramatized still, unfolding the themes of creation, existence and evolution in sync with the motion of the stars and of the seasons that accompany them. They are living myths, celebrated in remembrance of our heritage and lineage, in accord with ancient tradition, preserving and continuing humanity's role in the evolution of its own creative legacy.

Following a solar and/or lunar cycle, the rites of Eleusis and Diwali are also seasonal, as is the Scandinavian blót. None of these culturally diverse rites can be deemed Wiccan, despite sharing elements of structural form that has grouped various Craft traditions under that all-encompassing banner, readily applied by academics uncertain *how to properly apply a strict criteria*. Because of the failure to discern and process information more critically, the homogenous umbrella terms Wicca and neo-Pagan, have become meaningless.

Neither do any of the theological labels, used for comparative classification, confer typological universality – that is to say, to use the polytheistic belief of Heathenism, as an example of neo-Paganism, is to apply, by extension, neo-Paganism as a definition even to historical examples of polytheistic faiths from Sumer, to Scandinavia. This renders a great disservice to all faiths and beliefs. In fact, looking at the definition of non-revivalist forms of paganism, we discover that it was:

> A system of interlocking and closely interrelated religious worldviews and practices rather than as one indivisible religion.

And as such, consisted of,

> Individual worshippers, family traditions and regional cults within a broadly consistent framework.

One could say then, that pre-Christian forms of paganism, being largely prehistoric, and therefore devoid of texts, or, later, being concurrent with Christianity, are restricted by transmissions never based in textual form. Primarily dependent upon oral tradition via myth and legend, all artes of craft and tongue were disseminated and preserved mouth to ear, and hand to eye. Therefore, in matters of history, poetry, magick and arte, the spoken word has always been deemed superior to a written record, and in all cases preserved and defined the parameters of folk-lore, that is to say, *the Lore of the People*.

As revived or reconstructed forms of paganism, neo-Paganisms do not adhere to some of the older tenets of archaic belief systems from which they are derived. Specifically, these include generic forms of ancestral cults and clan systems including certain oath-bound allegiances, which are not the same thing at all as oath-bound secrets within other societies and occult systems.[75] Conversely, reconstructed paganisms that fully adhere to those former tenets of belief, should not be termed as neo-Pagan. Nor would they be Wiccan, despite post-dating Gardner.

Having explored all manner of praxis, in prose and verse relating to the correct classification of form and force, one final example is provided in another prayer, this time composed by an historical pagan.

Presenting a significant conundrum, if it were to be used within a revived tradition that post-dates Gardner, would its use within a modern context revert the classification of a revived tradition to a former, archaic paganism, or would the revived tradition maintain its neo-Pagan status in spite of the inclusion and expression of an archaic pagan prayer?

Or perhaps an academic might determine a Wiccan status for the prayer, based on the 1939 yardstick applied to its usage! In reality, in the round, *in praxis*, the definitions blur and account for nothing; they matter only to those who follow those tenets and subscribe to pertinent beliefs.

---

[75] Clan systems were typical across the ancient world, especially Europe, the Mediterranean, throughout India and even the Biblical World etc.

Prayer of The Sower (Finnish)

BLESSING to the seed I scatter,
Where it falls upon the meadow,
By the grace of Ukko mighty,
Through the open finger spaces
Of the hand that all things fashioned.
Queen of meadow-land and pasture!
Bid the earth unlock her treasures.
Bid the soil the young seed nourish,
Never shall their teeming forces
Never shall their strength prolific
Fail to nourish and sustain us
If the Daughters of Creation,
They, the free and bounteous givers
Still extend their, gracious favour
Offer still their strong protection.
Rise, O Earth! from out thy slumbers
Bid the soil unlock her treasures![76]

To add another premise to the mix, Traditional Craft is theologically distinct from Traditional Witchcraft. Because the terms Traditional Craft and Witchcraft have also become synonymous with each other over the last few decades, it does not mean either discipline has always been understood by the terms that now define them.

For this reason, many families and traditions have commonly (though not always) subscribed to the collective term – Craft. Various branches of folk-magic, crafts guilds, charmers, herbalists, cunning men/women and syncretic faith practises, are all further distinguished according to regional influences, within Britain especially, and were largely the province of the laboured classes. The range across the fields of philosophy and cosmology apparent within various craft traditions is considerable. A Mythos inculcated as Faith, invokes a cultural perspective that exists as a *lived* tradition.

---

[76] http://www.sacred-texts.com/pag/ppr/ppr17.htm

Of Craft, Clan, old Compton and Charlie Cardell.

Having delved deeply into the pitfalls of terminology, an exploration of Cochrane's early Craft forays will determine what influences shaped his Craft. Together with his wife Jane, Cochrane travelled exhaustively in pursuit of an elusive heritage, reaching up into the Staffordshire canals where they spent a few years during the mid-fifties of the 20th century. These steady communities opened a window into a new wealth of folk-lore and folk-magics. Immersed in their way of life, he felt an empathy, an instinct for their customs and lore. He was convinced they held clues to his ancestral roots. For a few years he was inspired and motivated by these quaint, close-knit repositories of less familiar folk-loric magics and of alternative beliefs that provided the grounding he'd long sought.

Tradition fuelled Cochrane's understanding of the diversity within all that is termed: Craft. The arduous search for heritage, once feared lost to him, drew to a close. Though oft quoted, Cochrane's explanation of a now defunct coven in old Windsor is frequently misunderstood, or distorted to fit another paradigm. Entirely unbidden, he described with discerning lucidity, a coven in old Windsor town his mother had known as a young girl. Cochrane awards the old coven no importance, emphasising the distinction between a defunct coven and the recent establishment of another, entirely separate coven *in his local region* of the *Thames Valley*.

Cochrane explained his own spiritual journey was tied to neither of these, but to another he'd begun in earnest to reclaim as a rightful heritage. His pride in that achievement is palpable. Fiercely, he defended the origins of his family tradition. Without equivocation, having declared his roots were *not* to be found in old Windsor, or the Thames Valley, but somewhere else entirely, he said: *"Our Craft, <u>comes from the Midlands</u>."* [77]

Turning his gaze northwards, Cochrane had sought contact and information from others within the Midlands able to assist his quest further. A rare unpublished thesis discloses a very personal reiteration by Cochrane to its author, regarding his long quest. And how, when quite young (as an early youth), his understanding of the

---

[77] Despite his immediate family living in London, he had many relatives in the Midlands, Some in Australia too.

Craft came from his Grandmother, who lived in Cannock Chase, Staffordshire.[78] Local history records a rather fascinating background for this area now confirmed as where his family sprang from.

Prior to 1974, Staffordshire was the very heart of England, bordered by five counties, some of which he refers to in his letters to Gray, Gills and Wilson: Shropshire, Cheshire, Warwickshire, Leicestershire and Derbyshire.[79] From these regions, he hoped to garner knowledge of his fore fathers in the Craft, literally and metaphysically, from any person willing to share it.

Historically composed of five regions, ancient Mercia is formed of natural hills and peaks that divided tribal regions, allowing settlement to valleys either side, which included the occupation of an iron-age hill fort above them. The valley on the *Tame* riverside (a slow flowing black-water, in likeness of the Thames) was later subsumed by Anglo-Saxons, namely the *Hwicce*, near to the fortified region of *Wodensbury* and the sheltered woodland of *Teottanhahl* (now *Wednesbury* and *Tettenhall*), containing estates of great mineral wealth in charcoal and salt production, and black *Leahs* that provided rich hunting grounds.

From one of those Leahs, a later and very wealthy princess of the *Hwicce* people, named Goda, [80] married into Norman Stock, from whom another family strain arose in those regions. Named *Ferrers*, they established a family name renowned for its horsemen and smiths.[81] Remarkably, it was also here that the Staffordshire Hoard was discovered in 2009.[82]

---

[78] A totally independent and unbiased 'Thesis' written by Michael Bampton in the 1960' on religions and cults of his era, which includes a personal account of his interview with Roy Bowers, aka Robert Cochrane. A copy of this work was viewed and discussed with Ken Rees in February 2016. Reference to it, and extracts from it reproduced here, are by kind permission of Ken Rees.

[79] In modern times those counties are all that remain of the Five Shires that bordered Mercia = East Anglia, Essex, Kent, Sussex and Wessex

[80] Theobald de Verdun, was the end of his line in 1316, whence it extended to the Talbots, one of whom is responsible for transcribing the runes in the 16th century Henry VI Scene vii '*The Shakespeare Name Dictionary*' by J. Madison Davis, Daniel A. Frankforter. E-book 2016

[81] After the Norman conquest, the Verdun family were awarded regions of land mainly in the Midlands around Staffordshire, but also those that bordered it in Leicester, Cheshire, Shropshire, Derbyshire, Warwickshire, and oddly the Saxon region of Farnham in Buckinghamshire that houses Slough, where Cochrane lived. Verdun married a legendary, Saxon princess named Goda, who held a residence in Farnham, though their main residence became established in Alton at Saxon Farley in the region of Staffordshire, from whence she hailed. These families coalesced their forces with those of another major Norman Lord – *de Ferrers*, whose lands within the Midlands established control between Cumberland in the North, to the outer reaches of the Capital in the South. The Midlands were connected to the London environs via the Thames and its tributaries, and most importantly the peoples who lived along them – the *Hwicce*. '*Staffordshire – Warwickshire*' by Thomas Cox, Anthony Hall, Robert Morden; *A History of Staffordshire*, Rev Plot; *The Shakespeare Name Dictionary*' by J. Madison Davis, Daniel A. Frankforter.

[82] https://finds.org.uk/staffshoardsymposium/papers/dellahooke

Armed with a handful only of these facts relating to an historical heritage for the peoples of these lands, and the culture that enriched them, Cochrane began reaching out to others who shared his hunger. In his first response to Joe Wilson,[83] he presented the notion that his Father had been a Horseman, and an expert horse whisperer. Again, both were signatures of Old Craft, rather than witchcraft, which is properly one of several forms of folk-magic preserved within the greater body of the Craft.

Cochrane questioned Wilson regarding the possibility of an extant Clan system in the Midwest, since some of his own family and other possible Craft families migrated there centuries ago. Ever assertive in his desire to raise the issue of legitimacy, Cochrane engaged Bill Gray in similar bouts of inquiry. Referring to the roots of tradition, he boasted of his ability to recall Craft connections back to the 18th century, with particularly regard to his great grandfather, claimed as the last Grand Master of the *Staffordshire* witches.

That tale continues through the actions taken by his own grandparents, whom Cochrane claims were cursed by that same ancestor for renouncing the Craft to become Methodists. The veracity of his statements may not find provable resolve in the legends, but his history has a parallel traceable within them. What is infinitely more interesting here, is how he used the legend as a vehicle to present the subject of *witch-blood* as a particular Virtue.

Composed of five artes (abilities), the fifth is the gift of the *blood*, one Cochrane had already asserted as his birth-right. One person's singular influence is witnessed quite distinctly during these formative years. Overlooked in other histories concerning the life, times and works of this great man, it is an oversight probably due to the fellow in question having his own name and reputation maligned and discredited, written off and dismissed by the Craft in its historical purge?

As an adult, Cochrane's immediate family lived in and around the Soho region of London. Eventually, they settled in Slough along the Thames Valley region circa 1960-1. Their previous abode

---

[83] Oates, 2016. *SCSIII* Op. Cit. Cochrane to Wilson #1, December 1965. p 396

in Soho had been conveniently close to where his own metal-crafting skills were put to use in his brief work on the underground stations.

Moving freely in the heady occult circles of the late 1950s, Cochrane and his friends and associates were far more familiar with one another than many today might suppose was possible for them. From his letters, Robert Cochrane references certain other names and places in cryptic terms that yield little that might aid in their positive identification. Full significance would quite naturally be granted only to the recipient of those letters.

One vague individual, the *old man of Westmoreland*, was a crucial correspondent, though his identity remains an unresolved enigma. Clues offer significant hints, although several other would-be candidates have been pushed forward to date by Michael Howard and John of Monmouth. Highest on their list of possible named suspects are Norman Gills, Bill Gray, and George Stannard/Winter. For various factual reasons, neither of these fulfil the role suggested in that mystery title.

Though older than Cochrane, George Winter's maturity, in common with other candidates, was relative to those around him. Winter could not really be considered as old in 1966, though he was certainly older than Cochrane.' A former member of *The Regency*, John of Monmouth, implemented a clever visual trick to promote Winter as the 'old man. Using a photograph taken of George Winter many years after these events had originally occurred, the resulting image implied a greater age than he actually possessed at the relevant time.[84] George Winter, variously listed as a clerical worker, a bookie, artist or musician, lived in the London area, quite close to where Ronald White was a teacher.

Monmouth dismissed all other possible candidates to promote George Winter, announcing: *"The Old Man - I know it was George Stannard,"* an insistence he validates with conviction alone. [85] We offer certain proofs with equal conviction he was not *the old man of Westmoreland*. First of all, George Winter cannot be connected to a Westmoreland context. Secondly, an instructional letter from

---

[84] Monmouth, John of. 2012. *Genuine Witchcraft is Explained* (UK: Capall Bann) The author of one of the books this critique repudiates for its false claims regarding the Robert Cochrane Tradition.
[85] YouTube Interview with Karagan. See *The Secret History of the Royal Windsor Coven & the Regency with John of Monmouth*. '9 Sep 2012 - Uploaded by WitchtalkShow https://www.youtube.com/watch?v=WpAAmBpF0Us

Cochrane to Ronald White and George Winter explains *to them*, information he'd received *from the* old man of Westmoreland. Cochrane would hardly need to explain anything to George Winter if Winter had been the real source of that information.

Another letter concerning the flawed execution of *The Broom and Sword Ritual* that ruined an entire ritual, was sent by Cochrane to Ronald White and George Winter, which berates them for failing to understand his instructions, not to mention the ethos of the rite. To proffer George Winter, as both the Westmoreland source and originator of *The Broom and Sword Rite,* highlights Monmouth's inability to comprehend the letter's instructional significance, and his own confusion concerning the Ethos and hierarchy of the Clan.[86]

Speaking of that particular bridging mechanism as something commonly used in Traditional Craft rites, Cochrane stated that a similar system might have been adopted into the practises common to the four noted regions where Wica was widely dominant. This suggests Cochrane was in contact with someone familiar with its system of operation. Perhaps the *old man* he referred to as being 'on the inside' was a Wican? Cochrane offered another easily overlooked clue as to who the *old man* was.

> Spinning without motion between three Elements" this was the way it was in Long Compton, Shropshire, Lancashire and the Isle of Man, and since *one of my informants is now a <u>very</u> old man*, who has been in it all his life - and understands both the Broom and the Sword - I should think it has been traditional for many centuries. [87]

With a nod towards mysticism and the Qabbala, Cochrane continued:

> I agree though about movement - but as you know movement of any spectacular sort is nearly impossible once "Bell tone" has been reached, since by then you are verging up on the other world and preparing to enter beneath the hall of the King. Forgive me for saying so but you seem to be confused slightly as to the actual making of power - this of course is not suggesting that you have

---

[86] YouTube Interview with Karagan. See *The Secret History of the Royal Windsor Coven & the Regency with John of Monmouth.* "9 Sep 2012 - Uploaded by WitchtalkShow https://www.youtube.com/watch?v=WpAAmBpF0Us

[87] Oates, 2016 *SCSIII* Op. Cit. Cochrane to Norman Gills #8 pages 377-9

failed in discovering power, but that you have discovered it instinctively - which will work for you, but for nobody else. The *Star of David* is, of course, the basic explanation of the *Sword and Broom* - do you know how to apply this principle, or have you followed your instincts? [88]

The main issue, however, resides in Monmouth's determined attempt to link Winter to a Craft family tradition, first of all through a couple named *Willum and Mary Maidenson*. Cochrane spoke of this elusive pair to Bill Gray in the past tense. [89] George had an alleged association with *Willum and Mary Maiden* from Norfolk that Monmouth claimed influenced the composite name *Will Maidenson*.

However, the relevance of this name and back-story does not bloom quite yet. What is more important is that the person Cochrane referred to as the *'old man of Westmoreland'* was very much alive and in frequent contact with him at that time, Willum's deceased status negated his and George's candidacy along with it. The second attempted link conflicts with Monmouth's story above regarding George's surname. Although Winter's real surname was Stannard, George had allegedly adopted Winter along the way from a gypsy lady he claimed mentored him in his youth and brought him into the Craft.

Another important factor concerns the very real probability that Cochrane was familiar in the late 1950s with more than one George, making any positive identification extremely problematic. Because conflicting descriptions of George differ so vastly in sources provided by independent people, it is no longer useful, productive or correct to presume that where a George is mentioned, it must automatically refer to George Winter. Several documents exacerbate this issue further; some have George as hand written headers on them, others have George W., as if to distinguish one from the other.

Valiente mentioned at least one another George, better known as Desmond Bourke, a former druid and freemason, and long

---

[88] Ibid.
[89] Oates, 2016. *SCSIII* Op. Cit. In letter VIII to Bill Gray, Cochrane referred to 'Willum' as 'a man I knew' which may have prompted Monmouth to cite Willum as the Old man. An impossibility for many reasons, not least of which because he had been dead for some years, and Cochrane continued to receive mail from the real 'Old man' of course. It is most curious that George Arthur '*Maidenson* '(as he signs himself on the W&C) shares the same initials as George Arthur Melachrino (a famous musician and father of 'Taliesin') p 217

standing friend of hers. Bourke was a good friend to many around the occult scene at that time, and knew Diane Richman very well. He may have known Aleister Crowley, and indeed, it is claimed he did.

At least two detailed descriptions are a match for Desmond Bourke, one of these was made by Hans Holzer, the American filmmaker. His description of the person introduced to him as 'George,' is not only complimentary, but fits Bourke's known profile: *'sophisticated, well-mannered, smart and of several occult factions including Freemasonry,'* [90]

Michael Howard worked hard to first introduce, then to maintain the identities of White and Winter in the public mind. To that end, Howard deliberately misinformed everyone on numerous occasions. An example offered in the following statement made by Howard demonstrates a significant disparity in his presentation of the commentary as if it were Holzer's own. It was not. Howard inserted different names into his adapted version which he gave as Stannard (Winter) and Marian Green. Holzer mentioned only 'George' and 'Anne,' no surnames were given.

> Following this meeting, Dr Holzer was invited back to attend a Hallowe'en ritual held by what he describes as a 'robed coven' to which George Stannard and Marian Green, later the editor of Quest magazine, belonged. This presumably was the 'inner circle' of The Regency. (. . .) it was not accessible by the general public and performed its rituals in secret. Everyone present was wearing black robes and the rite was led by a couple described as the Master and the Lady and assisted by a young woman known as the Maiden. At the b e g i n n i n g of the ceremony, all those present were lightly scourged to 'absolve them of their sins.' [91]

Connecting (Stannard)Winter with 'George,' implicated Winter's presence within those particular rites Holzer had witnessed. Howard's assertion that Winter was the 'George' Holzer had described, created a false persona for Winter, one at odds with the reality acknowledged by those who knew him personally. Holzer

---

[90] Michael Howard adapted a comment made by Hans Holzer in 1967, without a supporting reference. See Jones, E. J. *Roebuck in the Thicket* (ed) Michael Howard, Capall Bann, 2001 p 26. The description is of George Bourke, not George Winter.
[91] Howard, 2011. Op. Cit. *CoC.* p 107

leaves no doubt that he referred at all times to (George) Desmond Bourke.

Identifying Bourke through Holzer's high opinion of the 'George' he met, is supported in another estimation provided by an independent academic researcher whose description of George Winter is considerably distinct and does not reflect Bourke in any way. The 'George' that Bampton met when conducting his thesis on the Craft, refers to Winter's intellect as 'questionable,' and to his form and manner as *'stocky, and uncouth.'* [92]

This unusual corroboration totally contradicts Howard's claim that Winter, not Bourke was the person Holzer met. From everything relayed to the Clan by E.J.J., Bampton's account of the companion of Ronald White fits Stannard/Winter. By contrast again, Bampton opined that Cochrane was highly intelligent and singularly motivated, a mover and shaker of his generation. [93]

'Old' George hailed from Norfolk and was described as having a heart problem and experienced trouble with his foot, a condition Ken Rees confirmed could suggest George Stannard/Winter, who was known to suffer from these complaints a decade later when Rees knew him in London during the late seventies. [94] Certain people were evidently known to different people at different times. After E.J.J., Cochrane's closest friends and acquaintances were William Gray and Doreen Valiente. He shared with them a special bond and an enduring Craft relationship.

Rather curiously, Valiente used the spelling *'Chalkie,'* when she referred to Ronald White and she believed that George W. (Stannard/Winter) was a figure who featured *later rather than earlier* alongside Ronald White, which suggests that initially at least, White and Winter had not been active together. In fact neither White nor Winter were active in the Clan when Valiente and Bill Gray worked with Cochrane circa 1964-65, to the extent that a reference in Valiente's diary proposes Bill Gray did not know them, only *of* them; a matter raised by another, albeit for a very different purpose ie, the use of secret magical names. [95]

---

[92] Michael Bampton's Independent Research Thesis, Unpublished C/O Ken Rees
[93] Bampton. Ibid.
[94] Ken Rees – Private Correspondence February 2017
[95] Valiente. 1966 Notepads, Op. Cit. November.

And indeed it will be shown that more than one Jean, Joan, John, Ray, Anne, Diane/a and Bill were known in Cochrane's social circle, so the possibility of another Chalky, Ron, and George is not only acceptable, but highly probable – in some cases provable. [96] On all counts, the irregularities concerning old George/George W. and of Chalky/Chalkie invite further research.

Valiente's investigations of Stannard/Winter in July 1966, suggest her familiarity with him was considerably less than some others had previously expected. But it does reveal she knew well those who were actual members and those whose membership was merely presumed from their proximity to Robert Cochrane and to the Clan, throughout the sixties, and up to his death. George Winter received little or no mention in her diaries, whereas George Desmond Bourke features with some frequency.

Of the *Compton folk*, Cochrane said very little, except to assert *they* had taught him many things, including the secrets of *'wand and stone.'* Again, not to dismiss too hastily other considerations, Cochrane had far better cause to refer here to the canal folk – the Bargees who worked the canals around the Midlands, shifting southwards down to the Ridgeway regions of (what is now) Oxfordshire and along the Thames into London.

One idea currently in circulation on forums and websites that connects Cochrane with the Rollright stones at Compton, Oxfordshire, was instigated by Michael Howard.[97] Evidence to the contrary is found in the correspondence between Cochrane and Gills, that demonstrates a very clear rebuttal of that notion by Cochrane. Admonishing Gills for *his* presumptive error, Cochrane denounced any perceived activity for himself or his people in or near the region of the Rollright stones much favoured by Gills and several notable Wicans.

Cochrane explained to Gills that although the traditions of his people originated in the Midlands, they had never followed the path of the *Long Compton people*, and that their distinct source of wisdom and heritage lay elsewhere. *"Perhaps your Clan and mine could meet one day and discuss things. Staffordshire and Warwick don't come to Long Compton."*

---

[96] See Oates, 2016 *SCSIII* Op. Cit. p 92
[97] Jones, E, J. *The Roebuck in the Thicket* (ed) Michael Howard. (UK: Capall Bann, 2001)

The group's early development was mentioned to Gills, and Cochrane remarked cryptically about his fascinating mentor as an *'old guy from Westmoreland.'* [98] As the *recipient* of this information, Norman Gills is also removed as a candidate. Because his name was put forward by Howard in error of these facts, it increased the confusion along the chain of wagging tongues in the many years since. A few moments of solid research easily invalidates this fallacy.

Cochrane shared generously of his own knowledge with Norman Gills, boasting to him of his wife's skill as seer, his heritage and his Craft legacy. As a later and occasional guest of the Clan, Gills brought to the group his friendship and quaint fragments of cunning lore. Although it is clear they met only a little over a year before Cochrane's death, Gills became a person Cochrane was reliant upon in the last few months before his death in 1966. Plentiful exchanges relative to the lore of their Craft, caused them to pitch their wits. It is abundantly obvious that Gills was the greater beneficiary of their exchange.

Oddly enough, Norman Gills, remained without mention by Valiente until 1966, just after Cochrane's death, at which point she began her investigations into *his* background too. She was an excellent tracker, and pursued pseudonyms relentlessly in her search to discover their real identities. Because of the confrontational stance adopted by the controversial figure *Taliesin,* Valiente eventually proved him to be so much less than he seemed.

Like so many others, including White and Winter particularly, none of these men were major players in Cochrane's game, or indeed the Craft scene at large for over a decade after his death, and so barely received a mention in her diaries, or indeed anywhere else for that matter. After 1974, White and Winter faded into obscurity in the Shropshire hills.

All this information collectively disqualifies *George Winter, Ronald White*, and *Norman Gills*, and possibly even *Desmond George Bourke* and *Bill Gray* as contenders for the old man. None of these could possibly be considered as very old, none were *'born inside the faith,'* and only two of these were external advisory sources. They were all recipients *of* Cochrane's instructions *from* the old Man,

---

[98] Oates, 2016 *SCSIII* Op. Cit. See all letters to Bill Gray and to Norman Gills

(except Bourke, as far as we know) and finally, none of them had any association with Westmoreland.

One other person, John Score, had 'West Moore' in his home address, and is qualified in age and status of being *'inside the pale of the faith,'* his druidic influences add an attractive lure. But beyond their mutual interest through Valiente to establish a representative body for the Craft, nothing else found to date justifiably links Robert Cochrane with John Score.

The sensible thing, is to always work within the parameters set by Cochrane's own words and views in order to secure and harmonise a viable context for his life and work. There has been a general tendency to waiver, wandering into the realms of fantasy by other writers beholden to their personal agendas. Be aware and wary of these. The folk Cochrane met, and who may have influenced him are clearly those people of whom he personally affords credit or time to comment upon.

One other, noted previously as the strongest candidate by far, was Bill Gray, with whom Cochrane exchanged letters for a long time before they actually met. Gray's considerable occult and Craft information would no doubt have proved invaluable to Cochrane. Their exchanges also seem fairly well matched and balanced. Cochrane's manner was blunt, having occasion to bluff and bluster, but his tone still falls short of the approach one makes towards a beloved mentor.

Bill Gray was Inducted into the Clan in 1964 and would therefore have received a copy of the circular 'round robin' sent out to them, in which Cochrane discusses material and information he'd personally received from 'the old man' - *the old man of Westmoreland!* Clearly, there is a need to look further afield towards someone with some true age upon their years. There is so much more to the 'old man' Cochrane speaks of in his enigmatic portrayal as someone: *"Being born inside the pale of the faith who claims hereditary knowledge..."*

Restricted to just a few areas of the country that suggest actual locations for Westmoreland, it is fruitful to learn that Westmoreland and Cumberland formed Cumbria, together with very small parts of northern Lancashire and Yorkshire in 1974 after the new county boundary changes were implemented. Cumberland was the noted region of the border bandit John Armstrong Cochrane refers to elsewhere. It is a region very close to the alleged traditional, robed coven Eleanor Bone was linked to, though how much contact existed between them or around them is difficult to determine; they did have each other's telephone numbers however. Despite this, another, hitherto unexplored option exists within a plausible location much closer to home.

Worthy of a little scrutiny perhaps, several buildings and a couple of streets in London bear the title of *Westmoreland* that collectively encircle an area of London, not too far from the Soho underground stations Cochrane worked on, possibly near to where he'd once lived. George Desmond Bourke frequented that area of London, to visit friends known to those within Cochrane's circle of friends, to meet and socialise. A natural occurrence as they all lived in London at that time, not unusual in any sense. Bourke appears to present a strong candidacy – a druid, GD initiate, magus and of the right age. Very little information is available relating to his discreet Craft activities, so he is certainly worthy of further investigation.

Another candidate who might sensibly bear the title of the '*old man of Westmoreland*,' will not be the popular choice in this list. His story crosses all nodal points, intersecting Wyrd along Cochrane's trajectory, a design worthy of diversion on its merit alone. Stretching a three mile area towards Soho that parallels the canals and waterways as they navigate their way to the Thames, we arrive at *Old Compton St.*

Mentioned by Valiente in her notes, this is the location she'd overheard in enigmatic reference to a random event - a coffee bar opposite the *Star Restaurant,* where someone said she'd heard Cardell's name but could not recall from where. Cardell had offices on Queensgate, around the corner from the Old Brompton Rd, another distinctive location noted by Cochrane who seemed very aware of its proximity to occult and antiquarian shops frequented by a good number of named personages confirmed in Valiente's notes. [99]

---

[99] The region of London under the jurisdiction of Westmoreland sub post – office, encompasses locations flagged by specific inferences to them by Valiente and Cochrane, thereby suggesting deeper implications concerning the mystery of the Old Man of Westmoreland. Cochrane curiously mentions Westmorland and Westmoreland, both noted roads and streets close to the canals and road networks between the city environs and the county of Surrey where Charles Cardell lived. The Grand Surrey Canal was authorised by an Act of Parliament obtained on 21 May 1801. Surrey hosted inland waterway routes that led all the way from the River Thames down through the county towards Guildford before meandering through Sussex towards the south coast.

By some coincidence, Cochrane mentioned *Old Compton;* an area commonly assumed by Howard to refer to a quite distinct region of Oxfordshire better known for the location of the Rollright stones. However, that county border, at the opposite end to the county of Buckinghamshire as Cochrane knew it, was a county that would only later be changed to Oxfordshire in the boundary changes of 1974. [100]

Serendipity affords the surety that experience teaches the rule regarding coincidence. So it is quite unsurprising to discover that *Westmoreland* Road snakes within a couple of miles of Soho (where Cochrane once lived), before leading into a major link road heading towards Surrey, past the former Charlwood estate and onetime home to Charles and Mary Cardell.

On this estate, notorious events of the early 1960s provided a catalyst for so many personages active in the Craft and occult scene at that time! Many who ventured there were well known to Cochrane. Cardell lived at Charlwood through the 1950s & 60s, until bankruptcy forced him to sell in the 1970s, just a few years before his own troubled death in 1977 at the approximate age of 84.

Although contextual events present a strong and interesting candidate in Cardell *as* the old man, and the most probable of all others put forward to date, there is insufficient evidence to claim him *definitively* as such. With only circumstantial evidence, it is impossible to prove one way or the other. The possibility exists only because of the intriguing coincidences that link their paths. Several of Cardell's traits appear mirrored in Cochrane. These are again, beyond the realms of supposed co-incidence. Cardell, would be a wild card – someone seemingly incongruous at this stage.

See:
http://cyclingfromguildford.co.uk/RotherhitheGuide.pdf
http://walworthsociety.co.uk/attachments/article/151/WalworthRoad-HistoricAreaAssessment-02Sep15.pdf

https://en.wikipedia.org/wiki/Grand_Surrey_Canal

[100] Wiki: The **Royal** Borough of Windsor and Maidenhead is a Royal Borough of Berkshire, in South East England. It is home to Windsor Castle, Eton College, etc The borough was formed on 1 April 1974 as a non-metropolitan district of Berkshire, under the Local Government Act 1972, from parts of the former administrative counties of Berkshire and Buckinghamshire. It inherited royal borough status from Windsor, the site of Windsor Castle. It is the only Royal Borough outside Greater London. The **Royal** Borough of Windsor and Maidenhead contains the towns and villages of Old Windsor and (New) Windsor.

On Cardell's wooded estate in Charlwood, in 1961, a deeply nostalgic outdoor rite stirred in the forests imbued with emotive traces of a northern heritage. Presenting an authentic expression of a Northern *'þing,'* (Thing) that witnesses the *High Seat - Seiðr*, this unprecedented rite remains unmatched by any other contemporary with it, a verification of unique workings distinguished from the popular rites of other crafts and orders. [101]

Murray described a *hooded* coven of notable figures in attendance at the meetings at Charlwood, common enough attire in 21st century occult praxes, but not fifty years ago. [102] Surprisingly enough, at that time, unless coveners performed their rites naked, then all groups, Wiccen, Wican or Wiccan, tended to wear their ordinary clothes, both indoors and outside. Few Traditional folk subscribed to cloaks fifty years ago, but would maintain a low profile in dark and inconspicuous apparel.

Several photographs easily found on the internet bear witness to Lois Bourne, Eleanor Bone, Sybil Leek et al, freely circumambulating the Rollright Stones and other ancient sites, around a fire or central altar in high profile, high status silks and tweeds, bedecked with strings of pearls! The men were no less dazzling, strutting as peacocks in their smartly tailored suits and ties - clothing totally unsuited to rough ground and spitting fires, smoky woods and inclement weather; not a robe in sight! For indoor rituals all clothing was deemed an encumbrance, and became popularly bypassed in favour of the new, swinging, liberating trend of performing *sky-clad*. [103]

Prior to his job as a metal-worker in London, Cochrane and his wife Jane made no secret of the fruitful time spent working those waterways and canals bordering Long Compton in Warwickshire, but more especially where they adjoin Staffordshire, rather than Oxfordshire. Amongst the canal folk and the bargees, his interest in

---

[101] A folk/volk meeting of common law. The Scandinavian Clan or ætter/ätt (pronounced 'ætt:' in Old Norse) was a social group based on common descent or on the formal acceptance into the group at a *þing*. The Clan was the primary force of security in Norse society. Clansmen often held allegiances to preserve honour and name. Unlike the Scottish Clans, those of Scandinavia were not land based. A Clan's name was derived from an ancestor, indicated by its prefix to a typical 'ing' or 'ung' ending.
[102] Valiente, 1964. Op. Cit. Notepad Entry
[103] http://homepage.ntlworld.com/wisewoman/RB%20LIFE%201964.pdf

folk religions and their practises was obviously piqued and proved inspirational in the formation of subsequent groups.

Passing near to Regent's Park and the Regent Canal of the *Blomfield* area of London, the Old Compton road continues, reflecting the waterways and canals of Cochrane's family origins in the County of Staffordshire. Another significant factor is discovered that links the upper and lower regions of the Thames Valley; its relevance will soon become apparent. Those travellers of the waterways, the bargee folk, had enriched his on-going pilgrimage. In his eager obsession to correlate his lost heritage with his burning spirituality and thirst for the 'other,' Cochrane had sought them out.

Piecing together these fractured, personal histories of family and his Craft, especially through those early years, his sense of loss is tangible, but so is elation. One letter in particular, written to Norman Gills, makes oblique reference to this loss. Discussing his involvement in a recently formed local 'cuveen' (sic) in Slough, he was careful to distinguish it from another non-local coven defunct for some decades. Cochrane deliberately used soft archaisms, as if to impress Gills with the antiquity of his connections.

Recalling a certain 'Mrs' Blomfield, mentioned earlier to another of Cochrane's correspondents, it is obvious that Cochrane delighted in the tale of his mother as a girl, engaged in séances, held by a coven in the town of *'old Windsor.'* Its activities had ceased when 'Mrs' Blomfield, as the last surviving member of that quaint coven, finally died. [104] A little research into that lady's spiritual beliefs, raised yet more intriguing factors of supposed coincidence that reside at the heart of the Clan Mythos. The maxims that pre-dominate the fundamental tenets of Cochrane's Craft, are exemplified in the beliefs held by *Lady* Blomfield, (1859-1939) a renowned philanthropist,

---

[104] Quote by Cochrane from his letter of Introduction to Norman Gills, circa 1965 as stated by Joe Wilson. The quotation is interpolated with my own addendums in block parenthesis to elucidate the text for ease: *"I am a member of a* [current] *cuveen, and* [like my parents] *come from a Crafter family, in which the Craft has been practiced for many generations. The local cuveen* [in Slough] *is small, consisting mainly of men* [my friends]*, and of recent making since the* [old lady, Mrs Blomfield, who had been the] *last of the old Windsor cuveen died,* [a few decades ago]. *When my mother was* [merely] *a girl back in Victoria's time, my mother* [had] *helped her occasionally as a 'Maid' for scrying, but she did not tell her too much, and you may know her through reputation, her name was Mrs. Blomfield, and she was of high degree. As for my own Craft, it comes from the Midlands where my people originated. My family tell that my great-grand father was Grand Master for the whole of Warwickshire and Staffordshire, with some sixty 'witches' under his care."* Cochrane to Wilson www.1734-witchcraft.org.uk

champion of the Suffragette movement, humanitarian, noted peace activist and civil rights protestor. [105]

It is easy to see how a young and anarchistic Cochrane would feel inspired enough to take up her colours. All that had moved him as a young man during his otherworldly encounters, all that had bewildered him, began at last to make sense and to be relevant to his strange world. Her words gave vision to his Craft, and a living context for his Truth. As a deeply spiritual person, Lady Blomfield officially embraced the mystical *Bah'ai* teachings, combining her natural articulation of spiritualism through those vital tenets she reflected upon as *the* Faith. Coincidentally, this is the very same title Cochrane chose to express and model his own Craft upon, and one that espoused all the virtues held dear by Lady Blomfield.

Awarded the name *Sitarih Khanum'*(Persian for star lady), she held reverence for nine as a star, a precious symbol of all life and being in the *Bah'ai* faith. The nine pointed star or *nonagon* is a glyph made exemplary by Cochrane's description of the Compass as a (nine point) *Necklace* of stone. [106]

Furthermore, Lady Blomfield's *Bah'ai* faith focuses on the Ultimate Source – Truth, a singularity of deity, of belief, of creation, of existence, guided by avatars/prophets and enlightened priests. Their Word of Truth is explored though prayer, contemplation, and service (to humanity) for the spiritual evolution of the species. Seeking justice and peace, CTC recognise numerous parallels with the core principles of CTC via Robert Cochrane that resonate still with the following:

> When a human dies, the soul passes into the next world, where its spiritual development in the physical world becomes a basis for judgment and advancement in the spiritual world. Heaven and Hell are taught to be spiritual states of nearness or distance from God that describe relationships in this world and the next, and not physical places of reward and punishment achieved after death. [107]

---

[105] http://www.oxforddnb.com/templates/article.jsp?articleid=52531&back=
[106] Privately circulated material relevant to the basic Structure of the Craft. See Box 33 at the Museum of Witchcraft archives on Norman Gills.
[107] http://en.wikipedia.org/wiki/Bah%C3%A1%27%C3%AD_Faith

That Faith also shares a Covenant based on Virtue, and at the risk of pushing credulity to the limit, that as a religion of One, it finds expression through Seven doctrinal Valleys, (or books) fundamental to the core principles of Law. It has three tenets to its creed, and four further Valleys or mystical treatises pertaining directly to the pilgrim's journey. Their book, *Bahá'u'lláh* describes the qualities and grades of the four types of mystical wayfarers:

Those Who Progress In Mystic Wayfaring Are of Four Kinds.

1. Those who journey first in the valley of self-transformed to God-pleasing attributes.
2. Those who journey by rejecting self and patterning their lives after Divine reason.
3. Those who journey purely by the love of God.
4. Those who journey in what is termed a 'secret' and 'bottomless sea.'

This Last Is Considered The Highest Or Truest Form of Mystic Union.[108]

Expressing a common four-fold construct intrinsic to mystical faiths, there are further parallels below in Cochrane's formulated beliefs to the Faith held by Lady Blomfield's. The possibility these tenets inspired his article entitled: *The Faith of the Wise* is substantial:

> Devotion requires proof. Therefore that proof exists within the disciplines of the Faith. The nature of proof cannot be explained, since force can only be shown by inference and by participation, not by intellectual reasoning. The nature of the proof falls into many forms, but amongst the most common are these:
>
> (a) POETIC VISION, in which the participant has inward access to dream images and symbols. This is the result of the unconscious being stimulated by various means. Images are taught as part of a tradition, and also exist (as Jung speculated) upon their own levels. They are, when interpreted properly, means by which a lesser part of truth may be understood.

---

[108] http://en.wikipedia.org/wiki/The_Four_Valleys

(b) THE VISION OF MEMORY, in which the devotee not only remembers past existence but also, at times, a past perfection.
(c) MAGICAL VISION, in which the participant undertakes by inference part of a Triad of service, and therefore contacts certain levels.*
(d) RELIGIOUS VISION, in which the worshipper is allowed admission to the True Godhead for a short time. This is a part of true initiation, and the results of devotion towards a mystical aim.
(e) MYSTICAL VISION, in which the servant enters into divine union with the Godhead. This state has no form, being a point where force alone is present.

These are proofs, since having enjoined with such forces, there cannot afterwards be any doubts as to the nature of the experience. Man suffers from doubt at all times, but to the participant in such experience, the doubt centres around the reality of the external world, not the inner. The reality of such experience illuminates the whole life. Therefore it can be shown that the Faith is a complex philosophy, dealing finally with the nature of Truth, Experience and Devotion. It requires discipline and work; plus utter and complete devotion to the common aim.[109]

As a Faith that holds the symbology of the pentagram to represent the form of man, a microcosmic glyph of the glory or splendour of creation, it finds further expression through five stages of virtue as a lived testament to their Covenant. This reflects exactly no less than the magickal poesis espoused by Cochrane in *The Round of Life*.

The Faith is a belief concerned with the inner nature of devotion, and finally with the nature of mysticism and mystical experience. It has, in common with all great religions, an inner experience that is greater than the exterior world. It is a discipline that creates from the world an enriched inward vision. It can and does embrace the totality of human experience *from birth to death, then beyond.* It creates within the human spirit a light that brightens all darkness, and which can never again be extinguished. It is never fully

---

[109] 'The Faith of the Wise' #2 *Pentagram* August 1965. Republished in Oates, 2016 *SCSIII* Op. Cit. p 347

forgotten and never fully remembered. The True Faith is the life of the follower, without it he is nothing, with it he has contained something of all creation. [110]

Cochrane was thus shaped from the beginning by the archaic beauty expressed by gifted exponents of mysticism in his early forays into other realms and worlds. The die was cast, setting the seal upon which the Cochrane Tradition was founded. Writing to Bill Gray, Cochrane agreed emphatically with the opinions and theories expressed by Jacqueline Murray, a lady familiar with several of his acquaintances.[111] His enthusiasm is again palpable.

Murray had provided the main thrust and impetus into *The Atlanteans*, an innovative body promoting Aquarian phenomena specifically of arcane psychic abilities and spiritualisms. Cochrane deliberated those themes further, albeit somewhat obliquely throughout his missives to Joe Wilson. In turn, Wilson extrapolated some of what touched and inspired him, including it in his own composite teachings through the working ethos established in his 1734 philosophical (occulted) method.

Cochrane made it obvious to Gray that he found Murray's psychic research exciting and innovative. That she knew and worked closely with *Charlie Cardell*, cannot be overlooked. Though their relationship was professional through the research groups and its publications, Valiente was convinced Murray was also a primary member of Cardell's possible 'Queensgate' Coven.[112] It is therefore unsurprising that Cochrane and Gray freely discussed Murray's views and articles in *The Atlanteans*.

This tightly knit social network of people and of books, literature and lectures, highlights again, how anyone remotely interested in the occult during the 1960s was more or less bound to encounter everyone else at some point in time. All these people shared a common interest in scientific and psychical research, a mutual fascination that formed a significant bond between them.

The works of Charles Cardell are featured within the pages of Murray's journal, as an honoured guest of the *Society for Psychical*

---

[110] Ibid.
[111] See Oates, 2016 *SCSIII* Op. Cit. Cochrane to Gray #1 p 188
[112] Valiente, 1989. Op. Cit. pages 66-68, Valiente made several entries to her Notepads citing Murray

Study. It should come as no surprise to learn that Robert and Jane Cochrane were also committed members of the *Society for Psychical Study*. Even less surprising to discover, is that Cochrane's first article should appear within a leading magazine dedicated to psychical studies (1963 *Psychic News*). And though he does *suggest* he personally had *not* met Cardell, his comment is not altogether convincing, particularly when we recall from a later letter, his regrets concerning the way the Craft had treated Cardell. Even harder to imagine, is that he could have failed to make contact with Jacqueline Murray, either deliberately or accidently. He shared his indisputably *personal* impression of her with Bill Gray,.

    Valiente was likewise very well acquainted with Bill and Bobbie Gray, after meeting them in 1961 at specific occult events in London and Glastonbury. Both regions were the known haunts of the *Brotherhood of the Essenes* '(a society through whom she would later meet Cochrane in 1964), *The Atlanteans,* and the *Society of Psychical Research*. Papers were formally shared at these Conferences.

    Around this time, Valiente recorded her own tentative approach to Charlie Cardell. Several conversations over the phone were exchanged with him and later, she met both Charles and Mary at their consulting rooms in the fashionable Queensgate region of London. She also made personal contact with Raymond Howard, Cardell's former acquaintance and creator of the magnificently carved wooden-head of *Atho*. These and several other notable names are flagged repeatedly by Cochrane in his letters to Bill Gray and Joe Wilson. [113]

    Throughout her published and private works, Valiente confirmed these named figures as major players in the Craft scene and as people able to exhibit quite specific knowledge in matters of a traditional nature. She highlighted a private moment shared between Cochrane and herself regarding his mentor, when Cochrane had indicated towards an older gentleman seated upon a park bench in an old photograph, commenting that he was a member of his family. [114] This naturally conflicts with the tale of his 'Aunt' Lucy given to Joe Wilson some years later. [115]

---

[113] Oates, 2016. *SCSIII* Op. Cit.
[114] Valiente, 1989. Op. Cit. p 120
[115] #4 February 1966 http://www.1734-witchcraft.org/letterfour.html

When learning of this from Gills during his stay in the UK circa 1969, Wilson became disillusioned with Cochrane's works, though it should be remembered that any information, especially if it concerns intimate details, if shared with strangers, is rarely the same as that given to those held in deeper trust. And in this case, the story Cochrane told both Valiente and Jones, being close Clan members, was the same. It differed only to Wilson, as someone on the outside of that Clan.

When E.J.J. referred to this incident to current Clan members, he made it quite clear that the lady named as 'Aunt Lucy' was 'sister' to the old gentleman previously referred to on the park bench. As sister to his mentor, she would certainly fulfil the role of 'aunt.' [116] For a number of reasons that soon become apparent, it is quite plausible the persons referred to here are none other than Charles and Mary Cardell.

Cardell's initial friendship with Gerald Gardner and his *Bricket Wood* coven, eventually fell into enmity sometime in 1958, citing Gardner's excessive publicity-seeking as the cause. Perhaps in bitter, vengeful mode, Cardell, under the pseudonym of Rex Nemorensis, published a small booklet entitled *Witch* shortly after Gardner's death in 1964.

Deriding the works of those who'd been his former friends, the publication included extracts from G. B. Gardner's *Book of Shadows*. A vivacious beauty named Olwen Armstrong-Maddocks (aka Olive Greene) has been popularly cited as the spy in their midst, though it remains unproven which side she'd originally defected from, or to. The information she is credited as having stolen from Gardner, may have come from Cardell's own acquaintance with him and/or any speculative initiation he received at the hands of G. B. Gardner. The converse must also be recognised as a possibility.

During the summer of 1959, Charles Cardell claimed he was writing a book about magic and witchcraft, due to be published later that year, around autumn. Cardell, a veteran stage magician, was also an avid student of the psychology & philosophy of Gurdjieff, and well enough seasoned to deliver an influential lecture on Magic presented at the annual meeting of the *Marylebone Spiritualist*

---

[116] http://www.thewica.co.uk/Others.htm and See Oates, 2016. *SCSIII* Op. Cit. Cochrane to Gray #II p 200

Association. [117] Cardell followed on with further talks in October and November 1962 on the subject of *magick*, specifically, regarding his idiosyncratic perspective of it.

Established in the field of psychology, Cardell was well versed in how powerful and persuasive suggestion can be, the importance of words, and how they are used. To that end, his views were very pronounced on the distinctions between theatrical magic and spiritual magick. He loathed the former, perceiving it as an evil influence, delusional, something ruled by the head, and worse, that it induces paranoid schizophrenia. Stipulating that all acts should be ruled by the heart to counter those illusions of the mind, he claimed the most effective means of accomplishing this, were through the artes of *magick*, a purely occulted, emotive modality. A spelling Cochrane adopted when referring to this same principle.

Even so, Cardell was keen to assert that of itself, magick was no more than a romantic term for psychology - a more arcane term for the means of achieving an holistic state of well-being. Magick, first established as an alternative idiom by Aleister Crowley, was for Cardell, simply an awareness that induced calm and peace within. He affirmed how magick was the immediate, correct and instinctive response to a situation enacted without thought (intuition). Speaking from the heart rather than the head, he posited how: *"Magic is what intellectual people think magick is."* It is very interesting to note that Cochrane expounded a similar philosophy whereby: *"We must avoid the trap of intellectualisms."*

Speaking at some depth of these matters to Bill Gray, Cochrane explored the mechanisms employed in various forms of occultism that generate illusion. In particular, he notes why some of them are no longer applicable to the 20th century mystic, pagan or witch:

> Whoa, back Billy boy. Who said anything about contacting the forces of nature? That sort of witchcraft belongs to the shaman, not to us. Natural forces are means to us, not ends, and that sort of stuff dies out with the primitives, Scotch hill farmers and all that. The sort of stuff we practise has little or nothing in common with pantheism at that level. To the best of my knowledge, it has been

---

[117] Valiente, 1959. New Year. Op. Cit. Notepad entry. Museum of Witchcraft Archives.

out since the twelfth century at least, along with the group release of the primitive in tribal ecstasies. We have as about as much in common with it as we have with Catholicism, for that matter, more in common with Catholicism. That was primarily the reason for me being a little uppity about the explanation of the origin of the circle.

To work witch magic properly, one must work outdoors, buildings, unless ectoplasmic displays are required, are useless and destroy 'Virtue.' Outdoors is the law for us, and it is also the law of correspondence necessary to the higher ritual. Nudity, although we do not practise it, has a good psychological effect, for the uninhibited types who are the latter day pagans. I understand, although this may not be correct, that they also regard nudity essential as a means to what they describe as power. Obviously scourging is also strongly favoured because of this. It again is supposed to produce 'Power.' Probably something to do with the release of adrenaline and its decayed by-products to produce psychological effects.

Since they seem to run until they are in a thoroughly suggestive state, the suggestion plays a greater part in this than the scourge. I personally have very little time for such primitive behaviour from sub-topians. It is 'all in the blood,' as one of them told me. In the past, the whip was used because of its symbolic correspondence. The 'Devil,' or his Summoner chased the others in a grim game of 'Hare and Hound.' It is a good way of bringing home the attraction of death, as well as the attraction of life, and a better way of imprinting a 'party line' I have never yet come across. Once someone has learned the symbology, they are very unlikely to forget it again. Forbid that we should ever use it today though. Nothing can ever remain still. Thought must either grow or corrupt. To retain a primitive pattern, is to corrupt mind and souls. [118]

Sharing a mystical commonality with several gnostic fraternities, Cardell's personal symbol was a seven-pointed star. For him, it denoted the seven virtues of: humility, respect, trust, kindness, truth, honour and dignity. He was convinced that working

---

[118] See Oates, 2016. *SCSIII* Op. Cit. Cochrane to Bill Gray #1 p188

with these virtues ensured an absolute state of well-being and total harmony of the self.

A parallel view held by Cochrane echoes this remarkable concept perfectly, where he philosophically asserts that he has seen: *"Seven become one and one become seven."* Cochrane adds that *'Fate is the single name of all gods'* [119] suggesting a complex monolatry, bordering upon monism. For him, *The High Goddess* – the one in seven wisdom, again expresses sublime Sophianic gnostic archons.

Underscoring how the very *'mysteries of the Craft essentially oppose the mysteries of paganism Wica is based upon,'* Cochrane likewise explored the belief in an original, hoary, transcendental god – *"the unknown god, not of sun or fields, but one who represents the transcendental spirit of man"* and his relationship with the Creatrix.

Earlier, in 1958, being no stranger to magazine publications, Cardell had published an article in *Light*, entitled *The Craft of the Wiccens* inviting genuine enquirers to contact him. Valiente, intrigued by several comments the Cardells had made and artefacts held by them, was convinced at that time, they could be genuine Old Craft. Although, when she finally met Charles Cardell, she wrote of her disappointment in his claim to be an adherent and guardian of an arcane Celtic (sic) tradition.

She was markedly disconcerted with his use of the word Wiccen, to define his professed Anglo-Saxon beliefs. A moot point, since the word does exist, and Valiente is again correct to point out that Wiccen is not used to describe a witch. Modern translations that consider the relevance of contextual information demonstrate a better association for the word Wiccen with the reed huts lived in by workers involved in medieval salt production across the Midlands. Perhaps their folklore and beliefs merged with their Craft? And it should be remembered that Cardell did not favour the art or craft of witch and witchcraft per se.

Moving on to describe an icon of his patron deity, allegedly of his tradition, the tiny figure appeared to represent Thor rather than Cernunos. Of course, Valiente rightly asserts that Thor is actually a Scandinavian deity, and Cernunos is not.

And yet so many associations regarding the Northern pantheons have been misappropriated as generically Celtic in popular

---

[119] See Oates, 2016. *SCSIII* Op. Cit. Cochrane to Joe Wilson #2 p 364

culture. From Valiente's brief description, it better suggests neither Thor, nor Cernunnos, but Loki, the horned male deity depicted upon the *Gundestrup Cauldron*. Popular enough, this unique relic is all too frequently presented quite incorrectly as Celtic.

This Scandinavian artefact found in a peat bog in Denmark, even today, continues to confound and baffle many experts and academics. Serving to illustrate so many articles on Celtic related subjects, and for decades now, its erroneous association seems unavoidable. It is therefore entirely possible a misunderstanding, based in historical semantics arose between Valiente and Cardell, each correct by degrees of popular association in their identification of an Indo-European Horned God.

Gundestrup Cauldron

Curiously, both Cochrane and Valiente pursued the mythologies of a horned god in considerable depth at a time when the Goddess was the more popular deity of choice for many people in the early 1960s. As Valiente marked Cardell's public exposure and defamation in the Craft, Cochrane was finding his feet and his own media presence; his wilderness days were behind him, though they were destined to return.

With considered fascination Valiente followed the rise and fall of both enigmatic figures. She spent many years piecing together the puzzles that surrounded controversial affirmations of mysterious traditions, of deeper mysticisms both claimed were precedent to Gerald B. Gardner 's Wica.

Valiente's Notebooks are a tremendous reference resource, that offer numerous clues and insights into events and associations between people, in addition to confirming them. She had been especially keen to trace anyone who might have worked with Cardell 1950-1962, and more importantly, who may have known or worked with both Cardell and Gardner. Her list of suspects name: *Lois Pearson (Bourne), Jack Bracelin, Diane Richman, Charles Pace, Madeline Montalban, Olive Greene* and *Jacqueline Murray,* all of whom were known to have embraced fully or at least flirted with the *Wica* of G. B. Gardner, some as spies and informants, others as true dedicants.

Others, less certain include Raymond Howard & his estranged wife. Raymond Howard, an engineer by trade, went on to develop the *'Coven of Atho'* from the teachings Cardell shared with him during their brief and troubled acquaintance. Any misgivings regarding Cardell's Craft involvement and insight may dissolve in the beautiful phrase *"where two streams meet,"* used by Cardell to signify the Streams of Life and of Death, united as One in Truth is the main tenet of the bi-faced god, Janicot.

Although Raymond Howard did eventually confirm that his mentor, Charles Cardell had never actually seen his crudely carved wooden god mask of Atho, the dark one, Cardell's vision of a horned being of light very probably inspired the crude image fashioned by Raymond Howard. He failed dramatically to comprehend and translate to it the subtleties expressed in the mystical ethos of Cardell's personal insignia, which had been adopted from the *Monad of Dee*. First created in 1564, Dee's mystical sigil, the *Monas Hieroglyphica* signified the supreme glyph of the Universal, Catholic One.

The sigil represents the seven planetary angelic virtues within, encompassed within one overall virtue. Valiente had written in her notes that ATHO - *Addhu* or *Arddhu* might possibly be old Welsh for *The Dark One*, noting the diphthong transitional pronunciation, *dd* to *th*, making the word Arthur. Seims, a Wiccan historian, likewise intuits a connection between Arthur, the bear, the plough and the dark colour of earth.[120] Certainly, there is a strong

---

[120] http://www.thewica.co.uk/coven_of_atho%20article.htm Melissa Seims

connection to the plough, especially as a constellation, and of its seven stars, a lifelong fascination for Valiente, Cochrane and for the Cardells, it would seem.

Throughout 1962, Valiente had flirted with the correspondence course offered by Raymond Howard; from him, she received a great deal of conflicting information regarding Charles Cardell's work and beliefs and the authenticity and creation of the *Head of Atho*. Several years later she was able to piece together what had transpired between them to bring forth an unfavourable end for both men. Charles Cardell had denigrated Wica; Raymond Howard it seems, was an odious fraud. Having borne a grudge against the Cardells for supporting his wife in a divorce case, Howard invited the press to witness a rite held in the woods by the Cardells.

The exposure was as shocking as it was condemnatory, and as inflammatory as it was ignorant. Ironically labelled as *satanic* witches, the Cardells sued the Press for libel; an ill-considered act that eventually left them bereft and broken. Everyone had clamoured into the spotlight, eager for any media attention, desperate to prove witchcraft as an acceptable practice; yet ironically, it conformed to all the worst fears that had haunted medieval demonology.

Tragically, not a single person had actually paused to consider what the Cardells' were saying about their own beliefs, about their view of magick, as opposed to magic, or that the very principle of satanic blasphemy was anathema to their lofty philosophies. As far as the press were concerned, the Craft was simply Witchcraft, and as black as it came.

The tide of prejudice and public opinion was turned against them; there was nothing rational in the consequential wave of frenzied invective. The Cardells' own testimony was totally ignored, they stood as accused, branded with an image abhorrent to themselves. Shadowing the witch craft trials of others, hundreds of years before them. Alone in the dock, broken and in despair, both Charles and Mary Cardell panicked, confessing to seeking out the company of witches, albeit merely to expose them as practitioners of black magic, and as fakers or illusionists.

Cardell explained that his mission was to remove the superstitious fears that form mind blocks, inhibiting progress and evolution of the mystical Craft. Interestingly, during their trial,

Charles Cardell declared in his defence that: *"There are no witches, there never have been, and I don't think there ever will."* [121]

In fact, Cardell had offered to pay £5,000 to anyone who could produce proof of any performance relating one successful act of so called sorcerous or malignant witchcraft. Charles Pace was the only person to come forward, and nothing came of it. An appointed time and place were set up for Pace's demonstration, but the incident never happened. None-the-less, the Cardells lost everything, socially and financially. They both died broken and penniless.

A false rumour circulated after their trial which claimed the Cardells had been cursed and died soon afterwards. They did not. Years later, Michael Howard propagated that fallacy through his own magazine, *The Cauldron*.[122] Charles Cardell died a mere shell of his former self a decade later in 1977, and Mary Cardell, the lady who'd lived alongside Charles as his sister, followed him a few years later still in 1984.

Hindsight yields a measure of revealed wisdom. In revisiting what Cardell said of his beliefs, alongside those he'd shared with Valiente, what emerges is something totally removed from the diatribes Raymond Howard presented to the Press. There is simply no correlation between what Cardell believed and practised and what Raymond Howard accused him of, exemplifies how effective negative and accusative propaganda is against someone whose idiosyncratic beliefs set them apart from the herd. Raymond Howard's gross misinformation, and the tragic trial that it incurred, has overshadowed what was an altogether different exploration into natural, cultural magicks through the heritage of shamanic arte.

Back in March 1961, their evocative ritual in the woods took place, witnessed by several people whose identities have proven elusive, despite Valiente's stalwart efforts. Enveloped within a cove of large stones, several trees emblazoned with mystic symbols, formed a deep and sheltered glade. Mary Cardell, dressed in a deep red cloak served as the scrying Maid. Slowly she entered the clearing carrying a lamp, then she seated herself upon a specific tree, articulated by five sinewy tines. Charles Cardell, dressed in a black cloak, drew a boundary around her with his sword, before

---

[121] Seims, Op. Cit.
[122] Seims, Op. Cit.

withdrawing to silently observe subtle changes in her physical posture as she shifted into and out of trance. To close the rite, Cardell blew an antlered horn and shot an arrow from a longbow into the air.

What Raymond Howard relayed to the press, was a very different and damning tale. His carefully chosen barbs, utterly demeaned the significance of this most profound rite. Stating quite coldly that Mary Cardell was trying to communicate with spirits of their long dead brotherhood and that Charles Cardell was willing Mary to bring forth the voice of a dead Queen of their sect, from the mouth of the Witch Maiden, induced a furore of defamatory condemnation amongst the press and public. Accusations of Satanism were inevitable.

The irony is woeful. Diane Richman, a lady well acquainted with Cardell, boasted that she found Cardell's magick (sic) extremely effective. Discussing this rite with Valiente, Richman admitted her familiarity with the rite, better known to her as: *Man, Maid and Pupil*. Richman recanted her own brief foray into the dark artes, reaffirming her former faith as a Roman Catholic, a deed she claimed Cochrane condemned and cursed her for just days before Dame Fate swept him into the arms of death.

Of the many claims and controversial anecdotes, too few have some basis in fact, enhanced by natural means over time, while others are in stark contrast, offering nothing but fabrication. Contention feeds the drama of society. When it comes down to real work, Virtue speaks for itself - a factor Cochrane quickly realised.

> The nearer I grow to the original Old Craft, the more it points to a science that knew all the answers, but solved in different ways. [123]

Never the Twain

Early in 1963, just as the mood of the time was already turning, things were changing. Possibly due to a slight shift from elsewhere, or even boredom with the science of psychology as it shifted in para-psychology, Cardell's works were coincidentally

---

[123] Oates, 2016. *SCSIII* Op. Cit. Cochrane to Bill Gray #XI p 298-30

phased out, and remained unpublished by his former research associates. With curious synchronicity, Cochrane's works embraced another significant layer in their cumulative and unique complexity. His keen interest in matters connected to psychical research waned, then shifted, although he remained fascinated by the subtle bodies and the manipulation of virtue around them. Cochrane began experimentations into the deep mind, marking a significant shift from the etheric into the Ketheric *Other*.

As a young man, the exploratory aegis of that era, overwhelmed his enquiring mind. His experiences of new and exuberant phenomena, personal and transpersonal, were manifest within his next published article in the 1964 November edition of *New Dimensions,* entitled: *A Witches Esbat.* Something else occurred that garnered Cochrane's wide-ranging but chaotic knowledge into a new trajectory. That influence was generated through the person of Evan John Jones,[124] a kindred soul with whom he formed a deep friendship, impacting both their lives conclusively. Enduring time and tragedy, it had wrestled issues of ego, pride, folly and sorrow.

Of the man himself, E. J. J. held the impression his own *call of blood* lay across the border in Wales, close to his family village. His later involvement in the Craft increased as a gradual process through a youthful encounter, a sealed friendship with another, whose family held considerable farmland in Wycombe. His subsequent adoption into their tradition was to prove momentous in his own understanding of the Craft, impacting further generations of seekers, including the young and very impressionable Robert Cochrane.

Early in 1963, a fated meeting with Jane Bowers, led almost immediately to E. J. J.' rapid Induction then Admission as one of the People within Cochrane's growing *Clan of Tubal Cain.* After drifting around the peripheries of the Craft since the early 1960s, he later met several other crafters Cochrane had attracted to the Hearth, working with them until their own deaths swept them into other realms according to their beliefs, be that all manner of Heaven and Hel as Paradise, the Summer-lands, Tír-na nÓg, Valhalla etc. These were namely: Dick, 'Arthur', Sean Black, Peter (West?), George 'W' and Ronald White (all deceased).[125]

---

[124] Referred to hereafter as E.J.J.
[125] See their website resource: http://ronaldchalkywhite.org.uk/

Amongst those who later became members of the Clan, were *William Gray*, his wife *Bobbie* and Doreen Valiente. Select guests were befriended later still, included *Marian Green, Justine Glass Geoff* & *Louise Hampton-Cole*, and *Gerard Noel*, aka *John Math*, editor of the Occult Magazine – *Pentagram*. Well known to some in the occult circles, one other character, the noted cunning-man *Norman Gills*, herbalist and faerie photographer also attended a couple of rituals as a guest, as did several others who remained only distant associates. Some of these were involved in the establishment of The Regency1966/7.

The Craft scene during the 1960s was small enough to engender a certain familiarity with the various occult factions everyone belonged to. Due to his own familiarity with several Craft and occulted modalities, E.J.J. firmly believed there existed a common enough ground between all of them, to draw their directives closer together. And no-one worked harder than Valiente to persuade others in the Craft to support that view.

Running parallel to these events, several people who'd been particularly close to Cardell at one period or another, now engaged actively with others, to varying degrees. Obviously, within a limited occult society, this could not be avoided. Most, if not all, would, at some point vacillate between relationships and allegiances, for reasons of politics as much as they were personal. Of these, *Charles Pace, Eleanor Bone, Diane Richman, Roy Harris* and his wife *Christine, Lois Pearson* (parted from St Alban's coven in 64), *Gerard Noel* (a former member of Eleanor Bone's coven who left to instigate the *Witchcraft Research Association*) and *Jacqueline Murray* were regularly seen together.

These people were also amongst those closest to Robert Cochrane, and some were guests at his rites. Others are noted in scattered commentary as associates throughout his numerous letters, either by name or by inference. Within a wider Craft periphery, some of these included *Desmond Bourke, Celia Penny, Madge Worthington, Jack Bracelin, Patricia Crowther, Reginald Hinchcliffe, Frederick Lamond, Monique Wilson,* and *Madeline Montalban*. None of these people were strangers to each other, nor indeed to many on the Cardell list above, and most knew and interacted with those of Cochrane's circle of associates and Clan members.

Gathered from a variety of people, Cochrane's letters have finally been published within a much needed chronology, clarifying certain irregularities and misappropriations attributed to them.[126] Eleanor Bone and Lois Pearson/Bourne naturally, had Cochrane's telephone number, and were able to describe to Valiente certain aspects of his praxes, unknown to anyone not formally associated with his method of working.

Valiente's scribblings have provided invaluable background details relative to these matters. Most particularly, she noted how some of those people were able to highlight the significance of the Stang and the high Office related to the cloak. For a long time Valiente had pondered who'd served as mole. Although the circle of occultists at that time was slender by modern social media statistics, Cochrane obviously knew them all to a greater, or lesser extent.

Naming certain people, even if only briefly in his letters determines a time frame for the people known to him, and to what degree his involvement with them extended. In one letter to Bill Gray, penned towards the end of 1963, Cochrane invited Gray to go caving with himself and Jane in Wales, at Llangastock (Crickhowell) to hold a ritual there.

Cochrane had commented to Gray that the two men who'd recently joined the group as his apprentices - John (Evan John Jones) and 'Dick' (almost certainly Richard Swettenham), were not yet up to par for the forthcoming expedition. After flirting briefly with Traditional Craft, 'Dick' did not stay long at all, and very soon returned to his Gardnerian coven. Derek Boothby was also nicknamed 'Dick,' highlighting again yet another instance of repeated names.

Of Cochrane's own group, not all its members stayed, and others were merely guests at the hearth, so it could be justifiably said his influence was very much dependent upon time spent with him and the degree of proximity to the Clan. Anxious to expand his Clan and to reach more people, Cochrane later accepted Gray's invitation to meet Gerard Noel, the soon to be editor of *The Pentagram* journal, confirming that they too had not met prior to 1964.

Without guile, Cochrane informed Bill Gray that he kept a copy of the *introductory forms* required to join a group of the Wica,

---

[126] Oates, 2016. *SCSIII* Op. Cit. Those surfaced to date at least. Several remain in private collections.

specifically Eleanor Bone's Group, to prove for posterity the manner in which Wica, as a movement, sought to make the Craft acceptable. This confirms two things: One, that he had the necessary contacts to acquire those forms, and freely admitted it. And secondly, that he held no regard whatsoever for the Wica path; it held no lure for him at all. [127] Any speculative hint Cochrane had joined their ranks is easily discounted. The entire subject matter was steadfastly refuted by Doreen Valiente, Patricia Crowther and Jean Williams amongst others with the authority and knowledge to do so.

Valiente's notes refer repeatedly back to a specific and growing list of people who had worked with Charlie Cardell. Both Lois Bourne and Eleanor Bone were well known to Cardell and Bone was at one time a very good friend to him. Both ladies claimed Traditional Craft connections; therefore, it is very possible their interest in Cochrane was the common ground they all shared. This deepens further our understanding of his associations with these people, enabling us to dismiss unfounded allegations of a Wican Initiation based upon them.

After Gerald B. Gardner died in 1964, Lois Bourne, his Priestess of his coven at Bricket Wood, left Wica intending to form her own non-Wican group. Feeling restricted and tired of Wican politics, she became somewhat beguiled by Monica English, a beautiful would-be aristocrat who'd joined her coven at Bricket Wood. Entranced, she needed little persuasion to follow her back to a traditional coven in Norfolk where Monica English served as Magistra. [128] According to her notes, Valiente was aware of a growing number of experimental groups working outside the confines of Wica.

One confidant, described the people she worked with, remarking that her Priest and Priestess were married, and that the Leader & Summoner of their group would beat upon the dancers with strips of leather at their meetings Valiente refers to them as a *robed* coven who wore masks, met outdoors and worked silently. [129]

Though unconfirmed, it is highly unlikely the coven referred to here, was Wican. More likely, it was the one in Norfolk, where

---

[127] Oates, 2016. *SCSIII* Op. Cit. Cochrane to Gray #V & #VII, pages 267-271
[128] Bourne, Lois. *Dancing with Witches* (London: Hale 2006) pages 46-55 & 94-106
[129] Valiente. 1964. Notepad entry. December

Lois Bourne briefly dallied, or something more ad hoc, as noted by Valiente. Veiled in the desire for natural discretion, the known facts of this mystery were easily misappropriated.

Few were impervious to Cochrane's charm; opinions of those beyond his own immediate Craft, were not often favourable to him. An initiate of Lois Pearson Bourne, named Cynthia Swettenham, dismissed Cochrane as an *hysteric*. Jack Bracelin, thinking little better of him, described him as a *weirdo*. They were very evidently underwhelmed, a matter Valiente felt important enough to record in her notebooks.[130]

Michael Howard expressed very different views on these meetings and interconnected relationships. Ignoring the facts and the testimonies of everyone concerned, he declared:

> We know even Cochrane slipped off the traditional wagon and got himself a first degree Gardnerian Wiccan initiation! [131]

Howard repeated this claim as if it were accepted fact, always without evidence, and stated countless times in articles, books and online forums. Until finally, when pushed hard enough for proof, Howard responded to the meeting with Bracelin:

> Perhaps C was introducing the new initiate into Wicca to the HP of Gardner's old coven? 'I have no proof to offer on that so it remains speculative, but makes sense. [132]

Despite that lack of proof, and lack of sense, this was picked up and repeated by Doyle White, Barratt, Phillips and Monmouth. Another researcher of those times, its people and events, bears witness to these events. His perspective is very different from Howard's.

---

[130] Seims, 1966, Op. Cit.
[131] Selected & Abridged transcripts of exchanges between Shani Oates and Mike Howard on the 1734 forum in 2012-2014. Howard's contentious comment was presented as fact not opinion.
[132] Ibid. Meetings occur for a number of reasons and do not imply a pathway to Initiation. The reason for that meeting as proved, was due to their mutual interest in experimentation with hallucinogenics. Furthermore, everyone involved in Wica has firmly denounced any Wican initiation for Robert Cochrane.

All of Roy's group were offered initiation by *Bricket Wood*, <u>apart from Roy himself</u>' Cynthia Swettenham in conversation with me, 1974. Also, confirmed in the DV notebooks I remember, although I do not have the reference. Again, no puzzle here. Thus much of discussion re: Gardnerian Myth becomes redundant. 'Dick' could have been Richard Swettenham. [133]

Comments made by Cochrane in his letters indicate that 'Dick' Swettenham did not dedicate himself fully to Gardnerian Wica until at least 1963/4, when he left Cochrane's group and returned to Wica. Another interesting comment adds important context to this matter. Removing all ambiguity, confirmation is found elsewhere; Cynthia informed Rees that her :

> Magical partner Dick Swettenham (who died in 2001) was privileged for 35 years to be a member of the coven of which Gerald Gardner was also once a member. [134]

Swettenham could not possibly have initiated Cochrane prior to his presumed involvement with *The Thames Valley Coven*. Cochrane's letters referring to his membership of a coven that *'went over to Aradia'* indicate it occurred circa 1959–61. This suggests that when these people became of the Wica, Cochrane did not, tying it in with the report confirmed above (by Cynthia Swettenham), that everyone <u>but</u> Cochrane was offered and accepted a Wican initiation.[135]

Valiente had observed certain associations between some of these people, despite natural boundaries relating to opposing camps, which raised natural curiosity, and also foolish gossip. What needs to be established first of all are the reasons that caused for these diverse folk to meet up.

A rising and rather disturbing trend amongst fellow crafters caused Valiente no small measure of concern. It involved experimentation with certain entheogens and hallucinogenic fungi. Bracelin and several others, including Gardner, had embraced these mutual ventures with vigour. A letter from Cochrane to his Elders

---

[133] Ken Rees private email correspondence. Verified by Rees KIR/TH/Imbolc 2017
[134] Ken Rees private email correspondence. Verified by Rees KIR/TH/Imbolc 2017
[135] https://en.wikipedia.org/wiki/Robert_Cochrane_(witch)

around 1964/5 mentions his intent to introduce similar exploratory experimentation, albeit with certain tentative caveats.[136]

Diane Richman, a local police woman in the London C.I.D commented that several people within their particular social circle, were well-known drug abusers; Gerard Noel and Taliesin, especially. Others merely dabbled. In an era that is often retrospectively referred to with affection as the 'swinging sixties,' very few secrets existed. Wife swapping and drug induced orgies were regular social events during this liberating decade.

A proper appreciation of this level of hedonism is essential in order to understand the contextual psychology of their activities. It would however, be quite wrong to say this was accepted or embraced by everyone. Conflict and disapproval came in counter measure. In fact disagreement was no stranger to Cochrane's door and he faced down many internal squabbles and challenges to his authority. The disparity of opinion between himself and other strong-minded individuals did nothing to ease an already thorny path.

A Real People.

Changing tides, chaos, and hope tinged with despair became the cocktail of the 1960s - a corruptive decadence that frequently fuelled the tone of Cochrane's correspondence with Bill Gray circa 1963. With some optimism, Cochrane announced that finally, new people were forming the *"basis of a working group,"* one properly able to 'work' Clan rites. From a previous state of planning, rumination and rejection of ideas, it had finally moved to elements of praxis. Delighted that a commonality of vision allowed further development and exploration of a viable praxis, Cochrane's enthusiasm was unmistakable. In the letter cited below, he described this new and untried group, fixing a context for much that happened before and after it was written.[137]

Throughout their lengthy correspondence, Cochrane enjoyed a respectful familiarity with Bill Gray. Certainly he knew Gray well enough to take him into his confidence, when occasion required it.

---

[136] Oates, 2016. *SCSIII* Op. Cit. Documents 'ii' & 'hh' pages 334-337
[137] Oates, 2016 *SCSIII* Op. Cit. Cochrane to Bill Gray #II p 250

Cochrane had commented upon his former group in a previous letter to Gray, a marked distinction to a later reference to a *second* group. Immediately prior to when Doreen Valiente and Bill Gray joined the Clan, Cochrane commented on other new members to that *second* group:

> The *second group* seems to be organising itself around me, people are happily coming in from all nations and walk of life. My two apprentices have found others.

Cochrane's language is very specific. His reference was to an additional *second* group, concurrent to another *extant*, that is, present group. The existence of a second group within the Clan was not unknown, but it is important to show that Cochrane had made direct reference to them. That two groups were in play may help to explain why Bill Gray had never seen Ronald White and why Norman Gills only guested at one or two Clan Sabbats. Considerable confusion surrounding Cochrane's reference to a second group has led to speculative explanations that did nothing to bring clarity to those on the outside, looking in.

After a very unorthodox introduction, the mechanical genius, E.J.J., ushered the Clan towards a fruitful and productive synthesis of his considerable knowledge and skills with those Cochrane is noted for. Forging their individual traditions into a potent Mythos, the Clan's Egregore thrived. Supplemented by other subtle influences from respected Elders of the Craft, Cochrane's hidden fire was finally ignited, which inspired him to his greatest mystical insights.

The beneficiaries and avatars of this intoxicating core, the primal nucleus were and remain *The People of Goda, of the Clan of Tubal Cain*. What the Clan creates, it maintains. It is entirely whole and greater than the sum of its parts. A core is utterly distinct from an *inner faction* – the core forms the heart and soul of a group, the living macrocosm. An inner faction is a sub-set which is extraneous, peripheral - by default a separate entity. It is neither the source nor the expression of its Virtue, but something a 'part,' fractured from the whole, incomplete.

The next claim advanced by Howard and Monmouth further implicated Ronald White and George Winter as the source of

Cochrane's Tradition, his words and works, and more, that as an (alleged) 'inner faction,' White and Winter maintained the acumen and Virtue of Cochrane's Tradition after his death. Extraordinary and utterly unique, Cochrane's gift of genius was his own, as was his Tradition, Clan and Legacy.

Years of research and study confirm there never was a secret *inner faction* to Cochrane's Tradition, and never could be. That concept is as impossible as it is inimical to the ethos of his Clan. Secret orders and inner factions have their place within Cults where they are better disposed to thrive.

Breaking down the genius that both Howard and Monmouth widely pronounced as a Virtue they believed belonged to White and Winter, several areas of expertise ranging from elements of lore and custom, to knowledge and poesis, were explored in order to expose the claim as invalid.

Monmouth focussed upon specific elements of folklore, highlighting ritual methodology extrapolated from an obscure reference within one of the documents in the cache. Monmouth described it as the 'swing system.' From an historical Craft perspective, the subject of swing style is extremely fascinating.

Monmouth struggled, not realising that swing system and swing style had nothing in common. Because of that, after dedicating a substantial section of his book to explaining what he presumed 'swing system' is, he failed to explain it in terms that are actually relevant to Traditional Craft.

Drawing his own conclusion as to what such an enigmatic term might refer to, he freely admitted he knew nothing of it. Believing that the term referred to popular *Swing* style music of the 1950s that originated in the USA, Monmouth consulted a musician to explain Jazz rhythms at lengths. Grasping at connections that were simply never there, he grossly overcomplicated the matter. [138] Monmouth wrestled with the problematic association with Jazz music which cannot be explained in terms of *swing*. He neglected to add that the *swing element* of Jazz, actually describes the specific emphasis

---

[138] See: YouTube Interview with Karagan. *The Secret History of the Royal Windsor Coven & the Regency with John of Monmouth.* "9 Sep 2012 - Uploaded by WitchtalkShow
https://www.youtube.com/watch?v=WpAAmBpF0Us
and John of Monmouth via private email. Monday, 20 June, 2011.

placed on spasmodic (irregular) *off* beats designed for stimulating *jive* dancing.

What the term 'swing' actually refers to, has absolutely nothing to do with Jazz, off beats, or upbeats, nor to fast-paced dance moves. 'Swing' in a Traditional Craft context, correctly describes the threshing rhythm of a flailing tool beating the wheat and grains upon the ground! The consistent and unwavering *thud, drag, thud,* rhythm is completely incompatible with *swing* as a jive beat, as explained above, but wholly compatible with the Mill dances for circumambulation during ritual. The swing rhythm is exemplary in the *Lame God* Mill that Cochrane loved, and that E.J.J. passed on in turn to current CTC members.

Swing Poles - Threshing Rhythm

A fundamental tenet of ritual shared as basic training between mentor and student, is that which engages effective trance-inducing rhythm - simple, slow and steady. Monmouth credits George Stannard for introducing the 'swing system' (sic) into the rituals used by Robert Cochrane, a strange claim given that White and Winter were Monmouth's mentors.

If that knowledge had been theirs and not Cochrane's to pass on, Monmouth should not have been ignorant of its true meaning. Perhaps a realistic evaluation of independent works accomplished by those credited with Cochrane's genius should be undertaken, and compared alongside his works. Such an analysis would easily distinguish the true source from the false.

When studying CTC's works, follow only genuine sources. Cochrane cautioned Bill Gray against taking everything at face value. He advised him that despite frequent discussion of matters pertaining to CTC's Mythos with others outside the Clan, it maintained its core mysteries by means of a discreet veiling: *"Hekate, Saturn and Hermes are only close approximations of what we believe."* [139]

With regard to the limited elements of Clan mythos Cochrane shared with his guests and outsiders, they might have assumed a focus upon the *Horn-ed God*. To a fair extent, that is true, but ultimately, homage remains predicated upon the Divine Feminine - Fair *Diana, Herodias,* adored by *'Her darling crew.'* The Horn-ed One's manifest presence is always acknowledged via the Stang. Intrepid guardian of the *dancing floor, he is the bridge and link between realms* – the *Lord of the Dance,* no less!

Be aware in particular how these approximations of godhead are incorporated into CTC's beliefs. Bear in mind how these matters are explained by Clan members including Cochrane and E.J.J. Study how the hierarchy of its ancestry is structured and most especially, how the divine is understood and approached. This knowledge will provide a perceptive appreciation for inconsistencies that arise in the works of others, lacking in authority and authenticity.

Under the later auspices of Ronald White's leadership of *The Regency* (mark II), circa 1969, Graves' Celtic poesis was a major influence, providing the mythological structure for its seasonal rites. Alienated from the Clan, Ronald White plumbed his own obsessions with all things Celtic, including Graves' exploratory expositions of *Arthur* and *Robin*. Adopted by White as the central figures of *The Regency* (mark II), they formed the year twins in its mythos. [140]

Robert Graves was additionally mentioned by Cochrane as someone who greatly inspired him. Graves' *explanation of the process* of

---

[139] Oates, 2016. *SCSIII* Op. cit. Cochrane to Bill Gray #II p 250
[140] Monmouth, John of *Genuine Witchcraft Explained* (UK: Capall Bann 2012)

poesis provided Cochrane with a natural structure for the history of mythological thought, and the patterns and symbology therein. Cochrane brought these to bear experientially within his Craft workings.

Wilson, Gills, Ronald White and others, totally miscalculated Cochrane's admiration for Graves' propensity for lateral thinking, falsely presuming it to be an interest in Graves' Celtic bias, in spite of his repeated protestations to the contrary. They could not have been in greater error. It was not the Celtic mythology per se, of Arthur that fascinated Cochrane, but the greater mysteries of the grail, its mystical gnosis and transcendental poesis. More than anything he cherished a heritage in the Mysteries their secular life denied them, a view he expressed with conviction to Bill Gray.[141]

Clan rites and its methodologies are bound within archaic codes of law that evolved under the stricture of Cochrane's guiding hand. E.J.J. explained that although Cochrane had intuited the basic concepts, he had not worked out the relevant practicalities. People he'd encountered so late in life as contacts, were often unable to offer him very little beyond verbal knowledge, hinting only towards the mechanics of ritual in practise. His tragic premature death robbed him of the opportunity to tease out those mechanics over time.

Advancing slowly beyond its original foundations, its connections stretch from the Midlands to *The Thames Valley*. Within his numerous missives to the Clan, E.J.J. explained how traditional elements known to him before joining the Clan en-fleshed communal bones, gifts gleaned in varying degrees by Cochrane throughout his pilgrimages that articulated the basic structure of their Craft.

Working methods Cochrane utilised were again, very different to those employed by his contemporaries in the Craft, and by those who later established the working rites of *The Regency*. Cochrane favoured specific preparation of the ritual area, whereby the Clan's main working area was delineated by a shallow pit marked with ash and soot. This was for ease of sight only, not to create or suggest a finite boundary, but to effectively keep all participants together within the ritual landscape. The method was time-and energy consuming, as befits adult men in their prime. Today, rather

---

[141] Oates, 2016. *SCSIII* Op. Cit. Cochrane to Gray #1 p 188

than disturb the earth to this extent, the Clan use natural markers within the landscape around working sites to set the bounds. Sabbat-fayre remains traditional, consisting of easily transportable foods such as bread, meat, cheese, butter, apples, beer and mead.

The Clan's *Seasonal Rites* reflect to some extent, a Christianised calendrical round of folkloric celebrations and observances. Referred to as *knots* by the Clan, the *Telling of the Maze*, *The Skull and Mound, Crossing the Lethe,* are mnemonic pathways to reach Her Castle beyond – and it is this poesis that continues to beguile seekers within and without this stream.

One foremost Magisterial key imparted to Robin-the-dart, by E.J.J., his successor as Magister and leader of the Clan, involves the arte of *seidr*. This *Rite of Seeing* is one of the four *arts/aetts/airts* that pass between each consecutive Magister of the Clan. Demonstrated through the virtue of the rune *hagalaz*, the flux generated by continual change ensures the Cauldron is ever flowing – for it cannot *'Be Still.'* Established by the traditions it encompassed, the Clan mythos deepened further as knowledge and experience confirmed its philosophical tenets. Cochrane had been aware of the philosophy of *The Rose Castle* but unfamiliar with the rites behind it, an important element E.J.J. provided for him.

Encouraged by creative inclusion, George Winter shared the very basic threads of *a* generic cauldron rite, which should not be mistaken for *The Cave and the Cauldron* rite, one of the four key rites undertaken by Elders which stands outside general workings. Cochrane had knowledge of its philosophies and intent but not the rudiments of ritual procedure relevant to it. Its original form was deemed by E.J.J. as inadequate and little better than table rapping; what E.J.J. shared with the Clan changed the dynamic absolutely, having a resonance more akin to true Old Craft practices.

Everyone had been familiar with different versions of the *Stone Stile* as the *Boundary & Threshold Rite*. Development of *The Castle of the Four Winds* from its raw mechanics, common to the Old Craft, was again, a characteristic collaboration of Cochrane and E.J.J. Together they refined the salvaged vestiges of Craft lore with deeper ritual magicks, shaping its inherent symbolism in accordance with Clan mythos. Not all Clan members had understood its complexity or profundity. In fact, because Cochrane's term as leader of the Clan was so short, some of its members did not gain the experience necessary to undertake these special rites.

The mysteries of the Castle are not easily won; after Cochrane's death, without his or E.J.J.' guidance, Norman Gills and Ronald White were taxed most sorely in their efforts to fathom them alone. More than any other, *The Rose Beyond the Grave* in particular, required the exceptional ritual experience that E.J.J. gifted the Clan.

No definitive history of that period exists, and it is impossible to even consider one that would place everyone involved into the rigid camps desired for them today. Though comparatively few when compared to a modern demographic, their experiential ventures into the Craft, facilitated opportunities in companie all too often denied people involved in the modern Craft and Occult communities. Probably the last of their kind, they were people who *truly* shared their history and yet frustratingly, so many of them remain unknown to us today; their anonymity assured.

III) The Roots of Chaos

The Gardnerian Myth

Phillips' lecture pertaining to the history of Wica, proved to be a popular online document during the 1990s, so its many flaws have been overlooked.[142] Perhaps Phillips had never intended that her work should provide a definitive foundation for all that has been repeated since, and had simply placed too much faith in information received from her oral source, Michael Howard. By way of example, only the most pertinent errors are discussed below, accompanied by succinct, and direct refutations placed directly beneath each quoted comment for ease of comprehension.

---

[142] Initially, this document had cited that considerable information in it had been provided by Michael Howard, whom she had considered to be 'a good authority,' but he is no longer listed on her revised account. See: Julia Phillips - http: History of Wicca // www.sacred-texts.com/pag/wiccahst.txt

> D and C. S. are probably completely anonymous, and if it were ***not for the fact that C initiated Robert Cochrane***, they would probably stay that way! [143]

Anyone reading this might reasonably ask, what *'fact'* exactly, has confirmed this wild claim. To date: nothing at all has even been presented for perusal or consideration. And we have already ascertained from comments made by D &C S – Dick and Cynthia Swettenham, that everything indicates the alleged event was never more than specious rumour.

> Cochrane's origins are obscure, *'**but I have been told**'* that he was initiated into the Gardnerian tradition by C S, and met Doreen Valiente through a mutual acquaintance in 1964. When he met Doreen, however, he claimed to be a hereditary witch, from a different tradition to Gardner's......[144]

Everything that follows any assertion where: *"I was told,"* or *"someone told me,"* indicates only unsubstantiated rumour and should be summarily dismissed as nothing but empty conjecture. To date, and over several decades, this fiction has been ably repudiated by several ranking Wican High Priestesses, Valiente foremost of all. Presented by Howard across several media forums, requests for proofs of these supposed 'facts' from him generated only considerable hostility.

And yet despite Howard's prior knowledge and familiarity with the archived material in the *Museum of Witchcraft,* it was perplexing to witness his insistent yet cavalier references to them, out of context and very much distorted.[145] The following comments are mapped verbatim from Valiente's Notepads.

They reveal the extent of contrary information Howard disseminated based upon them, altered to comply with an agenda that was becoming ever more apparent. As names are mentioned elsewhere and remain within the *Museum of Witchcraft* archive for

---

[143] Ibid. See: Julia Phillips – http: History of Wicca // www.sacred-texts.com/pag/wiccahst.txt
[144] Ibid. See: Julia Phillips – http: History of Wicca // www.sacred-texts.com/pag/wiccahst.txt
[145] It should be observed that Michael Howard had access for many, many years in advance of Clan members. In fact, even when clan members finally did get access to the archives, it was in a limited capacity only. Salient pieces of research material were originally kept from the Clan by the then curator Graham King, a close friend of Michael Howard. Only after the Museum changed hands were we able to freely access all the relevant information.

public and private research, they remain here for clarity. Some of them disclose the names of initials referred to above in Phillips' comments.

- 8 -2-66: Ray Bone has 'Robert Cochrane's telephone number in her address book, given to her by someone called Jack Pilgrim. [146]

- Roy Bowers and Jane were brought to Bricket Wood by Cynthia Swettenham. [sic] Jack liked Jane but thought Roy a 'weirdie.' [147]

- Roy wrote a number of letters to Jack with what Jack called 'a load of drivel.' Jack not impressed favourably by Roy, so they drifted out/apart. [148]

Perhaps at this juncture, we need only to be reminded of Ken Rees testament that:

> All of Roy's group were offered initiation by Bricket Wood, ***apart from Roy himself***. Cynthia Swettenham in conversation with me, 1974. Also, confirmed in the DV notebooks I remember, although I do not have the reference. Again, no puzzle here. [149]

Decades after these events, and after Valiente, Jones, Swettenham *et al* were long passed the bar, Michael Howard repeated several confrontational claims regarding the alleged Gardnerian Initiation that Cynthia Swettenham was supposed to have presided over. The accounts provided by Valiente and Rees expose the impossibility of such an event, and ably dismiss it as fictional nonsense.

Referring to an alleged gift of two remarkable candlesticks. Michael Howard strongly asserted his *belief* they were hand-fashioned by Cochrane for Cynthia Swettenham, his alleged High Priestess. They were supposedly a gift for initiating him into Wica. However Swettenham's opinion of Cochrane was less than savoury, and her extreme contempt for him compromises Howard's claim; her

---

[146] Valiente Notepads. 23/5 Transcript ref: Melissa Seims. Held by the Museum of Witchcraft at Boscastle.
[147] Ibid.
[148] Ibid.
[149] Rees, 2017. Op. Cit. Imbolc -Personal Correspondence.

account is added to several others that expose it to be foundless. Devoid of source material and lacking in evidence, his remarks exhibit only wishful thinking. [150]

Claims are easy enough to make. To be taken seriously requires some measure of proof. It is not acceptable to simply make an open ended declaration without the ability to back it up with something. To have nothing and make such claims is specious and unprofessional. The Clan is fortunate to have other testimonies from those who actually knew Cochrane, and well enough to provide astute character profiles, better knowledge and corroborative comments concerning what he and others known to him, did and did not do.

Valiente's writings present Cochrane as more acquisitive than magnanimous.[151] This made him a keen 'borrower,' who gifted less than a handful of items amongst his dearest and closest friends. At best then, any item thus claimed as a gift from him, may be discussed as an item of curiosity with anecdotal application only. Too often these items are used to validate personal status by association. As in all things, it is perhaps advisable to observe considerable scepticism in the absence of proof.

Another Notepad entry by Valiente delves further into her own investigations into behind the scenes machinations and claims surrounding these much gossiped over people:

❖ Cynthia described to Jack the rituals performed by Robert Cochrane.* Said that they wore black robes and carried 'staffs,' and also used a skull placed upon a pole and practiced 'necromancy.' Cynthia knew that 'Robert Cochrane' is Roy Bowers.

*Valiente had observed that <u>Ronald White</u> was a very good friend of Cynthia Swettenham, and of Lois Bourne. Beyond Cynthia's intense dislike for Cochrane, this shows an intimate, more closely connected occult community than is often presumed in *our* time, for people of *their* time. No matter the tradition, almost everyone was

---

[150] Ken Rees remarks in a private email his observation that Michael Howard was a known fantasist. Op. Cit. Easter 2017
[151] Valiente. 1964. Op. Cit. Notepad entry, November. Doreen was asked to 'procure' certain ritual items for Cochrane. She also gifted him things of her own that he 'liked.'

known to one another, which again proves that acquaintance cannot be correlated with initiatory status. At any time, then or now, such an idea is absurd. Note the following comments by Valiente in this regard:

❖ 8/3/66 *Jack has had conversation with Cynthia Swettenham* [sic] *who knows "Chalkie White as member of Cochrane's* [Bowers] *coven." "Cynthia describes Roy as an hysteric." "L* [Lois Bourne, formerly Pearson] *said, that when **she** formed a group, Roy would be initiated in due course."*

Then again two weeks later when she was investigating strange rumours abound concerning a collaboration of a book project involving Cochrane:

❖ 27/3/66 Story about Roy and Cottie (Burland) collaborating on a book is apparently where Lois Pearson knows Roy, because Roy told me about how he and Jane had visited her.[152]

What can be extrapolated from this, is certainly *not* an initiation with Cynthia, but a very different and extremely fascinating understanding of the complexities of their lives:

❖ Robert Cochrane and his wife met with and were known by several folk from other Traditions.

❖ And that aside from those closest to him, or from his own tradition, almost all of those other people did not like Robert Cochrane, or had little time for him.

❖ That Chalkie (sic) is clearly stated by Doreen Valiente as being in Roy's group, *not* the other way around as Monmouth suggests with some frequency within his book. This point alone is of immense significance to the claims implicit throughout his text, especially when it is confirmed that everyone knew everyone else's business.

❖ That Cynthia's testimony to Ken Rees stands again here by her own admonitions. Which brings into question the alleged candlestick as the gift from Cochrane to her.

---

[152] Valiente. 1966. Op. Cit. Notepad entry - 27/3/66

❖ That 'L,' (Lois Bourne *would* be willing to initiate Robert Cochrane herself into 'a' group, which remains non-specific, if she formed one (in time). It should be emphasised that she had left Wica some time back, and was at that time engaged in a traditional coven. However, under the strained circumstances immediately prior to Cochrane's death in June, any such indulgence was hardly credible.

Looking into the realms of speculation, there is a possibility that as Cynthia Swettenham and her partner Richard (Dick) were also known to Cardell and to Ronald White, the generic coven they all worked in together could either have been Cardell's or White's, or Cynthia's, or Bourne's? Valiente nowhere adds further comment regarding such possibilities, nor that Cochrane had actuated an initiation, nor pursued further than this passing invitation from Lois Bourne.

Valiente privately confirmed to Clan members in 1999 that Cochrane had not pursued that offer. Patricia Crowther also confirmed the same, quite emphatically so, as did Evan John Jones and his own good lady. Naturally, these comments remain hearsay, as they were personally relayed and not recorded on paper. They merely support what Valiente records elsewhere, and what the absence of contrary evidence asserts.

Tolerance for another's path is the mainstay of all true spirituality. Cochrane was no stranger to any of the leaders or initiates of the Wica, being friendly with several of them until his death. He shared several of their interests, as aforementioned, which again, should not be overlooked when seeking motives for contact. In that same letter to Bill Gray, Cochrane hinted at a proposition he'd received from Eleanor Bone, and to the introductory forms. Having friendships with and receiving invitations from any organisation does not however, define nor confer membership.

As a movement so eagerly embraced by the liberated set, it was not unusual for those forms to be made available for enquirers seeking entry into the Wica.[153] Freedom of access to such information was much greater then. Secrecy was phased in gradually, particularly over the seventies, a reaction to so much bad press and exposure

---

[153] Oates, 2016. *SCSIII* Op. Cit. Letters # V & VII from Cochrane to Bill Gray pages 267-271

through several moles. No Introductory forms have been found or recorded, blank or otherwise.

For those of Gardner's line, this dearth is unheard of, especially sixty years ago when the crowd of initiates was still relatively small, certainly small enough for nothing *in house* to escape them. As a system, its data base is essential for affirming the veracity of its countless claimants covering decades of its history, there recorded for posterity. Of those few High Priestesses around at that time, had any one of them brought Robert Cochrane into Gardner's Stream, then someone would certainly have made a considerable hue and cry of his duplicity before now. Proofs to the contrary are most welcome; speculation is not. And to date, only the latter has been forthcoming.

There is a strange twist in the following comment by Howard, used before E.J.J.' death in 2003 and then again afterwards, several times beginning in 2007. Offered initially as a refutation, it appeared in the second book E.J.J. produced through Capall Bann that Howard edited. Later, after E.J.J.' death, the context of this statement was altered when Howard used it to promote the rumour as evidence for Cochrane being a Gardnerian.

> There has always been a persistent rumour that Cochrane belonged to Gardner's coven at Bricket Wood in Hertfordshire in the 1950s, in fact [Jean Williams], the High Priestess of that coven has told Michael Howard that there is no evidence Cochrane was ever a member. [154]

During privileged time spent with Doreen Valiente, the Clan discussed these and other similar rumours, and of deeper matters pertaining to shared commonalities. These included issues relevant to CTC, its histories, and of Wica and its histories. On the subject of Cochrane's alleged Initiation into the Wica, she soundly dismissed it as aberrant nonsense.

Taking that knowledge in addition to the refutation by several prominent ladies of the Wica, including Valiente, it would seem highly improbable the rumour ever had any basis in fact. Cochrane's remaining hand written letters to Norman Gills reveal his

---

[154] Jones, E. J. *The Robert Cochrane Letters* (Ed) Michael Howard (UK: Capall Bann 2003) p 26 and again as personal communication via letter from Michael Howard in 2007.

true state of mind at this point. March was the date given for Lois Bourne's gesture. And it was in March that the second great love of his life, A.M. abandoned him. A month later, his own dear wife and first love of his life, J.B. left with their son, leaving him quite alone. This scenario hardly presents a conducive context for seeking an initiation. [155]

As the group floundered about him, and friendships dissolved, bereft of all he loved in this world, in that moment of crisis in the final two months preceding his alleged suicide, it is beyond credulity he contemplated initiation into anything, especially into a stream of Wica he had so long derided, and by a woman who despised him. He would have been hard pressed to contemplate Bone's, Bourne's or Swettenham's alleged offer into another tradition at such a tragic stage in his life. In fact, according to everyone who knew him, at no time, at the beginning or the end, did Cochrane engage the path of the Wica.

Representing all he deemed to be an utterly false expression of the Craft, his frustration at his own inability to stem the tide of Wica, led him to develop a penchant for what is now dubbed - *grey magic*. It was a glamour based entirely upon obfuscation, preventing anyone, especially ones peers in the Craft, forming a true assessment about one's self. Somewhat harshly, this challenging technique sorely taxed those who began to entertain even a nominal interest in the Craft. Cochrane had allowed himself to bamboozle people until they lost all sense of truth.

Expertly he'd gathered his yarns to weave into all manner of circumstance, leaving the recipient bewildered and uncertain about where the boundaries of fact and fiction began and ended. Because of his propensity to tease the fabric of reality around people, several tall tales have built up around this legendary figure and his life, including the claims listed previously in Phillips' incomplete and inaccurate history.

Within his own contentious articles, Cochrane expressed the need for a radical overhaul of belief and for a return to a community based Craft. He'd long fostered strong opinions of what that community might and might not entail. His opinions found expression through his articles and his correspondence:

---

[155] Oates, Op. Cit. 2016. *SCSIII* p 410

> I am against the present form of Gardnerism, and all kindred movements (. . .) it could be something far greater.

This suggests he was not altogether unfamiliar with other forms of Craft traditions and systems, including Wica, possibly even the form espoused by Charlie Cardell, known as Wicce. Obviously, Cochrane was not fundamentally opposed to the concept of Wicce/Wica, merely how those who espoused its proponents, chose to present it. He recognised merit, but considered that it may be either hidden, or discouraged.

> The inherent philosophy of the Old Craft was always fluid and fluid it must become again before it gasps its last under a heap of musty nonsense, half-baked theology and philosophy. [156]

All too frequently, Valiente's own dogged tenacity to follow everything that transpired within the occult world, remains unheeded. She was incredibly keen to expose contradiction and hypocrisy where she found it, Gardner and Cochrane were no exception. Yet we are directed to suppose that she would ignore the most heinous example of all.

And despite the infamous incident of the *Night of the Long Knives,* that had so enraged Doreen Valiente, she and Cochrane maintained contact and on good terms, in contradistinction to current popular belief. Naturally she was furious with him. She saw all that she had worked so hard to achieve in *The Witchcraft Association* vanquished by public opinion and negative media attention in the wake of this debacle. But they did not remain at loggerheads with each other, Valiente did not share the entrenched vehemence held by others for Cochrane or his works.

Valiente's research concluded the rumour was fallacy, a view supported by CTC. However, there is *no* objection whatsoever to Cochrane's (alleged) Gardnerian initiation being proven as an actual fact, should that ever come to pass. On the contrary, if a man were willing to seek first-hand experience of something in order to be better informed about, that intent could only be admired.

---

[156] 'Witchcraft Today,' published in *Pentagram* #2 Nov.1964. Republished in *SCSIII* Oates, 2016. Op. cit.

Nothing here states, or even suggests the possibility of an initiation into a Gardnerian Coven; the accusation remains foundless and without supporting evidence. Objections oppose the presentation of malicious rumour as fact. Repetition does not validate nonsense, nor make fact of a fiction. A clever courtroom tactic is to place a comment in a person's mind, once there, it is impossible to remove. Rumours and fallacy expand this concept exponentially.

"Extraordinary claims require extraordinary evidence."

~ Carl Sagan

Lucifer – A spectre within the Clan?

Beyond Mind, resides the totality of Godhead. Having considered the feminine virtue – of Fate already, balance demands an equal exploration into the masculine virtues percolated as form, through and within the manifest realms. The Clan's Tutelary deity - Tubal Cain, presides over triune civilising arts of music, poetry and agriculture. Shadowed by His Tanist Self, the psychopompic god of death, a complex *Third* is yet formed through the divine smith, forging and annealing, tempering and shaping the very soul, She infuses with spirit.

Many perspectives of this principle exist, other expressions of the Tubal Cain avatar are widely familiar to most occultists, often in contra-distinction to that found within Clan cosmogony. A popular exoteric view germane to the *Cultus Sabbati,* and some others, was much promulgated by Michael Howard.[157]

They embrace a perspective that plumbs the depths of Biblical associations, presenting Cain as *'first murderer,'* and Tubal Cain as a dualistic artificer of metals.[158] As a subjective principle of belief, it is a view that must be noted as wholly incompatible with that of CTC's Ethos and Mythos.

By way of instruction and example, E.J.J. discussed this distinctive premise at length with Clan members. The following extract is summarised from his personal correspondence with Andrew D. Chumbley:

---

[157] Jones. 2003. Op. Cit. p 29
[158] Howard, M. & Jackson, N. A. 2000. *The Pillars of Tubal Cain* (UK: Capall Bann)

The earth-shattering idea as propounded by Chummy & Co that Tubal Cain can be equated with Lucifer is correct [only] in as much as he can be equated with all other metal deities, and so old, it's positively covered in lichen and cobwebs. All this was explored in the 1960s when it was, after much talk, decided that it was as much use in Clan sense as an udder on a bull. Having heard about it from you, I wouldn't be surprised if the next step will be to make the universe shattering discovery that Jesus in his own way, was a pretty good witch master too!

The only reason it has never appeared beyond a hint in any of Roy's work or mine, is because it was too damned trivial to bother with and didn't advance knowledge one iota, and having been around for so long. I'm baffled that people are so surprised by this, as I thought it would have been one of the basic things one was told when they came anywhere near the craft. It seems as though I called it wrong this time.[159]

Having arrived at this understanding decades ago of the true *Lucifer* as a virtue of illumination - in a spiritual sense of the *lamp within*, E.J.J.' frustration with its mis-appropriation and subjugation into a more primitive and superstitious mold, is unmistakable. He protested its use in this form, as either disingenuous or ignorant. Here again, E.J.J. clarified the Clan's deviation in its Mythos from any Abrahamic stance, and much favoured by Chumbley:

As I said to you on Sunday, the only reason Chummy goes on about Luciferian Craft, is because most people haven't a clue as to what he is on about. As for Roy's work a similar vein, not true. The Luciferian Cult was a Christian Heresy and had nothing to do with it, even though Roy thought Jesus would have made a good witch if he hadn't been born a yarmulke."[160]

Though perfectly acceptable to those workers who uphold this as a personal truth, it illustrates how easily those outside another's tradition or Clan presume false or incomplete understandings of matters that are held discreetly by those within.

---

[159] Oates. S, *TM: Legend* (Create Space, 2016) Personal Correspondence from EJJ to SLO (EJJ,L3): (ADC-1) 17/7/2001
[160] Oates. S, *TM: Legend* (Create Space, 2016) Personal Correspondence from Evan John Jones to Shani Oates (EJJ, L4): (ADC-2) 23/4/02

Far more than those limitations of exilic murderer and smith, who these *Mighty Men of Old* are to CTC, has been explained in depth, elsewhere. [161]

One tenet, taken up at length, explores the gnostic elements within Cochrane's Faith, and considers the veracity and origin of the Luciferian factor within his works. One academic's assessment of these tenets of belief within the Clan Mythos appears misguided by the resilient bias of his principle source, Michael Howard. [162] Doyle White asks if perhaps Cochrane was: "(. . .) *instead purporting a tradition of Luciferianism with underpinning Gnostic philosophies?* [163]

Yet Doyle White seemed determined to perceive a contrary view. Ignoring this acute insight, Doyle White imposed a caveat that he should perhaps reject it on the grounds that he, "*Cannot see any of these implicit references, but am an outsider who is neither a member of the Clan nor a practising occultist.*" [164] His lack of personal familiarity with the subject placed an overreliance on his external source, which led to a summary that is completely incorrect. He states that, "*from the evidence at hand, I am forced to the conclusion that this seems unlikely,*" [165]

Several immediate problems occur with that deduction, not least of which, the suggestion that the origin of the term itself, and its application within the Craft of CTC was a recent evolution and not induced by Cochrane. Attempting to draw parallels upon which to draft his conclusion, Doyle White admitted the Traditional Mythos of CTC is so unlike any other, there is no precedent to *categorise CTC in any genre but its own*.

And yet, he failed to do so, opting instead for a hypothesis based upon a biased interpretation of generic, exoteric works found in selected examples within the public domain. His conclusion was drawn from the criteria he had dismissed as unsuited to the task. For any comparative study there is no appropriate material, CTC are simply not aligned to any mode of work, most particularly none based in Luciferian **Witchcraft.**

---

[161] Oates. 2016 Op. Cit. *SCS I & II & III* and Oates, S. *Crafting the arte of Tradition* (Canada: Anathema Publishing 2016)
[162] Noted in Doyle White articles referenced below.
[163] *An Elusive Roebuck: Luciferian roots of the Robert Cochrane Tradition* - Ethan Doyle White www.ethandoylewhite.blogspot.com
[164] Doyle White. Op. Cit. www.ethandoylewhite.blogspot.com
[165] Doyle White .Op. Cit.

Had Doyle White paid closer attention to how the Craft element of CTC holds a deeply spiritual core, of principles influenced by those of *Luciferian gnosticism* (exactly that principle ethic he'd cast aside), a better and more accurate assessment would have been achieved. The distinction between the *practise* of Luciferian Witchcraft and the inherent *spiritual belief* of Luciferian Gnosticism within an evolving Craft as a lived tradition, is vast in theology and in history.

As a remarkable example, Doyle White's ironic statement that: *'Luciferian Witches consider their faith to be basically Gnostic,'* is deeply troubling, more for the fact that he fails to recognise it as an oxymoron, and therefore wholly inappropriate. Historically, Gnosticism was a dualistic, obsessive religious Faith, of pure spiritual intent; Witchcraft, a practise of destructive malefica based entirely in the corporeality of time and place – the magics of manifest results!

Lucifer shares no object in theology with the Master of Witchery – the Devil himself and neither should be confused with Satan; something to consider when making literal comparisons with that inimical ethos. It is hoped the measure of this work and others centred on this theme will encourage more stringent research. In time this will provide a better understanding, an informed opinion at least, regarding the Tradition and Faith of CTC.

Luciferian gnostic tenets and folk magics are imbedded within the Clan's works, from the early missive's written by Cochrane himself, to other more recent endeavours by those of his Clan who continue to evolve them. Though it is most flattering to be considered responsible for the introduction of Luciferian gnosticism as a core tenet of Clan Mythos, the honour must be declined in deference to those more worthy.

E. J. J.' blunt explanation of precisely how the figure of Lucifer does and does not apply to CTC's Mythos elucidates the origins of the Clan's Cosmology. It shares no force or form with any perspective sourced from an *Abrahamic religion*. Simple and succinct. his explanation has been *unheeded* by student and scholar alike:

> Getting on to your questions. The Mythos of the Fall is great story telling but in a clan and traditional sense, doesn't mean a thing as we have always held to the chaos theory where order came from chaos and things developed from there, so in that sense, Lucifer as

the fallen angel doesn't really fit into our Mythos. Mind you, one of the best stories I've heard concerning the Golden age and the fall is summed up by looking at the Garden of Eden as a perfect piece of espionage. The satanic serpent was an enemy agent operating under the cover as a reptile who enlisted Eve as an asset in place to destabilize the relationship between God and the Garden of Eden. It's a good an explanation as any. And to be honest with you Shani, I haven't a clue what the hell Chummy was on about. [166] I thought he was throwing me a crib just to see what I have to say, a bit of 'disinformation,' then sit back and wait for a reply. Where it is a case of deny and belittle yourself somewhat or claim what he'd known to be a lie. [167]

Lucifer, *"is not a fallen angel."* CTC do not hold to a Biblical premise of *The Fall*, neither of man, nor of an avatar, nor of the principle of Truth, nor in presumed deception and sin of Eve, nor the wilfulness and betrayal of god by humankind in the Garden of Eden. E.J.J.' choice of words suggest no ambiguity, the Abrahamic Mythos does not inform or inspire the Traditional Craft of his forebears, nor of the Faith upheld by the Clan. The Clan Cosmology is sourced in the chaotic creation myths of Northern Tradition.

Later, discreet gnostic influences permeated the philosophies that tutored humankind towards apotheosis, (as the true Luciferian principles upon which) our Craft thrives still. From those early foundations, a spiritual belief explores cognate mysteries and their absorptions during the several hundred years of its evolution.

Doyle White examined another of E. J. J.' works to unearth possible Luciferian references, or at least concepts he might agree falls outside his estimation of what is deemed to represent Wica or modern neo-Paganism. Focussing upon E.J.J.' chapter in *Sacred Mask, Sacred Dance,* Doyle White calls into question the origin and continuity of those ideas based upon information received from his source, external and contrary to them.

As an exposition devoted to the beliefs of Cochrane and his Clan, Doyle White, writes as a confessed non-occultist, a total outsider, which is a fair point to admit. Because of that, he placed too

---

[166] Oates, S. *TM: Legend* (Create Space, 2016) Reference to Personal Correspondence from A.D. Chumbley to E.J.J. Oct. 1998 See -(EJJ, L5) : (ADC-3) & (EJJ, L1)
[167] Oates, S. *TM: Legend* (Create Space, 2016) L2 Pers. Corr. 14th Dec. 1999 page 2 of 7. E.J. Jones to Shani Oates

much confidence in the views of Michael Howard when interpreting Clan theology. Compromised by an outsider's limited perspective to the ways of the Clan, Doyle White's understanding of Robert Cochrane's and E. J. J.' views has not increased. Doyle White's pronouncements on the beliefs of the Clan are based incorrectly in a neo-Pagan perception of: *The Old Horned God and Triple Goddess.* His simplistic expression of them using that yard-stick falls far from the mark not to mention his staggering arrogance in his assumptive summaries regarding tenets of Faith he is no party too.

Doyle White registers Cochrane's stress upon the existence of a Godhead behind all these deities, but fails to follow its correct theology. Doyle White insinuates that the Luciferian tenets appear as later innovations by E.J.J. or Shani Oates, as part only of, *"Jones' 'current' praxes, rather than the beliefs of Cochrane back in the 1960s."* [168] Doyle White's statements deliver an unqualified assault upon CTC's philosophic integrity. However, they remain unsubstantiated. Serious bias is evident in his presumptive declarations. The following comment exhibits both the source of the error and its impact upon Doyle White's critical analysis.

> Michael Howard has informed me that this book contained ideas that Jones had adopted from an Oxfordshire group separate to the Clan whom he believed had been founded in the 1940s, operating within a Northern European mythos. [169]

Strange though it may seem, CTC are extremely thankful to Michael Howard for this comment. As an outsider, he disclosed what had previously remained discreet information, shared with him by E.J.J. on trust. Howard's desire to use this information to imply that E.J.J. had somehow diverged from Cochrane's works after his death, is as false as it is cavalier. Primarily it overlooked the rather startling, but plainly obvious factor that E.J.J. belonged to an *extant* group in the 1940s *before* entering the Clan twenty years later!

Focussed intently on establishing a derisory premise that CTC's Traditional Mythos was something E.J.J. established *after* Cochrane's death, despite its free exposition throughout Cochrane's

---

[168] Doyle White *'An Elusive Roebuck'* www.ethandoylewhite.blogspot.com
[169] Doyle White *'An Elusive Roebuck'* www.ethandoylewhite.blogspot.com

entire corpus of works, Howard side-lined the incredible existence of a *pre-war craft Tradition*!

That understatement was repeated by Doyle White, again bereft of needful discrimination. E.J.J.' interactions with people of that old family tradition in 1940s Buckinghamshire through an old school chum, is of phenomenal import. E.J.J, was blooded as one of them! His school friend had naturally been born into an entrenched family tradition at least two decades *prior* to that, founded at a time indeterminable to outsiders.

Those rites and to some extent, the beliefs of this former *pre-war group* may have been taken up *by Cochrane*, finding unique expression through his extraordinary vision by his own and E. J. J.' works *before and after* Cochrane's tragic death, in Clan, and in continuance of its Ethos and Mythos. [170]

Doyle White's ready acceptance of the opinion of a person outside the Clan, not best informed as to its beliefs & practises, and as someone known for his hostility to it, is naturally disappointing. Using any outsider as a principle source for the Clan's Tradition and its Mysteries in preference to an authorised source from the *inside* of that Tradition, lacks academic rigour. Any conclusion based upon unprovenanced research is therefore void.

Had Doyle White extended his research into actual documents available to him from the Stannard/Monmouth cache, he might have come across the poem written by Bowers aka Robert Cochrane in a typed letter to Ronald White, illustrating his own perspective on Lucifer. [171]

This poem is the Tradition's provenance of continuity. It reflects idiosyncratic elements pertinent to both Luciferian and Northern Traditions, thereby completely exonerating E.J.J. on all counts. Lucifer's place within the Craft is not something E.J.J. expected Howard to misunderstand; within Clan Mythos, its very specific meaning is not something Howard should have expected to understand, or expect disclosure of, from E.J.J.

Within the poem, Cochrane acknowledged Fate, the Castle, gnostic twins, Sophianic Mysticism, occulted Qabalisms, the Pentagrammatic Star, arcane cosmology and archaic mythologies of

---

[170] See later explanations of certain Clan rites developed by E. J. Jones and Cochrane.
[171] Monmouth, 2012. Op. Cit. Doc. O. p 448

East and North. Defining quite succinctly his own summary of the complex precepts woven into the Clan's mythos, Cochrane's reference to the *Triple Goddess as the Mothers*, is exemplary.

Later confirmed in E.J.J.' own writings, if Doyle White had pondered upon these objectively, he might have arrived at a different conclusion. He would have found further benefit in descriptions of the Star-Crossed Serpent, specifically in relation to the role of the Horn-ed God's role as the Fated Lord and Master of the World - the Liberator and Initiator into magicks and mystery.

Failing this, Doyle White could so easily have discussed these matters with current Clan members, testing the integrity of its archives. He might have taken the advice that many of the works claiming to be of Clan, were fake, and should be treated with extreme caution and meticulously scrutinized. Doyle White might even have extended the Clan a courteous acknowledgement that its authority is the *only* source qualified to provide that crucial information. Having already insisted upon that courtesy elsewhere for the *Cultus Sabbati*, safeguarding their indisputable authority for self-expression, Doyle White was clearly familiar with such protocols.[172]

Transcription: *Speaking in Tongues —Robert Cochrane* [173]

> Three Mothers the Witch has,
> One of Air, One of Fire, One of Water.
> Three Mothers older than Time
> Each knowing the other,
> Turning aside the Male of Earth.
> A Triple stone upon a Hill,
> Five Knights in a circle still.
> One for Ether, at the top,
> Black faced Owl, Bitch on top.
> Two for Air, the horse rider now
> Eight —legged Ygdrassdill,
> Messenger Goddess of the Winds
> Speeding, spiral of the Night.
> Goddess of dark faced men and Night.

---

[172] Further articles and papers by Ethan Doyle White as an independent researcher appear online, and in various magazines in the US, including *The Pomegranate* (The International Journal of Pagan Studies) and *Wyrd* (Three Hands Press)
[173] Oates. 2016. *SCSIII* Op. Cit. pages 347-9

Fire Goddess, falling star, Luciferous,
Wondrous firefly.
Glowing in the night, the verity
Of deepest Sight.
Below the turrets reign,
Venus rising from the waves.
Water is water, Air is Air,
Fire makes ether, have some care.
For one is female, the others, female male.
Plunder the fern, look at the lion's tail.
At the back of God, is the Gate to the World.
And watching all, is the earliest bird. [174]

> "Three mothers the witch has
> One of air, one of fire, one of water.
> Three mothers older than time
> Each knowing the other,
> Turning aside the male of earth
> A triple stone upon a hill
> Five knights in a circle still.
> One for Ether at the top
> Black faced owl, bitch on top
> Two for air, the horse rider now
> Eight legged Ygirasedill
> Messenger Goddess of the Winds
> Speeding spiral of the night
> Goddess of dark faced men and night.
> Fire Goddess, falling star, luciferous
> wonderous firefly.
> Glowing in the night, the verity
> of deepest light.

---

[174] Composed by Robert Cochrane. A deeper explanation of this poem provided by Robin-the-dart in *Heritage* (ed) Shani Oates (UK: Create Space, 2016)

> Below the~~sextirns~~ turrets reign
> Venus rising from the waves.
> Water is water, air is air
> Fire makes either, have some care
> For one is female, the others female male
> Plunder the fern, look at the lions tail.
> At the back of God is the gate to the world
> And watching all is the earliest bird.

CTC have been called upon to defend Valiente's knowledge of the Clan's Luciferian, mystical strain from similar adverse claims made by Doyle White and Howard. Not only was she well versed in that knowledge from the Clan, but from her own pursuit of Truth. Valiente was a Craft occultist through and through. Her many moments of inspiration were dedicated to expressing the myriad forms and forces of the inexplicable that lies beyond all kenning. Despite this amazing piece of writing, Howard dismissed her output as definitively Wiccan, so did Doyle White. They were both remiss.

> Come to the Circle of power,
> This is the night and the hour.
> Now as of old be adored, **Lucifer,**
> light-bearing lord!
> Horned and hoofed as a beast,
> Come and inspire our feast.
> **Lucifer**, come to us now,
> At your dark altar we bow. [175]

Ultimately, Doyle White is another outsider, one amongst many who should not presume to pronounce upon the tenets or the beliefs of closed (living) traditions. Opinions may be freely formed, but should be respectfully expressed as such, and not as conclusive definitions. Most particularly, they should avoid paying too much attention to peripheral information, and to the partial scraps gleaned from external or secondary sources, especially if they are knowingly biased or hostile. Sharing factual information with researchers and

---

[175] Valiente, 1970. Op. Cit. Notepad entry 21/1/1970

interested parties to dispel these errors of limitation, is a courtesy CTC willingly extend; a better understanding is advantageous for everyone. Although with regard to the Clan and its works, E.J.J. wisely said;

> We do not *need* to prove anything to anyone. We know what we are, and what we do. Others can either take it or leave it. I don't care which. It is our thing and that is all that matters.[176]

To write assertively about another's tradition from beyond its aegis, is simply not good manners. Where misunderstandings occur, a genuine person with integrity will amend their work to reflect this. At worst, scant resources are an impedance to any reality in truth. That reality is the vital fundamental premise upon which the Craft is predicated, a principle E.J.J. upheld quite vigorously throughout similar discussions with Andrew D. Chumbley, with whom his views clashed exhaustively.

It perplexed E.J.J. enormously that Chumbley, as someone claiming a Traditional Craft heritage, should press so deeply into a foundation within *The Pentateuch*. Nonetheless, as stated above, E.J.J. sustained his views, unwilling to be drawn into the realms of grey magic. People often take-up the words and works of others, just to postulate their own.

What CTC choose to believe is best concluded from a reasoning mind tempered by a spirited instinct. But, as E.J.J. often said: *"Everything is always hidden in plain sight."* Drawn from historical, cultural philosophies, the origins of Traditional Craft are not to be found in the roots of secular religion but in the folk expressions of religous evolution. Be advised to seek elsewhere. CTC do not Craft their belief from that biblical source.

Subsequent influences aside, the founding fathers who formulated the terms and tenets of Luciferian and Sabbatic Craft, may be explored in the fascinating psycho-erotic forays and exploits of Blake's Sabbatian Mysticism that followed the teachings of Swedenborg's Moravian *Unitas Fratrum* during the 18th century. Their yogic techniques, mastery of Tantra and devotion to the Sophianic

---

[176] Personal Correspondence from E.J.J. to S.L.O. Nov. 2000.

current, bridges medieval gnosticism with 18th century occultism.[177] Genius, visionary, artist and poet, William Blake was a man out of his time.

As a mystic entrenched in the metaphysics of a new science fused at its hearth with the stoic faith of the ancients, Blake espoused a gnosis of the senses, a divine paroxysm of devotion within the mantic throes of passion. By those methods he believed humankind's primal corporeality generated the keys to open the mind-gate to gnosis. Their pioneering studies bore ripe fruit in a metaphysical paradigm, influencing the occult investigations of the 19th and 20th centuries.

So greedily were its praxes disseminated in vibrant verse and image; familiar terminologies, commonplace to our modern sensibilities were launched into circulation. And yet, the *Sabbatic Craft* for centuries remained an underground mystical stream, nourishing diverse strata of the Luciferian current. All modalities of belief radiate their arcane mysteries, falling as dew upon the tongues of those who would utter the words of Truth. Perhaps, through confusions of ignorance and fear, those currents became demonised of their purity and beauty, the jewels once sought by all mystical pilgrims.

Satanism and Luciferianism are ultimately, tragic terms, used interchangeably, bereft of the distinctions each applies to their separate avenues of belief. Adopted by many for a host of reasons ranging from ignorance (witting or otherwise), to a desire for notoriety, it is a perennial issue and unlikely to be resolved easily. People adopt names, titles and labels often because of what they assume them to mean. They judge and are judged by their affectations of the loaded terms: Satanist/Luciferian.

In modern parlance, those who follow diverse and unique visions, are often labelled under unsavoury categories. Finding an origin in culture, 'cult' has pejorative connotations and is thusly a negative term used to distinguish a factionalised group from its detractors. It is often centred from within another belief invariably in opposition to it. Demanding extreme subjugation and obedience, its tenets are innately restrictive; total surrender of free will and choice

---

[177] Schuchard, Marsha Keith *Why Mrs Blake Cried* (London: Century, 2006)

is mandatory. Such cultish mannerisms are exploitative and extortive of its adherents. Its leaders become gurus seeking fame and fortune.

Based on historical and topical observation it is apparent how even something as seemingly benign as *'the cult of the personality,'* inhibits its adherents a healthier, critical analysis of a person's life and works. There are a number of excellent online academic explorations into the various definitions (none of which are definitive) that clearly distinguish the theological expression of a cult from the sociological variants. From its original use as a term for things non-Christian, it is now more commonly applied to all subversive or non-mainstream factions deemed to follow a specific behavioural pattern.

Another popular notion is that dead men don't speak; yet they do, by insidious and vicarious means. Beliefs, thoughts, opinions *et cetera* continue to reach out to influence thought or deed, long after all bones are dust. Words, just as much as deeds, are a legacy to beloved kin held in amity, and conversely to those held in enmity. Words can easily be taken up and manipulated by others, extrapolated from their original context to en-flesh even a contra view. Mindfully absorb equally what is said, and all that is *not* said, and adhere more closely to phrases and comments that radiate a sense of truth. Even hidden agendas are revealed, eventually.

CTC appreciate Cain as the wanderer, the exile whose purpose as an innovator, is also to gift and guard all, and through him, all Craft. His Horn-ed child survived the flood, the one who evolved that principle yet further in all civilising artes. Tubal Cain is not simply a smith, he forges cities and faith, belief and gnosis: Tubal Cain is The Child of Hope, the stag of seven tines, born survivor of the flood. Transformed thereafter by it, he travels the world as the (next eternal) wanderer.

The stag as the Roebuck forms the inner mystery of the godhead relative to the principles of sacrifice and of gyfu alongside the mystery of 1734 as feminine numerals that form the ladle/cup/cauldron/grail.[178] Following a profound encounter with the Horn-ed God, Cochrane described his vision in more visceral terms than the simple goat-foot god of arcadia. Valiente notes his emphasis on the Old One as the Lord of Death seemed almost to verge on the obsessive, that he was a being so archaic, so primal; he appeared as:

---

[178] Oates, 2016. *SCSIII* Op. Cit. Cochrane to Joe Wilson #4 p.388

Some massive and ancient tree in the dark forest, brooding yet all sentient, smelling of dead leaves and newly turned earth, ...He was so Old, ...Old from the beginning of the world. [179]

Valiente compared this to Gerald B. Gardner's view of the Old One's form that encompassed other, more creative aspects of fertility holding a balance with those chthonic elements that preoccupied Robert Cochrane. Though the image had not generated fear, he had been immobilized, by the sheer awesome presence before him.

Prof. Hutton of Bristol University, after careful study of all that Cochrane has written, has pondered if these experiences may be considered as Fact or of Faith, asserting the greater reality of Truth in both, he concluded that Cochrane was either *'Genuine, or a Genius.'* [180] CTC believe he was both.

Opinion remains fundamental to levels of influence absorbed. Cochrane's clarity of vision served to invigorate and illuminate the disparate fragments of lore he ravenously consumed along the trail of his own tragic argosy. Valiente never ceased to believe in him:

> As his writings (which I still have) show, Robert Cochrane was a firm believer in re-incarnation. I share his belief, I think he will return to finish his work. As for the fruit from the tree of Avalon, this is the apple. Cut an apple in half across its width and you will see the sign of the pentagram, which in one of its meanings is the figure of the Goddess of Life standing with arms outstretched, She gives rebirth in due time, until we need this world and time no more. [181]

An independent observer recorded his own impressions of Robert Cochrane which includes a description of an iconic artefact crafted by Cochrane, possibly created after his experiential vision of the Horn-ed being, encountered in the woods.

---

[179] Valiente, D *Rebirth of Witchcraft* (UK: Hale 1989) p 124
[180] Hutton, Professor Ronald *The Triumph of the Moon* (Oxford Uni. Press 1999)
[181] Valiente. 1989. Op. Cit. p 136

> Rex was highly intelligent (. . .) in his late twenties, married with a child (. . .) His wife was older, wiser, calmer...and devoted to him. His personality was strong, overpowering and he showed symptoms of deep-seated neurosis. He talked incessantly and fast about his Craft. He seemed profoundly unhappy as a person, yet spent time telling me how happy the Craft made him. (. . .)
>
> A remarkable figure that at first I thought was a crucifix on the wall about 24 inches high, was a bearded male figure, arms outstretched, sculpted of cast sheet metal, naked having a large erect phallus. This Rex claimed, was the God of the witches – *'Cernunnos.'* It was beautifully made, somehow not obscene.[...] 'Rex' spoke of being an Hereditary witch, initiated at an early age. He went on to show he had read widely and understood what he had read. I tried hard to catch him out but was unable. He had a belief in magic, astrology, telepathy and the tarot. There was no talk of a *'return to nature'* cult.[182]

Out to impress his interviewer, Cochrane described an iconic metal sculpture as a representative of Cernunnos, labelled by many as the God of the witches. Both Cochrane and E.J.J. elsewhere refer privately to this figure as *Tomkins* – a household Wight or Elemental. Puck, rather than Cernunnos, illustrating exactly how the Clan employ generic names or masks when speaking to outsiders. These are terms that are *'mere approximations'* of their true nature. For purposes of impression, it was enough that the domestic virtue of all that is wild and untamed in any masculine deity, named or unnamed, was maintained in the more popular figure of Cernunnos - Lord of the Animals, supreme hunter and Lord of this World.

Around this same time, in November 1963, Cochrane correlated his philosophical musings, committing them to paper through a spate of articles for occult magazines. The first appeared in *Psychic News,* entitled *Genuine Witchcraft is Defended*. Others followed at regular intervals; the next, *A Witches Esbat* appeared in *New Dimensions* in the same year.

After the death of Gerald B. Gardner in 1964, Cochrane penned four profound articles during a period of exceptional angst

---

[182] Bampton, Michael. Unpublished Thesis, c/o Ken Rees

within the Craft, as evidenced in the accompanying articles and letters published throughout *The Pentagram series*.

Caught up in some very unsavoury polemics, Cochrane along with his associate *Taliesin*, reproached certain members of the Craft community for their courtship of the media, a vanity they perceived as a betrayal. Its short life was doomed. In particular, they crossed swords with a celebrity stage-magician and his wife, Arnold and Patricia Crowther. Gerald B. Gardner had blessed their marriage, granting them his support for a base in the north, which they established as *The Sheffield Coven*.

Another, hitherto unrecognised factor that fuelled passions in that fateful final year, is sourced in Cardell's ruinous state, a controversy that might feasibly have contributed to, or even precipitated *'The night of the long knives.'* Whether Cardell was in fact Cochrane's mentor, may be less significant than how he perceived the public evisceration of a senior member of the Craft, for simply not holding the party line. It may even have involved more personal matters within the Craft that cumulatively overwhelmed him.

Whatever the root cause, because of its effects upon him, he temporarily lost a staunch ally in Doreen Valiente, a lady he much admired and held dear. The strength and endurance of their friendship has been severely underestimated, leading to considerable misrepresentation by a few self-acclaimed authorities on Craft matters, Michael Howard especially. As groundless invective, it is easily dispelled. Valiente did not harbour contempt for Cochrane, there was no lasting enmity between them. Years later, when recalling those events, she graciously conceded her own loss:

> I have to give credit to Robert Cochrane for having given me the opportunity to take part in some of the best outdoor Sabbats I have ever attended. [183]

Grieving his lack of foresight, her anger had crucially related only to the immediacy of his volatile response, which to her seemed an immature impedance to the long-term vision she and others were focussed upon. At the time Valiente feared he was jeopardising the

---

[183] Valiente, 1989. Op. Cit. p 125

future of a Craft that impassioned all of them, one she had worked so hard to generate.

Held to the very last, she maintained her belief that *'what unites us, is greater than what divides us.'* She recognised that to have any hope of staving off prejudicial media attacks, the Craft needed a protective organisation, an acceptable representation and voice in society. Her vision was eventually realised in the founding of *The Pagan Federation*.[184] Twenty five years after Cochrane had crossed the bar to join his ancestors. Her regrets concerning what might have been, are quite poignant:

> Robert Cochrane's death was a great blow, not only to me, but to all who knew him. He was perhaps the most powerful and gifted personality to have appeared in modern witchcraft. Had he lived, I believe he would have been a great leader. Ironically, it was precisely because he wanted so much to be a leader that he died so prematurely. Time and experience would have mellowed him. He was tragically young when he died. When we are young and enthusiastic for a cause, we tend to see things in black and white. Age teaches us differently. We become more tolerant as we grow older, and a little wiser. Cochrane was a highly intelligent man, as a talented one, he would have learned judgment, and patience as the years went by. Had he lived, the history of modern Witchcraft might well have been different. [185]

Chaos Reigns

The death of a leader is an inconsolable loss. Invariably, factionalisation and despair are consequences of bereavement. Restoration of equilibrium is seldom swift. The interim often generates its own problems as attempts are made to deal with the grievous issue of trauma induced events connected to that death. Under pressure, we all learn how to make sense of such confusion, then how to restore order from chaos

A curious gift in the form of an unprovenanced cache of letters and documents facilitated an opportunity for deeper investigation of the activities of unknown people allegedly associated with Robert Cochrane. Where they had been for decades, remains a

---

[184] Initially known as - The Pagan Front.
[185] Valiente, 1989. Op. Cit. pages 135-6

mystery. An informed and logical process places them with Norman Gills rather than George Winter, a member of Ronald White's group within the Clan and later, of *The Regency*. Allegedly found in a carrier bag, the documents present considerable contradiction and mystery, resolving nothing. They demand thorough and protracted study and wide-ranging research: something attempted in the lengthy process of collating material for this biography.

Information found on a few of the documents within this cache relates to specific communications between certain people involved with or close to Robert Cochrane in the *years preceding and following his death*. The remainder are anomalies, their origin and context unknown.

This now archived material has offered yet another window into the workings of the Craft, and the people involved in it between 1960 and 1975, raising more questions than answers. Notwithstanding the attribution to Cochrane of numerous published works in circulatory distribution since the 1980s, general understanding of them remains at best partial, and adds little to any useful history concerning him.

Cochrane firmly believed he was *"Waiting for a dawn that will not come."* Meaning the future did not lay in his hands, but in those of his Clan, who would come after him. Evan John Jones (E.J.J), became the next Magister appointed to that duty, and in terms of Mythos and Ethos, E,J,J.' works and knowledge are in absolute accord with those tenets expressed by Robert Cochrane throughout his own works and letters.

After all, as he explained more than once: *"I was there in the room when he wrote most of them!"* [186] E.J.J. had witnessed the development of The Clan, and his mentor's death, a devastating event that impacted so many lives then, and since. Likewise, he observed the emergence of *The Regency* thereafter.

E.J.J.' instruction of Clan praxes, especially of its inner workings and usage of virtue, remain crucial to its development. His advice and information relative to the background of persons within this history, is no less so. Upon those early foundations CTC established a history of people it considers to be collective Craft ancestors, in the broader sense. Valiente had closely observed

---

[186] Personal Correspondence from E.J.J. to Dave and Ann Finnin 1998.

Cochrane's distinct passion for his Heritage, his lineage – his family tradition, and his conviction of *being blooded into the Craft*. This uncompromising context relates to an Induction into an existing (clan) family tradition. Such things happen where there is a clear indication of Virtue witnessed in the mark, the presence of something *other* overlaying the flesh.

Blood and bone, whence infused with spiritual flux, is taken as an indicator of the true gift of genius – the god within made manifest through Her, the external Muse. The *fifth arte*, referred to by E.J.J. (see appendices) is one that may not be claimed – only awarded as an imparted gift. It is shared virtue *viz a viz* a connection to the Egregore of that tradition and may be gifted to any sworn member, alighted upon in spirit, in like manner. Cochrane described this enigmatic process as: *"Having been blooded by..."* [187]

Appearing every second or third generation, a Clan family thus grows, securely bound within the aegis of its tutelary spirit. Where Cochrane remarks upon an hereditary group, he does not refer to a physical family *in* blood, but a family *of* the blood, a spiritual essence within it. Offering an understanding as to why his own family insist there are no links to witchcraft within it before him, it is also the reason he believed he could not die until he had passed on his (spiritual) Virtue. [188]

Monitoring the Clan's disintegration after Cochrane's death, Valiente made several personal notes that refer to a disagreement on matters of internal politics that focussed upon that element of Virtue. Essential cross-references occur in Valiente's delicate approach to all sensitive matters, some of which find more generic corroboration broader afield.

An incident from within this very *real*, secret history about the *People of Goda*, reflects her personal reactions to matters raised by E.J.J. during a visit shortly after Cochrane's death. Due to grief and shock, the unresolved tension between them is apparent when E.J.J. asked her if she knew the whereabouts of certain ritual items. Clearly perplexed, she was somewhat surprised at being caught off-guard.

---

[187] Oates, 2016. *SCSIII* Op. Cit. Cochrane to Bill Gray #X p 182
[188] That vital imperative is explored in greater depth in another chapter. See also Oates. S, 'Witch Blood: A Modern Heresy,' *The Arcane Veil* (UK: Mandrake of Oxford, 2012)

A somewhat protracted illness, and a brief hospitalisation, had left her a little out of the loop. Arriving home from Hospital, she had not yet caught up with all the events and their consequences. Expressing some bewilderment and scepticism, she faithfully marked their conversation. Adding very little more, she quickly became aware of all that had transpired within the Clan in her absence. With poignant relevance to recent, personal events. She stated quite baldly that *"John blamed Chalkie,"* and that he:

> Claimed he was carrying out Roy's instructions given a few days before his death, to get out and keep quiet, because a big bust-up was coming over Chalkie and George, and he advised me to do the same. [189]

Justine Glass informed Valiente of various strains of malicious gossip she'd heard, that claimed Cochrane's widow no longer wished to *"see anyone from the past."* The *actual* remark Cochrane's widow had vented so painfully, referred principally to Ronald White and George Stannard/Winter. A few others were included whose behaviour she deemed hostile or unwelcome. It *did not* refer to her dearest friends with whom she remained in contact.

Both E.J.J. and his good lady were likewise, *'no longer on speaking terms with those involved.'*[190] This discreet matter was conveyed to the Clan by E.J.J. in 1998, and is confirmed by Valiente's records of those times. E.J.J. deeply regretted the shock Valiente experienced when thrust into the midst of events she had not been privy to in her absence, and how those final traumas played out. She had of course been well aware of the tensions between Ronald White and Robert Cochrane, and between Cochrane and his wife, and by default, the others. But she had not witnessed the true extent of actions taken in those final few months after her departure.

These are the circumstances surrounding one of the numerous Craft traditions that surfaced during the turbulent decade following the repeal of the Witchcraft Act in 1951. Revelling in that liberation, their hedonistic indulgences might cause many in our own era to shudder. Decades have passed since those tragic events

---

[189] Valiente, 1966. Op. Cit. Notepad entry. 11th December.
[190] Ibid.

transpired, and because certain individuals made them public, along with the contents of his private letters, the media, and whoever is able to manipulate it, now pronounce upon his life and tradition with self-acclaimed authority. By making them commonplace, they forget that his legacy lives on through his Clan. And in the disregard for its better knowledge and true authority, fictions have arisen to pervade its sacred mysteries. Some more fanciful than others.

2 Re-Birth: The Eternal Mask

IV) The Phantom Royal Windsor Coven

Tattered Oaths and False Identities

Recent attempts undertaken by additional outsiders to explore the history and Tradition that became Cochrane's legacy to his Clan, are fraught with disturbing motivations. Subjective and unabashedly selective, Michael Howard in *Children of Cain*, John of Monmouth in *Genuine Witchcraft is Explained*, David V Barrett in *A Brief Guide to Secret Religions*, and Ethan Doyle White in *An Elusive Roebuck*, have collectively fractured all understand of Cochrane's works.[191] Their distortions seriously undermine Cochrane's intent, paring down his works to a mire of conflict and confusion. It is no coincidence that Howard was the source used by all these writers.

To understand the purpose in this, the point at which their spurious versions of Clan history were asserted must be established. Working backwards, step by step, sideways and forwards, it is possible to follow the strange meanderings of a thread that binds together seemingly unrelated events. Sometimes, these are excruciatingly random and obscure, complex and hard to track; at other times, they are blatant, startlingly simple, bold and painfully obvious.

The next major subject tackled is the supposed existence of a secret coven, the existence of which is relative to the first only through the people involved. Firmly denied by E.J.J., he insisted unto his own death, that CTC had never been known by any other

---

[191] See Bibliography

name and that *The Royal Windsor Coven* was nothing more than a fictitious name for a fantasy group that had *no existence as part of Cochrane's Tradition*. As the one person who would know, he demonstrated that Cochrane was not only the founder and leader of his Clan, but that its traditions and works were wholly distinct from everything else around him.

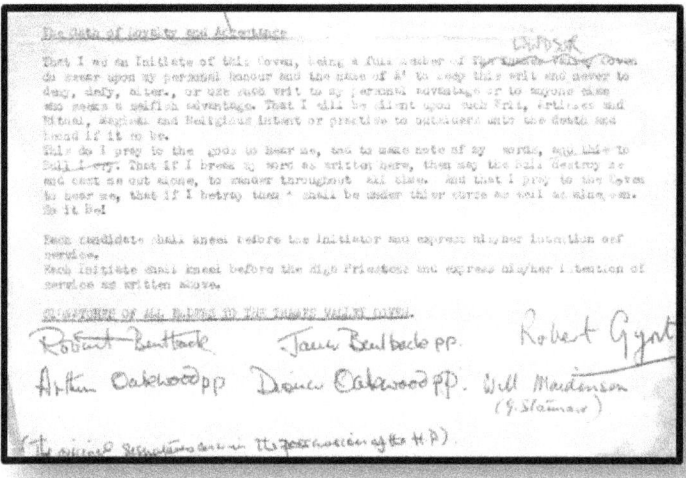

Oath of Loyalty and Acceptance to The Thames Valley Coven (AAA) A2

After E.J.J. joined CTC on the cusp of 1962-3, its organic development allowed all members to share its aegis through its Tutelary Egregore bound to its *People as* the *Clan of Tubal Cain*. [192] His notable testimony fully validates these grave matters, and through his own works, and those entrusted to him, a much needed clarity illuminates Cochrane's Tradition and Legacy. Supporting documents in their original form are available for study and scrutiny by any genuine seeker directly interested in the quest for Truth; and are published as transcripts and scanned excerpts in *Star Crossed Serpent III - The Complete Letters of Robert Cochrane*. [193]

Ponder deeply upon the clever use of this image (AAA) A2 by John of Monmouth to promote his belief in a Royal Windsor

---

[192] For decades Michael Howard has strived to convince people interested in CTC that E.J.J. was responsible for the CTC title *after* Cochrane's death, despite the fact that Cochrane makes clear reference to the CTC title in his own private letters to Gills, Gray, Wilson and *'ickle Deric.'*
[193] Oates, 2016. Op. Cit. *SCSIII.*

Coven.[194] Extracted from a document that clearly illustrates this is an *Oath to the Thames Valley Coven,* that name and fact is inexplicably ignored. Placed at the very forefront of his own book, Monmouth forced attention upon a named title and to certain people named upon it, that are contrary to what is clearly indisputable! Thereafter, Monmouth used this document as the basis for further fictions, cited to validate them. Yet within academic research, ideas and images presented at the forefront of any exegesis do so, for one of two reasons.

1. The usage and presence of motifs, images and documents *previously authenticated* by independent and external means, legitimate and/or academic, may validate and authorise all texts they accompany.

Or,

2. The motif, image or document is presented as an anomaly where validating facts within the accompanying text award authentication.

What Monmouth attempted, is *neither*. Rather, he devised an ingenious tactic, where *both text and motif* are presented as if they automatically validate each other by virtue of their existence alone, thus presuming a pre-established authenticity. This validation does not exist, it has no foundation in fact, though he bluffs his way through the entire text as if it does.

The *Writ & Constitution for a Coven to Diana* document, of which the oath forms a vital part, remains a contentious document. Its association with an alleged group named The Royal Windsor Coven is entirely spurious, as is the existence of any such coven in the lifetime of Robert Cochrane. To date, the author remains unknown. Without further evidence, it is impossible to authenticate. Had Monmouth acknowledged this fact, his book would have read very differently. Based upon this image (AAA) A2, observe Monmouth's direction to witness *"The beginnings of the Royal Windsor Coven"* with a bald notation beneath it: *"Witches signatures."* [195]

---

[194] Monmouth, 2012. Op. Cit. p 11
[195] Monmouth, 2012. Op. Cit. p 11

Absent of the necessary authenticating documentation, Monmouth applied confused logic to date this document as circa 1961. Nonetheless, the: *Writ and Constitution of a Coven to Diana,* finds a more realistic date somewhat earlier, around 1959. This date represents the time when we can firmly place Cochrane within another Coven in London. It speaks with clarity and authority regarding the former name of a group of people who thus far remain somewhat elusive, though we may be reasonably sure the coven was Arthur Everley's. At this stage however, more information is needed to properly investigate this coven and those who peopled it.

Although Fate had determined an exponential shift for Cochrane in his move to Slough and the establishment of his own working group, events prior to that need tracking backwards slightly to explore them fully, and in context. Of the four authentic names on that document, all of them are aliases. It is only a supposition that links any known person to them. For example, it is by no means certain that Cochrane and his wife should be identified with Robert and Jane Bentback. And if they are proved to be these other persons, their association with the enigmatic '*Arthur and Diane Oakwood,*' the two other mysterious signatories on the (AAA) A2 document, needs to be determined.

Scant documentation remains for this early period, and what has survived is without context or explanation. There are very few viable clues to possible associations, or time-lines. Monmouth, disregards this impediment, and freely speculates a history for the people involved. And though unknown, he tied them to names that occur nowhere else with associations for them that are not only unsupported, they have no precedent for plausible speculation. As the *original document no longer exists*, lost to time and circumstance, there is no way of knowing whose names were actually signed upon it. The best approach is to eliminate who they are *not*.

Importantly, it should be realised, the document (AAA) A2 is a photo copy of a transcript that was taken from the original. Because it is merely a photocopy, it has no legitimacy whatsoever. None. Furthermore, doc. (AAA) A2 bears witness only to a morass of surface graffiti that signify later edits and amendments in pencil and biro scribbled onto the page, *overwriting the <u>photocopied</u> text beneath.*

Large tracts of texts are similarly stricken through in pencil, leaving less than a third of the surface of this photo-copied document clear. Part of the original transcript is discernible in the photo-copied representation of it. This reveals an oath of allegiance made only to <u>The Thames Valley Coven</u>. This document should be considered in terms relative to The Thames Valley Coven and to the Oath ascribed to it, and not to any other. These are indisputable facts; there is simply no argument to the contrary.

Enticed by the photo-copied image of a transcript, it is too easy to falsely presume that what is seen, is the original document, that it is *not* actually dedicated to the name that appears on the document, and finally, that the document bears witness to *six, not four* legitimate names. It is not and does not.

According to this transcript copy, the original document bore only the inked names of *four* mysterious people in two neat columns, and was signed in the presence of an unknown senior official. It is reasonable to suppose the transcript once belonged to any one of those four named persons; though it is also possible each of the four named persons might have received a similar transcript, which might have been in the hand of the relevant dedicant. The bonafide transcription recorded by the *one* hand of Robert Bentback (whoever he proves to be) on behalf of the other *three* signatories is lost to time, as is the original *Writ & Constitution document* it was transcribed from.

No actual handwriting of Bentback's has survived for comparison, and no paper style to analyse for clues relative to the date of production. Despite its citation by Monmouth as documentary proof of the existence of his fictitious coven, it is prudent to note how *that* coven is *not mentioned anywhere on it*. Having ignored the real title, Monmouth's substitute title, could not be any less convincing in its alleged dedication to that phantom coven. As a document submitted to validate a phantom coven, it fails totally.

As a severely defaced copy, there are no clues as to whom this copy once belonged, before or after it was defaced. Even if those later pencilled edits were removed from the surface of this document, it remains nothing more than a photocopy of a transcript (copy) of an original document.

That aside, what is more useful about this much raddled copy document, is what it *is* able to reveal. Beneath the untidy scrawl, the overlay of mapped pencil marks illustrate which sections of the text were being salvaged by default at a considerably later date, when it became the inspiration for an extensive adaptation and rewrite. Free amendment and editing *overwrite* the text *beneath* to provide a working template for adaptive re-publication. The surface treatment is definitely what one might expect when a very old or discarded document becomes the basis of subjective revision at a different point in time. Failing to produce any proof or validation for his assertions regarding this document's provenance, Monmouth boldly uses it as his proof source to validate all further allegations based upon it throughout the book! This is both disingenous and unethical on an unprecdented scale and relies entirely upon the gullability and ignorance of his readers.

Having shown the correct title heading for the Oath of Loyalty assigned to *The Thames Valley Coven* and the *four* names only assigned to it, Monmouth bypassed everything to promote a very different statement. The perspective he promoted is that six legitimate signatures mark an *authentic* document. The two extraneous signatures were *added to the photo-copy* at a much later date, making this document and all claims for it, literally, fraudulent.

From the onset, all dedicants are referred to as *Witches,* a section of the photocopied transcription presents the six names as actual *Signatures,* and *The Thames Valley Coven* is referred to as *The Royal Windsor Coven.* However, those two incongruous signatures were *not on the transcript*, nor the original, that being the only document the four genuine people actually signed. Not only are the two extra names clearly out of line with the other four, penned in black ink and in neat rows, they are notably of an entirely different hand and pen to the single transcriber who'd recorded them on the original document. Unlike those four personages, the two extra new names appear only *on the actual surface* of this photocopied document, added on as part of the messy edits, and in biro. This information, empirically separates the two extra names from the other four by distances of time, blue biro and a photocopier.

Moving on to determine the identities of the people for whom the two pseudonyms are given as *Robert Gynt* and *Will Maidenson* (G. Stannard), Monmouth suggested they represent Ronald White and George Stannard/Winter. Without qualification he posits that all six named personages were therefore members of the *'Royal Windsor Coven.'* [196] Nothing actually written correlates with what the author claims the text says. Using the psychology of assertive and positive suggestion, Monmouth tried hard to convince the eye a different text exists. That projection clearly has no basis in any reality. It does not actually exist.

Everything document (AAA) A2 once alluded to, is nullified. Its oath defaced and reneged, its purpose lost, even the people involved are lost to us. The two extra signatures have no date or time or event to anchor them into the circumstances under which the original document was drawn up. It is illogical to ignore the uncomfortable realisation that anyone can scribble in names and change titles and sentences in the process of editing and copying; and at any time. [197]

To preserve a document laced with edits and present such to an initiate to sign is beyond absurd. For *anyone* to delete a Covenant to which they have laid oath and signature, is unthinkable. The text of the *Oath of Loyalty* [198] clearly states that for all time, those named persons are bound in oath to uphold and not defile or alter that Writ, which by mouth or deed is to be honoured and held as a sacred and holy writ; but more importantly, that failure to do so, calls upon the defiler all manner of horrors.

This five page document is quite precise and very complex regarding its inclusivity of all possible clauses. [199] It is therefore reassuring to show that none of the four original signatories defaced or defiled any legitimate oath-bound document beholden to them as *The Thames Valley Coven*. Perhaps Monmouth failed to consider the ramifications of his proposals for White and Winter as legitimate signatories; perhaps he did not understand them, or perhaps he simply ignored them, confidant everyone else reading them would do likewise.

Adjunct to his claims for doc. (AAA) A2, Monmouth goes to some trouble to convince the reader that it was created deliberately as nothing more than a draft document for edit, from which a final

---

[196] Monmouth, 2012 Op. Cit. p 15 Again it should be noted Chalky is Robert, not Robin, as referred to in (ooo)
[197] Monmouth, 2012 Op. Cit. p 11
[198] Monmouth, 2012, Op. cit. p 24 See: *Document of Oath and Loyalty* pp 277-281
[199] Monmouth, 2012, Op. cit. p 24 See: *Document of Oath and Loyalty* pp 277-281

document, contemporary with it was produced. However, Document (AAA) A2, even in its current state, bears witness to the fact that whatever document it is a representative copy of, was a fully completed, final document, legitimised by the four authentic and original names signed upon it. Monmouth pressed hard his belief that the photo-copied transcript document (AAA) A2 of the *Writ & Constitution,* is not a final, completed independent document, but merely a rough draft for another, entirely separate document - A4. [200]

There is no argument against doc. A4 being a finalised version of *an* initial draft, but that draft *was never* the original signed document that (AAA) A2 is a photo-copied representation of. It is entirely possible however, that the pristine A4 document *is* the final refinement of ideas drafted from the selected edits and revisions that now scar the surface of the photo-copied document (AAA) A2, which is a different thing entirely, and not unusual.

Older documents commonly serve as templates for later revisions.

To claim that the *signed and binding original* document the photo-copied document (AAA) A2 *represents,* was ever a *temporary draft* document, composed with the intention of discarding it after its purpose was served, once the final (non-existent) document (allegedly contemporary with it) was produced, is absurd.

In similar fashion to his claims tht every document is referred to as a Royal Windsor document, devoid of proofs or substantiating evidence, Monmouth asserted his assumptions were statements of fact. By labelling document (AAA) A2 as the intentional *draft copy of a separate finalised document,* he boldly claimed that (AAA) A2 [201] was created solely as a *draft* document,:

> By the time the draft 'Writ and Constitution' found its final form, it was one third of the length of the original document produced by Roy Bowers. [202]

---

[200] Monmouth, 2012, Op. Cit. pages 390-394
[201] Monmouth, 2012. Op. Cit. pages 277-281, A2 doc. *Writ and Const.* defaced photo-copy of lost transcript, being the signed *Oath of Loyalty to a Coven to Diana, The Thames Valley Coven*. Shown in Tubal's Mill biography as doc. (AAA) A2.
A true transcript of this document appears in Oates, 2016. *SCSIII* Op. Cit. p 127 Further unmodified scans and transcripts are available for study in *SCSIII,* presented in chronological order with explanations to assist and guide sensible research through the real time process between the redacted surface edits on doc. (AAA) A2 and the A4 documents.
[202] Monmouth, 2012. Op Cit. p 24

Monmouth's attempt to legitimise the two extraneous signatures upon it, achieves exactly the opposite. Moreover, draft copies do not require signatures. Final documents do not display the edits that led to their construction.

Specific factors do strongly suggest that doc. (AAA) A2 in its current state, *was* typically *re-used* as an inspirational (rather than an intentional) template some considerable time *after* Cochrane's death, during the years that followed, contemporary with *The Regency* (mark II or later). This process is investigated in the appropriate chapter. At this point, it is sufficient to note that the revision of pencilled edits on the surface of a photo-copied document were used to formulate an unsigned, updated version a number of years later.

Without reservation, it can be stated that the persons responsible for those later edits onto and over the copy document (AAA) A2, were *definitely not* present when its original composed and typed up, and consequently not amongst the four original persons who had signed their oaths individually on it. If they had, then any needful or required edits would have occurred at that time, and certainly before it was signed, and transcribed. Both acts confirm its use original as a completed document. That finalised, unique, legal document may be lost to us, but not its purpose.

Monmouth transformed its true intent as a textual witness to oaths taken for *The Thames Valley Coven,* into a nonsense, that is, if we accept his proposal that the persons involved decided to change the name of the coven immediately *after* putting their signatures to their oaths. Thinking laterally, would those Elders sign a binding oath upon a mere draft document, and then submit that draft document into the safekeeping of a HP, when a finished document is either available, or soon to be so? Someone later added those two extra names to the surface of doc. (AAA) A2. Whatever the purpose, and whomever it applied to, the original vow relating to it had not been taken. Those curious, enigmatic, named but unknown people, were not beholden by its tenets, and therefore had no compunction in inflicting graffiti all over it, an act that made a mockery and contradiction of its worth.

A single word - *windsor*, is scribbled in blue biro over the typed black text crossed out beneath it - *The Thames Valley Coven*. Howard and Monmouth both expanded upon 'Windsor' to make the title The Royal Windor Coven, which they then claim was the intended title of the coven the original signatories made their oaths to. This arrant nonsense has been repeated ever sonce, ad nauseum.

As mooted previously, *windsor* is amongst numerous other surface marks and comments that serve collectively as edits for the later revised document, A4. If the word does indicate a name or title, it would serve only those collective revisions that appear relevant to doc. A4, even so, there is no mention of a 'Royal Coven,' not as typed text or surface scribble, only *windsor*.

Should that word refer in any way to the Thames Valley region of Buckinghamshire, an important development occurred in 1974, which should be deliberated upon. Political boundary changes conferred the appellation 'Royal' upon the Windsor environs, making it a Royal Borough. Those factors therefore suggest a probable date for those edits appearing in doc. 'AAA' before those new titles came into effect circa 1974, but which become finalised as doc. A4, not too long after, circa 1975/6. This would coincide with Ronald White's stepping down from *The Regency*. Document A4 was probably created no later than 1981, because that name would not be relevant to Ronald White once he moved from London to Shropshire around that time.

Ronald White had undoubtedly been aware of the historical context for the defunct coven in old Windsor, Cochrane had referred to, and possibly had aspirations of reviving it. Nonetheless, this remains a speculative proposal, and though it may or may not have any basis in fact, it is possibly the presumption that instigated the rumour for the entire fiction it developed into. Namely, that *The Royal Windsor Coven* existed prior to 1974, as Cochrane's coven, and as the coven that White and Winter allegedly continued after his death clearly, it was none of these.

As a coven White and Winter 'may' have considered as part of their own journey in the Craft between 1976-81, it has nothing to do with Robert Cochrane and CTC, the vehicle he established to transmit his Tradition. Sidestepping these obvious impediments, Monmouth composed a very different tale.

Further impediments manifested in time, concerning paper size, and type style; the first as a span of around a decade that separates these two documents (in the middle of which Cochrane died); the second in the public availability of *A4* size paper; and thirdly, in the relevant authors and their typewriters. Ignoring these impediments too, Monmouth cited Roy Bowers aka Robert Cochrane as the author of both documents.

Described as doc.(AAA) A2, [203] the *Writ and Constitution* dedicated to *The Thames Valley Coven* and doc. A4 *The Final Version* of the *Writ & Constitution,* [204] nothing links these two documents together. It should be remembered at all times, that doc. (AAA) A2 is a photo-copy of a transcript that represents an original document that was a final version in its own right. The document A4 *Final Version,* is also an extant, original. Examination of the A4 [205] document scans reveals that it does not possess the vital section relating to *The Oath of Loyalty* and the signatures assigned to The Thames Valley Coven.

Monmouth's theory depends upon establishing a connection between these two documents that would legitimise them and the two extra signatures noted on doc. (AAA) A2, so he inserted the Oath section into the transcript version of the A4 document in his book GWiE (not on the actual document) which is therefore a composite created by him to deliberatley misinform.[206] This deceitful presentation created a false continuity between (AAA) A2 and A4. That is not all. He then changed the title of the coven in the *Oath of Loyalty* section from *The Thames Valley Coven* to *The Windsor Coven, and arranged the signatures so that equal emphasis is weighted on all six of them.*

The document is not a faithful transcript. The composite transcript A4 does *not* exist, it is a manipulation that *assumes* the appearance of a 'final version' it *could* be, if it truly *had* included the signed section of the oath, and if that oath had been dedicated to *The Windsor Coven*, and not to *The Thames Valley Coven*, and if the Writ and Constitution document had been a deliberate draft version. Disappointingly, *Genuine Witchcraft is Explained*, is not well served by its author, John of Monmouth. It presents a disingenuous account burdened with invalid addenda on its transcripts.

---

[203] Monmouth, 2012. Op. Cit. pp 277-281 doc. (AAA) A2 *Writ and Const.* defaced photo-copy of lost transcript, being the signed *Oath of Loyalty to a Coven to Diana, The Thames Valley Coven*. Shown in Tubal's Mill biography as doc. (AAA) A2 A true transcript appear in Oates, 2016. *SCSIII* Op. Cit. p127

[204] Monmouth, 2012. Op. Cit. doc. A4 pages 282-287

[205] Monmouth, 2012. Op. Cit. pages 282-87

[206] Monmouth, 2012. Op. Cit. pages 390-94

Other impedimenta expose unique typesetting, paper, card, print and ink in the alleged *Final Version,* that clearly demonstrate it is of more recent provenance, and therefore markedly distinct from all but one other document in this cache. These and numerous other inconsistencies presented by Howard and Monmouth made explanations of these documents extraordinarily complicated.[207]

Compounding those errors yet further, Monmouth referred to every person and document as being of *The Royal Windsor Coven.* Breaking down that artificial structure to expose discrepancies with workable references for study, aid further individual investigation and clarification.

- ❖ Scan of doc.(AAA) A2 pp 277-81 Image of the document <u>exactly</u> as it now looks, complete with all defacements pertaining to suggested edits, scribbles and amendments.

- ❖ A typed transcript of doc. (AAA) A2, is provided for clarity, pp 371-380. It maintains the integrity of (AAA) A2 complete with all line crossings and defacements. It reveals where '***The Thames Valley Coven'*** is crossed out by one of those surface edits for the scribbled edit *'windsor'* to appear above it.

- ❖ This transcript A3 is a 'generated' version, pp 381-389, presenting a re-typed version of doc.(AAA) A2 as it might appear without the surface graffiti, edits etc. now. It shows the unadulterated Oath section to **The Thames Valley Coven.** [naturally, therefore, the inserted edit *'Windsor,'* does not exist here, but the four signatures do, the extraneous two should not, however.]

- ❖ Doc. A4 the alleged *'Final Version of the 'Writ & Cons'* given on pp 282-87, is allegedly compiled from the edits on the (AAA) A2 (if used as) template. Although referred to instead by Monmouth as the *draft*, pp 277-281, it reveals anomalies. The A4 doc. is a much shortened, revised, streamlined and severely edited, document and bears some resemblance in content to the edits visible on the doc. (AAA)A2. Where it departs significantly is in *The Condition of Entrance Upon New Candidates* section.

---

[207] Monmouth, 2012 Op. Cit. pages 390-94

❖ The A4 *transcript* shown on pages pp 390-394, reveals quite a remarkable development from the A4 *scanned* document on pp 282-86 of the alleged 'Final Version.' The conversion from A4 scan to A4 transcript acquires an inserted section, copied in from the signed oath section from doc. (AAA) A2 that exists only on doc. (AAA) A2. The acquired section has also become subject to a name change from *The Thames Valley Coven* [p 281 & p 389] to *The Windsor Coven*, [p 393]

❖ The scan of the <u>actual</u> A4 document clearly demonstrates how the inserted section *does not exist*. On the A4 scan, the remaining page is blank. The *Oath of Loyalty* section is not there. That document correctly ends with the closing declaration that: "THIS IS THE LAW AND WRIT OF THIS COVEN"

To summarise the vital premise of these carefully articulated stages, Monmouth created an artificial composite for a document which then assumes an invalid existence through an alleged continuity. This provided a false context for *six* signatures to appear in, just to validate two signatures that should not be there. That document is then presented as if it were legitimately assigned to a coven, that is in fact named as something else entirely.

Another letter from the cache highlighted by Monmouth, also becomes relative to this fabrication through its association with a document named within it as the *Laws and Constitution*. Signed by *Robert Bentback,* the letter instructs Chalky, (also named as Robert Gynt at the end of the letter), to use an enclosed copy of the *Laws and Constitution* to procure signatures upon it from all forthcoming inductees to serve as a *personal* record and proof of their acceptance. Other than aliases, there is no indication as to *who* composed the *Laws & Constitution*, *when* that document was composed, or when this letter that accompanied it was written and by whom.

The similarity or relationship of that document to the *Writ & Constitution* doc. A2 (AAA) is therefore impossible to determine. Although Monmouth presumes the letter was written by Cochrane, there is nothing to support his assumption in logic, reason or by factual evidence, and so it remains unconfirmed. [208] Beyond Monmouth's desire, there is nothing to assume they are connected.

Whatever document described by Robert Bentback that once held the signatures of certain inductees, especially the lady referred to in the hand-written letter named Avril, it forms no part of this cache, and may no longer exist. Her signature is plainly absent on doc. (AAA) A2. It is reasonable to conclude that, irrespective of who Robert Bentback may have been, the *Law & Constitution* document he refers to, **is not** doc. (AAA) A2, the *Writ. & Constitution* for *A Coven to Diana*.[209]

An ambiguous time frame for the creation of the original document spanning Arthur Everley's group and Cochrane's first, tentative, abandoned coven, could have triggered a false trail for Monmouth, who failed to factor in so many other details by which he may have avoided that pitfall. A strong initiatory role appears central to the tradition referred to within all these documents, which removes their relevance to *The Regency* (mark I & II). Neither version endorsed initiation.

Focussing briefly upon the two extra names signed into doc.(AAA) A2, a purpose that would sensibly associate them with White and Winter should be established. It should be perceivable, rather than simply declared. As two of several surviving members of Cochrane's group after his death, irrespective of how that group defined itself, there would be no need for White and Winter to undertake initiations (back) into it. This is especially true, if, as alleged, they, rather than Cochrane, had been the real leaders of that group (CTC). As yet, the document cache cannot be wholly connected with and White and Winter as people, or as leaders of *The Regency* (mark I & II), its rites & rituals, or with Robert Cochrane and his Tradition.

Few options remain for this enigmatic cache of documents that might render them of some useful purpose. Aside from the

---

[208] Oates, 2016 *SCSIII* Op. Cit. pages 119-20 which discusses this particular document in considerable detail. The '*Laws & Const.*' doc.(d) pages 121-131 referred to in this letter does not actually exist. Monmouth has taken a huge leap in assuming that the document entitled Writ & Const. doc. is that doc. That they do not share an identical title, makes this very unlikely. We have no way of knowing what that missing document contained. It seems to be a very different document altogether. And this is now believed to be the case. The transcript (d) on pages 121-131 of *SCSIII* beneath the mislabelled heading '*Laws & Const.*,' is actually *The Writ & Const. for A Coven to Diana*. See also [GWiE –pages 277-281: Monmouth Op. Cit. 2012.]
[209] Oates, 2016 *SCSIII* Op. Cit. p 119

strong possibility that some of them are unrelated to the others, the bulk of them appear to have relevance only to *The Thames Valley Coven*. Two other documents stand out as incongruous to the remainder.

Of more recent composition, they focus on quite distinct matters, even their titles distinguish them. This might indicate their use by people who were probably responsible for the revisions evident between certain documents of note. The people responsible for their creation could have been *The Regency*'s third and final discreet form of select individuals formed after White retired to Shropshire.

Alternatively, that group of people might have been contemporary with CTC, formed of later members of *The Thames Valley Coven* before it folded, or even a group in which White and Winter were involved. It is simply impossible to confirm without further information.

One final example refers to another attempt for an impossible continuity in time sequences and of people. Nothing short of manufactured genius, the strategy was simple, but the procedure is convoluted. It requires considerable concentration to follow.

To uncover this tactical ruse, it is necessary to analyse a more recent, albeit undated document within the cache, entitled *The Final Rite of Initiation*. Monmouth drew attention to a pencilled annotation over the typed sheet which reads, *'consult Roy.'* [210] Without validation, support or proof of any kind, Monmouth assigns to that document an assumed date circa 1967. That premise allowed him to explain its existence as a 'final' document to a rough draft composed in pencil before Cochrane's death in 1966. Had that been true, then the typed up version, completed after his death would have no reason to carry over a previous edit from the draft to the final document - a pencilled directive to 'consult Roy.' If the edit from the draft was a memo to check something with Roy while he was still alive, then, it

---

[210] Monmouth, 2012 *GWiE* Op. Cit. p 15 This information remains vehemently disputed by us. Pencilled edits authenticate nothing. Monmouth refers to a document (The Full Rite of Initiation) that appears on pages 302-315 but provides nothing to support his presumptions regarding it. The document has no date or validating citation to authenticate it, or contextualise it. This means that any claim could be made for it. CTC have a copy of the original Rite of Initiation only as cited on pages 299-301, but not the alleged final version of it, named here by Monmouth as the 'Full' rite of initiation - this remains in Monmouth's care. This set of pages are considerably newer documents than all the others in this cache. Holding no relevance to Cochrane and CTC, they are relevant only to whichever group this initiatory rite belongs and whose rites this is extracted from.

was either done, or it was not. If not, then again, a pencil edit on a posthumously typed and completed document serves no purpose.

This is another example of the troubling inconsistencies apparent throughout Monmouth's explanations. They lack common sense, but more importantly, they lack purpose. The document's enigmatic directive is obviously *retrospective*. Post-dating Cochrane's death, it does not pretend to be contemporary with him.

The enigma is easily solved once the *purpose* of consultation is properly addressed. Though he cannot be consulted in person, his views, opinions, advice and directives may be studied via his works. Monmouth avoids any attempt to address why White and Winter would actually need to *'consult Roy'* on anything at all, if they and not he, were the 'real' brains behind the tradition as he repeatedly claims.

Monmouth jumps between a diary date in December 1966 for a meeting with two people he named Madge Worthington and 'George' (?) and later diary dates in 1968 that mention 'Belinda.'

Nothing is presented that could link them together, Monmouth presumed that Belinda was Madge Worthington.[211] Belinda, whoever that person might prove to be, is another pencil edit that could have been scribbled onto the document at any time, along with the phrase – *'consult Roy.'* As the document itself is undated, guessing when those comments were pencilled in is impossible. There is nothing to secure them in time or place, and nothing to indicate who Belinda is. Her actual identity is not relevant to this biography, nor to the Robert Cochrane Tradition. That her identity was used by Monmouth to assert time lines and associations between events is critical. Exposing those manipulations to be false claims within this biography is vital.

Despite Monmouth's ambitious claims for a comment allegedly found in White's diary: *'7.30p.m. / MADGES / THEN GEORGES / AGENDA / 1 23ʳᵈ / 2 INIT,'* [212] (discussed in full later), without

---

[211] Monmouth. 2012 Op. Cit. p 115 No evidence to supports that assumption. Ronald White's diary appointment 18ᵗʰ Dec. 66, names Madge only, no Belinda. In fact Belinda is not mentioned anywhere else. She is pencilled into the pages of this Rite only. Study the *Full Rite of Initiation* C3, pages 302-315 which is a considerably newer and more recently typed document. Monmouth claims it is a revision of the C2 pages 299-301. There is nothing whatsoever to link these documents. They are entirely dissimilar initiatory rites in , paper, age, content, form and style. The typewriter used in C3 is completely different to that used for C2. Neither of the two typewriters used by Cochrane produced C3 *Full Rite of Initiation*.

[212] Monmouth, 2012. p 114

context and visual scans to support his proposition, it offers only a wealth of ambiguity. Though obscure, a studied analysis of what is explained of this diary entry suggests a meeting to discuss initiatory material. What it *does not do*, is provide an anchor in the form of a year, nor offer clear names for positive identification of people, nor the coven it allegedly refers to, nor the events and circumstance for this meeting, nor even the context surrounding them. Taken in isolation, it is of little use.

Possible clues are found within Valiente's Notepads, consulted again for vital clues and possible cross-references. She referred to Wican specific initiations Madge Worthington was undertaking in this exact time-frame.[213] As Ken Rees' earlier comments maintain, Valiente's notes for 1964-6, additionally confirm that almost everyone around Cochrane, including George Stannard/Winter, Ronald White, Norman Gills and Gerard Noel was an initiate of Gardner's Wica, via Eleanor Bone, or Lois Bourne, or Cynthia Swettenham. Cochrane was the exception. He appears to be the only person *not* initiated into the Wica!

Practically everyone around him received verified initiations into Wica, so it is no small matter that no-one has been able to verify Cochrane's alleged initiation. Decades after these events, whence Valiente, Jones, and Swettenham had long crossed the bar, the matter became an issue of contention only when Michael Howard insisted upon it being fact. These and other confrontational claims remain unfounded, and without support.

Belinda, is nowhere else known or mentioned, a significant point when we remember that Valiente recorded Madge Worthington's initiations into Wica, from late 1966 through to 1968, identifying her as Fiona.[214] Apparently unaware of these authenticated facts, Monmouth presumed a contrary account of these events. He stated that document C3, upon which 'Belinda' is scribbled, marked her Initiation into The Royal Windsor Coven.[215]

Dissimilar to every other document from the cache, in terms of style, content, type face, paper, font and most particularly, its

---

[213] Valiente, 1966. Op. Cit. Notebook entry - 8/11/66
[214] Valiente, 1966. Op. Cit. Notebook. - 1966-70
[215] There is of course no means by which the existence of this group can now be proved. No-one qualified to do so remains alive to verify or authenticate this Full Rite of Initiation C3. As with so many things, anyone can create or forge a document to aid their own claims for validation.

newer status, it is noticeably distinct from doc. C2 upon which it is allegedly based. Coincidentally, the C3 document is the only one from the cache that refers to the otherwise phantom 'Royal' Windsor Coven. Standing apart from every other substantially older document, a tentative date may be plausibly suggested by the inclusion of the appellation - 'Royal,' a title that has no context *prior* to 1974.

Without means of proper validation, document C3 demonstrates the potential opportunity for its creation by almost anyone, and at any time since the 1974 at least. Taking two more unrelated documents, Monmouth tried to match them by intent and content, asserting a natural progression from one to the other. He suggested that Ronald White's disapproval of doc. C2 [216] led to its alleged refinement as doc. C3, the finished article.[217] Without provenance for either document, Monmouth presented his statement as pre-established facts. They are not. These two documents bear no relationship to one another, in terms of content, context or age, especially age.

Document scans are provided by Monmouth in his book, *Genuine Witchcraft is Explained,* in their extant state, followed by readable transcripts that include the visible edits, and a third time as reconstructions where the extensive edits are removed from the originals leaving a pared down 'final version.' A *Rite of Initiation*, which may be doc. C2, is referred to by 'Robert' in an unprovenanced letter.

Supposedly authored by Cochrane, the writer, 'Robert,' describes it as a *'simple rite,'* adding that a more complex rite would tax the coven such that they'd be, *"sure to mess things up."* [218] Robert, whoever he proves to be, wrote this letter to 'Chalky,' whoever he proves to be. If this 'Robert' is actually Cochrane, and this 'Chalky' is actually Ronald White, then as Robert is informing Chalky of the 'simple rite' *he* had just written, and was sending onto Chalky, White could not have drafted it.

---

[216] See Appendix of scanned documents in *Genuine Witchcraft is Explained* as an original source document, C2, pages 299-301. See also Oates, 2016. Op. Cit. *SCSIII* doc. (b) pages 113-118.
[217] Viewable in the Appendix of scanned documents in *Genuine Witchcraft is Explained* See next ref. C3, pages 301-315
[218] Oates, 2016. Op. Cit. *SCSIII* p 107 doc. (a) Both documents can be studied here.

This means that the Rite of Initiation, allegedly found in pencil as a rough draft along with its allegedly later typed version, are unrelated to Cochrane or his Tradition. This means that not only is the rite referred to in the letter extremely unlikely to be either doc. C2 or doc. C3, but that any refinement White and Winter, or indeed, anyone else, applied in their presumed revisions was *not* to the simple rite referred to in Robert's letter, enclosed for their use.

What should be realised here, is the significance of certain pieces of writing White created in the months following Cochrane's death that were overlooked by Monmouth, seeing something else in them. White's notepads for September 1966 exhibit rough drafts for *The Rite of Initiation* and *Basic Craft Theology*. [219]

These were certainly not composed for or implemented within the workings of *The Regency*. And if White had been preparing them at that time, just after Cochrane's death, they were clearly not created years earlier for an alleged phantom coven. More probably, it demonstrates his plans to form a new working group and recruit new initiates. That intent obviously changed when he later received a new epiphany at the Rollright Event at Hallow'en that year, to generate open, public gatherings instead. Perhaps when that dream had run its course, Ronald White returned to those notepads and developed his ideas in the private group he was rumoured to briefly hold in Shropshire.

Because the basic rite referred to in that letter is lost to time, any comparative analysis to either doc. C2 or doc. C3 is not possible. All that can be determined, relates to extant documents, not to those mentioned in other sources, without provenance or that have a speculative existence. What is certain, is that whoever composed C2, had no intention of it being a draft copy, but a completed document. Similarly, whenever C3 was composed, by whatever unknown party, it was typed up as an independent document a good number of years after C2. The previously discussed Document A4, as a drastic revision of (AAA) A2, bears resemblance to it; but doc. C3, bears no

---

[219] Monmouth, 2011. *GWiE* Op. Cit. p 97. Although Monmouth posits that some the information manifested in the Reading of the Festivals of the Year. A strange suggestion given that the document known as *The Reading of the Festivals of the Year* is actually a polished version of the ideas set out in the appropriate section of doc. (AAA) A2 for *The Thames Valley Coven*. This indicates White had later access to a copy of that early document. He had of course been a member of Everley's coven. So this may further link Everley to *The Thames Valley Coven*.

resemblance to C2 and is very clearly not a refinement of it. A few moments spent reading them side by side dispels any doubt.

The humble *three page* source document C2 is not a *draft* document, but forms part of the *Writ & Constitution,* it is lifted from. The *Writ & Constitution* cannot be the source for any document but itself, and readily appreciated as an original document. Bearing no resemblance to any other document, C3 is a sophisticated elaboration running to thirteen pages.

The two documents discuss totally different methodologies and modes of mentation, including language used, invocations and layout, which are fundamentally divergent. Different styles and methods of authorship can be detected for them, not least of which is relevant to the typewriters that produced them. Those are completely distinct; doc. C2 is typed on thin office *Large Post Quarto* typewriter paper, typical of the early sixties. C3 is actually a robust *A4* size paper, something of a mid-1970's phenomenon! [220]

Once more, this confirms that docs. C2 and C3 were created over a decade apart! Monmouth's speculative guess of a few months is off point by many years. The modern style of doc. C3 is similar only to one other document and that is Monmouth's assumed *A4 Final Version* for the *Writ & Constitution*.[221] To some degree therefore, although doc. C3 is more recent still than doc. A4, they appear reasonably contemporary with one another. Both are entirely incongruous to the much older, tissue thin and oddly sized documents in this cache.

Though Monmouth concedes the pencilled edits on doc. C3 are in the hand of Ronald White, he attempts to steer attention away from the evident similarities between docs. C3 and A4, which distinguish them from others by their more recent appearance. By suggesting an older date, c 1966 for doc. C3, he asserts an unnatural commonality with all the others, despite neither document being dated.

---

[220] 'A'4 paper size was set in 1975 and is based on a German standard originally from 1922. The UK entry into the common market in the 1970s introduced changes in the UK to comply with European standards which signalled the slow disintegration of all imperial measures and coin; our currency became decimal our weights and measures went over to metric, including the new metric paper sizes that adopted the ISO 216 standard 'A' series. This replaced foolscap and foolscap in offices across the UK within a couple of years, but the more popular 'foolscap folio' continued production and use into the 1980s. See Robin Kinross: *'A4 and before - Towards a long history of paper sizes'* http://www.nias.knaw.nl/Publications/KB%20Lecture/KB_06_Robert%20Kinross
[221] Monmouth, 2012. Op. Cit. A4 pages 282-287

Surface edits scribbled in pencil issue a directive to *'consult Roy,'* precisely at the point where the text begins to describe exactly where the *Building of the Bridge* is to be undertaken by the High Priest, *'using the correct formula.'* [222] At that part of the ritual, the officiating High Priest needed to *'consult'* (the formulae) *'Roy'* (had devised in *'The Bridge'* document) to understand how to proceed as directed!

By the contradictions Monmouth employs for his arguments, he loses them. Had White and Winter composed the 'Bridge' document they would have no need to consult anything directed towards 'Roy.' And Cochrane very obviously did not compose a rite after his death that requests he should consult his own earlier work about it.

Acknowledged by Cochrane as the major source of his knowledge, the *'old man of Westmoreland,'* had provided him with the basis of *The Broom & Sword* rite.[223] From that, Cochrane had composed a very explicit and specialised procedure, *Finding the Bridge*. [224] This entire rite is instrumental in *opening the gate*. At that juncture of initiation, the correct formula would indeed be crucial knowledge, without it, they could proceed no further. Since it was Cochrane's advice and counsel they needed, the *precedent set* over a decade earlier when Cochrane admonished 'Chalky' directly for failing to fulfil that exact procedure efficiently in a Clan rite around 1965, should be duly noted. [225]

Committed as ever to the search for truth, attention to an observable irregularity is required. Of all the documents within the cache, the *Writ & Constitution* doc. (AAA) A2, is a photo-copy. All the other documents and letters are originals. This is especially odd, given the Monmouth's claim that White and Winter were allegedly the (only) two surviving initiates of the phantom coven, a status he declared for them as the alleged foundation of all that followed. If that idea had even a semblance of possibility, would it not be reasonable to suppose that the *Writ & Constitution,* as *the* all important Initiatory document for their alleged coven of origin,

---

[222] Monmouth, 2012. Op. Cit. p 307 In addition to this fact, in common parlance, everyone refers to a 'named' source for instruction, especially deceased ones in such terms as 'consult Webster'
[223] Also referred to as 'Building the Bridge' as part of laying the Compass.
[224] Monmouth, 2012. Op. Cit. p 329-30
[225] See Oates, 2016. *SCSIII* p 244

would be an *extant original,* alongside the other original documents in this cache. And yet, it is not.

That mystery presents an uncomfortable predicament for Monmouth. Scribbled names on a photo-copy suggest either a very devious forgery, or rigorous revision of material discovered or acquired not of their own, therefore undertaken by individuals distinct in time and circumstance from those to whom the original once belonged and to those claimed by the Monmouth. As a document quoted in support of those claims, it actually illustrates only the existence of *another* coven entirely, displaying invalid signatures not contemporary with it. This lack of provenance is a huge issue. Everything hangs on it having authenticity and relevance to his claim for a phantom coven. It has neither.

In the first few pages of his book, Monmouth claims that White and Winter formed the coven that Cochrane joined and pushed his way to become its leader. Yet in a live You-Tube interview he made a contradictory comment to his own claim, when he admitted that in fact *'Ron White came to the coven.'* It was an unfortunate slip, but perhaps his focus had been on pressing the concept of a *coven* linked to Cochrane, so that he might then claim it as his fictional royal Windsor coven. [226] Of course, it was not a *coven*, but the *Clan* White joined.

Ghosts in the Machine.

Returning therefore to the events of 1959-60, and of Everley's Coven in London, Cochrane was involved with it, in some way . Fate may indeed have intervened as Cochrane often claimed, rendering time spent with Everley short, but significant. Referring later to these collective events in a letter to Bill Gray, Cochrane shared his disenchantment of antics witnessed in the previous coven he and his wife had attended. He went on to inform Bill Gray they had left under a cloud when tragedy and disagreement made it

---

[226] Cochrane never used the term 'Coven.' This usage is Monmouth's preference. YouTube Interview with Karagan . See *The Secret History of the Royal Windsor Coven & the Regency with John of Monmouth*. "9 Sep 2012 - Uploaded by WitchtalkShow
https://www.youtube.com/watch?v=WpAAmBpF0Us

uncomfortable for them to remain there. Valiente also notes that a lady named Diane died and that her partner, *Arthur* had followed Cochrane out when he left.

Leaving London to settle in Slough circa 1960, Cochrane soon set up his own coven, which *an* Arthur was part of, though it too appears to have been very short-lived, dissipating within a few short months. This course of events fails to distinguish which previous coven Cochrane and Valiente refer to; it could be the one Everley hosted in London, or Cochrane's first group in Slough.

As an anomaly it might help explain why the names of Robert and Jane Bentback on doc. (AAA) A2 are presumed to be those of Cochrane and his wife. Placed beside those of Arthur's and Diane's, they are collectively listed as the four Elders on *The Oath of Loyalty* document to *The Thames Valley Coven*. The Priest and Priestess listed in rank above the Elders, are not named and leave no signatures on this document. Only the four persons named above are validated Elders recorded there. [227]

Additional documents in the cache collectively present a greater conundrum than they solve, providing some small, but useful insight here, especially when studied closely. Significant amongst them, and noted already, the *Writ & Constitution* doc. includes a section that describes the *Hierarchies of the Coven*, a list of offices held by members of *The Thames Valley Coven*, which unmistakably places its Elders *below* the rank of Priest and Priestess.

Even supposing this could in any way relate to a coven of which Cochrane, his wife, White and Winter were members, any authority would again undisputedly fall to Cochrane and his wife. It would determine those traditions were from the outset, founded by Robert Cochrane, and run by himself as Head-Kinsman, thereby contradicting Monmouth's foundless proposition that fails to replace Cochrane with Ronald White. The existence of a coven's name is absolutely irrelevant *to that* basic premise. There is no means by which that changes in White's favour.

The inconsistencies deepen. If Cochrane and his wife had served as the Priest and Priestess of that coven, it might explain the absence of their names as Bowers or Cochrane amongst the four named Elders, a fact that would automatically negate their

---

[227] Oates, 2016 *SCSIII* Op. Cit. See Writ & Constitution doc. (d) p 121

identification as Robert and Jane Bentback. Conversely, if those identifications can be shown as correct for Robert Cochrane and his wife, then as Elders, they could not be Priest and Priestess. Lack of any other information at this time makes it impossible to properly determine if *The Thames Valley Coven* was Everley's, the group Cochrane and his wife left behind them in London, or the first coven they instigated in Slough, which as stated, disintegrated almost immediately. Enquiries regarding their identities amongst Craft Elders have gleaned little to advance a solution to the mystery, although, the following comment offers an interesting suggestion.

> I can alas offer no positive identification of Arthur and Diane Oakwood. On the other hand, I have encountered the name 'Oakwood' in a different context. Until they moved to Jean's Crouch End house in the 1970s, the old Bricket Wood coven used to meet at 'Fiveacres' - the Naturist Club in Bricket Wood, and this club is just off Oakwood Road. This may of course be entirely coincidental but I mention it in case it supports any other snippets you may have discovered.[228]

There is a letter in the cache that mentions a *Jean*. But at least two other leading ladies in the Craft were called Jean. Despite such speculation, all we know for sure is that around this time, Cochrane soon fell out with *Arthur,* and Diane died. If further research is able to prove *The Thames Valley Coven* was Everley's, and not Cochrane's, then it would certainly explain more of the current irregularities and help establish authorship for several other very early documents of a highly Wican and quasi-Masonic content. Significantly, the only certainty in either case, is that the documents would obviously <u>not</u> be authored by Cochrane, but by Arthur Everley.

      This would help explain why the handwriting in black ink is *not* in the hand of Cochrane or his wife and why at least one other letter in the cache of documents signed *Robert Bentback*, is of a very different style and tone to anything Cochrane has ever written. Enigmatic subject matter could be resolved more productively by this perspective. On the other hand, if future evidence is able to prove *The Thames Valley Coven* to be Cochrane's, it would need to explain

---

[228] Private Correspondence from Clive Harper to Shani Oates [email 7/31/16]

these and other considerable discrepancies right across this cache. It would definitely need to address the reason why there are two extra names on a document (AAA) A2 , where they do not belong, and are so very out of place.

There is a notable distinction between what is simply an *authentic document,* given some validity for its apparent form, age, and subject matter, its content etc and an *authenticated document* that can be verifiably attributed to a particular author's style, where it is accepted as an original or unique work by that author (i.e. neither a copy, nor a later original). All the documents in the cache have been examined by Prof. Hutton and by Marian Green, both of whom have agreed the *documents* are authentic. [229] And so they are, as far as the paper and possibly even the typewriters used, and how they relate to Craft history during the 1960s.

Nonetheless, these documents *have not* been authentically attributed to any specific author, nor are all of them original. How could they be. There are at least five, possibly six different people responsible for these documents, spanning a decade. Where any text is ambiguous or where any signature or name is absent, then the *sense* of a person's style might suggest a certain author; though of course, in other cases, it is easier to determine *who is not* the author by their inclusion in the body of text, or as its recipient/s.

Signatures *may* suggest an author, but handwriting styles raise significant alerts to authenticity. Faded stained papers veil the type beneath, yet are over-written in biro. If contemporary with the type, the writing would be similarly subject to the fading marks of time. Other documents are either dubious copies, or photocopies. [230]

Academic scrutiny alone will shed further light upon this cache of documents. If we are to have any hope of determining correct authorship and to securing rightful validation for this treasure hoard, irrespective of who the people involved are eventually proven to be; this should be embraced. To pretend otherwise, is to further obfuscate the search for truth. What these hastily appropriated but vital texts collectively posit, is an evolving history of the peoples that gravitated around a vibrant source, around *someone* endowed with

---

[229] Monmouth, 2012. Op. Cit. p 5
[230] Oates, 2016. Op. Cit. See *SCSIII*: Chronology of the Robert Cochrane Letters Doc: Study all letters in the chronology section.

conspicuous Virtue. As an inspiring genius, this quality is evidenced unequivocally throughout Cochrane's body of work.

The document entitled: *The Writ and Constitution of (the Thames Valley) Coven dedicated to Diana,* presents just a couple of discreet elements that may be recognised within some tenets of *Robert Cochrane's Clan Tradition,* whether by influence or design. Of course, this may be due to coincidence, a rare if not impossible quality; a commonality of shared interest in those matters is highly possible, or, they may just suggest direct influence – in Companie. This latter option is temptingly feasible, but we simply do not know. The matter is inconclusive, so remains hypothetical.

Tenets of Law and of Troth remain appropriate even today, readily understood by a person taking their *Oath of Loyalty and Acceptance* (Admission) into the Clan today. It is equally true to say these principles are common to all formal Inductions across a wide-ranging spectrum, including numerous modalities of Craft from the Horse-mans' Word to Freemasonry, occult systems and lodges.

As a personal record, it conveys what is meant by *The Constitution*, a gravid concept known to the Clan in perhaps more mystical terms as: *The Covenant*. All others tenets, laws, proscriptions and directives are however, totally alien to the Clan (CTC). Supporting documentation is sorely needed.

After Cochrane had moved on from Everley, aside from the Clan, his only other reference was to the *Society of Kerridwen*.[231] Forming a bewildering corpus of names, the interplay between them, over half a century ago, is overwhelming. Any attempt to unravel one from another is wrought with peril. To cite just one example - a lady sculptress, sponsored by Arthur Oakwood (identity unknown) is noted in one of the hand-written letters of the cache. She is also given scant mention by Valiente, who suggests the lady sculptress is Monica English.

CTC have painstakingly acquired more information of some relevance concerning this enigmatic lady from a variety of sources that lead back to Cottie Burland with whom Cochrane claimed to be planning to write a book together.[232] After Cochrane's death, Burland completed and published his book in which a lady named

---

[231] Cochrane to Bill Gray #
[232] Valiente, 1966. Op. cit. Notepad entry. Museum of Witchcraft Archives

Monica English features. Other writers, including Michael Howard[233] and Lois Bourne[234] have mentioned her in their writings. Hailed as Mistress of her own traditional coven in the late 1950s, she apparently joined the *Bricket Wood Coven* led by Lois Bourne, just long enough to analyse what Gardner's *Craft of the Wica* was all about.

After Gardner's death in 1964, Bourne left Bricket Wood. Persuaded by English to join her coven upon her return to Norfolk, Bourne did so, and remained with them for a while. A few years later in the very late 1960s, English retired and moved away to Hertfordshire with her husband, the coven's former Magister, leaving their intriguing activities in Norfolk behind them. Marian Green is described as one of several people from that circle of associates to have known Lois Bourne and Monica English well enough to have worked with them in Norfolk, although Marian Green emphatically denies this. [235]

A person matching Monica's profile is referred to in one of the hand-written letters to Chalky (allegedly by Cochrane) regarding a new recruit known to George. English is approximately the same age as George Desmond Bourke. This scenario is another in which all the major players are involved, adding as many anomalies as it offers possible resolutions. CTC have perhaps discovered the name of a person referred to in a letter, a letter that is unfortunately tampered with, so remains under suspicion. It is not known why English would pursue induction into another traditional coven at a time when, according to one source, she was allegedly the Mistress of her own.[236]

Well known by *a* George, to Lois Bourne, and possibly to Marian Green, but not to Robert Cochrane, at least not outwardly, there is little else to advance understanding of her motives. Though it should be remembered, it was not at all uncommon for people to move about and work with others in their era. She was out of Cochrane's societal league and strata of acquaintance. Hers was the world of twin-sets and pearls, sherry and cake, Cochrane despised.

What is certainly fascinating, is that English appears to have shared several tenets of Cochrane's distinctive, personal ethos concerning a belief in the Master of this World, and a Triune Aegis.

---

[233] Howard, Michael. *Children of Cain* (UK: Three Hands Press 2011)
[234] Bourne, Lois *Dancing with Witches* (UK: Hale, 1998)
[235] Howard, 2011. Op Cit.
[236] Howard, 2011. Op. Cit.

Both Cochrane and English acknowledged the Horsemen, the old craft and held reverence for silent workings, especially when engaging the *Other*, though it may simply example generic aspects of old Craft, witnessed in those covens.

The mystery continues. This critique is focussed intently upon Clan history, from inception to its current status. Some interesting points of its event time-line overlap with those of others that warrant further exploration where they appear to deviate from the primary focus. Of course, the history of *The Regency* is *not* Clan history. All explanations propose exposure of error, and are accompanied by unequivocal explanation, bringing clarity where confusion had previously prevailed.

Signatures are frequently inconsistent. Even the name Diane/a, one of the signatories on *The Oath of Loyalty* doc. (AAA) A2 document looks over-signed and tampered with on close inspection, possibly to conceal another beneath it? That of Fiona perhaps? One lady who knew all the major players quite well at this time, was Madge Worthington, a major figure in that history, and well known to Valiente.

Madge Worthington began her training in the mid-sixties into the *Craft of the Wica* and rose steadily through her degrees via a very mysterious figure, *Andrew Demaine*. Referred to as *Virgilio* by Valiente, he was an initiate of Celia Penny of the Bricket Wood Coven; Celia may have been initiated by Jack Bracelin.[237] Madge Worthington worked with Arthur Eaglan who was an initiate and High Priest of another of Gardner's ladies, Eleanor Bone, who died in 2003.

Madge Worthington established *The Merry Dancers* with Arthur Eaglan as her HP, a Wican lineage better known today as *The Whitecroft Line*. This was because Arthur's house was in Whitecroft Way. Associations between Madge W. and Arthur E. with Arthur and Diane Oakwood continue to be speculative, remaining possible, but unlikely. Perhaps the identity of Diane/a should be re-considered?

---

[237] Ibid. Valiente, Notepad entry, as per her former comment and date. M. W. who died in 2005. And our thanks go to *The Wiccan* readers' research project 2016. Details supplied by Clive Harper; personal communication 12 Sept 2017.

Valiente recorded someone by that name who suffered a tragic death just before Cochrane moved to Slough from Soho. And though it is tempting to assume this person is one and the same Diane known to Cochrane and his wife in Everley's London group, and who is potentially Diane Oakwood, it cannot be verified without further information.

Celia Matthews whose death is dated to 1958, presents the best candidacy for an enigmatic lady who continues to prove elusive. Pseudonyms were commonplace amongst these closely knit personages of the London occult scene, and it was not uncommon for several to be engaged simultaneously.

The *Witchcraft Museum Archive* holds a significant file submitted by Reginald Hinchcliffe, one of the initial leaders and founders of *The Regency* (mark I), a good friend of Joe Wilson and an initiate of Lois Bourne. A scrawled message on the cover on a manila envelope mentions Cochrane in connection with Everley, the obscure person with probable links to The Thames Valley Coven, and to the enigmatic figure of *Arthur Oakwood* mentioned in a couple of early documents in the cache.

Another letter from this cache dated March 9th 1962,* allegedly from Cochrane to *Ronald White,* notes the correlation between an impending initiation for someone referred to only as George, and the *Virgin Moon.* As the New Moon for that month in that year had already occurred, this letter is potentially spurious. [238] This letter should be set aside until it can be proven as a valid contribution to this history. Truth is rarely complicated.

Avril remains unidentified. Only Avril had that much in common with Monica English. Monmouth presumes first of all, that 'George' is undoubtedly George Winter, and secondly, that his mentors were *Arthur and Diane/a Oakwood*, a couple identified by Monmouth as Laurence and Avril. Resolving nothing, such compound speculation generated only further confusion. [239]

Several other candidates offer possible identities for Arthur and Diane/a Oakwood, including Ian and Diane Richman, or Geoff and Louise Hampton-Cole, John & Jean Score, or Roy and Christine

---

[238] Oates, 2016 *SCSIII* Op. Cit. #(a) p 104
[239] Oates, 2016 *SCSIII* Op. Cit. #(a) p 104. With regard to the name Diane on doc. (AAA) A 2. It should be spelled with the 'e' and not the incorrect 'a' applied by Monmouth.

Harris; all of whom were around 'the scene' in the early 1960s. If any of these people, under whatever names they chose to be known by, are to be considered as likely candidates for *The Thames Valley Coven*, their names would have been recorded alongside Arthur and Diane/a Oakwood's on *The Oath of Loyalty* document (AAA) A2. No other original names are authenticated on that copy document. [240]

Both persons are mentioned in another letter allegedly from Cochrane to Ronald White in which instructions are given to *Chalky* [241] concerning forthcoming ritual preparations.[242] The person writing the letter refers to *L & A.*, abbreviations without further expansion or explanation. The author of that letter also refers to a lady named Avril, whom the writer suggests is *'difficult'* and may need removing from the group.

This authority is extended from the writer of that letter to its recipient to implement in his name. With possibly two operative groups under his aegis, Cochrane was certainly qualified to make that statement, pass that judgment and to deputise others in his stead. Yet, the writer could just as easily have been Everley. Positive identification is not an option with such limited and unverified source material to consult.

With regard to the plethora of pseudonyms, eponyms, titles and nick-names, positive identification for almost everyone remains problematic. As indeed it should, according to the discretionary tenets of the Old Craft. So there is good reason to believe that *Robert* like its medieval equivalent, *Robin*, is a generic title for a *son of Elphame,* a priest of the Goddess, rather than an actual, legitimate forename. Nothing connects *Robert* Cochrane with *Robert Bentback*, nor to Robert/Robin Gynt, the three Roberts referred to, may be distinct people rather than multiple identities for one person.

Former Clan's people do not recall Cochrane ever using Bentback, nor to referring to himself as such. In any biographical account, positive identification of key players and characters is paramount. Without this key, the entire history is impossible to

---

[240] Private Letter and discussions with V** Jones confirms existence of The Thames Valley Coven, albeit a long before the time she and EJJ joined, which by then was the Clan. See Oates, Shani. *Tubal's Mill: Legend: A Companion Guide to Tubal's Mill.* (UK: Create Space 2016)

[241] Presumed by Monmouth and Howard to be Ronald White. Valiente referred to Ronald White as Chalkie.

[242] Oates, 2016 *SCSIII* Op. Cit. See: Chronology of the Robert Cochrane Letters Doc: 'hand written letter to chalky'(c) p 119

follow with certainty. Because so many incidents and interactions depend upon knowing who is who, almost everything becomes speculative by default. Presumption obfuscates all potential facts.

Knowing that two extraneous signatures were added to *the copy document* (AAA) A2, does not help to determine when or by whom during the 50 years that document had been absent from public exposure. Beneath the signature for the unidentified alias *Will Maidenson* (whoever that might be), is another for the person signing that name by proxy as G. Stannard.

In a letter to Gray, Cochrane passed comment on a shade Gray had envisioned. Cochrane believed the shade might possibly relate to a deceased person:

> The old chap you saw, I can't place him, except as a man I know as Willum, he was a Norfolk witch, and a great friend of a living friend (one of the Clan) of ours. He was the husband of a delightful old woman who initiated George (our friend) when he was a young man. George swears by Old Mary Maiden and Willum, they were his great friends. [243]

From this blank comment regarding *Willum and Mary Maiden*, with no positive identification of either person mentioned, Monmouth claimed an identity for George Winter as *Will Maidenson*, stated as fact. However, without exception, this idiosyncratic composite name form *does not* appear in Cochrane's letter to Bill Gray nor is it mentioned anywhere else, except as noted above, where it occurs as a suspicious addendum to a document that has no proven connection to Robert Cochrane and his Tradition. (*The Thames Valley Coven* doc. (AAA)A2). There is nothing to link anyone known, with the alias given as *Will Maidenson*.

What is most curious is that the signatory felt the need to add *G. Stannard* beneath it, as if to ensure the reader would not wonder about his identity and mistake *Will* for someone else, or George Stannard (Winter) for that matter. Cochrane confirmed only that *a* George was a member of the Clan. No certain identity is given for

---

[243] Oates, 2016. *SCSIII* Op. Cit. Letter from Cochrane to Bill Gray #VIII. p 281 Note the specific reference by Cochrane to the Clan, frequently overlooked by Monmouth, who insisted Cochrane's group was a 'coven,' and ignored by Howard who denied the association of the Clan with Cochrane, claiming E.J.J.' established it after Cochrane's death.

any of these people, and tracing them through alternative names or identities is exceedingly problematic.

By a series of presumptions, Monmouth insisted that *Ronald White = Chalky = Robert and Robin Gynt*. Certainty of this notion depends on specific facts. For example, the first thing that would have to be established is that when Cochrane referred to *Chalkie,* that person is the same person referred to as *Chalky*, which then requires further corroboration that Chalky, referred to Ronald White and not to someone else. Remembering that Valiente records in her note pads a definitive reference to Ronald White as *Chalkie*, but not Chalky, makes any alternative identification a wary and cautious action.

Following that, identification of Chalky with Robert and then Robert with Robin is essential, not merely implied or assumed, as Monmouth does. There is a single letter written to *Chalky, Robin Gynt*, but this happens to be the dubious letter that remains under suspicion. The letter also specifically mentions *Robin*, not Robert. Curiously, *Robert* Gynt is the second of two extraneous signatures that are surface mounted on the graffiti riddled photo-copied Oath of Loyalty to *The Thames Valley Coven* (AAA).

Again, both Monmouth and Howard freely espouse that *Chalky/Robin/Robert Gynt* is Ronald White, and that several of these letters either address Ronald White or are composed by him. This may yet prove to be true, and though probable, there are no precedents to secure this as fact.

Nonetheless, we should sensibly be alerted to the inconsistent references to Chalky, *Chalkie, Chalk, Ron, Robyn, Robin,* and *Robert*, all of which allegedly refer to Ronald White. Either everyone who'd known him could not make their mind up what to call him and how to spell it, or they were addressing different people, possibly even unknown from each other in time. Beyond opinion, nothing certifies anything as fact.

George Stannard/Winter is allegedly *Will Maidenson*, not to mention *Old George*. A reliable differentiation between *Chalkie* and *Chalky*, or *George from George W.* may prove impossible to achieve. Of course it is known for certain that George Stannard/Winter and Ronald White *did* eventually join the Clan circa 1963/4. But, due to their propensity for dropping in and out, a precise date remains indeterminable.

One other odd document in this curious cache of letters is addressed to Avril *and* Chalkie (sic) with no further clue as to who these people are. What the documents demonstrate very well, is that even collectively, because they fail as credible evidence, it is impossible to differentiate between aliases. Similarly, it is equally impossible to validate the true personas referred to within them. Realistically, nothing makes their identities conclusive.

Other names require some exploration, if only to emphasise the extraordinary task this entails, not to mention the impossibility of it in the face of such entanglements. What is known of this period in the late 1950s is that amongst this very small cliché of Craft and Occult people working in and around London, was a certain personage known then as *Laurence* Amos/Anton Miles, (1911-92)..

Laurence is mentioned in more than one letter by Monmouth as Arthur Oakwood. Despite ambiguous shadow, we are informed that his wife, named *Diane*, died circa 1958-9. She has the right name and the date is a fair contextual match to put them both forward as contenders for the aliases Arthur and Diane/a Oakwood, but still, it is not known if there are two persons named Laurence, or if they are one and the same.

Allegedly leaving England around 1959 for Australia, Laurence maintained a correspondence with Charles Clark,[244] secretary to G. B. Gardner, and close associate of both Lois Pearson (later Bourne) and Eleanor Bone. Laurence and his wife established a successful Wican group there dedicated to Pan and Diana, coincidently sharing a Tutelary deity with *The Thames Valley Coven*. Common enough in popular belief of course, but curious nonetheless.

Valiente made personal brief memos to herself, to send various rituals and documents onto Laurence for study and practise. That prominent Wicans were corresponding with him, builds a strong context for Melissa Seims' research. Seims states that according to her source, *Laurence* had his initiation in the *Bricket Wood* coven near St Albans in 1959. Seims did not derive this information from the High Priestess of that coven, *Dayonis*, but from Michael

---

[244] The person Eleanor Bone names as connected to the Traditional Witchcraft Group in Cumberland.

Howard.[245] Dayonis, (Bracelin's girlfriend) may have briefly served Bricket Wood Coven as the HPs after Valiente's departure in 1957 and before Lois Pearson (later Bourne) was instated in October 1959.[246] A positive identification of *this* Laurence as Arthur Oakwood remains elusive.[247]

A few years later, his studies in India drew him into the Tantric sect of *Uttarakaulas, Sahajiya* cult of Varanasi, and Laurence became the Chief Guru of the *Adinthas*. There, he changed his name to *Sri Gurudeva Mahendranath Mehendranath 999*.[248] He had known Aleister Crowley and was also a friend of Gerald Gardner. He was also allegedly Chief Guru to Andrew Chumbley in the *Uttarakaulas* sect. Certainly, the Laurence known as Anton Miles had a colourful history, which appears woven into that of the Clan. Given that crossing in Wyrd, it is needful to include coincidental occurrences that prove particularly relevant here:

> Andrew Chumbley was initiated into the Uttarakaulas as the Western Parampara or successor preceptor to Sri Vilasanath Maharaj. John Power (Sri Vilasanath Maharaj) was given the Uttarakaula succession by Sri Gurudeva Mahendranath Mehendranath 999 (Lawrence Amos Anton Miles), of the Northern Klan of Secret Tantriks of Ranchi, India. [249]

Andrew Chumbley and John Power did not agree on the issue of lineage. According to John Power, Chumbley did not share the fundamental premise of their belief, which concerned lineage and

---

[245] Seims, Melissa #116 May 2005 The Cauldron *'A Dedication to Charles Clark'.* It is necessary to draw attention to the repeated occurrence of Michael Howard as a named source in articles that feature in his own magazine particularly. Michael Howard rarely if ever, names *his* sources. And, where he does, as in the case of Julia Phillips, he is listed as their source! This creates the circular referencing system that always leads back to Michael Howard.

[246] Justine Glass, writing in *Prediction,* 1965, notes the 13 moons of Wica, as do many books and articles since. Between 1960-66, many newspapers and magazines [ref: Saga, Flash News, Daily Herald, The Sunday Telegraph, Life, Weekend Telegraph, Tit Bits and the Sheffield Star] featured sensationalist and defamatory articles on witchcraft, which led Valiente, Score and other to set up the WRA, for which Gerard Noel created *The Pentagram,* in 1964, as a hopeful media voice for it; but its potential quickly became utilised instead as a disparaging voice against Wica.
http://www.thewica.co.uk/Charles%20Clark%20Article.htm Melissa Seims.

[247] Tamara James. HPs briefly between Valiente and Bourne. Alongside her partner Richard James are the curators of Wican artefacts formerly belonging to G.B. Gardner (via Monique Wilson & Ripley's)

[248] http://www.shivashakti.com/dadaji.htm Anyone interested in Anton Miles may also find a small history in the previous reference by Melissa Seims.

[249] http://www.lashtal.com/forum/index.php?topic=5329.0

the *'passing of power upon the death of the Head Guru.'* Apparently, Chumbley was of the opinion that one need not wait until the head guru died for this to occur, and that it could be *passed* whilst he lived. Power's view on this is as follows:

> Andrew never really studied the system he was initiated in as successor, he more collected the initiation. As a result sadly he wasn't really in the second order of the system when he initiated others into it and without informing the head guru, John Power either those initiations need to be negotiated with John. Andrew declared war on his guru and though his guru tried to talk to him, he got blanked. [250]

Chumbley and Power were unable to resolve this tragic disagreement which occurred just six months before Chumbley died. This underscores once again, how the close proximity of the few occultists in and around London decades ago during the 1960s, no matter their denomination or occulted proclivities, has had far-reaching consequences into our own time, during the 21st century.

It is certain Laurence Anton Miles received an initiation in 1959, possibly just before he set out for his return to Sydney Australia in August; but by whom and where, remains undetermined. Seims claims it was Bricket Wood, but another source (independent of Michael Howard) merely states it somewhere near Watford. [251] The following elements of the rite noted by Laurence Anton Miles, stand out as totally incongruous to the general manner of the way Wican initiations are conducted. Laurence Anton Miles described the three tools that were presented to him, a knife, a cord and a lighted candle, all of which are strongly indicative of Clan Induction, as the following extracts demonstrate:

❖ a sharp knife for practical usage

❖ a cord, placed around his neck to indicate unswerving service (to the Master)

---

[250] http://www.lashtal.com/forum/index.php?topic=5329.0
[251] http://www.thewica.co.uk/Others.htm#anton

❖ and a candle, which he was instructed to 'take the flame', to light his own from the main altar candle to signify his own power is sourced and fed/nurtured by it, empowered by it as a continuous stream. He was then marked upon his forehead with coal. These are all initiatory hallmarks known by E. J. Jones for Induction in to a traditional group, and not typical at all of standard Wican practise. [252]

The description given on *The Initiation Rite* section of *The Writ & Constitution to a Coven to Diana*, bears an overwhelming similarity to Miles' expression of his highly experiential induction into 'something' in 1959.[253] Even though this information appears to support the probability that he and his wife Diane were the persons named on the original *Oath of Loyalty* within the *Writ & Constitution* composed for *The Thames Valley Coven*, it is insufficient to prove it. Certainty either way is unlikely.

Perhaps it is mere coincidence their paths converged at a time when Cochrane may have wished to form or inform an initial coven of like-minded souls to establish a working group. Cochrane's argument with someone named Laurence is validated in several sources noted already, including Valiente, White and Jones.

The identity of Arthur/Laurence and Diane/a is not crucial in any way to this biography of the Robert Cochrane Tradition, but it is of considerable interest to a shared history, known by Gardnerians, non-Wicans and Clansmen alike, especially with regard to untangling references made to other persons, and to the time-frames surrounding them. Making sense of the smaller mysteries allows us to create a context for the larger ones. Without context, all possibilities become meaningless and suspect.

In her history of Wicca, Julia Phillips made an interesting correlation, adding another dimension to this intriguing tale.

> We have two possible hereditary sources to the Gardnerian Craft: one, the *Horsa Coven* of Old Dorothy, and two, the Cumbrian Group into which Eleanor Bone claims to have been initiated before meeting Gardner. (. . .) Ray Bone: she was one of Gardner's HPSs, and her 'line' has been immensely important to

---

[252] Jones, E. J. *Witchcraft a Tradition Renewed* (Ed) Doreen Valiente. (UK: Hale, 1991) See chapter on Initiation.
[253] Oates, 2016 *SCSIII* Op. Cit. Doc (b) p 112.

the modern Wicca. (. . .) She ran two covens: one in Cumbria, and one in South London. (. . .) although her last coven moved to New Zealand many years ago, and she is no longer active. No-one has ever been able to trace the coven in New Zealand. [254]

Phillips raises an intriguing possibility that the coven in New Zealand is the one established by Anton (Laurence) and Diane, formed via a branch of Eleanor Bone's Traditional Craft connections in an older coven in Cumbria. Charles Clark had similar connections in Ayrshire and Lois Pearson in Norfolk. All of them, it seems, knew Laurence/Anton Miles, who knew Gardner, and very probably Robert Cochrane too.

If these fascinating connections can be validated with regard to the vague initiation undertaken by 'Laurence' at some point during 1959, they would anchor a date for the original *Writ & Constitution* doc. which certainly predates Cochrane's later friendships and Craft associations by several years, pushing back his viable history into the late 1950s.

Literary and oral sources would then combine in mutual support to bring clarity to Everley's London based coven Cochrane had joined, which had possibly been led by persons named in a hand written letter from the cache as Ray & Joan? It would assist a more certain identification of *The Thames Valley Coven,* and if this was Cochrane's first group, or one he'd joined.

Either would simultaneously explain why Ronald White and George Stannard/Winter were certainly *not* original signatories on the Oath document. These cumulative factors lend considerable weight to their absence in Cochrane's initial group, prior to forming the Clan around himself.

Remember, Cochrane had confirmed to Bill Gray, the problematic and traumatic disintegration of a former group and of a coven he had led, that had fallen apart after *'playing silly beggars,'* and before long, those who were left, had ended up *'going over to Aradia.'* After making this allusion to Gardner's Craft of the Wica, Cochrane bemoaned the weariness of leadership. He was obviously stinging from what he perceived as a betrayal of his leadership. The following

---

[254] http://www.sacred-texts.com/pag/wiccahst.txt Julia Phillips

comment refers to his vacillation between duty and personal pilgrimage:

> I am seriously considering leaving my group and working alone. I may sound dreadfully un-humble, but Jane and I have reached a stage when we can go faster by ourselves. The group is beginning to pull us backwards, and I for one would like to establish a new leader and move on myself. We had a brilliant 'flash of light recently that may lead to the end of an old era, and the beginning of a new one for us. The gods seem to favour us leaving also since they are going their hardest to stop new blood from coming in. We shall see whether it is meant that way, or whether the gods are just saying 'This is what it is like. See! You bumbling little worm.'
>
> The article I have written for New Dimensions[255] has been accepted and I received the magnificent sum of three nikker....well, well... I suppose now that I am considering moving on, hundreds of very suitable people will want to come crowding in. We have had trouble in the past with various unsuitable types, I was once in charge of a full and balanced cuveen, but they wanted to play at silly beggars, so I let them (we moved on). Net results, broken hearts and broken heads, but they still don't seem to have learned. The last I heard from them was that they had gone over to Aradia as 'it is so exciting' and have taken a vote to share the women out. Sex and Witchcraft Whee! The messes some people get into over that little bit of flesh. I suppose one cannot make silk purses out of sows ear'oles. [256]

A letter written by Cochrane to Norman Gills had referred to Evan John Jones and 'Dick' as his named candidates for the *two apprentices*,[257] not *Chalky and George*.[258] This provides a cross-reference for the two anonymous people Cochrane noted in a contemporary letter to Bill Gray.[259]

One of the recruits, drafted in by E.J.J. and 'Dick,' is significantly listed as a schoolteacher, the known profession of Ronald

---

[255] 'A Witches Esbat' *New Dimensions* November 1964 Republished in Oates, 2016. *SCSIII* Op. Cit. p 282

[256] Oates, 2016. *SCSIII* Op. Cit. Cochrane to Gray. #II p 250 This could very easily refer to the same people as mentioned already, Laurence, Ronald, George, Madge, Arthur, Monica etc.

[257] Oates, 2016 *SCSIII* Op. Cit. #6 Cochrane to Gills p 405

[258] Monmouth, 2012. Op. Cit. As suggested in his assessment of these documents.

[259] Oates, 2016. *SCSIII* Op. Cit. Cochrane to Gray #IV p 258

White.[260] Prior to that, during 1963, Cochrane listed himself and Jane amongst his (then) other members in an Esbat Rite he later published the following year in *New Dimensions*. The remaining men are named as: Arthur, Blackie, John and Peter.

Thus far, sufficient cross-referencing suggests these men are Arthur Oakwood, Sean Black, E. J. Jones and Peter West. E.J.J. needs no further introduction and Arthur has already been discussed. Peter was the husband of Sandra West, a lady well known to Cochrane and also to Bill Gray.

Sandra West was the writer of the *Devil's Prayer Book* under the pseudonym *'A Witch.'* Valiente suggested that West's rather controversial little book *'may be based on Ruth Wynn Owen's rituals.'* Sandra West was a close friend of Jacqueline Murray, Anne S. and George Bourke. West's husband Peter shared Cochrane's extreme left-wing politics. Sean Black, is a figure of whom very little is known.

A couple of vague references made by Valiente illustrate her plans to attend a Clan meeting in August 1964 and how she mapped out that journey. Noting a very special Pub favoured by Cochrane's wife, Jane, named *The Ploughshare* in *Pyecombe Valley,* a small window into their lives brings further clues as to who gravitated into their orbit. [261]

The O. S. co-ordinates scribbled on another letter indicate the High Mound of Newtimber, the stamping ground for the Clan in Cochrane's life time, and a place of annual pilgrimage for E.J.J. and Bill Gray for 20 odd years after Cochrane's death. Valiente records that she sometimes joined them in this annual vigil.

Sean Black was the smith in *Pyecombe*, a village in the vale below *Newtimber*. He may even have assisted Cochrane and E.J.J. to forge a sword, and very probably the iconic Horned god on his wall. Both these artefacts (observed earlier by Bampton), disappeared when Cochrane died.

Looking at the pattern of interaction between some of these people, their activities and familiarity with each other have been confused by John of Monmouth, who repeatedly referred to them as initiates of his phantom coven. When questioned about this by Clan

---

[260] Oates, 2016 *SCSIII* Op. Cit. Cochrane to Bill Gray #IV p 258
[261] Valiente, 1964. Op. Cit. Notepad entry date 25/11/1964

members, Marian Green, for example was able only to say that she'd heard of the (alleged) existence of the coven in question, but absolutely contests Monmouth's oblique explanation and false endorsement of her as a member of a Royal Windsor Coven, or anything else for that matter.[262]

Monmouth's insistence on the existence for that group, fails by its dearth of references contemporary to those persons allegedly involved. By way of contrast, abundant references and contemporary commentary *do* exist for Cochrane's *Clan of Tubal Cain*.

Valiente recorded her own later discovery that a lady named *Joan*,[263] the first wife of someone (also) named *Arthur*, died in tragic circumstances identical to the other aforementioned lady named *Diane/a*, an incident that had allegedly broken up the London group Cochrane had briefly belonged to.

Valiente wrote that, *'Roy had quarrelled with another man.'*[264] This information strongly implies that Arthur Everley and his wife Joan (?), who later died, are also possible candidates for the enigmatic signatories of the *Oath of Loyalty* doc. known as Arthur and Diane Oakwood, Elders of *The Thames Valley Coven*.

A rather curious letter is cited by John of Monmouth as one penned by Jane Bowers. Unmistakably signed off in a Wican manner, *'Blessed Be, Joan,'* it is *not* in Jane's hand.[265] The signature style is all wrong when compared to another validated example; nor is the style one she adopts when signing off. Moreover, she was never a *Joan*.

The letter to *Chalky* (not *Chalkie*) March 27th (no year date given), is very much a puzzle.[266] As noted, it is signed by *Joan*. Concerning a recent ritual flop, an embarrassing incident that had left everyone quite deflated, *Joan* mentioned *Laurence and Diana (rather than Diane)* by name, whose inability to cope with an impromptu ceremony had created the regrettable disruption. Joan also referred to someone named *Ray* whose laughter she believed was due to nervous anxiety. Ray is implied as her husband.

---

[262] Private Correspondence. Quoted, courtesy of Marian Green summer 2016/17
[263] Joan may be a generic name she uses for either a name unknown to her, or in place of a secret name.
[264] Suggested by several people as *Arthur* Everley, who is also named in Hinchcliffe's notes, who is confirmed as commercial artist there, and in Valiente's notebooks. Of course, 'Joan' may have been an alias Diane used – or vice-versa.
[265] Oates, 2016. *SCSIII* Op. Cit. 2016. (ooo) p 94
[266] Oates, 2016. *SCSIII* Op. Cit. 2016. (ooo) p 94

Several guests present during this rite, included Chalky/Robin and George (?), Norman (Gills?) and Jean, another lady who was possibly Norman's wife, partner or indeed, another lady by that name. This letter's inconsistencies when compared with known facts render it quite inexplicable.

Another Joan, (Hughes) was in Cardell's Coven. Eleanor (Ray) Bone's coven at that time included a lady named Joan Westcott. Certainly that some of the people mentioned in this particular letter were Wican initiates, mostly via Lois Pearson/Bourne and Eleanor Bone. They are the same people noted in connection with *Laurence* Anton Miles.

The letter's presumed relevance to *The Regency* or to the Clan, is completely unfounded. Any presumed connection should be rejected, as better evidence suggests it refers back to Everley's coven in London circa 1958-9. Obviously the people within this group though known to one another, were untested in the means of ritual work, and in group dynamics.

From descriptions provided, the work follows strictly Wican patterns, using terms that reflect this. Amongst Valiente's associates, several of these persons were known to her also. In her Notepads, she had listed more than one *Ray, Jean and Joan*. Aliases account for only some of these people, so tracking them effectively is almost impossible.

Cochrane's introductory letter to Gills very late in 1964, secures a cross-reference that provides unequivocal confirmation that Cochrane and his wife did not meet Norman Gills until the end of 1965. [267] Therefore, the *Joan* letter absolutely *cannot* refer to any coven in any time frame that places Norman Gills together with Robert Cochrane. And it is plain to see, that Ray and Joan, written quite clearly, *are not* Roy and Jane, and who are not even mentioned in this letter which seems to focus entirely upon Laurence and Diane.

It is tempting to conclude this letter refers to the actual Initiation of Laurence and Diane that allegedly took place in Bricket Wood.[268] If true, then how many other clues are linked to that needs to be determined. For example, if this is the *same* Laurence and

---

[267] Oates, 2016. *SCSIII* Op. Cit. See: Chronology of the Robert Cochrane Letters Bowers to Gills #1. p 289
[268] According to Michael Howard, who did not provide a reference to support this information.

Diane that may have previously signed the oath to '*The Thames Valley Coven*' as Arthur and Diane Oakwood, then what of the real identities of Robert and Jane Bentback.

If these do point towards Cochrane and his wife and not to others better suited for those names, then substantial evidence must also exist for their initiations alongside those of Miles and his wife, whose initiations *are* acknowledged and recorded. To leave them out makes no sense. But what makes better sense, is that those other two names refer to very different candidates.

What of the Norman and Jean cited in that letter, noted as Gills and his wife by that same authority; however, Valiente has Norman listed as a bachelor specifically, rather than widower, who lived alone with his Mother, and frequented by many ladies!

A radical approach is required to make any sense of this compound muddle. Norman and Jean are both familiar to Laurence, whose own letter in September 1963, mentioned by Monmouth, informs the reader of time spent with a *Norman and Jean* since their last meeting. It could very sensibly refer to someone other than Norman Gills. This would mean that Monmouth is mistaken in his identification of *Norman* with Norman Gills. Without access to the missing letter and a better understanding of the events noted in that letter, a true conclusion is not possible. In any event, whoever this particular Norman and Jean is, they were no part of Cochrane's circle of friends or associates before or after he also briefly joined *The Thames Valley Coven*.

Either way, questions remain. Monmouth makes far too many conjectural connections without evidence or support. He is undoubtedly way off in his assumption that Ray and Joan are *Roy and Jane* (Bowers). Everything here contradicts that completely.

As one of just a handful of documents that stubbornly remain elusive, and frequently pose more questions than they answer, the absence of any reference to Roy/Robert or Jane/****[269] leads to one of two immediate possibilities. If the letter is genuine, then the presence of these unknown people determines not just an earlier time

---

[269] Jane is not her real name, but an alias. Her real name is not referred to either in any of these letters or documents.

period, but an entirely different body of people to those suggested by other writers, by desire or error. [270]

This letter does not include nor concern Cochrane and his wife, it discusses matters within a group to which they were not party, and of a date unknown. Alternatively, it is simply not a genuine document, but a mere forgery. (see sample signatures in the Appendices). At this stage, until further information is gathered, an inclination towards the former is both cautious and logical. Greater confusion was to follow.

An Entangled Web

Other accounts for these peoples and the events that embroiled them have been commented upon, too often sensationalized, undertaken without recourse to legitimate source material. Over two decades ago, Julia Phillips' light-hearted *History of Wica,* included many colourful asides, tales that involved people in other areas of the Craft, including CTC.

Some of these people shared only temporary associations or occasional interactions, while others engaged themselves quite deeply, seeking variety where possible. Phillips' narrative speaks on occasion as if quoting directly from texts composed by the people concerned, particularly when speaking of Doreen Valiente, whose Notepads relate a very different prose. Regrettably, Phillips was not well served by her primary source. Had she chosen Valiente for that task instead of Michael Howard, she would have received accurate information. Because of that oversight, Phillips' lecture lost its full value.

Phillips made several strange addendums to Valiente's comments, inferring an intent not originally present within them. In some cases, comments are sandwiched between actual quotes, implying a continuity or connection not indicated by Valiente. It may not have been Phillips' intention to imply her own statements as the opinion of Valiente's, but the text is explicit. To avoid the possibility of any such ambiguity, Phillips should perhaps have distinguished Valiente's personal comments from her own poorly (mis) informed

---

[270] Oates, 2016 *SCSIII* Op. Cit. Ref: Chronology of the Robert Cochrane Letters

view. The first example occurs where Phillips inserts the implication that Valiente believed she was *'completely taken in by Cochrane,'* that he was a fraud and a false friend who had placed her under some measure of regret. These are not Valiente's words.

Valiente remarked at length on her 1964 Clan Induction as a member of the *People of Goda*. She named Cochrane as Magister of the Clan. Commenting on the number of men and women in the Clan, she expressed her belief the Clan was 'unbalanced.' [271] This reflects Cochrane's comment in a letter to Bill Gray regarding an imbalanced *Robin* (group-mind). As with many of Cochrane's expressions, this too, has been misunderstood.

Neither Cochrane nor Valiente had implied an imbalance of the *male to female ratio,* but something entirely distinct from the common understanding of that term amongst those more accustomed to the Wican system. What they had meant, involved the metaphysics of personality, spirituality and the simple manifest presence of virtue that different people exude. Cochrane had recognised that a strong group needed its members to possess complimentary qualities that find completion in each another. Any shortage of one virtue, or the abundance of one, will lead to an imbalance.

After leaving the Clan in 1965, Valiente's involvement with some of its members, namely E.J.J., his wife V.J., and Bill and Bobbie Gray, endured through ever deepening friendships. With others, namely guests and associates, Valiente dedicated herself to the shared vision and creation of the *WRA*, specifically with John Math, aka Gerard Noel, a Clan guest who attended some of *The Regency rites*.

> As well as White and Valiente, the *'Witchcraft Research Association'* meeting in 1964 John Math, founder of and editor of *Pentagram* magazine; Tony Kelly founder of the Pagan Movement, was also present. [272]

Cochrane's reasons for instigating the Clan system facilitated greater endurance for a heritage he felt the Craft was in danger of losing. Bearing in mind that *no outsiders* were accepted into the Clan

---

[271] Valiente, 1989. Op. Cit. p 117
[272] http://www.geraldgardner.com/History_of_Wicca_Revised.pdf This meeting also included Madge Worthington. John Score was Tony Kelly, and John math was Gerard Noel. The WRA was first, known as *The Pagan Front*, before it changed to *The Pagan Federation*.

without *Induction*, Monmouth's notion that Cochrane's occasional invitation to others to attend the Sabbat rites as guests *of the Clan*, marked the distinction between a coven and a Clan, is easily negated.

By comparison, *separate, autonomous* covens, each with separate leadership assert a *Wican* modality, something Cochrane was savagely keen to avoid. Both Clan and covens may choose to include *guests*; but this is entirely discretionary, and nothing to do with how the group is structured.

Cochrane frequently discussed certain aspects garnered from a variety of sources with his correspondents; in this way, he passed on a great deal of information. More than once, Norman Gills became the beneficiary of prized gnosis. Addressing Norman (Gills?) in one letter, Cochrane shared with him an open invitation: *"Your Clan and my Clan, should get together."*

As Norman Gills was certainly never a member of his Clan, it is clear that whichever *Norman* Cochrane addressed here, they had both understood very well how individual covens were also part of their own Clans only, and separate from the covens within another's Clan. Referring to this custom of groups bound together within a Clan, Cochrane had once boasted to White that *"Our two groups are kosher."*

Phillips tackled nomenclature, using information from her primary source, Michael Howard, which obfuscated the 'real' name of Cochrane's Clan tradition. Ignoring the testaments of Cochrane, Wilson, Jones and Valiente that completely void the false projections Howard asserted through her, Phillips accepted his advice, presuming as so many have done, that he was the authority he claimed to be. Few have realised his knowledge of Cochrane's Clan Tradition was as an outsider looking in, reliant upon information others also on the outside, have relayed to him.

And though Valiente's authority as a former member of Admission into his Clan, is much diminished by Phillips' insinuation, that *'for a while, she worked with him and 'The Clan of Tubal Cain,'* it is at least a statement that admits Cochrane named his Tradition CTC. Phillips' surprising inclusion of an actual quotation taken directly from Valiente's Notepads to complete the above statement: *"as he described His tradition,"* speaks volumes in its affirmation.

Despite Valiente's clear and singular endorsement of *The Clan of Tubal Cain* as Robert Cochrane's Tradition, Phillips repeated the unfounded speculation that The Clan of Tubal Cain *"was also known as The Royal Windsor Cuveen (. . .) and as 1734."* Neither of these titles represent that tradition – one is fictional, the other refers to an entirely separate tradition.

Phillips presented the comment as if Valiente had espoused it, listing her among its members. No reference to that fictional title exists throughout the entirety of Valiente's works. Published *or private*, her writings and research were dedicated to disputing fallacies and exposing them whenever she could.

Uncertain of the dynamics of Cochrane's Tradition, Phillips faltered, asserting that CTC was not part of the allegedly 'original' (phantom) coven. The following verbatim paragraph taken from Julia Phillips' talk, further examples needless inaccuracies. Phillips pressed hard the false premise that the *Royal Windsor Coven,* was not only Cochrane's working group, but that it somehow sourced *The Regency* under the leadership of a former member – Ronald White.

Phillips maintained her tangential perspective of CTC, both before and after Cochrane's death. She even repeated the erroneous assumption that Valiente had been a member of *The Regency*. Finally, Phillips added that other former members of that coven had joined *The Regency*:

> *The Royal Windsor Cuveen* had disbanded after Cochrane died, only to be reborn from the ashes at Samhain, that year under a new name – *The Regency*. All of its early members were from the *Royal Windsor Cuveen*, and they were under the leadership of Ronald White. Meetings were held in North London, at a place called Queens Wood.[273]

Every sentence in this statement is wrong. Strangely confused by her advisor, Phillips conflated the Clan that existed from the outset, with an imaginary coven that did not exist and therefore formed no part of Cochrane's Tradition. She referred to them however, as if they were one and the same. Cochrane's group, properly known as CTC (not a phantom coven) did not die and become reborn - the Clan *continued* through E.J.J.' Magisterial leadership.

---

[273] http://www.geraldgardner.com/History_of_Wicca_Revised.pdf

The *Regency* was in no sense even a remotely connected resurgence of The Clan, but a completely separate entity. After Cochrane's death, of all former Clan members, only White and Winter became instrumental in forming the Regency – no others. And in 1967 when *The Regency* was formed, it did not do so under White's leadership. He became its leader only in 1969, when public controversy brought it to its knees and almost all it major players left.

Some only of those people from within the generic Craft scene who had *guested* at the occasional CTC rite became attendees at a few Regency festivals. They had never been members of CTC. Howard and Monmouth's claims for these people as former members, is totally false.

These gross inaccuracies were challenged by myself, at source. Michael's Howard's response was quite explicit. For his part in proffering poor advice, he stated only *"that she* [Phillips] *did not always get things right and that the only part she had got wrong was saying that it* [the phantom coven] *had disbanded on his death."* [274]

Monmouth upheld a similar view regarding the phantom coven. Though he believed the part Phillips got wrong concerned how the (phantom) coven revived itself as *The Regency*. Monmouth remarked that Julia Phillips' 'History' is: *"a flawed and inaccurate, poetic fiction."* [275] Despite the marginal differences in Howard and Monmouth's perspectives, their agendas in this subterfuge are transparent.

Distortion of the facts appeared without relent throughout Phillips' lecture, especially where her focus and attention fell to Robert Cochrane and his Clan. Comments made regarding the importance of *The Regency* to the foundation of Wica, find balance in this response by Ken Rees, who believes that claim is absolute nonsense. [276] Likewise Ken Rees shared with CTC his kindly view regarding Phillips' claims throughout this lecture:

---

[274] Julia Phillips - *History of Wicca in England* www.geraldgardner.com her main source had quite deliberately mislead her, and a good number of others too, on this and several other statements she made in this study. Phillips' exposition as a respected writer and speaker on Craft matters is sorely tested in this lecture.
Personal Correspondence. Email quote is from Howard to Oates. 2009. Interpolated emphasis is by Shani Oates.
[275] Monmouth, 2012. Op. Cit. pages 94/95
[276] Ken Rees, 2017. Op. Cit.

> Julia Phillips *History of Wicca* is full of holes. Asked wrong people about everything (probably M. H). She is honest as the day but naïve in her statements. Not academic, no critical insight into secondary sources, hearsay, etc.[277]

The perpetuation of these errata by other writers who simply repeat Phillips' work without checking *her* sources for accuracy, continues to perplex the Clan. Her mistaken reference to Cochrane's Tradition as the 1734 Tradition, which is an entirely separate modality established by Joe Wilson, *not* Robert Cochrane, led onto another nonsense Valiente had struggled to dispel.[278]

> The figures 1734 have an interesting history. Doreen gives a rather strange account of them in *The Rebirth of Witchcraft*, which contradicts what Cochrane himself describes in a letter to Joe Wilson, dated '12th Night 1966,' where he says: *'...the order of 1734 is not a date of an event but a grouping of numerals that mean something to a witch.'* [279]

Nothing it seems, is too easy to explain as an unprovenanced gift, an item of heritage from one's mentor or supposed ancestor. This particular incident involved an alleged heirloom in one of Cochrane's many pranks. Valiente's attempts to bring clarity to the popular urban myth, fell on deaf ears. She eventually resigned herself to the fact that some people simply prefer to uphold a fantasy rather than concede to fact.

Having subjected the author Enid Corral (aka Justine Glass) to a simple hoax, Cochrane revelled in the publishing errors that gave the impression of the copper plate as a family heirloom.[280] Inscribed with the numerals *17_2_4,* he'd claimed the date was significant to his Tradition. Although he declared the whole affair was nothing more than a mix-up between the photo images and accompanying text descriptions at the time, it had not prevented him from befuddling all concerned.

---

[277] Ken Rees, 2017. Op Cit.
[278] Valiente, 1989. Op cit.
[279] http://www.geraldgardner.com/History_of_Wicca_Revised.pdf
[280] Glass. J. *Witchcraft, the Sixth Sense & Us* (UK: Spearman 1965) Chapter xi. p2. This plate was bought by Valiente as a psalter for Roy Bowers, from a Brighton antique shop. It had belonged to an old family house by the name of Shellys.

When challenged on this churlish behaviour by Valiente, Cochrane did not dispute his retrospective negative treatment of Corral, stating only his deep offence at the superficiality on Corral's part. He'd explained at length certain details of his Craft to Corral, and excused his reactionary behaviour as contempt for her lack of conviction, especially her subsequent indulgence of sensationalism and fantasy. She had failed to research his interpretive advice beyond its face value. For that, Cochrane berated the book as unworthy of reading.[281]

Valiente believed his treatment of Corral to be immature, a sour prank that turned it into the grossly misrepresented debacle that has persisted ever since. She did however, become firm friends with the author of the book the prank appeared in - Justine Glass (Enid Corral), going on to work with her for some time after. Cochrane had seized upon an enigmatic mystery as a prime opportunity to exploit his gift for allegory, analogy and mnemonic, all part of his *grey magic* tactic to construct a craft narrative for the symbols carved into a 17th century monolith in France.

Depicting the passion of Christ, the St Uzec narrative generated Cochrane's commentary in a letter to Joe Wilson, in which he also discussed the 1734 numerals and the *17<u>2</u>4.* plate incident. And though these three matters are not even remotely connected, they have been referred to in confusing and often relative terms that either links them, or conflates them, a foolish misappropriation added to by others over the years, and repeated without thought.

The numerals and digits are unrelated to each other, the name of the Clan, and to its tutelary deity. This is not contradicted by Cochrane, Valiente or Wilson. Cochrane is quite explicit in his self-defining assertion that he is: a member of the *People of Goda, of the Clan of Tubal Cain* – not 1734 and not anywhere a Royal Windsor Coven. Evan John Jones expressed considerable concern for these and other nonsenses too often instigated by those who had no knowledge of the events they were so eager to pronounce upon.

During the early blossoming of both Wica and Traditional Craft, it has been shown how many of its adherents worked freely with others, and that very few groups were what we might today

---

[281] Valiente, 1989. Op cit. See Chapter on Cochrane for full explanation of the plate, the book and Justine Glass. (Rebirth of Witchcraft).

consider *closed* or *stabled*. Cochrane's scathing comment to Bill Gray concerning acts of betrayal, highlights how his first group had reneged their requisite focus and dedication, leading to his current fears for the second group.

An article Cochrane published in *New Dimension* around November 1964, is briefly discussed with Bill Gray in one of his letters. This allows a confident date for the events of the article to the previous year and possibly beyond even that, coinciding with the time that Ronald White began his renewed interest and assimilation back into Cochrane's *troupe*.

White had not been present for the famous Esbat Caving Rite, and Cochrane's later appraisal of him later, indicated a lack of commitment to the Clan; his attendance had been casual to say the least. Valuable as all parts are to the whole, and as influential as all ideas are, pooled for the collective, it is not the information one brings into a working environment that counts so much as *how* that is assimilated and put into practice, amongst and for that collective. Even subtle influences are easily observed, shedding light on emergent threads that weave a partial story only.

Those threads continued in the years following Cochrane's death in 1966. Everyone in the US had initially received all their information from Joe Wilson and his wife Mara between 1970 – 1974, albeit at different periods. The people who gifted their knowledge to Joe Wilson, and then to Mara Wilson, were, primarily: Bill Gray, A. S., Norman Gills, Michael Howard and Ruth Wynn Owen. After 1974, some of the Regency people additionally shared brief and sporadic correspondence with Joe Wilson; he'd attended several of *The Regency* (mark II) rites during his time in the UK.

Most of the afore-mentioned people extended the same open hospitality to the Finnins during their visits to the UK, during the mid to late 1980s, providing them with background information on *The Regency* people especially. Michael Howard was the person they nominated as their advised informant in that period. They even stayed with him as extended guests. [282]

Upon the Finnins' return to the US, all previous knowledge of Robert Cochrane and his Clan Tradition became overlaid with the

---

[282] Personal conversations with both EJJ, M. Howard and Ann Finnin about their stay in the UK in 1982 & 1986-7

confused perspective they expounded. Their works advanced certain adaptations from various influences both side of the ocean, including Joe and Mara Wilson, Poke Runyon, Ed Fitch, Norman Gills and Michael Howard. By their own admission, the Finnins' works exhibit almost zero influence from E.J.J, whose opinions they never trusted. Rather than plumb the tremendous resource they had in E.J.J., even the information that related to Robert Cochrane came to them through Michael Howard's filter.

All false claims regarding secret enclaves, inner groups and phantom covens arose only after Cochrane, Valiente, E.J.J. and their friends and associates were no longer around to counter them, offer advice, or indeed to confirm fact. Crucial knowledge of those times and of the people involved is scant at best.

Sometime ago CTC began seeking out anyone who might have further knowledge and understanding of those times and of the rumours that encompass them. Just because a thing is *known*, or even popular, does not make it a fact or true. For example, Marian Green, a long-standing author and craft practitioner, attended a couple of Clan Rites in 1965 for which she is listed as a member of the phantom coven by Monmouth.[283]

Denying membership of any group or coven, Marian Green has referred to her memorable time with the Clan within her own writings, upholding them as highly experiential moments of real magick. When questioned about the existence of the phantom coven, her response, sensibly ambivalent, states that: *"As far as I am aware, the Royal Windsor Coven did exist, in the 60s/70s."* [284]

Rather non-committal, Green cautiously reiterates an assumed belief based on the strength of rumour. Failing to confirm or deny by direct knowledge or association, her response contradicts Monmouth's edict that placed everyone under an alleged oath of extreme secrecy. Monmouth declared that proof of the coven's reality lies in its *repudiation* by members when questioned!

As a historian of craft matters and member of *The Regency* in the late 1970s, Ken Rees, who had known Ronald White personally confesses to a knowledge of a Royal Windsor Coven as hearsay only. Making a concerted effort to recall and track down the first time it

---

[283] Monmouth, 2012 Op. Cit. p 32
[284] Personal Correspondence. From MG to SLO. 1/2/2016

was even *mentioned,* by anyone - even by those remotely connected to that time and circle of people, he conceded:

> I cannot honestly remember, but it might have been as far back as 1974, via Ruth Wynn Owen and/or via that journalist, Justine Glass' book. [285]

Decades later, when the rumour began to flourish, and vague references to it were widely circulated, he and many others laboured under the false impression The Royal Windsor Coven had been a real name used by a real group – by Cochrane specifically for his group. But no-one questioned why if its existence was the greatest 'alleged' secret, it was actually no secret at all. Everyone knew about it, if only as a rumour! Rees has observed how the original references to it are traceable to the same source, confirming our own conclusions for a single authority.

There are no first-hand accounts from anyone alleged to have been actively involved in the phantom *Royal Windsor Coven,* no affirmations, directly, or indirectly. Taking a radical departure from Monmouth's speculative conclusion regarding the meaning and purpose of the documents in this cache, it is sensible to scrutinise a few of them. As unsupported accounts, void of context and identity, Monmouth's interpretative errors, weighted heavily with misquotes and false addendums, collectively exhibit considerable prejudice on every page in his book, *Genuine Witchcraft is Explained.*

Written originally to flag the forgotten works of Ronald White and George Stannard, it was inappropriate to introduce a means of elevating them by the unnecessary denigration of Robert Cochrane and his works.[286] Two entirely separate traditions, *CTC and The Regency*, are presented as if founded from another, invented *third tradition,* despite copious evidence to the contrary. Scant sources inform the text in a self-validating loop, discussed as *pre-supposed* proofs, where none exist. Observe in this typical example, clear and abject misrepresentation of the facts:

---

[285] Personal Correspondence from KIR to SLO. 6/2/2016 Even this rumour did not manufacture any written evidence, not even as something alluded to between correspondents.
[286] Protests from CTC resulted only in a response that presented the option to remove CTC's submission altogether.

> After Roy Bowers' death, there were <u>only two remaining active members</u> of the *Royal Windsor Coven*: <u>Ron White and George Stannard.</u> [287]

In barely three lines, Monmouth established the entire premise of his claim, dismissed all opposition to it, asserted the names of those he wished to promote as legitimate and provided the (fictional) name of the coven they are to be associated with! Although it is presented casually, almost as an afterthought, this *entire* statement is a blatant deceit, with nothing offered to qualify or prove it as fact. Worse, it falsifies the *entire* history of Robert Cochrane's Tradition.

To counter what is claimed in these three lines, demands countless pages of explanation. The statement could be dismissed by an equally pithy retort, declaring with restrained economy that, *'it is entirely false.'* But it would not allow the *real* history to be told, nor the truth to reveal itself. Exposing deception through the context of real time, supported by factual evidence, persuades by better example.

Ronald White and George Stannard/ Winter were <u>not</u> the only active people of Cochrane's Clan to survive him. They continued to be active amongst their own circle of friends, just as some of those other Clan members also continued working together.

With Cochrane recently deceased, the Clan (and its tradition) *remained* in the hands of Jane Bowers, (Cochrane's widow), Lady of the Clan and also its Maid, and most important of all, E.J.J, the man she appointed to take authority and hold the Clan as its Magister thereafter. Contrary to Monmouth's claim, not only do two more people from the Clan continue after Cochrane's death, those two were its authorised Head-Kinsmen, the only people blessed with its continuance.

What Monmouth may not have been privy to, was the distressing incident that had caused Jane to *sever all ties* with White and Winter, just after Cochrane's tragic death. Forced to act on it, she declared their status as disavowed, negating any former rights to

---

[287] Monmouth, 2012. Op. Cit. p 114

use or share matters and works pertaining to the Clan, or to refer to themselves as Clan members.[288]

This, if anything provides reason in certain actions White and Winter instigated after Cochrane's death, from disguising their real status as exiled members, to falsifying the name for Cochrane's Clan, as 1734. Outwardly, this allowed them to eventually continue as a discreet side line without having to disclose it had no legitimacy. Inwardly, it meant that everything they did, tied them in ever tighter knots, and the need for secrecy.

For over a decade, Bill and Bobbie Gray, Doreen Valiente and others worked with E.J.J. and his wife, as Clan. Later, when Valiente and Gray moved onto other modes of working with new magical partners, E.J.J. maintained Clan workings with one or two discreet others over the years.

Popular and influential works have resulted from alliances formed through those who have peopled the neo-Pagan works of *The Regency, Y Plant Bran* and Joe Wilson's 1734. The claim that presumes the creation and development from a fictional coven, demeans the impetus of the genuine founders of those systems. Ruth Wynn Owen would sharply reject the notion that her tradition was instigated by Cochrane's tradition and works, or that those works initiated *The Regency*. Cochrane had as little to do with the creation of those independent systems, as Ronald White had to do with Cochrane's genius.

By far the greatest contribution to the modern neo-Pagan world was the conclave of leading craft persons formed from several craft modalities during the mid-sixties, that established *The Pagan Federation*. Their work was not in any way dependent on Cochrane, his Clan or *The Regency*, as Valiente was keenly aware of.

One denominating factor fed *The Regency, Y Plant Bran, 1734,* and possibly other minor groups influenced by them, and that is Ruth Wynn Owen. Her works are not sourced within Cochrane's, and have nothing in common with them whatsoever. No single coven or tradition should be credited as the source for the witchcraft traditions

---

[288] Oates, 2016. Op. Cit. *TM:Legend*. See (E.J.J:L 7). See also p 253 Tubal's Mill. E.J.J. makes it quite clear in this letter that they were effectively outlawed, exiled – anathema to the Clan. They were left to their own devices and cunning.

and neo-Paganisms that developed throughout the 1980s to the millennium, less still a fictional one.

Evolution of beliefs and praxes have extended in ways their founders would be unlikely to recognise. Naturally, there is a considerable difference between change required through popular culture, and growth obtained through changing culture. In that regard, to a limited extent only, should digression occur from an authentic source.

The principle of evolution championed by Cochrane, did not consist of deviations from core principles, merely growth. Hints that explain what a Clan is, or demonstrate its presence, find no expression in Monmouth's statements. He had no understanding of a Clan system in any sense, and falls down repeatedly on that subject; a matter very much reflected in his explanation of the Clan of Tubal Cain as something generated out of a coven, real or fictional. [289]

In defiance of history and tradition, Monmouth explained the distinguishing factors of a Clanship as something inclusive of guests/outsiders/non-initiates, in opposition to a coven with its closed system, exclusive of all guests. [290] Both may be closed or open as desired. A Clan, as previously explained, may consist of several groups of different families or traditions within a strictly enclosed, system of controlled inducted membership.

Monmouth's *modus operandi* began with the idea that Cochrane had a secret name for a secret enclave, which became a secret covine. (sic) After Cochrane's death, that secret coven was credited with generating *the Clan* (under E.J.J), *The Regency* (under Ronald White), 1734 (under Joe Wilson) and *The Roebuck* (under Ann and Dave Finnin).

Each carefully manufactured step is dependent upon the former being true and having a factual basis. And though these platforms are built upon presumption alone, the language used by Monmouth implies conviction. His statements sound convincing and authoritative despite having no basis in fact.

Monmouth advanced this notion to assert a startling pretext for the source of our tradition's inspiration, pressing hard his claim that it is falsely attributed to Cochrane, and should be accepted as the

---

[289] Monmouth, 2012 Op. Cit. p 18 See also the back page of GWiF.
[290] Monmouth, 2012 Op. Cit. p 92

work of others. This false promotion is repudiated. Several problems need to be addressed in Monmouth's dramatic claim that Cochrane's ideas were not his own and that his works were: *"Rituals he had been provided with by other members of the coven."* [291] Such a claim demands substantial evidence to back it up. None was offered.

Since Cochrane's death, no further examples of his work have been produced or replicated. They were not continued outside his Clan tradition. No-one may claim his unique insight, or form of expression. That lack, presented a significant problem for Monmouth's outlandish claim that Cochrane had merely been the spokesperson for the presumed but unproven genius in Ronald White and George Winter. No matter how many times the claim is mooted, that gift was never theirs. Cochrane's poetic genius expired with him, though his vital spark finds expression still though his Clan Tradition, through his People. Through their works, he lives on.

Recognising the value of pooled knowledge and how external influences fashion our growth spiritually and intellectually, Valiente recorded her shifting perceptions as they changed over time. In February 1966, a few months after she'd left the Clan, her Candlemas notes explore the absorption of ideas garnered from her time with Cochrane, which found expression through terminology more familiar to her. At this very special seasonal knot in the Clan Compass, E.J.J., his wife V.J., and another couple who had guested occasionally with the Clan, gathered alongside her in celebration.

> There are rites which are done by the whole coven. There are rites which are done by the innermost circle. And there are rites which are done by the Old Woman alone, which enable her to rule the coven, as the Goddess rules all things. These rites are with the Child of Art - the Egregore of the coven. The Old Woman contacts and gives commands to. She also opens the way for contact between the Child of Art and the inner planes. She invokes the Goddess, assumes her form, and in that form gives command and instruction to the Child of Art. An Egregore is not so much a group-soul as a soul-group. A group soul is that of animals, from which individuals differentiate. A soul-group is built

---

[291] Monmouth, 2012 Op. Cit. p 32

up by people who are 'of one mind'. This 'one mind' becomes a real thing, and can be influenced.[292]

With perfect understanding, Valiente described the three layers by which a Clan Compass is laid and its Mythos unfolded. That is, by everyone for seasonal workings, known as knots; by its Officers and Elders for the core rites, which are distinct again from those rites undertaken in all matters dealing with Fate directly – hence the Old woman, the Seer and the 'divil' (Robin).

Her description of the Egregore is wonderful. Composed of a hierarchical system, from its Head-Kinsmen through the Elders into the Companie, the separation between Inductees and those of Full Admission is explicit. Valiente clarified the notion of Virtue and how it is manipulated, accessed and shared amongst the Companie. There is no ambiguity in her explanations.

Emphasising the role of Fate within the Clan Mythos, Valiente confessed a shift that occurred in her understanding of the purposes of the knotted cord right after she joined the Clan. Speaking for the first time of a goddess in this context, she amended her earlier description of the cord as the rope that simply hanged them in the past, adding how that same cord (the witches' garter) could be the umbilical cord as well as the noose. Correctly, in this sense, it is the cord or thread spun by the Fates:

> The Triple Goddess is manifested as the Three Fates from very early times. The Fates of ancient Greece, the Norns or weird sisters of Saxon myth. etc. The Matres or Matronae to whom altars have been found in Britain.[293]

Her changing perspective provides a useful example of one of the major tenets of the Craft, that is founded upon logic as much as it is law. What any person of a Craft family may take with them upon departure or exile, is what they brought with them, and what they were *given* to *hold* - in terms of experience and memory, forming a fusion of all that comes to mean. Embracing that new understanding and finding expression for it, is how the Craft evolves, through productive, experiential growth. What is left behind, is the core, the

---

[292] Valiente, 1966. Op. Cit. Notepad entry dated Candlemas.
[293] Ibid.

heart and mind of that family, and its traditions they have partaken of, and may have once contributed to. In that sense, it is also true that no-one passes through without leaving something of themselves, for better or worse.

Since Cochrane's death, the writings of others familiar with, and to some sense, influenced *by his* works, have become mistaken *for his* works, generally by those who are not sufficiently qualified to assess either. Whilst the Clan remains the best qualified to determine such discrepancies in terms of content, it holds no such claim to any expertise regarding the correct analysis of handwriting style. Those essential skills must be employed in any true and scrupulous study. Without them, the task is impossible, and the authenticity and correct attribution of all works concerned are left undetermined.

Contradictions and inconsistencies litter the cache of letters and documents that Monmouth insisted should be linked to *Robert Cochrane's Tradition*. A strange assertion, given the clear relevance of some its later papers to *The Regency*. Other pieces defy explanation or identification. Additional notes, perhaps intended as edits or supplements on pre-existing documents, authored by another, present ambiguous attributions of identity. A shared typewriter further compounds the attempts to identify specific authors. Numerous typed works, *before and after* Cochrane's death were facilitated by that typewriter. A second yet very similar typewriter was also used for some of the letters in circulation between Cochrane and certain Elders of his groups before he died.

Valiente became involved in the whereabouts of a typewriter Cochrane had borrowed from George Winter just days before Cochrane's tragic death. Apparently his own was missing, although Valiente identified a letter from Cochrane's widow in September, typed on her late husband's typewriter. In the interim, George Winter had asked for the return of his own typewriter and ritual cup borrowed prior to Cochrane's death. Both items were believed to be in the safe-keeping of Norman Gills. A visit to retrieve them from Norman Gills, at some point after Christmas 1966 was arranged between E.J.J. and Valiente. But there is no confirmation they did, or indeed, if they were successful. [294]

---

[294] Valiente, 1966. Notepad entry for August-November.

The ability to distinguish authorship of individual documents within the cache depends upon effective analysis of content, subject matter and writing style, and is a more certain than presumptions based on the mechanical identification of unique typewriter keys. Letters typed on either of those typewriters after Cochrane's death by Gills and White, for themselves and for *The Regency*, are impossible to distinguish from those typed by Cochrane – *except* in content and style. This demonstrates the flawed methodology of validation according to typewriter only, and not by author in this particular and unusual circumstance.

It is not essential to have access to either Monmouth's book *Genuine Witchcraft is Explained* or to *Star Crossed Serpent III* in order to make sense of the arguments *there*, nor to follow the examples and references given throughout *this* critique. Access to them will, however, facilitate scrupulous research for the erudite scholar, where all contentions are put forward and clearly addressed. All relevant facts are provided in this biographical account.

Research continues to prove rewarding, bringing people and names to life in the struggle to understand their roles in this amazing but shrouded era of Craft history. Colourful journeys briefly crossed before departing on entirely tangential paths, whereas others formed enduring relationships over several decades. Very few people will be familiar with the rich resources provided by the documents and letters that recall a curious history for the Craft. Considered study will de-mystify the politicking and unrelenting ambition of the few ruthless individuals involved. The misappropriation of the document cache, Valiente's Notepads and Cochrane's letters that Howard and Monmouth plumbed repeatedly, has obfuscated the real history.

As part of a priceless Craft legacy, all these documents warrant deeper study alongside other archived works contemporary with them. CTC express an open invitation for others to pursue and ponder their true authorship. Sharing the research will hopefully bring better understanding and may even reveal the proper contexts for each document. The project is far from exhausted and remains open to amendment and possible correction where time and additional documentation allow for further study. As a prolific correspondent, there are many genuine letters and possibly documents Cochrane penned, yet to surface. Of course, the public legacy of *The Robert Cochrane Tradition* very much remains in its inspiration to others.

A Fine Ruse

Oblivious of Cochrane's visionary terms of expression and his verve for cultural tradition, Monmouth opposed established facts to press his bold claim that where ever Cochrane mentioned Clan, he really meant 'The Royal Windsor Coven.' The rumour concerning the phantom coven began decades after his death, at which point a past and secret existence was manufactured for it, retrospectively.

Without challenge, that fiction has been fuelled entirely by the sensationalism of (alleged) secrecy. Controversy in the Craft is sure to generate interest, people are naturally curious. Referring back to *The Robert Cochrane Letters* book, E.J.J. published with Howard as editor, the following well-known statement by Cochrane stands out:

> The local cuven is small, consisting mainly of men, and of recent making since the last of the old Windsor cuven died, when my mother was a girl back in Victorian time. [295]

Plain sight is ever the gift of hindsight. Howard included an insistent footnote that expressed *his* belief the statement referred to Cochrane's '*Royal Windsor Coven.*' Two assumptions made by him at that point conflict with E.J.J.' explanation, and went unnoticed by many. First of all, it presumes the existence of any group by that name is factual, and attributable to Cochrane. Secondly, that Cochrane was referring to that understanding in this quoted comment.

Cochrane, like E.J.J., understood all too well the invocation and alignment to fate a 'given' name holds over its people. To change a name is an insult of the greatest hubris. E.J.J. motioned more than once the folly of changing names – no matter what transpires, once declared in Troth, that name stays. Cochrane set his star on CTC and CTC it remains – it has never been anything else.

---

[295] Jones, E.J. *The Robert Cochrane Letters* (Ed) Michael Howard. (UK: Capall Bann 2002) p 115

This primary example shows how a simple statement finds new expression when reinterpreted by others outside the Clan, in this case, by Michael Howard. Cochrane's reference to a coven, was to the now defunct coven that had existed in the hunting grounds, and forested area of *'old Windsor.'* Cochrane then referred to another, quite separate untitled coven of *recent* making, local to where he lived in the *Thames Valley*, just north of old Windsor forest and very probably the aptly named *The Thames Valley Coven*. This may or may not have been Everley's group in London.

There is only a miniscule possibility the cuveen (sic) he referred to might have been his own, since it was – *'of* [very] *recent making, prior to his founding the 'Clan.'* The first (full and balanced) coven he started in Slough was short-lived and quickly disbanded. Better reason travails for a more logical and probable coven, mentioned for completion only in this biography, but without any implication of association or connection. In fact, several little groups were working all over, experimenting, as open but discreet units, some more rigid than others, extending from the libertine to the cultish. And all them were known to somebody in the Craft.

The only real secret is that which is never uttered, that no one hears of, and no-one knows of. Something can be discreet, about which little or nothing is known. Once something is known, it is no longer 'secret;' a secret does not feature on the spectrum between rumour and legend. Perceptible veiling, erring on caution at times, is keenly apparent within the correspondences Cochrane shared with others, and yet remains largely unappreciated.

Understood well enough by his contemporaries, Cochrane's boasts concerning personal connections in *Stafford and Windsor*, are woefully mis-abused by others in more recent times. Cochrane alludes only to the *regions* of *Stafford and Windsor,* referring to both equally as Craft landscapes where people once worked, whose beliefs and traditions generated the Craft he nurtured as a long and collective heritage. Pulled by the ties of history and of tradition, he spoke of heritage as *'the burden of ages.'*

He nowhere suggested or claimed his family were (of) the *Windsor* People; that is, a member of the old coven there.[296] Had he done so, then his comments might perhaps have included phrases

---

[296] Copy of this letter in author's personal possession.

denoting, *involvement with, allegiance to, admission of* or even, quite simply – belonging to. Instead, his simple reference of a *connection to*, signifies – through another, ie. his mothers work with Lady Blomfield. Being close to his heart, his Craft origins and who his people are, were matters he promoted, loud and clear. Cochrane quite distinctly described the region as *old* Windsor, a matter dealt with in a forthcoming chapter dedicated to those distinctions. The reader is advised to study those pages if necessary, to fully appreciate their import here.

> We teach by poetic inference, by thinking along lines that belong to the world of dreams and images. There is no hard and fast teaching technique, no laid down scripture or law, for wisdom comes only to those who deserve it, and your teacher is yourself seen through a mirror darkly. The answer to all things are in the Air – Inspiration, and the winds will bring you news and knowledge if you ask them properly. The Trees of the Wood will gave you power, and the Waters of the Sea will give you patience and omniscience, since the Sea is a womb that contains a memory of all things. [297]

Valiente again provides the basic information of this in her note-pads in the form of two clues. In December 1964, she received a letter from *'ickle Deric'* [298] which contained keys' for a book she was writing. He evidently had *'the full details regarding Windsor.'*

The second clue to that enigmatic statement occurred a few years later in Valiente's reference to a coven in Twickenham that had a branch at (old) Windsor (forest).[299] A lady named Sylvia was in charge of a cult named the *Mystic Forum.*

Valiente typically investigated these people, and in her report she described them as extreme occultists, a suggestion perhaps of their unpopularity and of the unpleasant undercurrents in their praxes.[300] Valiente's comments are brief but fascinating. She mentioned a Priest of the Horned God known by the title of *Stag*

---

[297] Oates, 2016. *SCSIII* Op. Cit. Robert Cochrane to Joe Wilson #3 p 370
[298] Rees, 2017. Op. Cit. Private Correspondence, Confirms identity of this person as Derek Hamer, who later attended the meetings of The Regency.
[299] Valiente, 1975. Notepad entry. 15th November. This info, came via Cynthia Swettenham.
[300] Valiente, 1975. Ibid. Other entries appear later that concern a Sylvia, [Campbell] or [Tatham] Valiente does not clarify which Sylvia, as it appears she knew at least three!

King, who was apparently *'fanatically loyal to Sylvia.'* This Stag King had other names: A. Damon and a general alias of Alastair Blackman.[301]

Although the group's active presence in Windsor was known to Cochrane, Valiente, and very few others, it was certainly private and discreet, but again, not secret. Once assimilated, this information achieves two things. It serves to distinguish the gulf between the existence of an actual working group in Windsor and a (phantom) coven fabricated upon rumour alone, given an amended title and identity.

More importantly, it shows how a false premise can be readily accepted (for want of factual information) where promoted and advocated by those within the Craft Community who profess to have knowledge of such things. As self-declared authorities on traditions not their own, Howard and Monmouth may have chosen to ignore this information. Howard certainly knew of it:

> By the way, Madeline Montalban knew Gardner during the Second World War (. . .) Rumours have swirled around for years that MM was Old Craft. (. . .) Despite this, my research has found no firm proof (unlike Cochrane's Gard initiation) that can be independently verified with the names of her initiator/s or confirm that she was ever in the OC. [Old Craft]. If that ever surfaces, and things don't remain secret for ever, I will no doubt write about in a book or The Cauldron.[302]

Going out on a limb to speak purely hypothetically, it is fanciful to speculate that this Sylvia 'may' refer to the Sylvia (Royals) who is better known as Doloras North, aka Madeline Montalban. Of course, it is also possible this Sylvia could be someone else entirely, despite the personality profile match. Howard noted on several occasions the persistent rumours that M.M. was 'Old Craft.' She certainly knew (and did not like) both Gerald B. Gardner and Charles

---

[301] A. Damon sounds remarkably similar to A. Demaine, the Initiator of Madge Worthington, and probably of Laurence Miles. Demaine had supposed links to traditional Craft. It is also rumoured that Madge Worthington did also. This may be nothing more than a curious coincidence. But it is an interesting speculation and worthy of investigation.

[302] Selected & Abridged transcripts of exchanges between Shani Oates and Mike Howard on the 1734 forum in 2012-2014. Howard was a member of the Luciferian Order of the Morning Star for a couple of years. 1967 to 1969. MM died in 1982.

Cardell, considering them both fakes. Howard claimed he met M.M. in 1967 around the same time *The Regency* had tentatively formed a group. Howard briefly joined her Luciferian Cultus, a closed group named the 'Order of the Morning Star.' Howard and Montalban parted company in 1969 when she expelled him after disproving of his Gardnerian Initiation.

This may or may not bring further understanding to this pressing inquiry. What does require further investigation is how some of the documents in the cache came to be edited and annotated so dramatically, for what original purpose, and if possible, by whom. For example – the *Oath of Loyalty* section refers specifically to *The Thames Valley Coven*, which forms part of the main *Writ & Constitution* doc. (AAA) A2 for *A Coven to Diana*. Its title is crossed out in one place and has *'windsor'* scribbled above it.

The content of that document and the description of its Initiation rites do not suggest any compatibility with Valiente's description of the *Mystic Forum* group at Windsor as 'extreme occultists.' But it does suggest that someone who knew of them either thought it did, or that they wanted others to believe it did. At the very least, they wished to bask in the kudos of a mysterious occult group of people known to work in Windsor by an assumed association.

This presents a possibility that the rumour or even a later independent existence for the phantom coven was instigated as something inspired by or founded upon *The Mystic Forum* group. It is one more enigma that may never be solved. How much is truth and how much is rumour is impossible to discern. From the information relayed by Valiente, Cochrane, E.J.J. et al, what can be established is that *The Mystic Forum* was not connected to Cochrane's Clan or Tradition.

There was certainly no logical reason for Cochrane to have referred first to the recent coven at Windsor, then go onto talk about his Clan without mentioning a connection between them, if one existed in reality. Having mentioned them, he had already abandoned the secrecy issue, if indeed there ever was one.

Cochrane's language is very specific on this; if he had intended to refer to a 'Windsor' coven *he* was currently associated with, then he would have simply used that exact descriptive –

'Windsor,' absent of new or old. And in his time, where he was, *'new'* Windsor was an actual but positively distinct region of 'Windsor.' New Windsor was a commercial and urban area completely apart from the traditional *'old'* Windsor town altogether, in terms of history, politics and its people. [303]

Knowledge of local geography, history and politics is an essential element in this puzzle, key in fact to solving it. And it should be realised that whatever Cochrane was part of before he established his Clan, he left it behind, and evolved something innovative and unique with the input of E.J.J. who continued that work after Cochrane's death.

Everything that was channelled into the creation and development of his Clan continues still. Whatever possible origins those influences had remain hidden by the obscurities of time and intent. Intrigue and desire should not lead to speculation and fantasy, which should always be discouraged.

The suggestion that Cochrane's group was secretly known as *The Royal Windsor Coven* is simply not sustainable. Faced with an unprecedented lack of supportive material wherein numerous facts reveal the premise to be false, it should be summarily dismissed. It ignores everything Cochrane declared for himself and the *People of Goda, of the Clan of Tubal Cain* throughout his entire corpus.

Cochrane abhorred the usage of the term coven (as verified by Valiente previously). The terms 'group' or 'society' were used by him in preference to it, defaulting to generic use in common parlance, that is, until better knowledge allowed him to replace it. Once he discovered the term 'Clan' and had applied it in principle and title, he never referred to his companie of people as anything else thereafter. This progression is verifiable fact and is particularly notable when studied correctly - chronologically. Only where those works have been deliberately jumbled up and presented without an observable time-line, do the terms appears random. [304]

Both Monmouth and Howard cast aside the Clan's legitimate titles assigned and used by Cochrane, declaring that E.J.J. had instigated that title (Clan of Tubal Cain) after Cochrane's death! This

---

[303] Wikiwand - The village of Old Windsor, just over 2 miles (3 km) to the south, predates what is now called Windsor by around 300 years; in the past Windsor was formally referred to as New Windsor to distinguish the two. [1]

[304] Jones, E. J. *The Robert Cochrane Letters* (ED) Michael Howard (UK, Capall Bann: 2003)

is simply one more claim so easily proved as false. By not consulting Cochrane's references to CTC throughout his own letters, they have failed to conduct essential research and failed to observe the facts.

Having established certain motivations of personal agenda, the persistence of unsupported speculation and the aggressive extent to which some of that spilled over into the public domain, may present a surprising challenge for anyone previously unfamiliar with the embedded politics. In play and developed over several years, substantial effort and study were required to collate the necessary information to expose and disprove those unfounded assumptions.

Persuaded perhaps by cumulative negative opinion, the prevailing consensus was too easily acquired. E.J.J.' authority and status gradually diminished throughout several editions of *The Cauldron*. No doubt, these concepts spread across into other forms of media, extending that perception beyond the magazine's readership. Evan John Jones' office as Magister of Cochrane's Tradition and keeper of its legacy was grossly misrepresented there, and by default, that of the Clan entire, something Howard keenly advocated as E.J.J.' creation after Cochrane's death.

As an attempt to side-line the genuine tradition from a fantasy construct, the ploy can be mapped back to its origins in the 1990s. Michael Howard, editor of *The Cauldron,* made disingenuous changes to how E.J.J was referenced, which specifically changed his status by subtle degrees. Consider the dates referenced below. Beginning simply, in his early articles, E.J.J. was described as the *author* – and

> A *past member* of **Robert Cochrane's** *group* in the 60s [305]

Between 1995 and 1999, the editor of *The Cauldron* mentioned Cochrane's *group and coven,* introducing E.J.J. tentatively as a member only, of that *group and coven.* Once the error was noted by E.J.J., it was (partially) corrected. With clear distinction the editor of *The Cauldron* presented E.J.J. as a '*former member of Cochrane's coven in the 1960s,*' rather than its *current Magister.* Howard slyly added, that 'today Evan John Jones is:

---

[305] #80 c 1995 Beltane. *The Cauldron* E.J.J. was referred to simply as '*the author.*'

The Magister of **Clan Tubal Cain** [306]

At first glance, this reference appears acceptable. Howard as effectively separated the existence and authority of Cochrane's 'coven' from the Clan, infering that EJJ's role of Magister of the clan (CTC), is not a continuity of the role Cochrane held in the same group. It is of course, but Howard's deliberate phrasing here was instrumental in his polemical verbiage that followed soon after John's death in 2003. The ambiguity may not be immediately clear, hopefully it should become so, once another excerpt is placed alongside it in which Howard described the position held by Shani Oates as:

The current Maid of the Clan of Tubal Cain, **a title inherited from Evan John Jones** [307]

Michael Howard was one of several Craft Elders E.J.J. had informed and notified in advance of the official appointment of Shani Oates and Robin-the-dart in May 1999 as the new Maid and Magister of Robert Cochrane's Tradition, to hold and maintain that legacy into the foreseeable future. Observe the date of *The Cauldron*, an edition that significantly marked the official handover of Cochrane's Clan legacy with the quotes noted above.

It is no coincidence that Cochrane's *Clan* Tradition was referred to thereafter as a separate *coven* by Howard. To emphasise this (false) origin and demarcation of Cochrane's heritage away from CTC, Shani Oates is described as:

The Maid of Evan John Jones' Clan of Tubal Cain!

The *Clan of Tubal Cain* thus became identified publically as something associated with E.J.J. only, separated entirely from Robert Cochrane and made independent of his legacy. As an entirely artificial pretext, it systematically removed E.J.J. from his true status as

---

[306] #82 c1996 Hallows. *The Cauldron* - "*The writer was a member of Robert Cochrane's group in the sixties and is currently a member of the Clan of Tubal Cain.*"
And #87 c1998 Eostre. *The Cauldron* - "*A member of Robert Cochrane's group in the sixties and today is the Magister of the Clan of Tubal Cain.*"
[307] #92 c1999. May. *The Cauldron* - "*The writer was a member of Robert Cochrane's coven in the 1960s and is a regular TC contributor.*"

Magister and lineage bearer of Cochrane's Tradition. [308] By removing the legitimate origin of the Clan heritage from Robert Cochrane, Howard replaced it with his legacy. The purpose of that embroidered fiction continued in all subsequent references to Shani Oates and Robin-the-dart as heirs only to "John's tradition -*whatever that might be!*" [309]

Confidant in his media misrepresentation of that transition, and of its subsequent diminishment of E.J.J. from Magister of *Cochrane's Tradition* (expressed through his *Clan*) to nothing more than a former member of *Cochrane's coven* (as a modality distinct from a Clan), the editor's full comment accompanied an article written by Shani Oates.

> The author is Maid of the Clan of Tubal Cain, an office she inherited from the late Evan John Jones - a member of Robert Cochrane's covine [sic] in the 1960. [310]

The false but popular history that fictionalised *The Royal Windsor Coven*, was actively promoted by Howard and Monmouth, who both professed it had continued in secret after Cochrane's death. An ironic twist occurred in the conflicting versions Howard and Monmouth presented thereafter.

According to Monmouth, the Coven (sic) relaxed its guard and became less secretive in 1963 when E.J.J. joined.[311] Despite that alleged openness, E.J.J., V.J. and Valiente repudiated the existence of any other name or status for Cochrane's Tradition –*The Clan of Tubal Cain*. As E.J.J. said, he was *"Roy's spiritual heir (Tanist) long before his death."* [312]

---

[308] #120 May 2006 *The Cauldron*
[309] In an online forum where we were attempting to explain this, the late Peter Paddon amongst others, made the sly comment, "*Shani Oates is heir to Evan John Jones' tradition, whatever that might be!*" For over a decade, whenever CTC were called upon to defend its Tradition and Legacy, Howard reacted as if that action had been a personal attack upon himself. His propaganda was quite successful as no-one questioned his behaviour or sought out answers supported by real facts.
[310] #120 May 2006. *The Cauldron* And #122 Nov. 2006. *The Cauldron* - Shani Oates: "*The author is the Maid of the Clan of Tubal Cain, a traditional group now based in Derbyshire*" And #123 Feb. 2007. *The Cauldron* - Shani Oates: "*The author is the present Maid of the Clan of Tubal Cain, an office she inherited through the authority of the late Evan John Jones, a member of Robert Cochrane's covine (sic) in the 1960s.*"
[311] Monmouth, 2012. Op. Cit. p 76
[312] To be clear: Robert Cochrane established the Clan (CTC). His praxes, knowledge and teachings, experienced within CTC, became expounded out of it. Cochrane and his widow as Clan Maid

Other writers have avoided the biased accounts given by Monmouth and Howard, presenting a balanced perspective to this history. Gavin Semple's meticulous research preserves irrefutable fact. He defers to a verifiable history, relating events associated with the genuine tradition founded by Cochrane and shared with E.J.J. [313] Semple reiterates some background history of the people closest to Cochrane. Following far better example, his work followed genuine sources, faithful to the extent it received approval by Jane Bowers and V.J.

After consultation with Bowers and Jones as primary authorities of all things related to that Tradition, Semple's perspective is very direct and in stark contrast to everything presented by Howard, Monmouth and writers who have sourced them. Semple refers to both *Roy* (Robert Cochrane) and *John* (E.J.J.) as equals, where each in turn had the same status as leader of their tradition, holding the title - *'Magister of the Clan of Tubal Cain,'* Semple also refers to E.J.J. as Cochrane's *'loyal student,'* a comment that conveys the depth of the relationship between Cochrane and Jones. [314]

For almost a decade Robert Cochrane's name had appeared everywhere, in numerous random journals, articles, online forums etc., always sourced by Michael Howard, directly or indirectly, and always associated with the phantom *'Royal Windsor Coven.'* The existence of any group of that name associated with Cochrane was rebutted by Evan John Jones until his own death in 2003, which followed just a few short years after Doreen Valiente had also crossed the bar in 1999.

Disagreements between CTC and Michael Howard became ever more vocal, noticeable on two particular public forums. [315] Called upon repeatedly to defend against repeated provocations based on falsehoods, conflict was unavoidable.

Responding to several commissioned articles that appeared in *The Cauldron* in the years after E.J.J.' death, each of which asserted a fictional existence for the phantom *'Royal Windsor Coven,'* E.J.J.' widow, V.J., wrote a letter to the editor, Michael Howard.

---

appointed E.J.J. to continue that heritage through their Clan; its traditions and legacy were deeded solely to him as befitting a Head-Kinsman, to preserve and continue.
[313] http://www.clanoftubalcain.org.uk/A_Poisoned_Chalice.pdf
[314] http://www.clanoftubalcain.org.uk/A_Poisoned_Chalice.pdf
[315] 1724 members forum and the Traditional Witchcraft forum.

Attempting to counter the continual stream of disinformation regarding the supposed existence of the phantom coven, her frustration was evident in this letter to Shani Oates.
It expresses her surprise that Howard had ignored her advice:

> I did try to refute (. . .) but Michael Howard did not seem interested. (. . .) both ***** and I feel the record should be put straight, I have done my best so far. [316]

Frequently obfuscated by misleading rhetoric obvious to kith and kin of the Clan, others looking in were mystified by elaborate claims and deceitful assertions. After two heated public exchanges, bewilderment amongst onlookers only increased. Unfamiliar with the facts, many could not comprehend a reality so contrary to the view carefully laid down by Howard over time. This may surprise those unaware of such incidents, and perhaps others, aware only of the peripheral detail at the time. Suffice to say, it forms an essential part of this Clan biography.

A different editor void of personal agenda might have truthfully presented E.J.J.' place in the schema of history, with focussed regard for his role as catalyst for the Clan's development alongside Robert Cochrane. A different person might even have promoted him as the archetypal unsung hero, the quiet man, and the only man from all those around Cochrane, to stand by him in life and death and beyond death. His input radically turned Cochrane around, honing his work into the genius all in turn have since been inspired by.

Ultimately, in that sense, CTC are the inheritors of both forebears - 'John' and 'Roy.' Their works generated *through* the Clan, forged a single legacy. They are neither distinct nor separate from each other, nor from the Clan they evolved together; it could not be otherwise - they are one and the same, both served and were served in turn by its Egregore.

Sourced predominantly from *The Cauldron*, a specious history for the *People of Goda, Clan of Tubal Cain* emerged, a history CTC are at continual pains to correct. Terms such as: '*Cochrane's Tradition,*' and '*Cochranite,*' have been thrown into the mix to further befuddle

---

[316] Oates, 2016. Op. Cit. *TM:Legend* Personal Correspondence. V. Jones to SLO. (L:31)

and discourage genuine interest or research. Designed originally to distinguish those *of* it, from those who assimilate it by aspiration, CTC are nonetheless, the former, and cannot be any other. The latter applies to nothing valid, though detractors have tried to place CTC in the latter category for the same reasons they tried to describe the Clan as E.J.J.' rather than Cochrane's.

Other leading remarks continued with only minor variation until 2009. Anxious to circumvent an alternative history for *The Regency* by the researcher Ken Rees from becoming common knowledge, Howard and then Monmouth intensified their references to the phantom coven across all media. Anticipating the supposed revelation within Monmouth's forthcoming book of a 'secret' coven as the genuine source and continuity of Robert Cochrane's Tradition, magazine articles and web forums began broadcasting brief references to the phantom coven. [317]

Believing the impetus for Monmouth's book, *Genuine Witchcraft is Explained,* was to assert an independent history for *The Regency,* the Clan initially encouraged, lending support to that project. That support was withdrawn once Monmouth's attempt to use it as a vehicle to appropriate Cochrane's tradition and legacy for Ronald White became transparent. And there, through a series of disingenuous sub-texts, Monmouth and Howard part company, each following their diverse claims to Cochrane's Clan Tradition. Monmouth also promoted a spurious fictional trajectory for E.J.J and the Clan:

> Evan John Jones eventually continued the traditions of *the coven* separately, transmitting them ultimately to Shani Oates, who now leads *the Clan*." [318]

Monmouth's intent to claim all was disclosed without ambiguity:

> The Royal Windsor Coven gave birth to the Cochrane Tradition in Witchcraft. The Regency was the first group to hold public pagan celebrations in Britain which culminated in the Stonehenge

---

[317] The official author was known as *Regency John*. This new title of JoM appears unnecessary.
[318] Monmouth, 2012. Op. Cit. p 99

Festivals. Together these groups gave rise to the Clan of Tubal Cain, Y Plant Bran, 1734 and Roebuck covens.[319]

However, the suggestion that even the Clan (CTC) evolved from (the phantom) Royal Windsor Coven, alongside the other groups merely influenced by Cochrane, his tradition and his Clan, is an absurdity beyond reckoning. Howard's and Monmouth have never been made fully accountable for this insidious deception. Yet is is their works that find constant expression and repetition rather than our own. This is the power of media under the manipulation of unscrutable people. Cochrane's Clan Tradition and everything properly attributable to it, have struggled on the peripheries of Craft media to retain their presence as Cochrane's *living tradition*. As the genuine source that has enriched the occult, folk and left-hand path traditions over recent decades, it is regrettable that media representations of CTC on forums, magazines, reviews, web sites and blogs, remain ambiguous at best in their references. Inaccurate perspectives reflect the bias established by Howard and Monmouth. Therefore, in order to relay Clan history, its people and its works accurately, the entrenched misconducts that occurred before and during guardianship of that legacy, must be exposed.

From within the document cache used to advance the notion of a Royal Windsor Coven, not a single document, letter, note or ritual refers to it, or cites it, by any member, guest or associate of CTC, before or after Cochrane's death. One document within this cache, entitled the *Final Rite of Initiation,* is the curious exception.[320]

Of more *recent* origin, a document of anonymous composition, sans date or context, references the phantom coven, distinguishing it from all other documents. Its only relevance to Robert Cochrane and Clan history concerns how it was used to generate a false history.

Should any valid proofs ever surface for the *actual* existence of a phantom coven, it could do nothing more than demonstrate its independent existence. That is to say, it could not and did *not exist* when Robert Cochrane was Magister of The Clan.

---

[319] Monmouth, 2012. Op. Cit. *GWiE* See comments and claims on the back cover page.
[320] Monmouth, 2012. Op. Cit. C3, pages 302-15 Image scan only. The actual Document is withheld from us. It cannot be examined and therefore cannot be validated. We have no means to provide a legitimate transcription of it in *SCS III.*

For all the reasons explored throughout this book, the fantasy that it did, is proven to be without grounds. The idea it could, has everything to do with craft politicking and ambition and nothing to do with facts or truth. Discernment is a virtue infrequently exercised by the disseminators of information, and by those eager to accept it, flawed or otherwise.

V) The Regency & 1734

A Compact Broken, A Compact Kept

> Witches cannot retreat from the world any longer, there is no room for us within this society unless we have something valid to offer it, and participate in its social evolution. [321]

When composing the original contribution for Monmouth's intended book project, Monmouth agreed that Shani Oates would write the introduction and closing summary. Later, once underway and permission to publish had been granted, the terms of the agreement were reneged by Monmouth when he decided to refine Clan commentary to a single chapter for the final published version. Protests were not well met, and it was made very clear the Clan should accept that decision or its contribution would be removed altogether from the final publication.

During initial discussions with John of Monmouth concerning the draft content of his own submission for the book, members of the Clan embraced congenial exchange with him, sharing knowledge of the documents in his care. There was a great deal of rudimentary information about White and Winter that was previously unknown to him. Disappointment and disbelief came in equal measure when that information appeared within his own commentary, relayed as first-hand knowledge.

Attempts were made to draw Monmouth's attention to signature anomalies, dating errors, copy documents, repeated or incongruous names, all of which were evident on key documents. But

---

[321] Robert Cochrane, 'The Craft Today' *Pentagram* #2 Nov. 1964. Republished in Oates, 2016. *SCSIII* Op. Cit. p 278

it was to no avail. Clan views differed enormously from his on several crucial issues, particularly those concerning the aforementioned surface edits on official documents, for example – (AAA) A2.

That incompatibility was pronounced when he began applying arbitrary dates for the documents in the cache that were not based in sensible logic, especially with respect to later edits by Ronald White personally. Monmouth deferred to his own summary of events, dismissing completely any *advice from the Clan*. He suggested the Clan should publish its own views in contra-distinction to his own, at a later time.

Obligation to the facts was certainly an essential task, and one undertaken with rigour. This Clan biography is the result of several years of research involving a wide network of people and events in order to finally bring them to bear in this book.

Specious presentations of personal histories are not new to the Craft. Such things have definitely occurred before and those who seek to manipulate Craft records do not go unnoticed. Valiente had followed closely the narcissistic behaviour of people naturally inclined to those paths of intrigue and manipulation, recording notes and comments here and there.

Her duty to the Truth is consistent throughout her life's works, recorded for all to witness. Valiente's remarkable Notepads cover her investigations into several scandalous events over three decades. These include the mysterious controversies that engulfed Charles Cardell, *The Coven of Atho,* and Alex Sanders. Most especially she cast her eye upon the real identities of two highly colourful personages known as *Taliesin* and *Galadriel.* Their exploitative machinations of the occult societal scene were followed most critically by her.

Valiente had cause to ponder deeply upon the words of her former friend and mentor. Her understated admiration of Cochrane's wisdom finds expression through his own words regarding his summary of the occult world as: *"Shoddy and sleazy,"* in which the obsession for the *"pursuit of money and status held no attraction for him."* She preserved Cochrane's remonstrations that in his opinion, the entire rot of the world could be encapsulated in one word – *"greed."*

[322] How little has changed. And yet despite all, Cochrane had the wit to see that:

> To close the human mind in order to protect it from outside circumstances that are hostile, is not a way to discover that, within oneself, which is most profound, but a return to a claustrophobic mother who will eventually smother the child.

Comments made by Monmouth that directly alluded to sections of text written by Cochrane are invariably out of context or in transparent contradiction with huge tracts of text he'd ignored. This tactic is exemplary in his claims that Cochrane was a misogynist. An abundance of material written by Cochrane negates that base claim. So easily countered, it takes but a moment to read any of his amazingly profound letters.

Across the decade of Cochrane's advancement from his early associations through to his final years, his works are notably reverential of the higher spirit that moves all. Even with true authority, humility to duty should be paramount. Over and again, Cochrane upholds the inspiring genius as a gift from the *Other*. He never claimed it for himself.

A remark in his long correspondence with Bill Gray dated circa 1963, affirms Cochrane as the Master of a small group of people. Without equivocation, he added that over the Clan, a higher authority than his, resides in the gift of two *Others*. The context and inflection indicated to Gray that Cochrane was not referring to two people, but to the tutelary spirits of his Clan. Sometime later, Cochrane reiterated this principle in a letter to Joe Wilson, offering a description of himself as Master of a Clan and a member of the People. His sense of duty is quite profound.

> Master is a term that we use, and use often. I myself, am a master of a small clan, the devil in fact. I, in turn, recognise the authority of others who are higher than myself, and that authority, once stated, is absolute, do what we may. Higher plane *adeptii*, or physical *adeptii* are terms that sit uneasily upon the witch. Master is the old word for the particular function we all (witches I mean) have to fulfil.

---

[322] Valiente. 1989 Op. Cit. p 120

My job is to train and organise, fulfil the letter of the law and to function, to discipline and to curse, as well as elevate and expound. To Jane, all men owe absolute allegiance, to myself, (or rather the law that I represent), they owe duty. We have to train new members up to certain standards, develop any hidden power they may have, and finally teach them the manipulation of various images of virtue.

We may be the very last of the old school, but we still uphold the old attitudes and expect the same things. Above we two rises another authority whose writ is far older than ours, to that authority we give absolute allegiance, and whose function is to train and work with us. I was in the fortunate position of having been blooded, therefore I have some hold on their ears. [323]

Despite the very evident immaturity in this letter which is similar to another, written to *'Chalky,'* where Cochrane intriguingly refers to a *High Priestess,* his voice and tone suggest transformative usage of old Craft terminology during an early stage of the Clan's development. A generic language obviously informed ritual structure and procedure, at least initially; it used a format common to both Traditional Craft and the more popular Wican model.[324] Slight similarities of terminology and expression could be explained as universal to the era.

Culled from a variety of sources, not all of which were mutual, Cochrane bemoaned the lack of deeper traditional elements identifiable in the emerging Craft. Another letter articulates well the system of Clanship and of his own duties and responsibilities towards his people as Head-Kinsman of his Clan: *"Although in some ways I have power over them, they also have power over me, and this is one of their decisions."*

Cochrane's charismatic nature had drawn people to him like moths to a flame. Gravitating to his undeniable magnetism, they were paradoxically repelled just as quickly by his frequent bouts of intolerance for others who did not share his vision, or who were not of his Craft.

---

[323] www.cyberwytch.com/roybowers
[324] Reflected further in the Wican status almost all of them achieved, as confirmed by Ken Rees. 2016. Op. Cit.

His drive to coerce them into a competent unit, compatible and able to face the *'Other,'* reveals his hitherto undiscovered talent for selectivity and adaptation, shepherding his flock, and even for refining and redefining their purpose and goals within the Clan. That position of authority is of long standing, and is reflected further in the listed hierarchy of the *Writ & Constitution* document for *The Thames Valley Coven*:

- Maid
- High Priestess
- Priest
- Elders &Musicians
- Red cords – Inducted members, qualified
- Green cords – Inducted members in training
- Neophytes (sic)

Whether influenced by this Craft document or not, as their Head-Kinsman, Priest and leader, Cochrane expressed himself as their superior in every sense of the word, labouring their deficiencies, reiterating that unless they shape up, and quite drastically, the Clan and all its aspirations are doomed to failure. There is no doubt of his leadership, nor of his person being the inspirational force that motivated the Clan and its works.

As to the listed hierarchy above, though fairly typical, it does share some ideology to the Clan's mythos. This document provides a curious insight to the roles and authority ascribed to them at each level.[325] The term and office of Elder was not understood by Monmouth, leading to some confusion on the matter.

Where Cochrane spoke deferentially of those with a higher authority than himself, of Others beyond the worldly flesh of humankind, Monmouth believed Cochrane had meant older and wiser Clan Elders. Cochrane spoke freely of his ancestral mentors as those who had gone before him, who exist in another place, accessible to him through having the ear of the gods, and by the grace of being blooded by them. Cochrane nowhere refers to ancestral beings, nor his gods, as *Elders*.

---

[325] Oates, 2016. *SCSIII* Op. Cit. p 121

An important directive entitled, *Beliefs and Practises* demonstrates Cochrane's authority as Magister. His escalating concerns were explained to those he considered *Elders of the Clan*, people of Full Admission who'd served their time as apprentices. Cochrane's *sub rosa* document addressed all *Clan Elders*, Ronald White included. Everything Cochrane did was imbued with the authority as Priest, and leader of his Clan, he was not in any way subordinate to its members, especially not to Ronald White and George Winter as Monmouth and Howard falsely impute. These are not the two Cochrane refers to as '*higher authorities.*'

When the letters and documents in this important cache and of those within the public domain are referred to and quoted from, proper regard should always be given to context. Beyond that, consultation with people familiar with those works directly – ie: the Clan, is recommended if a correct understanding is sought.

Monmouth was ill-advised to use these documents as the basis for his attempted displacement of Cochrane. Careful study of the entirety of the *Writ & Constitution* doc. (AAA) A2 confirms the authority of Priest is placed above Elder. This irrefutable fact places creative and administrative power with Cochrane and no other. [326]

Should the *Writ & Constitution* document ultimately prove to have no connection to Robert Cochrane and his Tradition (which seems probable), then his authority and Magisterial status remain precisely as credited by E.J.J., Bill Gray, Valiente and countless others, not to mention by himself as leader of his Clan (CTC). Cochrane's Tradition cannot be redirected away from its natural source authority. Cochrane was the leader, pure and simple. As E.J.J. stated in *Sacred Mask, Sacred Dance:*

> No-one knew what he was about, or what he would do. Whatever was shared or taught was won in the 'moment' of its relevance and of its becoming. [327]

Numerous examples confirm that Cochrane, not White issued directives and instruction to all members for the works he formulated as leader of the Clan. Aware that incompatible factors

---

[326] Cache of documents, A1 circa 1961
[327] Oates, Op. Cit. *TM Legend* (Create Space: 2016) Personal Correspondence from EJJ to SLO (L19) 1997.

prohibited development of the Egregore, he reminded them of their avowed duty, hoping to guide them away from distraction and conflict with the great work ahead. [328]

> To all <u>Elders,</u> the real fault at the heart of the group seems to be a lack of understanding of these basic principles. As long as this misunderstanding continues, we cannot create a group mind, therefore we cannot expect to work a group magick, irrespective of our [own] powers. [329]

A Grim prophesy. Fate had other plans for all concerned. This statement negates Monmouth's assertion that *Cochrane's personal pursuit for power* turned off all interest in his path. It is ironic to note that Monmouth failed to observe that fifty years later, Cochrane's Craft is turning people off precisely because *the pursuit for personal power* is deemed an allure the Clan do not hold in esteem. Cochrane emphasised the greater collective above the individual, in terms of duty and of desires in all magicks.

Ultimately, Monmouth's purpose to claim Cochrane's works as the legacy of White and Winter, and CTC as *"one of the creations of the Royal Windsor Coven,"* should have been abandoned along with the intention to create that alternative history. [330]

Present during those events and beyond, E.J.J. believed the greatest errors of comprehension were initiated by people who'd adopted Cochrane's words and works in the years *after* his death. Once his works became available, albeit in a limited capacity initially, their enigmatic content advanced the romantic notion of them as a *public* legacy, a belief that eventually manufactured a basis for nostalgic fiction.

Seizing it for their own, they overlooked the need for authenticity or even accountability. Legacies are bound by laws that ensure their continuity in an appropriate and designated manner. Heritage cannot be 'taken,' nor can it be assumed.

Those who follow disparate threads are taken ever further from the source, until what they have, becomes an heretical

---

[328] Oates, 2016. Op. Cit. *SCSIII* p 337 & Monmouth, 2012. Op. Cit. *GWiE* Doc T – Cache of previously unpublished material. p 350
[329] Monmouth, 2012. Op. Cit. *GWiE Beliefs and Practises* Doc T p 350 & Oates, 2016. Op. Cit. *SCSIII* p 337
[330] Monmouth, 2012. Op. Cit. p 18 See also Back Cover of *GWiE* for this audacious claim.

anathema, the very antithesis of its origin. Time is never a favourable ally. Degraded by half-lives, the original subject moves ever further into the subjective realms of fiction

From Ashes Rise

Returning to those first few chaotic months that followed the Summer of 1966 and the disconcerting inquest into Cochrane's death, a shift into Autumn brought a semblance of peace. Media controversy had died down, which allowed others to review and cultivate again an interest in a Craft mystique. Several theories have been put forward to rationalise the impetus and decision to form and name *The Regency*, ranging from the need to generate a link through to a perceived parent, to a reflection of a gregarious and egalitarian community.

Something had sparked the inspiration for the idea to germinate in the minds of people who for one reason or another, found themselves outside other mainstream occult, neo-Pagan and Wican groups at that time. In an online article, Monmouth penned this statement: *"The Cochrane Coven resurrected the Old Mystery Religion under the name of the Regency. It was so called because it could have no leaders; each of us is Regent to the deity!"* [331]

Valiente confirmed that no Clan member, herself included, wished to attend the meetings or rites of *The Regency,* an ad hoc group formed after Cochrane's death by a number of eclectic occultists. [332] She was most curious who did however, noting who amongst the Clan's former guests and its associates, became involved in Regency activities. Of course, none of them, at any time referred to, or commented upon a *'Royal Windsor Coven,'* which is to be expected as the rumour of it had not yet been instigated.

Valiente published her book, *The Rebirth of Witchcraft,* several years after her Craft peers (and associates within traditional groups and the Wica) became aware of the rumours attributed to the phantom Royal Windsor Coven. One good reason only excuses her fortitude in declining its mention thereafter, and for her failure to

---

[331] http://ronaldchalkywhite.org.uk/articles/the-regency-seasonal-meditations-rites-by-john-of-monmouth/
[332] Doreen Valiente, Jane Bowers, Evan John Jones (E.J.J.), V.J., and Bill & Bobbie Gray

mention it in her private Notepads or diaries. During privileged meetings with Valiente, several topics relative to the Clan and to other Craft matters including Wica and its own controversial history were discussed in private.

One of the subjects raised concerned the phantom coven, a rumour Valiente insisted should be dismissed as poor fiction. E.J.J. and his wife supported Valiente's appraisal, acutely aware the first whisper of it arrived well over a decade *after* Cochrane's death. Rather like the *Indian Rope Trick*, it would appear to have no basis in any reality except as a premise locked firmly into its own illusory legend.

Former members of the Clan, namely Doreen, Bill and Bobbie Gray, remained in contact with each other and with other close associates until their own individual deaths enforced departure from such illustrious company. Their personal contact with Regency people, was either negligible or non-existent. At this stage, it should be stated that *The Regency* and *The Clan of Tubal Cain*, cultivated their rich and diverse individuality with considerable depth and passion; they are *absolutely* distinct from one another, and neither are based in a fictional coven. E.J.J. sets an essential context with his comments on the works and legacy of the *Regency*.

> When it comes to *The Regency,* [mark II] it must be one of Chalky's ways of doing things As you know, I didn't go along with him when I saw the way he was running things, didn't like the way they were shaping up. *Of course he didn't dare use too much of Roy's material because he wasn't entitled to it as it had not been deeded to either George or him by Jane.* If they had done so, then there would have been no end of psychic trouble and nothing would have gone right for them. Tubal Cain has a way of protecting its own. [333]

These few examples confirm the facts *exactly* as Evan John Jones had posited, actualities he never deviated from. Throughout lengthy exchanges with E.J.J. in person and by letter, current Clan members were made aware that the concept for *a* Regency and for the eventual leadership (1969-76) of *The Regency* (mark II) by Ronald White and George Winter was, in his estimation, a deliberate

---

[333] (EJJ,L8)

manoeuvre, an act of politics designed to undermine the sole authority of CTC.

Their original intent to usurp the authority held by Cochrane's widow as Maid, Lady and Matriarch of the Clan, had been circumvented when that Lady instated E.J.J. as Magister of the Clan, pledged to continue its works and traditions, as per Robert Cochrane's edict. And though Monmouth emphatically ignores this, Michael Howard made note of it. [334]

Valiente confirmed White and Winter's initial plan to hold Cochrane's Tradition in trust for when his son came of age to claim as his *blood right* if he'd he so desired.[335] That intent proves unequivocally their full awareness of the true source of the Tradition and where it resided. Had White and Winter believed themselves to be the real source of that Tradition, as Monmouth and Howard have claimed for them retrospectively, their 'Regency' of Cochrane's son would have been a pointless contradiction. Jane Bowers' explicit response is confirmed by E.J.J. within this lengthy missive. [336]

> Getting on to the second part of the question. Jane long ago deeded me the whole thing and a very poor choice it was too even if I say so and the reason she did this, is to be found in *The Regency*. Chalky and George were part of the group who were constantly in hot water over what they thought should be done as opposed to what we were doing.[337] At times, the only thing that kept them in line, was good old fashioned fear of Roy. As soon as he was dead, they first of all disowned him and the group to the plods. Tried roping Jane as part of the <u>new Regency</u> and failed. Tried to bring both V** and I into the dammed thing and also help them with a little racket they had going. (. . .)
>
> When the idea was first mooted, Chalky and George more or less told Jane to her face, that they were taking everything over, and holding it for Roy's son Adrian and she could come along and be

---

[334] Howard, Michael. *Children of Cain* (US: Three Hands Press. 2011)
[335] 5/8/1966
[336] Monmouth's unsupported presentation of claims made for White and Winter conflict unfavourably with this first-hand account. His speculative conjecture fall away with this testimony – backed up by others who were also first-hand witnesses to these events. (see letter E.J.J:L 7 in Legend)
[337] Note here that E.J.J.' description in 1998, places White and Winter in a separate group within the Clan, and how he and Cochrane struggled always to instil the law and lore of the Clan tradition upon White and Winter – actions and consequences that generated considerable unease and bitterness.

the Queen Mother and let them do as they wanted with her and Adrian until they, in their infinite wisdom, would make him Magister. She never spoke to them again.

Who was left? The worse possible choice possible, me. Don't take my word for it, ask V** and Doreen when we manage to get into her den. Will explain in greater detail the how's and why's later, but rest assured, no-one but me can pass on the Clan Maid-ship to anyone. <u>No-one else has been vested with the authority to do so</u>. I was Roy's spiritual heir long before his death. Jane, Roy and I were that close to each other, even when V** and I met, we were still close. And we are the only ones Jane keeps in touch with even now.

In fact, as V** will readily tell you, when the cops questioned people over the circumstances of his death, none of them were actual members of the group, only observers, fact! What price loyalty? I honestly think Doreen would have been the only other one who would have stood by him in a Clan sense even though she wasn't a member having fallen out with him and had just come out of hospital at the time. Why do you think the Regency took the form it did? (mark I)

<u>Jane wasn't playing their little game and too many people knew about Tubal Cain for them to try to take it over and turn it into the Regency</u>, which they would have liked to have done, plus of course, they'd gone on record as denying the Clan membership, so what else could they do? The answer to quest. 7 as well Shani. [338]

With absolute precision, E.J.J. delineated historical matters of concern in this letter. His explanations became the subject of extensive discussion in person. White's ambition exhibited no restraint. Oblivious of the seething animosity initiated through their betrayals after Cochrane's death, White and Winter approached Cochrane's widow - Jane, E.J.J and V.J. for assistance and support to launch White's vision of a *Regency* into being. With some degree of acrimony, they all declined. [339]

---

[338] Oates, 2016. Op. Cit. *TM:Legend* Private letter from EJJ. to SLO. 1998 (EJJ:L7)
[339] Ronald White's failed ambition as Regent for a legacy held in abeyance for Cochrane's son became a perennial rumour dispersed by Howard and Monmouth. The folk who came together to establish The Regency (mark I) in 1967 were inspired by a very different vision, as noted by EJJ.' remark – '*why do think it took the form it did?*' Ronald White's private motivation was never the

Cochrane's widow exerted her full prerogative, and passed over all authority for *The Robert Cochrane Clan Tradition* (CTC) to *Evan John Jones* (E.J.J.). Her endowment of it to him as (the only) one she trusted to hold and maintain that authority with integrity, and with the humility to pay it forward, lay to some extent with her personal knowledge of E.J.J. Aware of the traditions he had brought within the body of the Clan and the knowledge he'd shared with Robert Cochrane in their efforts to fuel a common praxis, he was charged with their safe keeping. Jane Bowers' decree to continue Cochrane's tradition through E.J.J., should emphasise to what extent E.J.J. was a key figure in the Clan.

His devotion to those duties was ceaseless. Jane Bowers' avowed distance from Ronald White and George Winter, reveals her personal and contextual response to the situation, which may challenge anyone unfamiliar with the true cause of the enmity between them. Especially when those reasons are realised in their full unpleasant reality. Circulated for too long, the alternative version of events must cease in lieu of better information.[340]

Jane Bowers' just severance of White and Winter from filial allegiance to the Clan is another sharp reminder of the sense of duty expected within a Clan, a duty they failed dishonourably. By contrast, E.J.J. had placed his unequivocal allegiance with Jane Bowers. He remained steadfast and when questioned by the Police, E.J.J did not deny Robert Cochrane and their Clan.

To reiterate briefly, those who remained in the Clan after Cochrane's death were: Jane Bowers, John (E.J.J) and his good lady, V.J., supported thereafter by Doreen Valiente and Bill & Bobbie Gray until individual deaths parted their companie. Almost as an

---

shared intent or purpose of the founders of The Regency (mark I) in 1967. The 1966 date marks the date of *the inspiration for the idea of it only*, just as White stated. White's own comment is very different from what Monmouth and Michael Howard *claim* he said. Given that several ranking Wican's and other members of the Craft were the main founders of *The Regency* (Mark I) in 1967, it stretches credulity to presume they would accept or endorse a system set-up for the express purpose of nurturing Cochrane's legacy until his son came of age, to then comply with a pre-determined hand over. One of those founders, Reginald Hinchcliffe leaves no doubt of public opinion. His personal testimony accompanies re-typed copy letters from Cochrane's to his good friend Joe Wilson, and are without ambiguity. They expose who established The Regency, and what its true purpose had been. (See the Manilla envelope in Gills' Box. Museum of Witchcraft Archive) This is the reason Wilson left the UK perplexed by the lack of esteem Cochrane's tradition held at that time, especially by his Craft and Wican contemporaries.

[340] CTC's initial discretion fuelled media freedoms. Countering them now in favour of an accurate history, is the crucial and critical purpose for this biography.

afterthought to the tragedy, Valiente unwittingly delivered a vital clue in her summary of it. With regard to Cochrane's death and the Virtue of the Clan, she observed that it was another (meaning Jane, and not Roy), who held the real power of the Clan, and that when Jane left, *"it went with her."* [341] And so it did. Valiente's discreet remark relates to the beautiful mystery of the Virtue of the Egregore and how it resides always with the Maid. Only she may gift the Stang and appoint the hearth – no other. White and Winter had a fractured, limited understanding of this principle; Monmouth and Howard, none at all.

Her gift activates the spiritual transmission between one Magister and another, ensuring the direct transfer of the *Hamingja* - the fate and fortune of the Clan. Crucially held by the Head-Kinsman, the *Hamingja* allows him to protect the Clan through that aegis. As Clan's Magister after Cochrane, E.J.J. preserved and developed all works borne of the numerous experiences he'd shared with Cochrane during their short, but productive period together.

Uniquely distinct from the praxis and ethic of *The Regency,* CTC follows Cochrane's Spirituality, a vision matured under E.J.J.' guiding hand to focus upon the preservation of the Mystery Traditions of a Northern Heritage. That heritage maintains very specific idioms of law regarding Virtue. Addressing crucial issues raised with regard to a better understanding of the mechanics of these elements of Clan Mythos, E.J.J. began simply:

> Think in terms of the Pharaonic and matriarchal societies and you have witchcraft as the old craft should be but very rarely is. In our tradition, the Master leads the coven or Clan just as every Master does as well as heading the feminine mysteries. But, importantly, he leads them on sufferance from the Lady for as long as she wishes him to hold them.
>
> When women started to lose their status in society, the leaders of the groups made them subordinate, but where Roy is concerned, I suggest you try getting a copy of Doreen's book, the '*Rebirth of Witchcraft,*' reading in particular the chapter - Robert Cochrane, Magister. This was read by <u>V, Jane and myself</u> before it went into the book for our comments. If you can't get a copy, read mine when you come down again. After reading it, you'll see why I

---

[341] Valiente, 1989. Op. Cit.

stressed in the first book the role of the Lady, firmly believing that women should be restored to their true status rather than playing lip service to the concept.

Now, if people like Chummy (V's name for him[ADC]) claim they are devotees of our Lady and cannot accept that women are cast in Her image, making them special to Her – tough! A truth is a truth no matter how much it is denied. Roy did say he was equal to Jane and that no woman could lead a group, in a sense he was right. What he didn't say was more important though, he was leading the group because Jane let him, by making him her Magister. Hope this answers that question?" (. . .)

The idea and concept of the Maid has always been there in the old Tradition, but no Master pushed it because in the main, no man wants to play second fiddle to a woman. Why should he when he can be the great 'I am.' Now, if women were stupid enough to let them get away with it both now and in the past, who can blame a guy for trying it on? [342]

A Speculative Craft

The previous missive was written at a time of extreme disappointment concerning the behaviour of Ann and Dave Finnin in the US who had sought out then resisted the aegis of the Clan. E.J.J.' irritation at their failure to understand his teachings and their unfamiliarity with the subject matter proved to be a recurring challenge to them and countless others who recognise its deep truths.

Evan John Jones explained in an early letter to Dave and Ann Finnin in 1982, that (at the time of Cochrane's death) he was the only one who could legitimately continue Cochrane's Tradition.

At one time, five former members of the Clan, could in theory, *with the permission of the Magister*, form groups <u>within the</u> Clan, and bring people into them. As Ronald White and George Winter were two of those five people, any group formed by them, who might wish to claim descent from, or to be part of the Clan, *must first*

---

[342] Oates, 2016. Op. Cit. *TM Legend* Private letter from EJJ. to SLO. 1998. See (EJJ, L9 & L7). 'V' is VJ.

acquire *E.J.J.' permission,* as Magister of the Tradition and legacy holder. [343]

No other group is known to have been formed by Ronald White and George Winter, with his knowledge, or permission, as troth requires it, in order to continue within Cochrane's tradition. This certainly raises the subversive logic of a shadow group, now suggested by *'The all 'New' Regency,'* in pushing the alleged existence of the fictitious *'Royal Windsor Coven.'* Anything connected to Cochrane's Tradition must comply with the Law he established for it. To function under that Law any group seeking recognition must first seek permission from the Magister for its creation. Without that, *it is void of any claim to be part of the Clan, ergo Cochrane's tradition.* Conversely, if created and established with the Magister's knowledge and consent, it must, as stated above, offer its allegiance every seven years hence, to remain within the body of the Clan. That procedure was never undertaken.

Thwarted by Jane's rejection of original plans for a Regency, Ronald White had to rethink his strategy. Then, something very unique happened at the end of October in 1966, an event verified by Valiente in her Notepad entry dated November 1966. Norman Gills informed her that about fifty people were present to celebrate Halloween at a public gathering held at the Rollright Stones. [344]

Overwhelmingly impressed by this, Ronald White, who had been present, was eager to review his former plans and adapt them to a new and exciting venture. He raised this matter enthusiastically at the pub during the winter of 1966 with several other persons known to him. Having the genesis of an idea, several notable personages including Marian Green, 'George' Desmond Bourke, Justine Glass, Ruth Wynn Owen, George Winter, Norman Gills and Jill Hadden formed a slow and steady coterie. After several private planning sessions and meetings occurred, they were finally able to hold their first official meeting as *The Regency* in the Spring of 1967.

---

[343] Those two personages were exiled and put under the ban, by Jane Bowers' and E.J.J' authority. But, had they remained free of such unfortunate circumstance, their allegiance as hypothetical leaders of any group they'd established within the Clan must be given, and re-instated every seven years or be dissolved by default. E.J.J. made it very clear that neither The Regency, nor any other subsidiary groups it influenced over time ever came forward to request that authority or claim it.
[344] Valiente, 1966. Op. Cit. Notepad entry 8/11/66 Conspicuous by absence is any mention of The Regency, either as a formed idea or group prior to that securely dated event.

A very different version has been passed around the neo-Pagan community in the last decade. Monmouth exploited Valiente's remarks in carefully annotated and re-constructed comments that *imply he* is quoting *her* verbatim.[345]

His statement is a composition *based* upon comments Valiente made; they do not represent what she said, or her intent. It includes a reference to the Royal Windsor Coven, *totally absent* from Valiente's. He then turned E.J.J.' and his wife's obvious distrust of Ronald White into a disingenuous disaffection with his mentor Robert Cochrane and the Clan. At all times Monmouth referred to his phantom coven instead of using the terms employed by Valiente and E.J.J. – Clan. This detrimental and quite creative spin set the tone for Monmouth's version of events through the history he presented in *GWiE*.

> The first meeting of *The Regency* was held on 30 October 1966, four months after the death of Roy Bowers. John and V** Jones, disillusioned by events in the Royal Windsor Coven's recent history - decided not to attend. [346] John and Val Jones did not attend and they ceased to have any contact with Ron White and George Stannard. [347]

A similar comment was made by Howard, though it implied a different reason for their non-attendance. Placing emphasis upon a speculative break in E.J.J.' Craft activities, Howard inserted the specious reference to the phantom coven instead of CTC. He also suggested this alleged absence was due to his recent marriage and new arrival:

> John Jones and his wife were not interested in continuing with the 'Royal Windsor Cuveen' or getting involved with The Regency. White expressed disappointment about this turn of events and Valiente commented: *"I think they are just settling down to a 'normal' family life."* [348] Jones also told this writer that at this

---

[345] Monmouth 2012. Op. Cit. p 99
[346] Monmouth. 2012. Op. Cit. *GWiE* The reference to the phantom coven is Monmouth's interjection. It was not made by E.J.J.'
[347] Valiente, 1966. Op. Cit. Notepad entry 8/11/66
[348] Howard, 2011. Op. Cit. (pers. com from Dr Gillian Spraggs to MH, 4th August 2010, quoting letter from Doreen Valiente to Ronald White in her possession). p 84. Valiente's comment is taken out of

period he and his wife took time off from the Craft to raise their family.[349]

Naturally enough, E.J.J. did settle down with his new wife and child, though he did not deny or neglect his Craft involvement at any time. They are not mutually exclusive. On the contrary, he confirmed in his letters to CTC and others his continued duties in the Clan.[350]

Several people were persuaded to came on board in the following weeks, including Madge Worthington, Reginald Hinchcliffe, Charles Pace, John and Jean Score, Rosina Bishop and Tony Kelly. Over the winter of 1966/7, they discussed strategy and policy for the Spring Council Meeting that launched *The Regency* into the public arena.[351]

During that chaotic and troubled time, an unusual ritual working was undertaken in Ruth Wynn Owen's flat in London (where early *Regency* meetings and Esbats were held) which left her very disturbed. Referring to it as an act of necromancy, she declared it to be nothing less than 'black magic.'

Popular claims of necromancy and of summoning the shade of Robert Cochrane particularly, were made during this time, which continued into the decades following his death. Directed by Ronald White, the ritual seriously offended Ruth Wynn Owen's personal ethic. Given the scrutiny the Craft was under at that time by the press eager for sensationalism, she considered their dabbling especially reckless.

This presents a bewildering conundrum. With all the acknowledged grievances and resentments between Cochrane and many of these people, there is no reason for any of them to summon to their presence a person who was no friend to them, nor a leader, guide nor mentor to them? Cochrane's presence was the last thing they would want. Given Monmouth's assertion that White and Winter had been advising Cochrane, what possible use was his shade to them!

---

context. It's original intent is lost and it is tacked onto an unprovenanced comment E.J.J. allegedly made to Howard. Equally, CTC assert that E.J.J. told them the full story.
[349] Howard, 2011. Op. Cit. Unverified comment. p 84
[350] These are private letters but are available for sincere research.
[351] Marian Green Op. Cit. Private Letter.

Only as their former mentor and leader in the Clan, would that be plausible or needful. The notion of a Regency for Cochrane's son was equally contentious.[352] For certain the other founders of *The Regency* would have rejected any hint of themselves as Regents, holding a tradition in abeyance for that young man. Hence E.J.J.' comment, "*why do you think it took the form it did?*" Quite simply, <u>they couldn't do anything else</u>.

This genuine information seriously challenges the popular version of this history and these events. Inconsistencies dissolve within true context, and fact emerges from fiction. Those facts speak for themselves.

> What any of us knows, is not necessarily what can be proved. But if it is true, then facts will be found to support that Truth. If these cannot be found, then what we know, is false. ~ Robin-the-dart.

Ken Rees and others, including E.J.J have stated that over time, Ronald White's original intent probably never left him privately.[353] Some months passed before Valiente mentioned *The Regency* again. Having noted those in attendance, she added that "*Bill refused to join after one meeting.*" He left unimpressed, vowing never to return. Gray added that they: "*Worship the statue of Goddess with a slow circle-dance.*"

> The Regency meet in London flat of Yorkshire lady, of 'Welsh extraction (. . .) Has Welsh names (hyphenated ?) Wynn Owen.[354]

Monmouth observed that Ronald White and Bill Gray did not know each other by name and failed to realise the identity of one another.[355] This suggests their paths had not crossed previously, that is to say, they had not worked *together*. And yet they were both listed by name on a Clan circular following the *All Hallows* meeting of 1964.[356] This provides further support for the existence of two groups within the Clan, one of which may have been marshalled by Ronald White, who may or may not have been Chalky/ie.

---

[352] A theory/rumour Michael Howard is largely responsible for. See: Howard, 2011. Op. Cit.
[353] Ken Rees. Pers. Corr. 2017 Op. Cit.
[354] Valiente, 1967. Op. Cit. Notepad entry dated 30th September.
[355] Monmouth, 2012 Op. Cit. p 27
[356] Oates, 2016. *SCSIII* Op. Cit. See: Chronology of the Robert Cochrane Letters (z) p 305

An appreciation of the proper context in which *The Regency* was established is crucial. As an informal collective of those shared ideas, its renaissance was however, very short-lived. By 1969, suffering from internal friction and politicking, *The Regency* was under considerable pressure from inside and out.

One of their founding minds and major players, Ruth Wynn Owen, had abandoned the project in less than two years, strongly disapproving of what she believed were questionable witchcraft activities. She was evidently quite uncomfortable with the growing publicity in Craft matters. Although this was not focussed on her as a neo-Pagan, it did target her high profile Wican friends, *John Score, Charles Pace, Madge Worthington* especially. Her worst fears came to pass when several of her friends were subjected to months of harassment by the Press, eager for tales of sex and nudity.

During the media storm that finally erupted in the Spring of 1969, many fled from the public face of the Craft, fearful for their jobs and anonymity. From February 1969, that despicable coverage dragged on for several weeks throughout into the Summer. Everyone was under threat of exposure for alleged 'satanic' based witchcraft, especially. Understandably, none of them could face the slanderous detriment to their livelihoods.

Of grave concern to the Craft and to *The Regency*, those aggressive interjections were not incidental, nor random, but cyclic. Negative and inflammatory news coverage had preyed upon the Craft at three to four yearly intervals prior to this situation that reached its head early in 1969 after almost a year of intermittent exposés, *three years after* Cochrane's death. During the previous decade, Valiente and others recorded at least three similar circumstances where charges were levied against the Craft, citing many alleged cases of Black Magic, Satanism, Necromancy, Orgies and all manner of libertine and nefarious indulgences.

Monitoring this next sequence of events closely, especially from April through to the end of July, 1969, Valiente observed Ruth Wynn Owen's brave plea to the newspaper editors responsible for *The News of the World*, not to print inflammatory material. Wynn Owen's request for amnesty for her fellow crafters was refused, her efforts were to no avail. Many lives were devastated in the fevered exposure that followed; Madge Worthington and John Score were ruthlessly targeted. Disgusted by the whole media circus, Ruth Wynn Owen left the public arena. All the initial founders voted with their feet and left with her, utterly devastating the rank & file of *The Regency* (mark I).

Abandoned to their own devices Ronald White and George Winter were left with no impetus, no endorsements and no material to work with. Things looked very bleak for their short-lived enterprise. Recorded by Ronald White in his own diary, these events rang alarm bells that signalled the end of all he'd tried to accomplish. Monmouth referred to a significant handwritten diary entry, this time, by Ronald White. Dated to the middle of May 69, it falls at precisely this most crucial moment within these traumatic events. His alarmed hand-written response is in abbreviated form. It allegedly reads very simply as: *"End of RWO & possibly Reg. ESB."* [357]

Given the exceptional circumstances of these events, and the pressure placed upon everyone, a sensible understanding of what these abbreviations describe is immediately transparent. CTC propose that Monmouth focussed too selectively upon Madge Worthington, which caused him to miss the bigger drama at play. Ronald White clearly understood it: *"End of Ruth Wynn Owen and possibly Reg. ESB."*

Ruth Wynn Owen was a very significant mover and shaker within *The Regency*, associated with mark I version since its inception. With the end of her involvement and endorsement of *The Regency* (mark I), Ronald White witnessed its collapse before him. *The Regency* were no longer allowed access for meetings at her flat or the use of her grounds for rituals. Those who remained were forced to look elsewhere.

White's diary entry (noted above), reflects his natural trepidation and despair. Presented with an ambiguous abbreviation, it could have manifold interpretations, all dependent upon presentation and context. Unfortunately, Monmouth did not provide a scans, nor observe vital context. A study of how words and letters were formed

---

[357] Monmouth, 2012. Op. Cit. p 121 It is unusual to say the least that White should be cited using Reg. as an abbreviation for the Regency. His notepads, visible online show distinct use of *Rg Y*. Reg. is more probably an abbreviation of Reginald, who may have hosted the Events. https://ronaldchalkywhite.wordpress.com/tag/the-regency/

would indicate certain clues, including graphological verification.[358] That so many scans were provided in his book presents concern by this absence.[359]

Bewilderingly, Monmouth failed to see the obvious. His adoption of a wildly subjective view, elevated but one part of these unfortunate trials. A critical analysis of what he *has* provided, and what *he says* about it, is essential. What is actually written, is very different from what Monmouth implied White said. Looking carefully at Monmouth's alleged quote from White's diary, two names in particular ring out from those abbreviations: *"End of RWO and possibly Reg. ESB,"*

Ruth Wynn Owen and Reg Hinchcliffe made their exit from *The Regency* (mark I) precisely at that point in time, presenting a perfectly cross-referenced context with specific comments found in Valiente's Notepads. All of which are corroborated by the newspaper summaries that archived those contemporary events.

Hinchcliffe's departure is explained by him in a letter to John Score dated 17th July 1969, in which the intended motivation behind *The Regency* is outlined. The original founders had recognised the need for a *'pagan church.'* Hinchcliffe conveys his disappointment and how their initial optimism disintegrated when Wynn Owen turned her back on all of it and walked away

> At the time Ruth was involved. When she finally withdrew her support, so did a great many others, myself included. The Regency in its *original form* was a good thing because it served as a meeting ground for people of esoteric leanings and satisfied the need of people who were unsuitable for closed groups. This was realised by those of us who followed Ruth out.[360]

The Regency was left decimated. No doubt Ronald White felt its death throes once Wynn Owen and the others left; everything fell

---

[358] In the history of archived documentation, handwriting is the single highest causality for all misunderstandings acquired in the field of error. If wrong at source, the consequences render the statement useless on all counts. All handwritten documents must be authenticated to separate them from forgeries. Anyone can write anything and claim a curious provenance for it.

[359] Personal Correspondence from GS to SLO. A scan was requested of just that one sentence from G. S. who initially reviewed the diaries of Ronald White in the preparatory stages for Monmouth's book. G. S. kindly replied that she no longer has those letters and was unable to double-check or confirm the above. (By email. August 2015)

[360] Reginald Hinchcliffe. 17th July 1969. Museum of Witchcraft Archive. doc. 791

away from him. *Everything!* Completely disregarding these irrefutable facts, plus reason, logic and context, all fully supported by corroborative statements from key witnesses, Monmouth bypassed everything to propose that Ronald White's alleged diary abbreviation should be read as: *"End of Royal Windsor Coven and possibly Regency Esbats"*

Several distracting side issues are raised by this suggestion, that need just a moment to ponder before their dismissal. Perhaps in desperation for any hint of his phantom coven, Monmouth *may* have mis-read Ronald White's handwriting. Mistaking cursive letters would be an easy thing to do. For example an open letter that looks like this: *C* , could be and O or a C. If mistaken in this way, RW*O* *RWC* would appear indistinct from RW*C* *RWC*. Handwriting aside, there is *no precedent or context* to support his left-field assertion it has anything to do with a phantom coven - in fact, *no* evidence at all.

Monmouth's speculative suggestion is created outside the actual sequence of events and make no sense of them, it is alien to the circumstances. As for *'Reg.'* being interpreted as Regency, an example of White's hand writing negates that possibility. He always abbreviated Regency as *RgY.* [361]

To posit that the exit of so many notable personages from *The Regency,* implied an end to a phantom coven, is to make the corresponding presumption that Wynn Owen, Hinchcliffe, Worthington, Score et al, were also (secret) members of it, in addition to others Monmouth previously cited as members.

Following that line of thought, the insinuation which makes the people of *The Regency* the alleged members of a phantom coven, by default, would make them members of Cochrane's alleged coven, before his death! That is, if any of Monmouth's assumptions were correct. That Cochrane could have ever had so large a group, counters everything he, E.J.J., Valiente, Green, Gray and others have all stated as fact. In fact, that any of those people would have been members of a secret coven of which Robert Cochrane was Magister, is not even feasible – it is a complete non-event. [362]

---

[361] Monmouth, 2012. Op. Cit. p 121. It is odd that White should be cited using Reg. as an abbreviation for the Regency. His notepads, visible online show distinct use of *RgY.* Reg. is more probably an abbreviation of Reginald, who may have hosted the Events.
https://ronaldchalkywhite.wordpress.com/tag/the-regency/
[362] Even today, Cochrane's name is *persona non grata* to any member of Y Plant Bran,

If, however, Monmouth meant they had all joined that phantom coven *after* Cochrane's death, it could not have been *retrospectively* secret in his life time, not in any sense. An alleged secret coven either had nothing to do with Cochrane, or was properly secret, which means that no-one knew of it, ever. It would have died with him; or, if it was created after him, it would admit its independence of Cochrane, having no reason to fain false connection to him. If the former, it ceased to exist; if the latter, there would have been no need for that non-secret coven to have *'invented a religion'* for *The Regency*. In fact, there would have been no need for *The Regency* to have existed at all! Perhaps then, given these severe irregularities and absurd contradictions, none of which Monmouth addresses, he was a little over zealous in his initial presumption for this abbreviated diary entry.[363]

Monmouth had pointedly dismissed the notion of inner courts or inner circles for his phantom coven, but there is no reason the Esbats held for *The Regency* should have any bearing upon the alleged activities for that phantom coven, or *visa versa* for that matter. After all, it was *The Regency* that had been decimated by these events. To all intent and purposes, it was the 'end of The Regency,' in every way, not just its Esbats!

If Monmouth wished to excuse his own condemnation of an inner court, by claiming the same people were the leaders of both Regency and phantom coven, as separate modalities, then the same argument against that, remains. Both would cease to exist, and neither could be singularly or partially affected. That is to say, his statement could not differentiate by distinct reference only to Esbats held by *The Regency,* but would have to include The Regency itself. A projection of that hypothetical entry might read: *'End of Royal Windsor Coven and The Regency.'*

Usage of the term Esbat presumes the abbreviation ESB, to mean Esbat.[364] And it may, but it could also refer to a separate entry for that Esbat date, placed there in advance, in anticipation of it. It may have had no contextual relationship to what else was added to

---

[363] This seems an involved and convoluted explanation of the ramifications of what is simply not possible. But, while it is easy enough for Monmouth, Howard, et al, to state something 'is'. It is not acceptable to respond with a denouncement – to say, it 'is not', is never so readily believed, and proofs are expected of the latter but hardly ever of the former.
[364] Monmouth, 2012. Op. Cit. pages 120-121 & 132-3

the diary box for that date at a later time, which in this instance could have been on the actual day of his terrible realisation. This suggestion of that improbable connection is supported where the abbreviations are read as a reference to Ruth's and Reginald's names as a later comment written in alongside an Esbat date written there possibly several weeks previously. *"End of Ruth Wynn Owen and possibly Reg. ESB."* Though ESB may even refer to something else entirely, something as yet uncertain.

For an interpretation of any validity or purpose, a key is essential, one that establishes White's handwriting and his intention for his personal abbreviations. Both should have been supplied as diary scans.

After her acrimonious exit, Ruth Wynn Owen, formed *Y Plant Bran*, focussing her time and energy developing her inherent traditions into its works. [365] Ronald White assumed leadership of *The Regency* after its resounding blow. Having lost its priests and priestesses, theatrical costume designers, scriptwriters, festival organisers, poets, dancers, meeting house and dancing ground, it survived somewhat tenuously and much diminished as *The Regency* (mark II). A change of modus operandi was sorely needed.

Over a year later, in October 1970, Valiente noted that *The Regency (mark II)* were spotted on Hampstead Heath, and in much diminished numbers. Tenaciously, White and Winter hung on, plumbing readily accessible and highly popular resources such as Grave's *White Goddess,* and Aradia. Commented upon by Monmouth and Joe Wilson, since 1969 the works they were introduced to, were not the scripted rites, theatrical plays, or grand folkloric pagan revelries of old. Those had disappeared with Ruth Wynn Owen. CTC can state with absolute conviction, that the original *Regency* (mark I) prior to 1969, did not subscribe to Cochrane's works in any way; in fact, Ruth Wynn Owen especially would have considered them inimical to her Craft.

During the course of the remaining year, the Rites and Rituals of *The Regency* (mark II) were re-structured accordingly. Some of the material White and Winter pulled together after 1969 was

---

[365] Ken Rees. Private Correspondence. Sept. 2017. GS verifies a considerable rift between RWO and RW at this time. In GWiE, Monmouth chose to focus on Madge Worthington rather than RWO. A tactic that draws fire from the shift in leadership and the change between mark I and mark II

their own, garnered from early thoughts and musings on the Craft as witnessed in a few documents within the Cache. As noted above, their, *mark II* evolution of *The Regency* drafted in ideas from several traditions familiar encountered over several years.

For example, *The Round of Life,* which is a fundamental tenet in Cochrane's Tradition, became much adapted (albeit still recognisable) as the *Reading of the Festival of the Year*. [366] Information found in a couple of the documents from the cache witness elements of what Monmouth describes as White's working mythos, and certainly reflect the mind of Ronald White. [367]

What cannot be known with certainty, is *when* most of them were originally drafted; this may have been around 1958 when both White and Cochrane were in Everley's Coven in London, or during the years up to Cochrane's death in 1966, or even in the years after that. White may have had access to some of them for use amongst his personal ad hoc gatherings, or after 1969 for use in *The Regency* (mark II). Without documented dates, any guess is unacceptable. It should be reiterated that White's views were deemed incompatible with his own, as the remaining documents, works and letters affirm.

Some ideas were pooled from various sources. Once formulated by Cochrane, they briefly served as exploratory works for use by other members of the Clan during the initial stages of their early workings. Anyone wishing to emulate them, would have to trace them through the themes and beliefs continued and developed further by Ronald White in *The Regency* (mark II). These are preserved in *The New Pagans Handbook*.

Tangential to those early experimental works and beliefs, Cochrane concentrated his creative efforts into forging together the core elements gifted to him into a workable mystery tradition. With crucial input from E.J.J. and the old man of Westmoreland, Cochrane's works advanced exponentially. Other Clan documents, including Cochrane's papers and letters to Bill Gray, Gills, Wilson, Graves and others, reflect the unique style and genius Cochrane is best *known* for.

---

[366] Rees. Op. Cit. 2016/17. Ken Rees states his belief that the form used by White and Winter originated in Graves' *White Goddess*.
[367] Monmouth. 2012 p 31

By and large, the interests Ronald White and George Winter held were equally distinctive. Their diverse mythologies led them along a different route. E.J.J. confirmed how White had developed *The Regency (mark II)* according to his own vision, supplemented with other influential material he'd gathered, pre-Clan and post-Clan. [368]

During that difficult and transitional period for *The Regency*, Ronald White expressed certain provocative ideas in a magazine interview, claiming that *The Regency* had been his brain-child and creation as far back as 1966.[369] There is a marked discrepancy between that date and the 1967 date recorded by Valiente. [370]

Monmouth also pushed the notion of a 1966 for the inception of *The Regency*, a date which better reflects White's reference to the *genesis of the idea* of it, rather than the actual realisation of it. [371] This misunderstanding is a persistent discrepancy. Frequently overlooked when repeated in retrospective commentaries, conflicting versions of arose. This inconsistency is partially echoed in an article written by Ronald White and printed in Michael Howard's former magazine *Spectrum,* in 1974, where the earlier date of Halloween, 1966 is repeated.[372]

However, the 1967 date correlates perfectly with the first public (council) meeting, in the spring, and with source information gleaned from documented comments made at the time by Ronald White personally. In a missive sent to a contact in Ireland, dated 1970, Ronald White remarked on an annual celebration of *The Regency* following its inaugural meeting:

> This Hallowe'en marks The Regency's <u>third</u> year of worship in the open, as we meet in a local wood in London. This is in the Highgate area. [373]

---

[368] Oates. 2016. Op. Cit. *TM:Legend* Personal Correspondence EJJ to SLO (L10)
[369] The Messiah of Highgate Hill *Man, Myth & Magic* Frontiers/Purnell Publishers. #43 1969/70
[370] Valiente's Notepad entry 8/11/66 – April 1967
[371] Monmouth. John of, *Genuine Witchcraft is Explained* (UK:Capall Bann 2012) p83
[372] A Letter to the Pagan Movement in Britain and Ireland. Published in Spectrum, no. 2, Nov/Dec 1974 http://ronaldchalkywhite.org.uk/articles/a-letter-to-the-pagan-movement-in-britain-and-ireland/
[373] Published in *The Waxing Moon* new series, 1, Samhain 1970
http://ronaldchalkywhite.org.uk/articles/a-letter-to-the-pagan-movement-in-britain-and-ireland/

What this statement does not reveal or explain, is why the initial planning meetings held at various houses, especially Ruth Wynn Owen's prior to their first public meeting in Spring 1967, ceased. Ronald White's *Regency* (mark II) were forced to hold Esbat meetings for a while at Sally & George Bourke/Desmond's place, before finally taking to the woods around Highgate The letter continues:

> We used to meet indoors [at RWO], but being unable to find a place at one time [after RWO left] we adopted the wood as our temple (. . .) meeting on the seasonal festivals. [374]

Ronald White quickly adapted to the more generic Sabbats that became synonymous with *The Regency* (II) open festivals in the park between 1969 to sometime around 1975-6. During a massively publicised event, he ceded his *crown* to a younger and more *virile man*. White confirmed his seven year term was ended - 1967-1974, acknowledged as his personal, sacrificial reign [375] Before White retired in 1974, he had re-invented a rather new, colourful history for *The Regency*, somewhat diverse from its original format. Monmouth declared its mythos and modus operandi were therefore a synergy of those original minds who had created it. [376]

> Generally speaking, we follow the old pagan custom of worshipping the Mother Goddess - Creatrix of all things'(...) following the pattern of 'beliefs that regional and national (...) Arthur still sleeps in Avalon – hence the name 'Regency.'

White explained how the genesis of its religious beliefs and rituals were redeveloped over the course of that first year (1969-70).[377] Within his 1969 *Man, Myth and Magic* Interview, Ronald White declared: *"We decided to invent a religion."* [378]

---

[374] Published in *The Waxing Moon* new series, 1, Samhain 1970
http://ronaldchalkywhite.org.uk/articles/a-letter-to-the-pagan-movement-in-britain-and-ireland/
[375] Rees. Ken, *Investigating the Regency* '#121 2006 *The Cauldron* (based on earlier info from 1970s research with them) Monmouth mentions this incident. See Monmouth, 2012. Op. Cit. White handed his crown to Charles Whitehead, who acted as leader only briefly before passing it again to *Regency John* until *The Regency* itself finally ceased in London, circa 1975-6.
[376] White. 1969. Op. Cit.
[377] Purnell/Cavandish #43. 1970
[378] Ronald White 1969 *Man, Myth and Magic* Op. Cit.

How or why does one invent a religion? Because Monmouth insisted *The Regency* had <u>not</u> ever been an outer or inner court/group for anything, it held no greater or lesser Mythos to adapt for itself. If it had already been a legitimate part of any other group, it would have those tenets in place already, so there would be no need to invent anything.

Only where an extant group, in this case CTC, had expelled them from it, and *denied* them access to its tenets, would there be an actual need to 'invent' their own, and to develop it accordingly. Their own words confirm there was no *intent* to continue works engaged with Cochrane before his untimely death. To be deemed a 'new' religion, it would need to be independent – unconnected to anything that preceded it. In other words, *entirely distinct from Robert Cochrane's Tradition and Clan*, or indeed anyone else's group or work.

Unofficially, as Rees pointed out, the reality presented, was significantly different to what was popularly assumed for them. Far from being unique, they'd plundered the works of Ruth Wynn Owen's and others to, (including Cochrane's); despite having no permission to do so.

As a popular rite generally associated with *The Regency, The Reading of the Festivals of the Year* is, essentially, a conglomeration of two documents Monmouth attributed to Cochrane: *The Writ and Constitution* and *Theories of Witch Practice*. Ken Rees has good reason to identify Robert Graves as an influential source for White's, *The Reading of the Festivals of the Year*.

Even so, those two other named documents were very unlikely to have been penned by Cochrane. Who the author actually was, is far from clear, and almost impossible to prove without further evidence. Ronald White's self-acclaimed 'new' religion attributed to *The Regency,* was evidently not so new, but accrued from a variety of recent and familiar sources.

One of the places the 'new' Regency (mark II) worked, is given below - *The Rollright Stones*. Valiente had mentioned how this site was popular with Norman Gills and Joe Wilson, and certain groups of the Wica, but **not** by Cochrane and his Clan. Cochrane had emphatically made that clear to Norman Gills in their previous correspondence.

The Regency met, mostly, in Queen's Wood, Highgate, North London, where it had been given the right by the LCC (London County Council) to celebrate the seasonal festivals. It also met at the <u>Rollright Stones</u> in Oxfordshire, Runton Woods in Norfolk, and at various locations in Shropshire and North Wales. With the exception of one festival (Candlemas), all its meetings took place outdoors. It met to celebrate the quarter and cross-quarter days. It also met on Twelfth Night and at the start of Advent, when *'The Reading of the Festivals of the Year'* would be read. [379]

Summarised from his study of *The Regency,* Rees observed a failure in their rites to convey meaningful intent within a constructive, coherent mythos. Rees expressed concerns for their politics. Considered unsavoury in nature, these have been called to question since, creating further controversy. [380] Not everything was as it seemed, nor indeed, has been proposed for them since. As supposed old hands, experienced in the ways of ritual, it is odd to read White's description of their struggle to find their feet and make it work.

These factors do not indicate a tight, efficient well-seasoned group of operatives that formed an outer court as Howard claimed. It better describes a group of people who remained uncertain of leadership, how to organise ritual efficiently, and how their unfamiliarity with the demands of structure, caused their failure to underpin their work with an established Mythos?

It is evident that a small gathering of people sought to build their identity and create a new and independent existence in *The Regency* (mark II). They struggled to find it, and make it manifest. By default, this confirms the lack of a prescribed ritual format needful to build upon and develop according to their own vision, just as E.J.J. had said.

---

[379] Phillips, Julia 1993 - http://www.sacred-texts.com/pag/wiccahst.txt Comments Italicised, underlined or given emphasis are those of this author – Shani Oates.

[380] *The Regency* by Ken Rees Vol. I & II *The Wiccan,* Beltane 2004
Rees reiterates in his own, aforementioned article, his own attendance at several rites held by *The Regency* between 1974 and 1976 as it was winding down, dwindling under the auspices of a 'personal friend.'

An Operative Craft

The pattern of suggestion and presumption is self-evident. People are introduced and woven into the history retrospectively. Enormous leaps of faith are made, and in all cases, the *actual* history is ignored. Abbreviated diary entries made by Ronald White, span the winter of 1966/7, and relate to meetings with several people. Indicated by times and initials only, White's notations are taken completely out of context. This scant information is creatively enfleshed by Monmouth to presume unsubstantiated claims of initiations for those people into his phantom coven.

> At some point in the early autumn 1966, Gerard Noel was initiated into the 'Royal Windsor Coven,' taking the name Lance or Lancelot.[381]

First of all, the repetitious and retrospective use of this phantom coven's title, several times upon every page indicates a method of conditioning designed to persuade acceptance of the coven's existence as an unquestionable reality. Secondly, the use of inserted names and dates alongside it, imply further validation, without actually providing proof of them.

Other sources confirm that Ronald White had several meetings with Gerard Noel and others in that period usually at the pub, *The Whittington and his Cat,* Highgate Hill, where they very probably discussed the formulation of the group they eventually launched as *The Regency*.[382]

In neither account is the phantom coven mentioned. All names, titles, initiations and covens are *presumed* by Monmouth. For example: The entry made by White refers to a *meeting only* (with 'Lance'). Monmouth made a considerable leap to imagine the meeting with Noel's was his initiation into the Royal Windsor Coven, noted above. Nothing signifies this presumption and nothing is provided to verify his claims. They are simply stated as fact. White's diary entries clearly *post-date Cochrane's death*, further disassociating these people from anything related to the Clan or its continuing tradition.

---

[381] Monmouth, 2012. Op. Cit. pages 114-5
[382] Rees, K. 2016. Op. Cit. Imbolc. Private Correspondence, used by permission.

Gerard Noel and Ronald White had already been acquainted for a number of years. Gerard Noel had left Eleanor Bone's (Wican) coven in 1964. Then, after Bill Gray introduced him to Cochrane around 1965, Noel was an occasional guest only, never a member of the Clan. He chose to be independent and focus on the *Witchcraft Research Association* and co-Masonry, along with other notable persons such as Desmond Bourke between 1967-71 Noel's initiation is referred to by Valiente's in this context, and correctly dates it as 1967. [383]

Noel's active involvement with *The Regency* was brief, mostly confined to the mark I phase, and sporadic at best in mark II. [384] By 1969, Noel had long departed the Craft scene with several others who'd very quickly become disillusioned with it; Ken Rees confirmed Noel's occasional appearance as the guest of Charles Whitehead and Desmond Bourke during 1974. [385]

Monmouth laid considerable importance upon a list of titles provided in one of the documents: *Sir Will the musician, Sir Lancelot, the Summoner, and Sir Edmund, the Steward*. He made further presumptions, stating those specific identities were associated with the following men: *George Winter, Gerard Noel and Ronald White*. [386] None of these assignations have been verified.

The Identification of George *Winter* as Sir Will, the musician, implies musical ability, an automatic qualification that assigns to him the requisite experience to have advised Cochrane on dance and dance related issues, including music and song. Sir Will, could just as easily be George Bourke. [387] Because Bourke was never a member of the Clan, he is not in the running as a member of the fantasy coven it is meant to represent.

This does not discount the possibility that George Bourke was Sir Will, merely that as another alias of Bourke's, it held no relevance to any alleged former associations with Cochrane, his People, or his Tradition. Very little actually links George Winter to any assumed musical abilities. Beyond his nickname – 'bang-bang,'

---

[383] Valiente, 1964. Op. Cit. Notebook entry 6/7/1964
[384] Valiente, Ibid.
[385] Rees, 2016/17. Op. Cit.
[386] Monmouth, 2012. Op. Cit. *GWiE* p 114
[387] George Arthur Melachrino, the band musician for instance.

acquired due to his propensity to 'bang' together two old tobacco tins to beat out the rhythm for the Mill, no other connexion is evident.[388]

Almost everything Monmouth focused upon, occurred after 1966; the events *all post-date Cochrane's death*. No matter how hard he tried to factor particular pieces of information into Clan history, they remain external to it, relevant only to *The Regency* and its members. Cochrane invested the authority for his Tradition within the Clan, specifically, with its Head-Kinsmen, i.e. The Clan Matriarch (as Lady and Seeress/Maid) and her Magister.[389] Cochrane stressed this imperative in certain documents of the cache and within his letters. Jane, his widow and Clan Matriarch, demonstrated it when she authorised E.J.J. to continue their Clan, as did E.J.J. in turn with Robin-the-dart and Shani Oates in 1998.

As facts founded within the Cochrane Tradition, it is interesting to note that challenges to its authority are raised only by those *outside* it. In like manner, the information used by those external challengers regarding CTC's tenets of law and lore, are found in documents that have little to no bearing on those things. Reality finds better purpose for those documents in their relevance to the traditions of others.

According to Michael Howard, this *cache* was discovered in an old plastic carrier bag, allegedly in Winter's possession. Monmouth finds a more fanciful origin in a ceremoniously gifted package received from three mysterious old ladies dressed in black. There is no provenance for either.

A third and more probable solution is that they were in the possession of Norman Gills, a curator and collector of craft oddments and a person noted for dipping his toes here and there, and for his a hoc workings with different people. His archived material in the Museum of Witchcraft includes countless letters and documents, pieces, partial copies and hand-written transcripts. Several of these

---

[388] Personal conversations with E.J.J. & V. Jones, (1998) Doreen Valiente (1999) and Ken Rees (Feb 2016). In one of the handwritten letters to Ronald White, Cochrane asks him to remind George to bring his 'drums.' Both E.J.J.' and Roy's testimonies confirm a distinct view to Michael Howard's contrary history that explains the nickname was associated with Winter stamping the ground with his staff: p 26. EJJ., 2001. Op. Cit. This history by Howard witnesses many such errors.

[389] If clarity is needful at this stage, only actual members of Cochrane's Clan bear his Tradition, and the Clan are associated with no-one else. To be of that tradition, one has to be in the Clan. Not outside it. Once a person is out of the Clan, they are out of the tradition's aegis.

oddments are cut and paste composites, largely of Cochrane's letters to Gills and to Wilson, forming a most intriguing selection.[390]

An unusual letter and a delayed meeting add considerable weight to this third option, though its course to discovery thereafter is less simple. It began with Gills and completes in the correspondence between Iain Steele and E.J.J. Their focus was upon certain documents in Steel's possession that had belonged to his former, late wife A.F., a pupil of Norman Gills in the 1980s.

Steele was trying to find out the author of these documents, and the source of the information typed upon them. He wondered if they were Gills,' Cochrane's or something Gills had picked up from someone else. One of the documents from A.F.'s cache of teaching material she received from Gills, is mentioned in Steele's letter to E.J.J. It is entitled: *'The 8 spirits of The Moon.'* [391]

Apparently, Steele's former, late wife (A.F.) had told him, that Gills had told her, that it was Cochrane's. This document - *'The 8 spirits of The Moon,'* was amongst the document 'cache' Howard claimed was allegedly 'found in George's old carrier bag'; or, according to Monmouth, was allegedly a dramatic gift from 'three old ladies dressed in black'! That same cache of documents is cited and illustrated in Monmouth's book.[392] How A.F.'s material found its way to Monmouth is not determined and may only be surmised. It may have passed through one or several hands.

For a couple of years after E.J.J.' death in 2003, Steele had continued his efforts to contact prominent members of CTC to discuss his deceased wife's cache of documents, in addition to other Craft matters, but without success. Steele wrote to the editor of *The Cauldron* (Michael Howard), hoping to initiate contact through him. No messages were received by CTC.

A couple of years later, in 2007, Shani Oates met Iain Steele at a Conference in Ludlow. Steele expressed his regret and disappointment that he had not been able to find a way to make contact a few years earlier. Steele then explained he had been told by Howard that CTC did not accept correspondence. This was not true.

---

[390] This collection and its composites are the source of the many forgeries in circulation for over three decades. Some of them feature in Oates, 2016. *SCSIII* Op. Cit. p 429-

[391] Steele, Iain. 1998 Private Correspondence between IS and E.J.J. in Author's possession.

[392] Monmouth, 2012. Op. Cit. *Genuine Witchcraft is Explained: Secrets of the Royal Windsor Coven.*

A friendship was forged between Oates and Steele that endured until his death in 2011.

During that time, Steele revealed to Oates that Howard and Chumbley had visited his house to view the document cache. Afterwards, they advised him to submit the documents to the *Museum of Witchcraft* for their archives. Feeling it was where they belonged, Steele had wanted to pass them on to CTC; he felt that a living British Craft Tradition should have them, irrespective of their origin or provenance. He was not a well man, and knowing his time was short, was very reluctant to place them in the Museum. Eventually, he conceded to it, having failed in his repeated attempts to make contact with CTC.

Once secured there, Howard studied the document cache at length; eventually, the cache found its way to Monmouth as the resource for GWIE. This example exposes the extent a deception was undertaken to manipulate the flow of information, which was then used foremost in the specious histories presented by Howard and Monmouth for *The Robert Cochrane Tradition* and its people.

Further to that, forgeries of works claiming to be Cochrane's, or those associated with him are now commonplace, some have found their way into the Museum of Witchcraft archive. For a variety of reasons, those works have been employed by certain individuals, generally as teaching materials, but also for the purposes of self-aggrandisement, Norman Gills and Joe Wilson included. [393] Over numerous years, they have become part of the surfeit of fallacious material circulating the public domain, works that many researchers will assume are genuine. [394]

The many hands those documents have passed through is known, but the person or persons originally responsible for the creation of the documents in this particular cache may never be known. A substantial number of the documents remain without provenance, though several appear genuine. Given their subject matter, almost all of them are unrelated to Robert Cochrane or his Tradition and Clan. Few clues assist identification or dating and so they have proved to be a most taxing study.

---

[393] See Oates, 2016. Op. Cit. *SCSIII* Section on Composite Documents.
[394] See Oates, 2016. Op. Cit. *SCSIII* Section on Composite Documents.

After five years of continual evaluation and research, a greater portion of them defy identification. Some documents provide only ambiguity and confusion, so must be treated with reserve and an earnest degree of scepticism. Too few are clear, or easily attributable to their rightful authors, or to a time-frame that offers discernible context.

Monmouth could not have failed to notice the problematic content in these documents. He suggested that for some years after retirement in Shropshire and until his death in 1998, White had maintained a low-key format with a couple of discreet members to hold *The Regency* operative. And this may be true, certainly no mention was made of them again until a publicity campaign headed by Michael Howard began in earnest to promote them and their works, with all new levels of intrigue.

That campaign was achieved through a series of articles commissioned by him as editor of *The Cauldron,* during the late 1990s. Continuing into the early part of the new millennium, one of the most curious to appear in *The Cauldron* #112 (2004) was penned by 'FP' who claimed attendance in Regency Rites. Hinting rather clumsily at the possibility of an *'inner court,'* it referred to the public face of *The Regency*, as: *"The outer group of The Regency."* These and other comments provided by 'FP' are unreferenced and without useful citation. Both E.J.J. and Valiente separately confirmed that Howard knew Peter Larkworthy, despite Howard's denial to the contrary. Ken Rees, was able to provide a little more insight into this curious article.

> FP is P.L. Who, like Howard, had no participatory knowledge of the *Ry* and had not even heard of it before I showed him my script in 1981/82. (doc***) I knew Peter extremely well, (. . .) I wrote no article for publication on the *Ry* until 2004, Peter and I did, of course, discuss The Regency in the context of him giving me feedback on my proposed chapter in 1981.[395]

Peter Larkworthy (P.L.) was also a former initiate of *The Roebuck,* headed by Dave and Ann Finnin. They had initially worked with Joe Wilson, intrigued by his newly developed 1734 tradition in

---

[395] Rees, Ken. Private Correspondence. August 2017

the USA, a system which acquired some fairly basic and provisional ideas during his term over in the UK, 1969 – 1972/3. [396] Flitting around the social circles in the US and the UK as a go-between, Larkworthy gathered considerable amounts of gossip and rumour on all things alleged within the occult community. Larkworthy was responsible for the doc***, and its surreptitious circulation in the mid-1980s. Referred to by Ken Rees, (ref :326) doc*** collated fact and fiction in an account about Robert Cochrane and the alleged Royal Windsor Coven.[397] But from whom did he acquire his information?

Ken Rees was able to throw further light upon a few other factors of note. He explained that fallacious material had crept into academic works, supposedly trusted, reliable sources, referenced accordingly by students and researchers alike. Mentioned previously, Prof. Hutton was the unwitting recipient of specious material some years before when composing *The Triumph of the Moon*. [398] Rees had pointed out that Prof. Hutton was very much misinformed by his sources, *The Regency* had not ended in 1974. It petered out over the next couple of years. Ronald White had taken a back seat, having passed his metaphorical crown over to a younger man, Charles Whitehead, who soon abandoned it for pastures new. *Regency John*, or *John of Monmouth* as he is better known since the publication of his book, briefly held that crown in London.

> It was still going in 1976 because I went to a rite then. It continued as a more or less private, even 'family' group on the Welsh borders. This is how both George and Chalky came to be buried in Church Stretton cemetery. In fact, this shift partly forms the substance (and the speculation) of my article on *the Regency* based on the Ludlow talk! [399]

---

[396] Jane Taylor: Ann and Dave Finnin "worked with Joe Wilson briefly to understand the workings he came up with using the letters which 1734 is based upon. Their training consisted of working with Poke Runyon of OTA (Order of the Temple of Astarte) and membership in the order. They also worked with Ed Fitch briefly in Gardnerian outer court circle as well as a group called The Pasadena Coven. All of these influenced the formation of *The Roebuck*. March 2016 [private email and personal conversation]

[397] Rees, 2017. Op. Cit.

[398] Hutton, 1999. Op Cit. p. 318

[399] Rees, 2017. Op Cit. Imbolc.

Referring to Prof. Hutton's additional comment that *'former members and guests have subsequently given birth to a number of different groups.'* Rees substantially reduces their implied importance with his own remark confirming they *"were nothing more than, spontaneous, independent emergents."* - a true context that overwrites an unreliable source that had inflated their value. Three crucial foot notes for Prof. Hutton's comments on *Cochrane, the fictional Coven and The Regency* cite Michael Howard as the *'weak source,'* indicated by Rees. [400]

At that conference in Ludlow some thirty years after he'd witnessed the decline of *The Regency* and his own departure from it, Rees had announced his support of the venture to spur new groups engendered by collective persons working together in their re-construction of the open neo-Pagan community that had once formed the core tenet of *The Regency* (mark I &II).

Co-incidentally present in the audience, John of Monmouth, formerly Regency John, responded unexpectedly by heckling Rees, challenging him on all counts, but especially on the rights of leadership. Rees met his challenge fairly, pointing out that after all, a *'leaderless'* public gathering, rather than a select private few, was, in all fairness the objective expressed openly in *The Regency's* original 1967 statement of intent.

By the time the 1980s had begun, all these people had moved away from London and *The Regency* ceased to be a presence there, and according to Rees, was barely a presence in Shropshire thereafter, before petering out. Another source known to Rees, has confirmed that in Cornwall, where John of Monmouth retired, its presence is unknown and appears non-existent. If any activity there had continued between 1998 to 2008, it did so with unprecedented discretion. The London hey-days were long gone. [401]

Whether a Regency presence was low-key or non-existent in Shropshire, Cornwall, or anywhere else for that matter, there were no valid grounds exist for Monmouth's objections to Rees reviving a Regency presence. As a leaderless non-initiatory system that provided open public ritual, Monmouth did not have that authority.

---

[400] *"When I knew [Prof] Ron [Hutton] he did not know that I had been involved with the Regency so had no reason to ask me about them."* KIR/Easter 2017
[401] Rees, 2017. Private Correspondence. August

With regard to *The Regency* (mark II) and its real impact upon the neo-Pagan scene, its presence was not nearly so marked as that claimed for it. Nothing escaped Valiente's curiosity. Her vigilance and tenacity are legendary, as was her knowledge of the Craft and those who peopled it. She made it her business to know of everything that transpired around her. Her records illustrate that later claims for the popularity of *The Regency* should be treated with caution. They feature almost never in her Notepads. Her published books and articles witness a similar occurrence. Scant mention of them was made by anyone prior to Howard's and then Monmouth's later resurrection of their works over the course of the first decade of the 21st century.

Though much exaggerated over recent years, their public status was evidently less significant than some have professed for them. Ken Rees confessed his belief that Phillips' opinion of the Regency's influence and import is wildly exaggerated. Rees makes the difference between mark I and mark II very clear:

> But, in any event I was in a few of these [groups] from the '80s and they had little in common with Wicca. Few if any of their members had ever heard of the Regency so I don't think we can infer any direct influence. Even today in London few people I've spoken to have ever heard of the Regency unless through me, reading the very short account in Hutton's Triumph or, indirectly, through White's website.

With regard to *The Regency* (mark I) it is probably also fair to consider the possible *Wican* influences, that fuelled its initial popularity and then later, its relevance to a wider public as Wicca evolved to encompass the broader neo-Pagan tenets of non-initiatory Craft. More than a few of its founders and leaders were initiates of original Wica, a diverse and very contra stream of Traditional Craft modalities. Select notables were:

- ❖ Gerard Noel, via Eleanor Bone, 1964-7;
- ❖ Ronald White very probably by Cynthia Swettenham, 1965?
- ❖ Reginald Hinchcliffe, early sixties. Lois Bourne
- ❖ Norman Gills early sixties by CS?

- ❖ Rosina Bishop early sixties (A D?). Also a student of Norman Gills
- ❖ Madge Worthington, via 'A. D.' circa 1967-8
- ❖ Joe Wilson via Lady Alice circa 1970 (mark II)

Of course, other influences had nourished the vitality of *The Regency,* which collectively infused a strong neo-Pagan undercurrent, totally compatible with the romantic ideology of a Celtic twilight world dear to Ronald White and George Winter. Monmouth built upon this to create a deeply subjective back story for *The Regency,* which is to be expected to some extent, though unacceptable where it deviates into the fictions devised to promote the idea of a Royal Windsor Coven linked in any form to Robert Cochrane:

> The Cochrane Coven [sic] resurrected the Old Mystery Religion under the name of the Regency. It was so called because it could have no leaders; each of us is Regent to the deity within us. The cycle of seasonal rites provided the focus by which members of the Regency connected with the deity. Without the shamanistic techniques used by the Regency and the capacity for mystical identification amongst its members, the cycle of seasonal rites would have been no more than, what it was to observers, a cycle of 'seasonal dramas'
>
> The nature of these rites may be surmised from what I have written of the Regency's rites. They were separate from them. They are contained in the correspondence between Robert Cochrane and members of the Royal Windsor Coven. * This correspondence was intended to be destroyed once read and so will probably never be published. Nevertheless, I hope that, in these two articles, I have given sufficient guide to the path followed by members of the Regency that people today, who wish to follow that path, may not be led from it by the 'blind leading the blind'. *Hony soit qui mal y pense!* [402]

Major inaccuracies present in this statement concerning the phantom title allegedly used by Cochrane, though cumulative, have largely been addressed already. Cochrane's Clan and his Tradition

---

[402] John of Monmouth. 2009 http://ronaldchalkywhite.org.uk/articles/the-regency-seasonal-meditations-rites-by-john-of-monmouth/

were named 'for' a very specific aegis - *Tubal Cain*. No other title would actuate the Covenant its *People of Goda* are avowed to as a Clan. Private correspondences between Cochrane and his *Clan* members and with others outside the Clan, contain clear and unambiguous references to both the *People of Goda and CTC* – *nothing else,* as it should be. Neither he nor any of his Clan members had any connection to a fiction that developed into a fantasy construction over a decade after his death.

Monmouth drew from limited and tenuous resources, all of which effectively amount to nothing; Bereft of facts, his hypothesis has nothing to offer as support. All relevant documentary evidence needed to bolster Monmouth's broad claim is conspicuously absent. He asserted that all the rites for his phantom coven (that is to say, by definition, Cochrane's group) are essentially the same as those of *The Regency* - a rather remarkable feat as Ruth Wynn Owen, who had never been a member of Cochrane's Clan, had not composed them until after his death.

Only when those people came together as *The Regency*, did the requirement occur for her to compose its rituals, having no cause to do so before it even existed. Perhaps coming later to the party during the latter end of the mark II phase of *The Regency*, Monmouth was completely unfamiliar with the rites RWO had composed for *The Regency* (mark I), and for that matter, its true history.

Ken Rees, as a noted researcher on craft and neo-Paganism, had extended contact with Ronald White and George Winter circa 1975-6, until around 1978. He'd joined *The Regency* as a student to complete his thesis, and became familiar with its operations and principles.

Another source close to Ronald White for a good number of years, makes a very candid observation that *The Regency* (mark II) were *not at all* esoteric, and certainly not shamanic, a transparent feature noted within the rituals and works marked in their demonstration, as recorded in *The New Pagan's Handbook.* Composed during the early 1980s, *TNPH* serves as a collated record of White's creative impetus during his leadership of *The Regency* (mark II). [403] Rees recalls a bold comment made by a bewildered guest at the rites, who'd stated his belief they"...*suffered from over-theatricalness at times.*"

---

[403] Private correspondence by email. G. S. 1 October, 2008

Explaining the general uncertainty of purpose or what they hoped to achieve, Rees imparts the final impression relayed to him that even its central members appeared uncommitted. [404] Referring to his own unease regarding the mixing of mythologies of Robin Hood with King Arthur, as their '*Twin Gods,*' he adds that as an incongruous perspective, it had been noted by another. Of course it is worth stressing that these two archetypes do not feature in the Clan's mythos; created by Ronald White as a distinctive feature for *The Regency* (mark II) they are not relevant to the Clan in any way.

Monmouth attempted to portray a very different image, one focused on sacred kingship and a natural mysticism that has no basis in their works, and no testimony from those who worked them, to back him up. A description given in a separate earlier article offers a more pragmatic explanation of them as an (idiosyncratic) organisation that celebrates the folk-loric seasonal round, having a basis in what was believed to be Celtic mythology. [405]

That aspect of '*Celtica*' very much influenced both the Finnins and Joe Wilson in the US, and is unmistakeably evidenced within their works. Indeed the Finnins were later to name their tradition: *The Ancient Keltic Church,* when they registered it for charitable status around 1991.

By way of contrast, CTC's foundation resides within Northern folk traditions, and an inherent gnostic strain. Through them, it developed the Triune Male, Female and Priestly Mysteries centred upon the Stang, the Hollow Tree and Axis Mundi about which the (Tanist) Young King/Rascal and Old Horn(ed) King wax and wane as one. This is contra to alternative adaptations that instead refer to Twins or Brothers out of context, or to Shadow Kings or even aligned minor 'Celtic' (sic) gods.

CTC honour and engage the Divine Feminine, Diana - the Pale Leukothea, quite distinctly in Her Triune form of *Wyrd*. Within Cochrane's beautiful *Round of Life,* the Clan live through the virtues of *The Muse,* observing the tenets of Fate, Truth, Love and Beauty. Many patterns over time, were woven together and apart. Certain principles had deeply affected them all, inclusively and without precedent.

---

[404] Rees. 2009 #121 TC. Op. Cit. *Investigating the Regency*
[405] Feb. 2009 #The Cauldron 131

As an innovative and public group, *The Regency* certainly bridged the gap between standard Wica and neo-Paganism oriented Craft that proved very popular stateside. And this is to be applauded. As a research project into these origins, the anticipation of mixed emotions along the way has proved to be an understatement.[406] Valiente's disdain for *The Regency* (mark II) and in Ronald White as a *failed leader,* who *liked to use people,*[407] is very much in accord with other opinions that express concerns of White's *megalomania* [408] and his *fear of failure.* [409]

From the beginning, the Ronald White's direction was never in doubt. His vocation was ever clear and distinct. From the earliest dates and stages of their associations with Cochrane, these are precisely the bones of contention they long chewed upon. There was no point in Mythos or Ethos at which they could meet and harmonise, and no direction their trajectories would intersect, their praxes were truly irreconcilable.

Only Monmouth and Howard failed to accept this. Their contrary petitions have adversely influenced public opinion, working against knowledge and truth.[410] By their inconsistencies all are exposed. Believing that Ronald White and George Winter were more popular than Cochrane because Cochrane was too elitist and that their neo-Pagan based *Regency* rites reached more people, Monmouth maintains that Cochrane turned people off with his profound belief in mysticism, expressed throughout his works:

> Magic is only a by-product in the search for truth, and holds an inferior position to truth, it is a product of the soul in its search for ultimate knowledge, an afterthought upon a much larger issue, while searching for a more important aim within the self. [411]

---

[406] This Clan biography has not only been one the greatest undertakings of our lives, but has enfleshed many bones that previously offered little beyond their anomalous presence.
[407] Valiente. 1981. Op. Cit. Notepad entry. 24/6/81
[408] Ken Rees 1982- quoting from the Michael Bampton's Thesis concerning a time frame circa 1960/1. There does appear to be some confusion about roles and skills attributed by others when speaking of or referring to Ronald White and George Winter as Chalky/Chalkie and George/George W. They find themselves invariably listed as school teacher, artist, musician, and Summoner. Old, Middle-aged, hailing from Norfolk, from London etc. etc. These freely circulate without settling on a definite name, making a positive identification impossible.
[409] Valiente. 1981. Op, Cit. Notepads entry. 24/6/1981
[410] Michael Howard in the chapters on Robert Cochrane and the Regency in *The Triumph of the Moon* by Ronald Hutton. (Oxford Uni. Press 1999)
[411] 'The Craft Today.' *Pentagram #2* 1964. Republished in Oates, 2016. *SCSIII* Op. Cit.

Monmouth then made a contradictory statement by claiming that people dismissed Cochrane's works because they were too involved in the practical magics:

> Not to the taste of the readers [of his works in *The Pentagram*] drawn to witchcraft in search of magical power, nor to those who proclaim to possess it. [412]

This lack of cohesion typifies Monmouth's approach, which clearly defines his negative opinion of Cochrane, who appears to be *'damned if he does, and damned if he doesn't.'* As for which modality Monmouth believed White and Winter adhered to — *witchcraft* or *mysticism,* he did not clarify. Occasionally, he vacillated between those tenets, uncertain which to emphasise. The difference between Cochrane's and White's working praxes is apparent in another early document that explores *Dance forms and their Meanings*.

Cochrane's divergent ideology and philosophical musings provided considerable immunity from possible subtle influences that might otherwise have occurred indirectly from George Winter to Cochrane via Ronald White. Knowledge of remnant folk dances was information Monmouth credited to Winter. His experience there, informed the rites of *The Regency* (mark II), where they are best suited, and reflected.

An established chronology for Cochrane's works, ably demonstrates how his ideas developed, through whom and what influences they reflect.[413] They witness a higher and distinctly mystical aspiration that remained with him until his death.

Almost as soon as Cochrane's grasp of his own heritage took root, the group he formed, referred to initially as a Society, quickly developed into his *Clan of Tubal Cain.* Other works, including the purpose of the *Society of Kerridwen,* sections of the *Writ & Constitution* of *The Thames Valley Coven,*[414] and the *Witch Practise* doc., display unequivocal traits of neo-Paganisms. They also exhibit a quasi-masonic formality that leans substantially upon the *Craft of the Wica.*

---

[412] Monmouth, 2012. Op. Cit. p 87
[413] Oates, 2016. Op. Cit. See *SCSIII* : Chronology of the Robert Cochrane Letters
[414] A scan of the *Society of Kerridwen's* statement of intent is included in Monmouth's 2012 *GWiE,* Op. Cit. A transcript of it is published in Oates. 2016. *SCSIII.* Op. Cit.

As fundamental tenets later adapted by Ronald White during his leadership of *The Regency*, (mark II), several influential aspects later appear by default in *The New Pagans Hand Book*.[415]

Cochrane's personal angst and disaffection with Ronald White finds expression within his letters, especially those to Bill Gray, a trusted confidant. He conveyed to Gray how their irreconcilable differences ranged from leadership ethics to mythic aspects of belief. Examples of those rifts and dissension are reflected in the few identifiable documents in the cache. Attributions for the other documents remain in question. [416]

Of the few documents possible to verify, all indicate that Cochrane as Clan Magister, provided teaching materials to Ronald White and George Winter, backed with the authority to reprimand them for their failure to observe it, are startlingly unambiguous. A letter from Cochrane to Ronald White et al, informed everyone that the early works of *the Clan* were experimental, an effective mode used when people strive to achieve a fundamental commonality. Deemed unproductive, vague and superficial, they were henceforth abandoned by Cochrane and his wife, Jane. Cochrane's instructional letter confirms this sense of disappointment and dejection. It begins with admonishments and palpable disappointment:

> Obviously the real fault lies in communication, and not in the alteration of ritual. We decided to follow strictly traditional patterns, we have had to scrap nearly everything that we held valid previously. [417]

The letter is closed assertively with the resolve to work according to merit, measurable as real methods he and Jane had been working together for some time. Offering his Clansmen the option to advance with them, he advised their compliance, informing them that he and Jane would continue that way, regardless of their decision:

---

[415] This work is published in Monmouth's 2012, Op. Cit. *GWiE*.
[416] Oates. 2016. Op. Cit. *SCS III*.
[417] Monmouth. 2012 Op. cit. Doc H p 329

Anyway, I'm not bulldozing you into anything, but this is the way, both Jane and I have been working, and will work in the future; let us know what you think vide letter.[418]

White and Winter struggled to work under Cochrane's direction. The conflict and friction between them is very apparent. Monmouth's persistent attempts to remove rightful credit from Cochrane as the brains and authority of his tradition, to assign it to others, whom he deemed older, wiser and humbler, is brutal in its ruthless diminishment of Cochrane's singular genius. Monmouth's irresponsible use of available material where conjecture and opinion are presented as fact, is a matter of concern.

Pushing further the image of Cochrane as a dictatorial egotist, Monmouth proffers his opinion of White and Winter's approach to life in no small contrast, describing them in egalitarian terms. For example, he explained that White and Winter had the: *"Ease and strength of character to step back and let a 'younger' man lead."*[419] Moving on a little, he must have forgotten his previous statement when he announced somewhat defensively that White and Winter were *not* men to be *"easily led!"* [420]

There is no doubt these strong young men were at constant loggerheads, and that Cochrane fought hard to hold the Clan together. His authority was hard won and hard – pressed. Far from being a magnanimous gift from White and Winter: *"It was only good old fashioned fear of Roy that kept them in line."*[421] It is not subject to a difference of opinion. Coming late to that party several years after Cochrane's death, Monmouth *was not* privy to those incidents, nor to those relationships.

By contrast, E.J.J. was there, alongside all persons concerned. Documentary evidence, letters, and other testimonies of weight from others around at that time, all attest to E.J.J.' statement as factual. The same cannot be said of Monmouth.

---

[418] Note here, Cochrane is in no way behaving in a dictatorial manner, countering again Monmouth's assertions to the contrary. For true perspective, see entire doc (P) page 245 *SCSIII*
[419] Monmouth, 2012. GWiE, Op. Cit. p 24
[420] Monmouth, 2012. GWiE, Op. Cit. p 26
[421] Personal Correspondence. EJJ to SLO.

A mere handful of the letters and documents from this cache are actually relevant to the Clan, some to the later *Regency*. [422] Some of the people mentioned appear to be former attendees of Everley's London based group and possible members of *The Thames Valley Coven*; others simply remain too obscure to identify, even tentatively

These legacies were wrought, as are all things of the Craft, by a tenacity of spirit as uncompromising as it is anarchic. In surviving the passage of time, this important cache of documents is nonetheless a great gift. A few of those faded, pitted sheets glow still with the collated works of people known to Cochrane, and of their forays into what he dubbed *occult science*.

Monmouth and Howard succeeded in raising the profiles of Ronald White and George Stannard/Winter, which has rightfully established their *entirely separate* contribution to the contemporary history of the Craft. CTC fully support this, it was long overdue.

A Shift from the Shadows

Further attempts were made to undermine the credibility of the Clan's Head-Kinsmen. These are evident in the streamlining of all roles, duties and responsibilities away from Cochrane and his wife to present a democratic and less hidebound liturgy. That ideal has no reality. The Clan *is* hierarchical, and is *not* democratic. Monmouth's views lack any understanding of the fundaments of Traditional Craft within an hereditary family or Clan format.

> My own opinion is that this is the age of dreams, when somewhere from the inner planes, a war drum is beating, calling all men of good intent together and to arms before it is too late. Sooner or later, we must face the enemies of life and decide once and for all, who and what is going to be the guiding light of this planet. [423]

An odd occurrence with a newspaper reporter explores a bizarre thread in the very false history Monmouth struggled to portray. His attempt to rationalise the extreme secrecy he claimed

---

[422] Oates, 2016. Op. Cit. See *SCSIII* for a clear chronology of these and all former published, and some unpublished letters and documents spanning over a decade from 1958 to 1969.
[423] Oates, 2016. Op. Cit. *SCSIII* #IX Cochrane to Bill Gray p 174

was demanded regarding the existence of the (fictional) coven he promoted, failed. A gravid incident with the press was transformed into an incredulous tale it actually had nothing to do with. Though Monmouth does not provide the original context for this incident, this biography has already referenced the testimonies of E.J.J. and Cochrane's widow that relate to the aftermath of Cochrane's death.

Police investigators questioned everyone they believed connected to him. Repudiating any knowledge of his occult work or connections, both Winter and White confessed only to a casual acquaintance with him.[424] Their statements of denial went on police record. Their betrayal caused Cochrane's widow to shun them. Thereafter they were forbidden to use or associate themselves with CTC. When Monmouth referred to an incident with the press, he shifted that focus entirely to involve his fictional coven, claiming that:

> No mention is made of the fact that Chalky and George had been members of Robert Cochrane's [fictional] 'Royal Windsor Cuveen.' *Either they decided to keep quiet about this or the interviewer suppressed* it on the grounds that it would mean nothing to the general public. They are said to have previously had an interest in 'Gardnerian witchcraft, Druidism and Nature worship'. It is true that Chalky had dabbled briefly in Wica before joining Cochrane's group.[425]

Side-stepping completely the real press interview held at midsummer 1966, Monmouth implied a very different scenario, a later scenario, which allowed him to introduce the premise of continuity for his fictional coven. However, his deflection is not logical and holds no rationale. Given the prohibition Monmouth claims was in place to prevent confirmation or denial of the alleged secret existence for his phantom coven, why would White and Winter wittingly compromise themselves by voluntarily mentioning its existence in casual conversation with a journalist!

Adding an entirely implausible caveat to his version of events to explain how a possible indiscretion, in which Ronald White '*may have*' freely offered up an alleged secret, did not become public

---

[424] Oates. 2016. Op. Cit. *TM: Legend* Personal Correspondence from E.J.J. to SLO. (L7)

[425] Monmouth. 2012 Op. Cit. p 123 [Author's emphasis] They actually continued to engage in Wica.

knowledge in their time, was either because, in the end *"they decided to keep quiet about it,"* or, because *"the interviewer suppressed it"* on the incredible grounds *"that it would mean nothing to the general public!"* [426]

It is hard to decide which is the more unlikely, that an extreme secret would be disclosed to a reporter, or that the reporter would keep it a secret! One can but wonder and imagine that Cardell, Madge Worthington, Maureen Shepherd and Ruth Wynn Owen all wished they had encountered such a magnanimous saint of a news hound! If the first option had occurred, then why even mention this incident at all, except as a vehicle to suggest the existence of his phantom coven.

The second option is unquantifiably implausible, but again serves the purpose mooted in the first option. Either way, the proposition that White and Winter gave up a name Monmouth asserts they were forbidden to use, whilst denying a name they were completely free to use, becomes a clever ruse to cover up rumours concerning those gravid charges of disloyalty and misconduct in 1966. Supported by independent testimony, these uncomfortable realities are uncompromising and would later determine the names used for themselves, and relayed to others. [427]

Understanding this, helps explain why Joe Wilson, Mara Wilson and the Finnins were under some confusion regarding alternative names falsely associated with the Clan decades ago. Investigating the policies of *The Regency* in this context, requires a return to the 1969 *Man, Myth & Magic* interview where Ronald White explained the notion of a 'Regency:' *"The idea was that we would have no dogma, no creed and no leaders."* [428] In the 1974 *'Spectrum,'* article, Ronald White described *The Regency* as:

> An organisation with no organisation – a group as its name suggests with no leader, for who can be so great as to presume the power of the Gods? [429]

To emphasise this egalitarian principle in their manifesto, White added an echo of the earlier sentiment: *"What The Regency*

---

[426] Monmouth, 2012 Op. Cit. p 123
[427] See Oates, 2016. *TM: Legend* Scanned excerpts of E.J.J.' letters to SLO and A & DF
[428] White. 1969. Op. Cit.
[429] Published in *Spectrum*, no. 2, Nov/Dec 1974

expected and worked towards was the restoration of the gods within." [430] And yet his behaviour at *The Regency Council Meeting*, was considered by more than one observer as *dictatorial*. Rees pressed this further in his own synopsis of events, recalling to mind *The Regency* meeting during which Ronald White demanded that all present take an oath of allegiance to him and to his cause! [431] Two only, conceded to do so, an action that signalled the demise of *The Regency's* appeal and popularity.

Losing its popular fascination amongst the neo-Pagan communities in England, it slowly declined until it ceased to be operative in London by 1976. Founded originally as an organisation devoid of divine presumptions of godhood, oaths and sovereignty, it was a leaderless democracy, supposedly free of the encumbrances of ruler-ship. Ronald White's 'leadership' of *The Regency* (mark II) demonstrates a most curious inconsistency that contradicts the entire ethos of *The Regency* (mark I). Reflecting the mood of his inauguration as leader in 1969, White motioned his desire in 1974 to *'resign his kingly crown,'* to stand down in a rather theatrical gesture of *'bending his knee,'* to his successor. [432]

These important events occurred at the time Joe Wilson approached his own vision of 1734 Tradition with renewed vigour, over in the US. Within his personal study of them as a modern neo-Pagan group, Rees impresses the significance of this. At this juncture it is essential to meaningfully scrutinise the documents in the cache to determine the extent their contents were misrepresented in Monmouth's book, articles and media construction. Abundant examples express the obfuscation of original context, of significances never intended, nor indeed, ever claimed by others.

A dramatic claim is made for a hand-written letter by a person enigmatically named *Joan*. As yet unidentifiable in the craft scene, she mentions *scripts, and roles, and of rehearsing them* in time for the next ritual. Anyone familiar with Cochrane's works, or descriptions made about them by people who witnessed his rites will be aware that his rituals were never scripted, quite the reverse. A common complaint from those who worked alongside him was

---

[430] Published in *Spectrum*, no. 2, Nov/Dec 1974
[431] Ken Rees, 2004 *The Regency* Vol. I & II *The Wiccan*, # Beltane
[432] Rees, 2004. *Ibid.*

having no more than a theme to work with. Rituals were spontaneous and inspirational.

As a modus assigned to Cochrane specifically, and confirmed by several people in their written comments after attending Clan rites as guests, not to mention the well-known testaments of its actual members, it is unsettling to encounter this exact principle referred to by Monmouth as a factor that distinguishes the works of Ronald White and George Winter from *Cochrane's* methodologies.

Ruth Wynn Owen introduced scripted rites, seasonal plays and dramatic rehearsals, as the following comments verify, her own included. She alone should rightly be credited for the works generated by the early *Regency* (mark I). History has underestimated her contributions, quite markedly so.

In his treatise, Ken Rees again referred to this initial usage of scripted boards, albeit in occasional use during his term with them, during the mid-1970s. Monmouth agreed that *The Regency* had used scripted boards (mark I all the time, and mark II some of the time). However, he slipped in a remark that made further unsettling claims for its leaders.

> The Regency held public, pagan celebrations of the seasonal festivals that were open to anyone. Initially, these celebrations were scripted and held in the homes of members of the 'Cochrane Coven.' [sic] They soon moved outdoors, with a celebration of May Eve on Hampstead Heath in North-west London in 1967. [433] They also soon dispensed with the written scripts, which were counter to the spirit of the intention of the celebrations. [434]

Implications aside, the supposition that *The Regency's* activities were ever *'Held in the homes of members of the Cochrane 'Coven,''* (sic) presents a remarkable degree of error. Laborious references to the Clan as a coven seek to persuade by repetition of that astonishing misnomer. Cochrane's rituals were unscripted and held outdoors, not in London, but at selected regions beyond the city boundaries.

---

[433] A totally re-constructed, fictional account by John of Monmouth. Almost everything written here is unsupported and inaccurate nonsense, and has no basis in a factual history for the Clan, Robert Cochrane or *The Regency*. It undermines the credibility of all it seeks to advance.
http://ronaldchalkywhite.org.uk/articles/the-regency-the-cochrane-coven-by-john-of-monmouth
[434] Ibid.

CTC was never open to public admission, held no public rites, and was (is) certainly not pagan or neo-Pagan. Given the amount of contrary evidence in Cochrane's own works on these matters, to proffer such claims is nonsensical. Those facts are not for dispute.

The Regency did not come into being until after Cochrane's death, when two former Clan members went on to assist in the foundation of The Regency. That those two people did so as members of a phantom coven is a matter very much disputed *by* the facts. Nonetheless, Monmouth was *not* referring to the homes of White and Winter, but to *former guests* of the Clan, he presumes were members of it, and at a time when Cochrane was very much alive. Monmouth's bald statement is therefore factually incorrect on every account. *His own* statement which had insisted 'the coven' and its rites were entirely separate from *The Regency,* by default repudiate his own claims:

> By the time I joined The Regency in 1969, all that remained of the original organisation of the celebrations was the guidance of Ron White's The Reading of the Festivals of the Year. [435]

Alluding to the divergence of the '*new*' Regency (mark II) after Ruth Wynn Owen left them to their own devices, her opinion of how rites were conducted until she left in 1969, are in tandem with those Ken Rees summarised in 1978. Rees confirmed the use of scripts for *The Regency* (mark I):

> The ritual structure of The Regency was centred on the seasonal festivals of the Wheel of the Year. In the early days, when they were being held indoors, Rosina Bishop told this writer the rituals were usually produced by a 'committee'. Meetings were held beforehand to discuss what form they would take and once agreed 'scripts' would be typed up on sheets of paper and glued on to pieces of thin card. [436]

> These were then handed out to the celebrants who each took specific parts, under the guidance of a 'master of ceremonies,' in what was essentially the enactment of a ritualised drama based on role-playing.

---

[435] White drafted rough notes for The reading of the Festivals of the Year in an early pub meeting for The Regency in the Autumn of 1966 a couple of months after Cochrane's death., If this rite had been originally created by White, he would have had the rough draft already. More probably White was relaying on memory, having no papers to work from, as Cochrane's wife burned what few there were. (Cochrane preferred to work inspirationally with very little written material)

[436] Howard, 2011. Op. Cit. *CoC.* Personal conversation with Rosina Bishop. p 99

In practice the rites were fairly simple in nature and took the form of 'plays' based on the mythic theme of the festival and its seasonal symbolism. They have been described as 'a beautiful synthesis of earth mysteries, ritual drama and the natural year, becoming a vehicle of expression of pagan spirituality.' [437]

Marian Green composed a description concerning <u>Clan Rites</u> she had attended as a guest in 1965. Emphasising the prohibition on printed or written material for the rites, Green's statement is very similar to Ruth Wynn Owen's above. Green exposes a very distinct working method operated by Cochrane:

> Although <u>quite complicated rituals</u> were performed, <u>I was never given a 'script,'</u> but <u>a list of moves or prayers</u>, which had to be learnt by heart. A sacred space was marked out and the usually small group consisting of about 8-10 people, would gather to participate in the work of the night. It could be a seasonal celebration, or a <u>meeting to call on the ancestors, or the spirit of the land to give an oracle, for example.</u>
>
> There was always a bonfire, and in winter there would be several, so that they warmed the area and provided light an cooking facilities for the cauldron, which contained soup or stew. <u>The rituals were often very long, with stamping dances, invocations and prayers, building up to a powerful and magical atmosphere.</u>
>
> <u>They were far louder and wilder, and more 'primitive' than anything I have seen written down. In fact writing anything was pretty much forbidden</u>, so I don't have scripts or notes, from any of the meetings I attended, except for the odd bits of poetry I wrote inspired by the place and the feelings generated, and by the darkness and firelight. It was the feeling of raw and ancient energy. And the visions of things half-seen by bonfire light that have stuck with me, almost half a century later.[438]

These *Clan* rites could not be more different from those of *The Regency*. In light of this amazing description of the beautiful and mystical *Assumption of the Mask* together with those Doreen Valiente

---

[437] Howard, 2011. Op. Cit. *CoC.* Personal Correspondence from KIR to MH. p 99
[438] Jones. 2001. Op. Cit. p 37

records in her Notepads and books about *The Wild Hunt,* the fires and amazing visionary experiences she had with the Clan, Monmouth is isolated in his assumptions that the *Regency* rites were shamanic and mystical. That had never been their purpose or remit; his claim is contradicted by everything that has ever been said of and written about *The Regency* by all those who were members of *mark I* or who attended *mark II*.

Compare the observations made in the aforementioned 'Joan' letter regarding the use of scripts, and the comments Cochrane makes below regarding their usage.[439] Cochrane's opinion of a needful economy of words and his consequent directive for silence as requisite within the work was provided without ambiguity. Monmouth wished to apportion that intuitive and widely known trait of Cochrane's, to White and Winter. Just two examples illustrate the fallibility of that intent. The opposite is readily apparent.

> Confession: I suggest this should be much shorter than the statement Ron suggested. 'Fains, I have trespassed' covers it!' [440]

And:

> If possible, once there is a build-up, do not chant or makes sounds, but keep the hood pulled over the face. I suggest we all have a common image of the God that is like the figure on my wall. [441]

Marian Green also confirms this in her own moving testament to her experience in his rites.

> He really knew the way to work with the forces of the land, and with time, and with elemental beings in what feels like an authentic, ancient way. [442]

This is re-iterated by Valiente[443] and often by Evan John Jones who both remarked upon Cochrane's free and open manner. Describing his tumultuous almost shamanic approach to working the knots, and his unnerving unpredictably, they note his manner of

---

[439] Oates, 2017, Op.Cit. *SCS III* doc.(ooo) p 94
[440] Oates, 2016. Op.Cit. *SCSIII* p 137 or Monmouth, 2012. Op.Cit. (Doc A) Appendices p 277
[441] Ibid. (Doc A) Appendices Scanned Documents
[442] Jones, E. J. *The Robert Cochrane Letters* (ed.) Michael Howard (UK: Capall Bann 2003) p 10
[443] Valiente. 1989. Op.Cit. Chapter 8

keeping things close to his chest as nothing more than, *'typical behaviour for Roy.'*

> Cochrane's way of working used much less words than that of Gerald Gardner. Much of it was meditational and performed in silence. I think myself that this was more in keeping with the ways of our ancestors. [444]

Several other examples pepper numerous letters and accounts of others, but these few suffice to prove the point. As an experienced Priestess and long-standing occultist, Valiente naturally had considerable wisdoms to share with the Clan. Others less so. Some not at all.

Nonetheless, attempts to discuss *now*, the influences brought into the Clan *then*, would be a naive assessment of the unique construction of a Clan as a purpose filled and evolving body, where the past is only relevant in how it becomes woven into the now. And that was Cochrane's genius. His unique gift was to draw ideas together, to recognise the most profound, sacred thing – hidden in plain sight, and mold it into the mysteries. Through the poesis of tradition, his fire enflamed others and his insights inspired them.

Pushing further a desire to garner the source of influence, and to apportion them to White and Winter, Monmouth insisted that Cochrane had a propensity for laborious cant. He claimed that when Valiente joined the *'Royal Windsor Coven'* (sic – Clan), she refined Cochrane's overlong invocations into verse. Through her, Monmouth said, Cochrane's chants were -*"given a new lease of life."* Yet by Valiente's statement regarding Cochrane's silent invocations, this is proved false.

Monmouth's repetitious references to a phantom coven, and to everyone being an initiate of it accrue tediously, and do not shift beyond his assumptions. Cochrane's preference for silent working, or with minimal comment as shown above, dismisses Monmouth's projections as fanciful fiction. Monmouth somersaults on this point in his scathing remark, that the upsurge of invocations inspired *by* her, was an influence: *"almost entirely absent from the Regency."* [445] Anyone familiar with the rites of *The Regency,* will find this

---

[444] Valiente, Doreen. 1998. *A Witch Speaks* Pagan Dawn #128
[445] Ibid.

incomprehendible. Just as those who worked with Cochrane can attest to his abhorrence of cant, and of his insistence of silent Mill dances.

Perhaps Monmouth had forgotten his own dependence on the shared ethos of CTC and *The Regency as one within* his fictional coven. This oversight presented a considerable conundrum for his agenda. Keen to demean Cochrane's works, Monmouth tied himself in knots at every turn. Unable to sustain the thread of this tall tale amidst the considerable weight of contrary information, it is surprising he failed to realise this. From Valiente's well-documented *Admission into the Clan,* to Marian Green's confirmation that Cochrane's methods were shamanistic, all the information was known to him.

Disregarding source material in the cache, Monmouth's shift to claim the introduction of silent trance work was due to the influence of White and Winter, was a considerable folly. Silence was in fact highly unpopular with them; it was clearly never a modus of work they introduced or continued in the works of *The Regency.*

With respect to the title of Cochrane's working group, at this point, it might be prudent to recall that Valiente noted how since the break-up of his initial coven, that descriptive had left a bad taste in his mouth. Rejecting the notion of a coven, Cochrane expressed a preference for *group,* if an informal situation required it. But as a formal descriptive, he upheld the full title: The People of Goda, the Clan of Tubal Cain. [446] Upon visiting them at their home in Slough, Autumn 1964, Valiente made this distinction in her observation: *"He initiated his wife, and a number of other people who now formed his coven (. . .) his Clan was small."* [447]

Choosing to reject Valiente's private and published comments, Monmouth cast a slight upon her personal intellect and impeccable Craft knowledge. He described her Clan Induction in 1964, with the insinuation that Valiente had failed to grasp the name and nature of the oath she had sworn herself to. [448] Presuming he knew better, Monmouth declared that *"Doreen Valiente joined The*

---

[446] A matter resolved by utilising an abbreviation: CTC
[447] Valiente, 1989 Op. Cit. pages 117-118
[448] Valiente, 1989 Op. Cit. Chapter 8

Royal Windsor Coven." He'd substituted the *Clan of Tubal Cain* for a fictional title. [449]

Monmouth then went on to suggest that Cochrane decided to introduce the use of cloaks merely to impress her at that juncture. The reality is very different. Cochrane's instruction to Ronald White informed him of their need to adopt Cloaks, and how to wear them if he wished to join the Clan in ritual, something the Clan were obviously accustomed to, but evidently not White and his group.

Transcript of an extract from the Twelfth Night letter sent by Roy/Cochrane to Chalky *(aka Ronald White?)*:

> Dear Chalky, All is well! We meet at Doreen's place at approx. 10 pm. Here are some matters to clear things enclosed. We will have your cloaks etc with us, see how we dress and copy us. Fashion Bridge by binding sword and broom together with 8 three times on North gate of circle in forming X. [450]

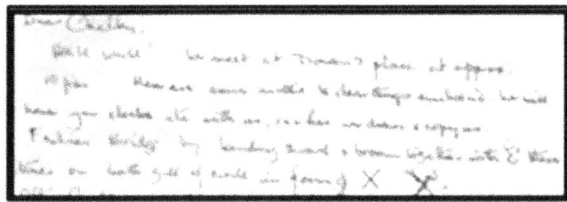

Note the tiny sketch of the bound sword & broom. A drawing of: *"how to dress,"* is included in the same letter. [451]

Letter from Roy to Chalky (aka Ronald White?)

Further instructions were provided by Cochrane to White and Winter on how to fashion *The Broom and Sword,* a process that relates to the Compass which on occasion is also referred to as *The Bridge.*

---

[449] Monmouth, 2012. Op Cit. p 47 His comment is made void of a reference, and remains totally unqualified. In point of fact, Valiente refers only to *Clan.* Please see her own references in her diaries and in *The Rebirth of Witchcraft* 1989 Chapter 8
[450] Oates, 2016. Op. Cit. See *SCSIII* for transcript of *Twelfth Night* doc. pages 312-314 or Monmouth. 2012. Op. Cit. *GWiE* for transcript of *'Hogmany'* doc. K pages 442-3, and letter scan of doc. K pages 335-6.
[451] Monmouth, 2012, Op. Cit. p 47 for a full image scan and transcript of letter, as above, see ref 368

As the second of two documents that reference this rite, the first, explored in depth in another chapter of this biography, is the *C3: Rite of Initiation (Final Version)* document that demonstrates a pencilled directive on its printed surface, an advisory edit to *'consult Roy'* about *The Bridge*. [452]

Cochrane gave White and Winter detailed instruction on where to bind the broom and sword, even how to use them. These directives illustrate beyond doubt that Cochrane taught those techniques to White and Winter, voiding another of Monmouth's claims that White and Winter had imparted the knowledge of those processes to Cochrane. Over and again this confirms what had long been known until a relentless campaign by Howard and Monmouth attempted to cast doubt on those facts. Cochrane taught, guided and instructed Ronald White and George Winter. Sharing his knowledge, he introduced these rites and techniques to them. That knowledge was never in their gift.

The instructions from Cochrane as Head-Kinsman to other members of his Clan intending to work together for this *Twelfth Night Ritual* are without ambiguity. As the second group within the Clan, they were required to conform to the patterns *already* adopted by Cochrane's people in order to present a more traditional anonymity - a coherent bond for the Clan in the Compass round.

Established as standard ritual procedure practise, these measures had derived from another source within the Clan, and some time previous to Valiente's arrival. Cochrane was *not* simply *"out to impress"* Valiente, a derogatory statement made by Monmouth to erode Cochrane's credibility. To impugn that he dressed up to impress anyone, reveals a considerable lack of familiarity with the real character of Robert Cochrane.

Hooded robes are described in the published *Witches Esbat Rite* of 1963, and in the instructions document on the preparation for ritual, both in the self and for the site, 18 months before this instruction letter was even written - an honourable credit strictly reserved for Evan John Jones. The accompanying sketch portraying the *Cloak and Apron* typically worn by members of the Traditional

---

[452] Monmouth, 2012. Op. Cit. *GWiE* for letter scan of doc. C3 p 307. Unfortunately he does not provide a transcript for this alleged Final version of Rite of Initiation. We do not have the document, and so were unable to provide a transcript.

Craft E.J.J. was familiar with, was for the benefit of Ronald White. Demonstrating E.J.J.' knowledge of Craft attire, it includes the highly significant item of ritual dress: the iconic Craft Apron, an item very distinctively noted in the diagram within Cochrane's letter. [453]

The large front pocket resembles a womb in that it becomes the symbol and repository for all tools of external creation. Hence the folkloric adage that all women and the *divil* only, wear them. As a Craftsman, the divil's arte sets him apart from other men. This is where the male and female mystery roles are exemplary: *A Maid* shares those creative artes with the men - *The Divil*, with the women. On the nature of his relationship with the Buckinghamshire (Oxfordshire) tradition, E.J.J. had little to share, initially. In an early letter he established a base line to advance from, in time, and with trust:

> When the West Wycombe lot wanted to get in touch with Roy, he was making something of a splash with his name. They weren't so much interested in Tubal Cain as such, more in his personality with the view of him bringing in some new blood. As for the reason they'd see me and not Roy in a face to face, he was in the Craft, I came with a personal recommendation as someone who had a foot in both. True, Roy and Jane did drag me into the craft and even gave me the title of the Worlds Worse Witch which as far as it goes, is true.
>
> No, I do not have any talent for improving magic, far from it. Intuition does play a strong part but there is also knowledge gained from sources other than Roy and were totally outside the craft and of a very, very different tradition. This stays very, very close to my chest as in the case of Roy, he knew some but less than half of it. One of these days, I might just sit down and write ' The Grimoire of Brother John of Oxford ' and really upset people. If you want to know more beyond this, then you will have to convince me that you really have a need to know because this doesn't actually lay within the remit of the Clan Shani." [454]

---

[453] Twelfth Night ritual at Newtimber Hill 1965. See Oates, 2016. Op. Cit. *SCSIII* for full transcript and explanation. pages 312-14
[454] Personal Correspondence From EJJ to SLO. 24th May 1999 page 1 of 4. (EJJ:L11)

E.J.J. shared more than he will ever receive credit for. In fairness to Monmouth, and others not actually present during the Clan's formative years over five decades ago, CTC appreciate it is impossible for them to know what transpired privately. This Clan biography should bring transparency. A careful study of the following message Cochrane expressed so passionately to White, confirms him as the genius of his own compositions and subsequently removes suspicion that he had relied on White for the introduction of poetic interpretation of myth. At some point in 1965, he wrote:

> It is all right, I haven't gone mad; this all makes sense if you can see what I am pointing to. Throw away all other ideas, and regard what I have written. There is no other way to explain what can be experienced. I have spoken with tongues the oldest poetry. It existed before syntax or logic. It is the sword in the stone, the philosopher's stone, the stone that makes lead into gold (...)One is seven, seven, seven.[455]

With apparent disregard for this beautiful statement, and without further qualification by way of support to contradict both its poesis and directive *from* Cochrane *to* White and Winter, Monmouth laboured his claim that Cochrane's entire genius was not his, but Ronald White's. Naturally, White's own literary talents are not to be denied. Nonetheless, the idea that Robert Cochrane was not the true author of his profound and prophetic works is inconceivable. It is more incredible still, that anyone would make the suggestion that White penned Cochrane's works, informed his mythos and generated his vision.

Though wild, this claim is easily rebutted by their own works, and especially by those works produced before and after Cochrane's death. There is nothing of Cochrane's Muse in the writings of Ronald White. Of George Winter's works, if there ever were any, none survive, and no-one has ever referred to them. There is nothing of the Clan in *The Regency*, and nothing to be found of Cochrane's works there.

---

[455] Oates, 2016. Op. Cit. See p 347 (jj) August 1965 *The Pentagram* Letter from Roy to Ron. It is in this letter the complex Poem by Cochrane illustrated on page 128 appears and its transcription may be witnessed in that document. (jj).

Whatever George Winter may have shared of his knowledge of folk-lore and folk-magicks would have been of some initial value to Cochrane, but of limited use within his extraordinary vision. Driven by an inherent mysticism, his focus wavered, vacillating between folk culture and its attendant natural magics, the metaphysical philosophies of hermeticism and the higher intimacies of Sophianic and Luciferian Gnosticism.

Whatever each person may have brought with them, *left with them*. As for what was shared, the contributions benefited *all*, meaning by default, none of them could undo their experiences, no more than they could un-learn them. Those things stay for life, and by varying degrees, inform the works of *all in turn,* thereafter. Certainly White and Winter could not dismiss what Cochrane and E.J.J. had shared with them. No-one may unlearn what they have been privy too: neither could Bill Gray and Doreen Valiente. The ways of a *People* are distinct and may not be mimicked; they thrive in continuity.

Within this history of *The People of Goda,* Clan, is a very explicit term - being the definition of a group of people united by a revered ancestor, which recognises kin-ship through birth or adoption into its family. Strictly hierarchical, the Head-Kinsman leads and holds the Law with considerable formality. Everyone within the Clan are under his protection and guidance; and all share a reciprocal bond, meted by oath, to a specific henotheistic deity, in our case - Tubal Cain. Throughout his few published letters, Cochrane noted the actuality of this (his) Clan system, making occasional reference to other Clans, besides his own.

Principally, he referred to the assignment of three small groups *within* the Clan who maintain specific working sites to ensure the preservation of ritual mechanics relevant to the three Mystery Rites of the Priesthood (the *godhi*). These are adjunct to the Male and Female Mysteries that collectively form the core Mythos of the Clan.[456] An inherent duty of care and clarity of expression falls upon those who continue to hold this stream, with particular regard as to how Virtue is disseminated through the tenets of kinship that define a Clan. Evan John Jones opened this concept further, taking it out to

---

[456] Jones, E. J. *The Robert Cochrane Letters* (Ed) M. Howard. (UK: Capall Ban. 2002) p 108

the occult community in his ground-breaking book *Sacred Mask Sacred Dance*.[457] He proposed:

> The hardest thing of all is coming to terms with and accepting the overwhelming all-embracing totality of the godhead trying to reduce it to mere simple terms and the one that Cochrane gave us, likened the godhead to a multi-faceted jewel, of which we see only one face. So to Cochrane and those of us who are members of the *People of Goda – the Clan of Tubal Cain*, the godhead is always expressed in terms of the Goddess, the mother of all creation and the giver of life and death.[458]

Of some significance to that privileged, sovereign Virtue, this final section on *The Regency* considers its impact on those beyond the enclave of Clan, a reflection that establishes a contemporary perception in time that is not retrospective in its consideration of all things related to Robert Cochrane, or believed to be.

An archived folder collated by Reginald Hinchcliffe of Cochrane's letters and works demonstrates a high measure of hostility towards Cochrane and his Clan Tradition and ultimately how that manifested in a deep suspicion directed towards *The Regency*.[459] Hinchcliffe's personal vehemence towards Robert Cochrane is evident in the extensive marginalia of a vitriolic nature on every page in this folder.

One letter therein, relates to the heated exchanges between Cochrane and Arnold and Patricia Crowther of *The Sheffield Coven*. Published in *The Pentagram* in 1965, the matter is familiar to many Wicans with whom Hinchcliffe corresponded, socialised, and circled. He goes on to claim spirit contact between Robert Cochrane and Patricia Crowther

From Hinchcliffe's transcript recording of a curious séance, extraordinary comments arise from a departed spirit identified by Hinchcliffe as Cochrane, firstly via a Ouija Board, and then through a Trance Medium, chosen for her psychic abilities. After a brief introduction the spirit they claim identified itself as Robert Cochrane,

---

[457] Jones, E.J. *Sacred Mask, Sacred Dance* (Ed) Chas Clifton. (US: Llewellyn 1998) pages 156, 159-160

[458] Oates, 2016 Op. Cit. *TM: Legend* Personal Correspondence from EJJ to SLO. 1998 (EJJ:L10) & (EJJ:L12)

[459] Reginald Hinchcliffe. 791 Archived section on Joe Wilson. Museum of Witchcraft. Boscastle.

apologised to Ms Crowther, and admitted that G.B. Gardner had been right all along!

The contact was brief, resulting in the following set of questions and answers that reveal a great deal about their contempt for Cochrane at that time, and their distrust for *The Regency* (mark II), specifically targeting White and Winter.[460]

❖ "What is the purpose behind the Regency?
"Just fooling about"

❖ Yes but what is the basic purpose of the men who control the Regency?
"Power,"

❖ Power for what?
"Just power!!!"

[technical difficulties necessitated a shift to a entranced subject psychic medium)

❖ Have you any further messages for us?
"Call on the Magister. Treat all with equal suspicion, beware of a new girl, frivolities are secondary to old and new."

❖ What is the underlying purpose of the Regency leaders?
"All are pissing about trying for power. Stay because witch not big enough."

❖ What on earth do you mean? What exactly are they up to? Do you know or not?
"Keep within your bounds you fool..................."

Contact lost - end of transcript....

Given the level of abhorrence Cochrane's name incited amongst Wicans, especially those Wican attendees of *Regency* meetings, why would Monmouth believe *The Regency* was constructed

---

[460] In 1969. Hinchcliffe makes a claim on his report, that Roy Bowers (aka Robert Cochrane) had been part of the St Albans coven, despite denials by all its HPs. See Museum of Witchcraft Archives. Boscastle.

to carry on Cochrane's works, his Clan's works? What led him to believe certain Wican's known to be Regency players were ever in the Clan, or that Cochrane was an alleged secret Wican initiate? It is a most perplexing matter.

In the end, what should matter, is that The Regency had been created in response to a need. It was recognised as a hopeful bridge between the Wica and more traditional practises within the Craft. The tragic failure of *The Regency* experiment breached a wall between both, that neither side wished to re-build. Caught in the middle of controversy, it served no-one. Lessons learned through reneged promises are ever hard to hold. Without a protective kinship or initiatory status, people found trust an impossibility. In a very much later letter, E.J.J. shared his unequivocal thoughts pertaining to the practises of *The Regency*, and what they were about:

> The snag with *The Regency* will always be – 'What are they working'? Chalky and George had their own system based on some of Roy's material and teachings, so if one wanted to be pedantic about it, they *could claim* to be kindred to Clan. Chalky and George *never claimed Clan status* for *The Regency* and neither do the *new Regency* people as far as I know. [461]

Two points worthy of note.

1. First of all is that E. J. Jones clarifies the once optional status *The Regency* (mark II) might once have wished to *claim* as 'kindred,' subject to the formalities of kin-ship – i.e. in allegiance to the Clan itself, no more, no less, which they *never* did. They never contacted E.J.J. to establish this status for the Regency. Even had they done so, he would never have reversed Jane Bowers edict rejecting White and Winter as disavowed.

2. Secondly, to his knowledge, that is prior to his death in 2003, he flagged the alert for claims of a deeper, more significant status by any member of *The Regency* as non-existent, that is, by its *former* members (mark I & II). They had made no attempt to authorise anything they might wish to do even remotely connected to

---

[461] Oates. 2016. Op. Cit. *TM: Legend* Personal Correspondence from EJJ to SLO . (EJJ, L9) & (EJJ, L11)

Robert Cochrane's Tradition. They were on their own and wanted to do their own thing.

And that, whatever it was, was theirs alone. Something John of Monmouth would have been wise to honour. Honouring one's ancestors, recalling their deeds and magics into the works continued in their name is an intrinsic tenet of Clanship. To that end, a solemn pilgrimage was made by Bill Gray, Evan John Jones, and on occasion, Doreen Valiente up to Newtimber Hill, at Midsummer every year to pay homage at the spot worked by the Clan under Cochrane's Magisterial auspices. For another twenty years, until Bill's death, they held vigil there, by the old Holly tree.

The Regency followed its own Wyrd, distinct from Clan. Significantly, the areas open for *The Regency* to work, did *not* overlap with those the Clan still mark for their own. The Clan's dancing grounds at Newtimber and Burnham Beeches were off-limits for White and Winter circa 1969. The *Regency* worked where they could initially, in friend's gardens, then in Windsor Park, before finally moving to Queens Wood in Highgate, London. Public rituals and celebrations were held there until 1976, at which point, *The Regency* ceased to be active there. [462]

1974: A Royal Jewel

At this stage, a digression into a different, less personal section of this complex history is needful. To matters of mystery, law and devotion the study must turn. The implications of context and the origin of names must be determined before meaningful progress in this Clan biography can be made.

The town of old Windsor, once a Saxon stronghold, was set within ancient woodlands and hunting grounds; named by the Saxons living there as Windsor (*Windlesora* - AS for crooked river). Eaton is a nearby village that serves as a good example of a Saxon name, describing here, the proximity of a sacred Mound. Windsor Castle had been built by William the Conqueror a few miles further

---

[462] Ronald White 'lingered' in the background for almost two more years before drifting off into obscurity and mundane life in Shropshire, working privately with friends.

upstream from the woodland Saxon settlement of old Windsor within the boundaries of Berkshire.[463]

Politically and socially, the old (Saxon) Windsor town remained quite distinct from William's recent settlement that created the 'new' (Norman) Windsor town[464] due to the later grant of charter in 1277. Thereafter, the area surrounding his Castle at Windsor, its hamlets and industries became officially and legally documented right through to the latter part of the 20th century as 'new Windsor.'

Matters of state, politics and boundary changes factor into this history, enabling specific deeds to be securely located to an anchor point in time, marked for posterity by the absence of precedent for its existence. This crucial imperative concerns an anonymous person, who, for reasons of their own, adopted *'at some unspecified point in time,'* the appellation – *'Royal,'* assuming its addition brought with it, the association of an historical precedent for the area known for centuries as 'new' Windsor. This desired association had a purpose.

Law statutes in 1974 established a momentous nationwide shift of local boundaries resulted in the absorption of both *old* and *new* Windsor into a <u>Royal</u> Borough. Mark, this *did not* occur until 1974, therefore it is exceedingly unlikely for anyone to claim an awareness and/or knowledge of any *'Royal'* label connected or attached to Windsor. Prior to 1974, the woodlands regions were known locally as old Windsor, and the town, as new Windsor. Prior to 1974, anything associated with the regional title 'Royal Windsor' could not exist.[465] Their attempts to re-shape history past, as well as present, in accordance with their individual fictions were convoluted, but not well done. A good story needs a credible plot. The bards and skalds of old knew this.

---

[463] The town is situated 21 miles (34 km) west of Charing Cross, London. It is immediately south of the River Thames, which forms its boundary with Eton. The village of *Old* Windsor, just over 2 miles (3 km) to the south, predates what is now called Windsor by around 300 years; in the past Windsor was formally referred to as New Windsor to distinguish the two.[1] And:
http://thehumanjourney.net/pdf_store/sthames/phase3/Resource%20Assessments/Post-medieval%20and%20%20Modern%20Resource%20Assessment.pdf
[464] http://www.tvas.co.uk/reports/pdf/RBE10-23dskreport.pdf
[465] This act transpired due to the reshuffling of county borders, drafting the jurisdiction of a newly created county borough. Several towns, including Old and New Windsor were amalgamated into this recently created 'Royal' Borough along with its new charter renaming it: 'The Royal Borough of Windsor and Maidenhead.' It is the only 'Royal Borough' outside Greater London, and this 'title' pertains to official, legal documents only.

Cochrane was justifiably convinced that Shakespeare *"knew a thing or two."* The Bard's erudition regarding the Clan systems and Tanist Traditions they operated under, is very evident in Macbeth and Richard III.[466]

As dynastic feudalisms replaced these archaic modes of kingship, those traditions were slowly eroded, a forgotten footnote within historical records. History has become a passé science, a discipline almost lost to less committed modalities that are symptomatic of post-modern homogenous isolationism. History affirms our place in the world, and sets the pattern of our lives; it determines who we are, and the destiny we might expect for our kind, which lies in the remit of fate, and of being in fate. Because those arcane laws are intrinsic to the Craft, it recognises still the principles upon which society and community are inter-dependant. Media is ever the key.

Then as now, popularity resides with farce and fantasy rather than the classics. Shakespeare's delightful comedy, *The Merrie Wives of Windsor,* is a rather quaint play often referred to by Monmouth and Howard, to impress the sense of a 'Royal' status upon elements of regional folk-lore. In turn, they add credence to the notion of a *'Royal' Windsor Coven,* as an historical reality. To secure that impression, *'Royal'* is inserted *by them* into the text when quoting from the passage that concerns *Herne the Huntsman*, whose shade is said to haunt *Great Windsor Park*.

Familiar perhaps with Howard's oft repeated comments on this subject, Monmouth wrote: *"William Shakespeare makes reference to the presence of Herne in the Royal Windsor Forest."* [467] Their attempt to establish a false precedent is exposed by the play itself. The word 'Royal' does not exist in any version of Act IV, scene IV. In Shakespeare's own words, there is merely – Windsor:

> There is an old tale goes that Herne the hunter,
> Sometime a keeper here in <u>Windsor</u> forest,
> Doth all the winter-time, at still midnight,
> Walk round about an oak, with great ragg'd horns: 30

---

[466] Still lawful and in operation until outlawed by James 1 of England, enforced in Scotland only after Culloden, a hundred years later.
[467] Monmouth, 2012 Op. Cit. p 14

Used by Howard and Monmouth as a deliberate ploy, the reference restores attention to the scribbled word <u>Windsor,</u> inserted above the crossed out title *The Thames Valley Coven*, making that amendment to the document entitled *'The Writ & Constitution to a Coven to Diana'* even more curious. The devil's advocate might suggest those edits to doc. (AAA) A2 began around 1974. The hand responsible for most of those edits, according to Monmouth, is Ronald White's own, though the date he proposes for that edit is as incorrect as the reason he supposes for it.[468]

For a number of reasons, his implausible date is underestimated by almost a decade. Boundary changes massively impacted topical and general references to local topography and geography. The appellation of 'Royal' is discussed in connection to the regions previously known as (old and new) Windsor. The new 'Royal' boundary date of 1974 is a significant jewel indeed and adds many facets and connotations yet to consider in this entanglement.

'Honi soit qui mal y pense'

Monmouth referred to specific aspects of heraldry to presume a relationship between (what is now known as the modern) *Royal* Windsor (post 1974) as a title for the alleged coven and the boar totem he believed connected the *Royal* Plantagenet banner to it. However, *neither* the Plantagenet (Angevin) banner, nor Richard the III's *personal* banner is connected to the region of Windsor itself.

This obscure connection was Monmouth's endeavour to justify details based within a letter from Valiente to *Chalkie* discussing his love of Plantagenet history. Monmouth claimed

---

[468] Monmouth, 2012. Op. Cit. p 14 The author cites 1961-62, stating that the dating of this document is one that 'might be plucked from the air' because it is 'natural' to do so, runs contra to the natural and academic basis of purpose, cause, reason. Lacking in supportive evidence, it becomes nugatory.

Ronald White had deemed the: *'boar standard'* of *'Windsor'* was therefore *'fitting continuity into the Royal Windsor Coven.'* [469]

Ken Rees confirms Ronald White's personal obsession with the Plantagenet boar, even to his assumption of the personage of Richard III.[470] The small 1974 Royal Heraldic Crest displays the arms given to the newly appointed *Royal Borough of Windsor and Maidenhead*, combining former elements from each contributing region, to generate this crest after that date.

However, because the boar was a personal emblem of Richard the III, and not a dynastic emblem, no boar is represented in the *Royal* heraldic crest of Windsor, nor the arms of old Windsor, which as a region is properly a demense of the crown. The House of Windsor did not become a named dynasty until 1917, so has no banners or crests prior to that; its Royal status is an entirely 'new' creation.[471]

> In the matter of Royal Arms, they usually signify the countries ruled, rather than the *family* symbols of the reigning monarchs. The history of England is largely portrayed in the periodical changes in the Royal Coat-of-Arms. (. . .) The Supporters *[saintly statutes of Virtue, namely patron saints]* of the Royal Arms, now the lion and unicorn, have had many changes. These were first added in the time of Richard II - Richard III *[had]* two boars. [472]

Perhaps Monmouth, being entirely unfamiliar with these changes to titles and emblems, confused the old (sovereign) demense[473] with the new (Royal) borough, and simply seized upon the inclusion of *Royal* in its title to suggest links that might secure his creation of an alleged *Royal* Windsor Coven.

The Plantagenet boar had featured only briefly on the English Coat of Arms, though long enough to assert sovereignty, that is, taxable land duty to the Crown. Even so, the boar remains

---

[469] Monmouth, 2012. Op.Cit. p 109
[470] Rees, Ken. Investigating the Regency' - *The Cauldron* # 121 August 2006
Others have disputed this as a tongue-in-cheek comment made to Rees, not to be taken seriously. Which may or may not be true. However, Valiente in particular seems very much of the opinion White was serious in this interest and obsession with Richard III.
[471]
https://archive.org/stream/royalhouseofwind031195mbp/royalhouseofwind031195mbp_djvu.txt
[472] See ref. 446 Op. Cit.
[473] Taxable land duty to the Crown

unconnected to Windsor per se, and this regrettable oversight serves only to underscore once and for all, that no source for the *Royal* appellation can be found prior to 1974, because it did not exist. Not historically, through a presumed and now proven non-existant link between the Plantagenet (ergo Royal) association, nor via the modern socio-political boundary changes that did not legislate Windsor as a *Royal* borough until after 1974!

Purely as a matter of interest, Valiente discovered a curious significance for the plantagenet boar in its historical association with Richard the III, specifically, how it relates to the role of *Regent*. It provides a logical context to link the Plantagenet Sovereign with Ronald White's ethic for both the *The Regency* and his personal allusions to himself as a re-incarnation of Richard III. [474]

As *arte* mirrors life, fate decreed Cochrane's widow should be estranged from Ronald White and George Winter after her husband's tragic death. Her actions dramatically altered the course of Ronald White's aspirations, and is probably why the man who could not be King, became Regent, and then a King after all. As a natural recourse, it was his only modus operandi, and one that followed the path of his hero, Richard the III, otherwise known as *Crookback*. [475] The similarity between *Crookback* and *Bentback* should be noted and is worthy of further investigation.

One other small curiosity history has gifted relative to the Clan Mythos, is witnessed upon the regional seals – the manifest impedimenta of the office of kingship. The old medieval Windsor seal used by William the Conqueror, portrayed a *Three Turreted Castle* nestled in ermine. The <u>new</u> 'Royal' (borough) seal draws inspiration from history in its design, portraying a Sovereign King, ensconced upon his throne, adorned with full state regalia. The history of a people and the land they occupy or relate to, is crucial to any tradition.

Examination of how ermine spots were used in medieval heraldry allow us to understand their early use by Saxon Earls as a guide to personal identification within the Germanic Hierarchy. [476] Glancing at no 39 on this chart, a symbol is visible that may be linked

---

[474] Op cit. Ken Rees – in his article concerning *The Regency*, Rees records Gerard Noel's disillusionment with Ronald White's increasing *'megalomania.'*
[475] Oates, 2016. Op. Cit. *TM: Legend* Personal Correspondence from EJJ to SLO (L7)
[476] http://www.ukrockfestivals.com/watchfieldfestival-menu.html

to Clan Mythos. Though reversed here, it undoubtedly mirrors Cochrane's personal sigil – the 'Tame' Stang and its coincidental significance offers intriguing connections.

Sourced historically from proto-heraldic ensigns used first by Saxons, and then later by William's knights to literally *flag* their distinctive allegiances – to fly their colours, and raise the Guiden Pole to their liege lord. Further investigations disclose a deeply profound bond between allegiances of Norman nobility with a Saxon family in the Midlands, of Old Mercia.

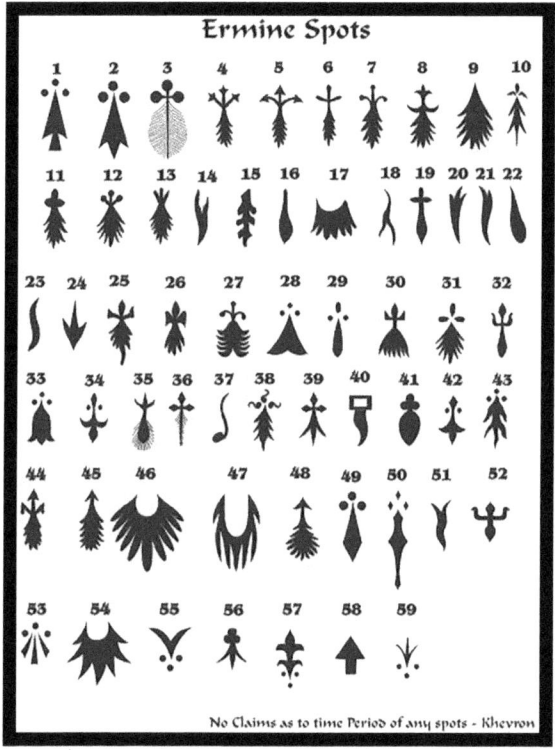

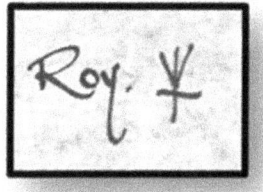

Cochrane's signature alongside his personal sigil. This sigil was adopted by Joe Wilson and transformed into the 1734 insignia.

'We come from the Midlands,' Cochrane had declared, hailing the roots of his tradition there. How amazing then to discover a high ranking knight *Robert de Verdun* bonded in wedlock to the Saxon princess Goda in Staffordshire. Details rarely offer significant correlations that increase understanding of the CTC heritage. It is far removed from Windsor, from Regents, Royal Boroughs and the ambitions of disavowed exiles, not to mention later exponents resurrecting their names in vainglorious ambition.

3 Love/Maternity: Fruition & Union

VI) The Eternal Pilgrim

1734 & Joe Wilson

Cochrane asked Wilson to consider the *"order of 1734"* - the notion of four digits that beheld a philosophical and poetic key to the mysteries. Importantly, he had not referred to them *as* the 'Order' of 1734. Hinting that it is *'not this, not that,'* Cochrane characteristically revealed, yet concealed all he shared. Those who mentor its teachings today as its Virtue holders would not disagree with Cochrane's explanation that it is not a tradition per se; it is, *not this, not that*. Perhaps its finest mystery is that which defies an absolute, descriptive classification.

Those drawn from Cochrane's current, face the reality of its practise, as sublime as it is deceptively simple. CTC therefore revel in his own alchemical application of this formulaic virtue of 1734 as: One Will to open the seven gates to the triune (three) god of the four square garden. Others who have taken up those digits in contemplation have placed an altogether different context for their exploration.

Several unusual events led to Wilson's development of 1734 during the few years that followed Cochrane's death. Joe Wilson was an American neo-Pagan keen to provide a community with a contact organisation where people could come forward with freedom from prejudice of their beliefs. With the help of his mentor 'Sean,' Wilson created his popular journal in 1965 entitled *The Waxing Moon*.

The following paragraphs are taken directly from Wilson's quite late biography *Warts & All*. His biography appears on the current website for the mentors of 1734; it was also serialised within several issues of *The Cauldron* magazine, compiled and edited by Michael Howard. [477] Joe Wilson's considerable interaction with all the leading names of the Craft, meant that he was familiar enough with more generic forms of Craft to properly understand the significance of Cochrane's tradition and its unique title as *The Clan of Tubal Cain*:

> In 1965 I listed an advertisement for *Pentagram* in TWM, and placed an advertisement for '*The Waxing Moon*' in that publication. I received about 30 letters from people in England who had read my advertisement. I recognized one of them, Robert Cochrane, as a regular contributor to Pentagram. His writings were mystical, and at odds with what he said was the simplistic approach the Gardnerian Wicca writers seemed to have. (. . .) <u>He called his group the "Clan of Tubal Cain."</u> (. . .) We corresponded for about six months before he died by his own hand.

During the years, 1969-72, he was stationed in the UK, with the U.S. Air Force in Oxfordshire, England, where he made good use of his time with several people he'd been in contact with for a few years. Mostly, these were people known in particular for their association with Robert Cochrane. Working relationships developed soon after, with key members of *The Regency*, and others he'd corresponded with, including Ruth Wynn Owen, although she had already separated from *The Regency* to form *Y Plant Bran* after the intense media harassment of the Craft through 1968-1969.

Alongside 'Sean' and Cochrane, Ruth Wynn Owen became the third and most major influence in his developing practice. These were later supplemented from articles published in Marian Green's *Quest* magazine.[478]

Wilson acquired his initiatory degrees within Gardnerian Wica, in the UK, with a High Priestess he refers to as 'Lady Alice.' Ruth Wynn Owen introduced Joe Wilson to Norman Gills, who also

---

[477] www.1734_witchcraft.org.uk
[478] Sandra West, alias 'A Witch,' author of *The Devil's Prayer Book*, occasionally wrote under the alias Elizabeth St George. She also worked on the Quest magazine with Marian Green.

maintained a curious interest in Cochrane's works. Gills apparently cautioned Wilson about Cochrane's tendency to mix *'truth with falsehood.'* Wilson was eventually introduced to Desmond Bourke, Gerard Noel, Reginald Hinchcliffe and John Score, with whom he'd corresponded through his newsletter, *The Wiccan.* He met White and Winter and attended a few *Regency* rites (mark II) and Tony Kelly, the Welsh poet with whom he launched his UK edition of his popular neo-Pagan magazine, attempting to recruit would-be Pagans.

Select members of *The Regency* (mark II) were significantly involved in the formation of *The Pagan Front* in 1971. It achieved considerable influence through the US outlet Wilson provided in *The Pagan Way,* extending its influence separately, which took root in *The Roebuck Coven.* [479] *The Pagan Front* is better known today as *The Pagan Federation,* of course. Wilson met several other influential people in those circles, namely Arthur E. & Madge Worthington, the well-loved Gardnerian founders of what is popularly referred to as the *Whitecroft* line of initiates in London. He also met Eleanor Bone briefly.

Under considerable stress for the next couple of years from his military commitments, Wilson finally retired from military life in 1973 and moved back to Los Angeles USA. Spending time in various magical lodges, he eventually settled into laying down the basics of his 1734 tradition.[480] Observe how Wilson referred to his time in the UK:

> The leaders of <u>*The Regency* (derived from Cochrane</u>) and [Y] Plant Bran covens in England. This led to the founding of the *"Pagan Front"* in the UK as a counterpart to the *"Pagan Way"* in America. While each initially worked together with the same aims, each evolved separately.
>
> 1734 is a Craft tradition which I established in the United States during the late 1960s and early 1970's. In its essence, it contains the teachings given to me by three sources. The first of these is a person who I will call Sean, who was my first teacher and who grounded me in the oral traditions of his family.

---

[479] http://www.oldways.org/paganway.htm
[480] Oates, 2016. Op. Cit. *TM: Legend* Personal Correspondence. 2/3/2016 Jane Taylor – *'Coven of the Ram'* in LA

Later I engaged in correspondence with Roy Bowers (alias Robert Cochrane) who, with Sean's approval and guidance, supplemented those initial teachings. The third source of inspiration and personal guidance was Ruth Wynn Owen, the matriarch of the Plant Bran. Sean provided the foundation, Roy provided some magical and mystical supplementation, and Ruth provided guidance for group workings.

Although the name I've used for this tradition, 1734, was inspired by <u>Roy Bowers, he is not the founder of the 1734 tradition</u>. Roy was knowingly teaching me that which would supplement the training that Sean had begun with me. <u>Roy did not call his tradition '1734' but rather "*The Clan of Tubal Cain*"</u> and although he used some elements from that tradition to illustrate some things to me, his intention was never to teach me that way but rather to help me to understand that which I already had. The Clan of Tubal Cain has a different orientation and practices, as it should. [481]

Wilson explained the three major influences upon him, their traditions, and the names he verifies were used *by them* for those traditions. Collectively, their works inspired the germination for his own systematic tradition named: 1734. This is confirmed by Wilson's own terminology regarding the information he'd been given mainly by Norman Gills.

Neo-Pagan elements synergised by Wilson were garnered from his time in the UK where he'd attended the rites of *The Regency* (mark II). Assigning Celtic deities to the cardinal points, Wilson refers also to the *Wind Gods*, which are the only inclusions that bear witness to any influence evident from within Cochrane's works. The winds feature quite dramatically in the previously mentioned in-house document sent by Cochrane to *All Elders* of his Clan. [482] Wilson referred often to the tenets espoused within the *Basic Structure of the Craft*, forming the basis of considerable philosophical discussion between 1734 members ever since.

Wilson constructed and birthed the 1734 Egregore, as something entirely his own. The current holders of the 1734 Virtue serve and are served still by that discrete Egregore. Passed one to another, they each presume a distilled reification in accordance with

---

[481] Joe Wilson http://www.1734_witchcraft.org.uk
[482] Oates, 2016. Op. Cit. See *SCSIII* page 337 (ii)

tenets pertaining to its own unique mysteries. In more recent years, this was widely expounded upon by Wilson himself, and by others who follow his stream. That aegis continues through those gifted with its guardianship and dissemination in the UK and the US. [483]

During 1974, Mara Wilson came to the UK seeking clarification of certain aspects in Cochrane's works, shared a few years earlier by Norman Gills et al with her then husband, Joe Wilson. Keen to expand and develop Joe's work, already founded in the US as 1734, she wanted to see for herself all available copies of materials and letters relevant to 1734. She returned to the USA a little jaded and bewildered.

To some extent Mara's mission was successful, though she did express some disappointment in the information she gleaned from Ronald White, Norman Gills and Mike Howard. Unimpressed by Norman Gills' questionable photographic interests, she considered his knowledge too vague and general, though she did learn that Gills was definitely not all he seemed and his *glamoured patter* often convinced people he knew more than he did. In fact, nothing any of them remembered or thought they'd understood, convinced Mara they knew anything at all. Seeing right through them, she later described Gills as a charlatan!

Mara discovered Gills had furnished Wilson with a good deal of false information tempered with nonsense, especially concerning the circumstances of Cochrane's death. She also discovered that a good portion of the material being passed off as Cochrane's, was Gills' own. Mara visited *Ruth Wynn Owen* too, and discovered the source of the greater body of the work Joe Wilson had used to establish his 1734 tradition back in the US.

Upon her return, she and Wilson separated. Influenced by the occult preferences of his next wife, Joe Wilson developed an interest in native shamanism, generating his shift in praxis he named Toteg. [484] Stuart Inman, one of the virtue holders for the 1734 craft legacy, briefly describes Wilson's ethic:

---

[483] www.1734_witchcraft.org.uk Joe Wilson and Stuart Inman have both refuted the insistent nonsense that '1734' is the Robert Cochrane Tradition, which is, as they know and have both asserted, - CTC. Not one person who actually knew Cochrane and his Clan, has ever claimed that his Clan or his tradition, was ever known as the Royal Windsor Coven! What's more, they have all offered their testimonies repudiating it.

[484] *A History of the Roebuck* 1993 by Ann Finnin - This was an online document, now archived. It has appeared in edited form in her book, *The Forge of Tubal Cain* (Pendraig Press: 1998).

> Joe Wilson was among the founding fathers of American Paganism, although he came to reject the label, observing the shallowness of much of the 'playgan' [sic] scene he had helped create, preferring to call himself an animist or a shamanist (to differentiate himself from a classic Shaman). [485]

In the early days during its own troubled history Joe, and others independently developed hybrid strains and sub-systems of Toteg and Metista. A candid account of a former student of Wilson's explains:

> It is my understanding and through working with Joe directly, that Toteg was not a stream of '1734.' It was separate as Joe's current wife at the time wanted nothing to do with it. Toteg, of course, was certainly influenced by the letters and Joe's experience. Toteg at the time was more akin to Native American shamanic workings mixed with interpretations of pagan worship. Totemic directional guardians as well as the Sky Father and Earth Mother. [486]

Wilson eventually coalesced all former sub-divisions of his 1734 related teachings into Metista, sometimes referred to as the (collective) 1734 streams. These teachings were based loosely around Wilson's personal understanding and development of the information gleaned from several sources, which included his shared correspondence with Cochrane, and the company of notable others within the Craft community both sides of the pond.

Once divorced from Joe, Mara independently developed her own version of the 1734 system tangentially to Joe's explorations of native and non-native shamanisms he'd become enamoured with (a system he named Toteg) For a while, Dave and Ann Finnin worked with Mara, absorbing her influences into their Roebuck ethos. With Mara's assistance, the Finnins were able to reconstruct *The Roebuck Tradition* in 1975, overlaying foundations formed by Poke Runyan and Ed Fitch. [487]

Although *The Roebuck Tradition* had been sourced originally in the basics of the 1734 system established by Joe Wilson, the Finnins

---

[485] Inman, Stuart. 2016 Personal Correspondence from S.I. to S.L.O. 14th Feb. Inman's emphasis in quote above.
[486] (This was in the early to mid 1980s) Jane Taylor
[487] American Wican's of eclectic lines of OTO et al

eagerly absorbed their new teachings, layer by layer. Wilson had found inspiration in Cochrane's letters and his teaching material had been supplemented with composites of Cochrane's works that had been re-constructed by Gills, interjected with snippets of his own knowledge of folk-magic.

Gills had not been part of Cochrane's Clan Tradition, he was never a member. As a guest only at a couple of rites, his unfamiliarity with Clan structure, meant that he could not furnish anyone with the correct format nor ritual mechanics relative to it. Gills' stated that Robert Graves' book, *The White Goddess* was a seminal text for grasping the mystery of 1734, a belief very much shared by Dave Finnin. The core Mythos of *The Roebuck Tradition* is demonstrably anchored within its pages.[488]

> Bowers' letters eventually became the secret text of a mysterious 'pseudo-tradition' that became known as 1734, which presented itself as a mystical alternative to standard Gardnerian Wicca. [sic].[489]

Nonetheless, due to repetition of error stated as fact, Wilson's 1734 Tradition and title have been spuriously referred to by others outside that tradition, as *The Royal Windsor Coven,* and on occasion, used interchangeably with it.[490] With only a limited knowledge of British Traditional Craft, and without the relevant ritual format and structure for a working praxis, his only option was to hang what had been interpreted and developed onto a Wican structure.

Ruth Wynn Owen's innovative impetus to the basic Wiccan form influenced the early stages of Wilson's praxis substantially. Wilson overlaid Wynn Owen's structure with a philosophical method around principles garnered in part, from the poesis of Cochrane's Ethic, before eventually abandoning the structural part.

That marked a considerable distinction between his and Mara Wilson's development of the 1734 system. Wilson asserted a coded name for the Goddess was hidden in Cochrane's Letters, accessed through solving its alleged riddles. Thereafter, in the USA, the 1734

---

[488] Finnin, 1993. Op. Cit.
[489] Finnin, 1993. Op. Cit.
[490] It does serve the point to look at the piece written by Julia Philips again, where she mentions the CTC, RWC and 1734 as one and the same! Julia Phillips - http: History of Wicca www.sacred-texts.com/pag/wiccahst.txt

stream flourished as the brainchild of Joe Wilson (developed by Joe and Mara) <u>not</u> by Robert Cochrane who was dead before its inception.

Cochrane and Wilson never met, and therefore obviously never worked together. No member of the Clan worked with Wilson or shared its tenets and praxis with him; the 1734 people and its traditions remain totally distinct from those of CTC.[491] CTC and 1734 are not connected and do not share origin, lineage, mythos, praxis, ethos on any level.

These facts have escaped many of Wilson's followers for decades, convinced there was more, even though Joe Wilson made it known that 1734 was never Cochrane's tradition. Beyond providing the inspiration through their brief but productive correspondence, Cochrane had no part in its creation.

Because falsified documents remain in circulation that perpetuate this nonsense, some people are quite convinced that Joe Wilson had been initiated by Cochrane and that he'd gifted his Tradition to Joe. Cochrane did not 'gift' Wilson anything beyond his knowledge freely shared in their correspondence.

The spurious document responsible for this false assumption was created from an edited extract of a private clan document circulated amongst Clan Elders.[492] A later, re-typed copy of the edited (cut & pasted) version entitled *The Basic Structure of the Craft*, has been found in Gills' effects, along with a written version in his own hand.[493] As an outsider, Gills had not been privy to discreet information directly, so could only have received a copy of the original or the edited version from someone who was a member, probably Ronald White.

The person responsible for putting together the falsified *Basic Structure of the Craft* document, or the extraneous inclusion that suggested this information ('*along with other things discussed*') should be gifted to Joe Wilson, has covered their tracks well, and may never be identified with surety. That inclusion does *not* appear on the original letter from Cochrane to Gills.

---

[491] www.1734_witchcraft.org.uk
[492] Oates, 2016. Op. Cit. See *SCSIII* p 337 (ii)
[493] Oates, 2016. Op. Cit. See *SCSIII* (ZZ) pages 442-451

Cochrane's Clan/Tradition had been briefly, but incorrectly known by the 1734 title, and though Wilson knew that it was not so, he liked it sufficiently to adopt it for his own modality. 1734 was never a title or name used by Robert Cochrane for his Tradition; The only name used by Cochrane was *The Clan of Tubal Cain*.

Nonetheless, it should be realised that in the UK and the US at this time, Cochrane's Clan was conspicuously referred to and known as 1734 by many people in the Craft, not close to the Clan, or to 1734. But it carried no hint of Windsor, royal or otherwise and no rumour of a covine/coven, or a fictional title had yet erupted. [494]

On this very matter, several years ago, it was baffling to learn that a substantial portion of the occult and craft community in the US particularly, and possibly even the UK too, remained under the impression that *CTC, 1734*, and the phantom *'Royal Windsor Coven'* were *one and the same reality*. Not *part of* the same thing, but actually THE same thing, and all by a name that has never held any association with Cochrane's Clan Tradition.

The rites and rituals that frequently appeared under such headings were either those of *The Regency*, or of *The Roebuck* covens; sometimes these were mixed up and distributed by unknown persons, and sometimes, over in the US, were spliced into E.J.J.' works, some of which had been adapted from CTC's rites for sharing with the public. Unfortunately, these have been taken up by other seekers, believing them to be authentic. They are not; they have no place in a history of Cochrane's Clan Tradition.

Why 1734, CTC, RWC et al, were names passed around in confusion, and by whom, at key dates over the last three decades and which aggravated the bad blood between Joe Wilson, the Finnins and E.J.J., is a matter that deserves resolve. Whether Wilson assumed the Clan was also named 1734, or whether Norman Gills, Ronald White or anyone else he encountered during his stay in the UK informed him that it was 1734, remains too well hidden to prove, or suggest with conviction.

One logical motivation for Ronald White leading Joe Wilson to assume that *1734* was another name for Cochrane's Tradition, or

---

[494] This remains a highly speculative supposition, as its extremities would require stringent proofs and authentication to take it beyond a 'theory.' There remains a gulf between possible and probable, and a greater gulf between probable and fact.

his own group within the Clan, would get him past having to explain why he was no longer entitled to consider himself as a member of CTC. He needed to keep his exclusion from the Clan a secret. If, as others have claimed, the tradition was theirs all along, but merely 'fronted' by Cochrane, that subterfuge would not have been necessary.

What *is* incredibly significant, is that Cochrane shared *the real name of his Tradition* within his correspondence to Wilson; that name and title was none other than *'The People of Goda of the Clan of Tubal Cain,'* Wilson initially chose <u>not</u> to share it with his protégés, initiates and students once he'd returned to the US!

Previously informed that Cochrane's group was named *1734*, Ann Finnin marked her considerable surprise when she Dave visited E.J.J in 1982, to learn that: *"The Clan of Tubal Cain was the actual name of Roy's group, <u>not</u> the order of 1734."* [495]

Once adopted into *CTC*, towards the end of the 1980s, the Finnins believed themselves very much elevated and advanced beyond the members of Joe Wilson's *1734*. These responses reveal their indirect acknowledgment that CTC was Cochrane's true tradition and legacy – not anything else, and not by any other name. [496]

Somewhat oddly however, rather than those other titles simply ceasing in their associations with Robert Cochrane and CTC, their separation merely generated rumours for non-existent groups. [497] In common with others suffering under poor advice, Ken Rees had initially referred to Cochrane as the leader of the 1734 and how: [498]

I. "Ron pointed out that a lot of people went to ground after the unfortunate death of the <u>1734 leader</u>." [499]

---

[495] *A History of the Roebuck* 1993 by Ann Finnin – A spurious version of this appeared as an unofficial online document, now archived. It later featured in much re-edited form in her book, *The Forge of Tubal Cain.* (Pendraig Publishing: 2008)

[496] Their aspirations to the 1734 title as a totally separate system has also witnessed considerable controversy, and again considerable elements of that history remain without validation.

[497] Hence the confusion in Mr Howards and Monmouth's variable descriptions.

[498] Contacting various people for his own research over several years, Ken Rees recalls that Ann Finnin had responded to him in 1982 to inform him of all she knew of Joe Wilson and (his wife Mara) whom they'd met in 1973. 1734 had been the only name associated with Robert Cochrane's Tradition at that time. Deleted pages on the Finnins' old website, describe their varied and very colourful history in the Craft, but there is still no mention of a Royal Windsor Coven at all from them.

[499] Rees, Ken. 'The Regency' – *The Wiccan vol. I & II Beltane 2004*

II. "A key element in the genesis of *The Regency*, however, is that of its own forerunner, usually known nowadays as the 1734 tradition." [500]

Ronald White's flawed explanation to Ken Rees, illustrates how conclusively he was aware that *Robert Cochrane, the man, not the fantasy coven later attached to his name, was the known and rightful genesis for all that followed.* Rees revisited his article in 2006, and made two subtle changes to the previous comments (I. & II.) based on a foundational assessment from a 1985 private synopsis. These significant changes substantially increase understanding of the enigmas surrounding Cochrane's Clan Tradition –

III. "Ron pointed out that a lot of people went to ground after the unfortunate death of Robert Cochrane." [501]

IV. "A key element in the genesis of *The Regency*, however, is that of its own forerunner, usually known nowadays in the States as the 1734 tradition, and in the UK as the Clan of Tubal Cain" [502]

When asked for clarification on the 2006 updates on his précis *Investigating the Regency* (TC#121) published two years earlier in *The Wiccan* (Beltane 2004), Ken Rees was kind enough to respond fully. His explanation removed previous misunderstandings.

> The Beltane 2004 *The Wiccan* text is my initial article on the Regency arising out of a talk I gave at Treadwells. In fact my article 2 years later in *The Cauldron* is substantially the same. I have both articles in front of me now as I type. Stuart Inman had corrected my nomenclature in the meantime so nothing intriguing about any changes. The Samhain 2004 Wiccan issue had carried an article on the Regency rituals (mark II) based on my field work. This was complemented by Paul Greenslade adding what he considered to be a Ry Mark I Hallowe'en rite.

Rees had made no reference whatsoever to *The Royal Windsor Coven,* only to *The Regency,* and to 1734. He correctly referred to

---

[500] 'The Regency' – *The Wiccan vol. I & II Beltane 2004*
[501] Rees, Ken. 'Investigating the Regency' *The Cauldron* # 121 Aug 2006.
[502] Rees, Ken. 'Investigating The Regency' *The Cauldron* #121 Aug 2006.

Supreme Fate. Most importantly he confirmed Cochrane's group as *The People of Goda, The Clan of Tubal Cain* [503]

Immortal Wisdom

Giving vent to his frustration, Cochrane bared his soul to share his deep ponderings with Joe Wilson, to emphasize how virtue is won, then maintained and assimilated - cumulatively. He had deduced how three basic ritual formats expressed perfectly the basic inter-locking mechanistic fundaments of the True Faith. Immensely driven, life gave his genius no ease. Many of the ideas he and E.J.J. discussed in their short but fruitful time together were en-fleshed over decades by E.J.J. who refined them and worked them until a deeper understanding could be realised.

Recognised and best exampled within the anchor Rites or Rings *viz a viz The Three Rites or Rings*, arcane links are formulated between the Mysteries proper and the core Mythos of CTC.[504] Frequently alluded to by Cochrane as the *Male and Female Mysteries* of the Clan of Tubal Cain, certain fundamental principles specifically mention the division of these rites. The Maid leads the Male Mysteries and The Magister leads the Female Mysteries, respectively. Cochrane declared a third section of the Faith, believed lost, had once encapsulated the Priestly Mysteries a long time ago.

Evan John Jones maintained this was simply Cochrane bemoaning an acute lack of spirituality within Craft practices extant during their own era, such that their recovery would present an arduous and gruelling heroic Quest. Apparently, even though these Mysteries were, of necessity, combined decades before Cochrane retrieved his legacy, it was his belief this somehow denuded their unique virtue. It remained his hope, a large enough community could be inducted into the Clan to allow theses distinctive mysteries to

---

[503] *Ibid.* Rees comments: *"A key element in the genesis of the Regency however, is that its own forerunner usually known nowadays in the states as the 1734 tradition (as per J.B. W.) and in the UK as the Clan of Tubal Cain......"* There is no mention of RWC. Verbatim copy of the article 'The Craft Today' written by Robert Cochrane, later appeared in #120 *The Cauldron* May 2006 except it is introduced by Michael Howard as written by the *"Magister of the Clan of Tubal Cain and The Royal Windsor Coven."*

[504] Oates, S. *Tubelo's Green Fire* (UK: Mandrake of Oxford 2010)

once again be taught separately within it, preserving the entire tradition, once more as a whole for posterity.

His determination to confirm the reality of a working philosophy, both compatible and in some ways comparable to the Kabbalah, became realised through specific terms quite unique to Traditional Craft praxes, but which are fundamental to CTC. Central to any understanding of the *Basic Structure of the Craft,* these profound Mysteries are embraced fully by CTC today.

As another generation in the history of the Clan to engage them, those concepts continue to evolve through an understanding of those early, tentative explorations. Insights freely gained within such vital core works, expand understanding and serve to complement and complete rather than challenge all that came before. Both Maid and Magister correctly embody the potencies of the Left and Right sides of the Tree of Life through the aegis of Severity under the Moon, and of Mercy under the Sun. [505]

Through this veil of mystery, many curious things continue still to dazzle in their revelation. E.J.J. cautioned always to be patient, to assimilate slowly the finer subtleties of an arte so inexorably woven into the fabric of the Clan, such that its indelible pattern pulsed instinctively to the soul's own rhythm. Drawing deeply from its fateful binding, the seven year cycle relative to it, is marked.

In real historical time, this metaphysical osmosis is embraced through the newly inherited Egregore, the very lifeblood of the Clan, in whose aegis all are nurtured and tutored in its Mysteries. No one may presume to teach, as indeed E.J.J. keenly espoused, especially not once the Mysteries are engaged. The best of us may only guide others to see truly for themselves what the Mysteries mean to them.

> Hopefully after the next cycle has transpired this may have evolved into wisdom. Through the work alone, does light dawn. [506]

Cochrane had noted how within one's own stream, the keys to understanding Truth, were the remit of the guardians of each

---

[505] *St Uzec* by Shani Oates: www.clanoftubalcain.org.uk/library
[506] *Ciphers and symbols* by Robin-the-dart: www.clanoftubalcain.org.uk/library

Tradition - discarnate ancestors and deific forms who benefit the next generation of spiritual heirs.

> Prayer is the ladder that binds the body to the earth whilst the soul ascends into the dizzying heights of the heavens.

The charge from one guide to the next, demands no less, and their task is no less exacting in the challenges this presents as they acquire the graft, literally and figuratively. Countless seeds planted during the seven years of study with Evan John Jones were to blossom later. The fruit they now bear is testament to an incredibly intense devotion; a labour of love for, and of, all concerned, one to another, in continuity. Each cycle, each shift, infuses the next generational speciation.

> I keep on getting the feeling that we are preparing the ground for a crop we will not reap, waiting for a dawn that will not come, but wait we must. We are [the] force for something else that is to occur, the creators of opinion for a new concept that is arising somewhere in the world. The St John the Baptists, hundreds strong, waiting, waiting, waiting. So far the new word hasn't come through, but it will, that I feel certain of. [507]

Cochrane understood the cyclic nature of wisdom, especially how its discovery: *"Creates the alchemy that brings forth an answer."* A Clan manuscript entitled the *Castle and the Cave*, written by E.J.J. during the 1990s, finally realised its due publication, in full, as *The Star Crossed Serpent I* in 2012. It had however, received fractured publication only, in 2001 as *The Roebuck in the Thicket*. [508] Within these texts, Evan John Jones expands upon Cochrane's comments concerning the male and female Mysteries, explaining how certain guardians operate within the Clans which he claimed:

---

[507] Oates, 2016 Op. Cit. *SCSIII* #IX Cochrane to Gray p 174
[508] Jones, E. J. & Cochrane Robert. *The Roebuck in the Thicket*, M. Howard [Ed] (Capall Bann 2001) p 161 First discussed in *Sacred mask, Sacred Dance* Jones, E. J. & Clifton Chas [Ed] Llewellyn pub. 1997 pages 159/60 and pages 156 and 160. Jones reiterates Cochrane's clear views on a single leadership wherein all cuveners [regardless of how many groups, cuveens (sic) or gatherings subsist within his Clan] owe allegiance and duty to The Maid and Magister respectively as pertinent to those Mysteries, & Jones, 2003. Op. Cit. *The Robert Cochrane Letters* p 108.

Had once been large enough to allocate a site specific to (each of three) particular (priestly) rites for smaller gatherings, (as) guardians within each Clan they were responsible for that sites maintenance and security. Knowledge of those distinct sites was even acknowledged externally between these and other Families or Clans prior to their dissociation, for fear of persecution.[509]

More probably, this was due to a decline in opportunity and interest in the post war aftermath of the 1950s. Prof. Hutton quoted Valiente's comment regarding her belief in the actual existence of several extant traditional covens before the explosion of the Wican (sic) popularity of the seventies and eighties. Discovered during her tenacious scouting and research ventures prior to 1962, she listed them as follows: *Sussex, the West Country, the Cotswolds, Lancashire, Yorkshire, Essex, Surrey* and the *New Forest*.[510]

Obfuscation beguiles, but also yields frustration in its confusion, which is not always productive. For this reason, as a mentor, E.J.J., attempted clarification of the querulous issue conjunct with the *Triune Mysteries* and the three working sites relevant to the (stellar) *Priestly Mysteries* only. Some of the old Traditional Clans (including CTC) had taught the (solar) Male and (Lunar) Female rites separately, held in various locations as the Mystery required. These commonly took place in *situ*.

The Priestly Mysteries required specific magickal locations, and the larger sacred sites were each maintained and shared by different Clans. Kindred groups within the Clan would maintain this duty on a more natural, localised scale. People shift through seasonal settlement dependent upon work and trade, demonstrating imperatives of communal motivation that contrast markedly with the modalities of 21st centuryWicca.

After more than five decades of that particular working model ingrained in mind, memory and media, the saturation of Wiccan praxes presents a now almost impossible challenge to any other viable option. It has set both precedent and mold. Nevertheless, alternatives do remain, even if they exist largely out of

---

[509] Jones. 2001. Op. Cit. Again the differences in the Traditional Compass, its purpose and symbology are emphasized as distinct from that now synonymous with Wicca. pages 126-7 and pages 148-151
[510] Hutton, Professor Ronald *The Triumph of the Moon*. (UK: Oxford Uni. Press 1999)

sight and out of mind, strong in their varied yet related practices of Traditional Craft, more so especially, where both Male and Female Mysteries were practiced separately.

The exception for that imposed separation, occurred when they embraced together the Nine Knots of the year, fulfilling the potencies of place with the dynamic of human interaction. Instruction of the arts and of Cosmology, occurs in-between seasonal rites. CTC maintain the necessary premise that only once this basic grounding is properly understood, may seasoned workers then engage the Priestly Mysteries, where the Stile encompasses the Cave, the Grave and the Castle. In closely couched terms, Cochrane reiterated this synergistic formulae to Joe Wilson, an American correspondent during those few and final months before his death in 1966, in the form of a poetic enigma.

> All things of This world belong to Him. Bring forth the Star Son, and you have Dionysus, the Horn Child and Jesus Christ in One – the True meaning of the Cauldron = Truth.

Of Clan and Compass

Thriving on testing those around him, especially seekers, Cochrane considered them fair game, and so his *grey magic* developed into quite extensive conundrums of poesy and lateral thinking. After the Menhir mnemonic and the 1734 riddle that beguile everyone to this day, Cochrane presented another to Joe Wilson, inviting him to consider the significance and methodology involved in *The Laying of the Compass*. Coaxing Wilson, he cast his magicks, dropping clues as to how a laid Compass is also referred to as the *Broom*.

Masking the *other* as angelic potencies, he moved with consummate ease over archaic mediaeval mysticisms to build a perception of unity and completion. A tease no doubt to determine if Wilson recognised those forms as indicative of the *seven stars* – the spokes in Her wheel or cart. Nerthus' Wagon/Carl's Wain; Carl is derived from the Saxon churl or ceorl, from the root stem that provides the Old Norse form, karl, meaning slave or servant - the one whose duty it is to pull Her around the Nowl.

The *order* is literal, as in the sequence of; deferring here to the manner of their manifestation, the order or stages of cumulative virtue as it flows within and throughout, a catalyst for transpersonal fusion. Within *Cochrane's Clan Tradition*, the digits 1734, refer to a quite specific *order* and diverge substantially from the understanding Joe Wilson attributed to them within his 1734 system. Below is a description for those of *Robert Cochrane's Clan Tradition* only.

- ❖ 1 is the 'Cauldron,' the literal 'vessel' of Truth - the 'Void' (of being) – Ginnungagap. Also Bran/Baal, god of* Fire, Time and Death the Stang, the Nowl (4th nail) axis, * God of Craft, lower magics, fertility and Death.

- ❖ 7 is the wheel of fate, of time [hence the hint at being the days of the week and all feminine) within eternity, hence 7+1 gives us the compass and why 7= 1 The lemniscate glyph ∞ is the union betwixt time and eternity, the 'still point', where it is possible: "....*to spin without motion upon three elements.*" The 'seven' stars whirl around the pole. The seven worlds/castles of the Mysteries.

- ❖ 3 are the Elemental Queens – the virtues of earth, air and water – the Three Wells of Fate – Hvergelmir, Mimr and Urdhr, (the three nails of fate). 3 are the trees of the broom, transmuted from the trees of the elemental mothers. Oak, Ash and Thorn of the Three Pillars, iconic totems and possibly of Uppsala too, become birch, ash and willow, faced in the broom. Three vowels. Tripod upon which sits the Pythian Sibyl, or more properly, the Seiðkona. (see illustration AA)

- ❖ 4 are the Queens of the Wind Gods – the Cardinal markers of the Sun cycle, Four vowels. The witch way of saying YHVH =1734 = ADOM (Greek Noktarion of Compass NSEW). Cross of Elements/crossed Arrows.

Cochrane's runic sigil, which became adopted as the 1734 glyph, is at its most discreet, a pictogram of the (reversed) broom. Composed of three runes, *Aiwaz, Iz and Gyfu,* it forms a bind rune. Three (vowels) trees in its composition and four (more vowels) points, in its construction, total seven separate elements. The cycle of the earth, the heavens and the great mill that grinds them, around the axis, the Nowl, churns the fate of all, for all eternity. These things, in the correct order, manifest the crossroads, the liminal point of entry to the *Otherworld*, where: *"Evening star and the dark of night meet."* Here origin meets completion, the beginning and the end, *'All is One and One is All and All Alone and ever more shall be so.'*

This cumulative expression evokes the primal levels of Yggdrasil, the principles of which Cochrane conveys to Bill Gray in their correspondence. [511] He explained how the *Broom, the Stang & Rods* each distinguish the *Tree of Life*, and that: *"All is One and the same thing'* in nature; therefore nothing can be *'supernatural.'* Of this, Cochrane said: *"We teach by poetic inference, the teacher is yourself, seen through a mirror darkly."*

Cochrane had previously discussed this mystery in some considerable depth with Justine Glass (Enid Corral), who had shown no love or appreciation for the Craft that burned his soul. She simply regurgitated everything he'd said without further research or engagement on any point; her eye only on its reportage. Both the plate and monolith were later featured within her book: *Witchcraft, the Sixth Sense and Us,* and in Cochrane's original article entitled: *A Hereditary Witch's Revelations* within it. [512]

She had not grasped the value of tutelage, nor the privilege afforded by it. A mentor is someone people are drawn towards for guidance and instruction, assistance and counselling, at least initially. God-like and Iconic, it is through the experiential challenges presented to them by students they also become, priest and warrior. Reciprocity places the Head-Kinsmen in dutiful service, across all three levels, sharing a trust, a bond, a troth, that is - a truth. No other Covenant may be witnessed in a more profound symbiosis.

Under Cochrane's tutelage, E.J.J. had served as the *Man in Black* within the *Clan of Tubal Cain*. Only after Cochrane's death, did E.J.J. assume the duty of its Magisterial post when Cochrane's wife, the Clan's Lady and its Maid, expressed her singular authority, bequeathing that mantle to E.J.J. to hold in troth. She established E.J.J. as the next guardian of the Mysteries of the Cochrane Tradition - the *Clan of Tubal Cain*. For many years after, E.J.J. served his Faith

---

[511] Oates, 2016. Op. Cit. *SCSIII* #3 Letter from Cochrane to Gray p 174
[512] Valiente. 1989 Op. Cit. p 122 Both these incidents may be explored in greater depth here.

with stoic mind-fullness, continuing to work its mysteries, preserving them for another, both he and Cochrane felt would come.

Disparaging comments raised over the years by Michael Howard brought attention to E.J.J.' role in the Clan, before and after Cochrane's death. Questioning E.J.J.' competence as Magister, the remarks attempted a trivialisation of the few years E.J.J. had spent with Cochrane. Yet the charge to become the next Clan Magister after Cochrane circumvents a very obvious fact. And that requires a reminder of how short a period *Robert Cochrane was himself the Magister of his Clan,* formed a mere year to 18 months before E.J.J. joined him! Together for almost four years, E.J.J. had served alongside him for almost three and a half of the five short years Cochrane had been Magister of the Clan before his death in 1966.

That brief time does not begin to compare with the decades of activity and work since Cochrane's death. The Clan has been well served by its loyal guardian and former Magister, - a mantle held in trust by E.J.J., despite ill-founded rumours to the contrary. A four volume work pays homage to the Faith and pioneering efforts of both these men, and to Robin-the-dart, who has worn that mantle for almost two decades since E.J.J' passed it on. Their works now continue under a new Magisterial auspice – as of the Winter Solstice 2017, Ulric 'Gestumblindi' Goding, former Tanist to Robin-the-dart, sustains that aegis.

Believing that Truth is variable, and that, *'what is true today will be not be tomorrow,'* all memories defeat reason. Locked within a distant moment, the elements that shape us were true only within that fleeting context. Yet it is memory that informs the path and keeps us true to it. Endearing and formative recollections of first contact with those who become mentors and guides in the flesh, are imprinted forever within the psyche, in the emotive metaphysics of the brain, where the alchemy of heart and mind are conjoined.

Seeing E.J.J. for the first time formed an impression never to be forgotten, and one that is cherished forever. Recognition was instant, a meeting of souls on a shared journey. When he crossed the bar to be with his ancestors seven fruitful years later in August 2003, he imparted blessings *'hael and hearty'* and the cautionary wisdom of *'weal and woe'* for the next generation of The People of Goda. Throughout his exacting, but invaluable friendship, he was a trickster to the end. He remains a constant source of inspiration to the People of the Clan.

Under E.J.J.' austere guidance the core teachings of the Clan were grasped. The rudimentary imperatives of its workings within the broader elements of Craft were taught, mouth to ear, as they should be. His mentorship was taxing. His Socratic method bewildering. Yet it proved enormously beneficent as he deftly juggled the roles of tutor, friend and guide, joking frequently that Robert Cochrane had named him – *'the worst witch in the world.'* Both had shared a deep love for their Pale Faced Lady, expressed poetically as the Goddess Diana. Having surrendered himself to Her, he cautioned:

> Once you embrace a dedicated magical path, you must live within its bounds; to forget that mundane and profane are one, to step out from its boundaries, is to invite chaos. [513]

Gregarious and astute, E.J.J. was not easily fooled, though he often personified that role, as is just, for *Roy's dirty rascal*. Being an Old School task master, his rigour was as unstinting as his expectations. Preferring a more direct and uncompromising expression of belief and practise, he saw glamour as illusion and grey magic as artful cunning, an unnecessary distraction from a more superstitious time. Pragmatic as ever, his advice for the best way to tackle a particular problem is succinct, as was his nature: *"No sense in wasting time and energy on spell craft or magic when a punch in the mouth works just as well."*

This was indeed his perennial philosophy; if it could be dealt with easily, or simply, then it should. He was not advocating violence, merely highlighting the obvious fact that physical matters pertaining to this realm, and of all things relevant to the mundane, as incidents of reciprocity, are often best addressed by physical means, where such a response is deemed imperative to it. And always, he asserted, real magick, belonged only to the realms of spirit. His wisdoms regarding detachment, are treasured still, and there is not a day marked, that lacks in an awareness of his voice, guiding, nurturing and challenging all thoughts, or action.

---

[513] Oates, 2016. Op. Cit. *TM: Legend* Personal Correspondence from EJJ to SLO August 2000 (L:14)

Induction and Full Admittance are essential way-markers in gaining sight of and entrance to the *Hearth and Halls of the Mighty Dead*, the *Mythos*, the *Mound and Maze* - all vital keys to the Mysteries undertaken by the Journeyman for recognition and acceptance into the Stream. And though such acts are of incalculable merit, even this does not automatically entitle them to any surety of their readiness, in the immanence of that moment.

Evan John Jones Summer 2003

Years of study offer no guarantee of success. Everyone must account for their own work in accordance with their measure of *gyfu*. Privilege is entirely the gift of the *other*, and not of any human agent. Poetry is certainly the Virtue of enchantment, and the Muse of sacred poetry, *Polyhymnia*, continues to inspire the fires of passion, enflaming the soul to experience elation. Pomegranates are the divine and golden fruit of Hesperides, the enchanted *Rose of Sharon*, gilded with nectar is the elixir of wisdom and immortality - the true tree of life and knowledge. The root and fruit of *both-as-one* are a twin curse and blessing, the coded and bonded word.

In the case of the Four Main Rites, the wording is only a vehicle for the concept. How you wish to word them, is up to you. The concept and the idea behind the concept is the important thing, does it have validity to you? Does it work well enough to satisfy you. The Rites must be your wording, your thoughts, your expressions; you are the only people who know what you are aiming for. The Craft has always been flexible enough to adapt to changing circumstances, rather than bogging down in an out-dated liturgy. Once the Craft rites expressed a fear of the unknown and the unseen, seeking protection in continuity. Today, the Craft explores the unknown and tries to understand it, instead of the practical order of the day, it's now mystical. You are the people doing the work, so what words you use to explain the concept, and work the rites, must be yours. ~E. J. Jones

The Celestial Rose

Frau Gode is the Clan Mother, *not* its Goddess. She is the spirit of mentation within it, a presiding genius of the Egregore – the soul connection maintained through the female family guardians as the Grandmothers of our ancestors. Their wisdom is the Saga of the People. It is Her Virtue that alights upon the Maid and Lady of the

Clan, and defines her as chosen by that ancestry to represent them. This is what defines her Clansmen, the *People of Goda,* as the priesthood of that presiding genius. i.e. *the godr lieged in troth to Gode* (the good spirit of the wise); *"We are the wise people, and wisdom is our aim."*

As a fundamental principle of heritage, it is a matter of Faith not fully understood by many in the Craft, the Finnins most particularly. Perceiving that aegis as a literal Goddess, they chose to pursue a false premise that has no relevance to the legacy and heritage of The Robert Cochrane Tradition. The Finnins elevated that Virtue, transformed and fully iconized as *Goda*, a tutelary goddess. Goda never was this. The Tutelary deity for the Clan is *Tubal Cain*, and is not paired with anything – as a duo-theistic premise, pairing is a concept sacred to Wiccans, though not exclusively so. Tubal Cain is a figure of Virtue far more encompassing than the smith-god eponym commonly assigned to him.

All notions relating to anything assumed to be 'Celtic,' should be appreciated as artificially constructed, ironically in lieu of rising nationalism of more recent centuries, made palatable by this obfuscation. Celtic is a term that only properly relates to a language grouping for various tribal people that remained distinct from their neighbours east of the Rhine, in Germania. Academia remains divided on the origin of the Fir Bolg in Ireland, but the Belgae tribes that breached both east and western borders of the Rhine are the strongest contenders. [514]

Politics of latter centuries, dogged by wars and sectarian prejudice, generated extreme and emotive sensibilities both for and against nationalisms. Despite the fiction, all things Celtic have become the acceptable face of nationalism. Speaking disparagingly to Bill Gray about the darkening tide of returning superstitions, believed lost when the more enlightened folk cast down the Fir Bolg millennia ago, Cochrane added:

> Again the Keltic [sic] mind is strongly addicted to nature worship, what is not so forthcoming is the alteration in personal perception so that we may see god. [515]

---

[514] http://www.davidkfaux.org/files/Belgae_England_R_U152.pdf
[515] Oates, 2016, *SCSIII* Op. Cit. #V Cochrane to Bill Gray p 267

Cochrane clearly saw a parallel rising inwards within his Clan: notably between himself and Ronald White. Neither faction was able to shift beyond that divergence concerning the principle of animism. These matters of form served only to exacerbate further the enmity between them. White stubbornly expressed his distinct preference for Celtic myth and open neo-Paganism. Fundamentally contra to Cochrane's vision, 'Keltica' was rejected by Cochrane soon after his brief exploration deemed it as romantic revivalism, a path without historical substance. Valorising the Virtue of the old gods within, Cochrane and E.J.J. observed a kindred spirit, declaring: *"I am Od's man, since in me the spirit of Od(hr) lives in me."* For them and for ourselves, it is *Holda,* not Keridwen, and *Oðin* not Dagda to whom CTC look to as examples of true myth and folk tradition.

> I have been thinking of holding it [The Rite of Calling] in Wales, instead of the Mendips, we will be in Dylan's territory, which for me is untried. [516]

The popularity for all matters 'Keltica,' (sic) which blossomed through the works of *The Regency, 1734* and *The Roebuck - 'Ancient Keltic [sic] Church,'* was therefore not shared by anyone of Cochrane's Tradition. His works and his Clan embrace the myth and ethic sourced in the histories of those earlier peoples east of the Rhine. Opting out of a strictly neo-Pagan ethos, Cochrane maintained a round of seasonal feast days and observances based in folk-lore, folk-magics, and remnants of the old religion that had fused within Traditional Craft. Evidenced within the 1961 edition of *Psychic News,* Lois Bourne (nee Pearson), HP's Gerald Gardner's St Albans coven after Valiente left in 1957, remarked how the: *"Four great festivals of the year are: May's Eve, August Eve, Hallow'een and Candlemas."*

This fascinating description correlates perfectly with those used by the Old Craft, but deviates from the names popularised by modern Wiccans in their Celtic resurgence instigated in the later 1980s. Previous folk oriented terms were replaced with titles deemed more pagan: *Lughnasadh, Samhain, Beltaine* and *Imbolc* became desirable replacements, popularised by modern practitioners.

---

[516] Ibid.

> In the 12th century the Roman Catholics and the paganism of the countryside were well and truly mingled, and each tolerated the other. But just before and during the first crusade, emissaries or wandering pilgrims from Persia landed in both Britain and Ireland, and what they had to teach was a development upon the Craft at that time.

And

> The highest pagan ethic of the 12th century was better and more defined than the best of the Christians, unfortunately Christianity and ignorance won. [517]

Cochrane's works developed obliquely to those of Ronald White and George Winter. There should be no confusion between them. Enriched by personal explorations into spiritual beliefs sourced in the predominant cultures of Northern Europe, Cochrane fused hermetic magicks with archaic philosophies that had left their mark in the intellectual revolutions that follow social dissention these isles are typically noted for.

From the crusading centuries to those of the industrial revolution, from land reform to psychic science, the collective arcana, culled from a cultural perspective of history, provided the balm his soul craved. Convinced this was missing in the contemporary beliefs of his peers and their praxes, he sought ever new and innovative ways to bring that awareness to them. His homilies shine as shattered jewels, strewn amongst his letters and articles written thereafter.

> I agree with you about the Gods from the east, but as you know, not all the Craft accepted the eastern gods. Many still preferred the Old Ones, and continued the ancient observances. I for one do not like the eastern star, but prefer the Mill as my ancestors did [518]

---

[517] Oates, 2016. Op. Cit. *SCSIII* #1 Letter from Cochrane to Bill Gray p 188
[518] Oates, 2016. Op. Cit. *SCSIII* #3 Letter from Cochrane to Norman Gills p 295

Enduring all trials of time, the Mythos of the Rose Castle, remains the heart of the Pentagrammatic *Compass Rose* that sources and vitalises the virtue of CTC (Clan of Tubal Cain). As a manifest Compass, it forms a reflection of its celestial counterpart, and the fundamental premise of Cochrane's *Round of Life*. Across the range of his works, from the folkloric language told in the hands, to the magicks of the Rings, to the ethic of its Law, the 'rosy knot' is ever present. Over several decades, many, including seasoned crafter's, have dismissed Cochrane's works, unable to grasp its more obscure elements, or fathom its mysteries. Gills was completely out of his depth. Gills was wrong. Labelling his puns and kennings as *grey magic,* and his works as *'something he made up,'* is to mistake the finger for the moon.

> When the shadow faces from the past draw close, and claim you for their own, you drift through past lives and places my friend, to seek the Castle and the Rose. [519]

4 Maturity: Realisation of Truth

VII) The Lapwing

The Ancient Keltic Church

Following the aspirations of his own mentor, E.J.J. had worked towards establishing a Craft community. Serving that purpose, he maintained a healthy network of contacts whose enquiries spanned almost all continents and hemispheres, drawn from North and South America, Australia, Africa and Eurasia. A good friend and advisor to many, especially to Nigel Jackson, his other correspondents include Andrew Chumbley, Stuart Inman, Tony Steel, Iain Steele and Caroline Tully. He was optimistic of their interest and encouraging it where expedient to do so. But unlike his mentor, E.J.J. believed the Craft could be of value to those whom Cochrane would never have considered as being *'of the blood,'* in the

---

[519] Oates, 2016. Op. Cit. *SCSIII* #3 Cochrane to *'ickle deric'* p 262

literal sense. They both held merit for all who had the 'mark' in the metaphysical sense.

Perhaps history records the ironies of our human failing and endeavours to do the right thing where the best of intentions are thwarted by Fate, or more often, because of it. In that regard, E.J.J. is probably best known for the controversy engendered by his adoption into the Clan of persons from America, people wholly unfamiliar with UK Tradition, custom and lore. No strangers to the Craft, they were leaders of their own successful group - *The Roebuck*, formed initially through their work with several well-known occultists in the US.

Once aware of influences from English Craft Traditions upon the convoluted and diverse history *The Roebuck* was founded upon, Ann and Dave Finnin were sufficiently intrigued to seek out the source in the UK.[520] An in-house private biography composed by them sometime in the early 1990s found its way online, albeit much amended by an unknown third party.[521] It discussed their independent attempts to make contact and to work its known rites as they had become available in the course of time through involvements with several people based mainly in the UK.

Labouring under the false impression that Gills had once been a member of Cochrane's group, their over evaluation of Gills, White and *The Regency*, predisposed Ann and Dave Finnin to think they'd been gifted with superior knowledge of Robert Cochrane's Tradition and works.

Norman Gills' limited understanding of the few works of Cochrane accessible to him at that time, generated subjective tangents in all works later shared with his students. Supplemented further from dubious and unreliable sources, Gills' personal adaptations of second-hand, garbled information on Cochrane were embraced by Ann and Dave Finnin, when they visited the UK.

Preferring the idiosyncratic perspective of those who had merely guested occasionally at the Clan rites, they placed no value on the advice of a co-founder of its traditions or guardian of its legacy. Mara Wilson discovered that Gills had never been an actual member

---

[520] See the Official 1734 Website: http://www.1734_witchcraft.org.uk
[521] An early, controversial draft circulated the internet, entitled *A History of the Roebuck Coven* which later formed the basis for Ann Finnin's own book *The Forge of Tubal Cain*

of the Clan at all, and that his personal works were entrenched in Faerie lore and Keltica, grafted upon a Wiccan ritualistic structure.[522]

It is unsurprising to observe those influences within the rites of *The Roebuck*. Rather than acting upon this information with discernment, the Finnins were charmed and flattered by Gills and also by Howard, with whom they stayed on one of their visits to the UK. Prior to contacting E.J.J., Ann and Dave Finnin had heard of Cochrane's Tradition, possibly through Peter Paddon or Joe Wilson.[523] They had not anticipated how divergent that information was from the actual tenets of Cochrane's Tradition.

In his attempts to guide them in the true ways of the Clan, E.J.J. unwittingly exposed himself to considerable frustration. This became further exacerbated when Bill Gray allowed the Finnins to photocopy private letters he'd received from Cochrane. Challenged by entrenched bias, the Finnins found themselves overwhelmed and unable to comprehend the information within them. This did not prevent their push towards acquiring a prestigious title as adoptees into The Clan.

A typical example of E.J.J.' directives is evident in the following extract[524] taken from an early letter to them. Aware of their unfamiliarity with its obscure tenets and operative mechanics, his initial exchanges with them expressed patience. Distinctive core mechanics emphasising the imperatives of duty, virtue, and allegiance to ***the*** Head-Kinsman, as sole and absolute authority of the Clan, were shared with them.

The Finnins found these concepts distinctly alien. They were extremely uncomfortable with the Head-Kinsman's jurisdiction over who may or may not join the Clan, in what capacity, and all matters pertaining to Clan Law. Cochrane's words ring truest in this instance: *"I do not believe they understand the power this gives to the HP."*

As Clan Magister, E.J.J. explained to them how the Clan may also operate as a body comprised of other groups and covens within it; with each group operating under a Marshal, and how each

---

[522] Summarised from the *A History of the Ancient Keltic Church* document, available in the online archives of the 1990s. A re-edited version of this biography appears in Ann Finnin's book *The Forge of Tubal Cain* (US: Pendraig Publishing 2008)

[523] Both Joe Wilson and Peter Paddon are now deceased

[524] Oates, 2016. *TM: Legend.* Op. Cit. Personal Correspondence from E.J.J. to A & D Finnin. See (EJJ, L15:F4)

of those groups are held in allegiance to *the one* Head-Kinsman as Magister of the Clan.

Their reticence generated a considerable stumbling block, a matter they could not resolve. They presumed that either E.J.J. or Cochrane had acted as a spiritual guardian and barred their progress. Responding to their distress at this impediment, E.J.J. advised them it was *not sourced* in the issues of the living; nor was that source human. In other words, their own, personal prejudices for specific tenets of the Clan ethos, established a natural barrier between themselves and the Clan Egregore. Their rejection of everything E.J.J. had introduced them to, both prior to their adoption and after it, is immensely significant. Stressing that as Master overall, he held his position at the behest of the Egregore, a force that resides with *the* Maid and Lady of her Clan, his words pulled no punches:

> Yes, there is a Clan of Tubal Cain, or the goat foot god. As for joining, you have to be invited to do so. At present, there are five people, who are entitled to initiate potential members of the Clan, and *with the permission of the Clan Magister can go off and form his or her own coven which in turn will be part of the main clan.* The five people who have the authority to form other covens as part of the clan are Chalky, George, Jane Bowers Doreen Valiente and myself. [525] So as you can see, there is no leg pull about it. Mind you there are certain rules and oaths that have to be taken firstly by you and David, after that you both will have to initiate your own people in the same way.
>
> As there is so much distance between us, David will have to act for me at first, until he has served a year and a day and then he can carry on, on his own. The other thing is, *as your present members advance within the clan so they and their allegiances to you both as head of the clan must be given.* This in turn gives you the right to call a full

---

[525] As clarified previously, through their own abjuration, Ronald White and George Winter had forfeited all Clan rights under its law. Their banishment was permanent, E.J.J. would never grant amnesty over Jane Bowers' decision. And indeed, he did not. They expressed no intention or desire to redeem their exiled status from the Clan. Doreen Valiente was keen to work independently, free to engage whom she wished, and when her own oath of allegiance expired naturally over time, it was not renewed. She belonged to no Clan, Creed or system, but was her own person. She did remain close to Clan members and worked with them on occasion to celebrate the knots, but this was always on an informal basis, strictly outside Clan prerogatives. Due to circumstances already explained, none of the previous Clan members therefore retained any authority to procure and mentor seekers with a view towards Clan Induction.

> meeting of all the covens in the clan as and when you feel like it. If you'd like to check the authority of this tradition, look up the man in black and there you have it in a nutshell.
>
> As I have said before, if this is a path you wish to tread, then I am willing to go along with it, but first of all your group must agree as you are a group, and not individuals wanting to join a coven. Any one after who wants to join you can be dealt with in the normal manner. Strange isn't it, things never quite work out the way you plan them in the circle. *No it was not Roy or me that stopped you, we may be good but we are not that good.* From what has been said I have the feeling that the Old man is with you and is working through your circle. Soon with any sort of luck you should get a clarification of him in the circle, or even better, outside of it. [526]

As an early insight into the relationship that was to blossom and then sour between E.J.J. and the leaders of *The Roebuck* in the US, this fascinating early missive lays the ground for much that transpired afterwards. Although E.J.J. stated his willingness to adopt *The Roebuck* into the Clan as a kindred satellite, it was another concept Ann and Dave did not understand on any level. They found this aspect of Clanship an objectionable affront to their independent sovereignty.

Characteristically, E.J.J. saturated his text with the present tense, even when referring to future events, discussed only as plausible things, as possibilities as yet unrealised, and then only in a nebulous manner. It was ever his way to blur time, to compress everything into the 'now;' his world-view was simply coloured by a faith he'd lived almost all of his life. All is Wyrd, and of a singular tense to him.

> What John wanted for them was merely to carry an interest in the Clan over to US and begin a legacy for its continuance over there as a public form of what HE HELD as Magister of the private, actual Clan, here in the UK. An adopted status can never be more than an outer form. This is why they never undertook the remaining rites that would have marked them as anything but that. And that John makes very clear, they just never saw it, because

---

[526] Oates, 2016. *TM: Legend.* Op. Cit. Personal Correspondence from EJJ to A & D Finnin, circa 1987-89. See (EJJ, L12:F-1) and (EJJ, L14:F-3).

they were 'reading' it differently. Nothing they had ever done or known helped them 'see' that distinction. And what John said was never the same thing they'd imagined, not in any way. [527]

In the following extract, the wording of the oath *to the Clan*, taken by Ann and Dave Finnin upon their own adoption *into the Clan* is without ambiguity; they were swearing to uphold their *oath to the Clan*.

> The Oath. First of all, I will transmit it to you Ann and then I will appoint David to act for me in all matters pertaining to the Clan for one year and one day. After the aforesaid time has passed, you are both free <u>to form your own group within the clan</u> of Tubal Cain and to <u>form other groups within the clan structure under your control</u>. [528]

This was not an oath that named them leaders of *The Clan*, only as leaders of any groups they may form within the Clan structure. Moreover, those oaths are to support and protect the laws and teachings of their Clan; that is, the *Clan of Tubal Cain and its People of Goda*:

> I also swear to hold true to the Clan of Tubal Cain, to regard all others of the Clan as my brothers and sisters of the faith, to aid them in time of need, to protect them in time of danger, to hold true to the Clan laws and secrets. [529]

Towards the latter end of the 1990s, in another letter, E.J.J. informed Dave and Ann Finnin of his plans for *Witchcraft a Tradition Renewed*.[530] What is obvious from this letter, is the understated reiteration by him, of his extant status as the Head-Kinsman to them, and their own, very different status' as heads of a Coven that *represents*

---

[527] Robin-the-dart. Equinox 2016.
[528] Oates, 2016. Op. Cit. *TM: Legend* Personal Correspondence from EJJ to A & D Finnin, circa 1987-89. See (EJJ, L12: F-2)
[529] Oates, 2016. Op. Cit. *TM: Legend* Personal Correspondence from EJJ to A & D Finnin, circa 1987-89. See (EJJ, L14: F-3) This was an oath they reneged in 2008, by which time they were already disavowed. Hence CTC invited them to re-take their oath, to be re-instated once again as a satellite. They declined. Shortly after, they allied themselves to C.J. and M.B.I. Neither faction were able to cede or share authority and their alliance broke down quite aggressively.
[530] Oates, 2016. Op. Cit. *TM: Legend* Personal Correspondence from EJJ to A & D Finnin, circa 1987-89 See (EJJ, L15: F-4)

the Clan's presence in the USA, (and how that Coven subsists within *the* Clan, headed by E.J.J. as Clan Magister, *here* in the UK).

He nowhere stated their Coven was anything but part of *the* Clan; nor to them as a separate Clan.[531] E.J.J. referred to them only as leaders of their own line of covens and groups affiliated to them under their aegis, just as they must in turn, remain under E.J.J., as Magister of the Clan of Tubal Cain. *For as long as they hold that allegiance sacred their status stands.* It is certainly a very British 'thing.' Peculiar it is, prejudiced it is not.

> So, now I've got his function down in respect to the covens of the Clan. This in turn led me to having to explain how individual covens relate to Clan traditions, what their rights are from the Clan and what their duties are to the Clan and how it is all joined together. In short, how to build up a network of Covens within the Clan tradition. This means that instead of finishing up within a couple of months with a couple of oaths and rituals, it looks as though I'm going to be doing it for the next year or so[532]

Entitled, *Witchcraft, a Tradition Renewed,* it is perhaps, E.J.J.' most widely acclaimed work. He could not have foreseen the impact it would have, and continues to hold. Another extract begins with a simple, unambiguous directive; one that informed Ann and Dave Finnin how interest generated by this new book, should it take off, may inspire interest, generating newcomers and seekers throughout America.

Initially E.J.J. was hopeful the Finnins would (eventually) become the leaders of such a group. He had not anticipated the problems he would have explaining how their sworn duty is deferred back to *the* Clan in all things,.[533] Exploring that idea yet further, E.J.J. described how the Finnins would *represent* the Clan's *'tradition'* in the USA. Note, they are neither *the* Clan, nor the Covenanted heirs of its tradition.

---

[531] At the very end, once they were disavowed and contact severed, John referred to their frustrating inability to grasp that they were not part of CTC, and of their insistence on being 'their own clan,' as a 'Keltic Clan' ie – the one they'd created for themselves from *The Roebuck* and the *Keltic Church*.
[532] Oates, 2016. Op. Cit. *TM:Legend* Personal Correspondence from EJJ to A & D Finnin, circa 1987-89. See (EJJ, L15: F-4)
[533] Oates, 2016. Op. Cit. *TM:Legend* Personal Correspondence from EJJ to A & D Finnin, circa 1987-89. See (EJJ, L16: F5)

If what I'm doing now, ever gets published and taken up by other groups, this will make the Roebuck titular head of any group set up in the states **a**nd that every one of them will have to take an oath of suzerainty to you before they can claim to be of the tradition. A mind boggling thought indeed, perhaps I'd better burn everything and take up fretwork instead, what do you think? Seriously though, think about it. Both of you took an oath on the hill to the tradition, so anyone wishing to form a group within **our** [note: not **your**] tradition, must take an oath to you. To hold true to the faith and to recognise your <u>Coven</u> as the mainspring [Clan's representatives] of the tradition in America.[534]

Upon that achievement *only*, would they be responsible for everyone drawn to them via the interest generated in the Clan's tradition as expressed to them and others within his new book, and whomsoever they might bring into their Coven/s in the US resulting directly from that. It seems clear enough, and yet it failed to convey his intent to them.

Retreating from the occult scene to concentrate on what they had created, they established themselves as King and Queen of their own Castle. Oblivious of its false foundations, they imparted a very insular craft to their initiates.[535] Only in more recent years has the source of their overwhelming confusion and misdirection away from *The Robert Cochrane Tradition*, been identified.

Other letters followed, each revealing a deepening failure of communication between E.J.J. and the Finnins. Certain traits evinced in CTC's customs were later deemed by them as indicative of British prejudice. Rather than follow E.J.J.' lead, finding much within it that conflicted her own ethic, Ann Finnin recorded these incidents in her own book *The Forge of Tubal Cain*, and again later in an email to CTC. Ann made it very clear that Dave and herself considered E.J.J.' authority a cultural impingement of their personal rights.

Ignoring their best and closest source, they chose instead to consult others, whose second and often third hand peripheral status, transmitted a very sketchy and flawed impression of Cochrane and his

---

[534] Oates, 2016. Op. Cit. *TM:Legend* Personal Correspondence from EJJ to A & D Finnin, circa 1987-89. See (EJJ,L16:F-5) [Author's emphasis]
[535] Private conversations with some ex members of *The Roebuck Coven*. March 2016.

works. Subsequently, the Finnins selected what appealed and did not compromise those sensibilities.

Reading the next statement made by Cochrane to Joe Wilson in his first letter to him in December 1965, with the gift of hindsight, it is obvious how easily Clan teachings are misunderstood. Certain archaic English folk beliefs are wholly incompatible with those inherent of American Craft. They are also so easily manipulated.

> I come from the country of the oak ash and thorn. I am against the present form of Gardnerism, and all kindred movements (. . .) my religious beliefs are found in an ancient song, green grow the rushes O, and I am an admirer and critic of Robert Graves. [536]

From the copies of letters supplied by Bill Gray of his own correspondence with Robert Cochrane and those of Norman Gills (given to Bill Gray by Norman Gills), the Finnins had created their own vision wholly at odds with the tutelage of the Magister of the Clan and its living Mythos.

What they had manifested and consolidated was a decisive shift towards the realisation of their own works within an organisation known and registered as the *Ancient Keltic Church,* a title composed of three words that bear no semblance or correlation to the legacy, culture or faith of the Clan of Tubal Cain, and are completely anathema to it.[537] A later missive reveals the irreparable breach between E.J.J.' view on 'Celtic' and the perspective taken up by Ann and Dave Finnin. [538]

> All the trouble seems to hinge on what you call the Clan and what Roy called the Clan are two different things, yours is Celtic in orientation, ours is English. [539]

Reliably informed by former Roebuck members, this move was to offer safety to its members under US Law, and to assure their protection from arrest when carrying their 'tools of arte' in public,

---

[536] Oates, 2016. Op. Cit. *SCSIII* #1 Cochrane to Wilson p 364
[537] Oates, 2016. Op. Cit. *TM:Legend* Personal Correspondence from E.J.J. to A &D Finnin. Feb. 1998. See (L17:F6).
[538] Oates, 2016. Op. Cit. *TM:Legend* Personal Correspondence from E.J.J. to A &D Finnin. Feb. 1998. See (L17:F6) and also (EJJ, L17) : (F-7).
[539] Oates, 2016. Op. Cit. *TM:Legend* Personal Correspondence from E.J.J. to A &D Finnin. [22/1/98] See (EJJ, L17 : F-6)

which might otherwise be considered inappropriate, or provocative.[540] This may have been prudent, but their adoption of a specious title was perceived by E.J.J. as a hostile rejection of his mentorship in favour of tenets inimical to the Clan.

Frustrated by Ann and Dave Finnin's refusal to uphold the founding principles of the Clan's Mythos, E.J.J. explained how their continued usage of the Clan name as a veneer to cover their overtly Celtic (sic) principles was not acceptable.[541]

Convinced they could not rise beyond their adoptive status as a satellite group to become fully admitted Elders of the Clan, E.J.J. was prompted to take judicious action. He told them quite bluntly, that as far as he was concerned, their workings remained irretrievably divergent from those of the Clan's. This incited open hostility and further disregard for his authority.

Confrontation was inevitable. E.J.J. severed their adoptive status entirely. His attempt to explain how he alone had the authority to bring them into that adoptive state, to induct and exile with impunity as its legitimate Magister, had failed. They did not understand this premise.

After a final protracted argument in 1998,[542] in which E.J.J. endeavoured to highlight their now voided status within the Clan as opposed to their assumed status, all contact ceased. Somewhat acrimoniously, *The Roebuck Coven* fought against its release from the Clan of Tubal Cain, refusing to accept that it had drifted so far away with their own 'creation' as E.J.J. called it. No point of accord remained between them:

> The root problem as I see it, stems from years back when the Roebuck and the Clan of Tubal Cain parted company. The first inkling I had of this, was the feedback I had after the publication of the book *'Witchcraft a Tradition Renewed'* when certain of your members asked the question 'why aren't we doing this?' and from what I was given to understand, you told people that you didn't need to do this and that in the book I tried to throw people of the

---

[540] Taylor, 2016. Op. Cit.
[541] Oates, 2016. Op. Cit. *TM:Legend* Personal Correspondence from E.J.J. to A &D Finnin. Feb. 1998. See (L17: F6).
[542] Oates, 2016. Op. Cit. *TM:Legend* Personal Correspondence. From E.J.J. to A &D Finnin. See (L18:F7)

scent concerning the Clan workings as well as baffle, maze and mystify.

You know full well that his isn't true and that everything in the book was factual, accurate and above all open. In fact, it is what I claimed it to be, the basic root source of all the Clan workings, it was then, and still is and will always be so, and if you attended one our workings today, you would find that we still open and close our meetings in the way so described. From other material supplied by you and from feedback of various sorts, including first-hand experience, the Roebuck workings have taken a decidedly Celtic turn compared to the line we over here were [and are still] following.

This in turn leads to the oath both you and Dave took. I may be getting old, but my memory is still good and of course I still have Peter who was present to check it with, and to the best of our memory, you swore to follow the tradition and mythos of Tubal Cain. Quite a simple oath, the sincerity of which was never doubted. At the same time, this did NOT name you as the sole inheritrix of the mythos and the Clan of Tubal Cain everywhere – *ONLY what YOU created and ran.*

Evidently, you have had a change of heart and decided to follow your Roebuck. Now I've certainly no quarrel with that, after all it is a free world, and people should work what they want to. Where the problem comes in, this, is what I pick up from the letters I get, is that the Roebuck is being called Tubal Cain, something it isn't and people are working the Roebuck under the impression that *they are working Tubal Cain, which they are not!* [543]

E.J.J. highlighted this breakdown, explaining each detail to current Clan members. He wished them to understand the true status of *The Roebuck* within the Clan, and how, as a satellite group it had existed with limited adoptive status. More than this, E.J.J. wished to illustrate Ann and Dave Finnin's failure to recognise his overall jurisdiction as Head-Kinsman and Magister of the Clan Tradition

---

[543] Oates, 2016. Op. Cit. *TM: Legend* Personal Correspondence from EJJ to A & D Finnin. See (EJJ, L17 : F-6) February 1998

itself. E.J.J. had overestimated Ann and Dave Finnin's understanding of English Craft and of Clanships. [544]

Twenty-five years ago, information on how Clanships were operated was scant. Very little was known to anyone outside its bounds. Even so, it was a substantial shock for E.J.J. to discover how uncommon that knowledge was in reality, even to those who espoused their superiority in that arena.

Amongst his private papers, E.J.J.' record of his regrettable involvement with Dave and Ann Finnin, reveals endless strife, his despair and ultimately, how he came to terms with their unrelenting grievances. [545] Their flagrant disregard for his views and advice led to irreconcilable differences which forced him to sever all lines of contact and relations with the Finnins. As to their confusion regarding Clan praxes and why they believed they were autonomous baffled him to his grave. [546]

Sensibly, of course, it should never have been an issue. The authority of a Magister to bring people into the Clan, does not evaporate with their Induction. Until relinquished through the Covenant, that status is irrevocable.

E.J.J. dismissed their American 'clan' as a self-styled creation that bore no authority or association with the *Clan of Tubal Cain* and its People. It had failed in every way to adhere to, or adopt any part of the centralizing core mythos as their own. The Clan Hearth is where the Egregore resides, and is served by its People; no Tradition endures or functions differently. [547] To live under the aegis of a name, requires rather more than playing lip service to it. A name is a spell shared in gyfu. It is a bond reciprocated, or it is a bond reneged. Addressing Ann and Dave Finnin, E.J.J. wrote:

> When people like Jim ask me about this, I tell them in all honesty, that we parted company years ago concerning Clan workings and that they have to make up their own minds as to what they want to do. If they work the Roebuck, then they must accept the rules of

---

[544] Oates, 2016. Op. Cit. *TM:Legend* Personal Correspondence from E.J.J to A & D Finnin. See (L12:F2)
[545] Private discussions with several former members of the Roebuck.
[546] Oates, 2016. Op. Cit. *TM:Legend* Personal Correspondence. From E.J.J. to A & D Finnin. See (F1-9) Excerpts from email. Dave Finnin dated November 2005.
[547] Oates, 2016. Op. Cit. *TM:Legend* Personal Correspondence from E.J.J to A & D Finnin. See (L18:F8) February 1998

the Roebuck without question. If they want to do something else, then they should leave and make it clear why they are doing so, the one thing that cannot do, is to be part of, yet at war within a group, this isn't fair on all concerned.

Certainly, the feeling over here with the Tubal Cain membership, is that we are so far apart in what both of us do, that there is little point in going on with any sort of association, and the best thing we could do, is to dis – associate ourselves fully from the Roebuck and let me tell you, I've come in for some stick over the last few years, for introducing you to the Clan in the first place. [548] One of the questions raised in the letters I've had, concerned the masked rites which I gather you dismissed as 'Brits playing cowboys and Indians.'

If you had been working the Clan Rites, then you too would have arrived at same point we have concerning the shamanistic elements in Roy's work, something others have commented upon more than once and which is now a generally accepted picture of what we do. So, once again, the difference between what we are doing and [what] the Roebuck are going is shown up [in the] aforementioned argument. All the trouble seems to hinge around the fact that what you call the Clan, and what Roy called the Clan, are two different things.

Yours is Celtic in orientation, ours in English in content, and never the twain shall meet, so to speak. *The Roebuck is the Roebuck (. . .) the only thing I can suggest to stop* **all this trouble, is that you drop the idea of the Clan of Tubal Cain** *and let The Roebuck stand on its own merits (. . .) wishing you all the best for the future as I don't suppose I'll be hearing from you again.* [549]

Their response to his former suggestion to concentrate on their *Roebuck Coven* and cease any pretence to its affiliation to the *Clan of Tubal Cain,* was unprecedented. [550] Astonished at their lack of

---

[548] Personal Conversation with E.J.J. concerning Jane Bowers' reluctance to endorse their status further.
[549] Oates, 2016. Op. Cit. *TM: Legend* Personal Correspondence from E.J.J. to A & D Finnin. 22/1/98 See (L17:F6).
[550] Their rude rebuttals are recorded without further comment. See *TM: Legend*

(respect) and comprehension, his final words convey unconcealed anger. As Magister, E.J.J. declared their previous status, void. [551]

All that remained, was the final undertaking of a very specific Clan Rite, one that executed needful severance, metaphysically and in law. Unable to conceal his indignation, E.J.J was shocked to have received a legal draft, complete with more than a dozen signatures from members of *The Roebuck,* not only protesting E.J.J.' decision, *but rejecting it.* [552] As a final response, E.J.J.' terse dissolution of their status is unsurprising.

> As for banishment, I can only that that this came from the letter I wrote to (. . .) where I mentioned the floating of the candle. If we shared any common ground whatsoever, you would immediately know that floating the candle over the falls is quite a common occurrence. Also, if Susan cared to read the letter properly, she would know that all this does is release Ann and Dave from their oath, thus separating the Roebuck and us over here from each other, nothing more, nothing less. At May's Eve when I pass on the stag's head wand over to someone else, I too will float a candle over the falls to signify that the oath of leadership has been dissolved and that I am no longer leading our Clan.
>
> You have your 'American Clan' [read: 'version'] of Tubal Cain and no-one here can strip you of that, even if they wanted too, which they don't, all we say is that you and I have grown so far apart we have nothing in common so we disassociate ourselves from each other and go our separate ways, thus putting a formal ending to what has been happening for years. As for being any part of my future, after your letter, I think not. [553]

From the beginning, the Finnins had not sought its wisdoms, only the shallow enterprise of a name, initially given in faith. The

---

[551] Oates, 2016. Op. Cit. *TM:Legend* Personal Correspondence from E.J.J. to A & D Finnin. See (L:F3) and (EJJ,L18:F-8).

[552] Oates, 2016. Op. Cit. *TM:Legend* Personal Correspondence from E.J.J. to A & D Finnin. See (EJJ, L19:F-9) Some of those persons have since come forward to express regret for their behaviour, now better informed of a situation in which they were subject to false impressions and only limited information at the time.

[553] Oates, 2016. Op. Cit. *TM:Legend* Personal Correspondence from E.J.J. to A & D Finnin. See (EJJ, L18:F-8) Literally, it was a business venture for them, not so much for financial profit as for kudos in the Craft. They 'traded' on the name.

Finnins' right to bear that name was withdrawn by E.J.J. as one they had first misunderstood, then dishonoured by deed of the *Ancient Keltic Church,* and finally rejected in their refusal to acknowledge his absolute authority under its law.

Floating the Candle was the ritual undertaken to delineate their demarcation from that of the Clan and its People, who continue to hold that title by right. As a manifest act, it releases those attached through prior friendships, no longer desired; or through oaths given by another, deemed to have failed. The act removes reciprocal duty and responsibility between the Clan and that person, dissolving attachments frayed by neglect, severed by grief or anger, or desired in freedom.

By returning the soul candle given at Induction, the Clan relinquish the original bond of troth, restoring individual Wyrd. Henceforth all such persons are independent of Clan Wyrd. In a sense, it recognises a shift within relationships, removing the dynamic that unites them. Depending upon context, the intent voids former status as one never actualised in fact or deed, as exampled below.

For all of these reasons, E.J.J. astutely distinguished the act of *floating the candle'* from an *act of banishment.* Both are quite formal acts, but to banish anyone from one's Clan, family, system or organisation, they must *first belong.* By his action, E.J.J. declared that by their own deeds and actions, Ann and Dave Finnin had removed themselves from all intended opportunity and invitation to Clanship, and had *never achieved status as Inducted members of* CTC.

They had simply never shifted beyond their status as a satellite group *adopted into* the Clan. Their duty as a *kindred group* to renew their oaths of fealty every consecutive 7th year to the Magister and Head-Kinsman of the Clan, was years overdue even before they'd arrived at this impasse in 1998.

E.J.J.' direct redress alerted them to the consequences of retaining an empty name, without authority or allegiance. He informed them that, on the forthcoming May's Eve, *'when the regalia is due to be handed over'* with full ceremony, another candle will simply and formally be floated, but on that occasion to denote the shift of leadership, a significant distinction to the candle floated previously for them at the Old Mill, drawing all association to an end.

Hopefully an understanding of Clan mechanics is sufficient at this juncture to appreciate that the legacy and tradition of a Clan cannot diverge within itself, or outwards through a coven that exists only as a subsidiary inner component part of its parent Clan. Most especially it may not diverge from within itself as a parallel stream.

Ignorance of these tenets intrinsic to a Clanship, flag again the impossible claims for even the idea, that any coven (secret or otherwise) could develop a Clan from within itself, and then continue an independent and autonomous existence. [554] Similarly, any group or coven claiming to be distinct from the Clan, even if once held in allegiance to it, has no recourse to its aegis or Egregore and may not adopt its name for their own. That remains with the Head-Kinsmen of the Clan Tradition at all times.

Simply stated, if any group formerly held within the Clan, ceased its allegiance, became independent, and diverged away from the Clan, it would become an entirely new and distinct body, without claim or association to the Clan. That group or coven would require a new name. With that comes the requisite to create its own aegis and Egregore. Whatever name it might decide to choose for itself, it could not, under any circumstances then claim to be of the tradition it is now independent of. [555]

By referring to the *Ancient Keltic Church* and *The Roebuck* groups as the *'American clan'* of Tubal Cain, E.J.J. clarified it as their own thing, their version via influence alone. He reminded them of his original instruction that *"what you created and ran with,"* was all they had. This effectively dismissed them, making them an entity wholly separate from the actual Clan. With earnest resignation, E.J.J. announced the causality of their own reverse thinking; an insistent oversight with ironic overtones. Their desire for independence, had awarded them exactly that, automatically!

---

[554] That is a tenet of Wica and does not apply to Clanships. To reiterate the distinction between Wica and Clan. Covens in Wica are independent. They extend outwards from a parent coven. The People held in Troth to a Clan, exist only within the Clan; never with-out it! A coven may exist within the Clan, but not be independent of it. As the Clan is the greater (parent) body, it cannot exist within a coven. Explained by E.J.J. many times in his writings; we are one named Clan only, within which all other groups or clans (of whatever different names and titles they hold) subsist collectively, headed by one Head-Kinsman only, bound under his singular status and authority. Not even a smaller clan may exist within a parent Clan unless it is becomes subordinate to it, as in days of old, when historical clans gathered for protection and where the main family name would then become theirs by adoption. Its name, aegis and Egregore are specifically aligned as one.
[555] To be clear, Robert Cochrane's tradition, continued only in his Clan – that is CTC. By contrast, in Wica, covens only extend outwards from a parent coven.

A Clan's name then, is a very literal *entitlement*. It declares for its people, a bond to and **of** *that Clan*, one to the other. Where they are not bonded thus, they are simply not of its People, its name not theirs to claim. In this instance, E.J.J. had asked them previously not to use the name, but to let it go as *something long beyond them*. He cannily expressed no desire to strip them of their status as head of all *they* have created, viz – their own Clan.   Sharing in no part of CTC's future, what they did was finally no longer his concern. Nonetheless, *The Ancient Keltic Church* continues to assert an attachment and association with CTC that is quite voided of authority and legitimacy.

These manoeuvres of the Spring of 1998 were finally drawn to a close in the months prior to the meeting that would initiate the next phase of the Robert Cochrane Tradition. Confirmed below, E.J.J.' initial cautions cross-reference the aforementioned incidents.

> I would have written sooner, but I've had no end of hassle from some people working in the states. I tried to get them working the rites of Tubal Cain and now I wish I hadn't, it's turned into a nightmare with personality clashes.[556]

A question raised on that long letter concerned the Finnins' *Book of Shadows* and their declarations regarding their assumed status. Posted by an unknown person onto the internet in the early 1990s, it was part of the private document that briefly surfaced there, available to anyone with a computer terminal. At that time, E.J.J. had only a word processor; he did not acquire a computer until after the millennium.

A copy of the document was shared with E.J.J. a few years later by CTC, which allowed him to give further comment upon the status and works Ann and Dave Finnin had circulated, and where they did and did not relate to information he'd shared with them concerning the working praxes of CTC.

Particular imperatives and distinctions were identified by E.J.J.' as points of failure on their part to uphold the tenets of Clanship. As part of their previous adoptive status, Ann Finnin had been appointed as a maid of her adopted kindred group. *The Roebuck Coven* had initially been introduced to the Clan Egregore through

---

[556] Oates, 2016. Op. Cit. *TM: Legend* Personal Correspondence. Letter from EJJ to SLO. February 1998 (EJJ, L19:F9).

their oaths of allegiance to it, to the Clan and to E.J.J. as CTC's Magister. E.J.J. explained how the aegis and Egregore of the Clan withdrew itself from all individual members if oaths were not maintained or honoured.

Significantly Ann Finnin had <u>not</u> been appointed as The Matriarch of CTC, nor its Lady and Seer, commonly referred to as the *Maid* of the Clan by *Virtue of the Old Covenant*. As Magister of CTC, he was required to search, recognise and formally declare that Virtue present within the appropriate person. E.J.J. had not deemed it present within her; the sacred office that elevates *a maid* within a Clan, to that of *Clan Matriarch*, had not been offered to her:

> Much of the Finnin material [from Ann's book where she discusses the use of a skull] on us is accurate especially the skull material, ours we named Eliza and we had the same feelings and contacts as Ann described with 'Stuart' [The skull used and named by the Roebuck]. But you can totally ignore what they said about being brought into the Clan. A long and involved story too it was, as Peter will vouch. It was a case of doing something just to shut them up from their constant nagging to do something.
>
> The 'lights over the city' etc is nothing more than a figment of her rather vivid imagination. The written material looks very much like material that formed their 'Book of Shadows' and could well be a prototype of it. Did have the original material, got rid of it as soon as I read the first four pages, I gather Peter did the same, <u>Tubal Cain it certainly wasn't</u>.
>
> By the sound of it, you've found an ideal place to work and I'm also glad that you have the foundations for a good working group. Should anyone question why it seems to be happening all of a rush where you and T**** [557] are concerned, tell them that where the *Rites of Tubal Cain* are concerned, after 1999, the Clan would cease to exist unless you were prepared to take it over and the coven regalia would be destroyed and along with it the Clan Spirit.
>
> When we leave the site, if we have got one, we usually chuck a 5p into the bushes as a token payment for the use of the site and that is

---

[557] The real name of Robin-the-dart, E.J.J.' Tanist and Magister of CTC.

all. The ritual is grounded at the feast that follows, will explain this in greater detail a little later. [558]

Just a few weeks after Robin-the-dart and Shani Oates were instated to their full duties with CTC, in the Autumn of 1998, E.J.J. was approached tentatively with several questions regarding the authority attached those recent attributions. As Magister and Head-Kinsman of CTC, E.J.J. had formalised those appointments by passing over the regalia of Clanship to his legitimate successors for the continuance of the Clan. With Jane Bowers' full knowledge, approval and blessing, the Clan Aegis was re-aligned in Shani Oates as the Maid appointed after her, in 1998.

And through deed of *The Old Covenant,* invoked as a compact of spirit, flesh, blood and bone, The *Rites and Airts of the Magister* were passed to Robin-the-dart as Tanist. Seeking full clarification of these procedures, it was important to acquire a correct understanding of everything that affected the Clan. Somewhat bemused by that candid request, E.J.J.' answers highlight the enormous gulf between the status of the new Maid and Magister of CTC and the adopted status he'd given the Finnins' a few years previously:

> 4) No, you don't need to renew your oath ever again, not unless you feel a personal and pressing need to. What you read in the book was for <u>kindred workings</u> where any group was akin to us, but not part of the true lineage. <u>You are that lineage until you feel the need to pass it onto someone else.</u>
>
> Where the regalia goes, so does the Office of the Lady of The Clan of Tubal Cain<u>. I had no lady as such, that's why I hold the Stang, cup etc</u>. Doreen, as well versed in the Craft as she is, wouldn't have been the one to carry on the tradition for various reasons.
> Ann Finnin (the American) would have used it in a bid to become Queen or King of all Witches in America (could never make up my mind which), plus the fact that she would have turned it into pan Celtic/Irish tradition with everyone costumed up to the eyebrows waving all sorts of cutlery in the air all for the greater glory of Ann and her oft quoted *"You're not ready for this yet,"* every time someone asked her a question.

---

[558] (Author's emphasis in parenthesis) See Oates, 2016. Op. Cit. *TM: Legend* Personal Correspondence from EJJ to SLO. 1998 (EJJ, L7:F:11)

<u>She was kindred, she's now history, forget her</u>. She took a kindred oath, full story when you meet up with Peter, the whole oath taking was so absurd that it's hard to believe. And I refused point blank to give the Roebuck any sort of certificate etc. stating she was more than just kindred in spite of being asked a number of times.

I've asked you twice, I will ask you once again, as simple as the ceremony was, do you feel within yourself that you are the Lady of the Clan, if the answer is yes, then you are. I have no doubts about it, nor will anyone else for that matter, you seem to be the only one a little uncertain about it. If you hadn't happened, <u>then eventually the regalia would have been destroyed and the fragments scattered out to sea and that would have been the end</u> of it all and very much sooner than you think. Don't think of the power as power in the sense of a tangible that can be transferred as such. The power you have, is within yourself, all it needed was a trigger which was pulled by making you our Maid.

I could have hallowed you as Maid twice nightly every Monday, Wednesday and Friday from here to the Second Coming and at the end of it, you still wouldn't be the Maid unless you had that certain something very special within you that sets you apart from the rest of us. **You have it.** [559]

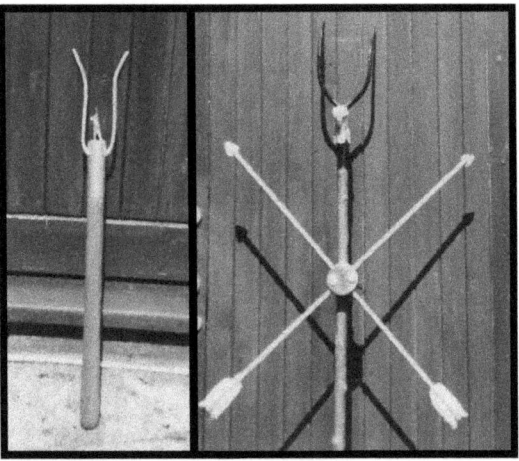

Stag's Head Wand / Magister's Handstaff & Stang and Crossed Arrows

---

[559] Oates, 2016. Op. Cit. *TM:Legend* Personal Correspondence from EJJ – SLO. Oct 98. See (EJJ, L7:F:12)

Unfortunate as this part of the biography is, relaying it facilitated an exploration of Clan dynamics, that in turn, allowed insights into its operative mechanics. Various explanations have covered slightly different scenarios, making it obvious that once any group or person from within the Clan had left, they were no longer members. For anyone to attempt to claim that in leaving, the heritage and legacy of the Clan went with them, suggests considerable self-deception on their part. As shown, this simply is not how a Clan Tradition operates.[560]

This lengthy explanation of traditional matters has eluded the understanding of numerous people in the Craft. With little or no experience of the ways of the old Craft and a greater familiarity with either neo-Paganism or Wicca, there are no precedents to assist comprehension.

Decades later, the 'Wiccan' model is the popular form known by the majority of people, whether they are Wiccan or not. And that system's mechanics and group dynamic, excellent in its own right, nonetheless remains totally at odds with those embodied in Clanships. A Clan's unique system and incumbent Ethos, is not easy to grasp in an occult world peopled and influenced by numerous forms of media.

Right at the beginning, Cochrane established the enigmatic *'Society of Kerridwen,'* referred to twice only: [561] once as a letter from the document cache, and again within a letter to Bill Gray in which he discussed the opportunity of inviting discourse and contact through an advertisement.[562] Cochrane developed his Clan from his vision of an occult society, *a community*.

He did not condone a coven structure, and avoided its use totally. Realising the limitations of the 'modern' coven system he *restored the Clan system of his fore-fathers*, a matter he mentioned to Wilson in one his letters to him. Controversial as this statement seems, it is an historical fact that the Clan system is far older. It has

---

[560] Cochrane, and none other, as Magister, held the Clan aegis, which continues decades later through his Clan today. To summarise, Ronald White and George Winter did not remain Clan members, nor in allegiance within it. Howard and Monmouth both claim that Cochrane's Tradition continued with Ronald White, an impossibility for a number of reasons as discussed re: Clan mechanics. Ronald White was also an exile to that Tradition.
[561] Monmouth, 2012. *GWiE* Op. Cit. Document 1. Republished in Oates, 2016. *SCSIII* Op. Cit. See Transcript Chronology.
[562] Oates, 2016. Op. Cit. *SCSIII* #III Cochrane to Gray p 174. A discussion of setting up the society and the possibility of advertising it in New Dimensions.

served all manner of communities, generic or Craft as lived cultural traditions when the idea of a coven was just a fantasy concocted to demonise the celebratory rites of older societies and folk cultures.

Almost no-one beyond the remit of the Clan had understood its status, or ethic, especially not White and Winter, who had clung stubbornly to their more familiar Wican and neo-Pagan teachings. Fragments of the Gills' and Wilson's letters began to circulate later still, until eventually, the facts of the matter became more widely available to the public. White's own group was separate from Cochrane's, and his familiarity with the Clan's *modus operandi* is not nearly so great as has been imagined or claimed for him.

CTC's attempts to bring that understanding forwards were thwarted, rather than assisted. The desire to bring clarity of these (previously hidden) mechanics met with serious hindrances, sometimes from surprising and quite unexpected quarters. There is a prevailing anxiety in transporting a Tradition beyond its origins. The gulf between details known in-house, including actual and vital fact, are in opposition to the mis-information that flows rather too easily through and around the occult and neo-Pagan world, seeking connections between all such Craft modalities.

In this, Monmouth's and Howard' understanding is the most remiss. Writing at length upon another's Tradition does not present a superior grasp of its mechanics. Their zeal should not be mistaken for authority, and their persistence should not be accepted as conviction. Knowledge is direct and experiential, it comes only from within.

> Take up works that are based upon Truth, and you are a condemned man, for the human race as a whole, does not want truth, but the comfort of illusion. [563]

Castles made of Sand

During his remaining years, E.J.J.' consternation surrounding the dogged persistence that Cochrane's group had once been named the *Royal Windsor Coven* did not wane. Curious as to

---

[563] Oates 2016. Op. Cit. *SCSIII* #VI Cochrane to Gray. p 207

where the rumour began, he was staggered that, despite *his personal* dismissal of the rumour it was prone to raise its head here and there - as fact!

Having heard vague rumours of it from Michael Howard, the Clan sought E.J.J.' valued opinion of this matter during an early visit in the Autumn of 1998. The manner in which the misinformation concerning the proposed existence of *that coven* acquired its genesis and impetus initially appeared ambiguous. Yet E.J.J.' unwavering conviction assumed the entire mechanic was a probable ruse, a notion of obfuscation used to disguise a more recent origin, to attempt a retrospective claim to Cochrane's works indirectly.

Soon afterwards, within days of the Clan meeting, a long and very detailed letter arrived from E.J.J.[564] Among other things, he'd learned of the mysterious appearance of a set of papers, forwarded by an unknown party to Prof. Hutton, who was at that time finalising his research for *The Triumph of the Moon.*' Professor Hutton had been sending out odd chapters to his peers for opinion and proof reading. Michael Howard received chapters on generic elements of Traditional Craft.

Particular irregularities within the mysterious papers sent to Prof. Hutton accompanied by unusual claims, and so Prof. Hutton made arrangements to discuss the problematic material with E.J.J. What deeply perplexed E.J.J., was the content, which claimed to represent the rituals of *The Royal Windsor Coven* a group he knew didn't exist in reality.

Many of those who had worked with Cochrane as a member or guest, had long 'crossed over to bar;' those who remained, were very few in number. Four members in fact, namely, E.J.J., his good lady, Valiente and Cochrane's widow. Valiente died a year later in 1999. Critically, then, three people only were qualified in varying degrees to identify their own works, and separate them from forgeries and false claims.

One other person, a guest at two or three rituals was Marian Green, who might also be consulted to pass opinion or express a limited perspective. This was why Prof. Hutton was quite anxious to engage E.J.J.' unique insight on Clan matters.

---

[564] Oates, 2016. Op. Cit. *TM:Legend* Personal Correspondence from EJJ to SLO. November 1998 (L13)

Knowing the claim to be false, E.J.J. conveyed that opinion to Michael Howard and to Prof. Hutton, immediately. Once he was able to review the documents he confirmed the works submitted with the claim, were principally his own. The bulk of the documents, written by E.J.J. had been lifted from his two books: *Witchcraft a Tradition Renewed* (published) and *The Castle & the Cave* (in ms form only at that time). They were supplemented with a few notes composed by the Finnins relating to their own works.

A draft version of *Witchcraft a Tradition Renewed* had been released to the Finnins as foundational knowledge in small sections from the late 1980s to the early 1990s. Scraps of information from his current ms *The Castle & the Cave* similarly appeared amongst the material; however, he had not shared it with them. As a work in progress, most of the text had been sent to Chas Clifton, the editor of a second project they were working on together, following their highly successful joint enterprise - *Sacred Mask, Sacred Dance*.

Some months later, the Finnins ended up with a full copy. Clifton was a friend of Dave and Ann Finnin, and though we may assume he could have shared some or all of that ms version with them, we simply do not know how they acquired this information.

Since that exposure thirty years ago, <u>no other material</u> has come forth from *any* source to support the (alleged) existence of that phantom coven. This means that to date, the only material produced even allegedly associated with the phantom coven, is either material relative to a different coven altogether (Thames Valley), or E.J.J.' works composed as Magister of the Clan, intended for publication. In neither case, were those works secret; they also had nothing to do with Monmouth's and Howard's phantom coven.

Rumour it appears, thrives on self-fulfilling speculation. Spurred on to write a long and informative letter to Clan members, E.J.J.'s explanation emphasised what had become the bane of his life. It reveals more than he'd initially considered when seeking the people responsible

> Unknowingly, the material you sent may provide a couple of pieces in the tale Mike Howard is trying to sort out, as well as

clearing up something that has been bothering me for quite a few years now. For that alone, very many thanks.[565]

Starting with Mike's tale, you have no doubt heard of Ronald Hutton. He's working on another book, and has been sending chapters to Mike to look at, and if there are any errors, put them right. One of the things Ron got very excited, was a mass of material he received from the *'Royal Windsor Coven.'*

> Mike was not terribly impressed and felt that he'd seen it all before, anyhow, he brought it down for me to have a look at. Apart from the material which you enclosed which was also included in this mass, there was page after page of material lifted from the first book, on top of this, they'd even used the bloody line drawings commissioned by Hales, and this is what [Michael Howard had told him] Ron [Hutton] was claiming [through the material presented] to be old traditional material.[566] When you were down here, you saw the original letter of Roy's where some of this material was lifted from, namely, the Castle.[567] *What they have done here, is to add a few bits of their own, and <u>pass it off as the Royal Windsor Coven material</u>.*

Both E.J.J. and Valiente had categorically repudiated the existence of that phantom coven but to little effect. The seed was sown, and nothing intrigues more than an alleged 'secret.' Popular opinion is a hard thing to dispel, though Valiente of course was no stranger to championing a fact against an opposing tide of speculation.

With some measure of disbelief, CTC have witnessed how the court of public opinion can easily become a three-ringed circus. A free for all that is at best an ego fest, at worst, a force of chaos and destruction. The very glamour of a lie is often alluring, and where it

---

[565] The 'material' referred to was sourced, downloaded and printed from the internet concerning *The Regency* and The Roebuck Coven in the US. E.J.J. did not have access to the internet, and did not know that the Finnins had posted up Cochrane's letters up there, nor, for a limited time, their own biography. Their content made sense of things that had previously elude him, or had confused him. They answered questions he'd long pondered over.

[566] E.J.J. was quoting Mike Howard in his reference to Professor Ronald Hutton here. Author's emphasis.

[567] This sentence is of immense importance, as it counters a claim made by Michael Howard in *The Children of Cain*, that E.J.J. did not know anything about the secret works of Cochrane's secret coven. To support his specious claim, Howard maintained that Cochrane had entrusted a letter to Norman Gills concerning a description of Lucifer, a Castles, and Clan Cosmology. When this letter was shown to E.J.J. Howard said *'he denied Roy had written it.'* He was absolutely right to do so! That letter was a fake, a composite fraud. E.J.J.' reference here to the authentic original is without ambiguity. See Oates, 2016. *TM:Legend* for a scan of E.J.J.' actual letter. See Howard, 2011. *CoC* for his comments.

feeds the popular notion of illusory empowerment, the element of self-delusion is palpable.

A strange conundrum had occurred. From the few limited people E.J.J. shared his work with, someone had set in motion a particular course of events, the consequences of which, necessitated this current Clan biography. Pondering on those events at their advent, E.J.J., was certain it made absolutely no-sense at all for Chas Clifton to have sent any of his work onto Prof. Hutton. That would have been an act as counter-productive as it was coincidental and would not have served him in any way to do so, nor would he have needed to do so anonymously.

If not Clifton, a few others only stand to gain by that action. As to who else might be considered, the list is short, but succinct. Of less than a handful, the main contender had been the Finnins, a possible reaction to provocations inflicted in their shattered relationship with E.J.J. They had an axe to grind at that point, E. J. J. had just presented them with his final letter, informing them of their disavowed status, severing their connection to CTC irretrievably.

Although E.J.J.' material had been modestly supplemented by interpretive works he presumed were attributed to Dave and Ann Finnin from their *Roebuck Coven* in the USA, E.J.J. nonetheless explained to Prof. Hutton and Michael Howard that *he held the Finnins only partially responsible* for their insistent misappropriation of a spurious title associated with Robert Cochrane.

Nothing, pointed back to them however. In fact, there was better reason to assume the Finnins had little or no part in the creation of this fiction. Having ignored E.J.J.' directives led to their subsequent severance from their former adoptive status within the Clan, though they obstinately strived to cling to any status linked to CTC's title.

If they had believed at any time that Cochrane's aegis resided elsewhere, for example within another coven/group of whatever name, they would most certainly have turned tail and claimed *that* rather than attempt to claim CTC's title to advance themselves. Privately, E.J.J. felt that Marian Green was somehow involved in the creation of the recent rumour. Hoping it would remain a short-lived hoax, E.J.J. confessed it was something he had not needed to pursue, initially.

Outraged by all this persistent subterfuge, E.J.J. stated very clearly that Michael Howard had said the *'Finnins were responsible for the rumour of its existence,'* something E.J.J. believed was extremely unlikely. Based on extensive research, his conviction seems well founded. More importantly, any initial, or superficial perspective the Finnins may have held, confirms an origin elsewhere, from someone who required those assumptions to be vocalised.

Notes and online documents, contained information that alluded to further connections arising between specific people. Having observed the manner in which information was disseminated for some time, these were discovered to be of a circular nature. [568] Prof. Hutton, keen to act appropriately, abandoned the inclusion of the falsely contrived material in his most excellent Craft History: *The Triumph of the Moon*. [569]

Of greater immediacy for E.J.J. was the project he and Chas Clifton were working on. The ms draft of *The Castle and the Cave,* was the hopeful means to address public folly, to finally end all speculation about secret covens and fictional titles. Clifton had made contact with Shani Oates apropos the shared book project with E.J.J., and he had happily accepted her personal foreword for it sometime at the beginning of 1999.

Under E.J.J.' advice and instruction, the intention was to introduce Robin-the-dart and Shani Oates to the Craft Community, to establish their unmitigated positions as guardians for the Clan. As Matriarch and Tanist, a public affirmation of their duties as Head-Kinsmen of the Clan in line after E.J.J. and Cochrane was required. E.J.J. was eager to see that notification published, though alas, it was not to be.

Things developed unexpectedly, and a very different course was determined. As soon as Michael Howard heard from E.J.J. in August 1998 about the planned appointments for the new leadership of the Clan, Howard expressed a desire to meet E.J.J. to discuss craft matters. He also wished to study Bill Gray's letters from Cochrane which E.J.J. had in his possession. Then, as delays on Chas Clifton's side created difficulties that were never properly explained,

---

[568] Oates, 2016. Op. Cit. *TM: Legend* Personal Correspondence from EJJ to SLO. Sept. 1998 (L7).
[569] Hutton, 1999. Op. Cit. See footnote 285. p 77 This confirms how everyone, including Ronald Hutton, when writing about Clan matters, have invariably quoted their source as Michael Howard (now deceased), either directly, or indirectly.

Michael Howard made a proposal to E.J.J., suggesting a way to resolve his publication problem. After three years of procrastination, the partnership between E.J.J. and Clifton eventually disintegrated sometime in 1999.

Howard's idea was to correlate the material previously submitted by E.J.J. to *The Cauldron* (specific extracts from his Castle & Cave ms) as articles circa 1995 onwards; to publish them with additional commentary as a means of presenting *The Robert Cochrane Tradition*. Exasperated with failing health, E.J.J. was anxious to see his work reach fruition and the fulfilment of his promise. Frustrated by increased delays, he did not need much persuading from Michael Howard to accept an offer to try his luck with Capall Bann. This he did, and the project moved forwards with Michael Howard. The 'Introduction' E.J.J. had planned so carefully with Clifton, purposefully commissioned for their original project, was replaced with a new introduction written by Michael Howard, the project's new editor. [570]

Just a few months later, E.J.J. was saddened further to receive a letter from Chas Clifton asking if he still wished to move towards publishing. Mysteriously delayed in his obligations, his interest remained strong. Contracted to Capall Bann, E.J.J. had no choice but to decline Clifton's offer.

As a promising venture, *The Roebuck in the Thicket*, was finally published in 2001. It included Cochrane's previous articles salvaged from the *Pentagram*. Strong on editorial opinion, *TRitT* contains several major factual errors and presents a number of unsupported claims. Failing to realise E.J.J.' hopes to affirm the new leaders of Cochrane's Tradition, no-one could have anticipated just how detrimentally that lost opportunity would impact the Clan a decade later. [571] Hindsight offers an unhindered perspective, though its retrospective analysis is a harsh indictment witnessed in real time.

Moving swiftly, Michael Howard and E.J.J. very soon after collaborated on the next publication, *The Robert Cochrane Letters*, which collated the correspondences between Cochrane, Gills, Wilson and Gray. Once again, though E.J.J. was immensely relieved at last

---

[570] John & Julia Day - Capall Bann Publishers - (John Day is now deceased.)
[571] Over a decade later, E.J.J.' original ms eventually found publication in its original totality as *Star Crossed Serpent, Vol. I*, restored & edited by Shani Oates. (Cochrane despised the term 'coven' as Valiente confirms in chapter 8 of *Rebirth of Witchcraft*.)

to have kept his promise to Bill Gray for those works to find public release.

Despite several discussions E.J.J. had with Michael Howard to address the numerous errors and misconceptions of Cochrane's history, E.J.J. was very disappointed to discover that specific errors were stubbornly manifest. Most vexing of all, was the insistent reference to the *Royal Windsor Coven*.

Howard had exercised his authority as editor to determine whether or not the rumour should be included, or denounced as fraudulent. And despite E.J.J.' objections, the publication went ahead with the rumour intact. Aware the rumour had begun some decades after Cochrane's death, E.J.J. was unable to comprehend the full complexity involved in Howard's obsession for false rumour. Although duty to the text was served, E.J.J. was troubled by this and he maintained his rebuttal of those inaccurate comments until his death, just a few months after publication.

Michael Howard had made a bold stance in his introductory piece in *The Roebuck in the Thicket*; he claimed that: *"Cochrane's old coven" was a thing distinct from the "modern Clan of Tubal Cain."* Further to this damning pronouncement, he added a single line comment that E.J.J, as Magister of the Clan had: *"since retired and handed over to younger hands, so the [Clan] tradition will continue into the future."* [572]

Too subtle for many unfamiliar with the actual tradition and its legacy, its slight was not observed or acknowledged until much later. Regretfully, it left the Clan wide open to a series of onslaughts, one after another in the decade that followed E.J.J.' death in 2003.

Tracking down the source of those rumours and errors before he died, was a final concern E.J.J. passed on to his Clan to resolve. A pattern emerged, of connections that leave no margin for doubt. These are reflected and fully supported in Doreen Valiente's Notepads. She too had freely pursued all suspicious activity, especially where they involved Taliesin and Galadriel.[573] Truly, *"where the light shines, the darkest shadows fall around them."*

---

[572] Jones, E.J. *The Roebuck in the Thicket* (Ed.) Michael Howard. (UK: Capall Bann 2001) p 39

[573] These notorious figures feature in Valiente's Notepads. For several years, she followed them, determined to discover their true identities. Her findings are mutually validated by those found by CTC, decades later. These facts have been glossed over and events covered up by others in recent years to disguise the truth.

Investigations initiated by Valiente and E.J.J. into incongruous associations surrounding Cochrane, are incorporated within this Clan history via their own primary sources. CTC have most carefully pursued their directional leads and lines of enquiry. And now, after a turn in the maze, all things return to the centre. Re-reading an early letter from E.J.J., its content is truly illuminating.

> Going back to the original, you sent to me, in the poem, *'I am She as Old as Time,'* this was something I wrote when I first knew Roy. It could only have come from three people, Chalky and George of the Regency, or Bill Gray who would have seen it with Roy. A long way back, Bill let the Finnins photocopy the letters, and 'somehow' they've turned into the tradition of the Royal Windsor Coven. <u>Mike thought all along it was the Finnins who were behind this</u>.
>
> But I had my doubts, putting it down to some others I knew of. Seemingly I was wrong, as the last page of the material now proves. Now comes the interesting bit. At the end of the letter, there is a mention of P/L/ who was at one time, a member of the Roebuck.
>
> Coming to my side of the story now, for years we've had <u>a constant leak of info pertaining to the Clan,</u> then being picked-up from some unusual sources on the way back to me. Now the one thing you can say about Peter is that he gets around, and knows a lot of people, including Mike Howard, who says he can't remember him, and old Doreen, who was a 'good friend' of his, and who only has a vague memory of him. From one or two meetings, they attended at the time.
>
> Having seen your material, especially the little piece at the end, the finger seems to be pointing to Peter as the loose-mouthed source. I don't mind Peter talking, or anything like that, what I object to, <u>is the way it is being used to undermine what I've tried to do over the years, it's just not on</u>. [574]

Contemporary events transpired between members of *The Roebuck* in America that had convinced E.J.J. of a conspiracy.

---

[574] Oates, 2016. Op. Cit. *TM: Legend* Personal Correspondence from EJJ to SLO. Oct. 1998. (EJJ,L6)

Someone known to him in the UK, was liaising with the Finnins to purposefully circulate fantasy as fact. This particular fantasy, related to the notion of a coven that had no existence, and which continued to be a bane to him in his remaining years. When questioned further on this matter, E.J.J.' response was candid:

> Royal Windsor Coven? <u>Certainly not Roy's group</u> and the bloody thing keeps cropping up. Originally, I think it came from the Finnins via Peter Larkworthy. Others have picked it up and it has spread from there. The 'Royal Windsor' material sent to Prof Hutton came from Los Angeles and had been lifted directly from the book of rites I first wrote. I know Peter knows something about this and Mike Howard is sniffing around as well. Sometime in the future, I shall with all sweetness and light, ask Peter what he knows about it, if the sweetness and light doesn't work, I'll try the good old fashioned splinters of burning bamboo under the finger nails. That usually works. If I get hold of more, you'll know. [575]

Despite Prof. Hutton's honourable gesture, the rumour was not quelled. It recurred until it manifested in Monmouth's book: *Genuine Witchcraft is Explained,* en-fleshed there as legend. With all due irony, the alleged existence of the 'secret' coven and its 'secret' name were widely broadcast as a revelation. The real back story had vacillated between exposure and discretion, manipulated retrospectively as necessity demanded of this tall tale. The matter of secrecy for the coven's presumed existence was a grand pretence.

Numerous contradictions within the legend are significantly compromised by compound error and the lack of material evidence. For example: Monmouth insisted that secrecy was so strict that all members were forbidden to acknowledge, refer to, speak of, or write of it, even to each other, not even to themselves in their private and most intimate diaries. Monmouth completely negated this maxim in an extraordinary online Interview, in which he described how this allegedly secret coven was not only *open to guests, but that they all contributed to the creation of its praxis!* [576]

---

[575] Oates, 2016. Op. Cit. *TM: Legend* Personal Correspondence from EJJ to SLO. Oct. 98 (EJJ, L7): (F-10) and (L15)
[576] You Tube Interview with Karagan. See *The Secret History of the Royal Windsor Coven & the Regency* with John of Monmouth.' '9 Sep 2012 - Uploaded by WitchtalkShow https://www.youtube.com/watch?v=WpAAmBpF0Us

This remarkable tale has raised important factors that need address. First of all there is *no material evidence* whatsoever for the flurry of creativity Monmouth claims the open 'secret' coven generated. Those texts allegedly written by those 'guests' to support this fantastic claim have not been found or provided for investigation. It is a fair assumption to state they do not exist.

As for non-textual evidence, such as advice, or information shared that may have contributed to elements of praxis. This is of course possible, though if that is accepted, then the claim for secrecy is lost. Such an extreme level of secrecy is in contradistinction with the claim that guests could contribute to 'secret' rituals for an allegedly secret coven! How can a group of people forbidden to acknowledge each other, accept guests into their midst and then, allow them to write rituals for a coven that every person within it must again deny exits, even to each other! These are immensely significant irregularities.

In every instance asserted or claimed, the base line premise has been overlooked. The simple fact of the matter is that *no-one else* except E.J.J. was authorised to continue Cochrane's Tradition after his death in 1966. Any attempt to do so, by deed of action, speech, or writing, is not undertaken legitimately. Without official sanction, all pretentions must be rejected by default.

The factual history of CTC has never been secret. It is well documented, publicised, shared, written about and commented upon when everyone concerned was still alive, including Ronald White. Faced with the wealth of fact and evidence that are sufficient to bury all rumour, the means by which the fallacy thrives must be exposed.

Since Cochrane's death, his few surviving written works, were hastily set down in irregular and often contradictory form *by others,* together with what endured in memory, to preserve them for personal exploration. To some extent, those perspectives have coloured the records, sometimes quite dramatically, and certainly to their detriment.

Conflicting ideas, extrapolated from these diverse sources, found their way to America, before returning to our native shores totally transformed. Embraced again in a new era, they found favour with those unaware the works are far removed from any genuine or original source. Where such presumptions are encountered, the genuine seeker is well-advised to disregard them without further consideration. Instead, they should consult official sources for factual information concerning *The Robert Cochrane Tradition*.

As a self-declared *Od's* man, Cochrane was fascinated by the runic vowels of the *aetts*, and explored their instruction relative to the sacred trees of our ancestors. Extreme cosmogonies are evident, exhibited as factions exemplified in the Wican/ neo-Pagan versus old Craft divide. Attempting to reconcile these widely opposing views in order to categorise them for academia, one study observes how marked this incongruence is manifest:

> Cochrane's Craft is now a magico-religious tradition that is divided along theological lines starker than the Catholic-Protestant divide within Western Christianity. [577]

This is almost true! Both E.J.J. and Cochrane likewise expressed with absolute clarity, their Tradition is not pagan, neo-Pagan, or 'Celtic/Keltic.'

A Cuckoo in the Nest

From the beginning E.J.J had stated with absolute conviction that we all; "*sooner or later find what we need rather than what we want.*" [578] As a mentor E.J.J. stated that everything of worth is coveted, and anything that is worth stealing, is equally, worth fighting for. No-one could ever have foreseen how the Clan would be called upon to defend what it had been given to hold – and so many times; though it is stronger and wiser for it.

In the late summer of 2003, just weeks before his death, E.J.J.' made his final official Clan visit to the Hearth which coincided with the Induction into the Clan of a former student of Marian Green. The young man received a special blessing from E.J.J. personally, a memorable occasion also witnessed by all Clan members. And as with all matters of fate, this event was marked with

---

[577] Ethan Doyle White *An Elusive Roebuck* –www.ethandoylewhite.blogspot.com
[578] Oates, 2016. Op. Cit. *TM:Legend* Personal Correspondence from EJJ to SLO. Sept. 1998 (L20)

particular significance. Soon after, almost as soon as E.J.J.' death was made public in August 2003, provocations from across the pond begin with earnest as Dave Finnin went online declaring himself the Magister of Tubal Cain.

Before a suitable response was generated, others had intervened, denouncing it completely. E.J.J.' widow and his daughter authoritatively repudiated the Finnins false claim, making it clear to them and others observing these events, that E.J.J. had appointed Robin-the-dart and Shani Oates with that authority,- none other.

In addition to learning of this incident from E.J.J.' widow and daughter, the Clan received a letter from Michael Howard. His missives commonly served as a media for sowing the seeds of discontent. Similar letters went to the Finnins, and many others too, each slightly different, and all designed for maximum mischief. Insisting on involvement, Howard reiterated the following:

> V. Jones tells me that they have had to correct the Finnins who published an obituary of John on their website. Apparently Dave Finnin has been claiming to be the Magister of the Clan of Tubal Cain, which is ironic as they didn't even get a proper initiation from John! [579]

The incident had been dealt with by the appropriate people and as a Clan matter, was not his concern. Though he was at liberty to denounce the Finnins, given the information E.J.J. had shared with him. But he did not. Notwithstanding the presence of enmity within the history of those once adopted as Clan across the pond, CTC's recent efforts to re-establish their allegiance to the Hearth, fuelled only further enmity and disappointing failure. The hand of friendship was not reciprocated, and the hope of their renewed allegiance was not won.

Shifting back a few years, to the previously mentioned visit by E.J.J. to the Clan's new Hearth in Sheffield in May 1999, the People of Goda Clan were summoned to witness a rare and auspicious rite. From E.J.J., Clan Magister since Cochrane's death in 1966, an historical gift of stewardship was passed to another,

---

[579] Michael Howard 2003. Personal Correspondence. 23rd November.

according to Clan Law. The journey brought him from Brighton to ritually hallow the new Hearth and complete all he'd set in motion privately a few months previously in the Autumn of 1998.

Through the *Old Covenant*, the next Head-Kinsmen of the Clan were charged to continue the *Robert Cochrane Tradition.*' His blessing declared Shani Oates as Clan Matriarch (and Seeress/Maid) and Robin-the-dart, as Tanist, the next Magister to be, to serve and uphold the honour of our *People of Goda, of the Clan of Tubal Cain.*

It was important to re-iterate this, because in order to affirm this momentous occasion, Evan John Jones had to inform all the old Craft families and relevant people in the occult and Craft world. This included Cochrane's widow (the former Clan Matriarch and Maid) and Doreen Valiente, both of whom granted their auspicious blessings. Several others were notified, including Michael Howard and Prof. Hutton.

Thereafter, he was visited often in Brighton by the Clan, at his family home. His health was failing fast, and the journey to Yorkshire had taxed him sorely. The new Head-Kinsmen preferred a discreet Craft presence, one that focussed on the task ahead, of the work and of gaining the experience to understand what was needed of them. A few years later, E.J.J. requested an interview for publication in *The Cauldron* magazine to make it widely known who he and Cochrane's widow had authorised to singularly continue *The Robert Cochrane Tradition* – CTC.

Evan John Jones and Shani Oates 1999

The Interview was published just a few months before his death.[580] In it, E.J.J. declared that if the continuity of that legacy *'had not happened,'* then that Tradition would fold with him and cease to be – there was simply no-one else he trusted or believed capable of continuing the Clan legacy. It is that simple. One of the things that E.J.J. sensed most acutely, was the destructive element within a community of people. He was all too familiar with the damage an unbalanced or malicious person can do from within and without. Having witnessed it when Cochrane was alive, he quickly realised there was one such person within the Clan whose presence was on sufferance alone.

He understood the extenuating circumstances for that, and how destructive the fallout is in their removal, how damaging for all concerned. He recalled all too vividly, the deep, personal grief that had shattered the Clan back in the 1960s. His support and guidance through the process that brought *'the person of conflict'* towards eventual expulsion, remains a valued life-lesson.

There was a cuckoo in the midst. As a member of the Clan, C.J. had been identified by E.J.J. as the malignant presence that needed to be repelled. Before her expulsion from the Clan could be achieved, time was needed to bolster against the consequences. The extent of her manipulative and unscrupulous activities required careful manoeuvring to ensure her threats to Clan members were rendered impotent. Their safety from the harm her behaviour threatened was paramount, a primary duty in fact. Though E.J.J. had hoped to see it carried out, that day did not arrive until two years after E.J.J.' death. It had been a waiting game.

In another time, things would have been dealt with very differently. Stealth, cunning, and kenning were the gifts of patience, and E.J.J. had taught their value well. Waiting for the right moment was an arte recognised 'in fate.' Even so, E.J.J.' frustration occasionally spilled out into his correspondence. Here are just a few extracts from E.J.J.' letters that confirm his directives relevant to C.J.'s (aka CSJ) unacceptable incidents.

---

[580] *The Cauldron.* # 109. February. See archived posts at www.clanoftubalcain.org.uk

Well, if you feel like reading C**** the riot act, fine, but don't be all that surprised if it doesn't sometime in the future [fail], promises like pie-crusts, are made to be broken. [581]

When C**** starts again, just point out to her that the Clan Law states, *"To the Master you owe duty under the law. To the Maid, total allegiance in all things."* Now if C**** cannot live with that, then tell her to F*** off pronto, as the rest of you have no time or inclination to deal with her tantrums. The last thing you need is someone fermenting trouble, it's far too corrosive. [582]

Make sure C**** does stick by the law this time, she has already cost you one good person who you could ill afford to lose, and make sure she understands that next time, it'll be 'Bell, Book and Candle in spades,' if she doesn't! The last thing you need is people being driven away by her. [583]

Bell, Book and Candle it was in 2005! All in accordance with Clan Law. Observing old craft protocols, CTC informed various craft persons of the occult and pagan community to be aware, and in this particular person's case, beware. Retaliation was expected, that inevitability was the reason for her expulsion. A great many personal details of that person's misdeeds and extraordinary activities have been omitted in this account; they do not add anything to the facts. Those details, some by her own hand, remain within Clan archives, including the podcast she made in 2008.

That date signified the launch of herself and her new partner, M.B.I. in their attempt to usurp CTC's authority with their carefully orchestrated fraud. A brief outline is sufficient for the understanding and reckoning of this brief inclusion in this biographical Clan history.

Between her expulsion in 2005 and her media outburst in 2008, she'd used her time to lay the ground with bitter seeds, spreading poison and falsehood, lie upon lie. Those deeply personal and equally false unpleasantries serve no good purpose to repeat here.

---

[581] Oates, 2016. Op. Cit. *TM: Legend* Personal Correspondence from EJJ to S.L.O. 2000 (L17) plus (EJJ,L24:CJ-1)
[582] Oates, 2016. Op. Cit. Personal Correspondence from EJJ to SLO. 2001. (L18) and (EJJ, L25: CJ-2)
[583] Oates, 2016. Op. Cit. Personal Correspondence from EJJ to SLO. 2002. (L19) and (EJJ, L 26:CJ-3)

Then, Michael Howard informed CTC via email that a person named C. J. and her partner M. B. I. were due to appear on a podcast. Hosted by his friend Peter Paddon, it was set-up to launch C.J.' claims that she had been deposed in 2001, by her 'upstart protégé', that she was the 'real' Maid of CTC, and that M.B.I. was her newly appointed Magister [584]

At that point, the Clan discovered that she had been working in the shadows for years, even before her exile, informing those she encountered in Craft circles that she was the real 'Maid.' Her bitter claim was but one more example of behaviour not unknown within the Craft. However, an attack upon known and accepted persons of authority, should always be approached critically and with due caution. If that procedure is not followed, then everyone is vulnerable, left defenceless against slander. Common sense should always prevail. And once again, it did not.

No-one observed the requisite protocols in response to their incredible claims. Once alerted, Elders of the Craft community should have tackled the matter officially and as discreetly as possible, prior to any media event. Then, if a media event was unavoidable, it should have been **CTC** Paddon hosted, not C.J. and M.B.I. to expose them as foolish pretenders. Because this did not happen, the public, confused and on the outside of these Clan matters, failed to offer their support. To them, C. J.' and M. B. I.' launch and acceleration through media channels, unchallenged by Craft Elders, implied a validity to their claims.

At the time, the Clan had not expected her to receive the publicity and support she did for her vicious attack. In retrospect, the reason they went so far without impedance is simple. No-one properly understood the issue and its exposure was unprecedented. Everyone underestimated the brevity of the situation as C.J. and M.B.I spread confusion and controversy with their false allegations. They led everyone to believe it was nothing more than petty in-fighting between egos, The facts of the matter were lost to theatre.

Morbid curiosity, the fascination others find in controversy is a strange and overwhelming media beast. It was surprisingly easy. No-one challenged her; no-one questioned the veracity of her claim.

---

[584] Though unnamed here for obvious reasons, their identities and profiles are easily found online, through our own websites and those of 1734, various forums and FB pages.

No-one asked the question that if her grievance was genuine, or why it was that E.J.J. had done nothing about it, or why she had waited until after his death?

If her claim had been true, and again, such things are known in the Craft, then usurping E.J.J.' chosen Matriarch and Maid was a grave concern, a matter he would certainly have wished to resolve face-to-face. Indeed, the perfect opportunity to present her alleged case arose during E.J.J.' final visit just weeks before his death in 2003, at the Induction he attended in Sheffield. The reason she did not, is again simple, her fictional back-story had not yet been created.

Over the 18 months that followed their brazen podcast, several people became involved in C.J.' and M.B.I.' excessive self-publicising promos and posturing; some even joined in the insidious slur campaign they launched against CTC. Others watched their performance, agog, confused, uncertain, unable to judge fact from fiction. Somewhat perplexed by this, and by the ambivalence of other people in the Craft, and of their lack of critical thinking, it was soon realised that media opinion was being influenced to the detriment of truth. An authoritative finger on the pulse is able to manipulate matters to their advantage. This is a primal lesson and not new to our times.

Initially, CTC had no means to combat their excessive and immature media attacks. CTC's former discreet workings had not required an online presence. Confident that enough people knew the truth, the matter was sure to run its course. People would soon get past the sensationalist behaviour and begin to think rationally, perhaps even begin to ask them questions. For some reason, this also did not happen.

The official declaration was made by E.J.J. a few years prior to this recent incident which had named the legitimate Clan Leaders, amongst his peers in the Craft. These included Chas Clifton with whom he'd wished to promote that continuity in his planned publication, and Michael Howard, whose magazine *The Cauldron* published the official announcement that should have been sufficient to expose C. J.' and M. B. I.' as frauds. And yet it did not. That these two people were nowhere mentioned in any official media, nor rang alarms, suggests disconcerting co-operation in its orchestration.

Since 1998, CTC had discreetly published books, articles, held Interviews and lectured on Clan and Craft matters. In the media frenzy, these were easily forgotten, as was E.J.J.' final testament, which had been no secret. It seems CTC's media status was severely compromised by having kept a low profile.

Concerns grew as it became apparent that someone was aiding C.J. and M.B.I.' attempt to diminish CTC's status and influence. For C.J. and M.B.I. to have been catapulted so far, so quickly without any supporting evidence, they were obviously supported by people of influence and with the right contacts to promote them. Had there been greater public knowledge about how Clans and Traditional Craft operate, that media storm could never have begun. As stated, historical precedent and logic demand that, when someone steps forward to pose a challenge to an pre-established and accepted figure of authority, the burden of proof – always *falls upon the challenger* to reveal grounds for any just cause or right to make those audacious claims, or else be dismissed immediately as imposters and charlatans.

No *established* person of influence or social standing is normally called upon to defend *their* position with provenances against their detractors. That authority is pre-disposed, accepted on the merit and fact of their *existing* position. Media hyperbole nonetheless ignored those protocols. A decade of authority was ignored, cast aside in favour of controversy.

To add insult to injury. CTC were called upon to defend *its* legitimacy, when that onus should have been placed entirely upon C.J. and M.B.I. to reveal the alleged proofs of claims to a status nowhere declared as theirs. They say that a lie gets half-way around the world before truth even gets her boots on. This has proven to be true in this case; there are no greater 'truths' or 'facts' than those held in public opinion. Falsehoods become embedded far too quickly.

Eventually, a rational man of laudable integrity, Stuart Inman, recognised that if C. J. and M. B. I. wished their claim to stand, then proofs *were* indeed needed by them.[585] After CTC had shared all the relevant background with him, he was quickly able to confirm how foundless C. J. and M. B. I.' entire fiction had been.

---

[585] The Cuckoo's Nest www.1734_witchcraft.org.uk

They did not disappear quickly or quietly, but issued an unrepeatable tirade of abuse.

With little other support from peers and Craft Elders, CTC stood almost alone. Despite requests made by CTC to Michael Howard, he declined to foreclose the situation. At the time his (self) acclaimed support appeared in confusingly ambiguous comments on his two forums, curious remarks that were subtle but damning in the long term. Publically, he stated that: *"He could not be seen to be involved, and must remain impartial."* [586] Lacking that impartiality in reality, his statement went unchallenged by all but CTC members.

Remembering that E.J.J. had informed Howard directly as to who he'd appointed as leaders of the Clan, Howard was in a privileged position to ensure the truth was widely disseminated. Aware of E.J.J.' former intention to publicize that information in Clifton's book, he could so easily have persuaded his good friend Peter Paddon to withhold hosting their podcast, at least until they were able to bring proofs to support their wild claims against CTC. Needless to say, he did not. [587]

As is often the case in these situations, certain individuals entirely motivated by self-interest, typically see an opportunity to raise their own profiles in the media. To that end, a handful of people were eager to promote C.J. and M.B.I. in two UK publications. - *The Pentacle* and *Pagan Dawn*. The editor of *The Pentacle*, at that time was Jon Randall. He allowed C.J. and M.B.I. to

---

[586] An odd comment. That same reticence was not extended in all other matters within the media eye. That 'impartiality' was never manifest on any forum post when he challenged CTC members. That same tenacity and forcefulness was never directed towards C.J. and M.B.I. Howard's few words of support were chosen very carefully, and very cleverly placed, and always to further the notion of the 'Clan' as E.J.J.' heirs, specifically, having no part in Cochrane's fictional Coven as the alleged repository of Cochrane's tradition. Howard used the media to mark his distinction between Clan (CTC), which he publically supported as E.J.J.', and Cochrane's Tradition, which he constantly challenged CTC members on. Howard became increasingly hostile when CTC were able to furnish proofs these were and have always been one and the same thing. After E.J.J.' death, Howard began to openly undermine and provoke CTC, leaving only the challenges witnessed on forums etc. CTC were forced to defend its position and Tradition. An extremely derisory, petty, book review against the publication, *SCSI*, by Shani Oates appeared 'anonymously' in the *Pagan Dawn*, repeated identically in *The Pentacle*. But in that latter magazine, the editor unfortunately left the name 'Gwyn' attached. Gwyn is the known pseudonym used by Michael Howard (a name acknowledged by Monmouth in GWiE and by Howard). When asked pointedly on the 1734 forum if he was the author of that review as 'Gwyn,' Howard declined to answer. Howard finally revealed his true opinion of CTC, manifesting his polemic in Children of Cain.

[587] This podcast #100 can still be found on the internet. CTC have an archived Disc copy. It is available for research.

publish their mission statement claiming to be the real CTC. That act further extended media involvement with the controversy .

When Randall was approached with testimonies from Clan members and associates of E.J.J.', with evidence to expose C.J. and M.B.I.' as frauds; he refused them even 'the right to respond.' Having already expressed significant support for *the pretenders*, Randall published an additional inflammatory piece of slander against Shani Oates and Robin-the-dart.[588]

His character, summarised by another who knew him well described him as an unsavoury person and *'a well - known con-man whose widely professed knowledge came entirely from Llewellyn publications.'* The Clan later learned of a reciprocal arrangement for his perjury. He'd received a Wiccan initiation from C. J. at Burnham Beeches, something he'd apparently long coveted, and pretended on occasion to already have.[589] Thankfully, both *The Pentacle* and *The Pagan Dawn* have new editors, from whom CTC has received gracious apologies.

Of the several witness statements and testimonies Randall declined to print, one came from a Clan member wishing to vouch for E.J.J.' presence at his own aforementioned Induction Rite held in 2003. Describing that very personal ceremony, he was able to provide an eye-witness account of the correct, factual hierarchy and office of all concerned. He confirmed the singular acknowledgement of Shani Oates by Evan John Jones as the Clan Matriarch and Maid, and that E.J.J. in accordance with Clan Law, upholds <u>one</u> Maid only as the Matriarch of her Clan. To that end, E.J.J., had neither appointed nor recognised any other.

He also verified that C.J. had been present at his Induction Rite, and that her status was observed and acknowledged by E.J.J. as *a member only*. His understanding of these matters made it known in no uncertain terms, that the person in question, C.J., was blatantly lying. [590] His incontestable testimony was fully supported by all Clan members, not to mention E.J.J' previous accounts.

Other matters fed that gulf. Though unnecessary to elaborate upon here, they remain legion. Due to copyright laws, a brief quotation only from C. J.' podcast and her own published works is

---

[588] Jon Randall, now deceased.
[589] Ken Rees. 2017. Op. Cit. Private Correspondence. Imbolc.
[590] See #36 in the Appendices. This person *was not* the very kind Marion Pearce but Jon Randall (now deceased). Please see Martin White's Letter to the Editor in the Scans within TM:Legend.

possible. A published letter written by C.J. in 2003 contradicts later claims presented in her 2008 podcast, affirming her perjury. Her self-incriminating claims made in 2008 that E.J.J. first appointed her as his Maid, and that she made Robin-the-dart her Magister, are particularly noted. Setting credulity aside for the moment, C.J. had overlooked a flippant comment, a quip to her ego within her 2003 response to an article against Cochrane that had offended her.

Published in 'The Cauldron,' 2003, she'd boasted of her *own Induction into the Clan*. Commenting initially on her own status as a (Wiccan) High Priestess, she emphasised her prestige as being the one to bring Robin-the-dart into the stream of Wicca. She announced her own authority to speak from the Cochrane Tradition as an *Inducted member* of the Clan *brought in by Robin-the-dart* – its Magister. She wrote:

> Robert's [Cochrane's] leadership was a divine gift, this applies equally to the present Magister, a man of extraordinary humility and quiet depth, <u>who welcomed me into his family in turn.</u> [591]

Because this was actually true, it was something that all Clan members, including E.J.J. reading in *The Cauldron* in 2003 would consider exactly in accord with the facts. After all, E.J.J. had not appointed C.J. in any capacity, he had not even brought her into the Clan, as stated above, Robin-the-dart did that. Just as C.J. had *not* been the one to bring Robin-the-dart into the Clan or appoint him as Magister. The only person qualified in status and with the authority in Clan law to appoint anyone, was Shani Oates.[592] Having forgotten about this previous 2003 article, she'd damned her own gambit in 2008.

C.J.' later claims and retractions were fabricated to comply with the new narrative. They presented nothing more than a wishful expression of her fantastic ambitions. In 2008, she claimed that in 2001, that is two years before she had written the above article, Shani Oates secretly deposed her, without protest or opposition to them or E.J.J! Reminded (in 2009), of the article written in 2003, C.J.

---

[591] #109 The Cauldron - August 2003. CJ' response to 'Barry Bow'
[592] Shani Oates, as Clan matriarch did this under advisement and acknowledgment from E.J.J., who jointly held the authority of Magister with Robin-the-dart at that time. Upon E.J.J.' death later that year, Robin-the-dart assumed that full title.

amended her claim to declare that in 2003, she had been forced under duress to write the article published in *The Cauldron*.

Putting aside the impossibility that a legitimate Matriarch of the Clan could be so easily deposed, she had momentarily forgotten E.J.J.' place in this equation.[593] Unable to think fast enough, she overlooked the fact that E.J.J., knowing who he'd appointed to that position, had read that article in 2003, and naturally found nothing untoward in it. Meaning that, because it was an accurate account, C.J.' fantastic excuse of being forced to write it, was a lie! Robin-the-dart was indeed the Magister who brought her into the Clan as a member. Every comment entrenched her further in deceit.[594]

Logic presumes that had she been forced to abdicate, or write these falsehoods, E.J.J. would have responded appropriately to that article by banishing Oates and re-instating C.J. Obviously that did not happen as the entire drama was fallacious fiction.

To counter this, C.J. threw another measure of confusion with the next claim that there were three separate Clans, with three separate maids heading them, all autonomous and all called CTC. For this she garnered the support of the Finnins, who shared a mutual interest and benefit in that fiction.[595]

At that vital point, the E.J.J.'s widow attempted to put these matters straight. V.J. wrote separately afterwards to Shani Oates, expressing concerns that she had been unable to right those wrongs, especially as her insights and advice asked for by Michael Howard, *had been ignored by him*. Responding somewhat apprehensively to Howard's request for verification of information he'd been provided with by E.J.J. years previously, V.J. was initially uncertain as to his motivation. Howard had involved her quite unnecessarily. It was insensitive. Unsettled since E.J.J.' death, V.J., his widow, had wished only to be left in peace. Her distress is implicit in this letter to Clan:

---

[593] See E.J.J. letter to SLO, in which he informs her that *no-one* can remove the Maid appointed under the Old Covenant, not even the Magister. She is the Matriarch and supreme head of the Clan. Hers is the only non-elective or renewable position. EJJ to SLO. Oct. 1998. (EJJ, L6 and L7)

[594] Peter Paddon (now deceased) had spear-headed a hate campaign against CTC on his Crooked-Path Forum, supporting both the Finnins and CJ & MBI's unwarranted and entirely unprovoked attack on the Clan and its singular authority. Before his own death, he was a very good friend of Michael Howard (also deceased). His forum and the transcripts and comments may be viewed on web archived searches.

[595] Their alliance was short-lived, and very soon fell to in-fighting. They parted acrimoniously. C.J. and M.B.I, likewise, soon after.

> I have heard of your former member causing trouble. Mike Howard has also been in touch with me over this. I will tell you, exactly what I told him. At no point has this person ever been in touch with John. She never met him or corresponded with him. [596] (VJ,L1:CJ-4)

There is no ambiguity in this letter. Michael Howard forwarded a copy of his letter from V.J.' onto Stuart Inman. Paraphrasing the information from it, Howard instructed Inman to use it when deemed appropriate and to *quote himself as the source*. Given that this information was neither new, nor unique to him, it was a strange request and served no *obvious* purpose. Howard's directive had quoted himself as the person in correspondence with E.J.J.' widow. Everything was engineered to steer the central authority in all things concerning Robert Cochrane, *away* from CTC. Howard's letter to Stuart Inman conveyed this message:

> Evan John Jones' wife has told me she has never heard of C****J****. She also tells me that the only *members of the Gardnerian coven* in Derbyshire who visited them in Brighton was Shani and her husband, and that John eventually passed to them the 'knife and cup.' Therefore, the only legitimate Maid and Magister of the Clan of Tubal Cain as chosen and appointed by Evan John Jones and Robert Cochrane's widow are Shani Oates and her husband. This confirms a conversation I had with John *when I visited him during the research for the books on Cochrane*. I had forwarded on Shani's introductory letter to him after she'd read his articles in TC, and he told me she was the 'Chosen One' and the person he wanted to be the Maid of CTC after he died. [597]

Though it may appear supportive, initial impressions can deceive. Howard does not deny who the legitimate leaders of CTC are, but he does sidestep it with a very clever caveat. The comments are full of incongruous detail; a sub text is implicit that in no sense lends support to Shani Oates and Robin-the-dart as bearers of *The Robert Cochrane Tradition*. On the contrary.

---

[596] Oates, 2016. Op. Cit. *TM:Legend* Personal Correspondence from VJ to SLO. 2008(L20)
V.J. regarded the intrusion particularly tactless and lacking in purpose. It had coincided at a time of deep personal grief and trauma.
[597] Copy of letter to Stuart Inman from Michael Howard. 2/7/2008. Three months had passed since Paddon's US Crooked Path Podcast 100. Media hype was at its height.

In blending selected facts such as E.J.J.' edict that Shani Oates *'is the Chosen One and the person he wanted to be Maid of CTC,'* with casual comments regarding Shani Oates and Robin-the-dart as the *'only members of the Gardnerian coven,'* to visit E.J.J, Howard's tactic is clear.

This manipulation presented a very false impression about everything concerned with CTC, who they, are, what they are, what they are working, and what all of that means. Every line of Howard's text was designed to affirm his own image and authority relative to Robert Cochrane, while equally distancing CTC's from Robert Cochrane. Howard's carefully worded (passive – aggressive) stance confirms that intention.

Several unnecessary inclusions were presented in his commentary above, details absent in V.J.' quoted comment. She does not refer to Wica, or Gardner, to a coven in Derbyshire, nor any other personal detail he laid emphasis upon. Howard insinuated that as Wiccans, Shani Oates and Robin-the-dart were somehow disqualified as authorities on Cochrane or his Tradition, and that he was better placed to be that authority.

Assigning emphasis on *"when I visited him* [E.J.J.] *during the research for the books on Cochrane,"* Howard did not acknowledge E.J.J. as an authority on Cochrane. Rather, he proffers himself as that authority, and in that capacity, called to see E.J.J. as one amongst many people in the course of putting the books together. In fact, E.J.J. *was the primary and central source* for the books referred to that Howard edited. Without E.J.J., those books would not have been written or published.

One other facet to this sentence is relevant, and that is that by stressing his research on 'Cochrane,' Howard deliberately omitted to mention CTC, thereby removing any connection between Cochrane and CTC. He then made explicit reference to CTC in terms of it being something E.J.J. was involved with alone, disconnected from Cochrane. In turn Shani Oates and Robin-the-dart were likewise, involved in CTC, not with Cochrane.

Finally, the implication is that *CTC is a Wiccan Coven.* By referring to Shani Oates and Robin-the-dart as Gardnerians, he implied that the separate, Wiccan Coven C.J. was HPS of, was the one set up as CTC. Altogether Howard's expansive comments, though completely in error on all counts, speak volumes about how he wished *E.J.J. and CTC,* to be perceived. His efforts to alienate them from possible supporters amongst Wiccans and Traditional Crafters with this tactic almost worked.

Wica had never been an issue for E.J.J. nor for other members of the Clan. Being on good terms with people of widely different practises, including Wica, and having respect for their traditions has no bearing on the legitimacy of the leaders of CTC. CTC cannot be separated from *The Robert Cochrane Tradition*, they are one and the same.

CTC realised it could stay in the shadows no longer, nor quiet, it needed to be heard. Fate intervened when another couple, who were long-term, but troubled members of Ann and Dave Finnins' *Roebuck Coven* and *The Ancient Keltic Church* in the USA, decided that upon consideration of all the recently uncovered facts, they needed to move away from the Finnins. Seeking truth, they acted on the facts and formed *The Coven of the Ram*, a kindred, satellite coven, legitimately affiliated to CTC.

In addition to their staunch support, they gifted the Clan a much needed gateway to the net. They constructed an official website presence, a media platform for factual information to be disseminated to all interested parties. Connected to the internet at last, CTC set about that task, and a brief history of circumstances and events were posted there. Over the next year, C.J.'s ploy was vanquished. Open conflict with them had been avoided. All that needed to be done, was done.

The controversy posed by C.J. and M.B.I. had simply dumbfounded everyone. Public understanding of how real Traditional Craft operates, and how distinct the Clan system is to any form of Wicca, was obviously something CTC needed to address. This charade remains a grim factor in CTC's history, an unpleasant memory, and a reminder how easily a lie can be promoted in cyberspace, and how vulnerable and credulous people can be. Too few exhibit critical thinking, or even a desire to follow common sense and logic. As an occult and folk alternative to Wica/Wicca, familiarity with its Ethos was sorely needed.

Destructive forces are perhaps the greatest enemy of community, decimating trust and belief. As old as humankind, this is nothing new. As a species, we have become no wiser to it over the course of evolution and civilisation. CTC survived the challenge, but not all who accompanied them did; burned along the way, some chose different paths, of quieter spiritualties.

Media Sorcery

Just as all the dust was settling from this folly, CTC were contacted by David V Barratt who was completing a book on religions and cults. He wanted CTC to approve a piece he'd written on the Clan. It could not have been more wrong on every count; it was little more than sensationalist gossip, presented as fact. Mr Barratt was asked who had provided him with such poor information, and that CTC wished to replace it with real facts. That advice was rejected in favour of another source. The only recourse was to decline the permission to publish, but Barratt responded with an assurance that he would not hold back the specious material.

His summary of *The Robert Cochrane Tradition,* featured in one of his series of books on secret religions, societies and cults, exactly typifies the inherent errata of the popular presses. [598] Following the advice of his undisclosed source, Barrett described CTC's Tradition as pseudo-Wiccan in its praxis, and its mythos as inspired largely by the presentation of the White Goddess in Robert Graves' volume of the same name.

Barratt denied the Clan its right self-define its own Ethos, a premise granted to *every other system* noted in his book. That was not the only distinction. Barratt compared the factionalising elements of the Bahá'í Faith to that of CTC, a mode of analysis he did not apply to other traditions covered in his book. CTC was the exception. Barrett completely ignored all contrary advice. Barratt's comment fully supported the fiction of the '*Three Clans of Tubal Cain,*' (sic) and the three versions of its history, asserting that the 'clan' headed by Shani Oates is out of step with the two other 'clans' (sic), which have an accord. He states only that: "*Some of its details are disputed by <u>one</u> of the three clans of Tubal Cain.*" (sic). [599]

---

[598] Barrett, V. David. *A Brief Guide to Secret Religions* (UK: Robinson, 2011) pages 303-8
[599] Barrett, V. David. *A Brief Guide to Secret Religions* (UK: Robinson, 2011) pages 303-8

CTC's attempt to explain to Barrett that the information provided by them is well recorded by both Cochrane and Jones, and therefore in full accord with legitimate, original sources, makes his disinterest all the more curious. Backed by historical facts regarding Clanships, explanations were provided as to why the notions presented by the false claimants represented a travesty of Clan law, and that it was impossible to have three maids and *'three clans.'* [600] Barratt simply rejected everything without consideration.

As an academic writer, an impartial, critical explanation from him, at the very least, might have observed instead, a reference to a Clan as a singular entity, citing each as: *'one of the three groups all claiming to be CTC.'* It is disappointing that his interest in the subject did not merit thorough research, and that he preferred to accept poor advice from his other source. That he declined to include information and evidence from CTC as a primary source, especially where it related to *why* it is an impossibility to have three Clans sharing the *same* title, remains a matter of concern.

Ultimately, all Barratt chose to include of the textual verifications and information submitted to him, was a selected extract, presented without its qualifying context. Used with deliberation, the snippet was the expression Shani Oates had shared within a significant explanation, which he declined to add. He cited the part where she had said there could be: *"Only one Clan."* [601] His redaction served its purpose well. Published without its essential justification, its use added credibility to the defamation asserted by Howard, M.B.I. and Paddon that Shani Oates is a *'megalomaniac.'*

Having ignored better intelligence from prominent members of CTC, he presented all *'three clans and maids'* equally, without qualification of legitimacy on any level. With regard to the subject brief relative to secret religions and beliefs, the following descriptions convey a summarised account of the intent each of the three notable persons submitted to Barratt:

---

[600] The only historical exception to this, removes autonomy of any individual clan that seeks shelter within another clan. It becomes subservient to a single Head-Kinsman overall, oath bound in recognition of that Head-Kinsman as their liege lord. This means that Multiple Clans do not exist alongside each other as separate independent entities if one name is shared by all three. That concept is an oxymoron. One name= one clan, of which there can be only one Head- Kinsman!

[601] Barrett, V. David. *A Brief Guide to Secret Religions* (UK: Robinson, 2011) pages 303-8

- In keeping with his directive, CTC offered a supplement that relayed CTC's none Pagan tenets, its lore, and law particularly, as principles of its belief within a Craft historicity. Barratt ignored this.

- Ignoring his directive, C. J focussed entirely on her personal ambitions within the Clan, asserting an erroneous autonomy for each 'clan' to excuse her own actions. Barratt included this.

- Ignoring his directive, Ann Finnin also spoke on a personal level, deriding the teachings of their mentor, by insinuating that what he'd shared with them, *'was not in accord with Robert Cochrane's views but his own.'* She cited the masked rites by way of example. As echoes from a 'good authority' those same words were repeated everywhere. Barratt included this.

Barrett's bias is all too evident in his summary where he asks: *"What is the real Clan of Tubal Cain?"* [602] Resilient to any contrary persuasion, Barratt's conclusion is quite remarkable, all the more so because he was an outsider, not privy to any pertinent knowledge, and lacking the authority to convey it. Having rejected all accounts from prominent legitimate Clan members, Barratt posited that their version of the beliefs of Robert Cochrane's Tribe (sic) were arrived at through E.J.J.' teachings, declaring they:

> Have developed so far away from the 1980s version (E.J.J. shared with the Finnins), that they include Gnostic Luciferian ideas.

This comment strangely echoes that frequently espoused by Michael Howard, whose views CTC have been forced to defend itself against repeatedly on line and more recently throughout their published works. CTC have ably dismissed this fallacy, citing referenced links back to the beginning of Cochrane's works.

Barratt ignored this, giving his opinion that CTC's views are extreme, which he implies do not originate with Cochrane. To support that view, he quotes Ann Finnin's rejection of genuine Clan praxes, relative to hers, believing they exhibit: *"Serious doctrinal issues."*

---

[602] Barrett, V. David. *A Brief Guide to Secret Religions* (UK: Robinson. 2011) 303-8

[603] They do, but not as implied, nor why. E.J.J. made it quite clear in his directives to the Finnins it was they who exhibited those issues: *"All the trouble seems to hinge around the fact that what you call the Clan, and what Roy called the Clan, are two different things."* [604]

Having little else to say on the matter, Barrett merely reiterates his opinion, that, in common with minor religious Cults, this typifies a *schism* within *The Robert Cochrane Tradition*.[605] CTC absolutely reject this; his conclusion presents the gravest error. Barrett's definition is seriously flawed academically and historically.

The Tenets of a (family) Clan Tradition may not be defined as *'a Cult.'* Nothing *within* a Clan Tradition, can be separated from itself, nor shared as multiples of itself, all with the same named title. A Clan is not diminished when members leave. Once they have left, they are no longer Clan. Because of this, it is not possible for a schism to occur.

The two other groups claiming the authority and aegis of the Clan title, were never legitimate to begin with, therefore the term schism does not apply. Even if Barrett, having no clear understanding of historical Clanships, perceived that a (non-existent) premise allows a tradition to be parcelled off into *independent factions*, and *legitimately*, then again, by these tenets, it has not fractured as a *schism*.

By definition, an actual schism must occur from within, as the rupture of a *whole into unauthorised factions,* of splinter groups that continue *independently* through *legitimate* persons formerly associated with that belief system. That is to say, they become *apart* from something they were once *a part* of. Recalling the specific premise that, one is either *in* the Clan, or *out* - there can be no *independent* continuity outside the Clan.

Barratt's insistent use of the term 'schism,' suggests an unwarranted legitimacy on the two false claimants for their groups. One group (C.J.') <u>never</u> held any legitimacy. Its brief and fraudulent existence had ceased even before Barratt's book went to print. Legitimacy for the Finnin's, group, had long since expired; its term of office revoked and annulled, therefore its previous adoptive status was no longer tenable even as an option.

---

[603] Ibid.
[604] E.J.J. See ref. 521
[605] Ibid.

Barrett was unconcerned his interpretations were damaging to the public perception of CTC and its Tradition. It was later discovered that Barrett was a very good friend of Michael Howard, he even privately admitted that Howard had supplied him with the information he used in his book to describe CTC and its Tradition.[606]

Other pseudo-academics have adopted a tendency to rely upon similar views supplied by Michael Howard, in preference to correct information from CTC as a primary source. Those biased and factually incorrect accounts are then re-quoted by Michael Howard and others, as references in their published works, disseminating the false impression those works are backed by academic research. This ingenious circular referencing system returns the reader back to the same self-validating resource, cited in turn to perpetuate a very singular opinion – Michael Howard's.

By a process of diffusion, the numerous false accounts and erroneous perceptions found their way into online media resources, though a cursory glance may witness nothing untoward. The casual observer may fail to note the steady erosion that has undermined CTC' credibility over recent years. And yet, true to the adage *'that everything is hidden in plain sight,'* with a little effort all ambiguities are easily spotted.[607]

A fair and critical work should always offer primary and secondary sources, sources that have reliable provenance, and which are preferably not of the circulatory mode. Failure to provide accurate sources, demeans the work as hearsay and speculation. Opinion, should fairly be presented as such, and not as fact. It does not become true simply because it is said, or written. But it does become known. And therein lies the danger. Nonetheless, hearsay will always be hearsay, and diametrically opposed to fact, ergo distinct from truth.

---

[606] Barrett, D. V. 2010/11. Personal Correspondence by several emails that ended in a heated exchange. Frustrated by his unyielding agenda, CTC requested that as the comments it had submitted were prejudicially edited, it wished them to be completely removed from the final publication. His response was that the book would be printed the way it was, or with his views, supplemented by those of C.J.; A.F. and of M.H. CTC reluctantly conceded, hoping that anyone reading his account might be intrigued enough to look further afield, perhaps to official and legitimate works, and thereby discover the reality of these matters. The sudden flurry of pseudo 'academic' interest in Clan matters at precisely the time it was battling to secure its identity, seemed a rather odd occurrence of either fate or undue external manipulation.
[607] Wikipedia pages concerning Robert Cochrane, Roy Bowers, CTC, RWC etc. are not official or approved. These pages should be avoided without exception by any serious researcher of the works, tradition and history of CTC.

Although Ethan Doyle White's research is caught up in the above mentioned circular loop, he rightly asserts that the best people to consult about their own histories, are those best informed - the practitioners themselves. Citing biographical works in examples he'd endorsed for *The Regency* and the *Cultus sabbati*, Doyle White nonetheless denied CTC that same self-defining privilege.

Then, based on E.J.J.' material, edited by Valiente in E.J.J.' in *Witchcraft a Tradition Renewed,* Doyle White claimed CTC is fundamentally Wiccan. Noted by both E.J.J. and Valiente as a book that *does not* claim to represent the beliefs of Robert Cochrane, nor his Clan's praxes, Doyle White appears to have overlooked some very important facts relative to it.

This was becoming a strange and perennial issue, especially as Doyle White should have realised that was an exoteric work. First of all E.J.J. was never a Wiccan, and by Valiente's own admission, she had long since ceased to consider herself a Gardnerian. She referred to herself as a folk-lorist and an occultist. Of the sixty years Valiente ventured into, researched and practised folklore, traditional craft and other occultisms, she'd been a HP's for G. B. Gardner for less than five years. Of any influence she might therefore impart, Wicca, would be the most unlikely.

What may or may not be considered a *'wiccan'* trait has been covered separately in an earlier chapter of this biography. Wicca is not an issue for CTC, only the cavalier appropriation of it and its false application where it can be shown to be otherwise. It cannot be applied purely because someone wishes it; supportive material must in all cases be provided as evidence. What is false cannot be true.

Doyle White failed to appreciate that as an author, Valiente used terms readily accessible and familiar to a generic readership familiar with her works. And she is not alone in this, many writers endorse this method for that reason. Popular terminology is of course, commonplace. With regard to *Witchcraft a Tradition Renewed*, this approach was specifically requested by the publisher and agreed by E.J.J. and Valiente herself. Even so, a published book does not a tradition reveal. No-one should imagine it could.

In his own letters to Ann and Dave Finnin, E.J.J. provides explicit examples as to why *that* book *does not* profess to express or expose the actual rites and beliefs of CTC. He nowhere claims it represents the beliefs and ritual praxis of CTC, his open explanation simply suggests it may prove influential and inspiring, without conflict to pre-existing or popular methods of working. He hoped neo-Pagans and Wiccans might absorb some of its tenets into their practises to develop them along more traditional lines. Valiente adds:

> However, the ideas and rituals in this book are mainly his. I have been glad to help it find publication, because I feel that it is an important book and unlike any other which has appeared on this subject, in fact it is the only book I know which is devoted <u>entirely to Traditional Witchcraft, as opposed to more modern versions of the Old Religion</u>. [608]

> A deeper and more serious book about witchcraft than most of the books on the subject on sale today (…) there is no doubt that Wicca has brought much enjoyment and enlightenment to many people, <u>but there is an older witchcraft and it is the latter that this book is about</u>.[609]

Given the clarity of her own words, it is a wonder how *any* contra opinion could ever have been taken seriously, less still by an academic. Coincidentally, within a particular two year span, a sudden and supposedly random flurry of interest focused on Clan history and its activities. Several academic papers, journals and book compilations became subject to the pervading views and opinions of Michael Howard, whom they perceived to be *'a good authority.'*

> One of the problems in discussing any of these traditions is that, unless one is an initiate of a particular tradition, one can only have an outsider's knowledge of that tradition and that does create a limit beyond which all is speculation.[610]

Precisely! No other, beyond the enclave of the Clan, is equally placed or better qualified to do so. It has proved to be a constant bewilderment to the Clan why anyone would not defer to its opinions concerning its own beliefs. CTC have actively encouraged respectful debate with interested parties from other traditions. No

---

[608] Jones, E. J. *WaTR* See Valiente's preface (UK: Hale, 1990)
[609] Jones, 1990. Op. Cit.
[610] Stuart Inman. 2012. 1734 Forum.

matter how well intended, those others are not best placed to demean by comparison, how the Clan is regarded.

> One day, they will all realise that reality is outside, not inside, and that reality hurts as well as teaches. [611]

The truly esoteric mysteries held by CTC, its Mythos and Ethos, are not privy to outsiders, and remain with the conclave of 'initiates,' or Members of Full Admission, to refer to them correctly. Their understanding of god-forms of spirit and of deity cannot possibly be pronounced upon by outsiders to the Tradition. It is true that a great deal of information has been published about *The Robert Cochrane Tradition*.

Until very recently, these were presumptive works, composed entirely by outsiders looking in. And true to Robert Cochrane's vision and praxes, even those things stated recently by actual members, do not express what remains properly esoteric.

As Cochrane once explained to Bill Gray: *"Hermes, Hecate, Saturn are only approximations of what we really mean. Enough said."* This means that privy as its people are to those sacred mysteries on different levels and via different internal keys, those mysteries are incomprehensible to everyone else. The Clan asserts its right to maintain what Cochrane's works mean *to its own people*.

Holding individual opinions as one's own truth of experiences and understanding is an honourable enterprise; professing those views as definitive over another's, without the authority to do so, is not.

Whatever is gleaned exoterically from Cochrane's works by others, are subject to an entirely separate modality, based accordingly upon their own uniquely individual perceptions. Anyone so inclined by that body of Craft, become benefactors of his genius. The depth and range of Cochrane's words and works have influenced so much of what is presented as Traditional Craft even now, decades later.

These grievous issues illustrate the most tenacious challenges that CTC have endured. They cannot be expunged or glossed over, and indeed should not be. They remain factors of change and growth within this biography. Nonetheless, observing the tenets of

---

[611] Oates, 2016. *SCSIII* Op. Cit. #IX Correspondence from Cochrane to Gray p165

discretion, a necessary economy of all but the salient facts is demonstrated. Nothing more is necessary.

"The spirit of change is the ever present hungry wolf, prowling the periphery of stagnation." [612]

Sleight of Hand

Though CTC could not have known or suspected at the time, within less than two years, another onslaught rose to erode the reputation and impression of the Clan. The charge that follows here is based entirely upon the force of suggestion alone, showing just how influential the wrong information can prove to be. A prejudicial attempt to re-write the history of the Clan was noted in the account given by Michael Howard in *The Children of Cain*. Almost immediately, that was followed by John of Monmouth's book, *Genuine Witchcraft is Explained*.

Countering the fallacious errors expounded principally in those two volumes, necessitated this in-depth historical biography. Howard used his Craft status to sway opinion directly. Monmouth employed a different method that depended more on structural and cumulative subtleties. To ensure that method was successful, Monmouth needed to do to:

1. Establish a single document as proof for the existence of *The Royal Windsor Coven*.

[Monmouth used the *Oath of Loyalty* doc. (AAA)A2]

2. Find one letter in the cache that can be positively linked to Cochrane.

[Monmouth used a letter from Robert to Chalky]

3. Declare that $1 + 2 =$ Cochrane's 'secret' Coven = a 'secret' tradition.

[Monmouth used two documents as mutually validating]

---

[612] Shani. Oates

4. Declare that because 1 + 2 = 3, *all* documents from the cache must also belong to *The Royal Windsor Coven*
[Monmouth projected automatic association between them]

5. Declare that because Cochrane died, White and Winter continued that 'secret' coven/tradition thereafter.
[Monmouth used the rumour as proof of this]

6. Declare that White and Winter had been the real 'secret' source of knowledge and inspiration for that tradition all along.
[Monmouth used *'the old man of Westmoreland'* story]

This tactic is seriously flawed, and easily revealed:

1. Once the first supposition is proven to be false (see AAA-A2), then 2, 3, 4, 5 and 6 are irrelevant. The entire presumption underpinning Monmouth's book fails and is then voided.

[The documents and letters used by Monmouth have not been verified as legitimate, nor even relevant to a phantom coven. Therefore the first supposition is proven to be false. All other points below become adjunct to this by default.]

2. One or two random letters in a boxful spanning over a decade, does not signify or prove they are all sourced in the same subject matter, nor that they were composed by the same person, or even that the person who now owns the box of letters was the original recipient.

[The undated letter used in this case has also not been authenticated nor proven as a letter written and signed by Roy Bowers aka Robert Cochrane, so remains invalid]

3. Two separate documents may not be identified in association with one another unless information regarding names or events that occur in one document,

is positively referred to in the other, even if both documents are separately authenticated and legitimate.

[The coven oath, is not made to *The Royal Windsor Coven*, and it is not signed by Robert Cochrane. The presence of a separate letter, signed by Robert Cochrane found amidst numerous other documents does not prove its relevance or association to any other in that cache.]

4. Suspending logic, reason and rational, even if, given a different set of circumstances, it were possible that 1, 2 and 3 could be determined as fact, it would not authenticate all documents in the cache as relevant to that person and the group that person belongs to. It is commonplace to have eclectic collections of documents that individually bear little or no association to each other, particularly those that span several or more years.

[These documents display several handwriting styles, signatures, typefaces, paper sizes, paper densities, variety of inks and degrees of aging in addition to non-associative subject matter. They are not mutually relative.]

5. History is replete with 'claims' of legacies, blood-lines, dynasties etc. Unless backed up with scrutable evidence, they are not taken seriously. No claim may be accepted as fact simply by declaring it is so.

[Monmouth's unsupported presumptions fall against Cochrane's appointment of E.J.J. as Tanist, Cochrane's Widow's appointment of E.J.J. as the next Magister of their Tradition, continuing through the legitimate name and proven title for that Tradition]

6. Any claim that presumes an alternative source for information, previously accepted as the work of the person associated with it, must again, present scrutable evidence to support it and be taken seriously.

[The information expressed by Cochrane regarding the *old man of Westmoreland* indisputably rules out White and Winter as candidates. Cochrane's other letters clearly demonstrate that it is he who instructs and informs White, Winter and Gills on mythos, ethos, praxis etc.

To be succinct: Monmouth claimed that *The Thames Valley Coven* is really *The Royal Windsor Coven*, that White and Winter had founded it, and that Cochrane joined it, and was allowed by White and Winter to head the Coven as its Magister. To that, he added a further claim that the documents in the cache represent the rites and rituals of *The Royal Windsor Coven.*

These claims are <u>entirely false.</u> They are without foundation or validation. They remain entirely speculative, being without evidence or proof of any kind. The rumour remains without precedent. As one of several fallacies linked to CTC, it is debunked in this Clan biography.

The fictional account of a *Royal Windsor Coven* along with claims that attempted to forge connections for it to Robert Cochrane became disproportionally advanced, elevated beyond common sense in Monmouth's history, as does Cochrane's alleged initiation within the Wican stream of Craft. Both were articulated with increased vigour through a sudden influx of articles that began to appear within pagan journals, publications, and forums. Tracing a distinctive narrative, barely discernible over a decade, it is obvious in hindsight. A brief summary illustrates Howard's and Monmouth's non critical methods:

- ❖ No person is able to verify the existence of the phantom coven, recalling only the rumour of it as a presumed reality.

- ❖ Disingenuous and repeated reference to a fictional title, pretends a pre-existence, presented everywhere as acceptable fact.

- ❖ Manipulation of source material, excessive misquotes, and false addenda, false associations, and application of tremendous 'leaps of faith.'

❖ No original/source documents exist that cite the name or title *Royal Windsor Coven,* before Cochrane's death. One much later undated text printed on 'A4' sized paper that does refer to the phantom coven was cited by Monmouth, but remains unavailable for examination. Until that is granted, its authenticity and date cannot be determined, nor can its value as a possible primary source document relating to a group arising in this time period (1980s). It may also be a completely specious document.

❖ The name *Royal Windsor Coven* does not appear even in any secondary source material until sometime in the mid. 1980s – circa 1982-3. At that noted entry point, a retrospective origin in the 1960s and back story were claimed for it.

Connections between *Royal* and *Windsor* did not become a regional reality until 1974. Because of current familiarity with changes made 50 years ago, very few people would recognise previous references to the area known only as Windsor, to the extent that even today all titles and names pre-1974 are described using 'Royal' inclusively and retrospectively with Windsor.[613]

It is now used to refer to particular items rather than the geographical region established for almost a thousand years. But those things were not named *royal windsor* when they were established. For anyone to have considered a 'Royal' Windsor coven prior to 1974, would be to suggest their coven at Windsor was literally 'Royal,' that they are part of a *Royal* coven of the Windsor family.

The precedents for 'Royal' as a title attached to Windsor, prior to 1974, were exceptionally scarce and did not in any way refer to the *region of Windsor,* nor to 'Royal' as a noun but an adjective. For example: Having checked numerous guide books from the library catalogue, less than a handful only of countless publications, have 'Royal' in the heading, suggesting their odd use of 'Royal' to refer to the residences and buildings in Windsor as 'Royal' - an adjective rather than a noun.

---

[613] Prior to 1974 all regiments etc were typically assigned a titular *'Royal'* to assert their crown status, as follows eg; The *Royal* Fusiliers *of* Windsor, *Royal* Chapel *At* Windsor, *Royal* Cemetery *At* Windsor etc. Post 1974, because the *region of* Windsor became *'Royal Windsor,'* the regiments etc are now popularly referred to as The *'Royal Windsor'* Fusiliers etc, even though the actual name has not changed, and remains – The *Royal* Fusiliers *of* Windsor. It is a natural appendage now, since 1974, but not before. Prior to 1974, Windsor itself is referred to only as new or old, but not Royal.

Other extremely rare adoptions of the title 'Royal' are used purposefully through commission or endorsement, of pottery or cutlery, to imply status to their product. Such commercial appellations of 'Royal,' refer to registrations, catalogue number, name, crest etc; they are not titular, and are again, not associated with the region of Windsor.

Given the dating legalities of regional boundary information, there would be no cause for anyone prior to 1974 to have considered a coven in or around the Windsor region, being of that region, with a 'Royal' appellation. And, having no trade to endorse or sell products associated with a presumed 'Royal' status , again, there would be no reason to refer to themselves in terms of 'Royal.'

Another idea was raised recently, which considered the possibility that an association with regional witches was desired, specifically in the region of Windsor, an area noted by Cecil Williamson claimed for craft activity when he [briefly] had a Witchcraft Museum there in 1953. [614]

This is conceivable; however, people from that region prior to 1974 would have referred to a local coven as a 'Windsor' Coven, not a Royal Windsor Coven, unless the people in it were members of the Royal family. Only someone outside that region, unfamiliar with its proper associations might invent that title before that date; even then, it is highly improbable they would do so before the boundary changes of 1974 occurred to present that notion to them. [615]

- ❖ *Genuine Witchcraft is Explained* and *The Children of Cain* present a false context and chronology of the history of events. They seriously misrepresent them, particularly with regard to how many and which members continued to work after Cochrane's death and in what capacity.

- ❖ References to ambiguous initiations within anonymous groups are presented as definitive proofs for specific people within the fictional coven, and are used in attempts to prove its existence. Cross references from validated sources reveal these to be spurious.

---

[614] Clive Harper. 2017. Personal Correspondence. November.
[615] Clive harper. 2017. Personal Correspondence. November.

❖ The testaments of Robert Cochrane, Jane Bowers, E. J. J, V.J., Reginald Hinchcliffe, Ruth Wynn Owen, Ken Rees, Ronald White, Bill Gray, Marian Green and Ann Finnin, supplemented and cross referenced by Doreen Valiente's record of events are in <u>complete</u> contra-distinction to Howard's and Monmouth's alternative, unsupported, conjectural history and interpretive accounts.

❖ V.J., fully re-iterated what E.J.J. had long upheld, confirming that Cochrane's Clan, they'd both belonged to, <u>was known only as CTC, not 'The Royal Windsor Coven.'</u> E.J.J., as a long established Full Member, stood alongside Jane and Robert Cochrane. Valiente also confirmed these facts.

❖ Even as a rumoured name, V.J. had not heard Royal Windsor Coven mentioned until its circulation began decades later through the Finnins. She confirmed her knowledge of the name and existence of *The Thames Valley Coven,* as a previous group that had ceased to exist, several years prior to her own Induction into the Clan along with E.J.J. [616]

Anything therefore that may confirm a connection between Cochrane and *The Thames Valley Coven,* is fleeting and had certainly ceased before 1960. Naturally, nothing exists to connect anything, or anyone to the phantom coven. Surviving members of CTC have confirmed Induction into CTC, *not* into a coven, and by no other name. All of them unequivocally denounce the fictional title.

This information was shared freely with Michael Howard by several Clan members including Valiente, E.J.J. and V.J. separately, as need arose, and repeated over several years in their attempts to dispense the re-occurrence of rumours regarding that fictional coven. Clan Inductions have been systematically misinterpreted and misrepresented by Monmouth as 'initiations' into the phantom coven.

---

[616] Oates, 2016. Op. Cit. *TM: Legend* Personal Correspondence. 2009 Scan of V. Jones letter to SLO. V.J. is claimed by Monmouth, along with her husband EJJ to have been initiates of the Royal Windsor Coven, and Valiente also. ALL of them utterly refute this as nonsense! They all make it clear that the fictional coven <u>never</u> existed in their time, and indeed, they had never heard of it in any reality. Valiente and EJJ began this investigation, and worked hard to discover the source of a great deal of misinformation over several decades.

Other referrals to 'initiations' for George (Desmond Bourke), Gerard Noel, Madge Worthington and 'Belinda' concern *people outside the Clan, and some years after Cochrane's death* and are therefore not relevant to Clan history or its People. These initiations, are therefore completely unrelated to Robert Cochrane and his Tradition. Though largely a mystery, those other small, mutable, unknown groups, possibly relate to the *ad hoc* groups Marian Green describes as typical for this period.

Despite the freedoms recently won, there were very few actual craft practitioners and many of them were happy to experiment across the range of occultisms open to them, with different people across that range of relevant practitioners. Those new, fledgling groups, were informal, and non-initiatory. Marian Green recollects that it was a time of:

> Magical friendships, not [closed]groups, lodges or covens, but [open] gatherings of friends with mutual interests in nature, magic and witchcraft.[617]

Not all those people were Wicans, but a good number were, even so, this does not mean they formed Wican style covens, merely that they made full use of their freedoms. Both Monmouth and Valiente confirm this. There is no doubt that Madge Worthington was involved with *The Regency* (mark I) before committing herself to Wica. Recent investigations into those early years have proven to be very fruitful. Some extremely interesting facts have been discovered that present a very different version of events to those Monmouth believes occurred.

His speculations are garnered from Ronald White's non-committal abbreviations within his diaries, which to date remain unavailable for examination. Without academic rigour, everything is speculative. CTC and others may only hazard a guess as to their true meaning. Madge Worthington's initiations were into a Wican group, corroborated by dates and persons involved. If Ronald White had been there, a supposition by no means proven, then however unlikely, he too was probably involved in that same *ad hoc* group, which may or may not have been strictly Wican in orientation.

---

[617] E.J.J. 2001. Op. Cit. p 36

White's diary entries suggest only his awareness of certain events, nothing more. His activities are rather less easy to cross-reference however; in fact no other source even mentions Ronald White until after 1969, and then only briefly. Valiente's prolific Notepads mention him twice in her own researches into him around the time of Cochrane's death. She mentioned him no more until 1969.

On a forum discussion group, Michael Howard mentioned *The Regency Committee*. He referred to them as a *secret inner court* group, aka the *Royal Windsor Covine*. (sic) Attempting to imply some measure of secrecy and mystique to a generic explanation of the general function of a committee, Michael Howard embroidered a substantially enhanced description. His belief in the alleged core (of *The Regency* mark I) supposedly operative as the phantom *Royal Windsor Covine,* is as follows:

> Rosina Bishop told this writer the rituals were usually produced by a 'committee.' Meetings were held beforehand to discuss what form they would take and once agreed 'scripts' would be typed up on sheets of paper and glued on to pieces of thin card. These were then handed out to the celebrants who each took specific parts, under the guidance of a 'master of ceremonies,' in what was essentially the enactment of a ritualised drama based on role-playing. In practice the rites were fairly simple in nature and took the form of 'plays' based on the mythic theme of the festival and its seasonal symbolism.[618]

And also

> These members attended special rites by private invitation only. In practice this *inner circle* was actually operating like a traditional covine. A few days before each of the seasonal festivals this group comprising a 'Committee of six' met privately. The purpose of this meet was to meditate on the action, roles, settings and props needed for the coming celebration.[619]

Another alleged former member, Marian Green, when asked about this phantom 'coven,' did not *confirm* its existence with first-

---

[618] Howard, 2011. Op. Cit. p 97
[619] Ibid.

hand testimony, less still offer any proof, nor did she *deny* the *rumour* of its existence, as Monmouth decreed she should as a supposed 'initiate.' Thankfully, she seems sufficiently untethered from its illusory bond to speak freely, but remains discreet enough not to comment further or be involved in protracted machinations.

One other thing Marian Green was kind enough to comment on, confirming the recollections of others, is that *The Regency Council* met once only in Winchester, and that it was nothing to do with an alleged coven or committee.[620] For the sake of completion, CTC have unravelled a tentative identity for a group of people who served in an official capacity as *The Regency Committee*. None of them were in Cochrane's Clan, and at best some were merely guests in it.

Howard made repeated comment and references about an inner circle of *The Regency*, claiming it formed after Cochrane's death from the secret 'inner circle' of the Phantom Coven, formed before his death. He further claimed its meetings were attended by particular guests and by private invitation only. As a claim, it presents an oxymoron. As noted previously, something that secretive its members can never speak of it and must deny upon all manner of peril, yet accepts guests by invitation, is an ill-conceived fiction. A description given by Monmouth in 2008 was used by Howard to suggest they had shared a compatible view concerning his own presumed belief in an *'inner secret group:'* Misrepresenting its context, Howard used the following excerpt as the basis for his manipulative deception.

> 'During the rituals the covine practised mediumistic trances and these were induced by either the use of psychoactive plants, chanting or walking silently around the circle to create a state of self-hypnosis.' It seems clear from this description of the group's activities that it was still following closely in the footsteps of Robert Cochrane. [621]

There is no mention of *inner groups* or *inner court* in Monmouth's text cited above. Yet Howard made the following summary: *"In fact it has been claimed that its Inner Circle was directly an*

---

[620] Marian Green. 2016. Private Correspondence with SLO. Ken Rees confirms this in Private Correspondence. Imbolc 2017

[621] Monmouth, 2012, Op. Cit. p 65. Holzer paraphrased by Monmouth.

evolution of the Cochrane Coven" ⁶²² Monmouth completely rejected any notion of *inner courts* for *The Regency* and for Howard's version of a phantom coven, emphasising the conflict between their opposing views. As far as descriptions go, the mood conveyed by the above comment appears evocative of the era, and so it should, it was taken from a generic description by Hans Holzer in 1969. ⁶²³

Based on what he saw during his visit to the UK, Holzer's summary of British Traditional Craft techniques regarding trance-mediumship, is invaluable to this biography. As for the claim that it sounds like it might describe similar techniques to those used by Robert Cochrane's group, it does! Holzer's informant was in fact Marian Green, who had been an occasional guest of the Clan in 1965.⁶²⁴ What should be appreciated however, is that this incident occurred three years after Cochrane's death. Guised as a broad sweeping statement, Howard pressed his claim further. Composed of information taken out of its original context, it was fused with opinion and presented as self-evident proofs. ⁶²⁵

> Also it seems that the rites and practices of the Inner Circle of The Regency were quite different from the more neo-Pagan festivals that were performed for the benefit of the public. This has, in fact, been confirmed to the writer by both Rosina Bishop and Evan John Jones. ⁶²⁶

No letter or document scan is provided as confirmation for Bishop's or Jones' alleged comments. Of course, such things are not always easy or possible to procure. And that tends to place an over reliance upon peripheral or external sources, or to take someone's personal comments at their word, which should not be mistaken for proof. But with full respect to the written word, without it, this comment is merely hearsay, and entirely worthless as a presumed presentation of fact.

---

⁶²² Howard, 2011, Op. Cit. p 107 quoting 'John of Monmouth.' Note the very early date here. 2008, four years before publication of *GWiE*. This 2008 date coincides with the much publicised claim by CJ and MBL And their podcast.
⁶²³ Holzer, Hans. *The Truth about Witchcraft* (UK: Arrow Books LTD, 1971) American occult film-maker and researcher who came to UK in 1969. p 201
⁶²⁴ Holzer, Hans. *The Truth about Witchcraft* (UK: Arrow Books Ltd, 1971) p 199
⁶²⁵ Rees, 2017. Private correspondence. Op. Cit. Feb. Amongst others, Rees has expressed the opinion that Michael Howard was a 'nothing more than a fantasist.'
⁶²⁶ Howard, 2011, Op. Cit. p 107

Where hearsay is offered as a discreet bolster to support other previously verified facts, it may be considered, but in the absence of any other proofs whatsoever, then its carries zero weight. When hearsay presented is contrary to what is known of a person's natural traits and beliefs, it should be treated with full measure of suspicion and due caution. When presented with opposing facts, hearsay should be completely disregarded.

In fact E.J.J. confirmed to Howard only that Cochrane worked in *that way*, and that it was *very distinct from contemporary paganisms*. He *did not* in any sense confirm the existence of the phantom covine (sic), or an alleged Inner Circle, despite Howard's careful phrasing to imply that he did. Still, there are a couple of important factors to consider further.

Principally, Howard insinuated the notion of scourging as a distinguishing factor that marks a practitioner as someone who follows the rites and traditions of Robert Cochrane. Aside from the extraordinary attribution presented in that claim in a general sense, the practise of scourging in Traditional Craft is exceptionally rare, and executed very differently to the style described by Holzer. Relevant to the tenets of Traditional Craft, it cannot be mistaken for the method employed by people of the Wica. Though Cochrane once suggested experimentation with the scourge, it was overruled by Jane. There is no scourging in CTC, and never was.

Second Point. If Holzer's description is taken as a *definitive* marker to identify every group that imbibed narcotics and exerted themselves in trance-inducing walking or dancing during the late 1960s-70s, as a 'Robert Cochrane influenced group,' then the number of alleged groups would number in the hundreds. To demean the complexity of CTC's mythos by this pithy description brings to light just how little Michael Howard knew about the actual Traditions and lore Cochrane and Jones infused into the Clan. Cochrane's Clan Tradition requires much, much more than walking around in (an alleged drug induced) trance. Cloak or no cloak. This is an incredible understatement.

Presumption of an entheogen based Mythos as a comparable criterion, introduces yet another premise taken out of context. The introduction of entheogens to Clan workings occurred as a *temporary* measure during a very brief experimental phase in late

1965, and formed no part of its Ethos or Mythos. And though it <u>was never part of the established praxes</u>, it expresses a certain irony as the drastic method introduced for the sole purpose of bringing White and Winter up to speed with Cochrane's grasp of the work , work they'd failed to grasp. More than anything Cochrane was desperate for a way everyone could coalesce their working focus to realise the Clan's Mysteries. All of this is vividly explained by Cochrane himself in his succinct address to *All Members*. [627]

Third Point. What Cochrane did was *no secret*, and Valiente provides a number of quite explicit in-depth, finely-detailed descriptions in her Notepads of selective pieces of Cochrane's Rites. Certainly enough was shared by those who had guested at his rites to provide a very basic, admittedly sketchy outline of his 'way' of working. This information was known and commented on, mostly by Wicans, the associates of Cochrane's guests. That small occult world they all revolved in was advanced by Cochrane's willingness to share. To advance knowledge collectively, was one of the things 'the Boys' had major issues with. They had wanted it kept secret, just for them.

Fourth point. Cochrane was never precious about what he did, <u>only why and how,</u> and that was never widely explained or practised outside that essential attendant Mythos and the relative underlying purpose for the Knot.

Without that information, all anyone could witness, or recall, was that people walked around in circles, munching sacred herbs, as indeed Rosina Bishop and at least several dozen other people could easily attest. E.J.J., might nod in amusement at this thought, but he would also shake his head in disbelief that so much could be so easily misappropriated.

Because the rumour of that Coven drifted over many decades, its definition needed to evolve with shifting circumstance. Lacking a foundation in reality, several descriptions expressed its purposeful progression, all with variable degrees of subtlety; some were more controversial than others. They are all cited where relevant in this biography. Here again is the comment Howard composed in 2011 for The Children of Cain: *"The Regency consisted of*

---

[627] Oates, 2016. *SCSIII* Op. Cit. For documentary proof of this, please see appropriate section in the Letters' Chronology. (hh) p 334

an 'inner circle' made up of people who had mostly been members of or were associated with the old covine [sic] founded by Robert Cochrane." [628]

To avoid the imposing contradictions that should have troubled him, Howard insisted the core leadership of The Regency, responsible for mundane tasks and organising its neo-Pagan rites and setting dates, was a committee *'composed of members of Cochrane's former covine (sic), its ex-members and its former guests.'* [629] He then claimed the non-secret committee was a secret covine (sic) whose purpose was to evolve Cochrane's work. [630] Because of that, the entire impetus of Monmouth's book falls down, as does the argument Howard presents in The Children of Cain.

Discovering the identities of the people involved in the committee will explain why Monmouth and Howard neglected to name them. Their identities reveal them to be very different people to those who were genuine members of Cochrane's Clan before he died. <u>The failure to correlate the committee members with real Clan members exposes the fantasy coven, Howard and Monmouth both claimed was Cochrane's 'group.'</u>

So which former members, ex members and guests, did Howard imply Cochrane's 'inner circle' was comprised of? Two former members, Ronald White and George Winter were known to drift about a bit, involving themselves with other people in a variety of occult activities, as confirmed by Marian Green, Valiente and Rees. Often absent, they did not attend *all* Clan rites and meetings.

Setting aside the important point that Monmouth and Howard separately referred to Clan members as 'initiates' of the fictional Royal Windsor Coven,' Valiente, correctly referred to the *'Magister and his wife,'* and to *'three other men.'* She withheld the identities of these five 'full' Clan members (Elders). Once fully Admitted, Valiente became the sixth member. [631]

The three men are presumed by Michael Howard to include White and Winter. They are not included. Though obscure, even before Cochrane's death, two of the mystery persons are not too

---

[628] Howard, 2011. Op. Cit. pages 85-6 (Rees: Spring Equinox 2003) p 99
[629] Used to express the concept of the coming together of different things, past and present to create the circumstances of their predicament.
[630] It seems needful to point out that for ease of understanding, please read both Michael Howard's and Monmouth's references to the people within the *Royal Windsor Covine* as members of Cochrane's CTC.
[631] Valiente, 1989. Op. Cit. p 182

difficult to track down. The third man, was Evan John Jones (E.J.J.).[632] The leaders were of course Robert Cochrane and his wife, Jane. Bill Gray and three ladies joined later that year: V.J.J., A. M. and Bobbie Gray (Bill's Wife).

These four people were *Inducted* (provisional) Members of the Clan; combined with the previously noted six Full Members, make up the ten people Marian Green referred to as the typical number present at Cochrane's Clan Rituals. Noel, Gills Hampton Cole and some others were occasional guests, as was Marian Green.

In his famous Esbat Rite (of 1963, published in 1964), Cochrane states *'he could feel all of the <u>Clan</u> within him, as one.'* Seven people attended that rite, himself, Jane, John (E.J.J.), and four, provisional (Inducted) members of <u>his Clan</u> (as Cochrane referred to it). Named by him as *Arthur, Peter, Dick* and *Blackie,* their early presence in the Clan was brief, in fact, two of them (Arthur and Peter) had left before Valiente joined, the other two, (Dick and Blackie) just after. Aside from White and Winter who did join the Clan, but rarely attended, who, if any, amongst those four people named above, became regular attendees and leaders of *The Regency*, forming a mundane planning committee? By their own accounts, four people can be dismissed with certainty; their identities, though partially vague, are discernible enough to remove them from any Regency involvement.

Arthur could be Eleanor Bone's high priest, or the Arthur known also as Laurence, whose own identity became confused with another, neither of whom were involved in *The Regency*. Peter is tentatively identified as Peter West, who also rejected the Craft and wrote a series of polemical attacks on it during the 1970s. Therefore, he can be dismissed from the list.

Admittedly, if 'Peter' was not Peter West, then Peter's identity was a possible alias for one of the other well-known members who would eventually make up the central *Regency* committee (of six, according to Howard). 'Dick' could be a number of people, including Richard, the former partner of Cynthia Swettenham, and later partner to Marian Green. As far as it is

---

[632] Valiente, 1989. Op. Cit. p 182 Relating to the previous nonsense, Valiente was hardly a 'secret' sixth member.

possible to know, Richard had a brief flirtation only with Traditional Craft before returning to Wica.

Alternatively, Dick could have been 'Dickie' (Derek Boothby), who was *not* a core member of *The Regency* (mark I). The final person from the entire list above, is 'Blackie', who was almost certainly Sean Black, the *Pyecombe* smith who also dropped away into obscurity. If Blackie's real identity can be proved as someone other than Sean Black, then this alias could be a potential committee member of *The Regency*.[633]

Former guests of the Clan offer a more promising selection, included Marian Green, Norman Gills, Geoff and Louise Hampton-Cole, Justine Glass, Gerard Noel and George Bourke. Of these, all but the last two people were only intermittent attendees of *The Regency* (mark I) and an even lesser presence in (mark II). Thus far, only four of the possible six committee members can be put forward for *The Regency* from Michael Howard's list of 'former (Clan) members, ex-members and guests of the Clan:' *Ronald White, George Winter, George Bourke and Gerard Noel*.

Two others who had never been members of his Clan, nor its guests, are already identified as definite key committee members for The Regency: *Ruth Wynn Owen, and Reginald Hinchcliffe*. As neither *Arthur, Peter, Blackie* or *Dick* could ever be guised as *Ruth Wynn Owen* or *Reginald Hinchcliffe,* nor mistaken for them, their actual identities remain irrelevant and serve no further purpose in this history.

Having established who amongst Howard's inaccurate list of supposed former Clan members, could not be Regency committee members, has allowed an informed guess as to who the six most probable candidates were: *Ronald White, George Winter, Desmond George Bourke, Gerard Noel, Ruth Wynn Owen,* and *Reginald Hinchcliffe*. Others might include *Madge Worthington* and *Rosina Bishop,* who were also never members of Cochrane's Clan.

Clearly, with the exception of White and Winter, no member (or past member) of the Clan, nor any of its guests, all named and noted above, were the people who formed the *Regency* planning committee and nothing else. Grossly exaggerated by

---

[633] These names and their true identities may be known by Marian Green, and sensibly, she is keeping them close to her chest.

Michael Howard, its function was exactly as mundane as Rosina Bishop had described. [634]

That is, a body of people who were already founders and leaders of *The Regency,* meeting periodically at Ruth Wynn Owen's flat in London to organise and plan its rites. A proper sense of the people involved, their probable identities, and what their proclivities of involvement were, establishes at last, a valid demographic for that time line.

What that information ultimately proves, is that none of these people have a parallel existence in a fictional coven that allegedly shifted from Cochrane's Clan to *The Regency* via an alleged committee or council, inner, outer, secret or otherwise. The entire fantasy construct is proven to be completely foundless; these facts totally subsume all contrary information presented through rumour.

5   Wisdom: Mirror of the Muse

VIII) Evolution

The Roebuck in the Thicket

At this juncture, it can finally be explained why Ronald White was so alarmed by Ruth Wynn Owen's exit, and by what connection an *'exit and an end to the Esbats,'* was formed. It is simplicity itself. When she walked away, so did the remaining (actual) *committee members.* As the organisers and hosts for those Esbat meetings, and as the organisers and planners for all rituals, then it would indeed be the *end of* everything that held *The Regency* together and allowed it to function.

Monmouth's lack of familiarity with the Clan system is obvious in his muddled explanations that fail to distinguish Clan from coven. Confusing 'private' with 'initiatory,' as a descriptive applied to the activities of people in the occult and Craft world that encompassed the lives of Cochrane and his peers, both Howard and

---

[634] Howard, 2011. Op. Cit. pages 85-6 (Rees: Spring Equinox 2003) p 99

Monmouth named their fictions as the <u>secret</u> *Royal Windsor Covine* (sic).

In that long-standing debate between principle members of the Clan and Michael Howard, his insistence that the *Royal Windsor Coven* was an *'inner court'* of *The Regency*, disregards several other equally significant factors. [635] For example, those persons he would put together in his phantom coven, were actually all diverse occultists who had never worked together, with or without Cochrane in any capacity. As demonstrated in the previous chapter, they had never been privy to, nor a part of his Tradition. The true members of his Clan have all been named.

Initially, Howard and Monmouth could not quite agree on how they should manifest their conceit, nor correlate their claims relative to this massive appropriation of another's Tradition. Monmouth refuted the suggestion of *The Regency* as an outer court for the *Royal Windsor Coven*; he also repudiated *The Royal Windsor Coven* as an *inner court* of *The Regency*, but ambitiously claimed it as a (non-secret) foundation from which the Clan and everything else grew out of. That claim Michael Howard also recognised merit in, and later adopted.

Both Howard and Monmouth eventually agreed to posit that illusory coven as the foundation from which the *CTC, The Regency, Y Plant Bran, The Roebuck Coven,* etc. evolved separately, continuing distinctly as itself - *The Royal Windsor Coven*. Because that claim relates to a very deliberate fabrication, they are naturally unable to account for any of the following factors, provided as examples of the discrepancies in this tall tale.

- ❖ In the first few years following Cochrane's death in 1966, a small and selective gathering of folk collectively formed the fledgling group named *The Regency*. <u>No-one in it had, desired or claimed any connection to Cochrane</u> or to his Clan, the 'People of Goda.' In, fact, for all the reasons explained in other chapters of this biography, that idea would have been anathema to them.

---

[635] 1734 Forum, 12th May 2012. Howard's claim shifted considerably from whence it was first made in 1982 concerning a few people wishing to continue the works of *The Regency* once it ceased its public ventures – to a retrospective claim two decades to 1962 as the foundation group from which Cochrane's Clan sprang. His agenda was clearly long-term.

❖ The *Regency* was non-initiatory in any of its renditions. Its attendees worked openly with other craft members* in brief informal '*ad hoc*' groups, verified by all the crafters of this period, in various letters housed at the *Museum of Witchcraft Archive*. *This includes, Reginald Hinchcliffe, Marian Green, Doreen Valiente, Madge Worthington, Ronald White, et al.

❖ Almost all the people who walked away from the joint leadership and organisation of *The Regency* in 1969 certainly went on to establish other groups and traditions; Ruth Wynn Owen, Joe Wilson, Lois Bourne, Gerard Noel, Reginald Hinchcliffe etc. are all primary, examples. None of these were in any way secret. Others attending the *single council meeting*, held at Winchester, advanced similarly away from *The Regency*, such as Bill Gray, who were uncomfortable with its ethic.

Ultimately, these people stand on their own merit, and for their own works that diverge completely from those of Cochrane's *People of Goda, of the Clan of Tubal Cain*. As they should and must. [636] After considerable time spent researching these events and people tangential to CTC' Tradition, almost exhaustively, very little headway has been made. Beyond suggestion which exists in abundance, speculation underpins almost all declarations advanced.

Returning attention to an entry in Ronald White's diary for 18 Dec 1966. Monmouth's projected perception that it concerns Madge Worthington's initiation into the phantom coven, is not actually suggested in this entry in any sense.[637] All it does say, is this:

MADGES/ THEN GEORGES/AGENDA/1 23 RD/2 'INIT.'

At first glance, an imaginative mind might initially mistake the flow of words, believing they could indicate an initiation for George (Desmond Bourke) and Madge (Worthington). Though of course *'Init,'* could be an abbreviation for almost anything. Without an understanding of how Ronald White contextualised his

---

[636] Personal Correspondence between EJJ and JB (L 9)
[637] Monmouth 2012 Op. Cit. *GWiE* p 114

abbreviations, all suppositions are equal. The hand written text itself also requires an accurate transliteration before any assessments are begun, or interpretations offered. For example: 1 23 RD could suggest the 23rd of January, or something else entirely.

Recent information acquired by extensive research, shows that a person named *Andrew Demaine* is verified as the priest who *did* initiate Madge into her 2nd and 3rd degrees in 1968, on dates Monmouth cites for her further advancement into *his* phantom coven. Madge Worthington had told a number of her initiates that her first degree was given by *Arthur Eaglan*, the former High Priest of *Eleanor Bone*, but it is more probable that *Demaine,* from the *Bricket Wood* line of Wica, was also responsible for administering her first degree sometime earlier. Valiente cites all this information correctly in her Notepads as Wican degrees 1*, 2*, 3*. Further investigations continue. [638]

Understanding these factors, advances the probability that White's diary entry exhibits another mistakenly read abbreviation. The letters Monmouth presumed to be 'RD' *RD* could just as easily be 'AD' *AD* (Andrew Demaine). There is no doubt concerning Madge Worthington's and Gerard Noel's initiations into *The Wica*, but nothing gleaned to date even hints this was a possibility for George Desmond Bourke. That does not mean Bourke was not, just that nothing suggests it beyond Holzer's remark that he was, though he could have been mistaken. [639]

Valiente places *Bourke, Worthington, Noel, Marian Green* and *Charles Pace* together as leading players in *The Regency* (mark I), including them in a very interesting section relating to Holzer's UK visit. Introduced to several people in the Craft, including Eleanor Bone, Monique Wilson and Alex Sanders, Holzer is witness to a couple of rites described as a hooded druidic coven of which Bourke is clearly stated as the leader.

Holzer mentioned that someone named Anne told him she had been with that particular coven (Bourke's people) for seven years, since her teens. At the time of meeting Holzer in 1969, she was in her late twenties. Her work with Bourke obviously pre-dates

---

[638] The Wiccan Readers' Research Project 2016, details supplied by Clive Harper; Personal communication 12 Sept 2017.
[639] Holzer, Hans. *The Truth about Witchcraft* (UK: Arrow Books Ltd, 1971) p 201

Cochrane's formation of the group Anne later guested at in 1965. The dynamic between Bourke, Anne and Cochrane is intriguing, especially with regard to the identity of *'the Old man of Westmoreland.'*

Although the <u>second rite</u> was held in Bourke's temple and was considered private, it was very obviously <u>not secret</u>. It involved *'Calling down Pan,'* something the group were apparently rehearsing for their weekend rite. Both rites were experimental and formed from exploratory occult themes.[640] This unique event is described by Michael Howard very differently; he was heavily focused upon his presumption of an *'inner circle:'* [641]

> Following this meeting, Dr Holzer was invited back to attend a Hallowe'en ritual held by what he describes as a robed coven to which George Stannard and Marian Green, later the editor of Quest magazine, belonged. This presumably was the *inner circle* of *The Regency* mentioned before that was not accessible by the general public and performed its rituals in secret. Everyone present was wearing black robes and the rite was led by a couple described as the Master and the Lady and assisted by a young woman known as the Maiden. At the beginning of the ceremony, <u>all those present were lightly scourged to</u> "*absolve them of their sins.*" Dr Holzer was told the coven was interested in researching the 'old traditions' so that the Craft did not die out.[642]

Howard was the only person to present Holzer's meeting in this way. The manner of his description is completely rejected by Marian Green, his assumption of an inner circle or of a secret coven especially. George Winter and Ronald White were *not involved* with this event. Holzer mentioned 'George' only, no surname. His

---

[640] Holzer, 1971 Op. Cit. p 204 *The Broom and Sword Rite* described by Holzer bears no semblance of the metaphysical and emotive rite ascribed to the Clan Rite of this name. It is an empty title.

[641] During 1967/8, the film-maker Hans Holzer solicited an organised, staged ritual. Fulfilled by known occultists in London at that time, *a private rite* was allegedly led by a High Priestess/Maid, who may have been Monica English and her partner. It may even have been Lois Bourne and her partner. Some of those in attendance were regular celebrants of *The Regency (mark I)* rituals. Given its themed description, nothing presumes a connection to anything Cochrane ritualised or believed in, not even remotely. And although Ruth Wynn Owen was still very involved in *The Regency* at this time, there is no mention of her presence. Linked through Eleanor Bone, Madge Worthington, attended some of the rituals by *The Regency (mark I & II)* and may also have been involved.

[642] Howard, 2011, Op. cit. p 97. See also Monmouth, GWiE, p 65, He claimed there that Madge Worthington was Belinda, the alleged Maid of his phantom coven. This Holzer ritual is conversely described by Marian Green as one performed by an *ad hoc* group of people, who knew each other and worked together occasionally, but which was definitely not initiatory, nor a working coven.

account is very specific and accompanied by an equally clear description of his host. That profile distinctly fits *George Desmond Bourke*, not George Winter. Valiente observed that Sally Bourke was amongst those present. [643]

No-one involved referred to an inner court or to the phantom coven. Holzer was first of all present for a *public* meeting, after which, he was privy to a more discreet rite. Holzer's description does not reflect the activities of a regular coven, nor of an actual coven rite. Instead, it was *"a rather unusual attempt to combine several rites, representing various sects."* [644]

Both rites are demonstrably eclectic in nature, but the second is grafted upon a format that by some accounts, would be considered Wican. [645] It does however refer to several elements that do set Wiccan rites apart from others. These are namely: the use of an unmistakable password that was uttered with a kiss when 'entering the circle,' the submission to ceremonial scourging, and finally, a description of 'cakes and wine' at the close of the rite. [646]

Believing it supported the construction of his fictional coven, Monmouth readily accepted it, convinced the separate, discreet rite was conducted by people from *The Regency*.

Elements from Holzer's account regarding guests present in the first rite, were purposefully selected by Monmouth to declare it represented a *Clan style* rite, for which he makes a distinction in his next claim that the second more private rite was led by a coven, specifically, his phantom Coven. It has been satisfactorily demonstrated already that the presence of guests at a rite, do not signify Clan in distinction to a coven.

However, Monmouth omitted to add that guests were in fact present at *both* rites. Reading Holzer's description directly, rather than accepting another person's impression of what it suggested to them, offers a pure perspective. [647]

---

[643] Monmouth, 2012. Op. Cit. p 95 Monmouth makes a confusing claim for two separate rites in Holzer's description in his 1971 *Truth about Witchcraft* book: the first public meeting was allegedly with George Bourke's coven, the second, with allegedly with his phantom coven. None of this is supported in Holzer's book.
[644] Holzer, Hans. *The Truth about Witchcraft* (UK: Arrow Books Ltd, 1971) p 201
[645] This comment refers back to the measures employed by Ethan Doyle White to determine if a modality is or is not Wiccan. His criteria for assessment are repudiated by CTC. They are in error.
[646] Holzer, Hans. *The Truth about Witchcraft* (UK: Arrow Books Ltd, 1971) p 201
[647] Ibid.

Essentially, the first Rite was an eclectic ritual to diverse deities, performed by celebrants dressed as a Mandarin, a Roman Senator, Arthurian maidens and a dark occultist. With or without guests, Monmouth's presumption garnered from *this* account is bewildering. His deduction is premature and demonstrates a lack of comprehension for a subject he so assertively fashions opinion upon. After describing the second rite as a closed and secret rite, Monmouth expressed his belief that it was performed by *The Royal Windsor* Coven.[648]

As with all previous scenarios used by him to assert this underlying claim, the problems are manifold, not least of which is the lack of a credible reason for that assumption. Failing that, some gesture of evidence to support his conjecture would not go amiss. There is absolutely nothing in either of these rituals that is even remotely similar to Cochrane's Praxes, not even as a loose description expected from someone on the outside of the Tradition.

No account given by Cochrane, E.J.J., Gray, Valiente, or Green of Clan rites, correlates with, or possesses elements that could inspire the descriptions offered by Holzer, Monmouth or Howard of those two Rites.

All the people mentioned by Holzer, appear to be connected to Bourke's group. Monmouth previously named Marian Green as a member of his phantom coven, and also Gerard Noel, George Bourke and Madge Worthington. Unwittingly perhaps, Monmouth's flawed logic implicates Bourke's group as the phantom *Royal Windsor Coven* by default – just one additional factor within a manufactured fiction, dismissed already by redoubtable fact. Marian Green's alleged presence in Bourke's group does not occur with any timeline connected to her later work with Cochrane. Marian Green has also stated firmly in several places, without ambiguity, that she was not a member of *The Regency*, its committee or any other coven.

By far the most significant irregularity, is that which concerns the matter of secrecy. The proposal that the status of an alleged ultra-secret coven that denies its own existence, forbids acknowledgement of it, even amongst members, would allow itself to be compromised by a rank outsider, a film-maker no less, a person invited to attend a

---

[648] Monmouth, 2012. Op. Cit. *GWiE* pages 96-97

meeting held by them, film them and write a book about them, is completely implausible.

Recalling those allegedly secret works submitted to Prof. Hutton for publication from that alleged secret coven, their appearance for inclusion in his study on Traditional Witchcraft does not exhibit the acclaimed denial of self – existence. Because Monmouth had insisted that premise was an intrinsic obligation to maintain its secret status, its sudden provision underscores a contrary existence, one very desirous of publicity.

Someone wanted that premise known, they wanted the rumour to appear manifest. At no point do any of these separate, alleged proofs, all leaked at different times, or summoned up in Howard's or Monmouth's book, corroborate the alleged demand for absolute secrecy and denial.

No problem of communication is evident between any of the people allegedly involved, and the outside world. Likewise, taking secrecy to levels of denial was never an edict between the people involved with Cochrane, and no mention of a phantom coven passed between them.

Extracts and draft copies of all written works were shared and approved by E.J.J. with other members of the Clan before publication. Valiente submitted her MS for *Rebirth of Witchcraft* to E.J.J., Jane Bowers and V.J. for approval and amendment. Only when someone outside the Tradition decided to use information garnered for their own advantage, by sending it on to Prof. Hutton through an unknown source, did it become transformed from something it never was, to be presented as something it never could be - the *secret* works of a phantom coven.

Monmouth dismissed this incongruity when claiming those rites for his fictional coven, a decade later. He also ignored the rationale that anyone abiding by an extreme oath of secrecy would never do this. His ill-considered opinions cannot be justified and are easily countered by the fact that those materials were confirmed as being lifted from unpublished works, authored by Evan John Jones.

Ironically, if *this* illogical fraud is followed through, it would conclude E.J.J. as the legitimate leader and the author of Monmouth and Howard's phantom coven, its tradition and its works! Not their intention of course. In reality as the Magister of Cochrane's *actual*

Tradition, authorised to lead the Clan, E.J.J. *is* all that and more, just as Cochrane and his widow declared sixty years ago. The distinction evaporates into thin air once the entire fiction is exposed.

Looking more deeply into the alleged secrecy issue, Howard edited and published an article in *The Cauldron*, 2006, written by Ken Rees at least six years before Monmouth published *GWiE* in 2012. [649] The article mentioned one of several recorded instances in circulation since the 1980s that have referred to the rumoured existence of the phantom coven. This is another fact that automatically contradicts any notion of supposed secrecy connected to it.

During the two decades that rumour was in circulation, no-one paid attention to it, or bothered to bring the matter up for discussion, not even discreetly between persons allegedly involved. Largely ignored, it seemed of no interest to anyone. The determination to change that resulted in the works in question arriving on Prof. Hutton's desk, setting in motion an incredible sequence of events, leading ultimately to this biography.

Not speaking of the private affairs of one's tradition is natural enough, and often expected. Like numerous others, the Clan's Tradition is occulted (hidden), but its existence is not secret! And in common with other occulted traditions, whatever is kept private from outsiders, is freely admitted amongst members. As an oath-bound Tradition, when amongst kin, all names are known and shared, of the individual, of the ancestors, its *Mighty Dead* and its gods.

It is inconceivable for any tradition to be so secretive that it would forbid such exchange amongst its members! That suggests a cult mentality, rather than occult. But this extra-ordinary level of secrecy was asserted by Monmouth to explain the denial he claims they were oath-bound to uphold. [650]

No oath worthy of expression, would be given to an invalid name, no signature would be inscribed upon an invalid document; that notion is anathema. The (AAA) A2 *Oath of Loyalty* declares dire consequences for reneging its status, a prime example of obligation and duty to uphold its tenets, principally it name 'which should not be changed.' By force of suggestion alone, those tenets were

---

[649] Rees, Ken, 2006. *The Cauldron* #121
[650] Monmouth, 2012. *GWiE*. Op. Cit. p 24

transformed into a terrible act, made into an awe-filled secret of such extreme, it must be denied.

Narrators of fine stories, like the bards of old, require a keen memory – and key points in Howard and Monmouth's arguments were repeatedly unheeded. The oath they claimed was imposed to *deny the coven's existence*, <u>does not</u> demand that in any way. Reading the initiatory oath cited by Monmouth for his phantom coven, presented in *The Full Rite of Initiation* doc., it is in fact quite succinct on this point:*" I will not even admit to its existence, <u>until confident that such knowledge will be respected by her or him to whom it is given.</u> All this I swear."* [651]

As a valuable resource at his fingertips, that document was discussed by Monmouth at length in *GWiE*. Once again, the uncomfortable premise faced at this juncture is that certain information was either unwittingly overlooked, or deliberately looked over, that is to say ignored. By this caveat, all claims are void. Amongst them, the incident regarding the *'discreet'* reporter, should be better understood in the true context provided already.

Other strange inconsistencies occurred regarding secrecy. Monmouth had admitted in his own preface to *GWiE*, that he was <u>not</u> a member of the fictional coven, but that it had shared its knowledge and existence with him as an uninitiated outsider. Of course, this was something he insisted could not be admitted or discussed between 'initiates.' He explained the reason for his 'exception' was to facilitate the inclusion of selected material used by the alleged secret coven *'to harness the exoteric aspect of the Royal Windsor Coven'* within *The Regency's* rituals (mark II). [652]

This statement exposes the principle contradiction of alleged secrecy Monmouth was at pains to extend to all levels of communication, and to all extremes of expression, even to denial, only to have them evaporate on such an insignificant premise. The Virtue of secrecy is woefully absent, just as truth is. The observation of secrecy appears entirely arbitrary.

Its capricious use is not determined either by trust, but when and where it is deemed useful to do so. For example, it was never secret when informing others of its name or members, intermittently

---

[651] Monmouth, 2012. Op. Cit. C3 p 312.
[652] Monmouth, 2012. Op. Cit. pages 122-128

between 1982 to 2012, across various media, or when attempting to claim another's tradition for itself. Involvements with various media, through journalists and filmmakers are hardly secret enterprises. Conversely, the only actual secret pertains to anything requested that could prove its reality.

Perhaps it is prudent at this stage to suggest a caveat to warn against advocating or setting up dangerous precedents whereby a secret origin can be claimed against *any* established group, society or tradition, allowing an outsider to engineer control over it, without requiring any proof of their entitlement to do so!

Both Monmouth and Howard had failed to consider one extremely important factor of the Craft when crafting their fantastic enterprise – that was the purpose of troth. As a People, the greatest gift is an oath. Its bond represents a divine reciprocity. Therefore, the most heinous act is a disavowal of an oath. The lack of awareness concerning this crucial tenant was asserted in Monmouth's opening attack: *"The beginnings of the Royal Windsor Coven: Witches Signature."* A hard thing to witness, knowing that such an important principle was lost on so many, who 'took it as read.' [653]

To this obfuscation of fact, a substantial contradiction was added when Monmouth declared that guests were present at those allegedly secret rites held by the phantom coven. Karagan, a craft practitioner, occult presenter and radio/podcast host in the US posed the following question to Monmouth in a you-tube interview about GWiE: *"Tell us a little bit about the early rituals of the Royal Windsor Coven."* Monmouth had replied:

> The early rituals are a composite of ideas that were provided <u>by the original members of the coven and also its initial guests</u> …like, .yeah…just as the Regency was open to anyone. In its early days it was by invitation only… so the Royal Windsor Coven, yes, right from the very beginning, in particular Norman Gills [654] and his wife, so his ideas can't be left out of the sort of the stewing pot.

---

[653] Another example of contradiction was given in his admission that *'Ron was not a witch, hated the word, and would not use it,'* yet he repeatedly says the Regency was set up for witches!

[654] Oates, 2016. Op. Cit. *SCSIII* 2016. Cochrane was married in 1951 pages 55-70

As for where Norman Gills fits in to Cochrane's history, there is no more lawful testament than a marriage certificate, quoted in Cochrane's own introductory letter to him, within which he remarked to Gills his, 'marriage of 14 years hence.' This absolutely anchors their first contact at the very end of 1965, they first met not too long after, but Norman Gills' presence in those early days was therefore impossible.

Some of the ideas appear from Gerald Gardner, from High Magics Aid. [655]

And there it is, by his own admission, Monmouth exposed his manipulation of the facts. Unable to form an articulate response to the question, he referred to *'members and guests' present in the rites held by his phantom coven.* Having previously declared his belief that *a Clan is defined by having guests present at its rites*, in contradistinction to a *coven that is closed to guests*, his intent to labour that definition to show that CTC is an offshoot from the phantom coven, failed and is proved false in this dramatic reversal of that imperative.

Moreover, Cochrane's Clan members and guests knew its name, and knew who composed its rites and works, and all accounts are without ambiguity. No guest ever claimed they had contributed to the creation of its rites. On the contrary, all guests to Clan Rites have commented on their complete mystification in the execution of those workings.

Without qualification, Monmouth added that Ronald White's vision to expand the concept of a Clan was realised in *The Regency* which affirmed Monmouth's confusion concerning what a Clan is. Again, if true, then it reveals how little both Monmouth and White actually know of the mechanics and modus operandi of a Clan. Michael Howard made exactly the same claim as Monmouth, but he implied that Ronald White and George Winter had stated this was the case in their *Messiah of Highgate Hill Interview,* in the weekly series of *Man, Myth and Magic* (published in 1970). [656]

Aside from all that is proven thus far to the detriment of that claim, Cochrane had made it perfectly clear to everyone who knew him, both inside and outside the remit of his own oath-bound People, that he was *Magister of a small clan, the devil in fact!* Scouring the article, it is easily discovered that White and Winter did not advocate this anywhere, least of all there.

Michael Howard had employed a characteristic tactic, whereby a personal interjection is sandwiched between comments paraphrased from the article, changing the overall inference

---

[655] 9th September 2012 '*The Secret History of the Royal Windsor Coven* and the Regency* with John of Monmouth' – Witchtalkshow on You Tube.
https://www.youtube.com/watch?v=WpAAmBpF0Us
[656] Howard, 2011. Op.Cit. p 85

substantially. It is disingenuous, but quite purposeful in its intent. Howard cited the date for the Interview incorrectly as 1968; it was in fact, 1969, around the time Ronald White became leader of *The Regency*.

As someone who was never there, and never properly knew the people concerned, Monmouth evidently struggled with the information he was clearly swamped by. His chances of understanding even a fraction of it were never good, which in part, may explain the contradictions that entrench his arguments.

During this revealing interview, Monmouth states that he had '*never heard of Cochrane*', yet he dedicated the entire interview (an hour and a half), and a full book, to denigrating the man and his works with personal comment, both accusative and judgmental. This suggests his views were neither impartial, nor uninformed. Yet, when asked to comment upon the character of his own alleged mentor, Ronald White, of whom he claimed to have shared a house with briefly, he was unable. Stumbling over a few repeated words, he mumbled twice nothing more than, *'he was a lovely man.'*

When asked what he felt Cochrane meant by his statement that the '*Mysteries were open to everyone*,' he was momentarily speechless! After spending so much time explaining that he believed Cochrane was an elitist, dictatorial, ego-driven, narcissist, he could hardly begin to counter that by any measure of altruism and humility implicit in the prompt.

The incongruence of the needful response to Monmouth's beliefs is apparent in his ill-considered reply that *"The Cochrane Coven resurrected the Old Mystery Religion under the name of the Regency."* This illogical suggestion that something separate from itself would need to generate anything, in order to fulfil its own mythos, removes the purpose for a fictional coven. In point of fact, it admits that Cochrane's Tradition simply continued as itself, with purpose intact, which of course it did as itself, that is - CTC.

Ground Zero

Drifting slowly away from the Clan some time before Cochrane's death, Ronald White and George Winter had no choice but to resign themselves to reflect upon their own beliefs and methodologies. So it can be imagined *they would wish* to set a new course, albeit built around a structure familiar to them. Robert Cochrane's Tradition was closed to them, emphatically so; Jane Bowers and E.J.J had seen to that, as E.J.J.' statement confirmed. Their only recourse was to ally themselves to associates known to them from within the Wican and neo-Pagan community. That option is evident in the appointments lists in White's diary that noted a flurry of activity amongst those who later come together as foundational leaders of *The Regency*. [657]

An unverified account claims that is what White did, though not immediately, not until he'd finished with *The Regency*, and possibly even with London. A handful of people were allegedly 'told' of White's ultra 'secret' coven over several years between 1974 and 1982, with no coven name known, or given. Ignoring context, the factual accounts, testimonies and even logic, Monmouth and Howard pressed the extraordinary assertion, that the *phantom coven* continued the works of Cochrane's original coven after his death.

True or false, those unverified people share Howard and Monmouth's status' as external sources to that alleged tradition and to CTC; these accounts are all unable to furnish more than speculative commentary. Their opinions are at best, hypothetical only. [658]

White had no official capacity whatsoever to form any group claiming connections to Robert Cochrane, and no authority from Cochrane, his wife, or E.J.J for it. It should not be forgotten that any group formed without this authority, would be forced to exist under extreme secrecy, real secrecy, not the false secrecy applied throughout Monmouth's fictional account of their history.

Over the years, CTC received several letters and emails from Michael Howard. Almost all of them were deliberately provocative, or were fishing mechanisms. This process was stepped up in expectation of public interest in Monmouth's forthcoming book - *Genuine Witchcraft is Explained*.

---

[657] Monmouth, 2012. Op. Cit. pages 114-116
[658] Anon. Private Correspondence.

> Apparently John [of Monmouth] is going to explain in his talk why Cochrane's covine was called the *'Royal Windsor Cuveen'* (something to do with Richard III I understand!?) and also discuss the alleged influence of the Regency on Wicca. Oh well.....should be fun. At the moment there is a rumour circulating that Madge Worthington was involved in founding The Regency and was actually present at the famous pub meeting with Chalky and George Stannard. I really don't know where this nonsense comes from.[659]

Refraining from comment, CTC received another almost identical email a week later, beginning with *"I can't remember if I mentioned it before, but 'John of Monmouth' is due to give a talk on the Royal Windsor Coven....."* The information that referred to Madge Worthington appeared incongruous but was raised again by Howard elsewhere, exposing his tendency towards duplicity:

> I was introduced to the late Madge Worthington in 1969 by my Gardnerian initiator Rosina Bishop, who was a friend of hers and a fellow member of the Regency's inner circle which was one of the continuations of Roy Bower's Royal Windsor Cuveen. Rosina had also met Cochrane (. . .) through her friendship with Doreen. In the conversations we had when she stayed for a weekend at our Welsh cottage in 1982 she never mentioned the Old Craft or the Regency. [660]

In order to lay claim for the phantom coven as the foundation of everything that followed, an exceptional boast is declared on the back cover of *Genuine Witchcraft is Explained*. The alleged origin of the phantom *Royal Windsor Coven,* is projected backwards by almost two decades, from 1982 to 1962. This was an attempt to secure a date immediately prior to when Cochrane's fledgling group became CTC. The Clan was founded by Robert Cochrane on the cusp as 1962 turned into 1963, immediately before E.J.J. joined:

> *The Royal Windsor Coven* gave birth to the Cochrane Tradition in witchcraft. *The Regency*, was the first group to hold public pagan celebrations in Britain which culminated in the Stonehenge

---

[659] Private email to SLO from MH. 13/09/10
[660] Selected & Abridged transcripts of exchanges between Shani Oates and Mike Howard on the 1734 forum in 2012-2014

festivals. Together, these groups gave rise to the *Clan of Tubal Cain, Y Plant Bran, 1734* and *Roebuck Covens.*" [661]

So now we have claims that even the Clan (CTC) was only a product of the the phantom coven, and furthermore, one democratised to the same level as those groups it (actually) later influenced. With the exception of *The Roebuck*, more properly associated with *The Ancient Keltic Church*, none of these other named traditions are *covens,* but very distinct occult modalities. Beyond that obvious fact, its expression admits an intent to deceive it aimed to achieve in that publication, and all without a valid evidence.

Around the same time, on the 1734 Forum dedicated to its mysteries, this very subject was raised by a long standing member, somewhat puzzled and unable to fathom the tangled associations between 1734, CTC, *The Regency* and the phantom '*Royal Windsor Coven.*' He was perplexed as to how they fitted together. Michael Howard, a guest on that forum, responded with the following statement:

> Perhaps the reason why they are put together in books, articles and on the Internet is that 1734, Roebuck and CTC all originated with and were <u>inspired by Robert Cochrane and his tradition.</u> However as they were founded by different people that might explain any differences in praxis and approach? [662]

What had not been immediately apparent to the 1734 members on that forum, was Howard's implicit intent. In this bold statement he declared that everyone's tradition, including CTC were each separately formed and founded *from* Robert Cochrane's Tradition, and were distinct *to* it, and *by* diverse people. Howard had refined his commentary over the previous decade to concentrate the impact this declaration would have on the status of those modalities relative to Cochrane's Tradition. This was a bold and public attempt to denigrate CTC to a side-lined group merely *inspired by* Robert Cochrane.

---

[661] Monmouth, 2012. Op. Cit.
[662] Selected & Abridged transcripts of exchanges between Shani Oates and Mike Howard on the 1734 forum in 2012 -2014

Unavoidably incensed by the acceleration of similar provocations, CTC rebutted this comment with an explanation that CTC *is* The Robert Cochrane Tradition. Because of the deliberate confusion generated over (several years now), by Howard regarding names and leaders, several people on the 1734 forum assumed that CTC were claiming the aegis of 1734. Thankfully, Stuart Inman, the site's moderator and Guardian of 1734, set those concerns at least to rest:

> Shani was not referring to 1734 at all, but the Clan of Tubal Cain and we really do need to retain and clarify the distinction between the two.

Another comment then expressed concerns that CTC obviously wished to monopolise the works, tradition and legacy of Robert Cochrane! As far as the *private* works, Tradition and legacy go, CTC do this by default, there is no getting around that, something this autobiography has established without equivocation. This does not extend to other legacies, public and private, founded upon the endurance and efforts of those *inspired* by his work and his tradition to establish their own; as indeed Joe Wilson did with 1734.

In retrospect, it is easy to suggest that Howard's views were accepted too readily, and that his self-declared authority should have been challenged by others when flaws and inconsistencies were apparent in his many claims. The absence of genuine sources in his writings and comments could have been queried. Likewise for Monmouth. Casual observation is rarely transparent. Had that occurred, then this biography might have been easier to write and easier to read.

Given Monmouth's insistence that White and Winter held the true genius' behind what he claims Cochrane passed off as his own, some might ponder why White and Winter would even wish to continue the *Cochrane legacy* in preference to their own. Suspending briefly what is now known, to accept White and Winter as the real creators of the inspiring works Cochrane is popularly accredited with, surely it would follow that once he was dead, the opportunity to promote *themselves*, and reclaim *their* own works, would be the natural inclination? And yet Monmouth posits they wilfully chose *not* to do that, preferring to perpetuate their genius under the guise of -

Robert Cochrane! This is all clearly such arrant nonsense, that it remains a wonder anyone was so easily taken in by it. many may not care, and that is fine, they are not obliged to, but believing this fiction really is inexcusable. The flaws and errors are abundant as the evidence for their claims is lacking.

Both Howard and Monmouth additionally claimed *The Regency* was created to continue the works of Robert Cochrane. But if those works were as claimed, the genius of White and Winter, then why would *The Regency* have been created at all? If only to continue Cochrane's works, they could in theory have done so through the phantom coven. Either way, one or the other would be superfluous.

And what of the Wican initiates who collectively formed *The Regency;* it is not even plausible they would happily embrace Cochrane's works, nor maintain his legacy? Certainly, Doreen Valiente, despite mourning for the loss of her dear friend and mentor, was nonetheless stinging from the recent Pentagram entanglement, not to mention *The Night of the Long Knives* debacle. As were countless others, all less forgiving at that time. For them, he was and to some extent, remains, public enemy number one.[663]

Monmouth overlooked another major issue. In his lament to John Score, Reginald Hinchcliffe clarified the intended purpose for *The Regency*; it was hoped the provision of a generic 'Pagan Church,' would fulfil the needs of the masses of non-initiates, unwilling or unsuitable to join closed initiatory covens.

After Cochrane's death, Winter did not feature in anyone's accounts and faded into obscurity. White's distinct works are evident in the *Regency* (mark II) and in *The New Pagan's Handbook* he eventually completed circa 1986 based upon them. In order to remove any rumour of presumed effective or productive influences from White and Winter upon Cochrane's works, it has been necessary to show that White and Winter shared no commonality of interest or philosophy with Cochrane.

Their history would have been more fairly and accurately recorded by others, Ken Rees for example, whose archival research

---

[663] CTC attended the recent book launch of Valiente's biography by Philip Heselton to offer our support and interest in the CfPS. It was a shock to hear Heselton voicing *his* personal belief in derisory comment against Robert Cochrane, announcing him as an unsavoury and mentally unstable individual, a fake, who had made his entire tradition up. Treadwells' Book Launch of ' Doreen Valiente - *Witch*.' 2016.

as a former member would never have embroiled it in the confused tale of a secret name and history for a fictional coven. Cochrane did not ever refer to his Tradition, works or legacy as anything but Clan - *The Clan of Tubal Cain,* and its members as the *People of Goda*. [664]

Refusing to acknowledge this indisputable fact, the person responsible for creating the deliberately distinctive title of a singular legacy as *'The Robert Cochrane Tradition'* was actually Michael Howard. Both Howard and Monmouth worked actively to remove Robert Cochrane from the 'Clan' tradition, by desire and design. Their continued insistence the Clan is not the real locus of Cochrane's Tradition, nor its people the real legacy holders of his works, is not a pleasant or comfortable realisation. Yet hard fact it remains.

Monmouth wished to pass that credit to White and Winter, Howard to a fictional coven that select surviving members continued <u>outside</u> the remit of the Clan. Without pretence of subterfuge, that purpose and intent to separate E.J.J. and CTC from Cochrane and to present them as separate traditions was finally and openly declared on a craft discussion group by Michael Howard:

> As I see it, what is also at issue here is differing perspectives of EJJ and how and when the CTC originated and whether or not it was a direct continuation of Cochrane's *Royal Windsor Cuveen* [sic]. In my personal opinion the new information in John of Monmouth's book suggests it wasn't. That role was taken by the 'inner circle' of *The Regency* founded in the summer of 1966, shortly after RC's death, by Ronald White, George Stannard and Gerard Noel. [665]

Countering this same argument on this and other forums, magazine reviews, articles and specious commentary published in recent books, was wearisome and in CTC's defence, fractious. Still, it is regrettable. Howard's responses were invariably passive-aggressive and hardly ever on point. His retorts were frequently disguised as further attacks veiled as clarifications or excuses:

> I never said that John Jones was not 'of the [Cochrane] tradition' as that would be very silly. I also clearly said in my posting that 1734,

---

[664] From Robert Cochrane, through Evan John Jones, to Robin-the-dart, to Ulric 'Gestumblindi' Goding.
[665] Michael Howard, 2012. 1734 Forum. May.

> Roebuck and CTC originated with Robert Cochrane and his tradition. I cannot be clearer then that as it is the truth. All were 'inspired' by that tradition (…) as I am aware 1734 makes no claim to be, the Roebuck Coven and the CTC are the public faces of the Cochrane tradition.[666]

In other words, Howard is here making an claiming that CTC is merely the public face (outercourt) group for a secret, (inner court) group, continued by others, distinct from CTC which continues merely as a group inspired by Robert Cochrane. That this astonishing claim (years in its planning) was not properly understood by those observing the exchanges on that forum at that time, remains a testament to his manipulations and feats of misdirection. As an indictment, this damning statement is in every sense incorrect. CTC could (obviously) never be a continuance of something that did not exist, and could only be itself, the creative legacy of Robert Cochrane. Monmouth was adamant that *The Regency* did not have an 'inner circle' of any description. His conviction on this matter is fully supported by ample facts. Howard's own responses were well-articulated confirmations of what he had previously stated:

> Firstly, and most importantly, I have never queried or denied Shani Oates rightful position as "the chosen one" - the heir to Evan John Jones — or her and *****'s right therefore to be the Maid and Magister of the Clan of Tubal Cain (CTC).[667]

Because so many were unaware of the real back-history of this subterfuge, and were pre-disposed to Howard's influence, his comment went unnoticed or remarked upon. Its significance largely eluded those witnessing this incredible statement. Attempting to draw sense of that heated discussion, apparently obvious only to ourselves, the list moderator Stuart Inman affirmed his own astonishment at the anger CTC had expressed in their response.

Inman reiterated Howard's support for *'John's Heirs to CTC'* against those made by the pretenders a few years ago. Focussing on *that* point, Inman initially overlooked the disingenuous subtlety of

---

[666] Selected & Abridged transcripts of exchanges between Shani Oates and Mike Howard on the 1734 forum in 2012-2014
[667] Ibid. In this statement, Howard publically revealed Robin's 'real' name. Within Craft Traditions, this is considered as the ultimate treachery.

Howard's comment, presented almost as a throwaway line. Inman later drew attention to the issue:

> However, the point made by Shani is quite different, and it is to do with the legitimacy and transmission of the virtue of the Clan of Tubal Cain, which is to say her own legitimacy. This all becomes both rather sad and peculiar, as Mike has previously affirmed her legitimacy as <u>Evan John Jones' heir</u>. [our emphasis]. He has not backtracked on this, but *recently has stated that EJJ*, and *not Roy Bowers*, founded the Clan of Tubal Cain. This is apparently based on his reading of the recent book by John of Monmouth. This claim has been echoed in an anonymous review of Shani's latest book *The Star-Crossed Serpent*, published in *Pagan Dawn* and, I think, in *Pentacle* as well (?). My problem with what Mike has written on this is that it is stated as fact rather than as a claim, as if it were proven rather than it being some kind of evidence if backed up.[668]

Frequently controversial, it was not the first or last time Michael Howard presented opinion as if it were fact and approved by 'people in the know.' He did not respond well to challenges to them. Roughly paraphrasing his response to being asked why he was singularly obsessed with *someone else's* Tradition, he'd said: *'It is true I am not part of the <u>present incarnation</u> of CTC.'* and there we have it. Howard's undeclared intention to belong not to CTC, which he'd attempted to diminish and discredit, but to its supposed incarnation - being The non-existent Royal Windsor Coven.

Inman pointed out that where claims concerning the traditions of others are discussed, there is a need to be mindful of their status as outsiders. They are not initiates, and therefore not privy to the same level of information. Anything discussed or suggested in the public arena should always be backed up with proofs. Inman reminded Howard that he (Howard) was ever quick to defend his own tradition from similar provocations.[669]

With regard to CTC's legitimacy, Howard's explicit claim is unprecedented. Few people understood its full implications. To remove residual uncertainties, doubt or confusion, clarity denounces Howard's semantic ambiguities. Howard had no part in CTC because

---

[668] Stuart Inman, 2012. 1734 Forum. May
[669] Stuart Inman, 2012. 1734 Forum. 2012-14

it was Robert Cochrane's Tradition, and had only itself in continuity of it. All other names and guises Howard and others have attached to it, are false, illusory and bear no existence in reality. He was never part of it. It was never his Tradition to claim.

As in every other claim made throughout this biography, Howard had never challenged E.J.J. nor questioned his authority, directly. Waiting until E.J.J. had crossed the bar, he began to openly challenge his successors, undermining the work and heritage of CTC time and again, hoping to convince others less knowledgeable that his version was correct. In the midst of a considerable tirade, stunned members of the forum overlooked this valuable snippet:

> Although I have been privately working a version of the Cochrane system for many years, it is perfectly true that I have not been initiated into any 'official' (sic) surviving Cochrane tradition or group - nor have I ever made that claim or led anyone to believe it is true. In that sense I may be an 'outsider.' [670]

Before this had time to sink in, it was quickly followed with further polemics. Monmouth and Howard pressed a corrosive attack on the credibility of a Craft pioneer, a true genius, and his Clan. Of that legacy, Cochrane was the first to share its knowledge to a wider community. Howard's and Monmouth's insistence that Cochrane had not named his group the *Clan of Tubal Cain*, nor referred to that name, is insupportable. It is efficiently repudiated here, and in *SCS III*. [671]

Other provocative claims declared by Howard on the same theme, were executed with minor variations. His insinuations were intimidating but foundless. No evidence, verbally or textual, was ever produced or shared in support of them. This lack, was the primary objection CTC raised and questioned Howard upon. His responses were never subtle, always retaliatory, and always loaded with further accusation. His past claims to secret information in his remit that had not been disclosed by anyone, were generally preceded by: *"I know where all the bodies are buried...."* For example, he'd previously stated:

---

[670] Selected & Abridged transcripts of exchanges between Shani Oates and Mike Howard on the 1734 forum in 2012-2014

[671] Oates, 2016. Op. Cit. *SCSIII* 2016 pages 50-60

> I also have documentary evidence that around the same time there was another group independently working the Cochrane tradition. It involved two people who were also associated with the old covine. While they could not have directly claimed to be Cochrane's heirs they were following the tradition. This suggests the situation after RC's death was more complicated than some people claim or want to believe, or indeed want others to believe.[672]

Designed for maximum damage, this contentious statement deliberately presented a false impression of the continuity of Cochrane's legacy. There is no doubt that many groups were inspired and initiated in response to Cochrane's works, especially if first-hand experience of them in action had been acquired through being a guest at one of his selected Rites.

But this is not what Howard *implied*, which was very different. His objective sought to undermine the integrity of the Tradition. Breaking down his sensational use of language, however, all that remains of Howard's statement, is that two former associates (guests) formulated *their own* working system based on what they witnessed as guests on one, possibly two occasions. As non-members, their status as outsiders placed them below that of novice or apprentice, being the first level of comprehension acquired after a person is Fully Admitted into the Clan. A very different impact indeed.

Aside from matters of legitimacy that are dealt with in the appropriate chapters, which distinguishes any group following (what they assume Cochrane's works to be) from the genuine Tradition, led legitimately, and sourced in the Egregore, the Mysteries, Mythos, Ethos and Praxes of the Tradition were not meted out to guests and associates.

In fact, Clan members were often left mystified. Valiente, E.J.J. and Gray's remarks conform how tightly Cochrane kept things to his chest. Relaying only what was needful, he preferred experience to soften the mind into an easier receptivity for the actual teaching

---

[672] Selected & Abridged transcripts of exchanges between Shani Oates and Mike Howard on the 1734 forum in 2012-2014

mechanisms that generally followed the rites, rather than preceded them.

Identities of Clan members and their number have similarly been covered in the appropriate chapters, thus voiding any possibility for the introduction of guests and associates as presumed members. They are all known and accounted for. Monmouth and Howard both claimed that Valiente and Bill Gray were members of the phantom coven, and that Cochrane was its Magister. Howard added one more lie: *"putting aside his membership of the Royal Windsor Cuveen, EJJ was a genuine member of the Old Craft."* [673]

Making sure that E.J.J. could not refute it, this was naturally claimed only after his death. The number of errors is staggering. One by one, each presumption falls to fact, logic and clarity, providing better information backed by authoritative knowledge in its stead.

As the Millennium approached, several old crafters crossed the bar, an irreparable loss to the Craft and for those remaining. Certainly, it was at that point Michael Howard began circulating that rumour with intent. Coincidently 1998 marked and witnessed a change of leadership, an event that occurs possibly twice only in a generational lifetime within Clan history. Its legacy, under Clan Law, was transferred to Shani Oates and Robin-the-dart. The Virtue had shifted and this marked that official point in its history.

Knowledge of that act impacted elsewhere, reverberating along unseen trajectories, initiating a sequence of events that encompassed many years, and involved numerous people. One figure in particular was moved to pronounce upon it, asserting an inappropriate demand to a Craft Elder.

Cutting a swathe in Traditional Craft circa 1998, Andrew D. Chumbley approached E.J.J., Magister of CTC, charged with ambitious purpose. Although Chumbley was a stranger and an outsider to the Clan, his arrogance was boundless. He sent a letter to E.J.J. which berated him for what Chumbley believed was a grave error of judgment. He advised E.J.J., the Clan's leader and bearer of Cochrane's legacy, that it should be rectified in his favour, the only person he deemed worthy to be the successor of Cochrane's legacy. In short: having made the wrong choice, E.J.J. should renounce Shani

---

[673] Selected & Abridged transcripts of exchanges between Shani Oates and Mike Howard on the 1734 forum in 2012-2014

Oates and Robin-the-dart and appoint Andrew D. Chumbley in their stead.

Chumbley was bold, though not for the first time. His sights were set high and had created waves of antagonism in other occult factions he was involved with. Chumbley's letter concluded with several misogynistic comments concerning the person E.J.J. had chosen, as Maid, both as a female and as the 'Chosen One.'

Needless to say, E.J.J. responded swiftly and with full measure of all that is just and proper in that given situation. Once rejected by E.J.J, Chumbley's aspirations set a subversive course ahead, steered by the personal bias of his supporters who consequently worked to undermine CTC. Others, having knowledge of the history of CTC and the machinations of current and past people in the Craft were included, namely Doreen Valiente. It was all part of what Michael Howard termed *'his damage limitation strategy.'*

Matters of ambition and retribution aside. What should be plain to see in Chumbley's action undertaken in 1998, is the recognition and acknowledgment by him of precisely *where* the authority and Tradition of Robert Cochrane *resided and continued*.

Significantly, Chumbley had demonstrated that he knew Cochrane's legacy resided with CTC through Evan John Jones, *not* Ronald White, and certainly not with an alleged secret coven.[674] Though his mission was unsuccessful, he had identified and acknowledged the source of Cochrane's Tradition. Because of that, a new directive followed his failed initiative. It was at this point that Howard created and initiated his plan of action, leading to years of convoluted deceptions and manouverings, that we as Clan, have spent years countering. Whilst observers saw only conflict, they failed to see why.

Several former associates, members and guests of the Clan, including Doreen Valiente and Ronald White, crossed the bar as these events unfolded over the 1998-99 period, leaving no voice but that of CTC to speak truly of these events. By 2008, Howard had successfully inflated Ronald White's alleged activities out of proportion and into the history of CTC. Howard's disregard for the

---

[674] Ronald White was alive when Chumbley advanced upon E.J.J. Chumbley had shown no interest in him or his work at any time. Ronald White crossed the bar at the end of that year. Soon after Howard began promoting Ronald White and The Regency.

facts, cast dubious opinion and misinformation upon the historicity of everyone involved in Cochrane's life and times.

At that point, Monmouth appeared, driven by his own purpose to promote his version of that history, especially where it concerned Ronald White and his leadership of *The Regency*. Areas of overlap between Howard and Monmouth's accounts were in conflict, but Monmouth's perspective partly redressed some of the inaccuracies of Howard's version of events.

Cumulative misinformation generated confusions Monmouth could not fathom in his construction of *GWiE*. His narrative explored a mass of conflated events relating to people and circumstances involved with Cochrane. Its inaccuracies are disingenuous to the extent that little remains of value.

As a former member of Cochrane's Clan, White's activities after 1966 were either, falsely misrepresented by himself to others, or by others, for him. Perhaps even a measure of both. Motivated by ambition, it was not beyond Ronald White's vanity to bypass Cochrane's Clan as a legacy long denied them, then at a later point, establish a coven that *assumed* a link to the old coven in Windsor, even if in title only - a *'Windsor'* Coven.

Such a venture would resurrect the kudos held by the 'old' coven in Windsor, long defunct even when referred to by Cochrane in his letter to Joe Wilson in 1966. Moving beyond the pale of acceptable glamour, White's ambition was long ago marked by Valiente as the *"aspirations of grandeur."* [675]

It is a great opportunity lost that Monmouth's agenda for *GWiE* was focussed entirely on an erroneous *back story*. Rather than trying to understand what the material evidence was *genuinely able to explain* concerning what had really transpired in the years between 1958 to 1998, he followed a fictional account. To this day, *no material evidence exists to show that a secret group ever existed*, less still what it named itself. An absence of evidence is not an evidence of lack of course.

Which means that if a secret group had existed, even if only for a short time, it could never be confused with a publically known, legitimate, extant, practising group, of declared title, with appointed

---

[675] Valiente, 1981. Notepads 24/6/1981. Winter's ambition is recorded, as was his willingness to use others to serve it.

leaders. The secret group would have to be entirely separate from such a group; any correlation between them whatsoever, would compromise it. Once compromised or revealed by time or circumstance, should any persons or material allegedly associated with a secret group become known, they must be verified to avoid speculative assumption.

With regard to the alleged phantom coven posited by Howard and Monmouth, an enormous hurdle has arisen in that all the facts confirm it as a misrepresentation of the extant group, CTC. Everything they brought forward in their attempts to manifest an existence for the phantom coven is conjectural, based on verbal opinion circa <u>1982</u>, therefore relevant only to a period some decades after Cochrane's death. The rumoured existence of a secret coven began then; its name and purpose were awarded later still. Its *retrospective* name was given as the (phantom) Royal Windsor Coven.

That year, 1982, when that rumour began its course was the same year the Finnins contacted E.J.J., the same year they visited Howard in the UK, the year White moved to Shropshire from London, the year Montalban died. A coincidental year for events that encompass Michael Howard.

The confused associations for *CTC* with 1734 and *The Royal Windsor Coven,* and for their muddled time-lines relied upon that retrospective speculation. By placing a fictional (Royal Windsor) coven central to all, its satellites became sourced by that fictional core. As a deceptive sleight of hand, it orchestrated an imaginary tangent for *The Robert Cochrane Tradition* in the minds of the public only, not in any reality. False declarations cannot affect what actuality is, or exists. They affect perception only – as an illusory facet and vain fancy of the mind.

Howard's singular objective advanced the activities of *The Regency* disproportionately to their actual popularity. His attempts to secure those opinions as definitive, are voided by his numerous contradictions and lack of substantive evidence. The natural instinct to defend when faced with hostile appropriation was exploited by Michael Howard. Using his authority, he curried favour from public opinion against CTC whenever its members responded to his provocations. This is a typical example of Howard's barely veiled snide:

However I would have thought that John of Monmouth's new book on the origins and history of the Royal Windsor Cuveen and The Regency would have put to rest the idea that the CTC was the only 'official' inheritor of the Cochrane tradition. All that is left now is for the different claimants to have an undignified fight over the bones.

With unnecessary sarcasm Michael Howard referred to CTC as: *"The 'official' holders of the Cochrane keys to the Castle."* Adding that:

Unfortunately I think they protesteth too much, some people are beginning to see their version of the castle has foundations made of sand.[676]

CTC *do* hold the keys to *that* Castle, naturally. How could it not? Each to their own, and rightly so. CTC's roots and foundations are strong indeed; it is not we, who stand upon sand. CTC exist as the *Robert Cochrane Clan Tradition*, all other presumed connections to it are finally addressed and resolved, proven throughout this autobiography as void. There are no factions, splinters, hiving-off, separations of any description. Robert Cochrane was wise when he established his Tradition as a Clan, affirming his recognition of an older system of unity and loyalty. He made absolutely certain that *only those in that Clan can claim to be of its Tradition.* And only those appointed from within it, may hold it and advance it in time. It is simplicity itself. To serve this intent requires critical clarification in a simple, definitive and quotable explanation ~ *'One is either Clan or one is not.'* There is no middle ground.

---

[676] Michael Howard – 1734 Forum. May 2012

For many reading *Tubal's Mill* and *Star Crossed Serpent III* & *Star Crossed Serpent IV* in tandem with *Genuine Witchcraft is Explained and Children of Cain*, the contrast of views may prove uncomfortable. It is hoped the presentation of facts will alleviate this. Howard's world are laced with accusations, opinion and conjecture alone. he offers no proofs. Monmouth's book is blatant fabrication and specious nonsense, again offering no proofs and masses of refutable 'evidence', which in fact is now proven contrary to the claims he makes within it. Howard worked toward the gradual diminishment of anyone able to counter his version of history, to erode their professional reputation by ridicule, or render them *'persona non grata.'* That list includes past and present members of CTC, especially its leaders E.J.J, Valiente. Other named associates include Ken Rees, Iain Steele and Nigel Jackson.

The loyalty and integrity of those people, Valiente and E.J.J. especially, find voice in their wealth of knowledge concerning these matters. Shared freely, their works offer direct validation of what is factual and true, providing context and good account of events. Their authentic documents and letters are included where possible, and are available for private study where appropriate.

Whatever the facts (and fantasies) are regarding the histories of *Ronald White, George Winter, The Regency* (in all its versions and incarnations), secret covens and groups of whatever name, *Marian Green, Madge Worthington, Desmond Bourke, Gerard Noel, Joe Wilson*, and every other *June, Joan, George, Lance, Laurence, Avril, Alice, Ruth, Diane, Ron, Roy, Ray, Arthur, Dick* and *Norman* who may or may not have ever claimed acquaintance with Robert Cochrane or each other, is left to themselves and to others to speak for them, according to wherever the authority to do so is bestowed.

Anything written here about any of these people, is mutable, subject to contrary evidence produced at any future point.[677] The history of CTC is likewise, not set, but has a solid foundation

---

[677] CTC have endeavoured to contact all relevant people for advice and information on this period and of any events or incident they may recall that might assist those enquiries. CTC have scrupulously researched archives, ms, documents and letters for five years to resolve all former variations of rumoured tales that attempt to remark upon anyone known to be associated (however remotely), or who are desirous of association with this history, in order that CTC may establish a boundary that separates what is known to be true and what is believed to be true. And to separate facts from fiction. Some anomalies remain with regard to others, where certain ambiguities remain, but they do not concern CTC or its actual history.

established by its People, and that history is concerned only with its People, of Admission and of Goda. Anyone not of the People is not the concern of CTC and has no claim in fact to a place in its history, its ancestry or its future.

To conclude, CTC affirm the singular authority of its Tradition. This history is theirs to hold and reveal by them alone. Because no-one else is qualified to do so, no-one else may pronounce upon it in contradiction of that fact. Neither the single, one-off Council meeting, the mundane non-secret planning committee that possibly led to the creation of *The Pagan Federation*, nor *The Regency*, *mark I, II*; not the later, small private Regency group in Shropshire, and finally, not even the all 'new' theoretical Regency instigated briefly by Regency John in Cornwall, had or has *any* connection to Cochrane's Clan Tradition, nor are they a continuance of it. As a *closed* Tradition, it cannot be otherwise.

> For our ancestors in the smithcraft, may *this* day bring honour to them, and may we make them proud. ~ Robin-the-dart

A Giant is Slain

Real Craft history is a sadly neglected area of any legacy, underestimated in misdirected focus elsewhere. It has witnessed the trials and struggles of a new wave of belief seeking to assert itself, Marshall and guide itself, and to observe safeguards and new protocols. The life and tragic death of Robert Cochrane, his Clan Tradition and its legacy, though of immense importance to his own *People of Goda*, and those it may influence and who may follow its interests, have generated a lapwing for those intrigued by its mysteries.

Other leading neo-Pagans and Wicans not preoccupied with Cochrane's legacy, had business elsewhere to attend to. For sure these people gathered to discuss how to approach and repair the public expression of the Craft. In disarray; if it could not be salvaged, then all the ground they had gained since 1951 would be lost.

Having exposed the regrettable factors that became entangled within this history, its processing generated a remarkable form of expression by which CTC is able to explain how that real history operates as a *lived* tradition. A direct working knowledge of Clan Tradition is something no previous author has grappled with. That familiarity taps the source in ways no fictional, or speculative account could ever hope to. Circumnavigating those fictions has been an education. Much has been discovered and the clarity borne from that is refreshing and illuminating.

Anyone may access Cochrane's public legacy to the Craft through his works, via the inspiration they induce and by gleaning what those works mean to *them*. What they mean to Cochrane's people through his Tradition, is very different. The real story of the people Howard and Monmouth have corralled into a homogenous 'lot' is not linear, it does not progress; each body of folk are independent from one another. Each group, coven, system or church engage different gods, call upon different ancestors, endorse different Mythos' and Ethos' etc.

The vast majority of people fifty years ago had not seen or read Cochrane's letters to Wilson, Gills or Gray. Even forty years ago very few people were aware that his actual group was in fact a Clan. Three decades ago, when CTC first began explaining the Ethos and Mythos within those letters, there seemed no common language by which their insights could be shared.

This provided room for presumption, for speculation, for fanciful interpretation, which built error upon error as the reality slipped further into obscurity. Fuelled by controversy and media attention, the facts were overwhelmed by personality. Six decades later, those facts remain a matter beyond the kenning of most. During the interim, that lack had been widely exploited by Howard, and to some extent by Monmouth also. Efforts to bring attention to these errors, proved sporadic and largely ineffective.

Contestable views and opinions pronounced prematurely upon Cochrane's Tradition by writers and researchers throughout this biography, namely:- Julia Phillips, David Barrett, Ethan Doyle White, Michael Howard, and John of Monmouth, and all others who refer back to them. Their attempts to rewrite the CTC Tradition, its history and the roles of its people, were executed through one very disturbing premise: that CTC should be removed from it.

In addition to informing Doyle White, Barrett, Phillips, et al, Howard furnished the Finnins and others with conflicting information on the fictional existence of the *Royal Windsor Coven*. There is even a footnote in one of Daniel Schulke's books that refers incorrectly to Robert Cochrane as a late Magister of the *Royal Windsor Coven*. [678]

CTC fully concur with Ken Rees on this:

> Who among all these people cited in an evidential way have had the kind of discipline, academic or otherwise, which makes them credible witnesses and accountants? Who among such have the kind of integrity and rigorousness needful for peer reviewed writing or publishing........? [679]

And also that:

> Howard was basically a fantasist, and driven by wish-fulfilment for decades. I met him twice in 1974 and, of course, nothing of the above was discussed simply because it did not exist and he had only third hand knowledge of both RWO [Ruth Wynn Owen] and *The Regency* (e.g. through Rosina Bishop). [680]

These candid explanations support the causes mentioned in this entangled biography. In works of fiction, Michael Howard had been free to create his own fantasy, drafting in characters from another history. What he could never change were the facts. As the years passed, his fictional convolutions grew exponentially, such that his threads were forcibly knotted ever tighter around himself and his creation.

Howard was Prof. Hutton's principle source for the information concerning the continuity of *Robert Cochrane's Tradition*, and the one who proposed connections between that legacy and *The Regency*. Both Howard and Monmouth strived to convince everyone that CTC are nothing more than a side-line. Prompted by better

---

[678] Schulke, Daniel. *Veneficium.* (US: Three Hands Press 2012) p 18 *"Knowledge of ritual poisons is also present in other traditional witchcraft groups. Robert Cochrane, past magister of the Royal Windsor Coven possesses knowledge in this area. See John of Monmouth's 'Genuine Witchcraft is Explained' and Gavin Semple's 'A poisoned Chalice,' 'The Cauldron' #114."*
[679] Rees, 2017. Op. Cit. Personal Correspondence. Easter
[680] Ibid.

intelligence received from E.J.J., Prof. Hutton was the only person to refute that advice from his principle source all those years ago,

What should have been obvious to everyone, was not. Others looking in with fresh eyes should have no problem at all in discerning this. Beyond that, an easily reconcilable test is to simply study and compare the beliefs, tenets, expounded philosophies, rites, and works produced by the Finnins, members of *The Regency* (any version), 1734, E.J.J. and Valiente too, not to mention recent works by current Clan members, with those of Robert Cochrane.

CTC are confident the results will confirm an unmitigated correlation only between the latter four. The former three groups of people exclude themselves, through a distinct divergence on all crucial matters. By default, 1734 was a conglomeration of ideas extended from it as an American system based on ideas it believed pertinent to both.

At this stage, CTC propose that the leaders and planning committee for *The Regency (mark I)* were the natural representatives of the neo-Pagan Community at large. [681] They just might have viewed that body as a potential revitalisation of the doomed and shattered *Witchcraft Research Association,* now broken by the politics and polemics of opposing factions and fraught agendas. As is so often the case, even this brave venture was doomed.

Just possibly, they may have aspired to fulfil its mission, rising from its ashes reborn anew. Moreover, the title of *Regency* would properly reflect this principle. Historically, the Regency Period was one that offered freedom from the old order, a comparative autonomy. It was a liberating and egalitarian flowering of the arts, a Renaissance of sorts that would suit well the sensibilities of its original very Bohemian set.

The co-existence and cross pollination between all paths no matter of whether their origins in Wicca or Traditional Craft, validates the progressive evolution of The Craft as a natural and un-contrived phenomena typical of how humans fashion their knowledge and skills through interaction with their environs and communities. This is nothing new, and is evidenced within and throughout the

---

[681] Initial council meeting attended for Regency by Madge, Rosina, Bill, John and Jean Score, Ruth and Tony and Marian. In 1970, several of these went on to attend the meetings for PF., including Joe Wilson during his stay in the UK.

history of the Craft itself over previous centuries, typifying occulted influences from many fields. That said, it is agreed that many do remain aware of these differing streams as outsiders to those traditions, abstaining from numerous initiations within them.

After the publicity of the American film producer died down, journalists and news-hounds quickly began to target everyone. Eventually, those brave pioneers became battle-weary and walked away. Sour publicity and media hyperbole events induced the dilemma of endurance in the face of adversity, or indulgence of a prior, natural inclination towards privacy and discretion. Returning to the comments made between Reginald Hinchcliffe and John Score who laid the seeds for the third time of a self-governing pagan community, a *Pagan Federation* generated circa 1971.

This heady climate had drawn Joe Wilson into the social circles of Ruth Wynn Owen, Reginald Hinchcliffe, John Score and Doreen Valiente, who had been instrumental in setting up the original WRA. And though Valiente had never been involved in *The Regency,* she and the aforementioned others were heavily involved in establishing *The Pagan Federation*. All of them were keen to avoid negative politics, notoriety and negative media attention.

That charged climate coincided with the visit to the UK just a few years later by Joe Wilson's wife Mara, when making her own rounds amidst the turmoil of the 1974 boundary changes that made Windsor into a *Royal* borough. The rumour of a 'secret' group did not yet exist until a deliberate act of mischief created it sometime later.

Taking much for granted now, it should be appreciated that back in the 1970s and early 1980s relatively few people knew of the Clan, or the true name of Robert Cochrane's tradition. Those who did, were either former members and guests of CTC, or amongst those close to them in the UK, plus a handful of people in the US Joe Wilson might have shared that info with from Cochrane's letters to him.

It is not crucial to this history to know for certain who amongst a select few people in the know, was responsible for giving the false impression Cochrane's Clan Tradition was 1734. Whether it was Norman Gills, or Ronald White, or someone else who furnished Wilson with that misinformation may never be determined.

Certainly, what we do know is Rees states that during his correspondence with the Finnins' during the very early 1980s, they'd also laboured under this false impression, and had initially referred to Cochrane's tradition as: *1734*. White's usage of the name 1734, to refer to Cochrane's tradition, rather than its natural and real name: '*People of (Goda) the Clan (of Tubal Cain)*,' not only confirms what Ann Finnin records herself previously, but that no-one, as yet, had referred to *The Royal Windsor Coven* in any capacity. That changed. Given the locus of false information thus far, an origin in Michael Howard could be posited, but without proof, that remains conjectural.

Certainly, what we do know is Rees recorded that upon their return from the next visit to the UK in the mid to late-1980s, Ann and Dave Finnin began referring to Cochrane's coven in their writings, as the '*old Royal Windsor Coven,*' (sic), and Cochrane as its *Grandmaster!* [682]

Several factors could be responsible for this error. It could have been mischief or a mistake. The confusion might have been a misunderstanding on their part, an idiosyncratic association with elements of his family history.

Cochrane's great grandfather was described as a grandmaster; his mother, as a scrying maid in the '*old Windsor coven.*' It may be an error of understanding on the part of the person relaying this information to them during a period when the appellation 'Royal' was topical.

Howard asked Ken Rees to produce an article for publication in *The Cauldron* based on the perceptions Rees had acquired through working with *The Regency*. Howard especially wanted Rees' impressions based on comments shared by Ronald White concerning Cochrane. [683] The article was printed in *The Cauldron* under the heading of '*The Royal Windsor Coven.*' [684]

---

[682] Rees. Ibid.
[683] Rees, Ken. 'The Royal Windsor Coven' *The Cauldron* #118 Nov. 2005. This is taken from a revised synopsis of his, dated 1985. Rees confirmed by email dated 6th Feb 2015, that Michael Howard commissioned this article, to write specifically about The Royal Windsor Coven which he informed Rees was the title of Cochrane's group. The text covers Cochrane's works, his influences, his letters, from which Rees quotes, extensively, even referring to *The People of Goda and the Clan of Tubal Cain*. Because Howard created a distinction in title and group, confusion followed.
[684] *The Cauldron*, 2005. #118 November.

That article led to some very interesting correspondence between CTC and Ken Rees. The misnomer of the alleged *Royal Windsor Coven* was broached, but with the exception of the title, Rees does not actually mention it in the article. Though uncertain of the origin of that title relative to CTC, Rees does not refer to the Royal Windsor Coven by that name within the text, except in the title, provided by Michael Howard. Rees refers only the Clan or to Cochrane's Tradition, showing again the general understanding that these meant the same thing and were not considered as 'separate' identities.

Initially rankled by certain factual errors within it concerning aspects of CTC's Mythos, which have since been amicably addressed, a better understanding of where the source of that misinformation originated, *shared with him* from another person - Peter Larkworthy was acquired later.

In retrospect, he, like many others simply had no idea how or why in-house views could be so divergent from those in the public domain, and CTC, had no idea why that should be so! In recent discussions with Ken Rees, shared aspects of research and resources have enabled CTC to piece together a very crucial sequence of events that revealed the source of that misinformation.

A private research document typed by KIR (Ken I. Rees) was reproduced with a summarised addendum composed by PL (Peter Larkworthy) dated 1985. This was circulated around various people in the Craft (without permission from Rees) and briefly ended up on the internet. The document reached the Finnins in the US, and was included with other highly sensitive material of a private and confidential nature, that somehow became 'leaked' online, without permission.

In recent correspondence with Ken Rees, the author (KIR) of that document, he expressed considerable surprise to learn of this. In earnest distress he explained the following:

> I never wrote anything on the Ry prior to 1981 and that was private. The only person who ever read it at that time was Peter Larkworthy. [PL.] That document, word for word appeared in *The Cauldron* #118 (2005), minus the addendum by PL, entitled *The Royal Windsor Coven.*

Rees further explains how that article came into being.

> The Cauldron #118 article has, in fact, two addendums (i.e. the end pieces) which are both my own written 20 years apart. I received some of the main body of the work from P.L who had kindly lent me an unpublished paper he labelled *The Royal Windsor Coven and its Practices* – Part One – Theory (. . .) I should say that by the time he'd written his piece he was already an inductee of the Finnin's outfit and had met EJJ more than once. This suggests that despite him knowing EJJ, PL misunderstood areas of the article originally penned by him!

Peter Larkworthy died immediately prior to the article appearing in TC#118, and so his own final addendum and name were not included in the published piece. Rees was absolutely correct, P.L. had been a close friend of the Finnins,' an initiate of *The Roebuck* in the 1980s and had worked loosely with E.J.J. during the 1990s. Here at last, the missing piece to this puzzle is discovered, and all very much as E.J.J. had believed from the beginning.

Rees was able to confirm that the person responsible for bringing the false title and impression of a *Royal Windsor Coven, to the public domain was Peter Larkworthy*. But this does not make him the creator of that idea. He'd relayed that misinformation from the Finnins, privately, who'd acquired it during their second visit to the UK in the late 1980s. [685]

Appearing later in *The Cauldron* #118, Larkworthy's source is circular via the Finnins, both of whom received the notion separately from a source in the UK. Valiente records a very curious aside in her treasured archive for that period, that Peter Larkworthy declared himself a close associate of Michael Howard, although Howard had informed E.J.J. he did not remember Larkworthy.

That rumour was then taken up anew by Michael Howard, when it returned to him via the Finnins, and passed on in turn to Ken Rees (via PL), onto Ruth et al. With regard to the generic usage of the name associated with the fictional coven, Rees admitted that, *"Yes, both the Finnins and myself used the title, the Royal Windsor Coven quite*

---

[685] A 1985 paper circulated without authority of the author Ken Rees. It has to be said, this article largely concerns the workings and beliefs of *The Regency*, interjected with garbled understandings of CTC. PL, was certainly confused by information he had from the Finnins and from Michael Howard.

innocently and unintentionally...." [686] At that time, neither of them had access to better information that might have alerted them to this deception. They had no reason to suppose the information was false.

Although most of the information in Rees' original article information had come directly from Peter Larkworthy and Ann Finnin, the chain of Chinese whispers led to compound error. [687] Everyone concerned should have checked the source of those inaccuracies. It has taken several years to untangle that thread.

This required tracking back to the person whose advice first mooted this idea, presuming a credibility beyond that of a rumour. Checking Prof. Hutton's listed sources for *The Triumph of the Moon*, Michael Howard is the noted person by Prof. Hutton for unverified information where he adds *'according to some.'*

Howard is sourced in two exchanges that occurred between them in *1997 and 1998* at the time when Prof. Hutton was summarising his research immediately prior to the 1999 publication for *The Triumph of the Moon*. [688] Howard is also the source that implies the construction of other groups from the demise of *The Regency* after 1974.

Documents <u>do</u> exist for *The Thames Valley Coven* and for *The Clan of Tubal Cain,* and even for *The Regency* that independently appear much later. All groups, whether secret or open, have their own documents and works. That none exist for the phantom Royal Windsor group should raise concerns. The only works brought forward for them, were those E.J,J. had written many years later, produced via a strange route into the hands of Prof. Hutton as research for *TToTM*.

Claimed as papers from *The Royal Windsor Coven,* they arrived from persons unknown in the early spring of 1998, a candidate for their submission is within reach. A confirmed context and time frame eliminates another mystery.

Based on Ann & Dave Finnin's awareness of the rumoured existence back in the 1980s for the phantom group having an alleged association with Cochrane through a proposed Windsor title, there

---

[686] Rees, 2017. Op. Cit.
[687] *The Cauldron* # 119, Feb. 2006
[688] See ref 31, from p 318 *Light from the Shadows* Gwyn (aka Michael Howard) plus personal comments by Michael Howard 28th November 1997 & 25th June 1998, *TToTM*.

was an unlikely assumption posited in 1998 that those papers were submitted by them. However, the Finnins are not known for sharing information *anonymously*; on the contrary, they make sure they are known and named for their deeds, especially of generosity.

Prof. Hutton was corresponding with Ann Finnin for information needed for his research, so the suggestion they would send something anonymously, makes no sense at all. The first rule in magic is based in the sleight of hand; it is imperative to get everyone looking somewhere else. Better sense now can be made in the recollection of a particular reference to the Finnins, E.J.J. made in 1998: *"<u>Mike said</u> all along, he thought it was the Finnins."* [689]

Time at last for two concluding testimonies, that finally draw together the few remaining tattered threads. Throughout the extensive but convoluted research for this biography, all threads track back to a single, unambiguous source. Personal and direct responses are noted where appropriate throughout this biography. All except this one, significant report. E.J.J.' widow offers her own testimony as a former Clan member and as a person steeped in the lives and histories of all persons concerned, including Cochrane's widow with whom she remains in contact. Confirming their joint knowledge of the existence of *The Thames Valley Coven,* V.J. states without equivocation:

The Royal Windsor Coven <u>never</u> existed [690]

It <u>never</u> existed! Not for CTC, nor its people. If and when it may have had some form of existence even as a fiction or fantasy, it was nothing to do with them. Yet the fiction began, somewhere. Tracing that notion back to the Finnins, they were the first people to refer to it via letter circa 1982. This was shortly after their visit in the UK, to where the locus of so many crossed threads occur.

A former member of *The Roebuck* candidly explains:

On their return to L A, [in the early 1980s] Ann & Dave were excited to tell us that Michael Howard had revealed to them

---

[689] Personal Correspondence from EJJ to SLO August 1998 Author's Emphasis.
[690] Personal Correspondence. V. Jones #31

several things about the former members of Roy's group and what they got up to after his death.

Some of them formed *The Regency*, but after a few years when the leader, Ronald White was tired of the large public rituals and wished to retire, some of its members said they'd like to set up a much smaller private group. **Howard said they called themselves** *The Royal Windsor Coven.* That would be in the late 1970s.[691]

All the pieces fall into place. Proof. Finally. Howard initiated that story in 1982, back played to the 1970s. Not until over a decade later did the notion of White's small, private group of retired ex-members of CTC with an aspirational title, evolve into Cochrane's original coven, complete with its adoption of that new title. His initial claims to kudos via fantasy connections to Robert Cochrane's works, legacy and Clan were forcibly expanded upon to legitimise a false foundation for Andrew Chumbley's foray into Traditional Craft, that were thwarted when EJJ passed the tradition to Shani Oates and Robin-the-dart. Not only are source and root cause explicitly connected, they are confirmed and validated as such, by two separate, vouchsafed references. That intelligence is fully supported by everything this biography has laid open for scrutiny. The evidence is unwavering.

Every source and directive falls back to, and originates in - Michael Howard. He was the self-proclaimed authority on all Craft matters, the circular source and expounder of *his own tale*. He is the one person everyone cites, directly or indirectly, and the one person who repeatedly ignored every obvious fact in favour of his contrary, personal opinion.

Within their respective chapters, two (possibly) independent groups of people, both known to Howard, were briefly introduced due to their tentative connections with Windsor. Both remain speculative, but relevant to this conclusive chapter.

The first concerns the 'Mystic Forum' branch at 'Windsor,'— the name coincidentally scribbled onto the *Oath of Loyalty to the*

---

[691] Jane Taylor. 2015 Op. Cit. Author's emphasis. The Finnins visit to Howard was in 1982 around the time Ronald White moved to Shropshire. (George Winter had moved to Shropshire a few years before Ronald White. He died before White moved there). It was also the year M. Montalban died.

'Thames Valley Coven.' doc. (AAA) A2. It may never be truly known how or if these disparate pieces fit together, or indeed who tried to make them fit, who fashioned them and put them into play.

Coming together after Cochrane's death, this occult group were perhaps chasing his light? Seeking some connection perhaps through his stomping ground? They were not the first or last to do so. Noted at the beginning, in the years that followed Cochrane's death, many sought to make contact with him, and many claimed they did. Many since have claimed that light for their own. Others have simply forged connections where none existed.

Someone was clearly motivated enough to radically embellish their activities and associations through a fictional name, in vain hope a real connection could at some future date be won and the two made one? Alas, this cult, working in the Windsor region after Cochrane's' death failed in their venture and the cult dissipated.

If indeed Montalban was the right 'Sylvia,' then perhaps it morphed into something else when Montalban died in 1982. That year presents another serendipitous revelation – the one noted above whence Howard informed the Finnins' of the phantom group he'd named 'The *Royal* Windsor Coven.' Before Howard's later retrospective claims that changed the details significantly, he'd informed the Finnins this was a new group, formed only after *The Regency* ceased its activities.

Even so, no amount of backward machinations would tie them together in origin with *The Robert Cochrane Tradition* and his Clan. Whoever they really were, they and their Cultic order belong to another totally independent modality. Neither they nor their works share any part in any reality or history with *The Robert Cochrane Tradition*.

The second rumour concerned the phantom coven having origin in the small, discreet group of people who worked privately together, very briefly in Shropshire after White retired there circa 1982. Howard and several others it seems, were aware of those *private* workings that occurred around that time. They too had invited guests, which appeared to have existed in a manner Marian Green recounts was very typical of that era, as an *'ad hoc'* meeting of friends, working loosely together.

There is nothing to indicate they had considered themselves anything other than a discreet continuance of *The Regency*, albeit in retirement in Shropshire. The Regency title was all they ever referred to. A rumour persists for a small, separate group so secret nothing is known of them to date, yet open enough that some unaccountable people claim they knew about it and were invited to join, but declined. They too apparently enjoyed only a brief existence for a few years.

The only person who ever suggested anything else for them, or about them, was Michael Howard, at a much later time when circumstances made it expedient for him to do so. Monmouth followed suit. Rather than press the simplicity of what was real, they confounded each other in their desire to present a specious back-story, with *nothing* to back it up.

Again, at this stage it is hard to know if the name Howard relayed to the Finnins was originally for vanity or mischief, to either appear in the know, or, simply to misinform. The latter caused trouble for the Finnins with E.J.J., ensuring they remained at loggerheads.

Whatever Howard's motivation was in the 1980s, the tentative platform he created allowed for his later campaign to undermine and attempt to appropriate a unique Tradition. Had it been a coven, it would have been lost several times over. With ingenious foresight, Cochrane's creation of a Clan, established an aegis that creates its own bulwark against such hostilities. E.J.J. had stated that, *'(Clan)Tubal Cain looks after its own.'*

Monmouth was adamant *The Regency* did not have an inner circle, faction or court of any description. This biography has demonstrated how all claims that proposed Cochrane's Tradition was practised by him and continued after him as anything other than CTC are undisputedly false. His Tradition remains as he named it – The People of Goda of the Clan of Tubal Cain.

Whatever information may eventually manifest relative to the rumour of a Windsor Coven, be it 'Royal' or otherwise, however unlikely, has again been shown to have no connection to CTC beyond aspiration and desire. The contortions both Howard and Monmouth enforced upon the narrative to make it fit their purpose are unprecedented.

Based entirely upon rumour, their fictions thrived in the media until factual evidence became a necessity to sustain them further. In that absence, the momentum finally halted, allowing reason and scrutiny to reveal the gulf between the real untold history and the false history made common by repetition and rumour.

Howards claim shifted considerably from whence it was first made in 1982 concerning a few people who'd expressed their desire to privately continue the works of The Regency once it ceased its public ventures in the 1970s – to a later claim for those people as having continued Cochrane's Tradition as a secret group since the 1980s. Both Howard and Monmouth retrospectively declared the secret group, named by them as The Royal Windsor Coven, was founded by Cochrane two decades previously in 1962.

To accommodate opposition as it arose, details were amended until a formal declaration established their intent to manoeuvre a separation of Coven from Clan, and Tradition from person. It was an aggressive tactic undertaken entirely without authority or legitimacy. The agenda has been long-term, and increasing in its plan to erode and undermine the validity and authority of CTC as the legitimate heirs to the only tradition founded and practised by Robert Cochrane.

Setting aside their numerous differences and fall-outs, without Cochrane's guidance and knowledge, White and Winter were utterly lost. Every action and non-action indisputably reveals that Robert Cochrane was the real leader and genius, deserving of the status craft historians, researchers, and people of the Craft have long acknowledged. Cochrane's works and Tradition stayed within their point of origin - his Clan.

These final source testimonies release the Clan from any fictional association with a phantom group. And whatever Ronald White may or may not have established in private, after *The Regency* ceased its operations when he retired to Shropshire, is no concern of CTC. Whatever that 'may' have been, was entirely independent of Robert Cochrane's legacy. As the master and genius of his own works Cochrane ensured his heritage would continue, fuelled by the tradition he established in and through his Clan of Tubal Cain. Long may it serve.

The duty of a Magister and Head-kinsman for the People of Goda, of the Clan of Tubal Cain, is to defend, to stand at this side of the gate, in Truth, to do whatever is necessary to maintain what all the Clan holds within that Truth. It does not concern itself with popularity, but with what is right by Clan Law. Our works advance its people towards fulfilment of their destiny. Together we meter the Be, Before and Beyond.

~Robin-the-dart

Dedicated to Evan John Jones: 1937-2003

"She will gather you up Home again."

Epilogue

The Wheel turns, and so it ends where it began, except all have trodden the *Mill in the Round of Life* and gained the first gleanings of Wisdom, of Truth, of Life, Faith, Love and Duty. Pressed hard by circumstance to seek a measure of these virtues exampled in life, CTC share information gained in that mission willingly, with all who care still for reality and for truth, in a shifting, uncertain world.

Countless words lost in the drone of public opinion are collated here. The many voices and claims raised along the journey offered only a confused cacophony. Michael Howard once accused CTC of wishing to 're write history.' What he meant but declined to say, was that he knew CTC sought to address *his entirely specious part* in that history.

Pushed aggressively for two decades, Howard's version of CTC's history required substantial correction. Research and focus is costly in time and energy. The machinations of others riding the tide caused obstruction. Witting and unwittingly they increased further the puzzles and challenges for CTC to resolve.

Extraordinary lengths were undertaken by a few determined people to appropriate by one means or another, something that was never fated to be theirs. Fate and Truth are the twin pillars of CTC, and it guards those virtues well.

Putting the titles and traditions of 'man' aside, the Mysteries of the Gods are open to everyone. No-one owns them. There are as many paths and doorways to that Truth as there are points upon the Compass, in the fullest sense. This small Clan Tradition is but one facet of a myriadic jewel.

Cochrane, Jones et al, placed enough in the public remit for anyone to peruse and adopt into their own workings should they so desire, if they are deemed to hold sufficient merit. But the name, CTC, the Clan and its (private)Tradition remain and serve no-one else. It is pointless to attempt to grasp what is transient in Fate. CTC produced this biography to lay the many issues to rest that led to its needful composition. Many restless ghosts may now find peace.[692]

---

[692] Where desired, this book may be read alongside the Children of Cain written by Michael Howard, and Genuine Witchcraft is Explained by John of Monmouth. Please also consult The Star Crossed Serpent series I-IV (I & III are vital) by Shani Oates to provide essential source documents and a full contextual and chronological history, written by Robert Cochrane, Evan John Jones, and Shani Oates & Robin-the-dart!

History is best served in the provision of a rationale that replaces the obscure and ambiguous with facts and context. The fabrication and deliberate falsification of events and circumstance are exposed and replaced with objective information, critical analysis, and substantial research to build upon. Understanding those works, according to their original intent, the people and their place in this history is primary.

Able now to shift beyond the veils of romance, illusion, myopia, opinion and hearsay, a clarity of purpose brings the mysteries a little closer to the genuine pilgrim. Hindsight gifts a freedom of perspective impossible to witness as events unfurl. The course of those events are fully supported by evidence and testimonies of everyone involved, be that centrally, or upon the peripheries. From every challenge comes strength, and knowledge. No experience is wasted - all is Grist!

The root cause and source for decades of aggravation is finally exposed. Howard generated obfuscation and false trails for all genuine research into *The Robert Cochrane Tradition,* better known as *The Clan of Tubal Cain.*

This truth brings resolution to E. J. J.' own conviction, held to his death, that it was a complete fabrication, made up by another. With truth comes peace, especially from the grave. With faint humour, both Cochrane and E.J.J. might shake their heads and nod to the Lapwing, observing the irony that Howard's desperate agenda to attach the Royal Windsor Coven title to Cochrane, was crossed by Monmouth's agenda to attach it to White and Winter (albeit credited with Cochrane's genius), making Cochrane's genius the *Roebuck in the Thicket*. Truth in the form of the 'dog' thwarts all.

APPENDICES

Bibliography

Books

Barrett, David. V. *A Brief Guide to Secret Religions* UK: Running Press 2011

Bourne, Lois *Dancing with Witches* London: Hale 2006

Finnin, Ann *The Forge of Tubal Cain* Pendraig Press. 2008

Glass. J. *Witchcraft, the Sixth Sense & Us* UK: Spearman 1965

Holzer, Hans. *The Truth about Witchcraft* UK: Arrow Books LTD, 1971

Howard, M. *The Children of Cain* US: Three Hands Press 2011

Howard, M. & Jackson, N. A. The Pillars of Tubal Cain. Capall Bann. 2000

Hutton, Prof Ronald. *The Triumph of the Moon* OUP: 1999

Jones, Evan John. *Witchcraft a Tradition Renewed.* (Ed) Doreen Valiente UK: Hale 1991

Jones, E. J. & Clifton, Chas. *Sacred Mask, Sacred Dance.* US Llewellyn Pub. 1997

Jones, E. J. *Roebuck in the Thicket* (Ed) Michael Howard UK: Capall Bann 2001.

Jones, E. J. *The Robert Cochrane Letters* (Ed) Michael Howard UK: Capall Bann 2003

Monmouth, John of. *Genuine Witchcraft is Explained* UK: Capall Bann 2012

Oates, S. *Tubelo's Green Fire* UK: Mandrake of Oxford 2010

Oates, S. *The Arcane Veil* UK: Mandrake of Oxford 2012

Oates, S. *Crafting the arte of Tradition* Canada: Anathema Publishing 2016

Oates, S. *Star Crossed Serpent Volume III* UK: Mandrake of Oxford 2016

Oates, S. *Tubal's Mill: Legend* (Companion to TM) US: Create Space 2016

Robin-the-dart *Heritage* (Ed) Shani Oates UK: Create Space, 2016

Schuchard, Marsha Keith. *Why Mrs Blake Cried* London: Century 2006

Valiente, Doreen. *The Rebirth of Witchcraft* UK: Hale 1989

Articles

The Messiah of Highgate Hill *Man, Myth & Magic* Frontiers/Purnell Publishers. #43 1969/70

Ken Rees, Investigating the Regency *The Cauldron* #121 2006 & Feb. 2009 #The Cauldron 131

Ken Rees, The Regency Vol. I & II The Wiccan, # Beltane 2004

Joe Wilson in *The Waxing Moon* new series, 1, Samhain 1970

Ronald White in *Spectrum*, no. 2, Nov/Dec 1974

Doreen Valiente. 'A Witch Speaks' *Pagan Dawn* #128 1998

Melissa Seims, #116 May 2005 'A Dedication to Charles Clark' The Cauldron

Justine Glass, 'Prediction,' 1965

Web:

Gavin Semple A Poisoned Chalice - http://www.clanoftubalcain.org.uk/A_Poisoned_Chalice.pdf

St Uzec by Shani Oates - www.clanoftubalcain.org.uk/library

Ciphers and symbols by Robin-the-dart - www.clanoftubalcain.org.uk/library

Ethan Doyle White *An Elusive Roebuck: Luciferian roots of the Robert Cochrane Tradition* - www.ethandoylewhite.blogspot.com

www.1734-witchcraft.org.uk

http://www.1734-witchcraft.org/letterfour.html

http://www.thewica.co.uk/Charles%20Clark%20Article.htm

http://www.shivashakti.com/dadaji.htm

http://www.sacred-texts.com/pag/ppr/ppr08.htm

http://www.sacred-texts.com/pag/ppr/ppr17.htm

http://www.lashtal.com/forum/index.php?topic=5329.0

http://www.thewica.co.uk/Others.htm

http://www.thewica.co.uk/Others.htm#anton

Julia Phillips - History of Wicca http://www.sacred-texts.com/pag/wiccahst.txt

http://www.thewica.co.uk/coven_of_atho%20article.htm

http://www.geraldgardner.com/History_of_Wicca_Revised.pdf

http://ronaldchalkywhite.org.uk/articles/a-letter-to-the-pagan-movement-in-britain-and-ireland

http://ronaldchalkywhite.org.uk/

https://ronaldchalkywhite.wordpress.com/tag/the-regency/

http://ronaldchalkywhite.org.uk/articles/the-regency-seasonal-meditations-rites-by-john-of-monmouth/

http://ronaldchalkywhite.org.uk/articles/the-regency-the-cochrane-coven-by-john-of-monmouth

http://www.oxforddnb.com/templates/article.jsp?articleid=52531&back=

http://www.ukrockfestivals.com/watchfieldfestival-menu.html

http://www.nias.knaw.nl/Publications/KB%20Lecture/KB_06_Robert%20Kinross

http://en.wikipedia.org/wiki/Bah%C3%A1%27%C3%AD_Faith

http://en.wikipedia.org/wiki/The_Four_Valleys

http://thehumanjourney.net/pdf_store/sthames/phase3/Resource%20Assessments/Post-medieval%20and%20%20Modern%20Resource%20Assessment.pdf

http://www.tvas.co.uk/reports/pdf/RBE10-23dskreport.pdf

https://archive.org/stream/royalhouseofwind031195mbp/royalhouseofwind031195mbp_djvu.txt

http://cyclingfromguildford.co.uk/RotherhitheGuide.pdf

http://walworthsociety.co.uk/attachments/article/151/Walworth Road- HistoricAreaAssessmen -02Sep15.pdf

https://en.wikipedia.org/wiki/Grand_Surrey_Canal

http://en.wikipedia.org/wiki/Germanic_peoples

http://fmg.ac/Projects/MedLands/ENGLAND,%20AngloSaxon%20&%20Danish%20Kings.html

http://www.bartleby.com/library/prose/218.html

http://homepage.ntlworld.com/wisewoman/RB%20LIFE%201964.pdf

https://en.wikipedia.org/wiki/Robert_Cochrane_(witch)

The Cuckoo's Nest www.1734_witchcraft.org.uk

You Tube Interview with Karagan. See *The Secret History of the Royal Windsor Coven & the Regency* with John of Monmouth.' '9 Sep 2012 - Uploaded by WitchtalkShow
https://www.youtube.com/watch?v=WpAAmBpF0Us

Unpublished Sources:

Valiente's Notebooks 1959-66 & 66-85

Ken Rees 1982 - quoting from the Michael Bampton's Thesis concerning a time frame circa 1960/1

The Wiccan Readers' Research Project 2016, details supplied by Clive Harper (personal communication 12 Sept 2017)

Museum of Witchcraft Research refs:

• Box 32 letters from Gills to Cochrane, and some logged under Reg: Hinchcliffe, HP in St Albans coven run by Lois Pearson, nee Bourne

• Box 33 [3386A-3386] a few pages entitled 'some extracts taken from the writings of Robert Cochrane which appear re-typed by Gills, collated and annotated, different layout to originals. Some of those cut and pasted with bits missing are photocopies.

• Box 33 in Witchcraft Museum, contains correspondence where Andrew Chumbley asks Iain Steele/Plummer in 2004, for provenance on the letters between Norman Gills and others, and the works attributed to him. Steele whose former wife Andrea Foreman, like Rosina Bishop (a lady very close to Michael Howard for some time) was another of Gills students prior to 1985. Steele responds, in the negative, confirming this was not possible; he further clarifies that despite their claims to the contrary, considerable amounts do not actually belong to Cochrane at all, though they are frequently mistaken for his. Lots of sketches and handwritten work by Gills of his own studies on Cochrane's work, in this box on poppets and fairy lore, spells and charms, and often mistaken for it.

Nota Bene: Although CTC retain original documents in its archive, scans of all letters and documents used to provide vital textual support that inform this book will be provided as an external addenda, a companion guide and key publication in *Tubal's Mill: Legend*. Full copies have been donated to the archives of the *Museum of Witchcraft* and the former *Centre for Pagan Studies* (now under the aegis of the Doreen Valiente Foundation, directed by Ashley Mortimer), for students and researchers to evaluate directly. We anticipate this gift will prove instrumental in the search for open and honest appraisals of Craft History. [694]

There is currently another folder housed in the Museum donated by John of Monmouth containing all the scans of the letters from the cache used in his own book *Genuine Witchcraft is Explained – a Secret History of the Royal Windsor Coven*. The folder is disingenuously entitled *'Royal Windsor Coven material/documents,'* which falsely assumes self-validation. Any researcher is already pre-disposed therefore to accept those documents as if they are from that coven. They are nothing more than a collection of disparate letters, many without provenance, others of dubious origins, and some only, acceptable as written by Robert Cochrane. <u>None of them name or discuss a coven named the Royal Windsor Coven.</u>

Researchers should be aware that none of them state, cite or support or hint at the existence of any group or coven by that name. The title of that folder is a misdirection and does not serve academic rigour. A more honest title could have been *'The Stannard Cache: Documents pertaining to the history of people associated with Robert Cochrane and the Regency'* – or bold but simple: *' Research papers proposed as material evidence for a Royal Windsor Coven.'* Certainly its documents

---

[694] These can be viewed, by request.

should avoid declaration as authentic source *for* or *from* a Royal Windsor Coven. Therefore, with the addition of our own material evidence entitled: *'CTC: A True Origin - Dispelling the Myth,'* we expect to balance and correct the prejudicial folder donated by Monmouth concerning the phantom 'Royal Windsor Coven.'

'Society of Kerridwen' formed c 63 only after the move to Slough circa 61/2

Chronological Publications for Robert Cochrane and CTC:

Psychic News: Nov.1963 -   <u>Genuine Witchcraft is Defended</u>
New Dimensions: Nov.1964 -   <u>Witches Esbat</u>
Pentagram: August-64 -   <u>The Craft Today</u>
                     March-65 -   <u>On Cords</u>
                     August-65 -   <u>Faith of the Wise</u>

NB: Gerard Noel - editor and creator of *Pentagram* magazine, it provided an initial outlet for the aspirations and ideas of the Witchcraft Research Association established by Noel, Valiente & Score.

Justine Glass 'A Hereditary Witch's Revelations' by Robert Cochrane in *Witchcraft, the Sixth Sense – and Us* (Neville Spearman: 1965)

Doreen Valiente 'Robert Cochrane, Magister' in *Rebirth of Witchcraft* (Robert Hale: 1989)

Evan John Jones *Witchcraft: A Tradition Renewed* (Ed) Doreen Valiente (Robert Hale:1990)

Evan John Jones *Sacred Mask Sacred Dance* (Ed) Chas Clifton (USA: Llewellyn St Paul: 1997)

Prof. Ronald Hutton 'The Man in Black' in *The Triumph of the Moon: A History of Modern Pagan Witchcraft'* (Oxford University Press :1999).

Evan John Jones and Robert Cochrane *The Roebuck in the Thicket: An Anthology of the Robert Cochrane Witchcraft Tradition*. (Ed) Michael Howard (Capall Bann: 2001)

Evan John Jones and Robert Cochrane *The Robert Cochrane Letters: An Insight into Modern Traditional Witchcraft* (Ed) Michael Howard (Capall Bann:2003).

Alan Richardson and Marcus Claridge *The Old Sod: The Odd Life and Inner Work of William G. Gray* (Ignotus Press :2003)

Oates, S. *Star Crossed Serpent Volumes I- IV* UK: Mandrake of Oxford 2016

Oates, S. *Tubal's Mill: Legend* (Companion to TM) US: Create Space 2016

Biography: Shani Oates (England, UK)

Occultist, Sophianic Mystic, Luciferian Pilgrim of the Forbidden Arts, Traditional Craft Practitioner, International lecturer, researcher, historian and writer of the Craft, Ancestral Tradition, particularly *The Robert Cochrane Tradition*, and the cultural Folk-lore and Folk-magicks of the UK and its Northern Heritage. Spae-wife and Matriarch of *The People of Goda, The Clan of Tubal Cain*. Student of Anthropology, Tantra, Philosophy and the arcane 'Other.' Exponent of the devil and all his works through the authorship of several books that write authoritatively on the myths, gods and archetypes that imbue and inform the Cults and Crafts of Witchcraft and Folk-Traditions, from the arcane to modern times.

Published books

- *'Tubelo's Green Fire'* launched through Mandrake of Oxford in 2010, followed by:
- '*The Arcane Veil,*' Mandrake of Oxford 2011
- *'The Star Crossed Serpent I & II, III & IV* in 2011 & 2012, & 2016, & 2017 also published by Mandrake of Oxford.
- *'A Paean for Hekate'* & [Create Space] and
- *'A Paean for Hekate'* (Artisan edition) Hell Fire Books - http://www.hellfireclubbooks.co.uk/Paean%20to%20Hecate.html
- *'The People of Goda'* [Create Space]. 2012

- *'Crafting the Arte of Tradition'* Anathema Publishing Ltd 'April 2016
- *Tubal's Mill: The Round of Life, A Critique of the History of 'The Robert Cochrane Tradition''* & *Tubal's Mill: Legend* [Create Space/Amazon] 2016
- *Tubal's Mill: The Round of Life, A Critique of the History of 'The Robert Cochrane Tradition''* *Revised and abridged – 2018*
- *'The Devil's Supper'* Anathema Publishing Ltd ' 2017

Essays published within other Journals and Anthologies:

- 'Pillars II: The Ebon Kteis' [Anathema Publishing]
- 'Genuine Witchcraft is Explained: Secret Tradition of the Royal Windsor Coven and the Regency'[Capall Bann]
- 'Serpent Songs' [Scarlet Imprint];
- 'The Wanton Green' [Mandrake];
- 'The Silver Wheel' [Lear Books];
- 'Ancestors of the Craft' [Copper Cauldron Publishing];
- 'Hecate: Her Sacred Fires' [Avalonia]
- 'Heritage' (Ed) [Create Space]
- 'Pillars IV The Scalding of Sapientia' [Anathema Publishing]

And the 2011 #2 of *The Abraxas Occult Journal* that features: 'Pashupati – A Cainite Trimurti' [Fulgur].

Pendragon, The White Dragon, Pentacle, The Goddess Alive, The Hedge Wytch, The Wytch's Standard, Brighid's Fire, Verdelet, Pagan Dawn, and The Cauldron.

The Clan of Tubal Cain can be fully researched and studied here on official Clan websites:

www.clanoftubalcain.org.uk.

https://www.facebook.com/clanoftubalcain/

http://clantubalcain.com/the-people-of-goda-the-clan-of-tubal-cain/

manofgoda.com

Persons relevant to the era and to the events mentioned in this Biography

NAME	ALIAS	COMMENT
Andrew Demaine		Early Wican HP. Under Research
Charles Cardell (Maynard) Surrey & Queensgate London		Headed a Coven on his estate in Surrey. Psychologist
Charles Pace		Known for cursing people who all allegedly died shortly afterwards, including the lover of Michael Juste's wife & Rollo Ahmed. Had relationships with Diana Richman and Lois Bourne and Eleanor Bone.
Charles Clark		Initiated Monique Wilson in Ayreshire
Celia Penny	Francesca	HPs of a coven under control of Monique Wilson
Celia Matthews	Diana/e	Initiate of a coven Roy Bowers belonged to before he formed his own. She died in 1958.
Cynthia		Said by some to have stood in

Name	Alias	Notes
Swetten-ham Surbiton Surrey		very briefly as HPs for St Albans after Lois Bourne left. Disputed.
Derek Hamer/James	'ickle deric'	Wrote to Cochrane and others in the craft. Wican Initiate Editor of 'Insight' magazine.
Diane Richman London	'Anat' Stella Trueman	Secretary to astrologer John Naylor. Initiate of Eleanor Bone and also of Cardell's Queensgate Coven
Marian Green		Involved in many groups, worked with several major craftspersons. Including Desmond Bourke, Bill Gray Robert Cochrane and Doreen Valiente.
Fred Lamond		Initiate of GBG.
Gerard Noel	John Math	Founder of WRA in 1964 Publisher and editor of the Pentagram. Initiate of Eleanor Bone
Jacqueline Murray		In charge after Celia Matthews' death? (of?) Editor of 'The Atlanteans' Initiate of Charles Cardell's Queensgate Coven
George Desmond Bourke		A Founder and leader of the Regency. Occultist and initiate of many orders and lodges. Freemason
Enid Corral	Justine Glass	Attended Regency. Rites Had connections to Bricket Wood Coven and Tony Melachrino Author of Witchcraft: the sixth sense and us
Kevin Wanstall		Assisted Charles Pace to publish his books.
Monique Wilson	Lady Olwen Perth	Initiate of Charles Clark Gardner's last HPs. She inherited a controversial legacy from G.B.G.
Lois Bourne, nee Pearson	Vivian Lennox 'Tanith'	Left St Albans's Coven in 1964 High Priestess, - Lady of the 'robed coven'
Michael Juste		Owner of Occult shop in

		London. Rumour that an occult group met there regularly in his basement: (Alfred Mills, Gerald Yorke, John Symonds, Ann Roberts & Stanley Laithwaite), is disputed
Monica English		Traditional Witch from Norfolk. A controversial figure as she briefly joined Lois Bourne's coven in Bricket Wood.
Madeline Montalban Lancs, later - London	Dolores North Madeline Alvarez and Nina del Luna. "The Witch of St. Giles"	Madeline Sylvia Royals; 8 January 1910 – 11 January 1982) In 1952 she met Nicholas Heron. From 1933 to 1953 she published articles on astrology and other esoteric topics in the magazine London Life, and from then until her death in the nationally syndicated magazine Prediction. These were accompanied by several booklets on astrology, released using a variety of different pseudonyms. Disliked both Cardell and Gardner equally. Founded the *Order of the Morning Star* (Luciferian occultism)
Madge Worthing -ton	Fiona	Established the line known retrospectively as the 'Whitecroft.' Her HP Arthur, had been a former initiate and HP of Eleanor Bone.
Olwen Maddox-Armstrong High Wycombe, Buckinghamshire.	Olive Greene	Initiate of both G. B. Gardner and Charles Cardell. Socialite, known to have worked with several high-ranking occultists and occult orders, Wica and Traditional Craft Groups
Peter West		Husband of Sandra West Later left the Craft
Peter Lark -worthy Devon UK		Initiate of the 'Roebuck' the Finnin's group in L.A. Also an inductee of the Clan under John's magisterial office. Initiate of the Wica from Madge Worthington
Eleanor 'Rae/Ray'	'Artemis'	HPs of GBG. Bricket Wood. Had Old Craft connections in

Bone Cumber-land		Cumbria. Sometime lover of Charles Pace who was a member of her coven.
Ray Harris		TV producer. Initiate in IOM
Raymond Buckland NY. US		Took Wica to the US – Established it there. Instigated Seax Wicca
Reginald Roberts Sussex		Friend of Alfred Mills in Staffordshire. Brother of Ann Roberts. Close associate of Joe Wilson. Of Lois Bourne's Wicca
Tony Mela-chrino Bucking-hamshire	Taliesin	Polemical articles in the Pentagram. Alleged leader of a traditional coven. An ex-boyfriend of Lois Pearson, possibly initiated by her. Son of George Arthur Melachrino, musician and bandleader in London.
Tammara James	'Annis'	Curator of GBG's artefacts in Canada
Zachary Cox & Jean Williams South-East UK		HP & HPs of Bricket Wood Coven

Letters – Evan John Jones

Letter #1 (EJJ,L1)

BY all means will do a spread as you asked but wouldn't like to guarantee it'll be all that accurate as I haven't touched the stones for quite a while. Not surprising that Terry comes up with a middle eastern connection for Pellar because there is a connection between gypsy craft and the old English craft from way back, in fact, if you look at it carefully there are a lot of common ground concerning the Gypsy Black Madonna and the Dark Goddess of the clan so somewhere along the line, someone must have taken something from someone else and wove t into their beliefs even though the Poles have token to the concept in a big way.

Why shouldn't the Four Horsemen share the same colours as the clan, after all. much of the clan philosophy is connected with life and death in an intimate way, we celebrate life and we also celebrate death as the clan law points out while the Horsemen represent death and disaster in various forms which way back, to us, would have been the punishment from the Old 'Uns for some breach of the law like having a bath more than three time in one life, I can just hear one of the old clan elders going on " I telled eee 'avin a bath last Hawkumcumstucly day three year ago 'ud cause trouble, now look what we've got.......the black death, its unnatural I tell eee, unnatural."

You'll have to straighten the London lot out on the Goda and point out the the Godi was a Saxon word for priest and that we are the people of the priesthood etc. God knows where these people get their ideas from, it mush be from Ann who missed out on so much after she left Roy.

Letter #2 (EJJ,L2)

they were, took their beliefs from various Indian mythologies and people of the calibre of Lobsang Rampa the famous Tibetan monk who turned out to be living with a collection of women in a caravan somewhere in Essex and the nearest he'd ever been to Tibet, was the far end of Margate pier plus of course the films based on the Wheatly horror stories. Then there were reissues of M.M. and Graves and so on, so people began to use these to give form to their beliefs. In America where people didn't have a tradition to turn to, they either became Gardnerians or started to wander around in the Celtic twilight because there were well documented source material from the Celtic revival period and of course this started go come back over here. Roy like so many other of the time wanted to distinguish our ways of working from that of the Gardnerians and the others and the easiest way to do that, was to lump them all together as pagans claiming we were the only true witches. As far as I was concerned, that attitude didn't hold true and it still doesn't, when I wrote those lines, I was stressing Roy's attitude to others. Its up to you if you feel that way about it, to make it clear that this no longer is the case.

Much of the early paganism followed much the same line as we did at the start of things, the one thing they didn't have though, was the concept of the Castle of the Goddess as being the place where we developed and built upon shaping it our beliefs and to where we go after death, most of them held to a rather nebulous Summer Lands. They also accepted the old Gods and Goddesses as we did but where we differed, was in the claiming that behind these, there was the one supreme deity and that the old ones were no more than aspects of this deity which to many Gardnerians and pagans of the time, was a total anathema as there was nothing beyond them and in some cases, having wandered off into the Celtic Otherworld, came back with even more Gods and Goddesses.

Question two. You are correct in assuming the Tree of the North is the stang and you have the meaning of the stang reading from bottom to top. Now, go round the pagans you know and ask them to read their stang and see how many see it the same way as we do. If you get the same answer as we have, then you can bet your bottom dollar they have taken it over. Originally it was clan and clan alone that linked the stang to the mystery of the Unknown Deity and Creator as the find aspect of the stang in a multiplicity of aspects so in fact, you don't have to justify it to anyone, this is how we work and this is what we believe in.

Question three. Once again you are treating the question with hindsight, something we didn't have in the 60's. You've read the letters so you must have picked up some of the attitudes expressed in them. At that time, there was ceremonial magic, black magic of the satanists and witch magic and then there were very few groups practising this form of magic and most of them had a claim to the old tradition. Remember, when this was being taught as part of our beliefs, Bill Gray hadn't even formulated the Sangreal rites, they were still in embryonic form and in his Seasonal Occult Rituals he used a certain amount of Roy's material, changed slightly but basically Roy's. So does this material used by Bill make the Sangreal magic witch magic or Sangreal magic ? We had our way of doing things, Bill with Roy's consent took some of it and developed it into his way of working magic and this frankly is the difference.

Question four. Telling the maze is something you have done already, it is the preparation and steps taken when someone crosses the river and on to the castle of the Goddess that spins without motion between two worlds. As you well know, you start in the circle then exit it in the west, go down the snaking path passing through two upright stones on either side of the path and on one of them there is perched a raven and I'm sure you don't need me to explain the symbolism of this. You go on down the path to the ferryman, cross the river and follow the path through the wastelands and into the castle and as you follow the path, the wastelands start to bloom, something you've already done in spirit when I took you through it.

So other pagans have a river that separates this world from the next which they cross in death, fine, but its not the same place we go to which over the years, others have created for us and which we have maintained for the others who will follow us. Most traditional crafters believe that once they are accepted into their clan or coven, this is what they will be reborn to time and time again until they no longer have to be reborn into this world. Try asking some of your pagan friends about reincarnation and ask them what they will come back to, in many cases the specifics will be rather vague and I should imagine that somewhere along the line, the idea of the next life will be moulded by their actions in this life will crop up. Roy believed that we will all come back into the clan because in the future the clan will know us and find us once again and the reason for this, over the years the clan, magic, faith and belief has created this in our spirit world as the fate we have to live out in the physical world. Now if others don't like this, tough, we're not asking them to accept it. As long as we accept and believe this is our reality, then this is what it will be because we have over the years created and maintained this.

No, you haven't missed anything, the fifth art is the art of the family bloodline something you and I cannot claim. Once upon a time it was important, today, less so because the family ties are no longer as close knit as they used to be, you only have to look at Roy's father realising that if Roy hadn't followed in the family line, it would have been long dead. In many cases, if outsiders hadn't been brought in stepping into what was once family shoes, then everything would have been lost. Roy's brothers were not interested and Roy's son is the same in spite of what Chalky and George had in mind with the Regency, eventually one of Roy's descendants will heed the call of the blood and if you have transmitted the tradition, seek the clan out once

Letter #3 (EJJ, L3:ADC-1)

17th July 2001.

Dear Shani,

Many thanks for yours. Val said thanks for letting her know you'd had her card.

It was nice seeing you again even if the pair of us were staggering round like a couple of old wrecks. I'll being seeing the doctor later this week and see what he intends to do about my right leg as I'm still having difficulty standing up as you know.

The earth shattering idea as propounded by Chummy and Co that Tubal Cain can be equated with Lucifer is correct in much the same way as he can be equated with all other metal associated deities and so old, its positively covered in lichen and cobwebs. All this was explored in the 60's when it was, after much talk, decided in a clan sense to be about as much use as an udder on a bull. Having heard about it from you, I wouldn't be at all surprised if the next step will be to make the universe shattering discovery that Jesus in his own way, was a pretty good witch Master too. The only reason it has never appeared beyond a hint in any of Roy's or my work was because it was too dammed trivial to bother with and didn't advance knowledge one iota and having been around for so long, I'm baffled that people are surprised by this as I thought it would have been one of the basic things one was told when they came anywhere near the craft, it seems as though I called it wrong this time. I thought we'd long got away from the day of ' how many beans make five ' or 'who killed cock robin ' and who ' hunted the cutty wren with knives and forks ' and ' I'm the king of the castle ' etc.

Letter #4 (EJJ,L4:ADC-2)

23/4/02

Dear Shani,

Glad to have found out you are feeling better after Sundays bad turn. Hope that the new pills you are being prescribed work better than the last lot did, you had us worried for quite a while.

You can tell Terry I've read Chummy's interview and perhaps the best way to describe it is an example par excellence of what is ejected through muscular contractions from a taurean aperture diametrically opposite the ingestion aperture, or to the uninitiated, unmitigated bull****. One is almost tempted to write to him and ask what the hell is he smoking and where can I get some,

Egg and spoon champion, fie on you, what's with this serious athletics stuff ? if greed is good then sloth is superb and I intend to be a serious student of it, I was the one who organised the worlds first works lay-in as opposed to sit-in over redundancies. Shame on you Shani, what have got against aliens and their headgear, everyone has some taste, a bit like salty pork sans the crackling actually, not that I make a habit of going round eating people, you're always stuck with a dirty great pile of leftovers, people having no taste indeed, whatever next.

As I said to you on Sunday, the only reason Chummy goes on about Luciferian craft is because most people haven't a clue as to what he is on about. As for Roy's work following a similar vein, not true, the Luciferian cult was a Christian heresy and had nothing to do with it even though Roy thought Jesus would have made a good witch if he hadn't been born a yarmulke.

....

Letter #5 (EJJ, L5 ADC: L3)   14ᵗʰ Jan 1999 p 2 of 5

> Getting on to your questions. The mythos of the fall is great story telling but in a clan and traditional sense, doesn't mean a thing as we have always held to the chaos theory where order came from chaos and things developed from there so in that sense, Lucifer as the fallen angel doesn't really fit into our mythos. Mind you, one of the best stories I've heard concerning the Golden Age and the fall is summed up by looking at the Garden of Eden as a perfect piece of espionage. The satanic serpent was an enemy agent operating under the cover of a reptile who enlisted Eve as an asset in place to destabilize the relationship between God and the Garden of Eden. its a good an explanation as any.
>
> to be honest with you Shani, I haven't a clue what the hell Chummy was on about and to be honest with you, I thought he was throwing me a crib just to see what I'd have to say, a bit of disinfo then sit back and wait for a reply where it is a case of deny and belittle yourself somewhat or claim what he'd know to be a lie. Now I'm not too sure, does he know something that I don't and after all,

Typed Transcript (for clarity):

Getting on to your questions. The mythos of the fall is great story telling but in a clan and traditional sense, doesn't mean a thing as we have always held to the chaos theory where order came from chaos and things developed from there so in that sense, Lucifer as the fallen angel doesn't really fit into our mythos.

Mind you, one of the best stories I've heard concerning the Golden Age and the fall, is summed up by looking at the Garden of Eden as a perfect piece of espionage. The satanic serpent was an enemy agent operating under the cover as a reptile who enlisted Eve as an asset in place to destabilize the relationship of God within the Garden of Eden.

It's a good an explanation as any. And to be honest with you Shani, I haven't a clue what the hell Chummy was on about, I thought he was throwing me a crib just to see what I have to say, a bit of disinformation then sit back and wait for a reply where it is a bit to deny and belittle yourself somewhat or claim what he'd know to be a lie.

Letter #6 (EJJ,L6) 21ˢᵗ August 1998

21st August 1998.

Dear Shani,

You may not be aware of this, but you are an angel, not only an angel but one who has earned herself a very large brandy or calvados, whatever. Unknowingly, the material you sent me provided a couple of pieces in the tale Mike Howard is trying to sort out as well as clearing up something that has been bothering me for quite a few years now. For that alone, very many thanks.

Starting with Mike's tale, you have no doubt hear of Ronald Hutton. Well, he's working on another book and has been sending chapters to Mike to look at and if there are any errors, put them right. One of the things Ron got very excited over, was a mass of material he recieved from the Royal Windsor Coven. Mike was not terribly impressed and felt that he'd seen it all before somewhere, anyhow, he brought it down for me to have a look at. Apart from the material you enclosed which was also included in this mass, there was page after page of material lifted from the first book, on top of this, they'd even used the bloody line drawings commissioned by Hale's and this is what Ron was claiming to be old traditional material. When you were down here, you saw the original letter of Roy's where some of this material was lifted from namely the Castle. What they have done here, is to add a few bits of their own and pass it off as R.W.C. material. Going back to the original you sent me, in the poem ' I am She as old as time ', this was something I wrote when I first knew Roy. It could have only come from three people, Chalky and George of the Regency, or Bill Gray who would have seen it with Roy. A long way back, Bill let the Finnin's photocopy the letters and somehow, they've turned into the tradition of the Royal Windsor Coven. Mike thought all along it was the Finnin's who were behind this but I had my doubts putting it down to some others I knew of. Seemingly I was wrong as the last page of the material now proves. Now comes the interesting bit, at the end of the letter there is a mention of a P.L. who was at one time, a member of the

Coming to my side of the story now. For years we've had a constant leaking of info pertaining to the clan then being picked up from some unusual sources on the way back to me. Now the one thing you can say about Peter is that he gets around and knows a lot of people including Mike Howard who cannot remeber him and old Doreen who was a good friend of his and only has a vague memory of him from one or two meetings they attended at the same time. Having seen your material especially the little piece at the end, the finger seems to be pointing to Peter as the loose mouthed source we've been having our spot of bother with and I think you must agree, there seems to be enough evidence pointing in that one direction to suspect this. Not that I mind Peter talking or anything like that, what I object to, is the way it is being used to undermine what I've tried to do over the years, its just not on.

F.F.F
and
Blessed be

P.S. Before I forget, have I your consent to pass one or two pages of the material you sent me along to Mike. I know he'd be very interested and it would be a little more help to him practise the grand old witch tradition of

"putting the boot in"

....

Letter #7 (EJJ,L7) 13th October 1998

Getting down to business, letter questions.

(1) Think in terms of the Pharonic and matriarchal societies and you have what the old craft should be but very rarely is. Any Master leads the coven or clan just as every Master does as well as heading the feminine mysteries. But, he leads them on sufferance from the Lady for as long as she wishes him to hold them. Remember, once upon a time, at May Eve he'd have his throat cut and the Year King and the blood mixed with water and sprinkled over the public gathering as a blessing when the sacrifice was re-enacted the next day. This is reflected in the number of May Day festivals where ' Jack in the Bush dances around the town disguised as a bush and is finally pushed over to kill it to let the spirit of summer free to spread over the land. Ask your friend in Hastings if she's ever seen their May Day celebrations, if not, I may still have the cutting about it that I could let you have. When women started to lose their status in society, the leaders of the groups began to hold their positions in their own right rather than of sufferance. In the end, the priestess became subordinate to the Magister instead of the power behind the throne and the feminine balance to his masculinity. Where Roy is concerned, I suggest you try getting a copy of Doreen's book ' Rebirth

of witchcraft ' reading in particular the chapter 'Robert Cochrane, Magister'. This was read by #### Jane and myself before it went into the book for our comments. If you can't get a copy, read mine when you come down again. After reading it, you'll see why I stressed in the first book the role of the Lady firmly believing that women should be restored to their true status rather than paying lip service to the concept. now, if people like Chummy (Val's name for him) claim they are devotee's of our Lady and cannot accept that women are cast in Her image making them special to her, tough, a truth is a truth no matter how much it is denied. Roy did say that he was equal to Jane and that no woman could lead a group, in a sense he was right, what he didn·t say was more important though. He was leading the group because Jane let him by making him her Master. Hope this answers that question.

(2) No problem with 'kindred groups' if they don't like it, then they can do something unspeakable to a rolling doughnut at the run. Any person present and future who hives off from your immediate group must accept your suzerainty without question. The same goes for any group that can trace its lineage back to you. Any people I bring in or with me now will also be in the same position because at present being active, I acknowledge and owe total fidelity to you and do so on their behalf.

(3) The idea and concept of the Maid has always been there in the old tradition but no Master pushed it because in the main, no man wants to play second fiddle to a woman. Why should he when he can be the Great I Am. Now, if women were stupid enough to let them get away with it both now and in the past, who can blame a guy for trying it on ?

(4) No, you don't need to renew your oath over again, not unless you feel a personal and pressing need to do so. What you read in the book was for kindred workings where any group was akin to us but not part of the true lineage. You are IT until you feel the need to pass it on to someone else, where the regalia goes, so does the office of Lady of the clan as she by tradition, is the keeper of it. I had no Lady as such, that's why I hold the stang, cup etc. Doreen as well versed in the craft as she is, wouldn't have been the one to carry on the tradition for various reasons. Ann Finnin (the American) would have used it in a bid to become Queen or King of all the witches in

America (could never make up my mind which) plus the fact that she would have turned it into pan Celtic/Irish tradition with everyone costumed up to the eyebrows waving all sorts of cutlery in the air all for the greater glory of Ann and her oft quoted "You're not ready for this yet" every time someone asked her a question. She was kindred, she's now history, forget her. She took a kindred oath, full story when you meet up with Peter, the whole oath taking was so absurd that its hard to believe and I refused point blank to give the Roebuck any sort of certificate etc stating she was more than just kindred in spite of being asked a number of times.

I've asked you twice, I will ask you once again, as simple as the ceremony was, do you feel within yourself that you are the Lady of the Clan, if the answer is yes, then you are, I have no doubts about it, nor will anyone else for that matter, you seem to be the only one a little uncertain about it. Brenda Bartholemew wouldn't have done even though she tried to get in, she was far too much in the pocket of Basil Wilby. Jan hasn't the personality to carry it off, foot soldier, yes, clan Maid, never. If you hadn't happened, then eventually the regalia would have been destroyed and the fragments scattered out at sea and that would have been the end of it all and very much sooner than you think.

(5) Don't think of the power as power in the sense of a tangible that can be transfered as such. Think of it more in terms of the sheriff appointing deputies to the posse before riding off into the sunset after the baddies in black 'ats (Gawd Jones, not the most mystic of language and concept). The power you have, is within yourself, all it needed was a trigger which was pulled by making you our Máid. I could have hallowed you as Maid twice nightly every Monday, Wensday and Friday from here to the Second Coming and at the end of it, you still wouldn't be the Maid unless you had that certain something very special within you that sets you apart from the rest of us. You have it.

Getting on to the second part of the question. Jane long ago deeded me the whole thing and a very poor choice it was too even if I say so and the reason she did this, is to be found in the Regency. When the idea was first mooted, Chalky and George more or less told

Jane to her face, that they were taking everything over and holding it for Roy's son Adrian and she could come along and be the Queen Mother and let them do what they wanted to her and Adrian until they in their infinite wisdom, would make him Magister, she never spoke to them again. Who was left ? the worse possible choice ever, me. Don't take my word for it, ask Val and Doreen when we manage to get into her den. Will explain in greater detail the how's and why's later but rest assured, no one but me can pass on the Clan Maidship to anyone. one else has been vested with the authority to do so, I was Roy's spiritual heir long before his death. Jane, Roy and I were that close each other, even when Val and I met, we were still close and we are the only ones Jane keeps in touch with even now. In fact, as val will readily tell you, when the cops questioned people over the circumstan of his death, none of them were actual members of the group, only observers, fact. what price loyalty ? I honestly think Doreen would have been the only other one who would have stood by him in a clan sense even though she wasn't amember having fallen out with him and had just come out of hospital at the time. why do you think the Regency took the form it did ? Jane wasn't playing their little game and too many people knew about Tubal Cain for them to take it over and turn it into the Regency which they would have liked to have done plus of course, they'd gone on record as denying the clan membership, as what else could they do ? The answer to question 7 as well Shani.

(6) Certainly not Roy's group and the bloody thing keeps cropping up. Originally, I think it came from the Finnin's via Peter Larkworthy. Others have picked it up and it has spread from there. The Royal Windsor material sent to Ron Hutton came from Los Angelese and had been lifted directly from the book of rites I first wrote. Now, Peter knows something about this and Mike Howard is sniffing around as well. Sometime in the future, I shall with all sweetness and light, ask Peter what he knows about it, if the sweetness and light doesn't work, I'll try the good old fashioned splinters of burning bamboo under the finger nails. That usually works. If I get hold of more, you'll know.

(7) Cock-up on the question front here. Shani, we very often started with a somewhat scripted rite then part of the way through, things would happen and it was all change. What you have to bear in mind when reading the book, the words in the scripted rituals are only there to convey the idea, they can be changed, left out, replaced with others and whathaveyou without affecting the end results. None of our rituals ever followed the way we set out to do them. I remember in one case, we were working on Bill Gray's problem and things were going well when all of a sudden, Roy changed the healing into a cursing and when Jane realized, she kicked him to one side and took over and finished it. Roy just couldn't explain what had happened because during the rite, he was miles away and I'd guess that at some point, the forces of chaos took him over. Chalky and George were part of the group who were constantly in hot water over what they thought should be done as opposed to what we were doing. At times, the only thing that kept them in line, was good old fashioned fear of Roy. As soon as he was dead, they first of all disowned him and the group to the plods. Tried roping Jane as part of the new Regency and failed. Tried to bring both Val and I into the dammed thing and also help them with the little racket they had

Letter #8 (EJJ,L8)

> Roy was with other people before he founded his own little group and he made no bones about it and of course, he also found them unsatisfactory in that they ended up by smoking pot

> You have the material Roy used plus of course the material I've added not because I wanted to but because there wasn't that much to leave. Roy himself admitted that what he had was not the sum total of Tubal Cain, he had two parts and there was one that had been lost. You have to bear in mind two things, one, there was no formal written work, it was all orally transmitted, two, when he died, everything was up in the air and nobody knew which was to turn that's why Chalky and George based the Regency on Roy's material and added a lot more of their own.

> I'm not sure what mask, prayer etc is when it comes to the Regency, must be one of Chalky's ways of ding things As you know, I didn't go along with him when I saw the way he was running things, didn't like the way they were shaping up. Of course he didn't dare use too much of Roy's material because he wasn't entitled to it as it had not been deeded to either George or him by Jane. If they had done so, then there would have been no end of psychic trouble and nothing would have gone right for them. Tubal Cain has a way of protecting its own So when it comes to Candlemas, you have a general guide with the book, all you have to do, is to feel your way through it and and do what your instincts tell you is right.

> No, have no idea who's running the Regency now, but to be honest with you, haven't been that much bothered. Whoever it is, I wish them the best of luck with it if only for the sake of the memory of Chalky and George who if my memory serves me right, were a right diabolical pair and well matched to each other.

Letter #9 (EJJ,L9)

Its not a question of lineage at all, anyone Doreen initiated after being with Roy wouldn't be clan because Doreen didn't work clan she returned to her Gardnerian roots. Peter, who worked with Doreen after Roy's death doesn't consider himself clan, far from it. The snag with the Regency will always be, what are they working ? Chalky and George worked their own system based on some of Roy's material and teachings so if one wishes to be pedantic about it, they could claim to be kindred to the clan and that's about all. I don't know why this question should have cropped up in the first place, Chalky and George never claimed clan status for the Regency and neither do the new Regency people as far as I know.

Marian was never fully initiated into the clan, full stop. This has nothing to do with chalices poison or otherwise, she just wasn't fully initiated. The Poison Chalice has nothing to do with clan initiation, this is something totally different as you well know. It is something a person can either undergo or not according to how they feel and it is not confined to the clan either, there are one or two other groups I know of that have the same tradition, bona fide initiation has never depended on this nor should it for obvious reasons so there was actually nothing to drop, it is still there is anyone wants to claim the right to it.

24/7/2000 (A. S. is Marian Green)

You'll have to straighten the London lot out on the Goda and point out the the Godi was a Saxon word for priest and that we are the people of the priesthood etc. God knows where these people get their ideas from, it mush be from Ann who missed out on so much after she left Roy.

16th April 2003

> Marion took the first steps for initiation then more or less left the picture mainly because we all felt she was rather young. As far as the lineage is concerned, Jane passed all to me and I've passed it on to you, about that there can be no doubt. You have been given specific material that others do not have because of that connection, others may be working something close to the clan but that doesn't make them clan no matter what they claim, Only one person has that right and that's you if you are going to follow the hereditary principle. It was just the same with old George Pickingill, the only groups who had his tradition were those he specifically authorised and no others.

> Question (1) No, Norman was never a member, he was a guest. Norman could never have been a full member as such, there was too much of the old cunning man in him, he and Roy used to play question games trying to find out just what the other knew etc.
>
> (2) The power passed back to Jane and from her to me then on to you.

Letter #10 (EJJ,L10)

> The final manifestation of the the Deity has always been the nameless formless cold remote Deity of Creation, the one who laid down the order of the building blocks of this universe by giving the electron its specific value while at the same time, creating the seeds for its total destruction. With the words " Let there be light " there was and this light came from the exploding matter that was the foundation of the expanding universe. In time, this light will cease to be and the universe will start to collapse in on itself until it coalesces into a mass of matter where light can no longer escape from, If this mass of pure energy and intelligence so decrees, the whole process of creation will start again with the words " Let there be light " followed by the big bang of a newly expanding universe.

Yes, we've always used the compass orientation we do now unlike many groups who focus on the east as their major point. The reason for this quite simple, it's the old Nordic tradition, the land of eternal ice and snow from whence come the bitter chilling winds of winter with the breath of death upon its icy blast. The distant realm of the wild goose that carries off the souls of the dead to the Castle of the Pale Faced Goddess. Bering the Goddess of life and death, her domain has always been the fabled lands of Ultima Thule. As Roy's work was based on Anglo-Saxon tradition, we would never ever think of working to any other quarter than the one the old magical lode stone indicated which gives an idea how old the tradition is,

When it comes to specifics like the Rose beyond the Grave, Roy had it as a concept but never got round to structuring it as such, we'd vaguely worked it once with no great success but I knew from past experience there was something akin to it in another tradition and with a modicum of cross-fertilisation came away with what we use today. The same thing happened with the Cave of the Cauldron, he too had that but in rather a vague form, old George who'd worked it in the past gave him the bulk of the information and I had to ferret out a suitable cave and put him right and what we could and could not do underground. I could go on and on all night pointing out where Roy had the basic mythos and concept but hadn't got round to working out fully how it would be worked. What you have to remember, is he came to the faith later in life than most people and the folks who brought him in were quite old and not actively working so they could only take him through things verbally rather than working them with him and of course, he died young. If he had lived longer either one of two things would have happened, he would have gone on to be a leading light of the faith or he'd have simply dropped by the wayside. You picked up quite an impression from his letters didn't you, so I'll leave you to work

the Castle along with Roy ? As far as I know, there is no connection whatsoever between the traditions, the nearest our lot got to Essex, was the Cambridge area and that was the lot that held the rite of the Cave and the Cauldron. Did you

Letter #11 (EJJ,L11)

promised them as yet, all the personal lore and rituals that I've gathered over the years stay with me. As you know, people do work outside the clan meetings either on their own or with their partner and gradually gather together a lot of material that is outside the remit of the clan like the famed Jones binding ritual and the three arrows rite, these are my person property in the sense that I'm the only one who works them even though the Maid has the absolute right to demand that I work them for any member who has a need for this particular rite. Shani, the bronze knife is yours after September because it is the coven one and is yours as of right and coven law, mine are mine to deed as I see fit and at present I haven't named anyone. So yes, you are my spiritual heir as per the clan and through both Jane and I Roy's as well but you are not my personal spiritual heir because you haven't been named as such. If I ever get round to naming anyone, then my personal lore and rituals will be transmitted verbally and will be for that person only. If I decide not to transmit them, them they die with me. Hope this clears up any misunderstanding concerning what is or isn't a spiritual heir, a lot of people get confused by this thinking in terms of only one and not two.

Did you read the chapter in Doreen's book on Roy ? In it she mentions Diana as well as the old man who was an uncle on his mothers side and whose photo Roy had shown her. The Diana who died was the same Diana I mentioned. Need I draw you a diagram of how it was passed on to Roy and you can be sure that the Aunt Lucy Roy mentioned in one of the letters you saw, would have known and agreed with it all. When someone tell you that in the past Tubal Cain was all sweetness and light from the word go, don't believe them. What I will stress is what it becomes now that you are the Maid/Lady of the clan is up to you and the people you work with.

Letter #12 (EJJ,L12:F1)

right, enough, codes, stop pissing. The Oath. First of all, I will transmit it to you Ann and then I appoint David to act for me in all matters pertaining to the clan for one year and one day. After the aforsaid time has passed you are both free to form your own group within the clan of Tubal Cain and to form other groups within the clan structure under your control.

Letter #13 = (EJJ,L12:F2)

and taking you up ...., help yo to leap across. Then in the circle David will light his candle and one 1 at your feet saying." I David do renounce my baptism and all other faiths that I hold and swear to serve Our Lady The Goddess in all her forms. I also swear to hold true to the Clan of Tubal Cain, to reguard all others of the Clan as my brothers and sisters in the faith. To aid them in time of need, to protect them in time of danger, to hold true to the clan laws and secrets."

Letter #14 (EJJ,L14:F-3)

Yes there is a clan of Tubal Cain or the Goat Foot God, as for joining you have to be invited to do so. At present there are five people who are entitled to initiate potential members. The clan was founded by Roy and in the family tradition any member of the clan with the permission of the clan Magister can go off and form his or her own coven which in turn will be part of the main clan. The five people who have the authority to form other covens as part of the clan are Chalky, George, Jane Bowers, Doreen Valiente and myself. So as you can see there is no leg pull about it. Mind you, there are certain rules and oaths that have to be taken firstly by you and David, after that you both will have to initiate your own people in the same way. As there is so much distance between us David will have to act for me at first until he has served his year and a day and then he can carry on on his own. The other thing is, as your present members advance within the clan so they go off and form their own groups and these in turn become part of your clan and their alleigance to you both as head of the clan must be given. This in turn gives you the right to call a full meeting of all the covens in the clan as and when you feel like it. If you'd like to check the authenticity of this tradition look up the man in black and there you have it in a nut shell. As I said before, if this is the path you wish to tread then I am willing to go along with it, but first of all all your group must agree as you are a group and not individuals wanting to join a coven. Any one after who wants to join you can be dealt with in the normal manner.

Strange isn't it, things never quite work out the way you plan them in the circle. No it was not Roy or me that stopped you, we may be good but not that good, from what has been said I have the feeling that the old man is with you and is working through your circle. Soon with any sort of luck you should get a manifestation of him in the circle or even better on the outside of it.

Letter #15 (EJJ,15:F-4)

Now that you've had a chance to settle down after the trip over here, how are things with you. Have you had a chance of looking over those rough rituals that you took back with you. Concerning them, I'm not too sure how you'll get on with them. Having done more along the same lines, taken on their own they'll be out of context with the main theme. I took your sujestion concerning the death of Roy to heart and treated it as an opening for a book. Since then all sorts of other things have been falling into place. One thing that I had no intention of bringing into them was the Man In Black or the Dark Stranger. Well, there was no way that he was going to be left out. So now I've got his function down in respect to the Covens within the Clan. This in turn led to me having to explain how individual Covens relate to Clan traditions, what their rights are from the clan and what their duties are to the Clan and how it is all joined together. In short, how to build up a network of Covens within the Clan tradition. This means that instead of finishing up within a few months with a couple oaths and rituals, it looks as though I'm going to be doing it for the next year or so. The trouble is that getting one thing down means that three others have to be gone into as well as they are all inter-related. A sort of How to become a Witch. How to form a Coven. How to build a Clan within the tradition. This is as well as setting down the Sabbats. Rituals for the Esbats. Coven tools construction and usage. Personal tools construction and usage. Method for the casting of the circle. Invocation for dedicating the circle (You have that). The meaning of the symbology used in it plus the woods used in the garlands for the altar. The method of dressing the altar and the meaning behind the alrar staff ect ect. I seemed to have lumbered myself with a major job and I'm not even sure I want to do it or if there is even a need for that sort of thing in the first place.

Letter #16 (EJJ,L16:F-5)

Thinking back over what I've just written, I've just realised the implications of what I've just said. If what I'm doing now ever gets published and taken up by other groups. This will make the Roebuck titular head of any group set up in the States and that every one of them will have to take an oath of suzeranity to you before they can claim to be o: of the tradition. A mind boggling thought indeed, perhaps I'd better burn everything and take up fretwork instead, what do you think.? Seriously though, think about it. both of you took an oath on the hill to the tradition so anyone wishing to form a group within our tradition must take an oath to you ' To hold true to the faith and to recognise your Coven as the mainspring of the tradition in America. A stray thought,

Letter #17 (EJJ,17:F-6) 1 of 2

Dear Ann,

Many thanks for yours read with great interest.

The root problem as I see it, stems from years back when the Roebuck and the clan of Tubal Cain parted company. The first incling I had of this, was the feedback I had after the publication of the book ' Witchcraft, a Tradition Renewed ' when certain of your members asked the question " Why aren't we doing this ?" and from what I was given to understand, you told people that you didn't need to do this and that in the book I tried to throw people of the scent concerning the clan workings as well as baffle, maze and mystify them. You know full well that this isn't true and that everything in the book was factual, accurate and above all, open. In fact, it is what I claimed it to be, the basic root source of all the clan workings, it was then, it still is and it will always be so and if you attended one of our workings today, you would find that we still open and close our meetings in the way so described.

From other material supplied by you and from feedback of various sorts including first hand experience, the Roebuck workings have taken a decidedly Celtic turn compared to the line we over here were following. This in turn leads on to the oath both you and Dave took. I may be getting old but my memory is still good and of course I still have Peter who was present to check it with and to the best of our memory, you swore to follow the tradition and mythos of Tubal Cain, quite a simple oath the sincerity of which was never doubted. At the same time, this did not name you as the sole inheritrix of the mythos and clan of Tubal Cain everywhere, only what you created an ran.

Evidentally , you had a change of heart and decided to follow your Roebuck, now, I've certainly have no quarrel with that after all, its a free world, and people should work what they want to. Where the problem comes in, this I pick up from letters I get, is that the Roebuck is being called Tubal Cain, something it isn't and people are working the Roebuck under the impression that they are working Tubal Cain, which they are not and the more Tubal Cain becomes known to outsiders, the more the difference shows up. When people like Jim ask me about this, I tell them in all honesty, that we parted company years ago concerning clan workings and that they have to make up their own minds as to what they want to do. If they work the Roebuck, then they must accept the rules of the Roebuck without question. If they want to something else, then they should leave and make it clear why they are doing so, the one thing they cannot do, is to be part of yet at war within a group, this isn't fair on all concerned.

Certainly the feeling over here with the Tubal Cain membership, is that we are so far apart in what both of us do that there is little point in going on with any sort of association and the best thing we could do, is to dis-associate ourselves fully from the Roebuck and let me tell you, I've come in for some stick for over the last few years for introducing you to the clan in the first place, but there again, a change of leader means a change of attitude which is not unexpected.

One of the questions raised in the letters I've had, concerned the masked rites which I gather you dismissed as Brits playing at cowboys and indians. If you had been working the clan rites, then you too would have arrived at the same point we have concerning the shamanistic elements in Roy's work, something others have commented on more than once and which is now a generally accepted picture of what we do. So once again, the difference between what we are doing and the Roebuck are doing is shown up formenting argument. All the trouble seems to hinge around the fact that what you call the clan and what Roy called the clan are two different things, yours is Celtic in orientation, ours is English in content and never the twain shall meet so to speak.

The Roebuck is the Roebuck and as you rightly point out, the people are happy with it or they wouldn't be working with you so why change a winning formula. The only thing I can suggest to stop all this trouble, is that you drop the idea of the clan of Tubal Cain and let the Roebuck stand on its own merits instead of tying it in to something that it is obviously not and something that will become even more apparent over the coming years. The Roebuck should be strong enough to stand on its own feet and so is Tubal Cain so why try to make both of them something the aren't and failing in the process ?

Anyhow, I'm going to finish up now by wishing you both all the best for the future as I don't suppose I'll be hearing from you again. F.F.F. and blessed be John

Letter #18 = (EJJ,L17) –(F-7)

Letter #19 (EJJ,L18:F-8)

As for banishment, I can only think that this came from the letter I wrote to   where I mentioned the floating of a candle. If we shared any common ground whatsoever, you would have immediately known that floating the candle over the falls is quite a common occurance. Also, if Susan cared to read the letter properly, she would know that all this does is to release Ann and Dave from t their oath thus separating the Roebuck and us over here from each other, nothing more or nothing less. At May Eve when I pass on the stage head wand over to someone else, I too will float a candle over the falls to signify that the oath of leadership has been dissolved and that I am no longer leading our clan. You have your American Clan of Tubal Cain and no one over here can strip anyone of membership of that even if they wanted to, which they don't, all we say is that you and I have grown so far apart that we have nothing in common so we disassociate ourselves from each other and go our own separate ways thus putting a formal ending to what has been happening for years.

As for being any part of my future, after your letter, I think not.

Letter #20 (EJJ,L19) :(F9)

> ✳ I would have written soon but I've had no end of hassle from some people I write to in the States. I tried to get them working the rites of Tubal Cain and now wish I hadn't, its turned into a nightmare with personality clashes. If any Californians come near you, I'd advise you to scream rape then run like hell becuase once they latch on to you, your lost and doomed to be plagued by them for the rest of your life.
>
> As I said, just a short note so I'll finish up for now by

Letter #21 = (EJJ,L7) -(F10)

> (8) Certainly not Roy's group and the bloody thing keeps cropping up. Originally, I think it came from the Finnin's via Peter Larkworthy. Others have picked it up and it has spread from there. The Royal Windsor material sent to Ron Hutton came from Los Angelese and had been lifted directly from the book of rites I first wrote. Now, Peter knows something about this and Mike Howard is sniffing around as well.

Letters #22 = (EJJ,L7) -(F-11), #23 (EJJ,L7) – (F12)]

And #24 = (EJJ,20)

> As you say, some people are drawn to the Clan because they are what they are, others will try to use the Clan for their own ends, but the Clan spirit in the end will reject them and they'll have to pay a high price for trying. The only trouble is, these people can cause a lot of upset and bother for the members before being shoved out as you well know. All

Letter #25 (EJJ,L21) – (ADC-4)

18th April 2000.

Dear Shani,

Many thanks for yours. Its just as well you got back promptly, I was going to post the hand staff off to you just after the 20th of this month. The new moving date has been noted.

I agree, a total change where Chummy is concerned that's why I sent it off to you. When it comes to the clan, as far as I'm concerned, he can go take a running poke at a rolling doughnut but it isn't my decision that's important, its yours. To respond or not respond is your prerogative and whatever you decide I'll go along with, as far as I'M concerned, he's a crass ignorant pompous pain in the gluteus maximus.

Letter #26 (EJJ,L22) – (ADC-5) 16th November 1999

Sorry, didn't bother to read Chummy, I never do, he's a pompous pillock, end of story. The only time I'll ever take any notice of him is when he starts walking on water and we know that our revered leader Tony is the only one allowed to do that. The only reason why he's got it in for the ' hereditaries'imaginary or otherwise is because they won't tell him anything which you must admit is a trifle off-putting when you're the next best thing to God or sliced bread. The only arcane knowledge he's ever possessed, has come from other people's books. Strange thing though, Mike wrote and told me that he thought a lot of him as an old soul in a young body and that he still wanted to get in tough with me yet, Nigel Jackson thought he was the pits and was terribly disappointed when he actually met and worked with him

Letter #27 (EJJ,L23) – (ADC-6) 16th November 1999

Getting right away from the subject. I've had another letter from dear Andrew D which I'm enclosing for you to make up your mind about. You tell me what you want us to take concerning him then I'll frame a reply along the line you want to take.

Before you make up your mind though, I think you should know the results of the ferreting about I did. For a start, he's still living with his parents and has never had a job or anything, it turns out that the three covens we've all heard so much about are really solitary person covens and if as he says he'll be bringing three people with him when we eventually meet up, that'll be all three covens and the Magister whatever. It seems as though he has a slight Neppoleonic obsession with centralization etc and is rather fond of the old Crowleyan/O.T.O. secret society thing that went out with the flintlock musket so Terry's estimation of him sounded bang on target. Anyhow, he's your problem now so you tell me what you want to do with him.

This Hallowe'en, will be thinking a lot about you all as I light my candle and raise a glass. Praying that whatever you are doing on that night meets with success, so until I hear from you again, all the best to you all, love respects and best wishes and above all,

P.P.P
and
Blessed be.
John.

Letter #28 (EJJ,L24) –(CJ-1)

Well, if you feel reading Carol the riot act will work, fine, but don't be all that surprised if it doesn't sometime in the future, promises like pie crusts are made to be broken. Anyhow, going to finish up for now by wishing all the best of luck over the coming months, Hope the Consultant is able to sort you out soon, in the meantime, luck, respects and,

FFF
and
Blessed be.
John

P.S. Who on the group was sounding off in the Wiccan ? Someone evidently didn't like it a lot and asked me who it was.

John

19th June 2000.

Dear Shani.

Many thanks for yours.

Actually, Jan and Peter hadn't seen the article, it was Mike Howard who asked me and no, there was nothing wrong with the article, only with the name.

My dear Shani, one doesn't so much screw the opposition as tear them to shreds then stamp the remains into the ground, don't get mad, get even.

I'm afraid my trip will have to be an overnighter this time round and would suggest as you are going away the 22nd of July, making it the 15th and 16th of the month, Can you confirm these dates soon so as I can book my ticket and find out what train I will have to change to.

At present Chas Clifton is rather a dirty word in this neck of the woods. After having the mss for two years his grand contribution made it here today and comprised of precisely 16 pages which works out at less than a page a month, I have told him to forget it and return my material and I'm going to rewrite the bloody thing and present it as a solo mss. Yes, I did drop Chas the tiniest of hints like Shani has the coven stang, cup and knife and from now on, she'll be running everything from Sheffield so God knows what he's playing at, perhaps he too finds it hard to believe that anyone would willingly hand everything over to someone else without actually dying as they did it. Be as open or closed as you like with him, mind you, after receiving my letter telling him to more or less get stuffed, he may not write to you again. The trouble is with Chas,

Have written to Chas requesting the return of my original material but so far, haven't heard a thing from him and strangely enough, Mike Howard was asking the same question, only he thought I should rework it it and submit it to some British publisher, he did give me a name but I've forgotten it. Might think about it in a

Heard from Chas in the end concerning the mss, either he hasn't had my letter or he's decided to ignore everything I wrote and carry on as normal. He also made an interesting suggestion, how about a foreword from you as the one who is taking it all over? if he does hold me to the verbal agreement we had, how do you feel about it? This should really kill off any challenges as to the validity of your taking everything over.

• • • • • • • • • • • • • • • • • • • •

November 1999

> The question of you being kosher or not will soon be solved once and for all. As you already know, where the coven regalia is, there also is the leadership. Subject to your agreement, I'm thinking of doing an article along the lines of this concept. Tart the concept up a bit and it could make an interesting article for T.C. and for those of the readership who don't follow our ways. Later on, if anyone should question your right, you can show them the article plus the letter from me deeding you the regalia. If they still question your right, the only thing left, would be to hammer it home in the skulls with a baseball bat

Letter #29 (EJJ,L24) – (CJ-2) - 23rd April 2002

> When Carol starts again, just point out to her that the clan law states, " To the Master you owe duty under the law. To the Maid, total allegiance in all things " Now, if Carol cannot live with that, then tell her to F*** off pronto as the rest of you have no time or inclination to deal with her tantrums. The last thing you need is someone fermenting trouble, its far too corrosive.

Letter #30 (EJJ,L25) – (CJ-3)- 24th June 2002

> Make sure Carol does stick by the law this time, she has already cost you one good person who you could ill afford to lose and make sure she understands that next time, it'll be Bell, Book and Candle in spades if she doesn't. The last thing you need, is other people being driven away by her.
>
> Hope you get on well with Caroline and something results from it, I don't know about you, but I had the feeling from her letters that she was an interested, well meaning person who had a thirst for the craft even though she had reservations on how it would transfer to Australia. Mind

Letters from 'V.J.' (Widow of E.J.J.)

Letter #31 (VJ,L1) – (CJ-4) 11/3/09

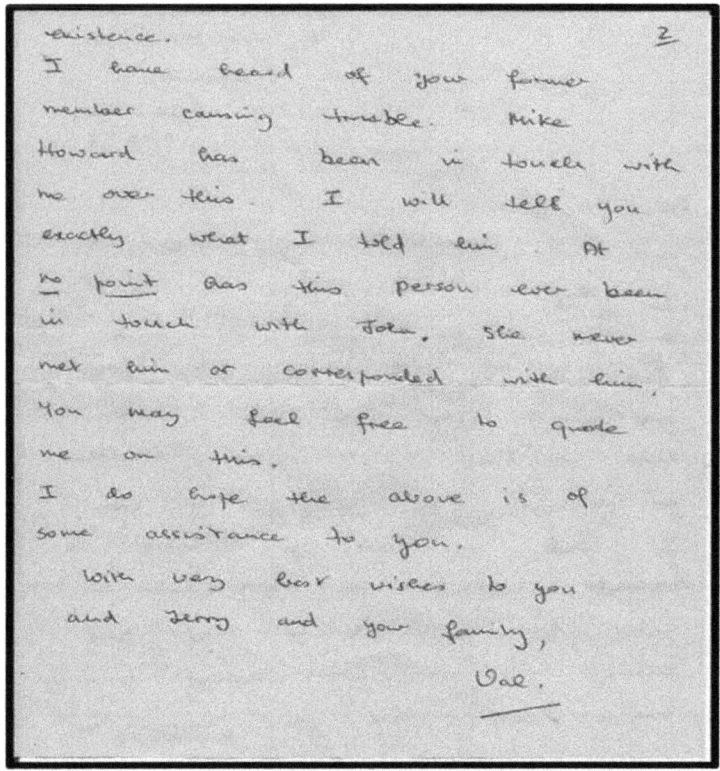

Letter #32(VJ,L2) – (RWC-1) 11/8/05

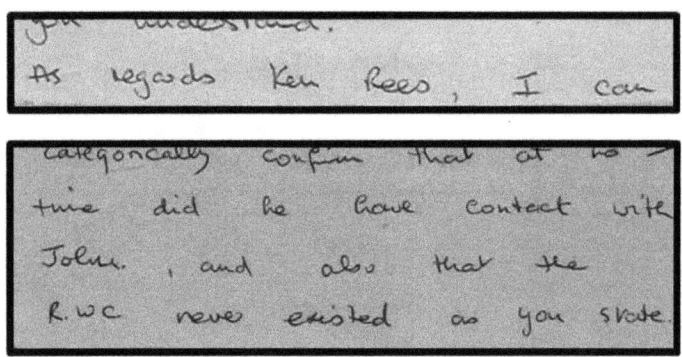

will eel you know.
I read your articles in "The Cauldron". I did try to defend Ken Rees (was that his name) but Mike Howard did not seem interested.
I hope you + Jerry and the rest of "Jeo Clan" are keeping well,
With best wishes.
Val

Letter #33 (VJ, L3)

As regards Anne, you are correct, she only attended a few rituals and was not admitted as a member.
I hope the above is of assistance to you, both Cathy + I feel that the record must be set straight. I have done my best so far. Both

Letter #34 (VJ,L4)

to examine them.
I know nothing about the letters from Cheeky & George, I was not around then. Roy never used the name "Bentback" as far as I know. I do not know who Diana & Arthur either. I did not know Dick either. I was not a member of the Thames Valley coven, I attended a couple of meetings, you can inform Mike Howard of this.

'Doc.A' : 1 of 2

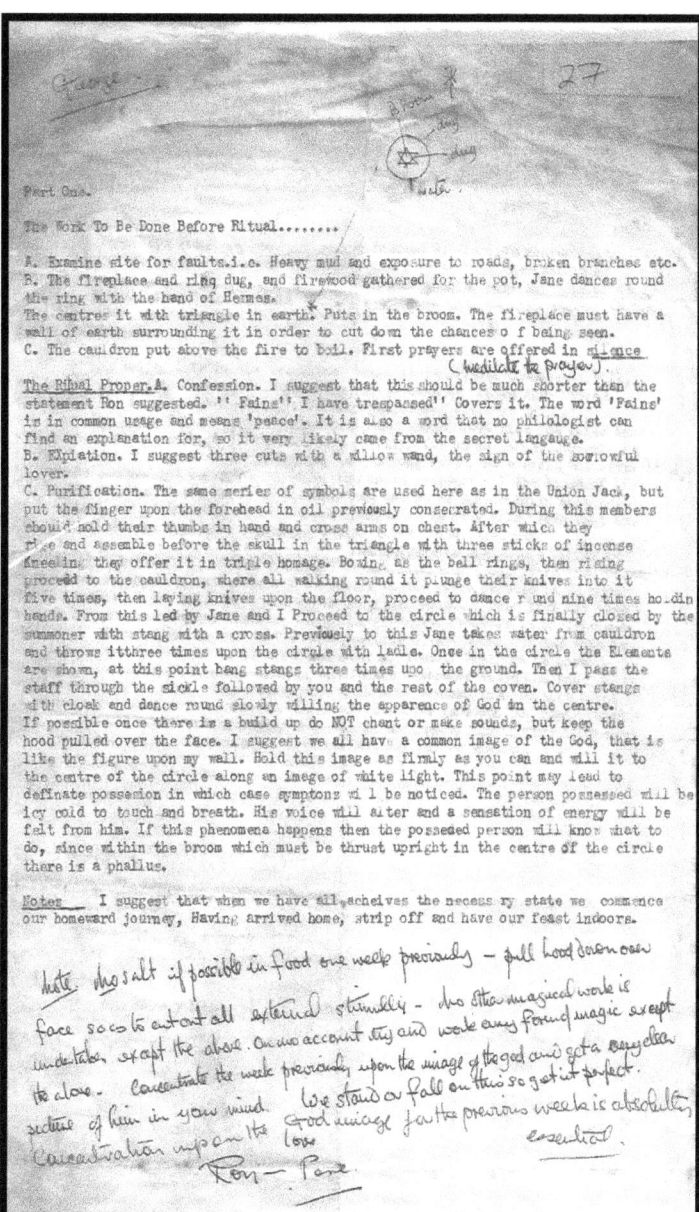

Part One.

The Work To Be Done Before Ritual........

A. Examine site for faults.i.e. Heavy mud and exposure to roads, broken branches etc.
B. The fireplace and ring dug, and firewood gathered for the pot, Jane dances round the ring with the hand of Hermes.
The centres it with triangle in earth. Puts in the broom. The fireplace must have a wall of earth surrounding it in order to cut down the chances of being seen.
C. The cauldron put above the fire to boil. First prayers are offered in silence (meditate the prayer).

The Ritual Proper. A. Confession. I suggest that this should be much shorter than the statement Ron suggested. '' Pains'' I have trespassed'' Covers it. The word 'Pains' is in common usage and means 'peace'. It is also a word that no philologist can find an explanation for, so it very likely came from the secret language.
B. Expiation. I suggest three cuts with a willow wand, the sign of the sorrowful lover.
C. Purification. The same series of symbols are used here as in the Union Jack, but put the finger upon the forehead in oil previously consecrated. During this members should hold their thumbs in hand and cross arms on chest. After which they rise and assemble before the skull in the triangle with three sticks of incense kneeling they offer it in triple homage. Bowing as the bell rings, then rising proceed to the cauldron, where all walking round it plunge their knives into it five times, then laying knives upon the floor, proceed to dance round nine times holding hands. From this led by Jane and I Proceed to the circle which is finally closed by the summoner with stang with a cross. Previously to this Jane takes water from cauldron and throws it three times upon the circle with ladle. Once in the circle the Elements are shown, at this point bang stangs three times upon the ground. Then I pass the staff through the sickle followed by you and the rest of the coven. Cover stangs with cloak and dance round slowly willing the appearance of God in the centre. If possible once there is a build up do NOT chant or make sounds, but keep the hood pulled over the face. I suggest we all have a common image of the God, that is like the figure upon my wall. Hold this image as firmly as you can and will it to the centre of the circle along an image of white light. This point may lead to definate possesion in which case symptons will be noticed. The person possessed will be icy cold to touch and breath. His voice will alter and a sensation of energy will be felt from him. If this phenomena happens then the possesed person will know what to do, since within the broom which must be thrust upright in the centre of the circle there is a phallus.

Notes. I suggest that when we have all acheives the necesary state we commence our homeward journey. Having arrived home, strip off and have our feast indoors.

Note: no salt if possible in food one week previously — pull hood down over face so as to cut out all external stimulii — No other magical work is undertaken except the above. On no account try and work any form of magic except the above. Concentrate the week previously upon the image of the god and get a very clear picture of him in your mind. We stand or fall on this so get it perfect. Concentration upon the God image for the previous week is absolutely essential.
Ron — Pax

The Tools. These are given magical properties instead of the more conventional properties of the simple rural craft. Incidentally it is from the failure of witches to develope thier ritual, that the failure of them to work any form of magic in recent years stems from. As such the tools are incorporated into magical rather than religious usages.
Reference: the Mask.

The Knife. This is the masculine tree. It represents Intellect, Will, and is symbolic of the search for knowledge and experience. It is also Choice, Love Physical, Mercy and Generousity. It also represents Craft or skill.

The Cord. This is the feminine tree, and should have five and three knots with a noose at one end. It is representive of FATE. The Noose formed properly is (a) Subjection to Hecate as Moria Hecate, the 'Strong Fate'. At a different level it represents the End and beginning of Life. The knots represent (a) the Round of Life *, (b) the Spirits of the Moon, (c) The Horn and the Noose and a third knot that depicts thepower of the Goddess over these things. It is from this cord that the practice of witches repeating a magical action three times camefrom.

Staff or Stang. This is the Supreme implement. It represents the middle pillar or Igrassdasll. It should be forked and bound at the base with iron. It is the Gateway, at the base or physical experience. The Chariot at the cntre because it is power and the treble Horns at thetop, the High spiritual endvour. Then from the base upwards it represents these factors. The Stone or Gate because it is phallic and because it representsHermes the Guide Next position is the Moon, because this is the path to the Mysteries. It is the Foundation of wisdom. Next. It is love because it represents the union of male and femAle, therefor attracton and counter attraction. Next it is Beauty, the Childe of Wisdom, then at this point it becomes the the Chariot or power. Its next attribute is death and destruction In this aspect it becomes the Lethe, Chronos, in fact mercy and Chronos in one. The next attribute at the horns is mystical and may not be written.

Sword   truth.
Sickle Judgment
Stone   mysteries
Pot   Inspiration Rebirth.
Fire   passion
Sickle The cruel mother, Death.
Cross   Elements +, X resurrection.
Platter Life forthcoming - choice, The world.
Cup   Abundance.
Cords (Binding twins) power over (Red) od, power over (blue) Hella,
Poppean Conjunction of my Heaven & Earth, The Code of the mysteries, long fertility,
Herbs Birch (life,) Vervian (love) Apple (Maternity) Fennel (wisdom) Willow (death)
                                            Maternity)

☆

'Doc.A' : 2 of 2 Letter to 'George' allegedly from Roy Bowers concerning the preparation of the ground for ritual. It exhibits quite a lot of handwriting, and a signature sample (a) which is very different to the authenticated sample (c)

Handwriting samples

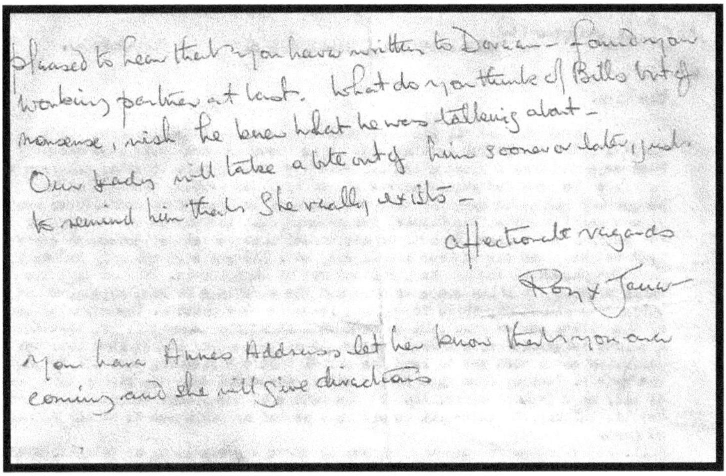

[handwritten note:]
Pleased to hear that you have written to Doreen — found your working partner at last. What do you think of Bill's bit of nonsense, wish he knew what he was talking about — Our Lady will take a bite out of him sooner or later, just to remind him that She really exists —

affectionate regards
Roy & Jane

You have Anne's Address, let her know that you are coming and she will give directions

First Edition signed review copy of Justine Glass's book. Allegedly to Roy Bowers

473

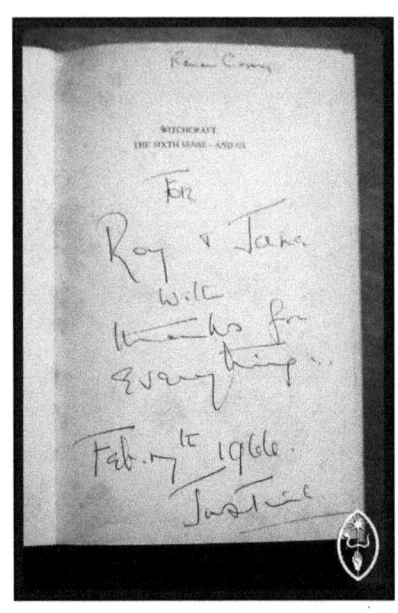

a) alleged

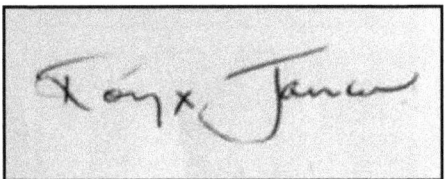

b) alleged

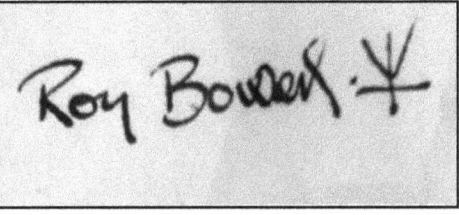

c) authentic

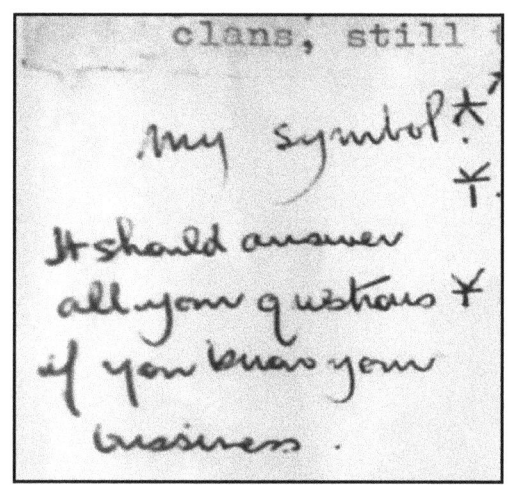

d) alleged

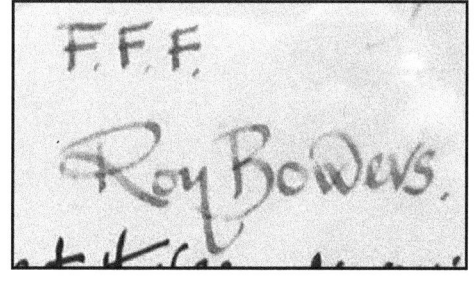

e) authentic

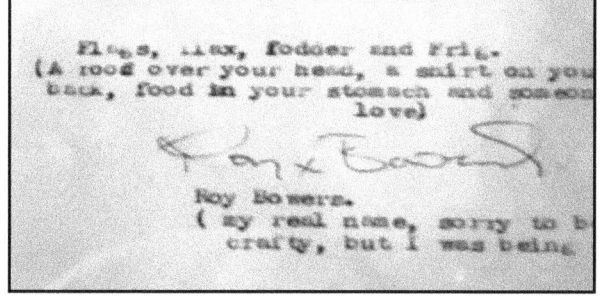

f) possibly authentic

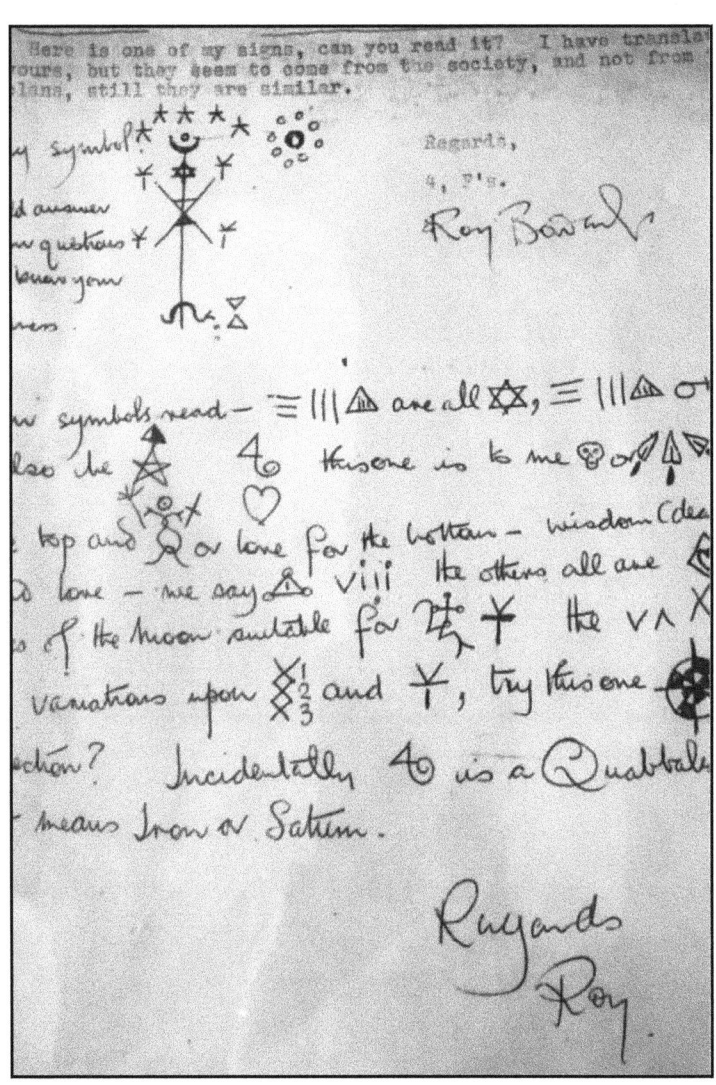

g) alleged

h) authentic

i)

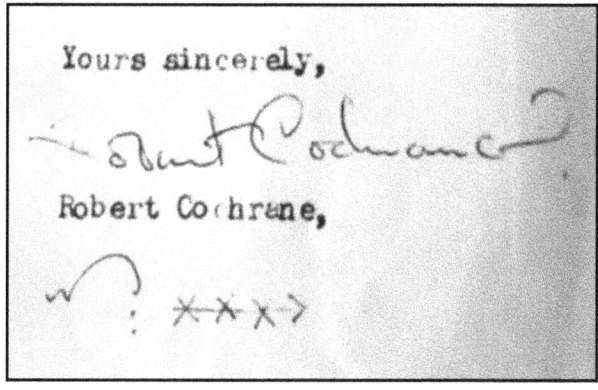

j)

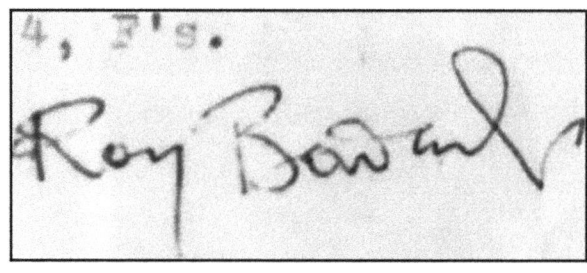

k)

(i), (j) & (k) alleged

> Lastly, the graduate is proclaimed to the Mighty Ones at the four quarters; and the words of dismissal are said.
>
> *This whole chapter is a tissue of lies!*
> *This ritual is only applicable to modern groups*
> *" It cannot be said of Trad".*

(l) & (m) are from inside the review copy and are claimed to be Bowers' annotations. Both are alleged.

> The 'old' witches claim that Dr Gardner's publicity campaign, far from helping the Craft, harmed it by cheapening it and making it a laughing stock: harm from which the more pessimistic cannot see it recovering from generations. Whether this is true or not, at least his impact on the Craft was such that it has to be considered in any assessment of witchcraft today.
> He was initiated into an hereditary coven in the New Forest area.
>
> 130
>
> *This is not true — New Forest have no knowledge of him at all, and deny this.*

m)

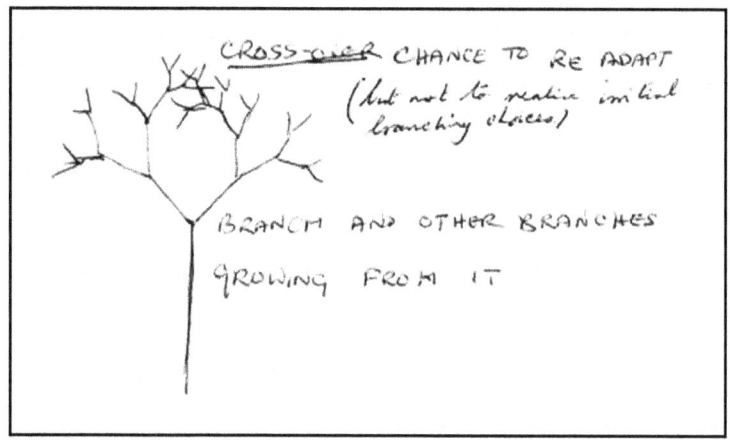

(n) & (o) are examples of Ronald White's handwriting

AAA Sample signatures of Roy Bowers

(Robert Bentback) ?

Ronald White (Robert Gynt) and George Stannard (Will Maidenson) have questionable presence on this document.

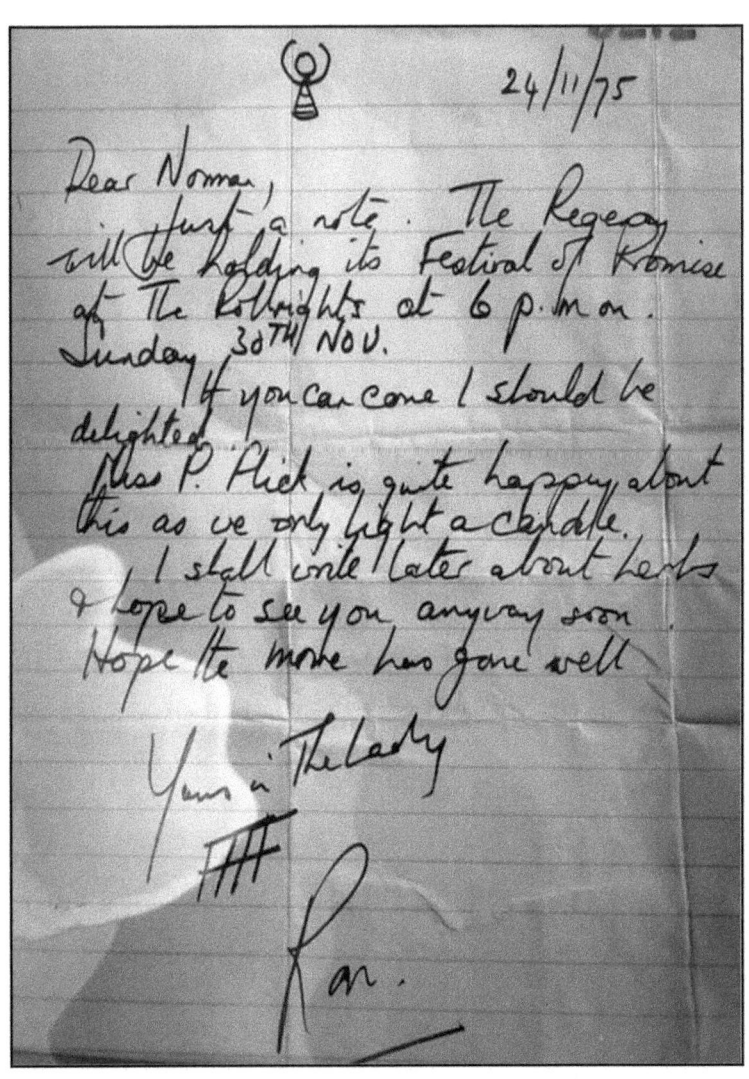

o) authentic – Ronald White

(p) & (q) are two more samples of Ronald White's hand

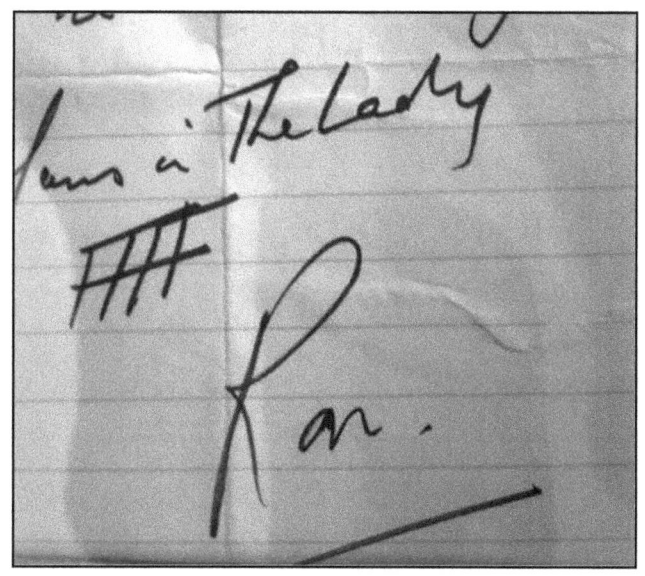

Authentic

r) Bowers (authentic)

> Dear Norman,
>
> Just a short line to ask whether you can bring the "black mirror", and a few suitable plants – since I only possess a small reflector made of quartz – and it would be of little value for work as a group because of its small size –
>
> See you on Saturday
>
> F.F.F.
>
> Roy Bowers.
>
> P.S. We will be there at three approx.

s) Bowers. (authentic)

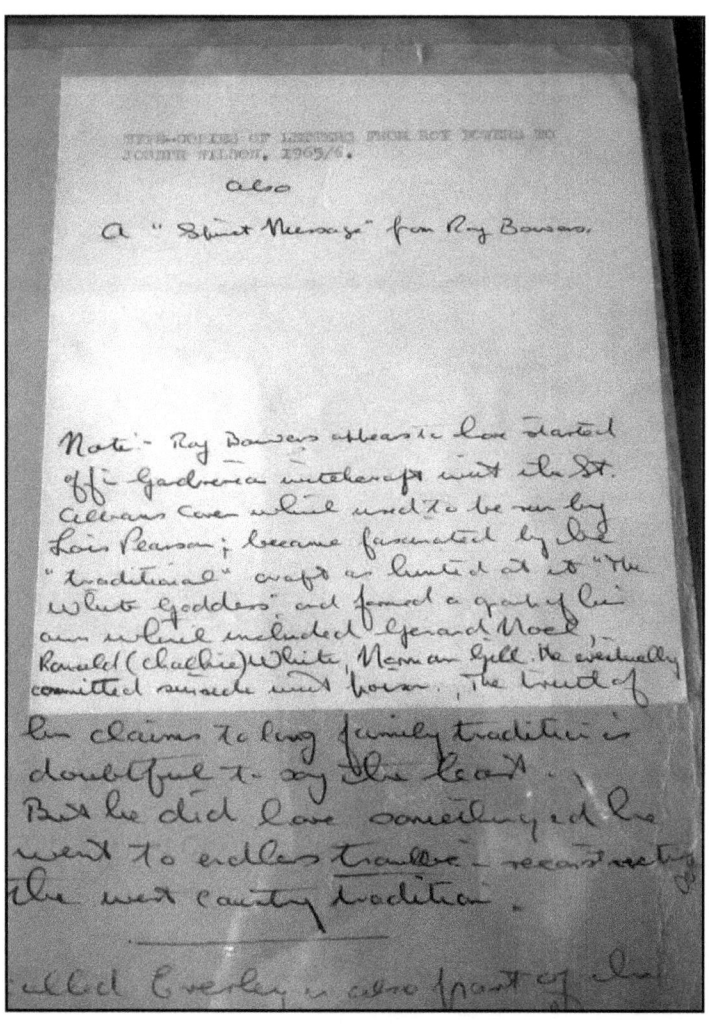

t) Reg Hinchcliffe (authentic)

Note that Ronal White is referred to as 'Chalkie' this spelling is verified by Valiente. Which means that 'Chalky' is either someone else entirely, or has been mis-spelled by someone attempting a fraudulent missive,

> everyone into confusion.
>
> Robin would you like to hold the official prayer book. You don't have to make them all up if you like can glean them from poems or ballads any source. I see from your letter that you are already doing this.
>
> Blessed Be —
>
> Joan.
>
> P.S. Ray feels awful about losing control and laughing. It is a sign of extreme nervousness and tension. He is very sorry. I hope Norman will be able to do something about this by hypnosis.
>
> J.

u) Letter from 'Joan' to Chalky. Monmouth cites the author as Jane Bowers (alleged)

Jon,

I read with interest your letter in the Imbolc '09 copy of the Pentacle referring to the Clan of Tubal Cain. I am prompted to write to you as I believe there are a few inaccuracies in the piece.

On the 24th July 2002 I was myself initiated into this clan. [Evan] John Jones made the trip to Derbyshire to attend, which I consider one of the greatest honours in my magickal life. Although I resigned from the Clan in 2004 I was a member long enough to know about its workings.

Hereditary covens such as this only appoint only one 'Maid' (the term used for the High Priestess) at a time; Hereditary Clans do not spawn new covens in the same way as a Gardnerian or Alexandrian one would by making new HP's. Hence, they do not grow beyond the titular auspices/authority of a single Clan.

That said, the Maid at the time of my initiation wasn't Carol Jones; she was one of the quarter officers (and my sponsor) on the evening. I don't believe there has been a change of Maid since.

It's a shame John isn't still with us to bear this out, but I can assure you that at the time of my initiation there was no doubt whatsoever from anyone attending who held which office and there was only one Maid. As I said, it was a wonderful evening for me, and the photo's I have of it take me right back there whenever I look at them.

I hope this helps to clarify the issue.

Martin White.

v) Clan member's letter to editor of Pentacle – JR. (authentic)

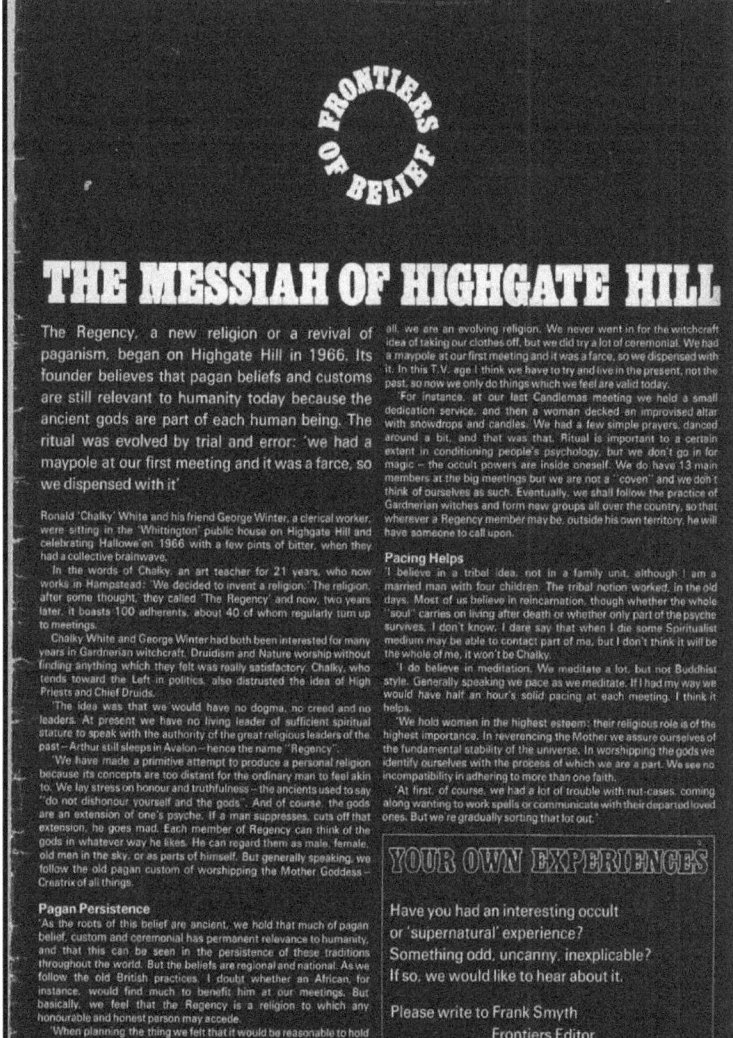

(w) Back page of Man, Myth & Magic' article by Ronald White on The Regency.

Other titles from Thoth Publications

HERITAGE An Anthology.
Clan Of Tubal Cain, by Shani Oates

"In Fate and the overcoming of Fate is the true Graal,
for from this, inspiration comes . . ."

ROBERT COCHRANE

Presented in prose and verse, this Clan Anthology of selected musings illustrates the poignant duty of all pilgrims in the Craft to explore and share their realisations and experiences in order to guide and shape those of others. Drawing upon our incredible legacy, we are bound by our troth to 'pay it forward.' Thus may we ensure the survival of its three sacred tenets – Truth, Love and Beauty (that parallel those of Freemasonry – Wisdom, Strength, and Beauty) for genera to come. Held within the lore of the folk, our insights regarding the Mysteries come direct from the source, and provide brief and thought-provoking comments on 'The Work.'

ISBN 978-1-913660-39-0

DION FORTUNE AND THE INNER LIGHT
By Gareth Knight

At last – a comprehensive biography of Dion Fortune based upon the archives of the Society of the Inner Light. As a result much comes to light that has never before been revealed. This includes: Her early experiments in trance mediumship with her Golden Dawn teacher Maiya Curtis-Webb and in Glastonbury with Frederick Bligh Bond, famous for his psychic investigations of Glastonbury Abbey.

The circumstances of her first contact with the Masters and reception of "The Cosmic Doctrine". The ambitious plans of the Master of Medicine and the projected esoteric clinic with her husband in the role of Dr. Taverner.

The inside story of the confrontation between the Christian Mystic Lodge of the Theosophical Society of which she was president, and Bishop Piggot of the Liberal Catholic church, over the Star in the East movement and Krishnamurti. Also her group's experience of the magical conflict with Moina MacGregor Mathers.

How she and her husband befriended the young Israel Regardie, were present at his initiation into the Hermes Temple of the Stella Matutina, and suffered a second ejection from the Golden Dawn on his subsequent falling out with it.

Her renewed and highly secret contact with her old Golden Dawn teacher Maiya Tranchell-Hayes and their development of the esoteric side of the Arthurian legends.

Her peculiar and hitherto unknown work in policing the occult jurisdiction of the Master for whom she worked which brought her into unlikely contact with occultists such as Aleister Crowley. Nor does the remarkable story end with her physical death for, through the mediumship of Margaret Lumley Brown and others, continued contacts with Dion Fortune have been reported over subsequent years.

ISBN 978-1-870450-45-4

HERE BE MAGICK
by Melissa Seims

This compelling account of eccentricity and Witchcraft in the 1950s and 60s revolves around two principal characters: 'Rex Nemorensis' (Charles Cardell), son of an internationally famous Victorian stage magician, and Ray Howard, owner of the Head of Atho – a representation of the Horned God of the Witches reputedly over 2000-years-old.

From the luxury of his country estate, Cardell trod his own unique path of modern Witchcraft, the reality of which was effectively put on trial in a High Court libel case brought against a major newspaper, following an article by two reporters who had hidden near Charles' sacred Grove.

What they witnessed, would change Cardell's life forever.
This book, based on new research, explores their fascinating lives and examines their writings and relationships with other witches including Gerald Gardner and Doreen Valiente.

For the first time, the writings of the Coven of Atho are reproduced. They reveal its previously hidden gems and provide a workable form of Witchcraft blended with Druidic influences.
The glistening strands of this story are woven into the larger history of the origins of modern Witchcraft in Britain. Here be Magick...

"I find two things especially appealing about this book. The first is the excellence of the research, by which so many details have been painstakingly retrieved concerning the people and rites concerned. The second is the author's readiness to see the best in those people, and to bring out their value and significance to the reader."
Ronald Hutton

"The author's unequalled, thorough and wide-ranging research techniques in both archives and personal contact are much to be admired and have uncovered the truth behind some of
the most enigmatic characters to be found in the history of modern magic and witchcraft, and their association with the mysterious Coven of Atho."
Philip Heselton

ISBN 9781913660338

WITCHFATHER: Into the Witch Cult - Volume 1
by Philip Heselton

From the author of the highly acclaimed "Wiccan Roots", this is the first full-length biography of Gerald Brosseau Gardner (1884-1964) - a very personal tale of the man who single-handedly brought about the revival of witchcraft in England in the mid 20th Century.

During a working life as a tea and rubber planter in Ceylon, Borneo and Malaya, he came to know the native people and was invited to their secret rituals. But it was only on his retirement to England, settling on the edge of the New Forest in Hampshire, that destiny took him firmly by the hand. Through various twists and turns involving naturist clubs and a strange esoteric theatre, he became friends with a group of people who eventually revealed their true identity - they were members of a surviving witch coven. One evening in 1939, as the hounds of war were being unleashed, he was initiated into the 'witch cult' by these people, who called themselves 'the Wica'. Gardner was overwhelmed by the experience and was determined that the 'witch cult' should survive. This book chronicles his efforts over the remaining quarter century of his life to ensure not only that it survived but that it would become the significant player on the world religious stage that it now
ISBN: 9781870450805

WITCHFATHER: From Witch Cult to Wicca Volume 2
by Philip Heselton
ISBN: 9781870450799

www.ingramcontent.com/pod-product-compliance
Lightning Source LLC
Chambersburg PA
CBHW050924240426
43668CB00020B/2420